CONTENTS

INTRODUCTION

Welcome to the 18th edition of the Robert Joseph *Good Wine Guide,* and the second to feature details and descriptions of 1,000 great and good value wines from the 2002 International Wine Challenge, the world's biggest wine competition.

The inclusion of these results helps to make the *Good Wine Guide* a wine drinker's companion that is really four books in one. In the first section – *The Basics* – you'll find all the grounding you need to get through a dinner party among wine buffs, set up a cellar, or choose a bottle in your local supermarket. There's guidance on grapes and regions, flavours and vintages. Wine and health and ideal marriages between food and wine are covered too, as are wine on the web and the pros and cons of wine investment for those who are feeling frustrated with the performance of their dot-com shares.

The A–Z of Wine – is an encyclopedia of some 3,100 wines, terms, regions, and producers, recommended examples, and the best way to pronounce the names of all those wines. So, you'll never have to pause before ordering a bottle of Ngatarawa from New Zealand.

Next come those International Wine Challenge wines – the 230 Gold Trophy winners and medalists and some 770 other Good Value award winners across a wide range of styles, and chosen for the flavour and character they deliver for the price tag they bear.

Having chosen your wine, you won't have to search to find it. The *Retailers* section includes over 250 wine merchants – from quirky one-man-bands, auctioneers, and fine-wine traditionalists to wine clubs, mail-order specialists, high-street chains, and supermarkets.

Taken as a whole, the *Guide* should (as a reviewer wrote of a previous edition) be the "only wine book you need" when choosing, buying, or drinking wine in 2003.

The 2003 *Guide* owes much to Margaret Rand, the Associate Editor of the A-Z, J.D. Haasbroek, the stalwart deputy editor who, again, kept the book on track and on schedule, and Josephine McLaughlin for A-Z research. Michael Florence, Birgitta Beavis, Richard Ross and Chris Mitchell were responsible for the International Wine Challenge content. Lavinia Sanders' organizing skills saved me from the asylum, and Charles Metcalfe and Anthony Downes provided moral support. I also have to thank Piers Russell-Cobb and, at Dorling Kindersley, Deirdre Headon, Louise Waller, Peter Luff, and Gary Werner. Richard Davies and Jane Brown at *WINE* and and Kim Murphy at the Wine Institute of Asia were as indulgent as ever. These people share any credit for this book; the criticism should fall on my shoulders alone.

THE
BASICS

News

HEARD IT ON THE GRAPEVINE

FREEDOM FIGHTERS

Imagine, if you will, an inexorably growing number of peas that have to be poured through a funnel whose neck is steadily becoming narrower. It's a picture that might reasonably be applied to the way wine is being made and sold today. New World wineries are launching new wines at a rate of one every couple of days. In Europe, producers who used to sell their wine in bulk are now eagerly beginning to bottle, label and – hopefully – sell it themselves. Italy, alone can boast over a quarter of a million estates and merchants with a licence to bottle. To complicate matters further, each of these can sell wines under several different labels.

So much for the peas. Now let's look at the funnel. Over the last few years the number of wine wholesalers and retailers has shrunk dramatically. In the US, there are a tenth as many wholesalers as there were 30 years ago; in the UK, one of the fastest growing wine markets in the world, 75 per cent of all the wine drunk at home is now bought at just half a dozen supermarket chains. With every year comes news of the purchase of yet another firm by a larger rival. In 2002 it was the turn of the Oddbins chain, regular winner of Wine Merchant of the Year awards, to be bought by the owners of Nicolas, France's biggest wine retailer.

The way wine is traded is changing too. Gone are the days when teams of skilled wine tasters scoured the world for tiny cellars full of vinous gems. Today, the deals that are being done far more frequently involve marketing deals (such as BOGOF - Buy One Get One Free) and listing fees that are out of the question for smaller producers. Perhaps the best and saddest illustration of the downhill slide was the decision by Unwins, Britain's last significant independent chain of wine retailers, to sack its entire buying team and hand the responsibility for wine selection to the beer buyer.

But irresistible forces and immovable objects tend to create reactions. Alternative funnels are being created in the shape of online wine retailing and wholesaling to accommodate the peas. Buying bottles over the Internet is still in its infancy, but after a euphoric birth and a sickly teething phase, the baby is beginning to look increasingly healthy. Plenty of ambitious would-be online wine merchants may have closed their electronic doors (or failed to open them) and ludicrous laws still prevent wine drinkers throughout the US from taking advantage of online retailers located beyond the borders of their state. Even so, sites like *wine.com wineandco.com*, *bbr.com*, *everywine.co.uk*, *virginwine.com* and a host of traditional wine merchants are all firmly established now. The UK-based *everywine.co.uk* offers some 22,000 wines on its site, while Tesco, the UK supermarket that has become the world's biggest online food retailer now offers small quantities of hard-to-find wines such as Cloudy Bay to its Internet customers. And, in the US, independent retailers throughout the country are attracting new customers through *wineaccess.com*. So perhaps there is hope for all those new wineries after all.

THE CAP FITS...

Tesco deserves credit too for taking another initiative in 2002. Over the course of a month, the chain's stores managed to sell over a million bottles of wine sealed with screwcaps. The novelty lay in the fact that these were familiar wines such as Bin 65 Chardonnay and good quality Chablis from la Chablisienne that had ever been sold in this way before. Top New World wine-makers such as Plumpjack in California, Kumeu River in New Zealand, Argyle in Oregon, not to mention nearly most of the producers from Australia's Clare Valley have lost patience with the inability of the cork manufacturers to offer corks that don't taint the stuff in the bottle. Their emphatic confidence in screwcaps is supported by the youthfulness of Australian Rieslings bottled in this way in the 1970s.

Industry estimates of the proportion of wines spoiled by bad

"Stelvin" screwcaps – rapidly gaining ground

corks range from the 0.6 per cent favoured by the cork manufacturers to the 15 per cent preferred by some winemakers. Out of the 12,000 bottles opened at the International Wine Challenge, the spoilage rate was 4.6 per cent. The cork manufacturers have responded strongly to the lack of confidence in their products – by spending £4m on a highly sophisticated public relations and advertising campaign aimed at the general public. Some winemakers and wine drinkers might prefer this money to have been devoted to solving the problem of cork taint rather than pretending that it doesn't really exist.

APPELLATION MOUNTAINS

A parallel crisis of confidence is just as apparent among the vineyards of Europe. As they confront increasing competition from winemakers in the New World, a number of producers are deciding that they no longer wish to be associated with the lumbering appellation systems in their countries. In Italy, high-profile producers like Gaja and Masi have simply removed wines from the official DOC/DOCG system. In Spain also, similarly famous producers such as the Marquès de Griñon are offering (delicious) Rioja made from a blend of traditional Tempranillo grapes and also far less than traditional Syrah, Cabernet Sauvignon, and Merlot. The German wine authorities have tried to

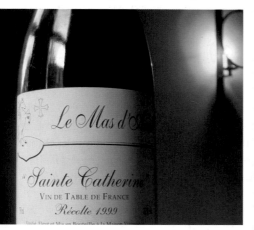

Outlaw of the French world - because of that vintage...

counter this anarchic trend – and the difficulty non-Germans have in deciphering traditional Rhine and Mosel labels – by introducing new "simple" designations of "Classic" and "Selection" for dry wines, and drawing up maps delineating the best vineyards in each region. Here, too, however, top winemakers like Bernard Breuer are sidestepping these official innovations by using equally simple labels of their own. In France, the move is towards labelling wines as Vin de Pays rather than Appellation Contrôlée, though a few braver producers are openly flouting the law by selling their vintage wine as "Vin de Table" even though it is officially illegal to use this term on a bottle bearing a year on its label.

All this talk of European laws and the challenges they face may strike some readers as arcane, but it's not. This readiness to question established and frequently cobweb-covered traditions is precisely what Europe needs to offer the kind of wine most of us want to drink.

PRICE FIGHTERS

And can afford to buy... There is a piece of good news this year for anyone who has been feeling nostalgic for wines they thought had slid forever beyond the reach of their wallet. In 2002, common sense – or at least a little of it – returned to the wine world. After an orgy of high pricing at the end of the 1990s, when the cost of Bordeaux exploded and previously unknown wines from the America, Australia and Italy hit the market bearing tags of £35-65, producers and merchants began to see sense. The 2001 Bordeaux were on offer as futures – *en primeur* – for over 25 per cent less than the 2000's, and prices of several high profile California wines slipped back from £45 or so towards a – relatively – more affordable £25. Many of these wines are still over-priced, however – especially when compared to the reds and whites to be found in some of the classic regions of Europe that have so far escaped the attention of wine gurus overseas. Great value is still to be found across the planet. Now is a good time to go looking for it.

STYLE VICTIMS

The choice of the wine you will buy, whatever its cost, will of course depend on its style. Sadly, the range of styles on offer today is less broad than it sometimes appears – as visitors to Bordeaux in April 2002 discovered when they had their first taste of the 2001 vintage. There were, of course, some lovely classic wines like Lafite, Léoville-Barton, Ausone and Vieux-Chateau-Certan that would delight traditionalists and modernists alike. But there were also a great many thick, dark, syrupy examples that tasted boringly as though they had all been drawn from the same toasty-oaky barrel.

The worrying thing about these immediately tasty wines which are unlikely to survive for long in a cellar, let alone improve over time, is the enthusiasm with which they were greeted by prominent US critics who prefer power to perfume. More depressing still was the resemblence they bore to similarly lauded wines from California, Australia, Italy, the Rhône and Burgundy.

The joy and magic of wine, like that of food, art, and music, lies in its variety and its potential to surprise. Life would be a lot less fun if all classical music had to sound like Wagner and every film had to resemble Titanic.

Personal Choice

An unashamedly quirky list of wines, out of the thousands I have tasted at the International Wine Challenge and elsewhere this year, that have particularly caught my attention. Prices are rounded off to the nearest pound. Stocks of many of these are limited, so it is likely that in some cases, the vintage mentioned may become unavailable during the lifetime of this Guide. Some others have yet to hit these shores.

REDS FOR DAILY DRINKING

1998 Temple Bruer Shiraz-Malbec, Langhorne Creek, South Australia (£7 Asda) A highly innovative Australian organic blend of grapes that might never have met in their homeland, France (where they are grown in the Rhône and the south west respectively). Lovely peppery stuff, packed with berry fruit.

2000 Quinta do Vale da Perdiz, Tinta Roriz, Douro, Portugal (Not yet imported) New wave Portuguese wine from the same region as the best vintage port, and made from a grape variety known in Spain as the Tempranillo. Rich, mulberryish, and strawberryish.

2000 Planeta la Segreta Rosso, Sicily, Italy (£8 Noel Young) Lovely wild berries and spices galore are on offer here in a wine from the family-owned Planeta winery, one of Italy's fastest-rising stars – and the increasingly exciting wine region of Sicily.

2001 Delicato Family Vineyards Shiraz, California, USA (£6 Ehrmans - 0207 418 1800) A producer that was once associated with very basic wine, but now offering some of the best value around.

2000 L.A. Cetto Petite Sirah, Baja California, Mexico (£5 Somerfield) From the part of California on the other side of the Mexican border, this is a very reliable, peppery, spicy wine made from a grape that is often confused with the Syrah of the Rhône and Australia. A perfect partner for fusion food.

REDS FOR SPECIAL OCCASIONS

1999 Henri Gouges Nuits St. Georges les Chaignots, Burgundy, France (£22 Howard Ripley) Built to last, this is top class red wine that is packed with raspberry and blackcurrant flavour and enough chewy tannin to make it worth keeping for a decade or more. Truly intense wine without the jammy character of so many New World superstars.

1997 Ch. Rauzan Ségla, Margaux, Bordeaux, France (£28 Justerini & Brooks) The 1997 vintage in Bordeaux was – very fairly – heavily criticised for being horribly over-priced. Five years after the harvest, however, some of the best wines are now offering far better value. This is classic claret to enjoy now, or over the next three or four years.

1999 Mas Igneus, Priorat, Spain (£20 Vintage Roots) Wonderfully intense, peppery, oaky, organic wine from the up-and-coming Spanish region of Priorato (or Priorat as it is known to its inhabitants). Serve with very hearty food – or sip it by itself.

1999 Sejana Merlot, Stellenbosch, South Africa (£12 John Armit) South African reds are finally beginning to live up to the enthusiastic hype they were prematurely accorded by well-wishers ever since Nelson Mandela won his election. This blend from several vineyards was made by a member of the Moueix family from Bordeaux and tastes like a plummy-cherryish New World answer to Pomerol.

2000 Grosset Gaia, Clare Valley, Australia (£15 Liberty Wines) Geoffrey Grosset is better known for his Riesling than his reds, but this stylish Bordeaux-like wine is a real star too. Grosset is so fed up with bad corks that he has also had the guts to seal his wine with a screwcap which should also allow its pure blackberry fruit to develop and last for well over a decade and maybe much longer.

1999 Miura Carneros Merlot, California, USA (not yet imported) A young rising star in California whose wines are still fairly priced. This is gorgeous, intense, damsony-spicy stuff that tastes good now but will keep well. Trophy Winner at the 2002 Vietnam International Wine Challenge.

1999 Vinedo Chadwick, Chile (not yet imported) The new top wine from the Errazuriz winery takes its name from the owner, and its style from somewhere between Bordeaux and California. Stylish and worth leaving in a cellar for a while.

1997 Brunello di Montalcino Vigna del Fiore, Fattoria dei Barbi, Tuscany, Italy (not yet imported) Wonderful, rich, herby, berryish yet delicate wine from a great vintage. Everything I want Italian wine to be.

1978 Salice Salentino, A. Ferrari, Piedmont, Italy (not yet imported) Extraordinary, nearly 25-year-old, spicy, port-like wine that is still vibrantly youthful – and only just released by its producer.

WHITES FOR DAILY DRINKING

2000 Thierry Matrot Bourgogne Blanc, Burgundy, France (£7 Booths) Now that some California wineries believe £15 to be a reasonable price to charge for their cheapest wines, it is refreshing to see a top Burgundy estate charging half that much for a classic wine like this. Produced in vineyards close to Meursault, it has much of the delicious, nutty, mineral character of wines from that village.

2001 Alamos Chardonnay, Argentina (£6 Bibendum)
Surprisingly subtle New Wave wine from the Catena winery, one of the biggest and most dynamic in Argentina. Good enough to beat far pricier efforts in the race for an International Wine Challenge Trophy.

1999 Clos d'Yvigne, Cuvée Nicolas, Bergerac, France (£7 Justerini & Brooks) Made by English-born winemaker Patricia Atkinson, this is a great value alternative to pricier white Bordeaux. It is richly dry and full of the flavours of peaches and fresh figs.

2000 Bodega Lurton Pinot Gris, Mendoza, Argentina (£5 Waitrose) Dry, creamy, peary wine, made in Argentina from a grape usually found in Alsace and Italy (where it's called Pinot Grigio) by a Frenchman whose home is in Bordeaux. Easy to drink by itself or with spicy food.

2001 Villa Maria Private Bin Riesling, Marlborough, New Zealand (£7 Waitrose) Proof that the Kiwis can compete with the Germans to produce great value, dry, fresh appley-grapey wine that would go perfectly with any kind of seafood or fusion food.

2001 Les Marionettes Marsanne, Vin de Pays d'Oc, France (£5 Somerfield) Great, lemony, limey dry southern French wine from a grape usually associated with white wines from the Rhône and the occasional success from Australia.

2001 Muscadet Sevre et Maine Domaine du Haut Banchereau, Auguste Bonhomme, Loire, France (£5 Anthony Byrne) Muscadet is woefully unfashionable now that we all want wines with fruit and oak – neither of which have much of a role in this style – but pour a glass of this and open a few oysters and you'll agree that fashion can be a less than helpful guide.

2000 Gorgo Bianco di Custoza, Veneto, Italy (£4 Oddbins) Creamy and gently floral, this modern Italian wine is great value and could be drunk in huge quantities with or without food.

1999 Arroyo Vista Chardonnay Single Vineyard, J Lohr, California, USA (£8 Enotria - 0208 961 4411) California is not good at making wines that offer good value for money at under £10. This is a good, rich, oaky exception to that rule.

WHITES FOR SPECIAL OCCASIONS

2000 Sancerre la Moussière, Alphonse Mellot, Loire, France (£11 Sainsbury) For a while, the New Zealanders seemed to have gained posession of the Sauvignon ball from the French, but the game is a lot more even now – as this classic Sancerre from a top producer proves. Fresh, dry, youthful with mouth-watering limey, gooseberryish stuff.

2000 Franz Haas Manna, Alto Adige, Italy (£12 Liberty Wines) Blending 50% Riesling, 20% each of Chardonnay and Gewürztraminer, and 10% Sauvignon in the cool conditions of the Alto Adige in northeast Italy makes for an extraordinarily aromatic, complex wine. The world needs many, many more wines like this.

2000 Viognier by Farr, Victoria, Australia (£15 Tanners) Garry Farr became famous as a champion Pinot Noir winemaker at the Bannockburn winery in the Australian region of Geelong. Now he's turned to Viognier under his own label, and produced a lovely, floral, peachy wine that would be delicious with or without food.

2001 Shaw & Smith Unoaked Chardonnay, Adelaide Hills, South Australia (£10 Martinez) Bored with oaky Chardonnay? This fresh, pineappley Australian wine from the Adelaide Hills is a perfect reminder that it is possible to make delicious wine from this grape without ever going near an oak barrel. One of my favourite wines with spicy food (though the same winery's Sauvignon comes close).

1991 Bründlmayer Grüner Veltliner Trocken, Alte Reben, Kamptal, Austria (Not yet imported) Lime and greengage are the key fruit flavours in this exciting wine, produced from a grape variety found almost nowhere outside Austria. Try this with any fish or poultry dish with vibrant fruit and spice flavours.

1999 Stony Hill Chardonnay, Napa, USA (Not yet imported) Arguably the least Californian of California Chardonnays, this is far more like a classic Chablis. It has delicate, white-plummy, stony flavours that have nothing to do with the big, oaky, butter-on-toast that is usually sold under the name of this grape.

2000 Tête de Cuvée Blanc Château Puech-Haut, Coteaux du Languedoc, France (£15 Lay & Wheeler) Pure Roussanne from southern France: delicious, rich, ripe, limey wine with a mixture of fresh blossom and peppery spice.

2000 Chateau Ste Michelle/Ernst Loosen Eroica Riesling, Washington State, USA (£15 Bablake Wines) A great joint-venture between Ernie Loosen of the Mosel, a top class German producer, and one of the big names of Washington State, which succeeds in bringing out the unique appley flavours of the Riesling grape.

SPARKLING WINES AND ROSÉ

Ba, Buenos Aires Brut, Argentina (£5 Majestic) Made by an outpost of Moët & Chandon (which also produces the excellent Terrazas still wines), this is easy drinking fizz that's at once fresh and rich.

Roederer Estate Quartet, California, USA (£16 Majestic) One of California's most reliable sparkling wines, this is very Champagne-like wine with a lovely, creamy quality.

1995 Billecart-Salmon Elisabeth Salmon Rosé Brut, Champagne, France (£60 Harvey Nichols) Impeccable pink Champagne to be sipped or enjoyed with food. Quite simply the best rosé, still or sparkling, that I've tasted in ages. And one of the best wines.

1990 Charles Heidsieck Blanc des Millénaires, Champagne, France (£37 Selfridges) Made by the late great Daniel Thibaut, frequent Winemaker of the Year, this is gorgeous, rich, maturing but still fresh wine, with toast and apples and hazelnuts and praline.

1996 Graham Beck Sparkling Pinotage, South Africa (£10 Bibendum) I'm not a fan of many of the still red wines made in South Africa from the Pinotage grape, but I really enjoyed this plummy sparkling version.

Jansz, Tasmania, Australia (£10 Oddbins) I know I recommended this in the 2002 Guide, but I enjoyed it just as much when I tasted it again this year, so I make no apology for including it again.

Clairette de Die Jaillance, S. France (£7 Waitrose) Juicy, grapey Muscat, with lovely intensity. This style – more usually found in Italy in the form of Asti – may be unfashionable, but so were flares, Tom Jones and Burt Bacharach before they were rediscovered in the late 1990s.

ROSÉ

2001 Fetzer Syrah Rosé (£6) Everything I want pink wine to be: fresh without being acidic and and fruity without being sweet. If only there were more wines like this to enjoy on warm summer days.

2000 Ch. Méaume Bordeaux Rosé (£5.50 Majestic) There is so much pale, weedy, watery, over-cropped – supposedly – red Bordeaux around that it's a delicious surprise to come across a wine from this region that is not only supposed to be deep pink, but also packs a punch of refreshing blackcurrant and redcurrant flavour.

2001 Inycon Cabernet Rosé, Sicily, Italy (£5 Enotria - 020 8963 4820) Italy should be a great source for bright, juicy rosé, but like Spain and Provence, it often offers up dull, bronze stuff that's as fresh as yesterday's news. This is a lovely blackcurranty exception to the rule.

SWEET AND FORTIFIED WINES

2001 Ch. Suduiraut, Sauternes, France (£30 - available from various merchants en primeur) Quite possibly the Bordeaux – red or white – of a truly great Sauternes vintage. Gorgeous, richly concentrated wine that will last forever and should be kept for at least a decade. But it will be all too tempting to drink in five years or so.

2001 Escherndorfer Lump Silvaner Eiswein, Horst Sauer, Franken, Germany (£55 Justerini & Brooks) From Franken – Germany's unsung wine region – and the Silvaner – its similarly unsung grape – this is stunning, intense, hedonistic wine, with layers of surprisingly delicate crystalised fruits, and more than a touch of the slatey, mineral character that comes from the soil.

de Bortoli Black Noble, New South Wales, Australia Exotic, dark, toffee'd late harvest wine with long-lingering flavours of super-ripe peaches, figs, sweet spice and mocha coffee.

2000 Ch. Tirecul la Gravière, Cuvée Madame, Monbazillac, France (not yet released) Better than all but the best Sauternes, this cult wine from the nearby region of Monbazillac deserves the praise it has received. Honeyed, rich marmeladey, with caramel and quince.

1999 Mitis, Amigne de Vetroz, Germanier, Valais, Switzerland (£20, wineandco.com) The Amigne is a very rare grape which is only found in Switzerland. This, the most famous and best example in that country, is lovely and peachy-mango-ey; it's lusciously sweet, but leaves your mouth feeling as though you have drunk a wine that was bone dry. Emphatically non-cloying.

FORTIFIED

1991 Moscatel Roxo, JP Vinhos, Portugal (£11 Harrods) Gorgeous, rich, grapey, honeyed Muscat to drink by itself or to drink with really good ripe peaches and high quality vanilla ice cream. Think of it as a super-charged Muscat de Beaumes de Venise.

2000 Niepoort Vintage Port, Douro, Portugal (£30 - available from various merchants en primeur) From a small but very highly-regarded family-owned port house, this may well be the most impressive port of a vintage that is one of the best the region has known for a while. Lovely, plummy, cherryish, and very intense.

Barbadillo Obispo Gascon Palo Cortado, Jerez, Spain (£22 D. Byrne) Savoury, nutty, dry yet honeyed sherry from a top class producer and made in a relatively unusual style that falls between Fino and Amontillado. The perfect accompaniment to really good olives.

Wine on the Web

THE NET WORKS

Early in 2002, IPC, part of AOL Time Warner and one of the world's largest magazine publishers, held its annual awards dinner, a glittering event at which its imprints' most finely honed features, most eye-catching covers, and most edifying editorials would all get the recognition they deserved. There was, however, one key difference from the dinner the same people had attended 12 months earlier. Back in 2001, the list of contenders for several key categories had included websites associated with IPC publications such as its wine magazine *Decanter*. This time around, almost the only reference to these sites was by journalists, many of whose online colleagues had recently lost their jobs when the publisher scaled back its online activities. The Champagne of the early Internet years had lost a lot of its fizz.

But, as anyone who has taken a level-headed look at the wine and Internet will have learned, all that has happened is that the hysteria has died down. Despite its smaller staff, *decanter.com* is still operational – and still one of the most useful websites for any wine lover in search of news and a reliable guide to the value of the wine in their cellar. Another publication, the *Wine Spectator* is not only still running a successful site, but has also launched a paid-subscription online news-letter aimed at US wine enthusiasts desperate to lay their hands on the latest ratings before the magazine hits the news-stands or subscribers' doormats. *Winespectator.com*'s online

Looking for older bottles at winebid.com.

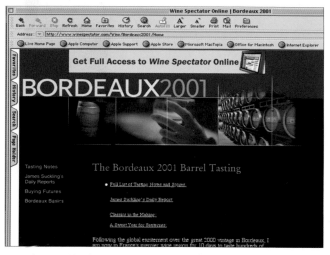

The Wine Spectator: essential reading for buyers of young Bordeaux.

reviews of the 2001 vintage in Bordeaux were eagerly accessed by professionals and amateurs alike – as were those of US guru Robert Parker's on his recently launched *erobertparker.com* and those of British authority Jancis Robinson (on *jancisrobinson.com*).

In the US, numerous efforts to run a profitable online wine retailer on the scale of *amazon.com* have been hampered by restrictive laws that outlaw the shipping of wine between many states of the Union, but wine drinkers there and in Europe and Australia are steadily becoming used to the idea of buying wine electronically. The rejuvenated *wine.com* in the US now competes head-on with the excellent *wine-access.com* which offers links to independent retailers. In the UK *virginwine.com*, *bbr.com* and *everywine.com* remained standing after others such as the Destination Wine Co's effort had fallen by the wayside, while France's *chateaux-online.com* and the new *wineandco.com* looked as though they had been built to last.

The traditional auction houses have been slow to establish a dynamic presence online, but the US-based sites like *morrellwineauctions.com*, *winebid.com,* and *brentwoodwine.com* are all doing well. Finally, and most usefully, perhaps, impartial, informative sites like *wineloverspage.com*, *wine-pages.com, bestwinesites.com, wineanorak.com* and the new *winereader.com*, all continue to offer lively information and links that are unavailable elsewhere.

Robert Joseph can be found at robertjosephonline.com *For a full list of recommended wine-related websites, see page 395.*

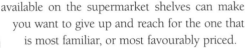

Tasting and Buying

SPOILED WITH CHOICES

Buying wine today has often become just like buying a gallon of paint. Just as the manufacturer's helpful chart can be daunting with its endless shades of subtly different white, the number of bottles and the information available on the supermarket shelves can make you want to give up and reach for the one that is most familiar, or most favourably priced.

If you're not a wine buff, why should you know the differences in flavour between wines made from the same grape in Meursault in France, Mendocino in California, and Maipo in Chile? Often, the retailer has helpfully provided descriptive terms to help you to imagine the flavour of the stuff in the bottle. But these too can just add to the confusion. Do you want the one that tastes of strawberries or raspberries, the "refreshingly dry", or the "crisp, lemony white"?

Arm yourself with a good corkscrew.

I can't promise to clear a six-lane highway through this jungle, but, with luck, I will give you a path to follow when you are choosing a wine, and one from which you can confidently stray.

THE LABEL

Wine labels should always reveal the country where the wine was produced (*see page 24*), and possibly the region and grape variety (*see page 48*) from which it was made. Both region and grape, however, offer only partial guidance as to what you are likely to find when you pull the cork.

Bear in mind the following:

1 Official terms such as Appellation Contrôlée, Grand or Premier Cru, Qualitätswein and Reserva are often as trustworthy as official statements by politicians.

2 Unofficial terms such as Réserve Personnelle and Vintner's Selection are, likewise, as trustworthy as unofficial statements by the producer of any other commodity.

3 Knowing where a wine comes from is often like knowing where a person was born; it provides no guarantee of how good the wine will be. Nor how it will have been made (though there are often local rules). There will be nothing to tell you, for instance, whether a Chablis is oaky, nor whether an Alsace or Vouvray is sweet.

4 "Big name" regions don't always make better wine than supposedly lesser ones. Cheap Bordeaux is far worse than similarly priced wine from Bulgaria.

5 Don't expect wines from the same grape variety to taste the same: a South African Chardonnay may taste drier than one from California. The flavour and style will depend on the climate, soil, and producer.

6 Just because a producer makes a good wine in one place, don't trust him, or her, to make other good wines, either there or elsewhere. The team at Lafite Rothschild produces less classy Los Vascos wines in Chile; Robert Mondavi's inexpensive Woodbridge wines bear no relation to the quality of his Reserve wines from Napa.

7 The fact that there is a château on a wine label has no bearing on the quality of the contents.

8 Nor does the boast that the wine is bottled at that château.

9 Nineteenth-century medals look pretty on a label; they say nothing about the quality of the 20th- or 21st-century stuff in the bottle.

10 Price provides some guidance to a wine's quality: a very expensive bottle may be appalling, but it's unlikely that a very cheap one will be better than basic.

A WAY WITH WORDS

Before going any further, I'm afraid that there's no alternative to returning to the thorny question of the language you are going to use to describe your impressions.

When Washington Irving visited Bordeaux 170 years ago, he noted that Château Margaux was "a wine of fine flavour – but not of equal body". Lafite on the other hand had "less flavour than the former but more body – an equality of flavour and body". Latour, well, that had "more body than flavour." He may have been a great writer, but he was evidently not the ideal person to describe the individual flavours of great Bordeaux.

Michelangelo was more poetic, writing that the wine of San Gimignano "kisses, licks, bites, thrusts, and stings...". Modern pundits say wines have "gobs of fruit" and taste of "kumquats and suede". Each country and generation comes up with its own vocabulary. Some descriptions, such as the likening to gooseberry of wines made from Sauvignon Blanc, can be justified by scientific analysis, which confirms that the same aromatic chemical compound is found in the fruit and wine.

Then there are straightforward descriptions. Wines can be fresh or stale, clean or dirty. If they are acidic, or overly full of tannin, they will be "hard"; a "soft" wine, by contrast, might be easier to drink, but boring.

There are other less evocative terms. While a watery wine is "dilute" or "thin", a subtle one is "elegant". A red or white whose flavour is hard to discern is described as "dumb". Whatever the style of a wine, it should have "balance". A sweet white, for example, needs enough acidity to keep it from cloying. No one will enjoy a wine that is too fruity, too dry, too oaky, or too anything for long.

The flavour that lingers in your mouth long after you have swallowed or spat it out is known as the "finish". Wines whose flavour – pleasant or unpleasant – hangs around, are described as "long"; those whose flavour disappears quickly are "short".

Finally, there is "complex", the word that is used to justify why one wine costs 10 times more than another. A complex wine is like a well-scored symphony, while a simpler one could be compared to a melody picked out on a single instrument.

TASTING

Wine tasting is surrounded by mystery and mystique. But it shouldn't be – because all it really consists of is paying attention to the stuff in the glass, whether you're in the formal environment of a wine tasting or drinking the house white in your local bar. The key questions are: do you like the wine? And is it a good example of what it claims to be? Champagne costs a lot more than basic Spanish Cava, so it should taste recognizably different. Some do, some don't.

See

The look of a wine can tell you a lot. Assuming that it isn't cloudy (which if it is, send it back), it will reveal its age and hint at the grape and origin. Some grapes, like Burgundy's Pinot Noir, make naturally paler wines than, say, Bordeaux's Cabernet Sauvignon; wines from warmer regions have deeper colours. Tilt the glass away from you over a piece of white paper and look at the rim of the liquid. The more watery and brown it is, the older the wine (Beaujolais Nouveau will be pure violet).

Swirl

Vigorously swirl the wine around the glass for a moment or so to release any reluctant and characteristic smells.

Sniff

You sniff a wine before tasting it for the same reason that you sniff a carton of milk before pouring its contents into coffee. The smell can tell you more about a wine than anything else. If you don't believe me, try tasting anything while holding your nose, or while you've got a cold. When sniffing, take one long sniff or a few brief ones. Concentrate on whether the wine seems fresh and clean, and on any smells that indicate how it is likely to taste.

What are your first impressions? Is the wine fruity, and, if so, which fruit does it remind you of? Does it have the vanilla smell of a wine that has been fermented and/or matured in new oak barrels? Is it spicy? Or herbaceous? Sweet or dry? Rich or lean?

Sip

Take a small mouthful and – this takes practice – suck air between your teeth and through the liquid. Look in a mirror while you're doing this. if your mouth looks like a cat's bottom and sounds like a child trying to suck the last few drops of Coke through a straw, then you're doing it right. Hold the wine in your mouth for a little longer to release as much of its flavour as possible.

Focus on the flavour. Ask yourself the same questions about whether it tastes sweet, dry, fruity, spicy, herbaceous. Is there just one flavour, or do several contribute to a "complex" overall effect?

Now concentrate on the texture of the wine. Some – like Chardonnay – are mouth-coatingly buttery, while others – like Gewürztraminer – are almost oily. Muscadet is a good example of a wine with a texture that is closer to that of water.

A brief look, then swirl the wine around the glass to release the aromas.

Does the wine smell fresh and inviting? Simple or complex?

Reds, too, vary in texture; some seem tough and tannic enough to make the inside of one cheek want to kiss the inside of the other. Traditionalists rightly claim tannin is necessary for a wine's longevity, but modern winemakers distinguish between the harsh tannin and the "fine" (non-aggressive) tannin to be found in wine carefully made from ripe grapes. A modern Bordeaux often has as much tannin as old-fashioned examples – but is far easier to taste and drink.

Spit

The only reason to spit a wine out – unless it is actively repellent – is simply to remain upright at the end of a lengthy tasting. I have notes I took during a banquet in Burgundy at which there were dozens of great wines and not even the remotest chance to do anything but swallow. The descriptions of the first few are perfectly legible; the 30th apparently tasted "very xgblorefjy". If all you are interested in is the taste, not spitting is an indulgence; you should have had 90 per cent of the flavour while the wine was in your mouth.

Pause for a moment or two after spitting the wine out. Is the flavour still there? How does what you are experiencing now compare with the taste you had in your mouth? Some wines have an unpleasant aftertaste; others have flavours that linger deliciously in the mouth.

SHOULD I SEND IT BACK?

Wines are subject to all kinds of faults, though far less than they were even as recently as a decade ago.

Acid

All wines, like all fruit and vegetables, contain a certain amount of acidity. Without it they would taste flabby and dull and go very stale very quickly. Wines made from unripe grapes will, however, taste unpalatably "green" and like unripe apples or plums – or like chewing stalky leaves or grass.

Bitter

Bitterness is quite different. On occasion, especially in Italy, a touch of bitterness may even be an integral part of a wine's character, as in the case of Amarone. Of course, the Italians like Campari too.

Cloudy

Wine should be transparent. The only excuse for cloudiness is in a wine like an old Burgundy whose deposit has been shaken up.

Corked

Ignore any cork crumbs you may find floating on the surface of a wine. Genuinely corked wines have a musty smell and flavour that comes from mouldy corks. Some corks are mouldier, and wines mustier, than others, but all corked wines become nastier with exposure to air. Around 8% of wines – irrespective of their price – are corked.

Crystals

Not a fault, but people often think there is something wrong with a white wine if there is a layer of fine white crystals at the bottom of the bottle. These are just tartrates that fall naturally.

Maderized/Oxidized

Madeira is fortified wine that has been intentionally exposed to the air and heated in a special oven. Maderized wine is stale, unfortified stuff that has been accidentally subjected to warmth and air.

Oxidized is a broader term, referring to wine that has been exposed to the air – or made from grapes that have cooked in the sun. The taste is reminiscent of poor sherry or vinegar – or both.

Sulphur (SO_2/H_2S)

Sulphur dioxide is routinely used as a protection against bacteria that would oxidize (*qv*) a wine. In excess, sulphur dioxide may make you cough or sneeze. Worse, though, is hydrogen sulphide and mercaptans, its associated sulphur compounds, which are created when sulphur dioxide combines with wine. Wines with hydrogen sulphide smell of rotten eggs, while mercaptans may reek of rancid garlic or burning rubber. Aeration or popping a copper coin in your glass may clear up these characteristics.

Vinegary/Volatile

Volatile acidity is present in all wines. In excess, however – usually the result of careless winemaking – what can be a pleasant component (like a touch of balsamic vinegar in a sauce) tastes downright vinegary.

Reading the Label

INTRODUCTION

Labels are an essential part of the business of wine nowadays, but even a century ago they barely existed. Wine was sold by the barrel and served by the jug or decanter. Indeed, the original "labels" were silver tags that hung on a chain around the neck of a decanter and were engraved with the word "claret", "hock", "port" or whatever.

Today, printed labels are required to tell you the amount of liquid in the bottle, its strength, where it was made, and the name of the producer or importer. Confusingly, though, labelling rules vary between countries and between regions. Labels may also reveal a wine's style – the grape variety, oakiness, or sweetness, for example. And lastly, they are part of the packaging that helps to persuade you to buy one wine rather than another. The following examples should help you through the maze.

CHAMPAGNE

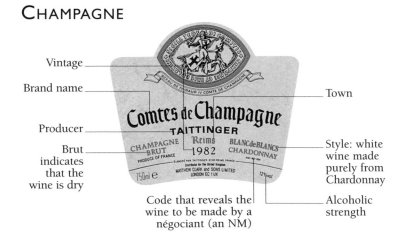

Vintage

Brand name

Producer

Brut indicates that the wine is dry

Town

Style: white wine made purely from Chardonnay

Alcoholic strength

Code that reveals the wine to be made by a négociant (an NM)

WHITES

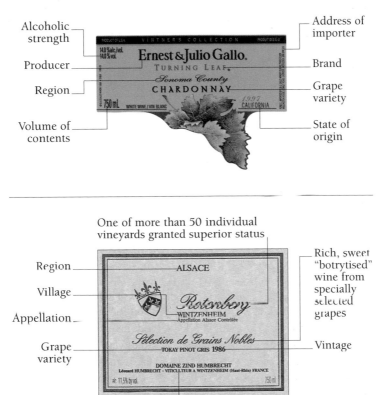

Alcoholic strength

Producer

Region

Volume of contents

Address of importer

Brand

Grape variety

State of origin

One of more than 50 individual vineyards granted superior status

Region

Village

Appellation

Grape variety

Rich, sweet "botrytised" wine from specially selected grapes

Vintage

Producer

Town/ Region

Year firm was founded

Vineyard

Village

Quality level

Region

Producer

Vintage

Grape

Sweetness

Volume of contents

Official identity number

REDS

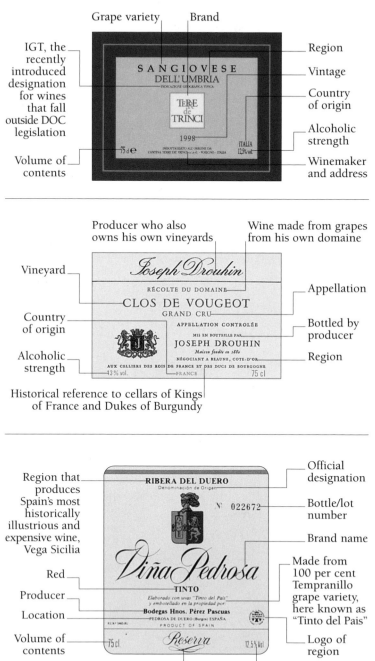

Grape variety Brand

IGT, the recently introduced designation for wines that fall outside DOC legislation

Region

Vintage

Country of origin

Alcoholic strength

Winemaker and address

Volume of contents

S A N G I O V E S E
DELL'UMBRIA
INDICAZIONE GEOGRAFICA TIPICA

TERE
de
TRINCI

1998

ITALIA
12.5% vol.

75 cl e

IMBOTTIGLIATO ALL' ORIGINE DA
CANTINA TERRE DEL TRINCI s.c.a.r.l. - FOLIGNO - ITALIA

Producer who also owns his own vineyards

Wine made from grapes from his own domaine

Vineyard

Country of origin

Alcoholic strength

Joseph Drouhin

RÉCOLTE DU DOMAINE
CLOS DE VOUGEOT
GRAND CRU

APPELLATION CONTROLÉE

MIS EN BOUTEILLE PAR
JOSEPH DROUHIN
Maison fondée en 1880
NÉGOCIANT A BEAUNE, COTE-D'OR
AUX CELLIERS DES ROIS DE FRANCE ET DES DUCS DE BOURGOGNE
13 % vol.
FRANCE
75 cl

Appellation

Bottled by producer

Region

Historical reference to cellars of Kings of France and Dukes of Burgundy

---

Region that produces Spain's most historically illustrious and expensive wine, Vega Sicilia

Red

Producer

Location

Volume of contents

RIBERA DEL DUERO
Denominación de Origen

N.º 022672

Viña Pedrosa
TINTO
Elaborado con uvas "Tinto del Pais"
y embotellado en la propiedad por:
Bodegas Hnos. Pérez Pascuas
PEDROSA DE DUERO (Burgos) ESPAÑA
PRODUCT OF SPAIN

75 cl

Reserva

12.5% Vol

Official designation

Bottle/lot number

Brand name

Made from 100 per cent Tempranillo grape variety, here known as "Tinto del Pais"

Logo of region

Red wine with a minimum of two years in barrel

Alcoholic strength

Sweet and Fortified

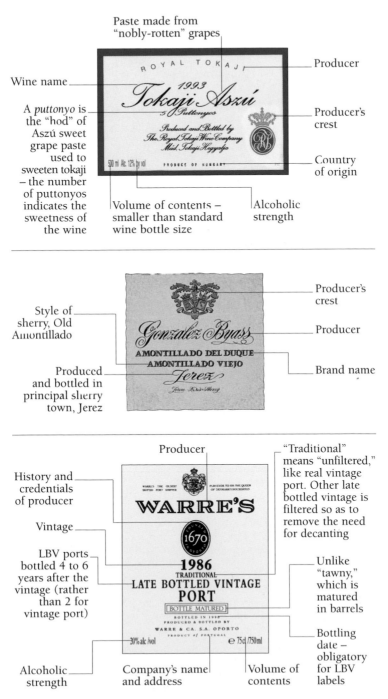

Paste made from "nobly-rotten" grapes

Producer

Wine name

A *puttonyo* is the "hod" of Aszú sweet grape paste used to sweeten tokaji – the number of puttonyos indicates the sweetness of the wine

Producer's crest

Country of origin

Volume of contents – smaller than standard wine bottle size

Alcoholic strength

Style of sherry, Old Amontillado

Produced and bottled in principal sherry town, Jerez

Producer's crest

Producer

Brand name

Producer

History and credentials of producer

Vintage

LBV ports bottled 4 to 6 years after the vintage (rather than 2 for vintage port)

Alcoholic strength

Company's name and address

Volume of contents

"Traditional" means "unfiltered," like real vintage port. Other late bottled vintage is filtered so as to remove the need for decanting

Unlike "tawny," which is matured in barrels

Bottling date – obligatory for LBV labels

Countries

WHERE IN THE WORLD?

Whatever the grape variety, climate, and traditions, the local tastes of the place where a wine is made still largely dictate its style. Let's take a whirlwind tour of the most significant winemaking nations. (For more information on grapes, terms, and regions, see the A–Z, starting on page 97.)

AUSTRALIA

> **Reading the label:** Late harvest/noble harvest – *sweet.* Show Reserve – *top-of-the-line wine, usually with more oak.* Tokay – *Australian name for the Muscadelle grape, used for rich liqueur wines.* Verdelho – *Madeira grape used for limy, dry wines.* Mataro – *Mourvèdre.* Shiraz – *Syrah.* Tarrango – *local success story – fresh, fruity, and Beaujolais-like.*

Over the last 12 months, Australian winemakers have been gratified to see their wines competing neck and neck with those of France for the biggest share of the British wine market. Quite an achievement for a country whose viticultural efforts were once the butt of a memorable Monty Python sketch – but maybe not very surprising, given the Aussies' 25-year master plan to dominate the global market for premium wine.

There are various explanations for Australia's success. The combination of cooperation, competitiveness and open-mindedness of its producers has been crucial. Where else would almost a complete region like the Clare Valley decide, for quality reasons, to switch from natural corks to screw-caps in a single vintage? (*See News*). Just as important has been the readiness to explore and exploit new regions – areas like the Barossa and Hunter valleys have now been joined by Orange, Robe, Mount Benson, Young and Pemberton – and styles – such as Semillon-Chardonnay and Cabernet-Shiraz blends. A more controversial factor has to be the dynamism and power of a quartet of giant companies – BRL Hardy,

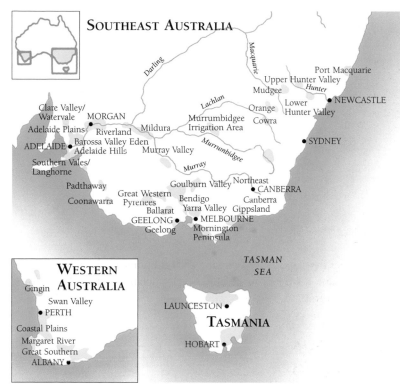

Mildara Blass, Orlando and Southcorp that collectively control over 75 per cent of the country's wines and approach winemaking in a way that is very reminiscent of the Japanese motor industry.

AUSTRIA

Reading the label: Ausbruch – *late-harvested, between Beerenauslese and Trockenbeerenauslese.* Erzeugerabfüllung – *estate bottled.* Morillon – *Chardonnay.* Schilfwein – *made from grapes dried on mats.*

The source of wonderful late harvest wines, dry whites (especially Grüner-Veltliner), and increasingly impressive reds (St Laurent). Names to look out for include Kracher and Willi Opitz.

CANADA

Reading the label: VQA (Vintners Quality Alliance) – *local designation seeking to guarantee quality and local provenance.*

Icewines, made from grapes picked when frozen on the vine, are the stars here, though Chardonnays and Cabernet Francs are improving fast. Okanagan in British Columbia seems to be the region to watch.

Eastern Europe

After a bright start in the 1980's, the Eastern European wine industry is now coming to terms with life under capitalism surprisingly slowly.

Bulgaria

The pioneer of good Iron Curtain reds, Bulgaria remains a source of inexpensive Cabernet Sauvignon and Merlot, as well as the earthy local Mavrud. Efforts to produce premium wines have yet to pay off.

Hungary

Still best known for its red Bull's Blood, Hungary's strongest hand today lies in the Tokajis, the best of which are being made by foreign investors. Reds are improving, as are affordable Sauvignons and Chardonnays.

Romania, Moldova, and Former Yugoslavia

Still struggling to make their mark beyond their own borders with better than basic fare. Romania has inexpensive Pinot Noir, Moldova produces aromatic white and Croatia can offer interesting reds from local varieties.

England and Wales

Despite an unhelpful climate and government, the vineyards of England and Wales are using recently developed German grape varieties to make Loire-style whites; high-quality late harvest wines; quirky reds produced under plastic poly-tunnels; and – most particularly – sparkling wines that win well-earned medals at the International Wine Challenge.

France

Reading the label: Appellation Contrôlée (or AOC) – *designation covering France's (supposedly) better wines.* Blanc de Blancs/Noirs – *white wine made from white/black grapes.* Cave – *cellar.* Cave des Vignerons de – *usually a cooperative.* Cépage – *grape variety.* Château – *wine estate.* Chêne – *oak barrels, as in* Fûts de Chêne. Clos – *(historically) walled vineyard.* Côte(s)/Coteaux – *hillside.* Crémant – *sparkling.* Cuvée – *a specific blend.* Demi-sec – *medium sweet.* Domaine – *wine estate.* Doux – *sweet.* Grand Cru – *higher quality, or specific vineyards.* Gris – *pale rosé, as in* Vin Gris. Jeunes Vignes – *young vines (often ineligible for* Appellation Contrôlée). Méthode Classique – *used to indicate the Champagne method of making sparkling wine.* Millésime – *year or vintage.* Mis en Bouteille au Château/Domaine – *bottled at the estate.* Moelleux – *sweet.* Monopole – *a vineyard owned by a single producer.* Mousseux – *sparkling.* Négociant (Eleveur) – *a merchant who buys, matures, bottles, and sells wine.*

Pétillant – *lightly sparkling*. Premier Cru – *"first growth", a quality designation that varies from area to area*. Propriétaire (Récoltant) – *vineyard owner/manager*. Réserve (Personelle) – *legally meaningless phrase*. Sur Lie – *aged on the lees (dead yeast)*. VDQS (Vin Délimité de Qualité Supérieur) – *"soon-to-be-abolished" official designation for wines that are better than* Vin de Pays *but not good enough for* Appellation Contrôlée. Vieilles Vignes – *old vines (could be any age from 20–80 years), should indicate higher quality*. Villages – *supposedly best part of a larger region, as in* Beaujolais Villages. Vin de Pays – *wine with regional character*. Vin de Table – *basic table wine*.

Still the benchmark, or set of benchmarks, against which winemakers in other countries test themselves. This is the place to find the Chardonnay in its finest oaked (white Burgundy) and unoaked (traditional Chablis) styles; the Sauvignon (from Sancerre and Pouilly Fumé in the Loire, and in blends with the Sémillon in Bordeaux); the Cabernet Sauvignon and Merlot (red Bordeaux); the Pinot Noir (red Burgundy and Champagne);

the Riesling, Gewurztraminer, and Pinots Blanc and Gris (Alsace). The Chenin Blanc still fares better in the Loire than anywhere else, and despite their successes in Australia, the Syrah (aka Shiraz) and Grenache are still at their finest in the Rhône.

France is handicapped by the unpredictability of the climate in most of its best regions and by the unreliability of winemakers, too many of whom are still happy to coast along on the reputation of their region and on *Appellation Contrôlée* laws that allow them to get away with selling poor quality wine.

Alsace

Reading the label: Sélection de Grains Nobles – *Sweet wine from noble rot-affected grapes.* Vendange Tardive – *late harvested.* Edelzwicker – *blend of white grapes, usually Pinot Blanc and Sylvaner.*

Often underrated, and confused with German wines from the other side of the Rhine, Alsace deserves to be more popular. Its odd assortment of grapes make wonderfully rich, spicy, dry, off-dry and late harvest styles. There is also sparkling wine and a little red Pinot Noir. This is my bet to follow the success of its spicy red counterparts in the Rhône.

Bordeaux

Reading the label: Chai – *cellar.* Cru Bourgeois – *level beneath* Cru Classé, *but possibly of similar quality.* Cru Classé – *"Classed Growth", a wine featured in the 1855 classification of the Médoc and Graves, provides no guarantee of current quality.* Grand Cru/Grand Cru Classé – *confusing terms, especially in St. Emilion, where the former is allocated annually on the basis of a sometimes less-than-arduous tasting, while the latter is reassessed every decade.*

For all but the most avid wine buff, Bordeaux is one big region (producing almost as much wine as Australia) with a few dozen châteaux that have become internationally famous for their wine.

Visit the region, or take a look at the map, however, and you will find that this is essentially a collection of quite diverse sub-regions, many of which are separated by farmland, forest or water.

Heading north from the city of Bordeaux, the Médoc is the region that includes the great communes of St. Estèphe, Pauillac, St. Julien and Margaux, where some of the finest red wines are made. The largely gravel soil suits the Cabernet Sauvignon, though lesser Médoc wines, of which there are more than enough, tend to have a higher proportion of the Merlot. For the best examples of wines made principally from this variety, though, you have to head eastward

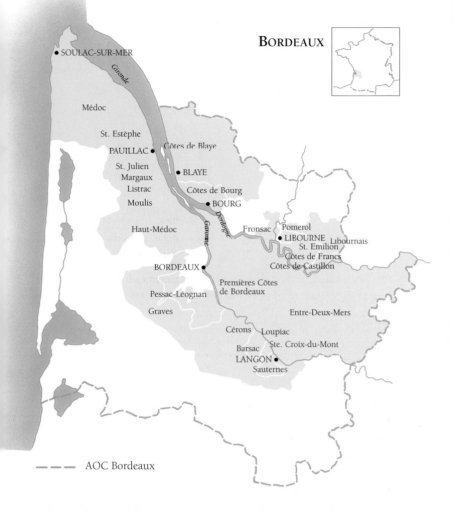

BORDEAUX

SOULAC-SUR-MER

Gironde

Médoc

St. Estèphe

PAUILLAC

Côtes de Blaye

St. Julien
Margaux
Listrac
Moulis

BLAYE

Côtes de Bourg

BOURG

Haut-Médoc

Garonne

Dordogne

Fronsac

Pomerol

LIBOURNE

Libournais

St. Emilion

Côtes de Francs

Côtes de Castillon

BORDEAUX

Premières Côtes
de Bordeaux

Pessac-Léognan

Graves

Entre-Deux-Mers

Cérons

Loupiac

Barsac

Ste. Croix-du-Mont

LANGON

Sauternes

– – – – AOC Bordeaux

to St. Emilion and Pomerol, Fronsac and the Côtes de Castillon, and
to the regions of Bourg and Blaye where the Merlot is usually blended
with the Cabernet Franc.

To the south of Bordeaux lie Pessac-Léognan and the Graves, which
produce some of Bordeaux's lighter, more delicate reds. This is also dry
white country, where the Sémillon and Sauvignon Blanc hold sway. A
little farther to the southeast, the often misty climate provides the
conditions required for the great sweet whites of Sauternes and Barsac.

Each of these regions produces its own individual style of wine. In
some years, the climate suits one region and/or grape variety more than
others. The year 2000, for example was better for the Médoc than for St.
Emilion. So beware of vintage charts that seek to define the quality of
an entire vintage across the whole of Bordeaux.

BURGUNDY

Chablis
AUXERRE ●
Sauvignon de St.-Bris
Irancy

Serein
Armançon
Seine

DIJON ●
Côte de Nuits
Gevrey-Chambertin
Côte d'Or
Vosne-Romanée Clos de Vougeot
Nuits-St. Georges
Volnay   ● BEAUNE
Côte de Beaune
Pommard   Meursault
Puligny-Montrachet
● CHALON-SUR-SAONE

Côte Chalonnaise

Mâconnais

● MACON
Juliénas
Chénas   St. Amour
Fleurie
Morgon
Moulin-à-Vent   Beaujolais
● VILLEFRANCHE-SUR-SAONE

▬ ▬ ▬ AOC Burgundy

Coteaux du
Lyonnais   ● LYON

Saône

Burgundy

Reading the label: Hospices de Beaune – *wines made and sold at auction by the charitable* Hospices de Beaune. Passetoutgrains – *a blend of Gamay and Pinot Noir.* Tasteviné – *a special label for wines that have passed a tasting by the* Confrérie des Chevaliers de Tastevin.

The heartland of the Pinot Noir and the Chardonnay and Chablis, Nuits-St.-Georges, Gevrey-Chambertin, Beaune, Meursault, Puligny-Montrachet, Mâcon Villages, Pouilly-Fuissé and Beaujolais. The best wines theoretically come from the Grands Crus vineyards; next are the Premiers Crus, followed by plain village wines and, last of all, basic Bourgogne Rouge or Blanc.

The region's individual producers make their wines with varying luck and expertise, generally selling in bulk to merchants who are just as variable in their skills and honesty. So, one producer's supposedly humble wine can be finer than another's pricier Premier or Grand Cru.

Champagne

Reading the label: Blanc de Blancs – *white wine from white grapes, i.e., pure Chardonnay.* Blancs de Noirs – *white wine made from black grapes.* Brut Sauvage/Zéro – *bone dry.* Extra-Dry – *(surprisingly) sweeter than Brut.* Grand Cru – *from a top-quality vineyard.* Négociant-manipulant (NM) – *buyer and blender of wines.* Non-vintage – *a blend of wines usually based on wine of a single vintage.* Récoltant manipulant (RM) – *individual estate.*

Top-class Champagne has toasty richness and subtle fruit. Beware of cheap examples, though, and big-name producers who should know better.

Loire

Reading the label: Moelleux – *sweet.* Sur Lie – *on its lees (dead yeast), usually only applied to Muscadet.* Côt – *local name for the Malbec.*

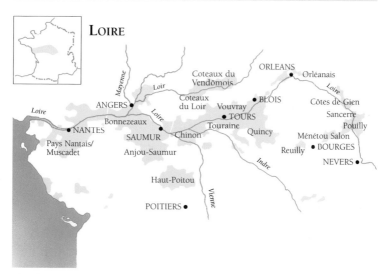

The heartland of fresh, dry Sauvignons and honeyed, sweet Quarts de Chaume, Coteaux de Layon and Bonnezeaux, and dry, sweet and sparkling Vouvray, all of which, like dry Savennières, display the Chenin Blanc at its best. The Chinon and Bourgeuil reds do the same for the Cabernet Franc.

Rhône

Reading the label: Vin Doux Naturel – *fortified wine, such as Muscat de Beaumes de Venise.* Côtes du Rhône Villages – *wine from one of a number of better sited villages in the overall Côtes du Rhône appellation, and thus, supposedly finer wine than plain Côtes du Rhône.*

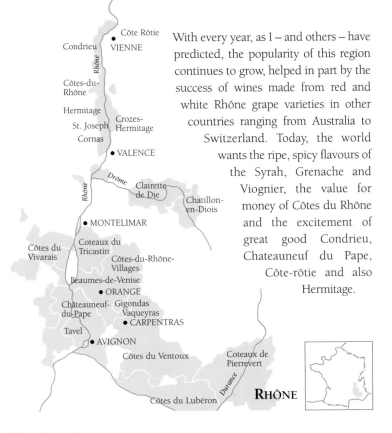

With every year, as I – and others – have predicted, the popularity of this region continues to grow, helped in part by the success of wines made from red and white Rhône grape varieties in other countries ranging from Australia to Switzerland. Today, the world wants the ripe, spicy flavours of the Syrah, Grenache and Viognier, the value for money of Côtes du Rhône and the excitement of great good Condrieu, Chateauneuf du Pape, Côte-rôtie and also Hermitage.

The Southwest

Reading the label: Perlé or Perlant - *gently sparkling, used in Gaillac.*

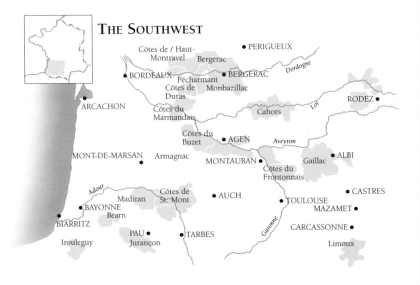

A region producing Bordeaux-like Bergerac, Pécharmant and Buzet, sweet and dry Jurançon, Gaillac, Cahors, and Madiran. Despite their fame among French wine buffs, these were often pretty old-fashioned.

Today, a new wave of winemakers is learning how to extract fruit flavours from grapes like the Gros and Petit Manseng, the Tannat, Mauzac and Malbec. These wines are worth the detour for anyone bored with the ubiquitous Cabernet and Chardonnay and dissatisfied with poor claret.

The South

Reading the label: Vin de Pays d'Oc – *country wine from the Languedoc region. Often some of the best stuff in the region. Rancio – woody, slightly volatile character in Banyuls and other fortified wines that have been aged in the barrel.*

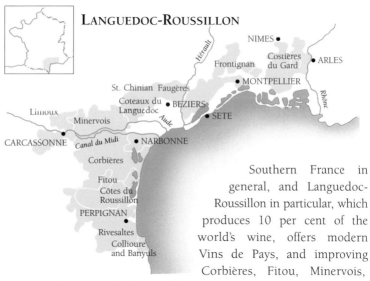

LANGUEDOC-ROUSSILLON

Southern France in general, and Languedoc-Roussillon in particular, which produces 10 per cent of the world's wine, offers modern Vins de Pays, and improving Corbières, Fitou, Minervois, Coteaux de Languedoc (especially Pic St. Loup) and Limoux (where Mouton Rothschild has a new venture). An ideal climate and increasingly dynamic winemaking are raising the quality here and in Provence, where classics such as Cassis and Bandol now attract as much attention as rosé.

Eastern France

Reading the label: Vin de Paille – *sweet, golden wine from grapes dried on straw mats.* Vin Jaune – *sherry-like, slightly oxidized wine.*

Savoie's zingy wines are often only thought of as skiing fare, but, like Arbois' nutty, sherry-style whites, they are characterfully different, and made from grape varieties that are grown nowhere else.

GERMANY

Reading the label: Amtliche Prüfungsnummer (AP number) – *official identification number.* Auslese – *(usually) sweet wine from selected ripe grapes.* Beerenauslese – *luscious wines from selected, riper botrytis-affected grapes (Beeren).* Classic – *new designation for dry wine from a defined region.* Erste Gewächs /Lage– *top vineyard.* Erzeugerabfüllung – *bottled by the grower/estate.* Halbtrocken – *off-dry.* Hock – *British name for Rhine wines.* Kabinett – *wines that fulfill a certain natural ripeness.* Kellerei/Kellerabfüllung – *cellar/producer/estate-bottled.* Landwein – *equivalent of a French Vin de Pays.* QbA (Qualitätswein bestimmter Anbaugebiete) – *basic quality German wine.* QmP (Qualitätswein mit Prädikat) – *there are five ripeness rungs of QmP, rising from Kabinett, via* Spätlese, Auslese, Beerenauslese *to* Trockenbeerenauslese *plus Eiswein.* Schloss – *(literally "castle" or "Château") estate.* Sekt – *basic, sparkling wine.* Selection – *new name for dry wine from a quality site.* Spätlese – *second step in the QmP scale, late harvested grapes,.* Staatsweingut – *state-owned wine estate.* Tafelwein – *table wine, only the prefix "Deutscher" guarantees German origin.* Trocken – *dry.* Trockenbeerenauslese – *wine from selected botrytis-affected grapes.* Weingut – *estate.* Weinkellerei – *cellar or winery.* VDP – *group of quality-conscious producers.*

Led by younger producers like Ernst Loosen and Rainer Lingenfelder and Phillipp Wittmann, a quiet revolution is taking place here. Sugar-watery Liebfraumilch is becoming a thing of the past – as are the aggressively acidic dry wines of the 1980s and early 1990s. Today, expect to find rich dry and fruitily off-dry whites (ideally but not necessarily made from Riesling), classic later harvest styles, and a growing number of good reds (especially Pinot Noir). The Pfalz, Mosel and Baden are regions to watch.

ITALY

Reading the label: Abboccato – *semi-dry*. Amabile – *semi-sweet*. Amaro – *bitter*. Asciutto – *bone dry*. Azienda – *estate*. Classico – *the best vineyards at the heart of a DOC*. Colle/colli – *hills*. DOC(G) Denominazione di Origine Controllata (e Garantita) – *designation, based on grape variety and/or origin*.

Dolce – *sweet*. Frizzante – *semi-sparkling*. IGT, Indicazione Geografica Tipica – *new designation for quality* Vino da Tavola. Imbottigliato nel'origine – *estate-bottled*. Liquoroso – *rich, sweet*. Passito – *raisiny wine made from sundried grapes*. Recioto – *strong, sweet (unless designated Amarone)*. Vino da Tavola – *table wine. Now replaced by IGT for top wines*.

Three facts about Italy: (1) It is more a set of regions than a single country; (2) There is a tradition of interpreting laws fairly liberally; (3) Style is often valued as highly as content. So when it comes to wine, this can be a confusing place. Producers do their own frequently delicious thing, using indigenous and imported grape varieties and designer bottles and labels in ways that leave legislators – and humble wine drinkers – exhilarated and exasperated in equal measure.

NEW ZEALAND

This New World country has one of the most unpredictable climates, but produces some of the most intensely flavoured wines. There are gooseberryish Sauvignon Blancs, Chardonnays, and innovative Rieslings and Gewürztraminers, and impressive Pinot Noirs.

Hawkes Bay seems to be the most consistent region for reds, while Gisborne, Marlborough, Auckland, and Martinborough share the honours for white wine (though the last, like Central Otago, produces classy Pinot Noir).

North Africa

Once the plentiful source of blending wine for French regions such as Burgundy, North Africa's vineyards have been hampered in recent years by Islamic fundamentalism. New investment is, however, now beginning to arrive from Italy and France (including a new venture in Morocco that is partly financed by Gérard Dépardieu).

Portugal

Reading the label: Adega – *winery*. Branco – *white*. Colheita – *vintage*. Engarrafado na origem – *estate-bottled*. Garrafeira – *a vintage-dated wine with a little more alcohol and minimum ageing requirements*. Quinta – *vineyard or estate*. Reserva – *wine from a top-quality vintage, made from riper grapes than the standard requirement*. Velho – *old*. Vinho de Mesa – *table wine*.

The sleeping beauty awakens. After far too long a period of conservative inertia, Portugal is introducing modern winemaking to its cornucopia of grape varieties, most of which are grown nowhere else (the Douro has over 80).

Innovators like Luis Pato, Jose Neiva, J Portugal Ramos, JM da Fonseca and Sogrape, with a little help from Australians Peter Bright and David Baverstock, and the ubiquitous Michel Rolland, are using varieties such as the Touriga Nacional in regions like Estremadura and Alentejo as well as better-known Douro, Dão and Bairrada.

Portugal

SOUTH AFRICA

> **Reading the label:** Cap Classique – *South African term for Champagne method.* Cultivar – *grape variety.* Edel laat-oes – *noble late harvest.* Edelkeur – *"noble rot", a fungus affecting grapes and producing sweet wine.* Gekweek, gemaak en gebottel op – *estate-bottled.* Landgoedwyn – *estate wine.* Laat-oes – *late harvest.* Oesjaar – *vintage.* Steen – *name for Chenin Blanc.*

The fastest improving country in the New World? No longer the source of "green" wines made from over-cropped and underripe grapes grown on virused vines, the Cape is now making terrific lean but ripe Rieslings and Sauvignons and delicious reds made from Cabernet, Merlot and the local Pinotage. Thelema, Boekenhoutskloof, Saxenburg, Plaisir de Merle, Rust en Vrede, Rustenberg, Naledi/Sejana, Zandvliet, Vergelegen, Fairview, Grangehurst, Kanonkop and Vriesenhof are names to watch – as are the up-and-coming regions of Malmesbury and Robertson.

THE CAPE

SOUTH AMERICA

Argentina

Reading the label: Malbec – *spicy red grape.* Torrontes – *grapey white.*

As it chases Chile, this is a country to watch. The wines to look for now are the peppery reds made from the Malbec, a variety once widely grown in Bordeaux and still used in the Loire. Cabernets can be good too, as can the juicy Bonarda and grapey but dry white Torrontes.

Chile

Reading the label: Envasado en Origen – *estate-bottled.* Carmenère/ Grand Vidure – *grape variety once used in Bordeaux.*

One of the most exciting wine-producing countries in the world, thanks to ideal conditions, skilled local winemaking, and plentiful investment. The most successful grapes at present are the Merlot and Cabernet, but the Chardonnay, Pinot Noir, Sauvignon and (the local) Carmenère, can all display ripe fruit and subtlety often absent in the New World.

SOUTHEASTERN EUROPE
Greece
After winning the confidence of a growing number of critics and wine-lovers in Britain, Greece's new wave of wine producers are beginning to make inroads elsewhere, both with "international" grapes and highly characterful indigenous varieties. Prices are high (so is demand in chic Athens restaurants), but worth it from producers like Château Lazaridi, Gentilini, Gaia and Hatzimichali.

Cyprus
Still associated with cheap sherry-substitute and dull wine, but things are changing. Look out for the traditional rich Commandaria.

Turkey
Lurching out of the vinous dark ages, Turkey has yet to offer the world red or white wines that non-Turks are likely to relish.

Lebanon
Once the lone exemplar of Lebanese wines overseas, Château Musar is now joined by the similarly impressive Château Kefraya.

Israel
Israel's best Cabernet and Muscat are produced at the Yarden winery in the Golan Heights – which raises interesting questions as boundaries are drawn and re-drawn in this troubled region.

SPAIN

Reading the label: Abocado – *semi-dry*. Año – *year.* Bodega – *winery or wine cellar.* Cava – *Champagne method wine.* Criado y Embotellado (por) – *grown and bottled (by).* Crianza – *aged in wood.* DO(Ca) Denominacion de Origen (Calificada) – *Spain's quality designation, based on regional style. Calificada (DOC) indicates superior quality.* Elaborado y Anejado Por – *made and aged for.* Gran Reserva – *wine aged for a designated number of years in wood; longer than for Reserva.* Joven – *young wine, specially made for early consumption.* Reserva – *official designation for wine that has been aged for a specific period.* Sin Crianza – *not aged in wood.* Vendemia – *harvest or vintage.* Vino de Mesa – *table wine.* Vino de la Tierra – *designation similar to the French "Vin de Pays".*

As elsewhere, the vinous revolution has arguably been most fruitful in regions that were previously overlooked. So, while traditionalists focused their attention on regions like Rioja, Navarra and Ribera del Duero and

SANTANDER
BILBAO ●
PAMPLONA ●
Navarra
Ampurdán
Costa Brava
Ribeiro Valdeorras Rioja Somontano
Ribera Ebro
del Duero BARCELONA ●
PORTUGAL Duero Cariñana Penedés
(see p41) Duero Terra Alto
Rueda Catalonia
MADRID ● Tajo
Mentrida
Utiel
La Mancha Requena ● VALENCIA
Valdepenas Valencia
Yecla
Jumilla Alicante
CORDOBA
Guadalquivir ●
SEVILLE ● Montilla
Guadalete ● GRANADA
Jerez Málaga
CADIZ ●
SPAIN

early modernists such as Miguel Torres looked to the Penedés, some of the most exciting fireworks have been seen in Galicia (source of lovely, aromatic white Albariño) and Priorat, an area that used to make thick red wine in which a spoon could stand unaided. Now, producers like Alvaro Palacios are making deliciously stylish wines there that sell easily for $100 in New York (but are, perhaps for this very reason, rather harder to find in London).

Elsewhere, Rioja is improving fast (thanks often to the addition of a little Cabernet to the red blend) and increasingly good wines are coming out of Navarra, Somontano, Toro and Rueda. Ribera del Duero offers some great reds (Vega Sicilia, Pesquera and Pingus) but is still home to far too many disappointing but pricy victims of poor winemaking.

SWITZERLAND

Reading the label: Gutedel, Perlan, Fendant – *local names for the Chasselas.* Grand Cru – *top designation which varies from one canton to the next.* Süssdruck – *off-dry, red wine.*

The only place in the world where the Chasselas produces anything even remotely memorable – and the only one sensibly to use screwcaps for many of its wines. Other worthwhile grapes are the white (Petite) Arvigne and Amigne (de Vétroz) and the red Cornalin, as well as the Gamay, Syrah, Pinot Noir, and Merlot, a variety that is used to make white wines here.

USA

Reading the label: Blush – *rosé.* Champagne – *any sparkling wine.* Fumé – *oak-aged white wine, especially Sauvignon (Blanc Fumé).* Meritage – *popular, if pretentious, name for a Bordeaux blend (white or red).* Vinted – *made by (a vintner, or winemaker).* White Grenache/Zinfandel, etc – *refers to the unfashionable rosé, slightly pink wines, sometimes also referred to as "blush".*

California

Despite the threat of an insect-borne disease that could wreck its vineyards (*see News, page 6*), the best-known winemaking state of the Union is still on a roll at the moment. The Napa Valley now faces serious competition from Sonoma (where the giant E&J Gallo is making some serious reds and whites) and southern regions such as Santa Cruz and Santa Barbara. The Merlot grape has now overtaken the Cabernet Sauvignon to become the most widely-planted red wine grape, but there

CALIFORNIA

is a growing trend towards making wines from the Pinot Noir (especially in Carneros and Russian River) and from varieties more traditionally associated with the Rhône and Italy.

Amid all this excitement, however, one problem remains. California may produce some of the very finest wines in the world, but its daily-drinking efforts still offer some remarkably poor value.

The Pacific Northwest

Outside California, head north to Oregon for some of the best Pinot Noirs in the US (at a hefty price) and improving, but rarely earth-shattering, Chardonnays, Rieslings and Pinot Gris. Washington State has some Pinot too, on the cooler, rainy, west side of the Cascade Mountains. On the east, irrigated vineyards produce great Sauvignon and Riesling, as well as top-notch Chardonnay, Cabernet Sauvignon, and impressive Syrah and Merlot

New York and Other States

Once the source of dire "Chablis" and "Champagne", New York State is now producing worthwhile wines, particularly in the micro-climate of Long Island, where the Merlot thrives. The Finger Lakes are patchier but worth visiting, especially for the Rieslings and cool-climate Chardonnays. Elsewhere Virginia, Missouri, Texas, Maryland, and even Arizona are all producing wines to compete with California and indeed some of the best that Europe can offer.

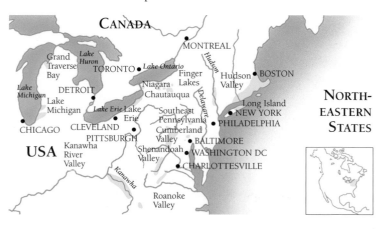

The Grapes

BLENDS OR SINGLE VARIETIES?

Some wines are made from single grape varieties – e.g. red or white Burgundy, Sancerre, German Riesling, most Alsace wines and Barolo – while others, such as red or white Bordeaux, California "Meritage" wines, port, and Châteauneuf-du-Pape, are blends of two or more types of grape. Champagne can fall into either camp, as can New World "varietal" wines, which, though generally labelled as "Chardonnay", "Merlot", "Shiraz", etc., can often – depending on local laws – contain up to 25 per cent of other grape varieties. Blends are not, *per se*, superior to single varietals – or vice versa.

WHITE WINE GRAPES

CHARDONNAY

The world's most popular and widely planted premium white grape variety, and the one whose name has become almost a synonym for dry white wine, is surprisingly hard to define. The flavour of any example will depend enormously on the climate, soil and the particular type of clone. Burgundy, and the best California examples (Kistler, Peter Michael, Sonoma Cutrer), taste of butter and hazelnuts; lesser New World efforts are often sweet and simple and often very melony (a flavour which comes from the clone). Australians range from subtle buttery pineapple to oaky tropical fruit juice. Petaluma, Giaconda, Coldstream Hills and Leeuwin show how it can be done. New Zealand's efforts are tropical too, but lighter and fresher (Te Mata, Cloudy Bay).

Elsewhere, Chile is beginning to hit the mark, as is South Africa (Jordan). In Europe, look around southern France (James Herrick), Italy (Gaja), Spain and Eastern Europe, but beware of watery cheaper versions.

CHENIN BLANC

Loire variety with naturally high acidity that makes it ideal for fresh sparkling, dry, and luscious honeyed wines; also raw stuff like unripe apples and, when over-sulphured, old socks. Most California Chenins are semisweet and ordinary. South Africans call it the Steen and use it for cheap dry and luscious sweet wines. There are few good Australians (but try Moondah Brook) or New Zealanders (try Millton).

GEWÜRZTRAMINER

Outrageous, oily-textured stuff that smells of parma violets and tastes of lychee fruit. At its best in Alsace (Zind Humbrecht, Schlumberger, Faller), where identically labelled bottles can vary greatly in their level of sweetness. Wines that guarantee luscious sweetness will be labelled as either *Vendange Tardive* or – the intensely sweet – *Sélection de Grains Nobles*. Try examples from Germany, Chile, New Zealand, and Italy too.

MARSANNE

A classic, flowery, lemony variety used in the Rhône in wines like Hermitage (from producers like Guigal); in Australia – especially in Goulburn in Victoria (Chateau Tahbilk and Mitchelton); in southern France (from Mas de Daumas Gassac); in Switzerland (late harvest efforts from Provins); and in innovative wines from California. At its best young or after five or six years.

MUSCAT

The only variety whose wines actually taste as though they are made of grapes, rather than some other kind of fruit or vegetable. In Alsace, southern France and northeast Italy it is used to make dry wines. Generally, though, it performs best as sparkling wine (Moscatos and Asti Spumantes from Italy, and Clairette de Die Tradition from France) and as sweet fortified wine. Look out for Beaumes de Venise and Rivesaltes in southern France, Moscatel de Setúbal in Portugal, Moscatel de Valencia in Spain and Liqueur Muscat in Australia (Morris, Chambers, Yalumba).

PINOT BLANC/PINOT BIANCO

As rich as Chardonnay, but with less fruit. At its worst – when over-cropped – it makes neutral wine. At its best, however (also in Alsace), it can develop a lovely cashew-nut flavour. When well handled it can also do well in Italy, where it is known as Pinot Bianco (Jermann), and in Germany (especially in Baden), where it is called Weissburgunder.

PINOT GRIS/PINOT GRIGIO

An up-and-coming Alsace variety also known as Tokay but unrelated to any other Tokay. Wines can be spicy, and sweet or dry. The perfumed, aromatic qualities are associated with later-harvest examples. In Italy it is called Pinot Grigio, and in Germany, Grauerburgunder. Look for examples from Oregon (Eyrie), California and New Zealand.

RIESLING

The king of white grapes. Misunderstood – and often mispronounced as Rice-ling rather than Rees-ling – it is often mistaken for cheap German wine made from quite different grapes. At its best, it makes dry and sweet, grapey, appley, limey wines that develop a spicy, gasoline character with age. Quality and character depend on soil – ideally slate – more than climate, and while the best examples come from Germany, in the Mosel (Maximin Grünhaus) and Rhine (Schloss Johannisberg), and Alsace (Zind-Humbrecht, Faller), this variety can perform well in such different environments as Washington State, Australia (Grossett, Tim Adams), and New Zealand (Matua Valley). Not to be confused with unrelated varieties such as Lazki, Lutomer, Welsch, Emerald or White Riesling.

SAUVIGNON BLANC

The grape of Loire wines, such as Sancerre and Pouilly Fumé, and white Bordeaux, where it is often blended with Sémillon. This gooseberryish variety performs wonderfully in Marlborough in New Zealand (where

Muscat

Sauvignon Blanc

the flavours can include asparagus and pea-pods), in South Africa (Thelema), and in Australia (Shaw & Smith, Cullen). Chile has good examples (from Casablanca) and Washington State can get it right, as can California (Cakebread, Frog's Leap), but many examples are sweet or overburdened by oak. Oaked US versions, wherever they are produced, are usually labelled Fumé Blanc, a term first coined by Robert Mondavi. Only the best of these improve after the first couple of years.

SÉMILLON

In Bordeaux – in blends with the Sauvignon – this produces sublime dry Graves and sweet Sauternes. In Australia there are great, long-lived dry pure (often unoaked) Sémillons from the Hunter Valley and (more usually oaked) Barossa Valley. Good "noble" late harvest examples have also been produced (by de Bortoli) in Riverina. Elsewhere in Australia the grape is sometimes blended with the Chardonnay. Progress is being made in Washington State and South Africa (Boekenhoutskloof), but most examples from California, New Zealand and Chile are disappointing.

VIOGNIER

A cult grape, the Viognier was once only found in Condrieu and Château Grillet in the Rhône, where small numbers of good examples showed off its extraordinary perfumed, peach-blossomy character, albeit at a high price. Today, however, it has been widely introduced to the Ardèche, Languedoc-Roussillon, and California (where it is sometimes confused with the Roussanne), and made with loving care (and often over-generous exposure to oak barrels) in Eastern Europe, Argentina, and particularly Australia (where Yalumba makes several good examples).

While examples of affordable Viognier are welcome, most lower-priced efforts are disappointing because this is a variety that performs poorly when asked to produce too much wine per acre. Clones of this grape vary widely too. Buy with care.

Sémillon   *Viognier*

RED WINE GRAPES

BARBERA

A widely planted, wild-berryish Italian variety at its best in Piedmont, where it is increasingly successful in blends with the Nebbiolo and Cabernet (look out for Elio Altare, Bava and Roberto Voerzio). Good in Argentina; making inroads into California and Australia (Brown Bros).

CABERNET SAUVIGNON

A remarkable success, associated with the great red wines of the Médoc and Graves (in blends with the Merlot), and the best reds from the New World, especially California, Chile and Australia. Eastern Europe has good value examples (Bulgaria), as does southern France (Vin de Pays). Spain is rapidly climbing aboard (in the Penedès, Navarra and – though this is kept quiet – Rioja). The hallmark to look for is blackcurrant, though unripe versions taste like a blend of weeds and bell peppers. There are some great Cabernets in Italy, too. Good New World Cabernets can smell and taste of fresh mint but, with time, like the best Bordeaux, they develop a rich, leathery "cigar box" character.

GRENACHE/GARNACHA

Freshly ground black pepper is the distinguishing flavour here, sometimes with the fruity tang of sweets. At home in Côtes du Rhône and Châteauneuf-du-Pape, it is also used in Spain (as the Garnacha) in blends with the Tempranillo. There are good "Bush" examples from Australia.

MALBEC

Another refugee from Bordeaux, this lightly peppery variety is used in southwest France (for Cahors), the Loire, and Italy, where it generally produces dull stuff. It shines, however, in Argentina (Zuccardi, Catena) and is finding a new home in Chile and Australia.

Cabernet Sauvignon   *Malbec*

MERLOT

The most widely planted variety in Bordeaux and the subject of (enthusiastic over-) planting in California. In Bordeaux where, in some vintages it performs better than Cabernet Sauvignon, it is at its best in Pomerol, where wines can taste of ripe plums and spice, and in St. Emilion, where the least successful wines show the Merlot's less lovable dull and earthy character. Wherever it is made, the naturally thin-skinned Merlot should produce softer, less tannic wines than the Cabernet Sauvignon (though some California examples seem to contradict this rule).

NEBBIOLO/SPANNA

The red wine grape of Barolo and Barbaresco in Piedmont now, thanks to modern winemaking, increasingly reveals a lovely cherry and rose-petal character, often with the sweet vanilla of new oak casks. Lesser examples for earlier drinking tend to be labelled as Spanna.

PINOT NOIR

The wild-raspberryish, plummy and liquoricey grape of red Burgundy is also a major component of white and pink Champagne. It makes red and pink Sancerre, as well as light reds in Alsace and Germany (where it is called Spätburgunder). Italy makes a few good examples, but for the best modern efforts look to California, Oregon, Australia, Chile, South Africa and, especially, New Zealand (Martinborough, Felton Road).

PINOTAGE

Almost restricted to South Africa, this cross between the Pinot Noir and the Cinsaut can, in the right hands, make berryish young wines that may develop rich gamey-spicy flavours. Poorer examples can be dull and "muddy"-tasting. Try Kanonkop, Grangehurst, and Vriesenhof.

Nebbiolo   *Pinot Noir*

SANGIOVESE

The grape of Chianti, Brunello di Montalcino, and of a host of popular IGT wines in Italy, not to mention "new wave" Italian-style wines in California and Argentina. The recognizable flavour is of sweet tobacco, wild herbs and berries.

SYRAH/SHIRAZ

The spicy, brambly grape of the Northern Rhône (Hermitage, Cornas, etc.) and the best reds of Australia (Henschke Hill of Grace and Penfolds Grange), where it is also blended with the Cabernet Sauvignon (just as it once was in Bordeaux). Marqués de Griñon has a great Spanish example, and Isole e Olena has made an unofficial one in Tuscany. Increasingly successful in California and Washington State and, finally, in South Africa. Surprisingly good, too, in both Switzerland and New Zealand.

TEMPRANILLO

Known under all kinds of names around Spain, including Cencibel (in Navarra) and Tinto del Pais (in Ribeira del Duero) and Tinta Roriz in Portugal, the grape gives Spanish reds their recognizable strawberry character. Often blended with the Garnacha, it works well with the Cabernet Sauvignon. So far, little used in the New World, but watch out for examples from Argentina and Australia.

ZINFANDEL

Until recently thought of as California's "own" variety, but now proved (by DNA tests) to be the same variety as the Primitivo in southern Italy. In California it makes rich, spicy, blueberryish reds (see Turley and Ridge Vineyards), "ports", and (often with a little help from sweet Muscat), sweet pink "White Zinfandel". Outside California, Cape Mentelle makes a good example in Western Australia.

Syrah　　　　　　　　　*Zinfandel*

OTHER GRAPES

WHITE

Albariño/Alvarinho Floral. Grown in Spain (delicious examples from Rias Baixas in Galicia) and Portugal, where it is used for Vinho Verde.

Aligoté Lean Burgundy grape, well used by Leroy.

Arneis Perfumed variety in Piedmont.

Bouvier Dull variety, used for late harvest wines in Austria.

Colombard Appley, basic; grown in S.W. France, US and Australia.

Furmint Limey variety, traditionally used for Tokaji.

Grüner Veltliner Limey. Restricted to Eastern Europe and Austria.

Kerner Dull German grape. Can taste leafy.

Müller-Thurgau/Rivaner Occasionally impressive; grown in Germany and England.

Roussanne Fascinating Rhône variety that deserves more attention.

Scheurebe/Samling Grapefruity grape grown in Germany and Austria

Silvaner/Sylvaner Earthy, non-aromatic variety of Alsace and Germany.

Torrontes Grapey, Muscat-like variety of Argentina.

Ugni Blanc/Trebbiano Basic grape of S.W. France and Italy.

Verdelho Limey grape found in Madeira and Australian table wine.

Viura Widely planted, so-so Spanish variety.

Welschriesling Basic. Best in late harvest Austrians. Like Lutomer and Laszki and Italico "Riesling"s, not related to the genuine Riesling.

RED

Bonarda Used in Argentina for juicy light wines.

Cabernet Franc Kid brother of Cabernet Sauvignon, grown alongside it in Bordeaux and by itself in the Loire and Italy.

Carmenère/Grand Vidure Peppery variety making waves in Chile.

Cinsaut/Cinsault Spicy Rhône variety; best in blends.

Carignan Toffeeish non-aromatic variety widely used in S. France.

Dolcetto Cherryish Piedmont grape. Drink young.

Dornfelder Successful, juicy variety grown in Germany.

Gamay The Beaujolais grape; less successful in the Loire and Gaillac.

Gamay Beaujolais/Valdiguié Pinot Noir cousin, unrelated to Gamay.

Mourvèdre (Mataro) Spicy Rhône grape; good in California and Australia, but can be hard and "metallic".

Petit Verdot Spicy ingredient of Bordeaux. Now being used on its own.

Petite-Sirah Spicy; thrives in California and Mexico. Durif in Australia.

Ruby Cabernet Basic Carignan-Cabernet Sauvignon cross.

Tannat Tough variety of Madiran. Better in Uruguay.

Touriga Nacional Plummy variety used for port and Portuguese wine.

Styles

STYLE COUNCIL

Wine can be separated into easily recognizable styles: red, white, and pink; still and sparkling; sweet and dry; light and fortified. To say that a wine is red and dry says little, however, about the way it tastes. It could be a tough young Bordeaux, a mature Rioja, or a blueberryish Zinfandel.

Knowing the grape and origin of a wine can give a clearer idea of what it is like, but it won't tell you everything. The human touch is as important in wine as it is in the kitchen. Winemakers vary as much as chefs. Some focus on obvious fruit flavours, while others – in France for example – go for the *goût de terroir* – the character of the vineyard.

In a world that is increasingly given to instant sensations, it is perhaps unsurprising that it is the fruit-lovers rather than the friends of the earthy flavour who are currently in the ascendant.

NEW WORLD/OLD WORLD

Until recently, these two philosophies broadly belonged to the New and Old Worlds. Places like California and Australia made wine that was approachably delicious when compared with the more serious wine being produced in Europe, which demanded time and food. Today however, there are Bordeaux châteaux with a New World approach and South Africans who take a pride in making wine as resolutely tough and old-fashioned as a Bordeaux of a hundred years ago.

Flying Winemakers and Consultants

These changes owe much to the "flying winemakers" – mostly Australians – and consultants – such as Michel Rolland – who help to produce wine all over the world. Today, you can choose between a Chilean white made by a Frenchman – or a claret bearing the fruity fingerprint of a winemaker who learned his craft in the Barossa Valley.

Fruit of Knowledge

European old timers like to claim that the Australians use alchemy to obtain those fruity flavours. In fact, their secret lies in the winemaking process. Picking the grapes when they are ripe (rather than too early); preventing them from cooking beneath the midday sun (as often happens in Europe while work stops for lunch); pumping the juice through pipes that have been cleaned daily rather than at the end of the harvest; fermenting at a cool temperature (overheated vats can cost a wine its freshness); and storing and bottling it carefully will all help a wine made from even the dullest grape variety to taste fruitier.

COME HITHER

If the New Worlders want their wines to taste of fruit, they are – apart from some reactionary South Africans and Californians – just as eager to make wine that can be drunk young. They take care not to squeeze the red grapes too hard, so as not to extract bitter, hard tannins, and they try to avoid their white wines being too acidic.

Traditionalists claim these wines do not age well. It is too early to say whether this is true, but there is no question that the newer wave red Bordeaux of, say 1985, have given more people more pleasure since they were released than the supposedly greater 1970 vintage, whose wines often remained dauntingly hard throughout their lifetime. A wine does not have to be undrinkable in its youth to be good later on; indeed, wines that start out tasting unbalanced go on tasting that way.

ROLL OUT THE BARREL

Another thing that sets many new wave wines apart has nothing to do with grapes. Wines have been matured in oak barrels since Roman times, but traditionally new barrels were only bought to replace ones that were worn out and had begun to fall apart. Old casks have little flavour, but for the first two years or so of their lives, the way the staves are bent over flames gives new ones a recognizable vanilla and caramel character.

Winemakers once used to rinse out their new casks with dilute ammonia to remove this flavour. Today, however, they are more likely to devote almost as much effort to the choice of forest, cooper and charring (light, medium, or heavy "toast") as to the quality of their grapes. Winemakers who want to impress their critics take pride in using 100 per cent new oak to ferment and mature their wine. Or more. Some pricey, limited-production red Bordeaux actually goes through two sets of new oak barrels to ensure that it gets enough rich vanilla flavour.

Oak-mania began when Bordeaux châteaux began to spend the income from the great vintages of the 1940s on replacements for their old barrels – and when New World pioneers like Mondavi noticed the contribution the oak was making to these wines. Ever since, producers internationally have introduced new barrels, while even the makers of cheaper wine have found that dunking giant "teabags" filled with small oak chips into wine vats could add some of that vanilla flavour too.

If you like oak, you'll find it in top-notch Bordeaux and Burgundy (red and white), Spanish *Crianza, Reserva,* or *Gran Reserva*, and Italians whose labels use the French term *"Barrique."* The words *"Elévé en fût de Chêne"* on a French wine could confusingly refer to new or old casks. Australian "Show Reserve" will be oaky, as will Fumé Blanc and "Barrel Select" wines.

RED WINES – FRUITS, SPICE, AND... COLD TEA

If you enjoy your red wines soft and juicily fruity, the styles to look for are Beaujolais; Burgundy and other wines made from the Pinot Noir; youthful Côtes du Rhône; Rioja, and reds from Spain; inexpensive Australians; young Pomerol and St. Emilion from Bordeaux; and Merlots from almost anywhere. Look too for Barbera and Dolcetto from Italy, and Nouveau, Novello and Joven (young wines).

The Kitchen Cupboard

Italy's Sangiovese is not so much fruity as herby, while the Syrah/Shiraz of the Rhône and Australia, the peppery Grenache and – sometimes – the Zinfandel and Pinotage can all be surprisingly spicy.

Some Like it Tough

Most basic Bordeaux, and all but a few wines from St. Estèphe and Listrac in Bordeaux, are more tannic, as are most older-style wines from Piedmont, California, and most traditional South African Cabernets and Pinotages. The Cabernet Sauvignon will almost always make tougher wines than the Merlot or Pinot Noir.

WHITE WINES – HONEY AND LEMON

If dry wines with unashamedly fruity flavours are what you want, try the Muscat, the Torrontes in Argentina, basic Riesling and Chardonnay, and New World and Southern French Sauvignon Blanc.

Non-Fruit

For more neutral styles, go for Italian Soave, Pinot Bianco, or Frascati; Grenache Blanc; Muscadet; German or Alsace Silvaner; and most traditional wines from Spain and Southern France.

Riches Galore

The combination of richness and fruit is to be found in white Burgundy; better dry white Bordeaux; and in Chardonnays, Semillons, and oaked Sauvignon (Fumé) wines from the New World.

Aromatherapy

Some perfumed, spicy grapes, like the Gewürztraminer, are frankly aromatic. Also try late-harvest Tokay-Pinot Gris – also from Alsace. Other aromatic varieties include Viognier, Arneis, Albariño, Scheurebe and Grüner Veltliner.

Middle of the Road

Today, people want wine that is – or says it is – either dry or positively sweet. The Loire can get honeyed *demi-sec* – semi-sweet – wine right. Otherwise, head for Germany and Kabinett and Spätlese wines.

Pure Hedonism

Sweet wine is making a comeback at last. The places to look for good examples are Bordeaux, the Loire (Moelleux), Alsace (Vendange Tardive or Sélection des Grains Nobles), Germany (Auslese, Beerenauslese, Trockenbeerenauslese), Austria (Ausbruch), the New World (late harvest and noble late harvest) and Hungary (Tokaji 6 Puttonyos).

All of these wines should have enough fresh acidity to prevent them from being cloying. Also, they should have the characteristic dried-apricot flavour that comes from grapes that have been allowed to be affected by a benevolent fungus known as "botrytis" or "noble rot".

Other sweet wines such as Muscat de Beaumes de Venise are fortified with brandy to raise their strength to 15% or so. These wines can be luscious too, but they never have the flavour of "noble rot".

PINK

Tread carefully. Provence and the Rhône should offer peppery-dry rosé, just as the Loire and Bordeaux should have wines that taste deliciously of blackcurrant. Sadly, many taste dull and stale. Still, they are a better bet than California's dire sweet "white" or "blush" rosé. Look for the most recent vintage and the most vibrant colour.

SPARKLING

If you find Champagne too dry, but don't want a frankly sweet grapey fizz like Asti, try a fruity New World sparkling wine from California or Australia. If you don't like that fruitiness, try traditional Spanish Cava, Italian Prosecco, and French Blanquette de Limoux.

Storing

LAYING DOWN FOR BEGINNERS

THE RESTING PLACE

Not so long ago, when winemaking was less sophisticated and there were fewer ways to counter tricky vintages, there were two kinds of wines: the basic stuff to drink immediately, and the cream of the crop that was left in the barrel and/or bottle to age. So, a good wine was an old wine. And vice versa. Young wine and old wine had as much in common as hamburgers and haute cuisine.

Today there are plenty of wonderful wines that never improve beyond the first few years after the harvest, and are none the worse for that. On the other hand, some wines – German Riesling, fine red Bordeaux and top Australian Shiraz, for example – by their very nature, still reward a few years' patience in the cellar.

While many of us live in homes that are ill-suited for storing wine, one can often find an unused grate or a space beneath the stairs that offers wine what it wants: a constant temperature of around 44–60°F (never lower than 40°F nor more than 68°F), reasonable humidity (install a cheap humidifier or leave a sponge in a bowl of water), sufficient ventilation to avoid a musty atmosphere, and, ideally, an absence of vibration (wines stored beneath train tracks – or beds – age faster). Alternatively, invest in a fridge-like Eurocave that guarantees perfect conditions – or even adapt an old freezer.

RACKS AND CELLAR BOOKS

Custom-built racks can be bought "by the hole" and cut to fit. Square chimney stacks can be used too. If you have plenty of space, simply allocate particular racks to specific styles of wine. Unfortunately, even the best-laid cellar plans tend to fall apart when two cases of Australian Shiraz have to be squeezed into a space big enough just for one.

If the size of the cellar warrants it, give each hole in the rack a cross-referenced identity, from A1 at the top left to, say, Z100 at the bottom right. As bottles arrive, they can then be put in any available hole and their address noted in a cellar book, in which you can record when and where you obtained it, what it cost and how each bottle tasted (is it improving or drying out?). Some people, like me, prefer to use a computer programme (Filemaker Pro or Microsoft Excel).

TO DRINK OR KEEP?

A guide to which corks to pop soon and which bottles to treasure for a few years in the rack:

Drink as Soon as Possible

Most wine at under £7.50, particularly basic Chardonnay, Sauvignon Blanc, Merlot, Cabernet and Zinfandel. French Vins de Pays and all but the best white Bordeaux; cheap red Bordeaux and most Beaujolais. Nouveau/Novello/Joven reds, Bardolino, Valpolicella, light Italian whites, almost all "blush" and rosé.

Less than 5 Years

Most moderately priced (£5–10) California, Chilean, Argentine, South African, and Australian reds and whites. Petit-Château Bordeaux and Cru Bourgeois, and lesser Cru Classé reds from poorer vintages (such as 1997); basic Alsace, red and white Burgundy, and better Beaujolais; Chianti, Barbera, basic Spanish reds; good mid-quality Germans. All but the very best Sauvignon from anywhere.

5–10 Years

Most Cru Bourgeois Bordeaux from good years; better châteaux from lesser vintages; all but the finest red and white Burgundy, and Pinot Noir and Chardonnay from elsewhere; middle-quality Rhônes; southern-French higher flyers; good German, Alsace, dry Loire, and finer white Bordeaux; most mid-priced Italian and Portuguese reds; most Australian, California, and Washington State; South African, Chilean, and New Zealand Merlots and Cabernets on sale at under £15. Late harvest wines from the New World and medium-quality Sauternes.

Over 10 Years

Top-class Bordeaux, Rhône, Burgundy, and sweet Loire from ripe years; top-notch German and Bordeaux late harvest, Italian IGT, Barolo, and the finest wines from Tuscany; best Australian Shiraz, Cabernet, Rieslings, and Semillon; and California Cabernet and finest Merlot and Zinfandel.

Serving

THE RULES OF THE GAME

"The art in using wine is to produce the greatest possible quantity of present gladness, without any future depression."

The Gentleman's Table Guide, 1873

The Romans used to add salt to their wine to preserve it, while the Greeks favoured pine resin (which explains the popularity of pine-flavoured Retsina today). Burgundians often refer to Napoleon's taste for Chambertin, but rarely mention that he diluted his red wine with water. A century ago, the English used to add ice to red Bordeaux – and in winter, in Europe today, skiers drink hot "mulled" wine, adding sugar, fruit, and spices. Today, Chinese wine drinkers apparently prefer their Mouton Cadet with a dash of Sprite. And why not? Millions of American wine drinkers got their first taste of wine in the form of a "cooler", – a blend of wine, sugar, and flavoured soda. I'm sure the addition of soda pop would do many a skinny Bordeaux a world of good – it's just a pity when it's added to a classier glass of Médoc or St. Emilion. It's well worth questioning accepted rules – especially when they vary between cultures. Have no fear, the advice that follows is based on common sense and experience – and offered only to help you to decide how you enjoy serving and drinking wine.

SOME LIKE IT HOT

Particular styles of wine taste better at particular temperatures. At many restaurants, though, white and sparkling wine are more often served too cold than too hot. Paradoxically, it is the reds that suffer most from being drunk too warm. Few of the people who serve wines at "room temperature" recall that, when that term was coined, there wasn't a lot of central heating. Be ready to chill a fruity red in a bucket of ice and water for five to 10 minutes before serving.

Red Wine

When serving red, focus on the wine's flavour. Tough wines are best slightly warmer. The temperatures given are a rule-of-thumb guide:

1   Beaujolais and other fruity reds: 50–57°F (an hour in the fridge).
2   Younger red Burgundy and Rhônes and older Bordeaux, Chianti, younger Rioja, New World Grenache, and Pinotage: 58–62°F.
3   Older Burgundy, tannic young Bordeaux, Rhônes, Zinfandel, bigger Cabernet Sauvignon, Merlot, Shiraz, Barolo, and other bigger Italian and Spanish reds: 62–67°F.

Rosé

Rosé should be chilled at 54–57°F, or for five to 10 minutes in a bucket of ice and water.

White Wine

The cooler the wine, the less it will smell or taste. Subtler, richer wines deserve to be drunk a little warmer.

1   Lighter sweeter wines and everyday sparklers: 39–46°F (two or three hours in the fridge or 10–15 minutes in ice and water).
2   Fuller-bodied, aromatic, drier, semi-dry, lusciously sweet whites; Champagne; simpler Sauvignons; and Chardonnays: 46–53°F.
3   Richer dry wines – Burgundy, California Chardonnay: 54–57°F.

Don't cook your reds – or freeze your whites...

THE PERFECT OUTCOME

The patented Screwpull is still the most reliable way to get a cork out of a bottle. The "waiter's friend" is the next best thing, especially the modern versions with a hinged section designed to prevent corks from breaking. Whatever corkscrew you choose, avoid the models that look like a large screw. These often simply pull through old corks. These fragile stoppers are often most easily removed using a two-pronged "Ah So" cork remover. I find these really tiresome for younger wines, however.

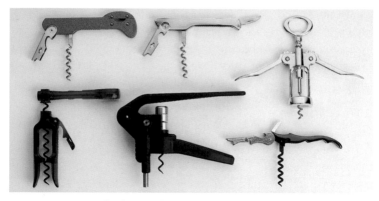

Good corkscrews all have spirals rather than screws.

WHICH GLASSES?

On occasions when no other glass was available I have enjoyed great wine from the glass in my hotel bathroom. I suspect, though, I'd have gotten more out of the experience if something a bit more stylish had come to hand.

Glasses should be narrower across the rim than the bowl. Red ones should be bigger than white because whites are best kept chilled in the bottle rather than warming in the glass. If you like bubbles in your sparkling wine, serve it in a flute rather than a saucer from which they will swiftly escape. Schott, Spiegelau and Riedel are among a number of companies that now produce attractive glasses that are specially designed to bring out the best in particular styles of wine.

Wines definitely benefit from custom-designed glasses like these.

TO BREATHE OR NOT TO BREATHE?

After what may well have been a fairly lengthy period of imprisonment in its bottle, many a wine can be a bit sulky when it is first poured. Giving it a breath of air may help to banish the sulkiness and bring out the flavour and richness, which is why many people tend to remove the cork a few hours before the wine is to be served. This well-intentioned action, however, is almost a complete waste of time (the contact with oxygen offered by the neck of the bottle is far too limited). If you want to aerate a wine, you'd be far better off simply pouring it into a jug and back into the bottle just before you want to drink it. Broad-based, so-called "ship's decanters" not only look good, but also facilitate airing wine as it flows down the inside of the glass in a fine film. Alternatively, small devices are now available that bubble air into wine to mimic the effect of decanting.

As a rule, young red and – surprisingly perhaps – white wines often benefit from exposure to air, especially when the flavour of a white has been temporarily flattened by a heavy dose of sulphur dioxide. Older red wines, however, may be tired out by the experience and may rapidly lose some of their immediate appeal.

Mature red Bordeaux, Rhône and port, for example, may need to be decanted in order to remove the unwelcome mudlike deposit that has dropped to the bottom of the bottle. This initially daunting task is far easier than it seems.

Simply stand the bottle for up to a day before decanting it. Pour it very slowly, in front of a flashlight or candle, watching for the first signs of the deposit. Coffee filters suit those with less steady hands.

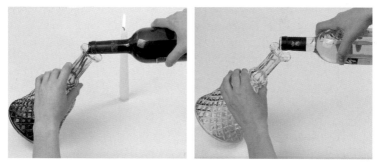

Decant red – or white – wine to bring out the flavour.

ORDER OF SERVICE

The rules say that white wines and youth respectively precede red wines and age; dry goes before sweet (most of us prefer our main course before the dessert); the lighter the wine, the earlier. These rules are often impossible to follow. What are you to do, for example, if the red Loire is lighter-bodied than the white Burgundy? Can the red Bordeaux follow the Sauternes that you are offering with the foie gras? Ignore the absolutes but bear in mind the common sense that lies behind them. Work gently up the scale of fullness, "flavoursomeness," and quality, rather than swinging wildly between styles.

Investing

LIQUID ASSETS

If you had bought a case of 1995 Château Margaux as a future (still in barrel) in 1996 and resold it in soon after taking delivery of the bottles 1997, you would have made a profit of £1,400 on an original investment of just £600. If, on the other hand, you had held onto the wine for another five years until 2002, your profit would have dropped back to around £1,000. The moral is simple: wine can be a first class investment, but it suffers from the same highs and lows as stocks or shares.

YOUTH BEFORE AGE

For most of the 20th century, the only wines worth investing in came from "blue chip" estates with long pedigrees such as the Bordeaux of Châteaux Latour, Cheval Blanc, and Haut-Brion; the Burgundies of the Domaine de la Romanée-Conti and Taylor's port. Wines that lacked the potential to improve with 10-20 years in the cellar were not taken seriously, and a bottle from a good vintage that had been matured for a decade or so would carry a significantly higher price tag than one made from grapes picked a couple of years ago.

Today, the auction rooms are full of newcomers, both among the wines and the bidders. There are Bordeaux from small estates (such as Clinet) and recently launched "microwines" or "garage" wines produced in tiny quantities, such as le Pin and Valandraud, and examples from New World regions such as the Napa and Barossa valleys. The common quality of these wines tends to be a rich, seductive, fruity, oaky character that was rarely encountered in traditional Bordeaux that traditionally required years to lose the tannic character of its youth. These immediately enjoyable young wines now often carry bigger price tags than earlier vintages. Their capacity to age – and retain their early value is far less certain.

THE RULES

1) Wines command different prices in different countries **2)** Unlike works of art, wines don't last forever. **3)** Tread carefully among microwines with unproven potential. **4)** When buying futures/*en primeur*, deal with financially solid merchants. **5)** At auction, only buy wines that have been carefully cellared. **6)** Store wines carefully – and insure them. **7)** Follow their progress – read critics' comments and watch auction prices. **8)** Beware of falling reputations for wines and vintages. **9)** When bidding at auction, take note of the buyer's premium. (15-17.5%) and the possible increase in cost from local sales tax (VAT) and delivery charges. **10)** A diamond brooch is more easily converted into cash than a prize Bordeaux.

FRANCE
Bordeaux

Châteaux Angélus, Ausone, Cheval Blanc, Cos d'Estournel, Ducru-Beaucaillou, Eglise-Clinet, Figeac, Grand-Puy-Lacoste, Gruaud-Larose, Haut-Brion, Lafite, Lafleur, Latour, Léoville Barton, Léoville Las Cases, Lynch-Bages, Margaux, la Mission-Haut-Brion, Montrose, Mouton-Rothschild, Palmer, Pétrus, Pichon Lalande, Pichon Longueville, le Pin, Rauzan-Ségla, Valandraud. Vintages: 1982, 1983 (Margaux), 1988, 1989, 1990, 1995, 1996, 1998, 2000. 1999 and 2001 (top properties only).

Burgundy

Drouhin Marquis de Laguiche, Gros Frères, Hospices de Beaune (from Drouhin, Jadot etc), Méo-Camuzet, Romanée-Conti (la Tâche, Romanée-Conti), Gouges, Lafon, Leflaive, Leroy, Denis Mortet, Roumier, de Vogüé.

Rhône

Chapoutier, Chave, Guigal (top wines), Jaboulet Aîné "La Chapelle."

PORTUGAL (PORT)

Cockburn's, Dow's, Fonseca, Graham's, Noval, Taylor's, Warre's.

CALIFORNIA

Beaulieu Private Reserve, Diamond Creek, Dominus, Duckhorn, Dunn, Harlan Estate, Howell Mountain, Grace Family, Matanzas Creek, Robert Mondavi Reserve, Opus One, Ridge, Spottswoode, Stag's Leap.

AUSTRALIA

Armagh, Clarendon Hills, Ch. Tahbilk 1860 Vines Shiraz, Henschke Hill of Grace, Cyril Henschke, Mount Edelstone, Penfolds Grange and Bin 707, Petaluma Cabernet, "John Riddoch," Virgin Hills, Yarra Yering.

Vintages

TIME WILL TELL

Thirty years or so ago, good wine was only produced when the climate was just right. Man had yet to develop ways – physical, chemical, and organic – of combating pests and diseases. Really disastrous years are a rarity now, however, but some places are naturally more prone to tricky vintages than others. Northern Europe, for example, suffers more from unreliable sun and untimely rain than more southerly regions, let alone the warm, irrigated vineyards of Australia and the Americas. A dependable climate does not necessarily make for better wine; grapes develop more interesting flavours in what is known as a "marginal" climate – which is why New World producers are busily seeking out cooler, higher-altitude sites in which to plant their vines.

IT'S AN ILL WIND

Some producers can buck the trend of a climatically poor year – by luckily picking before the rainstorms, carefully discarding rotten grapes, or even using equipment to concentrate the flavour of a rain-diluted crop. In years like these, well-situated areas within larger regions can, in any case, make better wines than their neighbours. France's top vineyards, for example, owe their prestige partly to the way their grapes ripen. The difference in quality between regions can, however, also be attributed to the types of grapes that are grown. Bordeaux had a fair-to-good vintage for red wine in 1997, but a great one for Sauternes. Similarly, there are vintages where, for example, the St. Emilion and Pomerol châteaux have already picked their Merlot grapes in perfect conditions before rainstorms arrive to ruin the prospects of their counterparts' later-ripening Cabernet Sauvignon in the Médoc, only a few miles away.

The following pages suggest regions and wines for the most significant vintages of this and the past century.

OVER 50 YEARS OF WINE...

2002 (SOUTHERN HEMISPHERE)

Australia and New Zealand had their best vintage in a while and good wines were made in Chile and Argentina. Fires and intense heat affected South Africa, making for patchy quality and often disappointing whites.

2001

Good red Bordeaux but great sweet and dry whites. Whites are better than reds in Burgundy and the Northern Rhône and most good Loires were sweet. Piedmont and Tuscany produced great wines, as did Tokaji and the best sites in Germany. Spanish wines were not outstanding, but there will be some high quality port. Chile and South Africa and New Zealand did well and there were signs of brilliance in California

2000

Good-to-great Bordeaux, (Médoc). Red Burgundy, Sauternes, and most of Northern France fared less well. Spain saw one of its largest harvests ever; and Portugal produced fine table wines and vintage port. Italy saw its best results in the south and also in the whites of the northeast, while 2000 was not as spectacular as 1999 in Germany, but Tokaji was great. Australia's best wines were from Western Australia and the Hunter Valley.

1999

A patchy year, with great Sauternes, but red Bordeaux was very variable. There were great red and white Burgundies and worthwhile Rhônes, Loires, and Alsaces. Look out for top Italians – especially Chianti – German wines from the Mosel-Saar-Ruwer and Tokaji. The vintage in Spain was good rather than great. Australia's stars were from Coonawarra and Victoria. New Zealand, Chile, and Argentina did well.

1998

Untimely rain made for a mixed vintage throughout the northern hemisphere. There were some great red Bordeaux (St. Emilion, Pomerol, and top Médoc and Graves), lovely Sauternes and Alsace, and fine white Burgundies (especially Chablis) and ports. California reds were varied.

1997

Bordeaux produced light reds and brilliant sweet whites, and Burgundy had great whites and variable reds. Alsace, Germany, and Austria made terrific wines, as did the port houses of the Douro and producers in the US, Australia, and New Zealand. Italy had a truly great year.

1996

Classic Bordeaux (especially Médoc, Graves, and Sauternes), white Burgundy and the Loire. Patchy Alsace, Rhône and Germany and fair in Italy, Spain, and Portugal. California, New Zealand, and Australia produced top-class red and white wines.

1995

Classy red Bordeaux and white Burgundy. Italian and Loire reds, Rhône, Alsace, German, Rioja, and Ribera del Duero are all good, as are Australia, New Zealand, South Africa, and North and South America.

1994

Unripe red Bordeaux, fine northern Rhône reds, fading red Burgundy, and great Vintage port. Average-to-good Italian reds and Germans; California had a great vintage, and Australians were good to very good.

1993

Red Bordeaux is tiring now. There are excellent Tokaji, Alsace, and Loires (red and white), good red Burgundy and top-class whites. Wines were better in South Africa and New Zealand than in Australia.

1992

Poor Bordeaux but good white Burgundy. Fading red Burgundy. Taylor's and Fonseca produced great vintage port. Fine California Cabernets.

1991

Maturing Bordeaux and good Northern Rhône reds. Fine port and good wines from Spain, South Africa, California, New Zealand, and Australia.

1990

Great Bordeaux, Champagne, Germans, Alsace, Loire whites, red Rhônes, Burgundies, Australians, Californians, Barolo, and Spanish reds.

1985–1989

1989 Great red and good white Bordeaux and Champagne. Stunning Germans and red Loires; excellent Alsace. Good red and superb white Rhône, good red Burgundy. **1988** Evolving red Bordeaux and Italian reds, fine Sauternes and Champagne, Tokaji, German, Alsace, Loire reds and sweet whites, good Rhône, and red Burgundy. **1987** Fading red Bordeaux and Burgundy. **1986** Fine red and white Bordeaux, Australian reds, white Burgundy. **1985** Reds from Bordeaux, Rhône, Burgundy, Spain, Italy and Champagne, port, Champagne, Alsace, sweet Loire.

1980–1985

1984 South African and Australian reds, and Rieslings. **1983** Red Bordeaux, red Rhône, Portuguese reds, Sauternes, Madeira, vintage port, Tokaji, Alsace. **1982** Red Bordeaux, Australian, Portuguese and Spanish reds, Italian reds, Burgundy and Rhône. **1981** Alsace. **1980** Madeira, port.

1970–1979

1979 Sassicaia, sweet Austrians. **1978** Rhône, Portuguese reds, Bordeaux, Burgundy, Barolo, Tuscan and Loire reds. **1977** Port, sweet Austrians. **1976** Champagne, Loire reds and sweet whites, sweet Germans, Alsace, Sauternes. **1975** Top red Bordeaux and port, Sauternes. **1974** California and Portuguese reds. **1973** Napa Cabernet, sweet Austrians. **1972** Tokaji. **1971** Bordeaux, Burgundy, Champagne, Barolo and Tuscan reds, sweet Germans, red Rhône, Penfolds Grange. **1970** Port, Napa Cabernet, red Bordeaux, Rioja.

1960–1969

1969 Red Rhône, Burgundy. **1968** Madeira, Rioja, Tokaji. **1967** Sauternes, Châteauneuf-du-Pape, German TBA. **1966** Port, Burgundy, red Bordeaux, Australian Shiraz. **1965** Barca Velha. **1964** Red Bordeaux, Tokaji, Vega Sicilia, Rioja, sweet Loire, red Rhône. **1963** Vintage port, Tokaji. **1962** Top Bordeaux and Burgundy, Rioja, Australian Cabernet and Shiraz. **1961** Red Bordeaux, Sauternes, Champagne, Brunello, Barolo, Alsace, red Rhône. **1960** Port, top red Bordeaux.

1950–1959

1959 Red Bordeaux, Sauternes, Tokaji, Germans, Loire, Alsace, Rhône, Burgundy. **1958** Barolo. **1957** Madeira, Vega Sicilia, Tokaji. **1956** Yquem. **1955** Red Bordeaux, Sauternes, port, Champagne. **1954** Madeira. **1953** Red Bordeaux, Tokaji, Champagne, sweet Germans, Côte Rôtie, Burgundy. **1952** Red Bordeaux, Madeira, Champagne, Barolo, Tokaji, Rhône, Burgundy. **1951** Terrible. **1950** Madeira.

1940–1949

1949 Bordeaux, Tokaji, sweet Germans, red Rhône, Burgundy. **1948** Port, Vega Sicilia. **1947** Bordeaux, Burgundy, port, Champagne, Tokaji, sweet Loire. **1946** Armagnac. **1945** Port, Bordeaux, Champagne, Chianti, sweet Germans, Alsace, red Rhônes and Burgundy. **1944** Madeira, port. **1943** Champagne, red Burgundy. **1942** Port, Rioja, Vega Sicilia. **1941** Madeira, Sauternes. **1940** Madeira.

ANNIVERSARY WINES

1903 Madeira. **1913** Madeira. **1923** Madeira. **1933** Madeira.

Wine and Health

BETTER RED THAN DEAD?

"Wine is fit for man in a wonderful way, provided that it is taken with good sense by the sick as well as the healthy."

Hippocrates

"Drink a glass of wine after your soup. Steal a rouble from your doctor."

Russian proverb

SAVOIR VIVRE

Around 2200 BC, a Sumerian clay tablet recommended wines for various ailments. In 1890, an Irish physician attributed the well-being of the French to red wine. A century later CBS television's *60 Minutes* "French Paradox" programme revealed that Gallic wine drinkers were healthier than Anglo-Saxon teetotallers.

WHITE WINE AND LUNGS

In early 2002, a survey of 1,555 New Yorkers by Dr. Holger Schunemann of the University of Buffalo uncovered an apparent link between the consumption of white wine and better lung function. Anti-oxidants in the wine appear to prevent the creation of free radicals, harmful molecules that damage lung tissues. If further research supports these findings, white wine sales may get the boost red wine enjoyed when it was announced that it was good for the heart.

RED WINE AND HEALTHY BLOOD

Numerous credible reasons have been given for the link between wine and health, including the simple fact that alcohol relieves stress that might otherwise cause disease. (This would help to explain why moderate consumption of other alcoholic drinks also appears to be beneficial.)

However, several of the leading scientists who gathered at the University Victor Segalen in Bordeaux in April 2001 believe that a complex mixture of 200 phenolic compounds to be found in red wine may be effective against a number of ailments, ranging from heart disease to cancer and Aids. Many of these come from the skins and seeds that are used in the making of red wine, but discarded when producing white. White wine has a tenth as many of these compounds as red.

RED WINE AND HEART DISEASE

According to Université de Bourgogne researchers, people who daily drink up to four glasses of red wine have higher levels of HDL (high density lipoproteins) – "good" cholesterol that escorts "bad" cholesterol away from artery walls. Prof. Ludovic Drouet of the Hopital Lariboisière in Paris believes that wine may also act against the furring of arteries because polyphenols aid cell proliferation and hinder blood clotting. Heart attack victims are now advised to drink wine while convalescing. A recent study published in the British Journal of Pharmacology additionally associated the relaxation of blood vessels and reduced blood pressure to red wine consumption.

Resveratrol, an anti-fungal compound found in high concentration in grape skins has been shown to improve the lipid profile of volunteers drinking three glasses of red wine a day for two weeks. Resveratrol appears to be 20 times more powerful in its antioxidant affect than Vitamin E. Prof. Joseph Vercauteren of the University Victor Segalen in Bordeaux suggests that the polyphenols mop up damaging chemicals in the body called free radicals more effectively than vitamins C and E because phenolic compounds found in red wine are fat soluble, while others can be dissolved in water.

WINE AND AIDS

Red wine may also be used to augment the treatment of Aids, according to Dr. Marvin Edeas of the Hôpital Antoine Béclère in Clamart, who is studying the way the polyphenols rejuvenate blood. It may also be effective against diseases such as sickle cell anaemia and thalassaemia.

WINE AND DIGESTION

Wine of both colours counters both constipation and diarrhoea, while white wine in particular stimulates the urinary functions. Wine also kills cholera bacteria and combats typhoid and trichinella, the poisonous compound in "bad" pork. Surprisingly, one researcher, Dr. Heinrich Kliewe, actually recommends that moderate amounts of wine can counteract some of the side effects of antibiotics.

WINE AND AGEING

Marie Antoinette apparently used to wash her face in red wine to protect the skin against wrinkles, and a Bordeaux health spa (at Château Smith-Haut-Lafitte) makes great use of extracts from grape seeds. Today, though, most researchers are more concerned with the way antioxidants in red wine appear to inhibit the effects of degenerative oxidation, such as strokes. Wine may also offer protection against Alzheimer's Disease; moderate wine drinkers in their 70s and 80s seem to remain more alert than their more abstemious contemporaries.

WINE AND VIRUSES

Apart from any beneficial effects of wine against the Aids virus, it may also combat other viruses. According to Drs. Jack Konowalchuk and Joan Speirs of the department of microbial hazards in Canada, the polyphenols in tannic red wine are effective against such viruses as those that cause cold sores, and may even act against genital Herpes 2.

WINE AND PREGNANCY

Despite the fears it arouses, the warning notices and the embarrassing scenes that have occurred in bars and restaurants between pregnant women and waiters, the risks associated with drinking wine while expecting a baby are actually very low. Fetal Alcohol Syndrome is rare outside the poorer inner cities of the US. In 1997, the UK Royal College of Obstetricians and Gynaecologists reported that up to 15 units of alcohol per week should do no harm to a foetus.

WINE AND CALORIES

There is no difference in calories between a Muscadet and a red Bordeaux (around 110 per glass). More alcoholic wines, such as California Zinfandels, Australian Shirazes, and some red Rhones, with strengths of 14 per cent will have more calories, while sweeter, but less alcoholic German wines such as Liebfraumilch, that weigh in at 9 per cent, have less than 80 calories. A Stanford University survey suggests the action of the wine on the metabolism somehow makes its calories less fattening.

WINE AND CANCER

Alcohol has been linked to rare occurrences of mouth and throat cancer – but only among smokers. In fact, as a British research team at the De Montfort University in Leicester has recently announced, there are clear indications that red wine may act against cancer. Lead researcher Gerry Potter has discovered that a tumour cell enzyme called

CYP1B1 transforms the resveratrol naturally found in red wine into piceatannol which, in turn destroys cancer cells. Thse findings support the belief of Dr. Francis Raul of the University Louis Pasteur in Strasbourg that Resveratrol inhibits the proliferation of human intestinal cancerous cells and the formation of tumours in mice predisposed to intestinal tumours. Prof. Djavad Mossalayi of the Victor Segalen University has tested it on human cells, both normal and cancerous, and found it to be toxic to both. He thinks the action of wine on cancer cells may not be linked to its antioxidant properties but to the way it acts on the basic process of cell division. Red wine is also rich in gallic acid, an acknowledged anticarcinogenic, and wine's role in reducing stress has been associated with a lower incidence of certain forms of cancer.

HANGOVERS

All alcohol is hangover fare. The best way to avoid this fate is to drink plenty of water before going to bed. Vitamin B (Berocca tablets from Roche) are useful on the Morning After, as is toast with Marmite or Vegemite yeast paste if these are available. Otherwise, go for protein and refreshing orange juice diluted with sparkling mineral water.

WINE AND MIGRAINE

Red wine, like chocolate, can inhibit a useful little enzyme called phenosulfotransferase-P, or PST-P, which detoxifies bacteria in the gut. An absence of PST-P is linked to migraine, which is why some people complain of headaches after drinking a glass or two of wine. Other people have found that red wine is also associated with episodic skin allergies. Sufferers from wine-related allergies may be encouraged to know that some of these conditions can come and go over time. Interestingly, there also seems to be differences in the effects of particular styles of wine. Makers of Chianti, for example, take pride in the fact that their wine seems to have lower amounts of histamines than reds from other regions. So, while awaiting the results of further research into wine-related allergies, it may be worth sampling small doses of various kinds of wine.

WINE AND ASTHMA

One side effect of wines that are heavily dosed with sulphur dioxide (used to combat bacteria in most dried, bottled, and canned foods) is an incidence of asthma attacks among those who are susceptible to this condition. Red wines in general, and New World and organic wines in particular, have lower sulphur levels. The highest levels of sulphur will be in sweet white wines and wines with low alcohol levels.

Food and Wine

MATCHMAKING FOR BEGINNERS

One of the most daunting aspects of wine has always been the traditional obsession with serving precisely the right wine with any particular dish – of only ever drinking red with meat and white with fish or shellfish. It may be reassuring to learn that some of these time-honoured rules are just plain wrong. In Portugal, for example, fishermen love to wash down their sardines and salt cod with a glass or two of harsh red wine. In Burgundy they even poach fish in their local red.

On the other hand, the idea that a platter of cheese needs a bottle of red wine can be trashed in an instant. Just take a mouthful of red Bordeaux immediately after eating a little goat's cheese or Brie. The wine will taste metallic and unpleasant because the creaminess of the cheese reacts badly with the tannin – the toughness – in the wine. A dry white would be far more successful (its acidity would cut through the fat), while the Bordeaux would be shown at its best alongside a harder, stronger cheese. If you don't want to offer a range of wines, try sticking to one or two cheeses that really will complement the stuff in the glass.

Don't take anything for granted. Rare beef and red Bordeaux surprisingly fails the test of an objective tasting. The protein of the meat somehow makes all but the fruitiest wines taste tougher. If you're looking for a perfect partner for beef, uncork a Burgundy. If it's the Bordeaux that takes precedence, you'd be far better off with lamb.

The difference between an ideal and a passable food-and-wine combination can be very subtle. Most of us have after all happily quaffed red Bordeaux with our steak, but just as an avid cook will tinker with a recipe until it is just right, there's a lot to be said for making the occasional effort to find a pairing of dish and wine that really works. Like people who are happier as a couple than separately, some foods and wines simply seem to bring out the best in each other.

A Sense of Balance

There is no real mystery about the business of matching food and wine. Some flavours and textures are compatible, and some are not. Strawberry mousse is not really delicious with chicken casserole, but apple sauce can do wonders for roast pork.

The key to spotting which relationships are marriages made in heaven, and which have the fickleness of Hollywood romances, lies in identifying the dominant characteristics of the contents of both the plate and the glass. Then, learn by experience which are likely to complement each other, either through their similarities or through their differences.

Likely Combinations

It is not difficult to define particular types of food and wine, and to guess how they are likely to get along. A buttery sauce is happier with something tangily acidic, like a crisp Sauvignon Blanc, rather than a rich, buttery Chardonnay. A subtly poached fish won't appreciate a fruit-packed New World white, and you won't do pheasant pie any favours by pulling the cork on a delicate red.

What to Avoid

Some foods and their characteristics, though, make life difficult for almost any drink. Sweetness, for example, in a fruity sauce served with a savory dish seems to strip some of the fruitier flavours out of a wine. This may not matter if the stuff in your glass is a blackcurranty New World Cabernet Sauvignon, but it's bad news if it is a bone-dry white or a tough red with little fruit to spare.

Cream is tricky, too. Try fresh strawberries with Champagne – delicious; now add a little whipped cream to the equation and you'll spoil the flavour. Creamy and buttery sauces can have the same effect on a wine and call for a similarly creamy white – or a fresh, zippy one to cut through the fattiness.

Spices are very problematic for wine – largely due to the physical sensation of eating them rather than any particular flavour. A wine may not seem particularly nasty after a mouthful of chilli sauce; it will simply lose its fruity flavour and taste of nothing at all – which, in the case of a fine red seems to be a pity. The way a tannic red dries out the mouth will also accentuate the heat of the spice. The ideal wine for most Westerners to drink with any spicy dish would be a light, possibly slightly sweet, white or a light, juicy red. Chinese palates often react differently to these combinations, however. They like the burning effect of the chilli and see no point in trying to put out the fire with white wine.

Always Worth a Try

Some condiments actually bring out the best in wines. A little freshly ground pepper on your meat or pasta can accentuate the flavour of a wine, just as it can with a sauce.

Squeezing fresh lemon onto your fish will reduce the apparent acidity of a white wine – a useful tip if you have inadvertently bought a case of tooth-strippingly dry Muscadet. And, just as lemon can help to liven up a dull sauce, it will do the same for a dull white wine, such as a basic Burgundy or a Soave, by neutralizing the acidity and allowing other flavours to make themselves apparent. Mustard performs a similar miracle when it is eaten with beef, somehow nullifying the effect of the meat protein on the wine.

Marriage Guidance

In the following pages, I have suggested wines to go with a wide range of dishes and ingredients, taking the dominant flavour as the key point. Don't treat any of this advice as gospel – use it instead as a launchpad for your own food and wine experiments.

And, if no wine seems to taste just right, don't be too surprised. Heretical as it may seem, some dishes are actually more enjoyable with other drinks. The vinegar that is a fundamental part of a good relish, for example, will do no wine a favour. Even avid wine lovers might well find beer a far more pleasurable accompaniment.

Cooking with Wine

Finally, a word or two about how to make the best use of wine in the kitchen (apart from its role as refreshment following a vigorous session of egg-beating, and as a tranquilizer for the moments when sauces curdle and soufflés refuse to rise). The first (and most often forgotten) rule to remember is that wine that's not good enough to drink is probably not good enough to pour into the frying pan or casserole. At least, not unless you take a perverse pleasure in using and eating substandard ingredients. On the other hand, despite the advice of classic French recipes, your "coq au vin" won't be spoiled by your unwillingness to make it with a pricy bottle of Grand Cru Burgundy. A decent, humbler red will do perfectly well, though it is worth trying to use a similar style to the one suggested.

Second – and just as important – remember that, with the exception of a few dishes such as British sherry trifle or zabaglione, in which wine is enjoyed in its natural state, wine used as an ingredient needs to be cooked in order to remove the alcohol. So, add it early enough for the necessary evaporation to take place.

A

Almond Liqueur Muscats or Beaumes de Venise.
  Trout with Almonds Bianco di Custoza, Pinot Blanc.
Anchovies
  Fresh Anchovy (Boquerones) Albariño, Vinho Verde, Aligoté.
  Salade Niçoise Muscadet, Vinho Verde, or Beaujolais.
  Salted Anchovies Rioja red or white, Manzanilla or Fino sherry.
  Tapenade Dry sherry or Madeira.
Apple
  Apple Pie or Strudel Austrian off-dry white.
  Blackberry and Apple Pie Late harvest Riesling, Vouvray demi-sec.
  Roast Pork with Apple Sauce Off-dry Vouvray or Riesling.
  Waldorf Salad Dry Madeira.
Apricot Late harvest Sémillon or Riesling, Jurançon Moelleux.
Arroz con Pollo (Chicken and Rice) Côtes du Rhône, young Zinfandel, Navarra or Rioja "Joven."
Artichoke White Rhône.
  Artichoke Soup Dry Loire whites, Pinot Gris.
Arugula Pinot Grigio, young Viognier.
Asparagus
  Asparagus Crêpes au Gratin Muscadet, Vinho Verde, Cider.
  Asparagus Soup Fresh dry whites, Sauvignon Blanc.
Aubergine
  Stuffed Aubergines Beefy spicy reds like Bandol, Zinfandel, a good Southern Rhône or a full-bodied Italian.
Avocado
  Avocado with Prawns Champagne, Riesling Kabinett, Sauvignon Blanc, Pinot Gris, Australian Chardonnay.
  Avocado Vinaigrette Unoaked Chardonnay, Chablis.

B

Bacon Rich Pinot Gris or Alsace Riesling.
  Bacon with Marinated Scallops Fino sherry or mature Riesling, Shiraz-based Australians, Zinfandel from the US, or a heavy Cape red.
  Warm Bacon Salad New World Sauvignon Blanc, California Fumé Blanc, or a good Pouilly Fumé.
Banana
  Flambéed Banana with Rum Jurançon, Tokaji, Pedro Ximénez sherry, rum.
  Banoffee Pie Sweet Tokaji.
Barbecue Sauce Inexpensive off-dry white or a simple, fruity Cabernet.
  Spare Ribs with Barbecue Sauce Fruity Australian Shiraz, Grenache, or Zinfandel; spicy Côtes du Rhône from a ripe vintage; or an off-dry white.
Basil Slightly sweet Chardonnay (i.e., California, commercial Australian).
  Pasta in Pesto Sauce New Zealand Sauvignon Blanc, Valpolicella.
Beans
  Bean Salad Spanish reds – Rioja and Rueda – or New Zealand Sauvignon Blanc.

Baked Beans Light Zinfandel, Beaujolais, dry rosé, or beer.

Cassoulet Serious white Rhône, Marsanne, or Roussanne; or reds including Grenache and Syrah from the Rhône, crunchy Italian reds, or Zinfandel.

Beef

Beef with Green Peppers in Black Bean Sauce Off-dry German Riesling or characterful dry white, like white Rhône or Marsanne.

Beef with Scallions and Ginger Off-dry German Riesling or one of the more serious Beaujolais Crus.

Beef Stew Pomerol or St. Emilion, good Northern Rhône like Crozes Hermitage, Shiraz or Pinot Noir from the New World.

Beef Stroganoff Tough, beefy reds like Amarone, Brunello di Montalcino, Barolo, Côte Rôtie, or really ripe Zinfandel.

Beef Wellington Top Burgundy, Châteauneuf-du-Pape.

Boeuf Bourguignon Australian Bordeaux-style, Barolo, or other robust reds with sweet fruit.

Boiled Beef and Carrots Bordeaux Rouge, Valpolicella Classico, Australian Shiraz.

Bresaola (Air-Dried Beef) Beaujolais, Barbera, and tasty reds from the Languedoc.

Carpaccio of Beef Chardonnay, Champagne, Cabernet Franc, and Pomerol.

Chilli con Carne Robust fruity reds, Beaujolais Crus, Barbera or Valpolicella, spicy reds like Zinfandel or Pinotage.

Corned Beef Loire reds from Gamay or Cabernet Franc.

Corned Beef Hash Characterful spicy reds from the Rhône or Southern France.

Creole-Style Beef Cheap Southern Rhône reds or Côtes du Rhône, Zinfandel.

Hamburger Zinfandel or country reds from Italy or France, e.g., Corbières.

Hungarian Goulash East European reds – Bulgarian Cabernet or Mavrud and Hungarian Kadarka – or Australian Shiraz.

Meatballs Spicy rich Rhône reds, Zinfandel, Pinotage, and Portuguese reds.

Panang Neuk (Beef in Peanut Curry) New World Chardonnay; New Zealand Sauvignon Blanc; or a spicy, aromatic white Rhône.

Pastrami Zinfandel, good Bardolino, light Côtes du Rhône.

Rare Chargrilled Beef Something sweetly ripe and flavoursome, but not too tannic. Try Chilean Merlot.

Roast Beef Côte Rôtie, good Burgundy.

Steak Pinot Noir and Merlot from the New World; Australian Shiraz; Châteauneuf-du-Pape; good, ripe Burgundy.

Steak with Dijon Mustard Bordeaux, Cabernet Sauvignon from the New World, or Australian Shiraz.

Steak and Kidney Pie/Pudding Bordeaux, Australian Cabernet Sauvignon, Southern Rhône reds, or Rioja.

Steak au Poivre Cabernet Sauvignon, Chianti, Rhône reds, Shiraz, or Rioja.

Steak Tartare Bourgogne Blanc; Beaujolais; Bardolino; or, traditionally, vodka.

Thai Beef Salad New Zealand or South African Sauvignon Blanc, Gewürztraminer, Pinot Blanc.

Beer (in a sauce)

Carbonnade à la Flamande Cheap Southern Rhône or Valpolicella.

Beetroot
>*Borscht* Rich, dry Alsace Pinot Gris; Pinot Blanc; or Italian Pinot Grigio.

Black Bean Sauce
>*Beef with Green Peppers in Black Bean Sauce* Off-dry German Riesling or characterful, dry white like white Rhône or Marsanne.

Blackberry
>*Blackberry and Apple Pie* Late harvest Riesling, Vouvray demi-sec.

Black Cherry
>*Black Forest Gâteau* Fortified Muscat, Schnapps, or Kirsch.

Blackcurrant
>*Blackcurrant Cheesecake* Sweet, grapey dessert wines.
>*Blackcurrant Mousse* Sweet sparkling wines.

Black Pudding Chablis, New Zealand Chardonnay, Zinfandel, or Barolo.

Blueberries
>*Blueberry Pie* Tokaji (6 Puttonyos), late harvest Semillon or Sauvignon.

Brandy
>*Christmas Pudding* Australian Liqueur Muscat, tawny port, rich (sweet) Champagne, Tokaji.
>*Crêpe Suzette* Asti, Orange Muscat, Champagne cocktails.

Bream (freshwater) Chablis or other unoaked Chardonnay.

Bream (sea) White Rhône, Sancerre.

Brie Sancerre or New Zealand Sauvignon Blanc.

Broccoli
>*Broccoli and Cheese Soup* Slightly sweet sherry – Amontillado or Oloroso.

Butter
>*Béarnaise Sauce* Good dry Riesling.
>*Beurre Blanc* Champagne Blanc de Blancs, dry Vinho Verde.

Butternut Squash
>*Butternut Soup* Aromatic Alsace Gewürztraminer.

C

Cabbage
>*Stuffed Cabbage* East European Cabernet.

Cajun Spices Beaujolais Crus.
>*Gumbo* Zinfandel or maybe beer.

Camembert Dry Sauvignon Blanc or unoaked Chablis.

Capers Sauvignon Blanc.
>*Skate with Black Butter* Crisply acidic whites like Muscadet or Chablis.
>*Tartare Sauce* Crisply fresh whites like Sauvignon.

Caramel
>*Crème Caramel* Muscat or Gewürztraminer Vendange Tardive.

Carp Franken Sylvaner, dry Jurançon, Hungarian Furmint.

Carrot
>*Carrot and Coriander Soup* Aromatic, dry Muscat, Argentinian Torrontes.
>*Carrot and Orange Soup* Madeira or perhaps an Amontillado sherry.

Cashew Nuts Pinot Blanc.
>*Chicken with Cashew Nuts* Rich aromatic white, Pinot Gris, or Muscat.

Cauliflower
Cauliflower Cheese Fresh crisp Côtes de Gascogne white; Pinot Grigio; softly plummy Chilean Merlot; or young, unoaked Rioja.

Caviar Champagne or chilled vodka.

Celery
Celery Soup Off-dry Riesling

Cheddar (mature) Good Bordeaux, South African Cabernet, port.

Cheese (general – also see individual entries)
Cheeseburger Sweetly fruity oaky reds – Australian Shiraz, Rioja.

Cheese Fondue Swiss white or Vin de Savoie.

Cheese Platter Match wines to cheeses; don't put too tannic a red with too creamy a cheese, and offer white wines – which go well with all but the hardest cheese. Strong creamy cheeses demand fine Burgundy; blue cheese is made for late harvest wines; goat cheese is ideal with Sancerre, Pouilly Fumé, or other dry, unoaked Sauvignons. Munster is best paired with Alsace Gewurztraminer.

Cheese Sauce (Mornay) Oaky Chardonnay.

Cream Cheese, Crème Fraîche, Mozzarella, Mascarpone Fresh light dry whites – Frascati, Pinot Grigio.

Raclette Swiss white or Vin de Savoie.

Cheesecake Australian botrytized Semillon.

Cherry Valpolicella, Recioto della Valpolicella, Dolcetto.
Roast Duck with Cherry Sauce Barbera, Dolcetto, or Barolo.

Chestnut
Roast Turkey with Chestnut Stuffing Côtes du Rhône, Merlot, or soft and mature Burgundy.

Chicken
Barbecued Chicken Rich and tasty white, Chardonnay.

Chicken Casserole Mid-weight Rhône, such as Crozes-Hermitage or Lirac.

Chicken Chasseur Off-dry Riesling.

Chicken Kiev Chablis, Aligoté, or Italian dry white.

Chicken Pie White Bordeaux, simple Chardonnay, or else a light Italian white.

Chicken Soup Soave, Orvieto, or Pinot Blanc.

Chicken Vol-au-Vents White Bordeaux.

Coq au Vin Shiraz-based New World reds, red Burgundy.

Curry Chicken Gewürztraminer, dry white Loire, fresh Chinon.

Devilled Chicken Australian Shiraz.

Fricassée Unoaked Chardonnay.

Lemon Chicken Muscadet, Chablis, or basic Bourgogne Blanc.

Roast/Grilled Chicken Reds or whites, though nothing too heavy – Burgundy is good, as is Barbera, though Soave will do just as well.

Roast/Grilled Chicken with Sage and Onion Stuffing Italian reds, especially Chianti; soft, plummy Merlots; and sweetly fruity Rioja.

Roast/Grilled Chicken with Tarragon Dry Chenin (Vouvray or perhaps a good South African).

Saltimbocca (Cutlet with Mozzarella and Ham) Flavoursome, dry Italian whites – Lugana, Bianco di Custoza, Orvieto.

Smoked Chicken Oaky Chardonnay, Australian Marsanne, or Fumé Blanc.

Southern Fried Chicken White Bordeaux, Muscadet, Barbera, light
    Zinfandel.
Tandoori Chicken White Bordeaux, New Zealand Sauvignon Blanc.
Chicken Liver (Sauté) Softly fruity, fairly light reds including Beaujolais,
    Italian Cabernet or Merlot, or perhaps an Oregon Pinot Noir.
Chicken Liver Pâté Most of the above reds plus Vouvray Moelleux,
    Monbazillac, or Amontillado sherry.
Chilli Cheap wine or cold beer.
Chilli Con Carne Robust fruity reds, Beaujolais Crus, Barbera or
    Valpolicella, spicy reds like Zinfandel or Pinotage.
Hot and Sour Soup Crisply aromatic English white, Baden Dry.
Szechuan-Style Dry, aromatic whites; Alsace Pinot Gris; Riesling; Grenache
    rosé; beer.
Thai Beef Salad New Zealand or South African Sauvignon Blanc,
    Gewürztraminer, Pinot Blanc.
Chinese (general) Aromatic white – Gewürztraminer, Pinot Gris, English.
Chives Sauvignon Blanc.
Chocolate Orange Muscat, Moscatel de Valencia.
Black Forest (Chocolate and Cherry) Gâteau Fortified Muscat or Kirsch.
Chocolate Cake Beaumes de Venise, Bual or Malmsey Madeira, Orange
    Muscat, sweet German, or fine Champagne.
Chocolate Profiteroles with Cream Muscat de Rivesaltes.
Dark Chocolate Mousse Sweet Black Muscat or other Muscat-based wines.
Milk Chocolate Mousse Moscato d'Asti.
Chorizo (Sausage) Red or white Rioja, Navarra, Manzanilla sherry,
    Beaujolais, or Zinfandel.
Cinnamon Riesling Spätlese, Muscat.
Clams Chablis or Sauvignon Blanc.
Clam Chowder Dry white such as Côtes de Gascogne, Amontillado sherry,
    or Madeira.
Spaghetti Vongole Pinot Bianco or Lugana.
Cockles Muscadet, Gros Plant, Aligoté, dry Vinho Verde.
Coconut (milk) California Chardonnay.
Green Curry Big-flavoured New World whites or Pinot Blanc from
    Alsace.
Cod Unoaked Chardonnay; good, white Burgundy; dry Loire Chenin.
Cod and Chips (French Fries) Any light, crisp, dry white, such as a
    Sauvignon from Bordeaux or Touraine. Alternatively, try dry rosé or
    Champagne. Remember, though, that English-style heavy-handedness with
    the vinegar will do no favours for the wine. For vinegary fries, stick to
    beer.
Cod Roe (smoked) Well-oaked New World Chardonnay.
Lisbon-Style Cod Vinho Verde; Muscadet; light, dry Riesling.
Salt Cod (Bacalhão de Gomes) Classically Portuguese red or white – Vinho
    Verde or Bairrada reds.
Smoked Cod Vinho Verde.
Coffee
Coffeecake Asti.
Coffee Mousse Asti, Liqueur Muscat.
Tiramisu Sweet fortified Muscat, Vin Santo, Torcolato.

Coriander
Carrot and Coriander Soup Aromatic, dry Muscat.
Coriander Leaf Dry or off-dry English white.
Coriander Seed Dry, herby Northern Italian whites.
Corn Rich and ripe whites – California Chardonnay.
Corn on the Cob Light, fruity whites – German Riesling.

Courgette
Courgette Gratin Good dry Chenin from Vouvray or South Africa.
Crab Chablis, Sauvignon Blanc, New World Chardonnay.
Crab Cakes (Maryland-style) Rias Baixas Albariño.
Crab Cioppino Sauvignon Blanc, Pinot Grigio.
Crab Mousse Crisp dry whites – Baden Dry or Soave.
Deviled Crab (spicy) New World Sauvignon, Albariño.

Cranberry
Roast Turkey with Cranberry and Orange Stuffing Richly fruity reds like Shiraz from Australia, Zinfandel, or modern Rioja.

Crayfish
Freshwater Crayfish South African Sauvignon, Meursault.
Salad of Crayfish Tails with Dill Rich South African Chenin blends or crisp Sauvignon, white Rhône.
Cream When dominant not good with wine, particularly tannic reds.

Curry
Beef in Peanut Curry New World Chardonnay; spicy, aromatic white Rhône.
Coronation Chicken Gewürztraminer; dry, aromatic English wine; or a fresh Chinon.
Curried Beef Beefy, spicy reds – Barolo, Châteauneuf-du-Pape, and Shiraz/Cabernet – or off-dry aromatic whites – Gewürztraminer, Pinot Gris. Or try some Indian sparkling wine or cold Indian beer.
Curried Turkey New World Chardonnay.
Tandoori Chicken White Bordeaux, New Zealand Sauvignon Blanc.
Thai Green Chicken Curry Big New World whites or dry Pinot Blanc from Alsace.

D

Dill Sauvignon Blanc.
Gravlax Ice cold vodka, Pinot Gris, or Akvavit.
Dover Sole Sancerre, good Chablis, unoaked Chardonnay.
Dried Fruit Sweet sherry, tawny port.
Bread and Butter Pudding Barsac or Sauternes, Monbazillac, Jurançon. Muscat de Beaumes de Venise or Australian Orange Muscat.
Mince Pie Rich, late harvest wine or botrytis-affected Sémillon.
Duck Pinot Noir from Burgundy, California, or Oregon, or off-dry German Riesling.
Cassoulet Serious white Rhônes, Marsanne, or Roussanne; or try reds including Grenache and Syrah from the Rhône, berryish Italian reds, or Zinfandel.
Confit de Canard Alsace Pinot Gris or a crisp red like Barbera.

Duck Pâté Chianti or other juicy herby red, Amontillado sherry.
Duck Pâté with Orange Riesling or Rioja.
Peking Duck Rice wine, Alsace Riesling, Pinot Gris.
Roast Duck Fruity reds like Australian Cabernet, a ripe Nebbiolo, or
  Zinfandel.
Roast Duck with Cherry Sauce Barbera, Dolcetto, or Barolo.
Roast Duck with Orange Sauce Loire red or a sweet white like Vouvray
  demi-sec.
Smoked Duck California Chardonnay or Fumé Blanc.
Duck Liver
  Foie Gras de Canard Champagne, late harvest Gewürztraminer or Riesling,
  Sauternes.

E

Eel
  Smoked Eel Pale, dry sherry; simple, fresh white Burgundy.
Egg
  Crème Brûlée Jurançon Moelleux, Tokaji.
  Eggs Benedict Unoaked Chardonnay, Blanc de Blancs, British Bucks Fizz,
    Bloody Mary.
  Eggs Florentine Unoaked Chardonnay, Pinot Blanc, Aligoté, Sémillon.
  Spanish Tortilla Young, juicy Spanish reds and fresher whites from La
    Mancha or Rueda.

F

Fennel Sauvignon Blanc.
Fig Liqueur Muscat.
Fish (general – also see individual entries)
  Bouillabaisse Red or white Côtes du Rhône, dry rosé or peppery dry
    white from Provence, California Fumé Blanc, Marsanne, or
    Verdicchio.
  Cumberland Fish Pie California Chardonnay, Alsace Pinot Gris, Sauvignon
    Blanc.
  Fish Cakes White Bordeaux, Chilean Chardonnay.
  Fish and Chips Most fairly simple, crisply acidic dry whites or maybe a rosé
    or Champagne (See Cod). Go easy with the vinegar.
  Fish Soup Manzanilla, Chablis, Muscadet.
  Kedgeree Aligoté, crisp Sauvignon.
  Mediterranean Fish Soup Provençal reds and rosés, Tavel, Côtes du Rhône,
    Vin de Pays d'Oc.
  Seafood Salad Soave, Pinot Grigio, Muscadet, or a lightly oaked
    Chardonnay.
  Sushi Saké.
Frankfurter Côtes du Rhône or beer.

Fruit (general – also see individual entries)

Fresh Fruit Salad Moscato d'Asti, Riesling Beerenauslese, or Vouvray Moelleux.

Fruit Flan Vouvray Moelleux, Alsace Riesling Vendange Tardive.

Summer Pudding Late harvest Riesling – German or Alsace.

G

Game (general – also see individual entries)

Cold Game Fruity Northern Italian reds – Barbera or Dolcetto – good Beaujolais or light Burgundy.

Game Pie Beefy reds, Southern French, Rhône, Australian Shiraz.

Roast Game Big reds, Brunello di Montalcino, old Barolo, good Burgundy.

Well-hung Game Old Barolo or Barbaresco, mature Hermitage, Côte Rôtie or Châteauneuf-du-Pape, fine Burgundy.

Garlic

Aïoli A wide range of wines go well including white Rioja, Provence rosé, California Pinot Noir.

Garlic Sausage Red Rioja, Bandol, Côtes du Rhône.

Gazpacho Fino sherry, white Rioja.

Roast/Grilled Chicken with Garlic Oaky Chardonnay or red Rioja.

Roast Lamb with Garlic and Rosemary Earthy soft reds like California Petite Sirah, Rioja, or Zinfandel.

Snails with Garlic Butter Aligoté and light white Burgundy or perhaps a red Gamay de Touraine.

Ginger Gewürztraminer or Riesling.

Beef with Onions and Ginger Off-dry German Riesling, one of the more serious Beaujolais Crus.

Chicken with Ginger White Rhône, Gewürztraminer.

Ginger Ice Cream Asti or late harvest Sémillon.

Goat Cheese Sancerre, New World Sauvignon, Pinot Blanc.

Grilled Goat Cheese Loire reds.

Goose A good Rhône red like Hermitage, Côte Rôtie, or a crisp Barbera; Pinot Noir from Burgundy, California or Oregon; or even off-dry German Riesling.

Confit d'Oie Best Sauternes, Monbazillac.

Gooseberry

Goosberry Fool Quarts de Chaume.

Gooseberry Pie Sweet Madeira, Austrian Trockenbeerenauslese.

Goose Liver

Foie Gras Best Sauternes, Monbazillac.

Grapefruit Sweet Madeira or sherry.

Grouse

Roast Grouse Hermitage, Côte Rôtie, robust Burgundy, or good mature red Bordeaux.

Guinea Fowl Old Burgundy, Cornas, Gamay de Touraine, St. Emilion.

H

Haddock White Bordeaux, Chardonnay, Pinot Blanc, single-vineyard Soave, Australian unoaked Semillon.
Mousse of Smoked Haddock Top white Burgundy.
Smoked Haddock Fino sherry or oaky Chardonnay.
Hake Soave, Sauvignon Blanc.
Halibut White Bordeaux, Muscadet.
Smoked Halibut Oaky Spanish white Rioja, Australian Chardonnay, oaked white Bordeaux.
Ham
Boiled/Roasted/Grilled/Fried Ham Beaujolais-Villages, Gamay de Touraine, slightly sweet German white, Tuscan red, lightish Cabernet (e.g., Chilean), Alsace Pinot Gris, or Muscat.
Braised Ham with Lentils Light, fruity Beaujolais; Côtes du Rhône; Rioja or Navarra Crianza.
Honey-Roast Ham Riesling.
Oak-Smoked Ham Oaky Spanish reds.
Parma Ham (Prosciutto) Try a dry Lambrusco, Tempranillo Joven, or Gamay de Touraine.
Pea and Ham Soup Beaujolais.
Hare
Hare Casserole Good Beaujolais Crus or, for a stronger flavour, try an Australian red.
Jugged Hare Argentinian reds; tough Italians like Amarone, Barolo, and Barbaresco; inky reds from Bandol or the Rhône.
Hazelnut Vin Santo, Liqueur Muscat.
Warm Bacon, Hazelnut, and Sorrel Salad New World Sauvignon Blanc, California Fumé Blanc, or a good Pouilly Fumé.
Herbs (see individual entries)
Herring
Fresh Herrings Sauvignon Blanc, Muscadet, Frascati, or cider.
Roll-Mop Herring Savoie, dry Vinho Verde, Grüner Veltliner, Akvavit, cold lager.
Salt Herring White Portuguese.
Sprats Muscadet, Vinho Verde.
Honey Tokaji.
Baklava Moscatel de Setúbal.
Horseradish
Roast Beef with Horseradish California Pinot Noir or mature Burgundy.
Houmous French dry whites, Retsina, Vinho Verde.

I

Ice Cream (vanilla) Try Marsala, Australian Liqueur Muscat, Muscadelle, or Pedro Ximénez sherry.
Indian (general) Gewürztraminer (spicy dishes), New World Chardonnay (creamy/yogurt dishes), New Zealand Sauvignon Blanc (Tandoori).

J

Japanese Barbecue Sauce
   Teriyaki   Spicy reds like Zinfandel or Portuguese reds.
John Dory   Good, white Burgundy or Australian Chardonnay.

K

Kedgeree   New World Sauvignon Blanc.
Kidney
   Lambs' Kidneys   Rich, spicy reds – Barolo, Cabernet Sauvignon, Rioja.
   Steak and Kidney Pie/Pudding   Bordeaux, Australian Cabernet Sauvignon,
      Southern Rhône reds or Rioja.
Kippered Herrings   New World Chardonnay or a good fino sherry. Or, if
      you are having them for breakfast, Champagne, a cup of tea, or Dutch gin.

L

Lamb
   Casserole   Rich and warm Cabernet-based reds from France, or California
      Zinfandel.
   Cassoulet   Serious white Rhône, Marsanne, or Roussanne; or reds including
      Grenache and Syrah from the Rhône, berryish Italian reds, or Zinfandel.
   Cutlets or Chops   Cru Bourgeois Bordeaux, Chilean Cabernet.
   Haggis   Beaujolais, Côtes du Rhône, Côtes du Roussillon, Spanish reds,
      malt whisky.
   Irish Stew   A good simple South American or Eastern European Cabernet
      works best.
   Kabobs   Modern (fruity) Greek reds or sweetly ripe Australian
      Cabernet/Shiraz.
   Kleftiko (Lamb Shanks Baked with Thyme)   Greek red from Nemea,
      Beaujolais, light Cabernet Sauvignon.
   Lancashire Hotpot   Robust country red – Cahors, Fitou.
   Moussaka   Brambly Northern Italian reds (Barbera, Dolcetto, etc), Beaujolais,
      Pinotage, Zinfandel, or try some good Greek wine from a modern
   producer.
   Roast Lamb   Bordeaux, New Zealand Cabernet Sauvignon, Cahors, Rioja
      reserva, reds from Chile.
   Roast Lamb with Thyme   Try a New Zealand Cabernet Sauvignon or
   Bourgeuil.
   Shepherd's Pie   Barbera, Cabernet Sauvignon, Minervois, Zinfandel,
      Beaujolais, Southern French red.
Langoustine   Muscadet, Soave, South African Sauvignon.
Leek
   Cock-a-Leekie   Dry New World white, simple red Rhône.
   Leek in Cheese Sauce   Dry white Bordeaux, Sancerre, or Australian Semillon.

Leek and Potato Soup Dry whites, Côtes de Gascogne.

Vichyssoise Dry whites, Chablis, Bordeaux Blanc.

Lemon

Lemon Cheesecake Moscato d'Asti.

Lemon Meringue Pie Malmsey Madeira.

Lemon Sorbet Late harvest Sémillon or sweet Tokaji.

Lemon Tart Sweet Austrian and German wines.

Lemon Zest Sweet fortified Muscats.

Lemon Grass New Zealand Sauvignon, Sancerre, Viognier.

Lemon Sole Chardonnay.

Lentils Earthy country wines, Côtes du Rhône.

Chicken Dhansak Sémillon or New Zealand Sauvignon.

Dhal Soup Try Soave or Pinot Bianco.

Lime Australian Verdelho, Grüner Veltliner, Furmint.

Kaffir Lime Leaves (in Thai Green Curry, etc.) Big-flavoured New World whites or Pinot Blanc from Alsace.

Thai Beef Salad New Zealand or South African Sauvignon Blanc, Gewürztraminer, Pinot Blanc.

Liver

Calves' Liver Good Italian Cabernet, Merlot, or mature Chianti.

Fegato alla Veneziana Nebbiolo, Zinfandel, or Petite Sirah.

Lambs' Liver Chianti, Australian Shiraz, or Merlot.

Liver and Bacon Côtes du Rhône, Zinfandel, Pinotage.

Lobster Good white Burgundy.

Lobster Bisque Grenache rosé, fresh German white, Chassagne-Montrachet, dry Amontillado sherry.

Lobster in a Rich Sauce Champagne, Chablis, fine white Burgundy, good white Bordeaux.

Lobster Salad Champagne, Chablis, German or Alsace Riesling.

Lobster Thermidor Rich beefy Côtes du Rhône, oaky Chardonnay, or a good deep-coloured rosé from Southern France.

M

Mackerel With Vinho Verde, Albariño, Sancerre, and New Zealand Sauvignon.

Smoked Mackerel Bourgogne Aligoté, Alsace Pinot Gris.

Smoked Mackerel Pâté Sparkling Vouvray, Muscadet.

Mallard Côte Rôtie, Ribera del Duero, or Zinfandel.

Mango Best eaten in the bathtub with a friend and a bottle of Champagne! Otherwise, go for Asti or Moscato.

Marjoram Provençal reds.

Marsala

Chops in Marsala Sauce Australian Marsanne.

Mascarpone

Tiramisu Sweet fortified Muscat, Vin Santo, Torcolato.

Meat (general – also see individual entries)

Cold Meats Juicy, fruity reds, low in tannin, i.e., Beaujolais, Côtes du Rhône, etc.

Consommé Medium/Amontillado sherry.

Meat Pâté Beaujolais, Fumé Blanc, lesser white Burgundy.

Mixed Grill Versatile uncomplicated red – Australian Shiraz, Rioja.

Melon Despite its apparently innocent, juicy sweetness, melon can be very unfriendly to most wines. Try tawny port, sweet Madeira or sherry, Quarts de Chaume, late harvest Riesling.

Mincemeat

Mince Pie Rich, sweet, late harvest wine or botrytis-affected Sémillon.

Mint Beaujolais, young Pinot Noir, or try a New Zealand or Australian Riesling.

Thai Beef Salad New Zealand or South African Sauvignon Blanc, Gewürztraminer, Pinot Blanc.

Monkfish A light, fruity red such as Bardolino, Valpolicella, La Mancha Joven, or most Chardonnays.

Mushroom Merlot-based reds, good Northern Rhône, top Piedmontese reds.

Mushrooms à la Greque Sauvignon Blanc or fresh, modern Greek white.

Mushroom Soup Bordeaux Blanc, Côtes de Gasgogne.

Risotto with Fungi Porcini Top-notch Piedmontese reds – mature Barbera, Barbaresco, or earthy Southern French reds.

Stuffed Mushrooms Chenin Blanc, Sylvaner.

Wild Mushrooms Nebbiolo, red Bordeaux.

Mussels Sauvignon Blanc, light Chardonnay, Muscadet Sur Lie.

Moules Marinières Bordeaux Blanc or Muscadet Sur Lie.

New Zealand Green-Lipped Mussels New Zealand Sauvignon Blanc.

Mustard Surprisingly, can help red Bordeaux and other tannic reds to go with beef.

Dijon Mustard Beaujolais.

French Mustard White Bordeaux.

Steak with Dijon Mustard New World Cabernet Sauvignon or Australian Shiraz.

Wholegrain Mustard Beaujolais, Valpolicella.

N

Nectarine Sweet German Riesling.

Nutmeg Rioja, Australian Shiraz, or, for sweet dishes, Australian late harvest.

Nuts Amontillado sherry, Vin Santo, and Tokaji.

O

Octopus Rueda white or a fresh, modern Greek white.

Olives Dry sherry, Muscadet, Retsina.

Salade Niçoise Muscadet, Vinho Verde, or Beaujolais.

Tapenade Dry sherry or Madeira.

Onion

Caramelized Onions Shiraz-based Australians, Zinfandel from the US, or a good Pinotage.

French Onion Soup Sancerre or dry, unoaked Sauvignon Blanc; Aligoté; white Bordeaux.

Onion/Leek Tart Alsace Gewürztraminer, New World Riesling, or a good unoaked Chablis.

Orange

Caramelised Oranges Asti, Sauternes, or Muscat de Beaumes de Venise.

Crêpe Suzette Sweet Champagne, Moscato d'Asti.

Orange Sorbet Moscato or sweet Tokaji.

Orange Zest Dry Muscat, Amontillado sherry.

Oregano Provençal reds, red Lambrusco, serious Chianti, or lightish Zinfandel.

Oxtail Australian Cabernet, good Bordeaux.

Oysters Champagne; Chablis; or other crisp, dry white.

Oyster Sauce

Beef and Snow Peas in Oyster Sauce Crisp, dry whites like Muscadet or a Northern Italian Lugana or Pinot Bianco, white Rhône, Gewürztraminer.

P

Paprika

Goulash Eastern European red like Bulgarian Cabernet or Mavrud, Hungarian Kadarka, or Australian Shiraz.

Parmesan Salice Salentino, Valpolicella.

Baked Chicken Parmesan with Basil Chenin Blanc, Riesling.

Parsley Dry, Italian whites – Bianco di Custoza, Nebbiolo, or Barbera.

Parsley Sauce Pinot Grigio, Hungarian Furmint, lightly oaked Chardonnay

Partridge

Roast Partridge Australian Shiraz, Gevrey-Chambertin, Pomerol, or St. Emilion.

Pasta

Lasagne Valpolicella, Barbera, Teroldego, Australian Verdelho or Sauvignon.

Pasta with Meat Sauce Chianti, Bordeaux Rouge.

Pasta with Pesto Sauce New Zealand Sauvignon Blanc, Valpolicella.

Pasta with Seafood Sauce Soave, Sancerre.

Ravioli with Spinach and Ricotta Pinot Bianco/Grigio, Cabernet d'Anjou.

Spaghetti with Tomato Sauce California Cabernet, Zinfandel, Chianti.

Spaghetti Vongole Pinot Bianco, Lugana.

Tagliatelle Carbonara Pinot Grigio or a fresh, red Bardolino or Beaujolais.

Peach Sweet German Riesling.

Peaches in Wine Riesling Auslese, Riesling Gewürztraminer Vendange Tardive, sweet Vouvray.

Peanuts

Beef in Peanut Curry New World Chardonnay; an aromatic, white Rhône.

Satay Gewürztraminer.

Pepper (corns)

Steak au Poivre Cabernet Sauvignon, Chianti, Barbera, Rhône reds, Shiraz, or Rioja.

Peppers (fresh green, red) New Zealand Cabernet, Loire reds, crisp Sauvignon Blanc, Beaujolais, Tuscan red.

Peppers (yellow) Fruity, Italian reds – Valpolicella, etc.

  Stuffed Peppers Hungarian red – Bull's Blood; Zinfandel; Chianti; or spicy, Rhône reds.

Pheasant Top-class, red Burgundy; good American Pinot Noir; mature Hermitage.

  Pheasant Casserole Top class, red Burgundy; mature Hermitage.

  Pheasant Pâté Côtes du Rhône, Alsace Pinot Blanc.

Pigeon Good red Burgundy, rich Southern Rhône. Chianti also goes well.

  Warm Pigeon Breasts on Salad Merlot-based Bordeaux or Cabernet Rosé.

Pike Eastern European white.

Pine Nuts

  Pesto Sauce New Zealand Sauvignon Blanc, Valpolicella.

Pizza

  Fiorentina Pinot Bianco, Pinot Grigio, Vinho Verde, Sauvignon Blanc.

  Margherita Pinot Grigio, light Zinfandel, dry Grenache rosé.

  Napoletana Verdicchio, Vernaccia de San Gimignano, white Rhône.

  Quattro Formaggi Pinot Grigio, Frascati, Bianco di Custoza.

  Quattro Stagioni Valpolicella, Bardolino, light Chianti, good Soave.

Plaice White Burgundy, South American Chardonnay, Sauvignon Blanc.

Plum

  Plum Pie Trockenbeerenauslese, Côteaux du Layon.

Pork

  Cassoulet Serious white Rhône, Marsanne, or Roussanne; or reds including Grenache and Syrah from the Rhône, berryish, Italian reds, or Zinfandel.

  Pork Casserole Mid-weight, earthy reds like Minervois, Navarra, or Montepulciano d'Abruzzo.

  Pork Pie Spicy reds, Shiraz, Grenache.

  Pork with Prunes Cahors, mature Chinon, or other Loire red, or rich, southern French wine such as Corbières, Minervois, or Faugères.

  Pork Rillettes Pinot Blanc d'Alsace, Menetou-Salon Rouge.

  Pork and Sage Sausages Barbera, Côtes du Rhône.

  Pork Sausages Spicy Rhône reds, Barbera.

  Pork Spare Ribs Zinfandel, Australian Shiraz.

  Roast Pork Rioja reserva, New World Pinot Noir, dry Vouvray.

  Roast Pork with Apple Sauce Off-dry Vouvray or Riesling.

  Saucisson Sec Barbera, Cabernet Franc, Alsace Pinot Blanc, or Beaujolais.

  Spare Ribs with Barbecue Sauce Fruity Australian Shiraz, Grenache, or Zinfandel; spicy Côtes du Rhône from a ripe vintage or an off-dry white.

  Szechuan-Style Pork Dry, aromatic whites; Alsace Pinot Gris; Riesling; Grenache rosé; beer.

Prawns White Bordeaux; dry, Australian Riesling; Gavi.

  Prawn Cocktail Light, fruity whites – German Riesling.

  Prawns in Garlic Vinho Verde, Pinot Bianco.

  Prawn Vol-au-Vents White Bordeaux, Muscadet.

  Thai Prawns Gewürztraminer; dry, aromatic Riesling; or New Zealand Sauvignon Blanc.

Prunes Australian, late harvest Semillon.

Pork with Prunes and Cream Sweet, Chenin-based wines or good Mosel Spätlese.

Prune Ice Cream Muscat de Beaumes de Venise.

Q

Quail Light, red Burgundy; full-flavoured, white Spanish wines.

Quince Lugana.

Braised Venison with Quince Jelly Rich and fruity Australian or Chilean reds; good, ripe Spanish Rioja; or a Southern French red.

R

Rabbit

Rabbit Casserole Red Burgundy, New World Pinot Noir, or mature Châteauneuf-du-Pape.

Rabbit in Cider Muscadet, demi-sec Vouvray, cider, or Calvados.

Rabbit with Mustard Franken wine or Czech Pilsner beer.

Rabbit in Red Wine with Prunes Good, mature Chinon or other Loire red.

Roast Rabbit Tasty, simple, young Rhône – red, white, or rosé.

Raspberries New World, late harvest Riesling; Champagne; Beaujolais; demi-sec Champagne.

Raspberry Fool Vouvray Moelleux.

Ratatouille Bulgarian red, Chianti, simple Rhône or Provence red, Portuguese reds, New Zealand Sauvignon Blanc.

Redcurrant (Cumberland sauce) Rioja, Australian Shiraz.

Red Mullet Dry rosé, California, Washington or Australian Chardonnay.

Rhubarb

Rhubarb Pie Moscato d'Asti, Alsace, German or Austrian late harvest Riesling.

Rice

Rice Pudding Monbazillac, sweet Muscat, Asti, or California Orange Muscat.

Roast Lamb with Garlic and Rosemary Earthy soft reds like California Petite Sirah, Rioja, or Zinfandel.

Rocket Lugana, Pinot Blanc.

Roquefort The classic match is Sauternes or Barsac, but almost any full-flavoured, botrytized sweet wine will be a good partner for strong, creamy, blue cheese.

Rosemary Light red Burgundy or Pinot Noir.

Rum

Flambéed Banana with Rum Jurançon, Tokaji, Pedro Ximénez sherry, and rum.

S

Saffron Dry whites especially Chardonnay.
> *Bass in Saffron Sauce* Riesling (German, Australian, or Austrian), Viognier.
> *Paella with Seafood* White Penedés, unoaked Rioja, Navarra, Provence rosé.

Sage Chianti, or country reds from the Languedoc. Otherwise Sauvignon
Blancs are great, especially Chilean.
> *Roast Chicken, Goose, or Turkey with Sage and Onion Stuffing* Italian reds,
> especially Chianti; soft, plummy Merlots; fruity Rioja; and brambly
> Zinfandel.

Salami Good, beefy Mediterranean rosé; Sardinian red; Rhône red; Zinfandel;
dry, aromatic Hungarian white.

Salmon
> *Carpaccio of Salmon* Cabernet Franc, Chardonnay, Australian reds, red
> Loire, Portuguese reds, Puligny-Montrachet.
> *Grilled Salmon* White Rhône (especially Viognier).
> *Poached Salmon* Chablis; good, white Burgundy; other Chardonnay;
> Alsace Muscat; white Bordeaux.
> *Poached Salmon with Hollandaise* Muscat, Riesling, good Chardonnay.
> *Salmon Pâté* Best white Burgundy.
> *Salmon Trout* Light Pinot Noir from the Loire, New Zealand; good, dry,
> unoaked Chardonnay, Chablis, etc.

Sardines Muscadet, Vinho Verde, light and fruity reds such as Loire,
Gamay.

Scallops Chablis and other unoaked Chardonnay.
> *Coquilles St. Jacques* White Burgundy.
> *Marinated Scallops with Bacon* Fino sherry or mature Riesling.
> *Scallops Mornay* White Burgundy, Riesling Spätlese.

Sea Bass Good white Burgundy.
> *Bass in Saffron Sauce* Riesling (German, Austrian, or Australian), Viognier.

Seafood (general – also see individual entries)
> *Platter of Seafood* Sancerre, Muscadet.
> *Seafood Salad* Soave, Pinot Grigio, Muscadet, lightly oaked Chardonnay

Sesame Seeds Oaked Chardonnay.

Shrimps Albariño, Sancerre, New World Sauvignon, Arneis.
> *Potted Shrimps* New World Chardonnay, Marsanne.

Skate Bordeaux white, Côtes de Gascogne, Pinot Bianco.

Smoked Salmon Chablis, Alsace Pinot Gris, white
Bordeaux.
> *Avocado and Smoked Salmon* Lightly oaked Chardonnay, Fumé Blanc, or
> Australian Semillon.
> *Smoked Salmon Paté* English oaked Fumé Blanc, New Zealand
> Chardonnay.

Smoked Trout
> *Smoked Trout Paté* Good, white Burgundy.

Snapper Australian or South African, dry white.

Sole Chablis, Muscadet.

Sorbet Like ice cream, these can be too cold/sweet for most wines. Try
Australian fortified Muscats.

Sorrel Dry Loire Chenin or Sauvignon Blanc.

Soy Sauce Zinfandel or Australian Verdelho.
Spinach Pinot Grigio, Lugana.
  Eggs Florentine Chablis or unoaked Chardonnay, Pinot Blanc, Sémillion.
  Spinach/Pasta Bakes Soft, Italian reds (Bardolino, Valpolicella), rich whites.
Spring Rolls Pinot Gris, Gewürztraminer, or other aromatic whites.
Squab Good, red Burgundy; rich Southern Rhône; or Chianti.
  Warm Squab Breasts on Salad Merlot-based Bordeaux or Cabernet Rosé.
Squid Gamay de Touraine; Greek, Spanish, or Italian white.
  Squid in Batter Muscadet.
  Squid in Ink Nebbiolo or Barbera.
Stilton Tawny port.
Strawberries – No Cream Surprisingly, red Rioja, Burgundy (or other
    young Pinot Noir). More conventionally, sweet Muscats or fizzy Moscato.
  Strawberries and Cream Vouvray Moelleux, Monbazillac
  Strawberry Meringue Late harvest Riesling.
  Strawberry Mousse Sweet or fortified Muscat.
Sweetbreads Lightly oaked Chablis; Pouilly-Fuissé; or light, red Bordeaux.
  Sweetbreads in Mushroom, Butter, and Cream sauce Southern French
    whites, Vin de Pays Chardonnay.
Sweet and Sour Dishes (general) Gewürztraminer, Sauvignon Blanc
    (unoaked), or beer.

T

Taramasalata Oaked Chardonnay or Fumé Blanc.
Tarragon White Menetou-Salon or South African Sauvignon Blanc.
  Roast/Grilled Chicken with Tarragon Dry Chenin Blanc, Vouvray, dry
    Chenin.
Thyme Ripe and fruity Provençal reds, Rioja, Northern Italian whites.
  Roast Lamb with Thyme New Zealand Cabernet Sauvignon, Bourgeuil.
Toffee Moscatel de Setúbal, Eiswein.
  Banoffee Pie Sweet Tokaji.
Tomato
  Gazpacho Fino sherry, white Rioja.
  Pasta in a Tomato Sauce California Cabernet, Zinfandel, Chianti.
  Tomato Soup Sauvignon Blanc.
Tripe Earthy, French country red; Minervois; Cahors; Fitou.
Trout Pinot Blanc, Chablis.
  Smoked Trout Bourgogne Aligoté, Gewürztraminer, Pinot Gris.
  Trout with Almonds Bianco di Custoza, Pinot Blanc.
Truffles Red Burgundy, old Rioja, Barolo, or Hermitage.
Tuna
  Carpaccio of Tuna Australian Chardonnay, red Loire, Beaujolais.
  Fresh Tuna Alsace Pinot Gris, Australian Chardonnay, Beaujolais.
Turbot Best white Burgundy, top California or Australian Chardonnay.
Turkey
  Roast Turkey Beaujolais, light Burgundy, and rich or off-dry whites.
  Roast Turkey with Chestnut Stuffing Rhône, Merlot, or mature Burgundy.

V

Vanilla Liqueur Muscat.
   Crème Brûlée Jurançon Moelleux, Tokaji.
   Custard Monbazillac, sweet Vouvray.
Veal
   Blanquette de Veau Aromatic, spicy whites from Alsace or from the
      Northern Rhône.
   Roast Veal Light, Italian whites, or fairly light reds – Spanish or Loire;
      St. Emilion.
   Wienerschnitzel Austrian Grüner Veltliner or Alsace or Hungarian
      Pinot Blanc.
Vegetables
   Roasted and Grilled Light, juicy reds; Beaujolais; Sancerre; and Sauvignon
      Blanc. Unoaked or lightly oaked Chardonnay.
   Vegetable Soup Pinot Blanc, rustic reds such as Corbières, or southern
      Italian reds.
   Vegetable Terrine Good New World Chardonnay.
Venison Pinotage; rich red Rhône; mature Burgundy; earthy, Italian reds.
   Venison Casserole Australian Shiraz, American Zinfandel, South African red
      (Pinotage).
Vinegar
   Choucroute Garnie White Alsace (especially Riesling), Italian Pinot Grigio,
      or Beaujolais.
   Sauerkraut Pilsner beer.

W

Walnut Tawny port, sweet Madeira.
Watercress
   Watercress Soup Aromatic dry Riesling (Alsace or Australia).
Whitebait Fino sherry, Spanish red/white (Albariño, Garnacha, Tempranillo),
   Soave.

Y

Yams Depends on the sauce. When subtly prepared, try Pinot Blanc.
Yogurt Needs full-flavoured wines, such as Australian Semillon or
   New World Chardonnay.

Z

Zabaglione Rich sweet Marsala, Australian Liqueur Muscat, or a fortified
   French Muscat.

A–Z OF
WINE

HOW TO READ THE ENTRIES

① **②**

🍷 **Ch. l'Angélus** [lon jay-loos] (*St. Emilion Grand Cru Classé, Bordeaux*, France) Flying high since the late 1980s and especially popular in the US and Asia,, this is a lovely, plummy *St. Emilion* to watch. The *second label* Carillon d'Angélus is also well worth seeking out.
★★★★★ 1990 $$$; ★★★ 1991 $$$ 95 96 00 01

③ **④** **⑤** **⑥**

①

Names of wines are accompanied by a glass symbol: 🍷
Grape varieties are accompanied by a bunch of grapes: 🍇
② Wine regions appear in burgundy type.

Words that have their own entry elsewhere in the A–Z appear in italic.
③ Recommended wines may also be cross-referenced.

Throughout this section, examples are given of recommended vintages, producers, or wines which represent good examples of the region, style
④ or maker.

Recommended wines are accompanied by stars:

    ★★★★★   *outstanding in their style.*
    ★★★★   *excellent in their style.*
⑤   ★★★   *good in their style.*

Prices are indicated using the following symbols:

⑥   **£** *under £7*   **££** *£7–£15*   **£££** *£15–£30*   **££££** *over £30*

Additional recommended vintages for particular wines may be listed in bold, where appropriate.

PRONUNCIATION GUIDE

All but the most common words are followed by square brackets [ ], which enclose pronunciation guides. These use the "sounding-out" phonetic method, with the accented syllable (if there is one) indicated by capital letters. For example, **Spätlese** is pronounced as ***SHPAYT-lay-zuh***. The basic sounds employed in this book's pronunciations are as follows:

a *as in* **can**	**ah** *as in* **father**	**ay** *as in* **day**	**ur** *as in* **turn**
ch *as in* **church**	**kh** *as in* **loch**	**y** *as in* **yes**	**zh** *as in* **vision**
ee *as in* **see**	**eh** *as in* **get**	**g** *as in* **game**	**i** *as in* **pie**
ih *as in* **if**	**j** *as in* **gin**	**k** *as in* **cat**	**o** *as in* **hot**
oh *as in* **soap**	**oo** *as in* **food**	**ow** *as in* **cow**	**uh** *as in* **up**

Foreign sounds To represent sounds not common in English, the following spellings are used in the pronunciation guide: **eu** is like a cross between **oo** and **a**; an italicized **n** or **m** is silent and the preceding vowel sounds nasal; an **ñ** is like an **n** followed by a **y** (as in **Bourgogne**); an italicized **r** sounds like a cross between **r** and **w**; **rr** sounds like a rolled **r**.

A

ℤ Abacus (*Napa,* California) An innovative (for California) concept by the long-established *ZD* winery of blending tiny quantities of different red vintages. (*Vega Sicilia* in Spain did it first.) Quality is high but prices are astronomical.

ℤ Abadia Retuerta [ah-bah-dee-yah Reh-twehr-tah] (Spain) Close to *Ribera del Duero,* this large new venture benefits from the expertise of Pascal Delbeck of *Ch. Belair* in *St. Emilion.* Several equally recommendable cuvées, including Palomar, Pago Negralato, Valdebon, and Campanario1. ★★★★ 2001 Abadia Retuerta Primicia £; ★★★★ 2000 Abadia Retuerta Rívola £

ℤ Abazzia Sant'Anastasia [ah-baht-zee-yah San-tan-nah-stah-zee-yah] (*Sicily* Italy) The hottest new star in Sicily, this estate makes a Cabernet – Litra – that can beat the *Super-Tuscans,* and some pretty fine *Chardonnay* – Baccante – as well as reds from the local Nero d'Avola.

Abboccato [ah-boh-kah-toh] (Italy) Semi-dry.

ℤ Abel-Lepitre [ah-bel luh-pee-tre] (*Champagne,* France) The wine to look for here is the Réserve Blanc de Blancs Cuvée C.

Abfüller/Abfüllung [ap-few-ler/ap-few-loong] (Germany) Bottler/bottled by.

Abocado [ah-boh-kah-doh] (Spain) Semi-dry.

ℤ Abreu Vineyards [Eh-broo] (*Napa,* California) Cult St. Helena winery with vineyards whose grapes go to such top *Napa* names as *Harlan Estate.* Don't bother to go looking in the stores, though; to lay your hands on a bottle, you'll have to be on the mailing list.

ℤ Quinta da Abrigada [keen-tah dah ah-bree-gah-dah] (Alenquer, Portugal) Reliable estate making characterful wines. **97,98.**

Abruzzi/zzo [ah-broot-zee/zoh] (Italy) Region on the east coast, with often dull *Trebbiano* whites and fast-improving *Montepulciano* reds. **Castello di Salle; Dino Illuminati; Gianni Masciarelli; Di Majo Norante; Eduardo Valentini.**

AC (France) See *Appellation Contrôlée.*

ℤ Acacia [a-kay-shah] (*Carneros,* California) Long-established, but often underrated producer of *Chardonnay* and *Pinot Noir, Viognier* and *Zinfandel.* Under the same ownership as *Chalone, Edna Valley,* and *Carmenet.*

ℤ Accordini [a-kor-DEE-nee] (*Veneto,* Italy) New *Valpolicella* star with fine vineyards.

Acetic acid [ah-see-tihk] This volatile acid (CH_3COOH) features in small proportions in all wines. Careless winemaking can result in wine being turned into acetic acid, a substance most people know as vinegar.

Acidity Naturally occurring (*tartaric* and malic) acids in the grapes are vital to contributing freshness, and also help to preserve the wine while it ages. In reds and many cool region whites, the malic is often converted to lactic by a natural process known as *malolactic fermentation,* which gives the wines a buttery texture and flavour. In hotter countries (and sometimes cooler ones) the acid level may (not always legally) be adjusted by adding *tartaric* and citric acid.

ℤ Ackerman-Laurance [ah-kehr-man Loh-ronss] (*Loire,* France) One of the Loire's most reliable sparkling wine producers. Privilège is the top wine.

Aconcagua Valley [ah-kon-kar-gwah] (*Central Valley,* Chile) Region noted for blackcurranty *Cabernet Sauvignon.* The sub-region is *Casablanca.* Grapes from both are used by many Chilean producers. **Concha y Toro, Errazuriz.** ★★★★ 2001 Errazuriz Wild Ferment Chardonnay ££

ℤ Tim Adams (*Clare Valley,* Australia) Highly successful producer of *Riesling,* rich peachy *Semillon,* and deep-flavoured Aberfeldy *Shiraz* and intense peppery Fergus *Grenache.* ★★★★★ 1999 Shiraz by Sorby ££; ★★★ 2000 The Fergus ££; ★★★ 2000 Tim Adams Semillon ££

ℤ Adanti [ah-dan-ti] (*Umbria,* Italy) Star producer of spicy reds and herby Grechetto whites.

Adega [ah-day-gah] (Portugal) Winery – equivalent to Spanish *bodega.*

Adelaide Hills [ah-dur-layd] (*South Australia*) Cool region, with classy, lean *Riesling, Semillon, Sauvignon Blanc* and *Chardonnay*, sparkling wine, *Pinot Noir* and even *Zinfandel*. *Lenswood* is a new sub-region *Ashton Hills;* Chain of Ponds; Grosett; Heggies; Henschke; Mountadam; Nepenthe; Penfolds; Shaw & Smith; Geoff Weaver.

Weingut Graf [graf-ah-del-man] (*Württemberg,* Germany) Top estate, making good reds from grapes such as the *Trollinger,* Lemberger, and Urban. Look for Brüssele'r Spitze wines.

Adelsheim [a-del-sime] (*Oregon,* USA) Classy, long-lived *Pinot Noir, Chardonnay,* and *Pinot Gris*

Age [ah-khay] (*Rioja,* Spain) Big, modern, highly commercial winery.

Agiorghitiko [a-gee-yor-jee-ti-koh] (Greece) Spicy, plummy red grape grown in the Peloponnese for *Nemea.* Best at high altitudes.

Aglianico [ah-lee-AH-nee-koh] (Italy) Thick-skinned grape grown by the Ancient Greeks. Now used to make *Taurasi* and *Aglianico del Vulture.*

Aglianico del Vulture [ah-lee-AH-nee-koh del vool-TOO-reh] (*Basilicata,* Italy) Tannic liquoricey-chocolatey blockbusters made in Southern Italy on the hills of an extinct volcano. Older examples are labelled as Vecchio (3 years+) and Riserva (5 years+). Armando Martino; D'Angelo; Basilium; Paternoster.

La Agricola (*Mendoza,* Argentina) One of this go-ahead country's most go-ahead wineries. The top wines are sold under the "Q" range. Picajuan Creek and Santa Julia are labels that are also worth looking out for.

Agricola vitivinicola (Italy) Wine estate.

Ahr [ahr] (Germany) Northernmost *Anbaugebiet,* making light-bodied reds.

Ajaccio [ah-JAK-see-yoh] (*Corsica,* France) Very mixed fare, but *Comte Peraldi* makes intense reds and whites. See also: Gie Les Rameaux.

Aigle [eh-gl'] (*Vaud,* Switzerland) The place to find fresh, floral *Chasselas* (known here as *Dorin*). The *Pinot Noir* can be good too. Baudoux, Testuz.

Airén [i-REHN] (Spain) The world's most planted white variety. Dull and fortunately more or less restricted to the region of *La Mancha.*

Ajaccio [a-jax-yoh] (Corsica, France) Good reds, especially from the Sciacarello grape, come from this region named after the capital of *Corsica.*

Alban (*Central Coast,* California) *Edna Valley* winery with exciting *Rhône*-style reds (esp. *Grenache*) and whites.

Albana di Romagna [ahl-BAH-nah dee roh-MAN-yah] (*Emilia-Romagna,* Italy) Inexplicably, Italy's first white *DOCG.* Traditionally dull but improving white. Passita, sweeter whites are best. Celli; Umberto Cesari; Gruppo Cevico; Conti; Ferrucci; Fattoria Paradiso; Madonia; Uccellina; Zerbina.

Albariño [ahl-BAH-ree-nyoh] (*Galicia,* Spain) The Spanish name for the Portuguese *Alvarinho* and the peachy-spicy wine made from it in *Rias Baixas.* Lagar de Cervera; Martin Codex; Pazo de Barrantes; Salnesu; Valdamor.

Castello d'Albola [KAS-teh-loh DAL-boh-la] (*Tuscany,* Italy) Top Tuscan Estate belonging to the increasingly dynamic firm of *Zonin.*

Alcamo [ahl-Cah-moh] (Sicily) Distinctive, rich, dry white made from the local *Catarratto* grape. Rapitalà is the name to look for.

Alcohol This simple compound, technically known as ethanol, is formed by the action of yeast on sugar during fermentation.

Aleatico [ah-lay-AH-tee-koh] (Italy) Red grape producing sweet, *Muscat*-style, often fortified wines. Produces *DOCs* A. di Puglia and A. di Gradoli.

Alella [ah-LEH-yah] (*Catalonia,* Spain) *DO* district producing better whites (from grapes including the *Xarel-lo*) than reds. Marfil; Marqués de Alella; Parxet.

Alenquer [ah-lehn-kehr] (*Oeste,* Portugal) Coolish region producing good *Periquita* reds and *Muscat*-style *Fernão Pires* whites. Also making successful efforts from French varietals. Quinta da Boavista; Quinta de Pancas.

Alentejo [ah-lehn-TAY-joh] (Portugal) Improving province north of the Algarve with five *DOCs*: Borba, Portalegre, Redondo, Reguengos, Vidigueira. This is the region where *JM da Fonseca* makes Morgado de Reguengo, *JP Vinhos* produces Tinta da Anfora and *Ch. Lafite* has its Quinta do Carmo. Alianca; Borba; Cartuxa; Cortes de Cima; Esporão; Herdade de Mouchao; Pera Manca; *Quinta do Carmo*; Redondo, Jose de Sousa; Sogrape.

Alexander Valley (*Sonoma*, California) *Appellation* in which *Simi, Jordan, Murphy-Goode*, and *Geyser Peak* are based. *Turley* makes big *Zinfandels* here too. Alexander Valley Vineyards; Arrowood, *Ch. St Jean; Clos du Bois; Geyser Peak;* Godwin; *Jordan; Marcassin;* Murphy-Goode; Seghesio; Silver Oak; Simi; Stonestreet; Turley.

Algarve [ahl-garv] (Portugal) Huge, officially denominated region whose wines are – just about – worth drinking while in the region on holiday.

❦ **Caves Aliança** [ah-lee-an-sah] (Portugal) Modern *Bairrada, Douro,* and better-than-average *Dão*. ★★★★ **1999 Quinta da Terrugem ££**

Alicante (*Valencia*, Spain) Hot region producing generally dull stuff apart from the sweetly honeyed *Moscatels* that appreciate the heat.

❦ **Alicante-Bouschet** [al-ee-KONT- boo-SHAY] Unusual dark-skinned and fleshed grapes traditionally used (usually illegally) for dyeing pallid reds .

❦ **Aligoté** [Al-lee-goh-tay] (*Burgundy,* France) Lesser white grape at its best in the village of *Bouzeron*. **G&J-H Goisot; Jayer-Gilles; A&P de Vilaine.**

❦ **Alión** [ah-lee-yon] (*Ribera del Duero*, Spain) New venture by the owners of *Vega Sicilia*, with fruitier, more modern wines.

❦ **Alkoomi** [al-koo-mee] (*Western Australia*) Fine *Sauvignon* and *Riesling*. ★★★★ **1999 Shiraz ££**

Allan Scott (*Marlborough*, New Zealand) Well made whites.

❦ **All Saints** (*Rutherglen,* Australia) Good producer of *Liqueur Muscat* and *Tokay*.

❦ **Allegrini** [ah-leh-GREE-nee] (*Veneto*, Italy) Top-class producer of single-vineyard *Valpolicella* and *Soave*. Now often doing so without recourse to the *DOC/DOCG* system. ★★★★★ **1998 'La Poja' ££££**

❦ **Thierry Allemand** [al-mon] (*Rhône,* France) Producer of classic, concentrated, single-vineyard *Cornas* from a small 6-acre (2.5-hectare) estate.

❦ **Finca Allende** [ah-lyen-day] (*Rioja*, Spain) Excellent, pricy new wave *Rioja* bottled earlier for more fruit, freshness, density. Aurus is the top wine.

❦ **Allesverloren** [ah-less-ver-lor-ren] (South Africa) Old-established estate making solid wines, especially port styles, *Cabernet, Shiraz, Tinta Barocca*.

Allier [a-lee-yay] (France) Spicy oak favoured by makers of white wine.

❦ **Almaviva** [al-mah-vee-vah] (*Maipo*, Chile) New, pricy red co-production between *Mouton Rothschild* and *Concha y Toro*. ★★★★★ **1999 £££**

Almacenista [al-mah-theh-nee-stah] (*Jerez,* Spain) Fine unblended sherry from a single *solera* – the sherry equivalent of a single malt whisky. **Lustau.**

❦ **Aloxe-Corton** [a-loss kawr-ton] (*Burgundy*, France) *Côte de Beaune commune* with tough, slow-maturing reds (including the *Grand Cru Corton*) and potentially sublime whites (including Corton-Charlemagne). Louis Latour's pricy whites can be fine. d'Angerville; Arnoux; *Bonneau du Martray;* Denis Bousse; Capitan-Gagnerot; Chandon de Briailles; Marius Delarche; *Drouhin;* Michel Gay; Antonin Guyon; Jadot; *Patrick Javillier;* Daniel Largeot; *Leflaive;* Prince de Mérode; André Nudant; Comte Senard; *Tollot-Beaut;* Michel Voarick.

Alsace [al-sas] (France) Region whose warm microclimate makes for riper-tasting wines that are named after the grapes – *Pinot Noir, Gewürztraminer, Riesling, Pinot Gris, Pinot Blanc* (known as Pinot d'Alsace), *Sylvaner,* and (rarely) *Muscat*. In the right hands, the 50 or so *Grand Cru* vineyards should yield better wines. *Late harvest* sweet wines are labelled *Vendange Tardive* and *Sélection des Grains Nobles*. Albrecht; J Becker; *Léon Beyer;* Paul Blanck; *Bott-Geyl;* Albert Boxler; *Ernest J & F Burn;* Joseph Cattin; Marcel Deiss; Jean-Pierre Dirler; *Dopff au Moulin;* Faller; Hugel; Josmeyer; André Kientzler; Kreydenweiss; Kuentz-Bas; Albert Mann; Meyer-Fonné; *Mittnacht-Klack;* René Muré; Ostertag; *Rolly Gassmann;* Schlumberger; Schoffit; Bruno Sorg; Marc Tempé; Trimbach; Weinbach; Zind Humbrecht.

A

🍇 **Altano** [al-tah-noh] (*Douro*, Portugal) Appealing newish red table wine from the Symington Group of port fame. **99,00.**

🍇 **Elio Altare** [Ehl-lee-yoh al-TAh-ray] (*Piedmont*, Italy) The genial, Svengali-like leader of the *Barolo* revolution and inspirer of *Clerico* and *Roberto Voerzio*. Tragically lost most of his 1998 harvest to mouldy corks.

🍇 **Altesino** [al-TEH-see-noh] (*Tuscany*, Italy) First-class *Brunello di Montalcino*, *Cabernet* ("Palazzo"), and *Sangiovese* ("Altesi").

Alto Adige [ahl-toh AH-dee-jay] (Italy) Aka Italian Tyrol and Südtirol. *DOC* for a huge range of whites often from Germanic grape varieties; also light and fruity reds from the *Lagrein* and Vernatsch are particularly successful here. **Cant. Prod. di Cortaccia; Cant. Prod. di Termeno; Cant. Vit. di Caldaro; Gaierhof; Giorgio Grai; Franz Haas; Hofstätter; *Alois Lageder;* Maddalena; *Pojer & Sandri;*San Michele Appiano; Sta Maddalena; Niedermayer; *Tiefenbrunner;* Thurnhof; Viticoltori Alto-Adige.** ★★★★★ 2000 Loacker Pinot Grigio "Isargus" ££

🍇 **Alvarinho** [ahl-vah-reen-yoh] (Portugal) White grape aka *Albariño*; at its lemony best in *Vinho Verde* and in the *DO* Alvarinho de Monção.

🍇 **Alvear** (*Montilla-Moriles*, Spain) Large producer of *Montilla*; quality is good.

Amabile [am-MAH-bee-lay] (Italy) Semi-sweet.

🍇 **Castello di Ama** [ah-mah] (*Tuscany*, Italy) Brilliant small *Chianti* estate. Great single vineyard Vigna l'Apparita wines and very fine *Chardonnay*.

Amador County [am-uh-dor] (California) Intensely-flavoured, old-fashioned *Zinfandel*. Look for Amador Foothills Winery's old-vine *Zinfandels* and top-of-the-line stuff from *Sutter Home* and *Monteviña*. *Quady*, Vino Noceto. ★★★★ 1999 Ravenswood Amador County Zinfandel ££

🍇 **Amarone** [ah-mah-ROH-neh] (*Veneto*, Italy) Literally "bitter"; used to describe *Recioto* wines fermented dry, especially *Amarone della Valpolicella*. **Accordini; Allegrini; Begalli; Brigaldara; Luigi Brunelli; Tommaso Bussola; Corte Sant' Alda; Masi; Angelo Nicolis; Quintarelli; Romano dal Forno; Tedeschi; Viviani; Zenato.** ★★★★★ 1998 Amarone della Valpolicella Classico Brigaldara £££

🍇 **Amberley Estate** (*Margaret River*, Australia) Not one of the top stars of *Margaret River*, but a reliable name. ★★★ 1999 Semillon ££

🍇 **Fattoria di Ambra** [fah-toh-ree-yah dee am-bra] (*Tuscany*, Italy) Leading *Carmignano* estate. Look out for single vineyard *Elzana* and *Vigne Alte*.

🍇 **Bodegas Amézola de la Mora** [ah-meh-THOH-lah deh lah MAW-rah] (*Rioja,* Spain) Eight-year-old estate producing unusually classy red *Rioja*.

🍇 **Amigne** [ah-meen] (*Valais*, Switzerland) Unusual white grape that makes traditional (non fruit-driven) wines in Vétroz. *J-R Germanier; Imesch.*

🍇 **Amity** [am-mi-tee] (*Oregon*, US) Maker of very high-quality berryish Pinot Noir, good dry *Gewurztraminer* and *late-harvest* whites.

Amontillado [am-mon-tee-yah-doh] (*Jerez*, Spain) Literally "like Montilla." Often pretty basic medium-sweet *sherry*, but ideally fascinating dry, nutty wine. **Gonzalez Byass; Lustau; Sanchez Romate.** ★★★★★ NV Lustau Almacenista Amontillado del Puerto ££

🍇 **Ampelones Vassilou** [am-peh-loh-nehs vas-see-loo] (*Attica*, Greece) Producer of good new-wave Greek wines.

🍇 **Robert Ampeau** [om-poh] (*Burgundy*, France) Traditional Meursault producer whose Perrières is worth looking out for.

Amtliche Prüfungsnummer [am-tlish-eh proof-oong-znoomer] (Germany) Identification number on all *QbA/QmP* labels.

Anbaugebiet [ahn-bow-geh-beet] (Germany) Term for 13 large regions (e.g. *Rheingau*). QbA and QmP wines must include the name of their *Anbaugebiet* on their labels.

Anderson Valley (*Mendocino*, California) Small, cool area, good for white and sparkling wines including the excellent *Roederer*. Do not confuse with the less impressive Anderson Valley, New Mexico. **Edmeades; *Roederer; Steele; Williams Selyem.*** ★★★★★ 1999 Hartford Pinot Noir Velvet Sisters

🍇 **Anderson Vineyard** (*Napa*, California) Stag's Leap producer of intense blackcurranty Cabernet and rich, full-flavoured Chardonnay.

Andrew Will (*Washington State*) Superstar producer of some of *Washington State's* – not to say North America's – best *Merlot, Cabernet Sauvignon*, and ("Sorella") Bordeaux blends.

Ch. Angélus [on jay-loos] (*St. Emilion Premier Grand Cru Classé, Bordeaux, France*) Flying high since the late 1980s, this is a plummy, intensely oaky *St. Emilion*. The *second label* Carillon d'Angélus is worth seeking out.

Marquis d'Angerville [don-jehr-veel] (*Burgundy, France*) Long-established *Volnay* estate with rich, long-lived traditional wines from here and from *Pommard*. ★★★★★ 2000 Volnay 1er Cru Clos des Ducs £££; ★★★★★ 1999 Aloxe-Corton 1er Cru Les Fournières 1999 £££

Ch d'Angludet [don gloo-day] (*Cru Bourgeois, Margaux, Bordeaux, France*) With a reputation built by the late Peter Sichel of *Chateau Palmer*, this is classy cassis-flavoured, if slightly earthy, wine that can generally be drunk young but is worth waiting for.

Angoves [an-gohvs] (*Padthaway*, Australia) *Murray River* producer with reliable, inexpensive *Chardonnay* and *Cabernet* and great brandy. Wine quality is now being helped by a move into *Padthaway*. ★★★★ NV Stoneridge Shiraz Cabernet Sauvignon £; ★★★ 2001 Kanarie Creek Cabernet Sauvignon £

Weingut Paul Anheuser [an-hoy-zur] (*Nahe*, Germany) Strong estate with good *Riesling, Ruländer* and *Pinot Noir*.

Finca la Anita [feen-kah lah an-nee-tah] (*Mendoza*, Argentina) Organic, small-scale winery to watch. Innovative wines include a tasty *Syrah-Malbec* blend.

Anjou [on-joo] (*Loire*, France) Dry and *Demi-Sec* whites, mostly from *Chenin Blanc*, with up to 20 per cent *Chardonnay* or *Sauvignon Blanc*. The rosé is usually awful but there are good, light reds. Look for *Anjou-Villages*, in which *Gamay* is not permitted. Within Anjou, there more specific ACs, most importantly *Savennières* and *Coteaux du Layon*. M. Angeli; Arnault et Fils; Baudoin; Bise; *Bouvet-Ladubay;* Ch. du Breuil; Dom. du Closel; Deslesvaux; Donatien Bahuaud; Ch. de Fesles; Gaudard; Genaiserie; V. Lebreton; Ogereau; Ch. de Passavant; J. Pithon; Renou; *Richou;* Dme de la Sansonniere; Soucherie; Y. Soulez; Ch. la Varière. ★★★ 2000 Renaissance Loire Anjou Blanc Donatien Bahuaud ££

Anjou-Coteaux de la Loire [Koh-toh duh lah Lwarh] (*Loire*, France) Small, lesser-known appellation for varied styles of Chenin Blanc, including quite luscious late-harvest examples. Do not confuse with *Coteaux du Loir*. Ch. de Putille.

Anjou-Villages [on-joo vee-larj] (*Loire*, France) Increasingly famous red wine appellation, thanks partly to Gérard Dépardieu's presence here as a (seriously committed) winemaker at Ch. de Tigné, and partly to the impressive quality of the juicy, potentially long-lived Cabernet-based red wines. Bablut; Closel; Ch. de Coulaine; C. Daviau; *Ch. de Fesles;* Dme Les Grands Vignes; Ogereau; *Richou;* Rochelles; Pierre-Bise; J-Y. Lebreton; V. Lebreton; Ogereau; de Putille Montigilet; Richou; Dom. de Sablonettes; *Pierre Soulez;* Ch. de Tigné.

Annata [ahn-nah-tah] (Italy) *Vintage*.

Roberto Anselmi [an-sehl-mee] (*Veneto*, Italy) Source of classy dry *Soave* Classico wines as well as some extremely serious sweet examples.

Antinori [an-tee-NOR-ree] (*Tuscany*, Italy) Pioneer merchant-producer who has improved the quality of *Chianti*, with his Villa Antinori and Pèppoli, while spearheading the *Super-Tuscan* revolution with *Tignanello, Sassicaia*, and *Solaia*, and producing around 15,000,000 bottles of wine per year. There are also joint ventures in California (*Atlas Peak*), Washington State, and Hungary ★★★★ 1997 Chateau Ste Michelle Col Solare Piero Antinori Stimson Lane Washington State ££££; ★★★★ Antinori Vino Santo ££

A

℧ **Anubis** (Argentina) Appealingly juicy reds come from this joint venture
bet\ween Italian Alberto Antonini and Argentine Susana Balbo.

AOC (France) See *Appellation Contrôlée.*

AP (Germany) See *Amtliche Prüfungsnummer.*

Appellation Contrôlée (AC/AOC) [AH-pehl-lah-see-on kon troh-lay]
(France) Official designation guaranteeing origin, grape varieties, and method
of production and – in theory – quality, though tradition and vested interest
combine to allow pretty appalling wines to receive the rubber stamp.
Increasingly questioned by quality-conscious producers.

℧ **Aprémont** [ah-pray-mon] (Eastern France) Floral, slightly *petillant* white
from skiing region. **Marc Portaz; B&C Richel; Ch. de la Violette.**

Apulia [ah-pool-ee-yah] (Italy) See *Puglia.*

℧ **Aquileia** [ah-kwee-lay-ah] (*Friuli-Venezia Giulia,* Italy) *DOC* for easy-going,
single-variety wines. The *Refosco* can be plummily refreshing. **Tenuta
Beltrame; *Zonin.***

℧ **Agricola Aquitania** [ah-gree-koh-lah ah-kee-tah-nee-ya] (*Maipo,* Chile)
Estate founded by Paul Pontallier (of Ch. Margaux) and Bruno Prats (formerly
of Ch. Cos d'Estournel), overlooking the city of Santiago and close to
premium housing land. Early vintages of the *Cabernet* were rather forbidding
(and suffered from being unoaked). More recent efforts are richer, thanks
partly to older vines and partly to a stay in cask. The top wine is Paul Bruno
and the second wine, Uno Fuero.

Aragón [ah-rah-GONN] (Spain) Slowly up-and-coming region in which are
situated Campo de Borja, Cariñena, Somontano.

🍇 **Aragonez** [ah-rah-goh-nesh] (Portugal) Synonym for *Tempranillo.*

℧ **Arbois** [ahr-bwah] (Eastern France) AC region with light *Trousseau* and *Pinot
Noir* reds and nutty dry Savignan (not to be confused with the Sauvignon)
and *Chardonnay* whites. Also *sherry*-like *Vin Jaune,* sweet *Vin de Paille,* and
sparkling wine. **Aviet; Ch d'Arlay; Bourdy; Dugois; Fruitière Viticole; Lornet;
Overnoy; la Pinte; J Puffeney; Rijckaert; Rolet; A&M Tissot; J Tissot. ★★★** 2000
Jean Rijckaert Arbois Pré Leveron

℧ **Ch. Archambeau** (*Bordeaux,* France) Good-value Graves reds and dry whites

℧ **Ch. d' Arche** [dahrsh] (*Sauternes 2ème Cru Classé, Bordeaux*, France)
Greatly improved, but still slightly patchy.

℧ **Archery Summit** (*Oregon,* USA) A recent venture in Yamhill County in
Oregon by Gary Andrus of *Pine Ridge* in Napa. Both Pinot Noir and Pinot
Gris are impressive – if pricey.

℧ **Viña Ardanza** [veen-yah ahr-dan-thah] (*Rioja,* Spain) Highly reliable, fairly
full-bodied, long-lived, classic red Rioja made with a high proportion (40 per
cent) of *Grenache*; good, *oaky* white, too. **★★★** 1994 Rioja Reserva ££

℧ **d'Arenberg** [dar-ren-burg] (*McLaren Vale,* Australia) Excellent up-and-
coming producer with memorably named, impressive sweet and dry table
wines, and unusually dazzling fortifieds. **★★★★★ 2000 The Coppermine
Road Cabernet Sauvignon ££; ★★★★ 2001 The Olive Grove Chardonnay ££**

Argentina Fast up-and-coming nation with fine *Malbec.* It is also good for its
Cabernet and *Merlot,* which have a touch more backbone than many efforts
from Chile; and there are interesting wines made from Italian red varieties.
Chardonnays and grapey whites from the *Muscat*-like *Torrontes* are worthwhile
too. La Agricola; Finca la Anita; *Leoncio Arizu; Balbi; Luigi Bosca;* Canale; *Catena;
M Chandon* (Paul Galard; Terrazas); Esmeralda; *Etchart; Lurton; Morande;*
Navarro Correas; *Norton; la Rural;* San Telmo; Santa Ana; *Torino; Trapiche; Weinert.*
★★★★★ 2000 Alamos Chardonnay Nicholas Catena Mendoza £

℧ **Tenuta di Argiano** [teh-noo-tah dee ahr-zhee-ahn-noh] (*Tuscany,* Italy)
Instant success story, with top-class vineyards, and lovely juicy reds.

℧ **Argyle** (*Oregon,* US) Classy sparkling wine and still wines from Brian Croser
(of *Petaluma)* Now (laudably) innovating with screwcaps.

🍇 **Arinto** [ah-reen-toh] (Portugal) High quality white grape with good acidity and
the ability to age in bottle. The flavour is lemony and peachy.

A

🍷 **Arietta** [ahr-ree-yeht-tah] (Napa, California) Maker of classy Bordeaux blends which, unusually, mimic Cheval Blanc by marrying *Merlot* with *Cabernet Franc*.

🍷 **Ch. d'Arlay** [dahr-lay] (*Jura*, France) Reliable producer of nutty *Vin Jaune* and light, earthy-raspberry Pinot Noir.

🍷 **Leoncio Arizu** [Ah-ree-zoo] (*Mendoza*, Argentina) Variable, old-established producer. Also owns *Luigi Bosca*

🍷 **Dom. de l'Arlot** [dur-lahr-loh] (*Burgundy*, France) Brilliant, award-winning *Nuits-St.-Georges* estate under the same ownership as *Ch. Pichon-Longueville*. Delicate modern reds (including impressive *Vosne-Romanée*) and a rare example of white *Nuits-St.-Georges*.

🍷 **Ch. d'Armailhac** [darh-mi yak] (*Pauillac 5ème Cru Classé, Bordeaux*, France). The wines from this château come from the same stable as *Mouton-Rothschild*, and show similar rich flavours, though never the same elegance.

🍷 **Dom. du Comte Armand** [komt-arh-mon] (*Burgundy*, France) The top wine from the Canadian-born winemaker here is the exceptional *Pommard* Clos des Epeneaux, but the *Auxey-Duresses* and *Volnay les Fremiets* are fine too.
★★★★ Pommard Clos des Epeneaux 1er cru £££

🍇 **Arneis** [ahr-nay-ees] (*Piedmont*, Italy) Spicy white; makes good, young, unoaked wine. Deletto; Ceretto; Funtanin; Malvira; Serafino; Voerzio.
★★★ 2001 Contea di Castiglione Roero Arneis Araldica Vini ££

🍷 **Ch. l' Arrosée,** [lah-roh-say] (*St. Emilion Grand Cru Classé, Bordeaux*, France) Small, well-sited property with fruity intense wines.

🍷 **Arrowood** (*Sonoma Valley*, California) Fine *Chardonnay*, *Merlot*, *Pinot Blanc*, *Viognier*, and *Cabernet* from former *Ch. St. Jean* winemaker.

🍷 **Ismael Arroyo** [uh-Roy-oh] (*Ribera del Duero*, Spain) A name to watch for flavoursome reds.

🍷 **Arruda** (*Estremadura*, Portugal) Both a sub-region and its eponymous co-op cellar, with a reputation for good value. ★★★ 1997 Arruda Tinto Adega Co-op £

🍷 **Artadi** [ahr-tah-dee] (*Rioja*, Spain) Up-and-coming producer with particularly good *Crianza* and *Reserva* wines – and fast-rising prices.

🍇 **Arvine** [ah-veen] (Switzerland) Delicious, spicy white indigenous grape which has reminded some visiting Italians of their *Arneis*. Bonvin; Chappaz; Provins; Rochaix

🍷 **Bodegas Arzuaga** [Ahr-thwah-gah] (*Ribera del Duero*, Spain) One of the growing number of new-wave estates in Ribera del Duero, with large acreage of vines and emphatically modern winemaking that is catching the attention of US critics.

🍷 **Matteo Ascheri** [ash-sheh-ree] (*Piedmont*, Italy) Pioneering producer. Impressive single-vineyard, tobacco 'n berry wines, also *Nebbiolo*, *Syrah*, and *Viognier* and Freisa del Langhe. ★★★★ 2001 Dolcetto d'Alba Vigna ££; ★★★ 2000 Barbera d'Alba Vigna Fontanelle ££

🍷 **Ashbrook Estate** (*Margaret River*, Australia) Excellent quality; look for *Chardonnay, Semillon, Verdelho, Sauvignon, Cabernet*.

Asciutto [ah-shoo-toh] (Italy) Dry.

Assenovgrad [ass-seh-nov-grad] (Bulgaria) Demarcated northern wine region with rich plummy *Cabernet Sauvignon, Merlot*, and *Mavrud*.

🍷 **Ashton Hills** (*Adelaide Hills*, Australia) Small up-and-coming winery producing good Pinot Noir as well as subtle, increasingly creditable *Chardonnay* and *Riesling*. ★★★★ 1999 Three Sheds Red ££

Assemblage [ah-sahm-blahj] (France) The art of blending wine from different grape varieties. Associated with *Bordeaux* and *Champagne*.

Assmanhausen [ass-mahn-how-zehn] (*Rheingau*, Germany) If you like sweet Pinot Noir, this is the place to come looking for it.

🍷 **Asti** (*Piedmont*, Italy) Town famous for sparkling *Spumante*, lighter *Moscato d'Asti*, and red *Barbera d'Asti*. Bera; Bersano; Contratto; Fontanafredda; Gancia; Martini. ★★★ 1998 Barbera d'Asti Croutin Reserva Personale Scrimaglio ££££; ★★★ 2001 Villa Lanata Moscato Cardinale £

Astringent Mouth-puckering. Associated with young red wine. See *tannin*.

A

Aszu [ah-soo] (*Hungary*) The sweet syrup made from dried and "nobly rotten" grapes (see *botrytis*) used to sweeten *Tokaji*.

☿ **Ata Rangi** [ah-tah ran-gee] (*Martinborough*, New Zealand) Estate with high-quality *Pinot*, *Chardonnay*, and *Shiraz*.

☿ **Atlas Peak** (*Napa*, California) Antinori's US venture is proving more successful with Cabernet than with Sangiovese.

Attica (Greece) Demarcated region round Athens; produces a lot of *retsina*.

☿ **Au Bon Climat** [oh bon klee-Mat] (*Santa Barbara*, California) Top-quality producer of characterful and flavoursome *Pinot Noir* and particularly classy *Chardonnay*. ★★★★★ 1999 Knox Alexander ££££; ★★★★★ 1999 Chardonnay Reserve Le Bouge D' à Côté £££

☿ **Dom. des Aubuisières** [day Soh-bwee-see-yehr] (*Loire*, France) Bernard Fouquet produces impeccable wines ranging from richly dry to lusciously sweet.

Auckland (New Zealand) All-embracing designation which once comprised a quarter of the country's vineyards. Often derided region, despite the fact that some vintages favour it over starrier areas such as *Marlborough*. **Collards; Coopers Creek; Goldwater Estate; Kumeu River; Matua Valley;** Sacred Hill; Stonyridge.

Aude [ohd] (Southwest France) Prolific *département* and traditional source of ordinary wine. Now *Corbières* and *Fitou* are improving as are the *Vins de Pays*, thanks to new grapes (such as the *Viognier*) and the efforts of firms like *Skalli Fortant de France, Val d'Orbieu,* and *Domaine Virginie*.

Ausbruch [ows-brookh] (Austria) Term for rich *botrytis* wine which is sweeter than *Beerenauslese* but less sweet than *Trockenbeerenauslese*. ★★★★★ 1999 Vinum Saxum Traminer Ausbruch Weingut Kugler ££

Auslese [ows-lay-zuh] (Germany) Mostly sweet wine from selected ripe grapes, usually affected by *botrytis*. Third rung on the *QmP* ladder.

☿ **Ch. Ausone** [oh-zohn] (*St. Emilion Premier Grand Cru Classé, Bordeaux,* France) Ancient (Roman) hillside pretender to the crown of top *St. Emilion*. Until the wine-making was taken over by *Michel Rolland* in 1995, the wine lacked intensity. The 2000 and 2001 were my wines of the vintage.

Austria Home of all sorts of whites, ranging from dry *Sauvignon Blancs*, greengagey *Grüner Veltliners*, and ripe *Rieslings* to especially luscious *late harvest* wines. Reds are increasingly successful too – particularly the *Pinot-Noir*-like *St. Laurents*. Bründlmayer; *Feiler-Artinger; Freie Weingärtner;* Holler; Juris; Knoll; *Alois Kracher;* Alois Lang; Münzenrieder; Nicolaihof; *Willi Opitz;* Pichler; Johan Tschida; *Prager; Ernst Triebaumer;* Umathum.

🍷 **Auxerrois** [oh-sehr-wah] (France) Named after the town in northern *Burgundy*, this is the Alsatians' term for a fairly dull local variety that may be related to the *Sylvaner, Melon de Bourgogne,* or *Chardonnay*. South Africa's winemakers briefly planted it under the misapprehension that it was *Chardonnay*. In Luxembourg it is called the *Luxembourg Pinot Gris*.

☿ **Auxey-Duresses** [oh-say doo-ress] (*Burgundy*, France) *Côtes de Beaune* village best known for buttery whites, but producing rather more rustic, raspberryish, reds. A slow developer. **Robert Ampeau; Dom. d'Auvenay; Dom Chassorney;** *Coche-Dury; Comte Armand;* Jean-Pierre Diconne; *Louis Jadot; Olivier Leflaive; Michel Prunier;* Vincent Prunier; Guy Roulot.

AVA (US) Acronym for American Viticultural Area. American *appellation* system. It makes sense in smaller, climatically coherent *appellations* like *Mount Veeder* and *Carneros*; less so in larger, more heterogenous ones like *Napa*.

☿ **Quinta da Aveleda** (*Vinho Verde*, Portugal) Famous estate producing fair-quality dry *Vinho Verde* and varietal reds.

Avelsbach [ahr-vel-sbarkh] (*Mosel*, Germany) Ruwer village producing delicate, light-bodied wines.

☿ **L'Avenir** [lah-veh-near] (*Stellenbosch*, South Africa) A new and fast-rising star in the *Cape*, thanks to a – for the region – historically unusual obsession with ripe fruit. The big fruit-salady *Chenin Blanc* is a star, as are the rich *Cabernet* and *Pinotage*. Some people will find the *Chardonnay* just a touch too hefty.

B

Ⅰ **Avignonesi** [ahr-veen-yon-nay-see] (*Tuscany*, Italy) Ultra-classy *Vino Nobile di Montepulciano, Super-Tuscans* such as the Grifi *Merlot*. There are also serious *Chardonnay* and *Sauvignon* whites – plus good *Vin Santo*.

Ⅰ **Avontuur** [ah-fon-toor] (*Stellenbosch*, South Africa) Increasingly dynamic estate. ★★★ 1999 Avontuur Baccarat ££

Ⅰ **Ayala** [ay-yah-lah] (*Champagne*, France) Underrated producer which takes its name from the village of Ay. ★★★ 1996 Ayala Brut Millesime £

Ayl [ihl] (*Mosel*, Germany) Distinguished *Saar* village producing steely wines.

Azienda [ad-see-en-dah] (Italy) Estate.

B

Ⅰ **Babcock** (*Santa Ynez*, California) Classy single-vineyard *Chardonnays* (*Mount Carmel*), *Pinot Noirs, Sangioveses, and Sauvignon Blancs*.

Ⅰ **Babich** [ba-bitch] (*Henderson*, New Zealand) Family winery with wines from *Auckland, Marlborough*, and *Hawkes Bay*, source of the rich "Irongate" and Patriarch *Chardonnays*. The *Sauvignon Blanc* is good too.

Ⅰ **Quinta da Bacalhõa** [dah ba-keh-yow] (*Setúbal*, Portugal) The innovative *Cabernet-Merlot* made by *Peter Bright* at *JP Vinhos*. ★★★ 1999 £

Ⅰ **Masia Bach** [mah-see-yah bakh] (*Penedes*, Spain) This producer's speciality is unusual sweet and dry white

🍇 **Bacchus** [ba-kuhs] White grape. A *Müller-Thurgau-Riesling* cross, making light, flowery wine. **Denbies; Tenterden.**

Ⅰ **Dom. Denis Bachelet** [dur-nee bash-lay] (*Burgundy*, France) Classy, small *Gevrey-Chambertin* estate with fine cherryish wines.

Ⅰ **Backsberg Estate** [bax-burg] (*Paarl*, South Africa) *Chardonnay* pioneer, with good, quite Burgundian versions.

Bad Dürkheim [baht duhr-kime] (*Pfalz*, Germany) Chief *Pfalz* town, producing fine whites and reds. *Kurt Darting;* Fitz-Ritter; Karl Schäfer.

Bad Kreuznach [baht kroyts-nahkh] (*Nahe*, Germany) The chief and finest wine town of the region, giving its name to the entire lower *Nahe*. Paul Anheuser; von Plettenberg.

Ⅰ **Baden** [bah-duhn] (Germany) Warm southern region of Germany, with dry (*Trocken*) whites and good *Pinot Noirs*. The huge *Winzerkeller* cooperative makes good wines, as do: Becker; Dr Heger; Karl Heinz Johner; R Zimmerlin.

Ⅰ **Baden Winzerkeller (ZBW)** [bah-den vin-zehr-keh-luhr] (*Baden*, Germany) Huge coop, reliable but perhaps a trifle dull.

Ⅰ **Badia a Coltibuono** [bah-dee-yah ah kohl-tee-bwoh-noh] (*Tuscany*, Italy) One of Italy's best *Chianti* producers. Pure *Sangiovese* and *Chardonnay*. Great mature releases.

Ⅰ **Badia di Morrona** [bah-dee-yah dee Moh-ROH-nah] (*Tuscany*, Italy) Up-and-coming estate with a notable *Super-Tuscan* in the shape of the N'Antia Cabernet-Sangiovese blend.

🍇 **Baga** [bah-gah] (*Bairrada*, Portugal) The spicy red variety of *Bairrada*.

Ⅰ **Ch. Bahans-Haut-Brion** [bah-on oh-bree-on] (*Graves, Bordeaux*, France) The *second label* of *Ch. Haut-Brion*.

Ⅰ **Bailey's** (*Victoria*, Australia) Traditional, good Liqueur *Muscat* and hefty, old-fashioned *Shiraz*.

Ⅰ **Bairrada** [bi-rah-dah] (Portugal) *DO* region south of *Oporto*. Revolutionary producers like *Sogrape, Luis Pato*, and *Aliança* are proving what can be done. Look for spicy blackberryish reds and creamy whites.

Baja California [bah-hah] (Mexico) Home to the Santo Tomas, Casa de Piedra, and *LA Cetto* wineries. ★★★ 1999 Santo Tomas Duetto ££

Balance Harmony of fruitiness, *acidity, alcohol*, and *tannin*. Balance can develop with age but should be evident (even if hard to discern) in youth.

Balaton [bah-la-ton] (Hungary) Wine region frequented by *flying winemakers*, and producing fair-quality reds and whites.

B

Anton Balbach [an-ton bahl-barkh] (*Rheinhessen,* Germany) Potentially one of the best producers in the *Erden* region – especially for *late harvest* wines.

Bodegas Balbás [bal-bash] (*Ribera del Duero,* Spain) Small producer of juicy *Tempranillo* reds, *Bordeaux*-style *Cabernet* blends, and a lively rosé.

Balbi [bal-bee] (*Mendoza,* Argentina) Producer of good, inexpensive modern wines, including particularly appealing *Malbecs* and dry rosés. ★★★ 1999 Barbaro ££; ★★★ 2000 Cabernet Sauvignon Reserva ££

Ch. Balestard-la-Tonnelle [bah-les-star lah ton-nell] (*St. Emilion Grand Cru Classé, Bordeaux,* France) Good, quite traditional *St. Emilion* built to last.

Balgownie Estate [bal-Gow-nee] (*Bendigo,* Australia) One of Victoria's most reliable producers of lovely, intense, blackcurranty *Cabernet* in *Bendigo.* *Chardonnays* are big and old-fashioned, and *Pinot Noirs* are improving. ★★★★ 1999 Shiraz ££; ★★★ 1999 Cabernet Sauvignon ££

Bandol [bon-dohl] (*Provence,* France) *Mourvèdre*-influenced plummy, herby reds, and rich whites. *Ch. de Pibarnon; Dom. Tempier;* Dom. Tour de Bon; Pradeaux; Ch. la Rouvière; Ch. Vannières.

Castello Banfi [ban-fee] (*Tuscany,* Italy) US-owned producer with improving *Brunello* and *Vini da Tavola.* ★★★★ 2000 Banfi Col di Sasso £

Bannockburn (*Geelong,* Australia) Gary Farr uses his experience at *Dom. Dujac* in *Burgundy* to produce concentrated *Pinot Noir* and *Shiraz* at home. The big *Chardonnay Bordeaux* blends are impressive too.

Bannockburn by Farr (*Geelong,* Australia) Gary Farr's own label – also worth watching out for.

Banyuls [bon-yools] (*Provence,* France) France's answer to *tawny port.* Fortified, *Grenache*-based, *Vin Doux Naturel,* ranging from off-dry to lusciously sweet. The *Rancio* style is more like *Madeira.* L'Etoile; Dom. Mas Amiel; Dom. du Mas Blanc; Clos de Paulilles; *Dom. de la Rectorie;* Dom. la Tour Vieille; Vial Magnères.

Antonio Barbadillo [bahr-bah-deel-yoh] (*Jerez,* Spain) Great producer of *Fino* and *Manzanilla.* ★★★★★ Obispo Gascon Palo Cortado £££

Barbaresco [bahr-bah-ress-koh] (*Piedmont,* Italy) DOCG *Nebbiolo* red, with spicy fruit, depth, and complexity. Approachable earlier (three to five years) than neighbouring *Barolo* but, in the right hands – and in the best vineyards – of almost as high a quality. *Gaja;* Rino Varaldi; Castello di Neive; *Paitin; Pelissero; Alfredo Prunotto;* Albino Rocca. ★★★ 1999 Barbaresco Coste Rubin Fontanafredda £££

Cascina la Barbatella [kah-shh-nah lah bahr-bah-teh-lah] (*Piedmont,* Italy) Rising star, focusing its attention firmly on the *Barbera* (as Barbera d'Asti and single-vineyard Vigna di Sonvico and Vigna dell'Angelo) as well as a good Cortese-*Sauvignon* blend called Noè after one of its makers.

Barbera [Bar-Beh-Rah] (*Piedmont,* Italy) Grape making fruity, spicy, characterful wine (e.g. B. d'Alba and B. d'Asti), with a flavour like cheesecake raisins. Now in *California, Mexico,* and *Australia* (at *Brown Bros.* and "I").

René Barbier [Ren-nay Bah-bee-yay] (*Penedès,* Spain) Dynamic producer of commercial wines and fine *Priorato.* ★★★ 1998 Cabernet Sauvignon Larga ££

Barco Reale (*Tuscany,* Italy) The lighter, younger, *DOC* red wine of the *DOCG* region of *Carmignano.* ★★★ 2001 Tenuta di Capezzana ££

Barca Velha [bahr-kah vayl-yah] (*Douro,* Portugal) Portugal's most famous red, traditionally made from port varieties by *Ferreira,* now getting a quality boost. Also look out for Reserva Especial released in more difficult years.

Bardolino [bar-doh-lee-noh] (*Veneto,* Italy) Cherryish red. Can be dull – or a fruity alternative to *Beaujolais.* Also comes as Chiaretto Rosé. Best young unless from an exceptional producer. *Boscaini; Fabiano Masi;* Portalupi.

Gilles Barge [bahzh] (*Rhône,* France) Son of Pierre who won an international reputation for his fine, classic *Côte Rôtie.* Gilles, who now runs the estate, has also shown his skill with *St. Joseph.*

Guy de Barjac [gee dur bar-jak] (*Rhône,* France) A master of the *Syrah* grape, producing some of the best – and most stylish – *Cornas* around.

B

♈ **Barolo** [bah-Roh-loh] (*Piedmont*, Italy) Noble *Nebbiolo* reds with extraordinary berryish, floral, and spicy flavours. Old-fashioned versions are dry and tannic when young but, from a good producer and year, can develop extraordinary complexity. Modern versions are oakier and more accessible. *Elio Altare; Batasiolo; Borgogno; Chiarlo; Clerico; Aldo Conterno;* Giacomo Conterno; *Conterno Fantino; Fontanafredda; Gaja; M Marengo; Bartolo Mascarello; Giuseppe Mascarello;* Pio Cesare; *Pira; F Principiano; Prunotto; Ratti; Sandrone; Scavino; Vajra;* Vietti; *Roberto Voerzio.* ★★★ 1997 Barolo Monforte D'Alba Aldo Conterno 'Cicala'

♈ **Baron de Ley** [bah-Rohn Duh lay] (*Rioja*, Spain) Small estate whose wines, French oak-aged, can be worth waiting for. ★★★ 1997 Rioja Reserva ££

♈ **Baron Philippe de Rothschild** (*Bordeaux*, France & Chile) This Bordeaux merchant is the name behind the improving but generally unexciting branded Mouton Cadet and a range of fair AC wines from *Pauillac*, *Margaux* etc. The Chilean range Escudo Rojo and expensive Almaviva (the latter a joint venture with Concha y Toro) is better and Opus One (with Mondavi) is fine. Baron Arques, a venture in Limoux has yet to dazzle. ★★★★★ 1999 Almaviva ££££; ★★★ 2000 Escudo Rojo ££

Barossa Valley [bah-ros suh] (Australia) Big, warm region north-east of Adelaide which is famous for traditional, old-vine *Shiraz* and *Grenache*, "ports", and *Rieslings* which age to oily richness. *Chardonnay* and *Cabernet* make subtler, classier wines along with *Riesling* in the higher altitude vineyards of the *Eden Valley* and *Adelaide Hills. Barossa Valley Estate; Basedow; Bethany;* Charles Cimicky; *E&E; Elderton; Wolf Blass; Grant Burge; Hardy's; Henschke; Krondorf;* Peter Lehmann; *Melton; Orlando; Penfolds; Rockford; St. Hallett; Turkey Flat; Yalumba.*

♈ **Barossa Valley Estate** (*Barossa Valley*, Australia) Top end of BRL Hardy with good old-vine *Barossa* reds. ★★★★★ 2000 Mamre Brook Shiraz ££

♈ **Daniel Barraud** [Bah-roh] (*Burgundy*, France) Dynamic producer of single-*cuvée Pouilly-Fuissé.*

Barrique [ba-reek] (France) French barrel, particularly in *Bordeaux,* holding about 58 gallons (225 litres). Term used in Italy to denote (new) barrel ageing.

♈ **Jim Barry** (*Clare Valley*, Australia) Producer of the dazzling, spicy, mulberryish *Armagh Shiraz* and great, floral Watervale Riesling. ★★★★★ 1999 The Armagh ££££; ★★★ 1999 McRae Wood Shiraz ££

♈ **Barsac** [bahr-sak] (*Bordeaux*, France) AC neighbour of *Sauternes* with similar, though not quite so rich, *Sauvignon/Sémillon* dessert wines. *Ch. Broustet; Ch. Climens; Ch. Coutet; Ch. Doisy-Dubroca; Ch. Doisy-Daëne; Ch. Nairac.*

♈ **Ghislaine Barthod-Noëllat** [jee-lenn Bar-toh] (*Burgundy*, France) Top class *Chambolle-Musigny* estate.

♈ **De Bartoli** [day bahr-toh-lee] (*Sicily*, Italy) *Marsala* for drinking rather than cooking from a revolutionary producer who has voluntarily removed his Vecchio Samperi from the DOC system.

♈ **Barton & Guestier** [bahr-ton ay geht-tee-yay] (*Bordeaux,* France) Highly commercial *Bordeaux* shipper. ★★★★ 2000 Cabernet Premium £

♈ **Barwang** [bahr-wang] (*New South Wales*, Australia) *McWilliams* label for cool-climate wines produced near Young in eastern *New South Wales.*

♈ **Basedow** [baz-zeh-doh] (South Australia) Producer of big, concentrated *Shiraz* and *Cabernet* and ultra-rich *Semillon* and *Chardonnays.*

Basilicata [bah-see-lee-kah-tah] (Italy) Southern wine region chiefly known for *Aglianico del Vulture* and improving *IGT wines.* Basilium.

Basket Press Traditional winepress, favoured for quality reds by Australian producers such as *Chateau Reynella.*

♈ **Bass Philip** (*Victoria*, Australia) Fanatical South *Gippsland* pioneer Philip Jones's fine *Burgundy*-like *Pinot.*

♈ **Von Bassermann-Jordan** [fon bas-suhr-man johr-dun] (*Pfalz*, Germany) A traditional producer with fabulous vineyards and fine *Trocken Rieslings.*

B

▼ **Ch. Bastor-Lamontagne** [bas-tohr-lam-mon-tañ] (*Sauternes, Bordeaux,* France) Remarkably reliable classy *Sauternes*; inexpensive alternative to the big-names, often offering comparable levels of richness and complexity. Fine in 2000.

▼ **Ch. Batailley** [bat-tih-yay] (*Pauillac 5ème Cru Classé, Bordeaux,* France) Approachable, quite modern tobacco-cassis-cedar *claret* from the same stable as Ch. Ducru-Beaucaillou. Shows more class than its price might lead one to expect. ★★★ 1999 Château Batailley ££

▼ **Bâtard-Montrachet** [bat-tahr mon-rah-shay] (*Burgundy,* France) Wonderful, biscuity-rich white *Grand Cru* that straddles the border between the appellations of *Chassagne* and *Puligny-Montrachet*. Often very fine; invariably expensive. *Cailot; Colin-Deleger; Joseph Drouhin; Jean-Noel Gagnard; Gagnard-Delagrange; Dom. Leflaive; Ch. de la Maltroye; Pierre Morey; Michel Niellon; Ramonet; Sauzet.* ★★★★★ 2000 Jean-Noël Gagnard Bâtard-Montrachet; ★★★★★ 2000 Etienne Sauzet Bâtard-Montrachet

▼ **Batasiolo** [bat-tah-see-oh-loh] (*Piedmont,* Italy) Producer of top-class *Barolo,* impressive cherryish *Dolcetto,* fresh *Moscato,* intense berryish *Brachetto,* and a subtle *Chardonnay.* ★★★ 1997 Barolo Cerequio £££; ★★★ 2000 Barbera d'Alba Sovrana ££

▼ **Dom. des Baumard** [day boh-marh] (*Loire,* France) Superlative producer of great *Coteaux du Layon, Quarts de Chaume,* and *Savennières.*

▼ **Bava** [bah-vah] (*Piedmont,* Italy) Innovative producer making good *Moscato Barbera,* reviving indigenous grapes such as the rarely grown raspberryish *Ruche* as well as a rather wonderful traditional curious herb-infused *Barolo Chinato Cocchi.* Try it with one of Roberto Bava's other enthusiasms: dark chocolate.

▼ **Béarn** [bay-ar'n] (*South West,* France) Highly traditional and often dull region. Lapeyre is the name to look out for.

▼ **Ch. Beau-Séjour (-Bécot)** [boh-say-zhoor bay-koh] (*St. Emilion Grand Cru Classé, Bordeaux,* France) Reinstated in 1996 after a decade of demotion. Now making fairly priced, greatly improved wine.

▼ **Ch. Beau-Site** [boh-seet] (*St. Estèphe Cru Bourgeois, Bordeaux,* France) Benchmark *St. Estèphe* in the same stable as *Ch. Batailley.*

▼ **Ch. de Beaucastel** [boh-kas-tel] (*Rhône,* France) The top *Châteauneuf-du-Pape* estate, using organic methods to produce richly gamey (for some, too gamey) long-lived, spicy reds, which reflect the presence in the blend of an unusually high proportion of Mourvèdre. There are also rare but fine creamy-spicy (*Roussanne-based*) whites. The Coudoulet Côtes du Rhône are a delight too. ★★★★★ 2000 Châteauneuf-du-Pape ££££

▼ **Beaujolais** [boh-zhuh-lay] (*Burgundy,* France) Light and fruity *Gamay* red. This wine is good chilled and for early drinking. *Beaujolais-Villages* is better, and the 10 *Crus* are better still. With age, these can taste like (fairly ordinary) *Burgundy* from the *Côte d'Or. Beaujolais Blanc,* which is made from *Chardonnay,* is now mostly sold as *St. Véran.* See Crus: *Morgon; Chénas; Brouilly; Côte de Brouilly; Juliénas; Fleurie; Regnié; St. Amour; Chiroubles; Moulin-à-Vent.* ★★★★ 2000 Brouilly Domaine de Mondenet ££

▼ **Beaujolais-Villages** (*Burgundy,* France) From the north of the region, fuller-flavoured and more alcoholic than plain *Beaujolais,* though not necessarily from one of the named *Cru* villages. *Duboeuf; Dubost; Foillard; Ch. es Jacques; Janin; Large; Pivot; Dme des Terres Dorées.* ★★★ 2000 Beaujolais-Villages Vieilles Vignes Mommessin £

▼ **Beaulieu Vineyard** [bohl-yoo] (*Napa Valley,* California) Historic winery getting back on its feet after years of neglect by its multi-national owners. The wines to look for are the Georges de Latour Private Reserve *Cabernets,* which have been consistently good (as a recent tasting of old vintages proved), and the new Signet ranger. Recent vintages of the Beau Tour *Cabernet Sauvignon* have been good too. Other wines are unexciting. ★★★★ 1997 Beaulieu Vineyard Georges de Latour Cabernet Sauvignon ££££

♀ *Beaumes de Venise* [bohm duh vuh-neez] (*Rhône*, France) *Côtes du Rhône* village producing spicy, dry reds and sweet, grapey, fortified *Vin Doux Naturel* from the *Muscat*. **Dom. des Bernardins;** *Chapoutier;* **Dom. de Coyeux; Durban; de Fenouillet;** *Paul Jaboulet Aîné;* **la Soumade;** *Vidal-Fleury*.

♀ **Ch. Beaumont** [boh-mon] (*Haut-Médoc Cru Bourgeois, Bordeaux*, France) Estate performing well again since 1998.

♀ **Beaune** [bohn] (*Burgundy*, France) Large commune that gives its name to the *Côte de Beaune* and produces soft, raspberry-and rose-petal *Pinot Noir*. As in *Nuits-St.-Georges*, there are plenty of *Premier Crus*, but no *Grands Crus*. The walled city is the site of the famous *Hospices* charity auction. Reds are best from *Michel Prunier, Louis Jadot, Bouchard Père et Fils* (since 1996), Ch. de Chorey, Albert Morot, and *Joseph Drouhin –* who also make an ultra-rare white. Other good producers: **Robert Ampeau; Arnoux Père et Fils;** *Pascal Bouley;* **Dubois; Génot-Boulanger; Germain (Ch. de Chorey);** *Michel Lafarge;* **Daniel Largeot; Laurent;** *Jacques Prieur;* **Rapet Père et Fils; Thomas-Moillard;** *Tollot-Beaut*. ★★★ 1999 Louis Jadot Beaune Boucherottes £££

♀ **Ch. Beauregard** [boh-ruh-gahr] (*Pomerol, Bordeaux*, France) Estate producing juicy oaky *Pomerol*.

♀ **Ch. Beauséjour-Duffau-Lagarosse** [boh-say-zhoor doo-foh lag-gahr-ros] (*St. Emilion Premier Grand Cru Classé, Bordeaux*, France) Traditional tough, tannic *St. Emilion*.

♀ **Beaux Frères** [boh frair] (*Oregon*) *Pinot Noir* winery launched by wine guru Robert Parker and his brother-in-law (hence the name).

♀ **Graham Beck** (*Robertson*, South Africa) Associated with *Bellingham* and producer of some of South Africa's best sparkling wines. A Coastal Range of still wines are looking good too. ★★★ 2000 Coastal Pinotage £

Beerenauslese [behr-ren-ows-lay-zuh] (*Austria/Germany*) Sweet wines from selected, ripe grapes (Beeren), hopefully affected by *botrytis*.

♀ **Ch. de Bel-Air** [bel-Ehr] (*Lalande-de-Pomerol, Bordeaux*, France) Impressive property making wines to make some *Pomerols* blush.

♀ **Ch. Bel-Orme-Tronquoy-de-Lalande** [bel-orm-tron-kwah-duh-la-lond] (*Haut-Médoc Cru Bourgeois, Bordeaux*, France) Highly old-fashioned estate and wines. Under the same ownership (and philosophy) as *Rauzan Gassies*. Made a good 2000, but still has plenty of room for improvement.

♀ **Ch. Belair** [bel-lehr] (*St. Emilion Premier Grand Cru Classé, Bordeaux*, France) Classy, delicate, long-lived *St. Emilion* with a very impressive 2000. Don't confuse with the *Lalande-de-Pomerol Ch. de Bel-Air* (or any of the countless lesser Belairs scattered around *Bordeaux*).

♀ **Bellavista** (*Lombardy*, Italy) Commercial Franciacorta producers of classy sparkling and still wines. The Riserva Vittorio Moretti, which is only produced in top years, is the star of the show.

♀ **Albert Belle** [bel] (*Rhône*, France) An estate that has recently begun to bottle its own excellent red and – oaky – white Hermitage.

♀ **Bellet** [bel-lay] (*Provence*, France) Tiny *AC* behind Nice producing fairly good red, white, and rosé from local grapes including the Rolle, the *Braquet*, and the *Folle Noir*. Pricey and rarely seen outside France. **Ch. de Bellet**.

♀ **Bellingham** (South Africa) Commercial winery that is focusing increasingly on quality. *Cabernet Franc* is a particular success. Look for the Premium range. ★★★ 2000 Shiraz £; ★★★ 1999 Spitz Cabernet Franc ££

Bendigo/Ballarat [ben-dig-goh] (*Victoria*, Australia) Warm region producing big-boned, long-lasting reds with intense berry fruit. *Balgownie;* Blackjack; Heathcote; *Jasper Hill; Mount Ida; Passing Clouds;* Water Wheel. ★★★★★ 1999 Mt Ida Shiraz ££

B

✠ **Benziger** [ben-zig-ger] (*Sonoma,* California) Classy wines from the family behind *Glen Ellen.* Look for the *Zinfandel* and *Chardonnay,* which are both stars.

✠ **Berberana** [behr-behr-rah nah] (*Rioja,* Spain) Producer of a range of fruitier young-drinking styles, as well as the improving Carta de Plata and Carta de Oro and Lagunilla *Riojas,* plus sparkling Marquès de Monistrol.

✠ **Bercher** [behr-kehr] (*Baden,* Germany) Dynamic estate, producing impressive, modern, *Burgundy*-style reds and whites.

Bereich [beh-ri-kh] (Germany) Vineyard area, subdivision of an *Anbaugebiet.* On its own indicates *QbA* wine, e.g. *Niersteiner.* Finer wines are followed by the name of a (smaller) *Grosslage,* better ones by that of an individual vineyard.

✠ **Bergerac** [behr-jur-rak] (France) Traditionally *Bordeaux's* "lesser" neighbour but possibly soon to be assimilated into that regional *appellation.* The wines, though often pretty mediocre, can still be better value than basic red or white *Bordeaux,* while the best *Monbazillac* can sometimes outclass basic *Sauternes.* Ch. Belingard; Court-les-Muts; *des Eyssards;* Grinou; la Jaubertie; de Raz; Tour des Gendres. ★★★ 1999 Chateau des Eyssards Cuvee Prestige Bergerac Rouge £

✠ **Bergkelder** [berg-kel-dur] (*Cape,* South Africa) Huge firm best known for its *Stellenryck* wines. Its cheaper *Fleur du Cap* range is likeable enough and the best of the *JC Le Roux* sparkling wines are first class.

✠ **Beringer Vineyards** [ber-rin-jer] (*Napa Valley,* California) Big Swiss-owned producer, increasingly notable for its single-vineyard *Cabernet Sauvignons* (Knights Valley, *Howell Mountain, Spring Mountain,* and Private Reserve), *Cabernet Francs,* and *Merlots; Burgundy*-like *Chardonnays;* and *late harvest* wines. ★★★★★ 1996 Beringer Merlot Bancroft Ranch Howell Mountain ££; ★★★★★ 1997 Beringer Cabernet Sauvignon Private Reserve ££

Bernkastel [berhrn-kah-stel] (*Mosel,* Germany) Town and area on the *Mittelmosel* and source of some of the finest *Riesling* (like the famous Bernkasteler Doktor), and a lake of poor-quality stuff. Dr Loosen; JJ Prum; Von Kesselstadt; *Wegeler Deinhard.* ★★★ 1998 Bernkasteler Badstube Riesling Spatlese Dr Thanisch ££; ★★★ 2000 Bereich Bernkastel Josef Brader £

✠ **Bernardus** (*Monterey,* California) Producer of rich, unsubtle, fairly-priced, unashamedly New World-style *Sauvignon Blanc, Chardonnay,* and *Pinot Noir.*

✠ **Beronia** [beh-roh-nya] (*Rioja,* Spain) Good, traditional reds and more modern whites from this small *Gonzalez-Byass* owned bodega. ★★★ 1998 Altozano Crianza Bodegas Beronia £

✠ **Dom Bertagna** [behr-tan-ya] (*Vougeot,* France) Estate offering the rare, (relatively) affordable *Premier Cru Vougeot* alongside its *Clos de Vougeot Grand Cru.* ★★★★★ 2000 Clos St Denis Grand Cru

✠ **Bertani** [behr-tah-nee] (*Veneto,* Italy) Producer of good *Valpolicella* and innovative wines such as the Le Lave Garganega-*Chardonnay* blend.

✠ **Besserat de Bellefon** [bes-ser-rah duh bel-fo'hn] (*Champagne,* France) Elegant, light Champagnes of good quality but not always for long keeping. ★★★ NV Besserat de Bellefon Cuvee des Moines Rose £££

✠ **Best's** (*Victoria,* Australia) Under-appreciated winery in *Great Western* making delicious concentrated *Shiraz* from old vines, attractive *Cabernet, Dolcetto, Pinot Noir, Colombard,* and rich *Chardonnay* and *Riesling* ★★★ 1997 Best's Great Western Shiraz Bin No.0 ££

✠ **Bethany** [beth-than-nee] (*Barossa Valley,* Australia) Impressive small producer of knockout *Shiraz.* ★★★★ 2001 Bethany Grenache £; ★★★ 2001 The Manse Semillon Riesling Chardonnay £

✠ **Bethel Heights** (*Oregon,* California) Long-established winery, now a rising star, with good *Pinot Noir* and particularly impressive *Pinot Blanc* and *Chardonnay.*

✠ **Dom. Henri Beurdin** [bur-dan] (*Loire,* France) The estate at which you'll find benchmark white and rosé *Reuilly.*

B

Ⓘ **Ch. Beychevelle** [bay-shur-vel] (*St. Julien 4ème Cru Classé, Bordeaux,* France) A fourth growth that achieves the typical cigar-box character of *St. Julien* but fails to excite. The *second label Amiral de Beychevelle* can be a worthwhile buy. Better than usual quality in 2000. Not great in 2001

Ⓘ **Léon Beyer** [bay-ur] (*Alsace,* France) Serious producer of lean long-lived wines.

Ⓘ **Beyerskloof** [bay-yurs-kloof] (*Stellenbosch,* South Africa) Newish venture, with Beyers Truter (of Kanonkop) producing some of South Africa's top *Cabernet* and *Stellenbosch Pinotage.*
★★★★★ 1999 Beyerskloof Cabernet Sauvignon ££

Ⓘ **Bianco di Custoza** [bee-yan-koh dee koos toh-zah] (*Veneto,* Italy) Widely exported *DOC.* A reliable, crisp, light white from a blend of grapes. A better-value alternative to most basic *Soave.* **Gorgo; Portalupi; Tedeschi; le Vigne di San Pietro; Zenato.** ★★★ 2000 Amedeo Bianco di Custoza Cavalchina ££

Ⓘ **Maison Albert Bichot** [bee-shoh] (*Burgundy,* France) Big *négociant* with excellent *Chablis* and *Vosne-Romanée,* plus adequate wines sold under a plethora of other labels. ★★★ 1999 Andre Simon Gevrey Chambertin £££; ★★★ 1999 Andre Simon Nuits-Saint-Georges £££

Ⓘ **Biddenden** [hid-den den] (*Kent,* England) Producer showing impressive mastery of the peachy *Ortega.*

Bierzo [bee-yehrt-zoh] (*Castilla y Léon,* Spain) Up-and-coming region close to Galicia. Fresh whites made from the local Mencia grape are worth looking out for. Drink young. **Pérez Caramés**

Ⓘ **Bienvenue-Batard-Montrachet** [bee-yen-veh-noo bat-tahr mon ra-shay] (*Burgundy,* France) Fine white *Burgundy* vineyard with potentially gorgeous biscuit-like wines. **Carillon; Henri Clerc; Dom Leflaive; Sauzet.**

Ⓘ **Weingut Josef Biffar** [bif-fah] (*Pfalz,* Germany). *Deidesheim* estate that is on a roll at the moment with its richly spicy wines.

Ⓘ **Billecart-Salmon** [beel-kahr sal-mon] (*Champagne,* France) Producer of the stylish winners (the 1959 and 1961 vintages) of the Champagne of the Millennium competition held in Stockholm in 1999 at which I was a taster. Possibly the best all-arounder for quality and value, and certainly the *Champagne* house whose subtle but decidedly ageable *non-vintage, vintage,* and rosé I buy without hesitation. Superlative.

Ⓘ **Billiot** [bil-lee-yoh] (*Champagne,* France) Impressive small producer with classy rich sparkling wine.

Bingen [bing-urn] (*Rheinhessen,* Germany) Village giving its name to a *Rheinhessen Bereich* that includes a number of well-known *Grosslage.*

Binissalem [bin-nee-sah-lem] (*Mallorca,* Spain) The holiday island's demarcated region. José Ferrer's and Jaime Mesquida's are the best producers.

Bío-Bío (Chile) The coolest, wettest and most southerly wine region in Chile. Has potential for whites and perhaps for Pinot Noir. ★★★ 2001 Cono Sur Gewurztraminer £; ★★★ 1999 Porta Grand Reserve Pinot Noir £££

Ⓘ **Biondi-Santi** [bee-yon-dee san-tee] (*Tuscany,* Italy) Big-name estate making absurdly expensive and sometimes disappointing *Brunello di Montalcino* that can be bought – after a period of vertical storage at room temperature – at the local trattoria.

Biscuity Flavour of savoury crackers often associated with the *Chardonnay* grape, particularly in *Champagne* and top-class mature *Burgundy,* or with the yeast that fermented the wine.

Ⓘ **Bischöfliche Weingüter** (*Mosel-Saar-Ruwer,* Germany) Large and historic *Mosel* estate, now making top quality again.

Ⓘ **Bitouzet-Prieur** [bee-too-zay pree-yur] (*Burgundy,* France) If you like classic *Meursault* and *Volnay* built to last rather than seduce instantly with ripe fruit and oak, try this estate's 1997 Volnay Caillerets and 1997 *Meursault Perrières.*

B

 Dom. Simon Bize [beez] (*Burgundy,* France) Intense, long-lived, and good-value wines produced in *Savigny-lès-Beaune.* ★★★★ 1999 Savigny lès Beaune 1er Cru Vergelesses £££

 Blaauwklippen [blow-klip-pen] (*Stellenbosch,* South Africa) Recently sold, large estate, veering between commercial and top quality. The *Cabernet* and *Zinfandel* are the strongest cards, but the *Chardonnay* is improving fast.

 Blagny [blan-yee] (*Burgundy,* France) Tiny source of unsubtle red (sold as Blagny) and potentially top-class white (sold as *Meursault, Puligny-Montrachet,* Blagny, Hameau de Blagny, or la Pièce sous le Bois). Ampeau; Chavy-Chouet; *Jobard;Thierry Matrot.* ★★★ 2000 Domaine Matrot-Wittersheim Blagny 1er Cru La Pièce Sous le Bois

 Blain-Gagnard [blan gan-yahr] (*Burgundy,* France) Excellent creamy, modern *Chassagne-Montrachet.* ★★★★ 2000 Bâtard-MontrachetGrand Cru

Blanc de Blancs [blon dur blon] A white wine, made from white grapes – hardly worth mentioning except in the case of *Champagne,* where *Pinot Noir,* a black grape, usually makes up 30–70 per cent of the blend. In this case, *Blanc de Blancs* is pure *Chardonnay.*

Blanc de Noirs [blon dur nwahrr] A white (or frequently very slightly pink-tinged wine) made from red grapes by taking off the free-run juice, before pressing to minimize the uptake of red pigments from the skin. Paul Bara; *Duval-Leroy (Fleur de Champagne);* Egly-Ouiriet.

 Paul Blanck [blank] (*Alsace,* France) Top-class *Alsace* domaine, specializing in single *Cru* wines.

 Blandy's [blan-deez] (*Madeira,* Portugal) Brand owned by the Madeira Wine Company and named after the sailor who began the production of fortified wine here. Excellent old wines. Younger ones are less exciting.

 Blanquette de Limoux [blon ket dur lee-moo] (*Midi,* France) *Méthode Champenoise* sparkling wine, which, when good, is appley and clean. Best when made with a generous dose of *Chardonnay,* as the local *Mauzac* tends to give it an earthy flavour with age.

 Wolf Blass (*Barossa Valley,* Australia) Part of the huge Mildara-Blass operation (and thus owned by Fosters), this brand was founded by a German immigrant who prides himself on producing "sexy" (his term) reds and whites by blending wines from different regions of *South Australia* and allowing them plentiful contact with new oak.   98

 Blauburgunder [blow-boor-goon-durh] (Austria) The name the Austrians give their light, often sharp, *Pinot Noir.*

 Blauer Portugieser [blow-urh por-too-gay-suhr] (Germany) Red grape used in Germany and Austria to make light, pale wine.

 Blaufränkisch [blow-fren-kish] (Austria) Grape used to make refreshingly berryish wines that can – in the right hands – compete with the reds of the *Loire.* ★★★★ 2000 Marienthal Blaufränkisch Haus Marienberg ££££

 Blockheadia Ringnosii (*Napa,* California) Despite the wacky name and label, this is a source of serious *Sauvignon* and *Zinfandel.*

 Quinta da Boavista [keen-tah dah boh-wah-vees-tah] (*Alenquer,* Portugal) Starry estate producing a range of red and white wines, including Palha Canas, Quinta das Sete, and Espiga. ★★★★ 2000 Casa Santos Lima Merlot £

 Bobadilla [booh-bah-dee-yoh] (*Jerez,* Spain) Fine Sherry *bodega*

 Boccagigabbia [Bbok-kah-ji-gah-bee-yah] (*Marche,* Italy) Top class estate, producing delicious *Pinot Noir* (Girone), *Cabernet* (Akronte), and *Chardonnay.*

Bocksbeutel [box-boy-tuhl] (*Franken,* Germany) The famous flask-shaped bottle of *Franken,* adopted by the makers of *Mateus* Rosé.

Bodega [bod-day-gah] (Spain) Winery or wine cellar; producer.

 Bodegas y Bebidas [bod-day-gas ee beh-bee-das] (Spain) One of Spain's most dynamic wine companies, and maker of *Campo Viejo.*

 Bodegas y Viñedos del Jalón [bod-day-gas ee veen-yay-dos del kha-lohn] (Calatayud, Spain) Good value reds and whites, especially Poema Garnacha, made by Scotswoman Pamela Geddes. ★★★ 2001 Poema £

B

Body Usually used as "full-bodied", meaning a wine with mouth-filling flavours and probably a fairly high alcohol content.

♚ **Boekenhoutskloof** [ber-ken-hurt-skloof] (*Franschoek*, South Africa) Marc Kent's little winery is the source of the Cape's – and one of the worlds' – best Semillons. The Syrah and Cabernet are terrific too. Porcupine Ridge is the second label. ★★★ 2001 Porcupine Ridge Sauvignon Blanc £

♚ **Jean-Marc Boillot** [bwah-yoh] (*Burgundy*, France) Small *Pommard domaine* run by the son of the winemaker at *Olivier Leflaive*, and offering really good examples from neighbouring villages *Puligny-Montrachet* and *Volnay*. ★★★★ 2000 Gevrey Chambertin Carougeots £££

♚ **Jean-Claude Boisset** [bwah-say] (*Burgundy*, France) Dynamic *négociant* that now owns a long list of *Burgundy négociants*, including the excellent *Jaffelin* and the improved though still far from dazzling *Bouchard Aîné*. Boisset also makes passable wines in *Languedoc-Roussillon*.

♚ **Boisson-Vadot** [bwah-son va-doh] (*Burgundy*, France) Classy, small *Meursault domaine*.

♚ **Bolgheri** [bol-geh-ree] (*Tuscany*, Italy) Increasingly exciting and recently officially recognized region that was originally made famous by red superstars such as *Antinori's Sassicaia* and *Ornellaia*. Other impressive producers now include: *Belvedere*, *Grattamacco*, *Tenuta dell'Ornellaia*, *Le Macchiole*, and *Satta*, and there are some top-class whites made from the *Vermentino*.

♚ **Bolla** [bol-lah] (*Veneto*, Italy) Producer of plentiful, adequate *Valpolicella* and *Soave*, and of smaller quantities of impressive single vineyard wines like Jago and Creso. ★★★ 1998 Bolla 'Creso' Cabernet Sauvignon ££

♚ **Bollinger** [bol-an-jay] (*Champagne*, France) Great family-owned firm at *Ay*, whose full-flavoured wines need age. The luscious and rare *Vieilles Vignes* is made from pre-*phylloxera* vines, while the nutty *RD* was the first late-disgorged *Champagne* to hit the market. The 1988 RD is a current star. ★★★★ Bollinger Special Cuvée £££

Bommes [bom] (*Bordeaux*, France) *Sauternes commune* and village containing several *Premiers Crus* such as *la Tour Blanche*, *Lafaurie-Peyrauguey*, *Rabaud-Promis*, and *Rayne Vigneau*.

🍇 **Bonarda** (Italy, Argentina) Several red grapes in northern Italy use the name of Bonarda: most make quite rich, deep wine of no great complexity. The Bonarda grown in Argentina may be the same as one or more of these, or it may be different again. Properly ripe Argentine Bonarda can be very good.

♚ **Ch. le Bon-Pasteur** [bon-pas-stuhr] (*Pomerol, Bordeaux*, France) The impressive private estate of *Michel Rolland*, who acts as consultant – and helps to make fruit-driven wines – for half his neighbours, as well as producers in almost every other wine-growing region in the universe.

♚ **Domaine de la Bongran** [bon-grah] Good Mâcon from Jean Thévenet.

♚ **Henri Bonneau** [bon-noh] (*Rhône*, France) *Châteauneuf-du-Pape* producer with two special *cuvées* – "Marie Beurrier" and "des Celestins" – and a cult following. ★★★★★ 1999 Corton-Charlemagne

♚ **Dom. Bonneau du Martray** [bon-noh doo mahr-tray] (*Burgundy*, France) Largest grower of *Corton-Charlemagne* and impressive producer thereof. Also makes a classy red *Grand Cru Corton*.

♚ **Bonnes Mares** [bon-mahr] (*Burgundy*, France) Rich *Morey St. Denis Grand Cru*. **Dom d'Auvenay; Bouchard Père; Clair Daü; Drouhin; Dujac; Fougeray de Beauclair; Groffier; Jadot; Laurent; Roumier; de Vogüé.**

♚ **Ch. Bonnet** [bon-nay] (*Bordeaux*, France) Top-quality *Entre-Deux-Mers château* whose wines are made by *Jacques Lurton*.

♚ **F. Bonnet** [bon-nay] (*Champagne*, France) Reliable producer under the same ownership as *Charles Heidsieck*. ★★★ 1996 £££

B

⏺ **Bonnezeaux** [bonn-zoh] (*Loire,* France) Within the *Coteaux du Layon,* this is one of the world's greatest sweet wine-producing areas, though the wines have often tended to be spoiled by heavy-handedness with sulphur dioxide. *Ch. de Fesles;* Dom. Godineau; Les Grandes Vignes; René Renou; Sasonniere; Ch. la Varière. ★★★ 2000 Bonnezeaux les Melleresses Château la Varière £

⏺ **Bonny Doon Vineyard** (*Santa Cruz,* California) Randall Grahm, sorcerer's apprentice and original "Rhône Ranger", also has an evident affection for unfashionable French and Italian varieties, which he uses for characterful red, dry, and *late harvest* whites. The sheep-like Californian wine industry needs more mavericks like Grahm. ★★★★ 1999 Le Cigare Volant £££; ★★★★ 2001 Malvasia Ca'Del Solo ££

⏺ **Bonvin Jean** [bon-van] (*Valais,* Switzerland) Top producer of traditional local varieties.

⏺ **Bonterra** *Fetzer's* recommendable organic brand. ★★★ 1999 Sangiovese ££

⏺ **Tenuta Bonzara** [bont-zah-rah] (*Emilia Romagna,* Italy) *Cabernet Sauvignon* and *Merlot* specialists producing "*Super-Emilia-Romagnans*".

Borba [Bohr-bah] (*Alentejo,* Portugal) See *Alentejo.*

⏺ **Bordeaux** [bor-doh] (France) Largest (supposedly) quality wine region in France, producing reds, rosés, and deep pink *Clairets* from *Cabernet Sauvignon, Cabernet Franc, Petit Verdot,* and *Merlot,* and dry and sweet whites from (principally) blends of *Sémillon* and *Sauvignon,* with a little *Muscadelle. Bordeaux Supérieur* denotes (relatively) riper grapes. The rare dry whites from regions like the *Médoc* and *Sauternes* are (curiously) sold as *Bordeaux Blanc,* so even the efforts by Châteaux d'Yquem and Margaux are sold under the same label as basic supermarket white. See *Graves, Médoc, Pomerol, St. Emilion, etc.*

⏺ **Borgo del Tiglio** [bor-goh dehl tee-lee-yoh] (*Friuli,* Italy) One of the classiest wineries in this region, hitting the target with a range of varieties that includes *Sauvignon Blanc, Chardonnay, Malvasia,* and Tocai Friulano.

⏺ **Giacomo Borgogno** [baw-gon-yoh] (*Piedmont,* Italy) Hitherto old-fashioned *Barolo* producer that is now embracing modern winemaking and producing fruitier, more immediately likeable wines.

Palacio de Bornos [pah-lah-thyo day bor-noss] (*Rueda,* Spain) Leading producer of unusually good Spanish *Sauvignon Blanc* and *Verdejo.*

⏺ **De Bortoli** [baw-tol-lee] (*Yarra* and *Riverina,* Australia) Fast-developing firm that startled the world by making a *botrytized,* peachy, honeyed "Noble One" *Sémillon* in the unfashionable *Riverina,* before shifting its focus to the very different climate of the *Yarra Valley.* Top wines here include trophy-winning *Pinot Noirs* and impressive *Shirazes.* Windy Peak is a second label. ★★★★ 1996 Rare Dry Botrytis Semillon ££

⏺ **Bodega Luigi Bosca** [bos-kah] (*Mendoza,* Argentina) Good producer with good *Sauvignons* and *Cabernets.* ★★★ 2000 Pinot Noir ££

⏺ **Boscaini** [bos-kah-yee-nee] (*Veneto,* Italy) Innovative producer linked to *Masi* and making better-than-average *Valpolicella* and *Soave.* Look out for individual-vineyard wines such as the starry Ca' de Loi Valpolicella. ★★★ 2000 San Ciriaco £

⏺ **Boscarelli** [bos-kah-reh-lee] (*Tuscany,* Italy) The star producer of *Vino Nobile de Montepulciano* is also the place to find its own delicious Boscarelli *Super-Tuscan* and the exciting new De Ferrari blend of *Sangiovese* with the local Prugnolo Gentile.

⏺ **Boschendal Estate** [bosh-shen-dahl] (*Cape,* South Africa) The place to find some of the *Cape's* best sparkling wine and one of its most European-style Shirazes. Watch out for the new *Pinot Noirs* too. ★★★ 2001 Merlot ££

⏺ **Ch. le Boscq** [bosk] (*St. Estèphe Cru Bourgeois, Bordeaux,* France) Improving property that excels in good vintages, but still tends to make tough wines in lesser ones.

B

❧ **Le Bosquet des Papes** [bos-kay day pap] (*Rhône,* France) Serious *Châteauneuf-du-Pape* producer, making a range of styles that all last. The pure *Grenache* example is particularly impressive.

❧ **Botobolar** (*Mudgee,* Australia) Organic winery making characterful reds and whites.

Botrytis [boh-tri-tiss] Botrytis cinerea, a fungal infection that attacks and shrivels grapes, evaporating their water and concentrating their sweetness. Vital to *Sauternes,* the finer German and Austrian sweet wines, and *Tokaji.* See *Sauternes, Trockenbeerenauslese, Tokaji.*

❧ **Bott-Geyl** [bott-gihl] (*Alsace,* France) Young producer, whose impressive *Grand Cru* wines suit those who like their *Alsace* big and rich. The oaked (*"barriques"*) *Pinot Gris* is quite unusual.

Bottle-fermented Commonly found on the labels of US sparkling wines to indicate the *Méthode Champenoise,* and gaining wider currency. Beware, though – it can indicate inferior *"transfer method"* wines.

❧ **Bouchaine** [boo-shayn] (*Carneros,* California) Much improved *Carneros Chardonnay* and *Pinot Noir*

❧ **Pascal Bouchard** [boo-shahrr d] (*Burgundy,* France) One of the best small producers in *Chablis.*

❧ **Bouchard Aîné** [boo-shahrr day-nay] (*Burgundy,* France) Once unimpressive merchant, now taken over by *Boisset* and improving under the winemaking control of the excellent Bernard Repolt. ★★★★ 1999 Meursault Les Charmes £££; ★★★ 2000 Signature Fixin La Mazière ££

❧ **Bouchard-Finlayson** [boo-shard] (*Walker Bay,* South Africa) Burgundy-style joint-venture between Peter Finlayson and Paul Bouchard, formerly of *Bouchard Aîné* in France. ★★★ 1999 Tête de Cuvée Pinot Noir ££££

❧ **Bouchard Père & Fils** [boo-shahrr pehrr ay fees] (*Burgundy,* France) Traditional merchant with great vineyards. Bought in 1996 by the *Champagne* house of *Henriot.* The best wines are the *Beaunes,* as well as the La Romanée from *Vosne-Romanée.* Also doing wonders in *Chablis* at *William Fèvre.*

❧ **Vin de Pays des Bouches du Rhône** (*Midi,* France) Dynamic region around *Aix* in *Provence,* focusing on *Rhône* and *Bordeaux* varieties. Top wines here include the great *Dom. de Trévallon.* Dom. des Gavelles.

❧ **Pascal Bouley** [boo-lay] (*Burgundy,* France) Producer of good, if not always refined, *Volnay.*

Bouquet Overall smell, often made up of several separate aromas. Used by Anglo-Saxon enthusiasts more often than by professionals.

❧ **Henri Bourgeois** [on-ree boor-jwah] (*Loire,* France) High-quality *Sancerre* and *Pouilly-Fumé* The top wine is called "la Bourgeoisie"). Also owns Laporte. ★★★★ 2000 Sancerre le M.D. de Bourgeois £

❧ **Ch. Bourgneuf-Vayron** [boor-nurf vay-roh] (*Pomerol, Bordeaux,* France) Fast-rising star with deliciously rich plummy *Merlot* fruit.

Bourgogne [boorr-goyñ] (*Burgundy,* France) French for *Burgundy.*

❧ **Bourgueil** [boorr-goyy] (*Loire,* France) Red *AC* in the *Touraine,* producing crisp, grassy-blackcurranty, 100 per cent *Cabernet Franc* wines that age well in good years. Amirault; Boucard; *Caslot-Galbrun;* Cognard; Delaunay; Druet.

❧ **Ch. Bouscassé** [boo-ska-say] (*Madiran,* France) See *Ch. Montus.*

❧ **Ch. Bouscaut** [boos-koh] (*Pessac-Léognan, Bordeaux,* France) Good, rather than great *Graves* property; better white than red.

❧ **J. Boutari** [boo-tah-ree] (*Greece*) One of the most reliable names in Greece, producing good, traditional red wines in Nemea and Naoussa.

❧ **Bouvet-Ladubay** [boo-vay lad-doo-bay] (*Loire,* France) Producer of good *Loire* sparkling wine and better *Saumur-Champigny* reds. "Les Non Pareils".are top-quality mini-cuvées.

✹ **Bouvier** [boo-vee-yay] (Austria) Characterless variety used to produce tasty but mostly simple *late harvest* wines.

Bouzeron [booz-rron] (*Burgundy,* France) *Côte Chalonnaise* village known for *Aligoté.*

B

Bouzy Rouge [boo-zee roozh] (*Champagne,* France) Sideline of a black grape village: an often thin-bodied, rare, and overpriced red wine, which can occasionally age well. **Paul Bara; Barancourt; Brice; Ledru.**

Bowen Estate [boh-wen] (*Coonawarra,* Australia) An early *Coonawarra* pioneer proving that the region can be as good for *Shiraz* as for *Cabernet.*

Domaines Boyar [boy-yahr] (*Bulgaria*) Privatized producers, especially in the *Suhindol* region, selling increasingly worthwhile "Reserve" reds under the Lovico label. Other wines are less reliably recommendable. ★★★ **2001 Barrique Chardonnay £**

Ch. Boyd-Cantenac [boyd-kon-teh-nak] (*Margaux 3ème Cru Classé, Bordeaux,* France) A third growth performing at the level of a fifth – or less.

Brachetto d'Acqui [brah-KET-toh dak-wee] (*Piedmont,* Italy) Eccentric *Muscatty* red grape. Often *frizzante*. **Banfi; Batasiolo; Marenco.**

Braida [brih-dah] (*Piedmont,* Italy) A big producer whose range includes *Barberas* galore and some highly recommendable *Dolcetto* and *Chardonnay.*

Dom Brana [brah-nah] (*Southwest,* France) One of the best producers of Irouleguy.

Ch. Branaire (-Ducru) [brah-nehr doo-kroo] (*St.-Julien 4ème Cru Classé, Bordeaux,* France) New owners are doing wonders for this estate.

Brand's Laira [lay-rah] (*Coonawarra,* Australia) Traditional producer, much improved since its purchase by *McWilliams.* Delving into the world of *Pinot Noir* and sparkling *Grenache* rosé.

Ch. Brane-Cantenac [brahn kon teh-nak] (*Margaux 2ème Cru Classé, Bordeaux,* France) Often underachieving *Margaux*; made a better wine than usual in 1999. The unprepossessingly named second label Ch. Notton can be a good buy.

Branon [brah-no'n] (*Graves, Bordeaux,* France) The first "Garage Wine" in the Graves, made in 2000 by Jean-Luc Thunevin and given an orgasmic response by critics who enjoy intensity and oak. Predictably pricey.

Braquet [brah-ket] (*Midi,* France) Grape variety used in *Bellet.*

Brauneberg [brow-nuh-behrg] (*Mosel,* Germany) Village best known for the *Juffer* vineyard.★★★★ **2001 Max Ferd Richter Brauneberg Juffer Sonnenuhr Riesling Auslese**

Brazil Large quantities of light-bodied wine (including *Zinfandel* that is sold in the US under the Marcus James label) are produced in a rainy region close to Puerto Allegre. The Palomas vineyard on the *Uruguayan* border has a state-of-the-art winery and a good climate but has yet to make exciting wine.

Breaky Bottom (Sussex, England) One of Britain's best, whose *Seyval Blanc* rivals dry wines made in the *Loire* from supposedly finer grapes. ★★★ **1999 Breaky Bottom Brut ££**

Marc Bredif [bray-deef] (*Loire,* France) Big, and quite variable *Loire* producer with still and sparkling wine, including some good *Vouvray.*

Breganze (*Veneto,* Italy) Little-known *DOC* for characterful reds and whites. Maculan is the star here.

Palacio de Brejoeira [breh-sho-eh-rah] (*Vinho Verde,* Portugal) Top class pure *Alvarinho Vinho Verde.*

Bodegas Breton [breh-tonn] (*Rioja,* Spain) Small, new-wave producer to watch for his Dominio de Conté single-vineyard wine.

Ch. du Breuil [doo breuh-yee] (*Loire,* France) Source of good *Coteaux de Layon,* and relatively ordinary examples of other *appellations.*

Weingut Georg Breuer [broy-yer] (*Rheingau,* Germany) Innovative producer with classy *Rieslings* and high-quality *Rülander.*

Bricco Manzoni [bree-koh man-tzoh-nee] (*Piedmont,* Italy) Non-*DOC* oaky, red blend made by Rocche dei Manzoni from *Nebbiolo* and *Barbera* grapes grown in *Monforte* vineyards that could produce *Barolo.*

Brick House (*Oregon*) A small organic slice of *Burgundy* in Yamhill County founded by a former television reporter. The *Gamay* can be as good as the *Pinot* and the *Chardonnay.*

B

Ⓘ **Bricout** [bree-koo] (*Champagne*, France) A cleverly marketed range of good-to-very-good wines including the Cuvée Spéciale Arthur Bricout.

Ⓘ **Bridgehampton** (*Long Island*) Producer of first-class *Merlot* and *Chardonnay* good enough to worry a Californian.

Ⓘ **Bridgewater Mill** (*Adelaide Hills*, Australia) More modest sister winery and brand to *Petaluma*. ★★★ 1999 Cabernet Sauvignon ££

Ⓘ **Peter Bright** Australian-born Peter Bright of the *JP Vinhos* winery produces top-class Portuguese wines, including Tinta da Anfora and Quinta da Bacalhoa and a growing range in countries such as Spain, Italy, and Chile under the Bright Brothers label. ★★★★★ 1999 The Harvey Shiraz ££

Ⓘ **Bristol Cream** (*Jerez*, Spain) See *Harvey's*.

Ⓘ **Jean-Marc Brocard** [broh-kahrr] (*Burgundy*, France) Very classy *Chablis* producer with well-defined individual vineyard wines, also producing unusually good *Aligoté*. ★★★★ 2000 Chablis Premier Cru Vaucoupins ££

Ⓘ **Brokenwood** (*Hunter Valley*, Australia) Long-established source of great *Sémillon*, *Shiraz*, and even (unusually for the *Hunter Valley*) *Cabernet*. Look for the "Cricket Pitch" bottlings. ★★★ 2000 Rayner Vineyard Shiraz ££

Ⓘ **Castello di Brolio** (*Tuscany*, Italy) Historic *Chianti* estate now being revived. Look out for Castello di Brolio, Rocca Guicciarda and Casalferro, a blend of Sangiovese, Cabernet and Merlot. Wines labelled Barone Ricasoli are generally not from the estate. ★★★★★ 1997 Chianti Classico

Ⓘ **Brouilly** [broo-yee] (*Burgundy*, France) Largest of the 10 *Beaujolais Crus* producing pure, fruity *Gamay*. *Duboeuf; Cotton; Sylvain Fessy;* Laurent Martray; Michaud; Piron; Roland; Ruet; Ch. des Tours.

Ⓘ **Ch. Broustet** [broo-stay] (*Barsac 2ème Cru Classé, Bordeaux*, France) Rich, quite old-fashioned, well-oaked *Barsac* second growth.

Ⓘ **Brown Brothers** (*Victoria*, Australia) Family-owned and *Victoria*-focused winery with a penchant for new wine regions and grapes (including several from Italy). The sparkling wine, the *Shiraz* and the *Liqueur Muscat* are good and The *Orange Muscat* and *Flora* remains a delicious mouthful of liquid marmalade. ★★★★ 1998 Limited Release Cabernet Sauvignon ££

Ⓘ **David Bruce** (*Santa Cruz*, California) Long established *Zinfandel* specialist whose fairly-priced *Petite Sirah* and *Pinot Noir* are also worth seeking out.

Ⓘ **Bruisyard Vineyard** [broos-syard] (*Suffolk*, England) High-quality vineyard.

Ⓘ **Alain Brumont** (*Madiran*, France) Leading producer of modern wines from the traditional Tannat grape. Look for Ch. Montus and Domaine Bouscassé.

Ⓘ **Le Brun de Neuville** [bruhn duh nuh-veel] (*Champagne*, France) Little-known producer with classy *vintage* and excellent rosé and *Blanc de Blancs*. ★★★ Cuvee du Roi Clovis £££

Ⓘ **Willi Bründlmayer** [broondl-mi-yurh] (Austria) Oaked *Chardonnay* and *Pinots* of every kind, *Grüner Veltliner*, and even a fair shot at *Cabernet*.

Ⓘ **Lucien & André Brunel** [broo-nel] (*Rhône*, France) The Brunels' "Les Caillous" produces good, traditional, built-to-last *Châteauneuf-du-Pape*. ★★★ 1999 Les Cailloux Châteauneuf-du-Pape ££

Ⓘ **Brunello di Montalcino** [broo-nell-oh dee mon-tahl-chee-noh] (*Tuscany*, Italy) DOCG red from *Sangiovese*. *Altesino; Argiano; Villa Banfi;* Barbi; *Tenuta Caparzo; Costanti;* Lambardi; Col d'Orcia; *Poggio Antico;* Talenti; Val di Suga.

Brut [broot] Dry, particularly of *Champagne* and sparkling wines. Brut nature/sauvage/zéro are even drier, while *"Extra-Sec"* is perversely applied to (slightly) sweeter sparkling wine. ★★★★ NV Taittinger Brut Reserve £££

🍇 **Bual** [bwahl] (*Madeira*) Grape producing soft, nutty wine – wonderful with cheese. *Blandy's; Cossart Gordon; Henriques & Henriques.* ★★★★★ Henriques & Henriques 10 Year Old Bual £££

Ⓘ **Buçaco Palace Hotel** [boo-sah-koh] (Portugal) Red and white wines made from grapes grown in *Bairrada* and *Dão*. They last forever but cannot be bought outside the Disneyesque hotel itself.

Bucelas [boo-sel-las] (Portugal) *DO* area near Lisbon, best known for its intensely coloured, aromatic, bone-dry white wines. *Caves Velhas.*

B

Buena Vista [bway-nah vihs-tah] (*Carneros,* California) One of the biggest estates in *Carneros*, this is an improving producer of California *Chardonnay, Pinot Noir,* and *Cabernet*. Look out for Grand Reserve wines.

Bugey [boo-jay] (*Savoie,* France) *Savoie* district producing a variety of wines, including spicy white *Roussette de Bugey*, from the grape of that name.

Reichsrat von Buhl [rike-srat fon bool] (*Pfalz,* Germany) One of the best estates in the Pfalz area, due in large part to the success of vineyards like the *Forster Jesuitengarten*.

Buitenverwachting [bite-turn-fur-vak-turng] (*Constantia,* South Africa) Showpiece organic *Constantia* winery making tasty organic whites.

Bulgaria Still relying on its country wines and affordable *Cabernet Sauvignons* and *Merlots*. *Mavrud* is the traditional red variety and *Lovico, Rousse, Iambol, Suhindol,* and *Haskovo* the names to look out for.

Bull's Blood (*Eger,* Hungary) The red wine, aka Egri Bikaver, which helped defenders to fight off Turkish invaders, is improving now thanks to winemaker *Tibor Gal*.

Bernard Burgaud [boor-goh] (*Rhône,* France) Serious producer of *Côte Rôtie*.

Grant Burge (*Barossa Valley*, Australia) Dynamic Shiraz specialist and – since 1993 – owner of *Basedows*. The Holy Trinity Rhône is fine but the oaky Meshach gets the attention. ★★★★ **2000 Filsell Old Vine Shiraz ££**

Burgenland [boor-gen-lund] (Austria) Wine region bordering *Hungary*, climatically ideal for fine sweet *Auslese* and *Beerenauslese*. *Feiler-Artinger; Kollwentz-Römerhof; Helmut Lang; Kracher; Opitz; Wachter*.

Weinkellerei Burgenland [vine-kel-ler-ri boor-gen-lund] (*Neusiedlersee,* Austria) Cooperative with highly commercial *late harvest* wines.

Bürgerspital zum Heiligen Geist (*Wurzburg,* Germany) One of *Wurzburg's* ancient charitable institutions, making often very good wine.

Alain Burguet [al-lan boor-gay] (*Burgundy,* France) One-man *domaine* proving how good plain *Gevrey-Chambertin* can be without heavy doses of new oak. ★★★ **2000 Gevrey Chambertin Cuvée Tradition ££**

Burgundy (France) Home to *Pinot Noir* and *Chardonnay*; wines range from banal to sublime, but are never cheap. See *Chablis, Côte de Nuits, Côte de Beaune, Mâconnais, Beaujolais,* and individual villages.

Leo Buring [byoo-ring] (*South Australia*) One of the many labels used by the Southcorp (*Penfolds* etc.) group, specializing in ageable *Rieslings* and mature *Shiraz*.

Weingut Dr. Bürklin-Wolf [boor-klin-volf] (*Pfalz,* Germany) Impressive estate with great organic *Riesling* vineyards and fine, dry wines.

Ernest J&F Burn [boorn] (*Alsace,* France) Classy estate with vines in the Goldert *Grand Cru*. Great traditional *Gewurztraminer, Riesling,* and *Muscat*.

Buttery Rich, fat smell often found in good *Chardonnay* (often as a result of *malolactic fermentation*) or in wine that has been left on its *lees*.

Buzet [boo-zay] (*Southwest,* France) Eastern neighbour of *Bordeaux,* using the same grape varieties to make generally basic wines. **Buzet; co-operative** (Baron d' Ardeuil); Ch. de Gueyze; Tissot. ★★★ 1998 Domaine de la Croix Vieilles Vignes Les Vignerons de Buzet £

Byington [bi-ing-ton] (*Santa Cruz,* California) Fine producer of *Chardonnay* (Spring Ridge Vineyard) and *Pinot Noir,* and a rare example of good California Semillon.

Davis Bynum (*Sonoma,* California) Producer of interesting single vineyard *Pinot Noir* and *Chardonnay*.

Byron Vineyard [bi-ron] (*Santa Barbara,* California) Impressive *Santa Barbara* winery with investment from *Mondavi,* and a fine line in *Pinots* and (particularly good) subtly oaked *Chardonnays*. ★★★★ 1997 Pinot Noir Sierra Madre Vineyard ££

C

Ca' del Bosco [kah-del-bos-koh] (*Lombardy*, Italy) Classic, if pricey, *barrique*-aged *Cabernet/Merlot* ("Maurizio Zanella") blends and fine *Chardonnay Pinot Noi* ("*Pinero*"), and *Pinot Bianco/Pinot Noir/Chardonnay Méthode Champenoise Franciacorta*. Look out also for the new Carmenero, made from the *Carmenère*.

Luis Caballero [loo-is cab-i-yer-roh] (*Jerez*, Spain) Quality *sherry* producer responsible for the *Burdon* range; also owns *Lustau*.

Château La Cabanne [la ca-ban] (*Pomerol, Bordeaux,* France) Up-and-coming *Pomerol* property.

Cabardès [cab-bahr-des] (*Southwest*, France) Recent appellation north of Carcassonne using Southern and Bordeaux varieties to produce good, if mostly rustic, reds. Confusingly, some are Cabernet-Merlot dominated, while others lean toward the Rhône. **Cabrol; Pennautier; Salitis;Ventenac.**
★★★ 1999 Chateau Salitis Cabardes £

Cabernet d'Anjou/de Saumur [cab-behr-nay don-joo / dur soh-moor] (*Loire*, France) Light, fresh, grassy, blackcurrant rosés, typical of their grape, the *Cabernet Franc.*

Cabernet Franc [ka-behr-nay fron] Kid brother of *Cabernet Sauvignon*; blackcurranty but more leafy. Best in the *Loire,* Italy, and increasingly in Australia, California, and Washington, of course, as a partner of the *Cabernet Sauvignon* and particularly *Merlot* in Bordeaux. See *Chinon* and *Trentino.*

Cabernet Sauvignon [ka-ber-nay soh-vin-yon] The great blackcurranty, cedary, green peppery grape of *Bordeaux*, where it is blended with *Merlot*. Despite increasing competition from the *Merlot*, this is still by far the most successful red varietal, grown in every reasonably warm winemaking country on the planet. See *Bordeaux, Coonawarra, Chile, Napa,* etc.

Cabrière Estate (South Africa) Reliable produce of *Cap Classique* sparkling wine. The wines are sold under the Pierre Jordan label

Marqués de Cáceres [mahr-kehs day cath-thay-res] (*Rioja,* Spain) Modern French-influenced *bodega* making fresh-tasting wines. A good, if anonymous, new-style white has been joined by a promising oak-fermented version and a recommendable rosé (*rosado*), plus a grapey *Muscat*-style white.

Ch. Cadet-Piola [ka-day pee-yoh-lah] (*St. Emilion Grand Cru Classé, Bordeaux,* France) Wines that are made to last, with fruit and *tannin* to spare.

Cadillac [kad-dee-yak] (*Bordeaux,* France) Sweet but rarely luscious (non-*botrytis*) *Sémillon* and *Sauvignon* whites. Ch. Fayau is the star wine. Its *d'Yquem*-style label is pretty chic too. **Carsin; Cayla; Fayau; du Juge; Manos; Memoires; Reynon**

Villa Cafaggio (*Tuscany*, Italy) Characterful *Chianti Classico* and IGT Toscana wines from an estate that has never taken its eye off the ball, quality-wise. San Martino is based on *Sangiovese*, Cortaccio on *Cabernet*; the top Chianti is *Riserva* Solatio Basilica. ★★★★ 1998 Chianti Classico Riserva

Cahors [kah-orr] (*Southwest,* France) Often rustic wines produced from the local *Tannat* and the *Cot* (*Malbec*). Some are *Beaujolais*-like, while others are *tannic* and full-bodied, though far lighter than in the days when people spoke of "the black wines of Cahors". **Ch. de Caix; la Caminade; du Cèdre; Clos la Coutale; Clos de Gamot; Gautoul; de Hauterivem; Haute-Serre; Lagrezette; Lamartine; Latuc; Prieuré de Cenac; Rochet-Lamother; Clos Triguedina.**
★★★★ 2000 Château Croze de Pys Cahors Domaines Roche £

Ch Caillou (*Bordeaux*, France) *Second Growth* Barsac property making elegant and increasingly good wine. As always in Bordeaux, there is an unrelated property of the same name in Graves, a Le Caillou in Pomerol and a dry white, Caillou Blanc, from the Médoc's Ch. Talbot.

Cain Cellars (*Napa*, California) Spectacular *Napa* hillside vineyards devoted to producing a classic *Bordeaux* blend of five varieties – hence the name of the wine.

C

℥ **Cairanne** [keh-ran] (*Rhône*, France) Named *Côtes du Rhône* village known for good peppery reds. Dom d'Ameilhaud; Aubert; Brusset; Oratoire St-Martin; Richaud; Tardieu-Laurent. ★★★★ 2000 Cuvée Eloise Dme Grands Bois ££

℥ **Cakebread** (*Napa*, California) Long-established producer of rich reds, very good *Sauvignon Blanc, Chardonnay*, and improving *Pinot Noir*. ★★★★ Cabernet Sauvignon Vine Hill £££

Calabria [kah-lah-bree-ah] (Italy) The "toe" of the Italian boot, making Cirò from the local Gaglioppo reds and *Greco* whites. *Cabernet* and *Chardonnay* are promising, too, especially from *Librandi*. Watch out for new wave *Aglianico*. ★★★ 1999 Magno Megonio Librandi £££

℥ **Calem** [kah-lin] (*Douro*, Portugal) Quality-conscious, small *port* producer. The speciality *Colheita tawnies* are among the best of their kind.

℥ **Calera Wine Co.** [ka-lehr-uh] (*Santa Benito*, California) Maker of some of *California's* best, longest-lived *Pinot Noir* from individual vineyards such as Jensen, Mills, Reed, and Selleck. The *Chardonnay* and *Viognier* are pretty special too. ★★★★ 1997 Pinot Noir Reed Vineyard Mount Harlan £££

California (US) Major wine-producing area of the US. See *Napa, Sonoma, Santa Barbara, Amador, Mendocino*, etc., plus individual wineries.

℥ **Viña Caliterra** [kal-lee-tay-rah] (*Curico*, Chile) Sister company of *Errazuriz*. Now a 50-50 partner with *Mondavi* and co-producer of *Seña*. ★★★★ 1999 Arboleda Cabernet Sauvignon £££

℥ **Callaway** (*Temecula* California) An unfashionable part of California, and a deliciously unfashionable style of – unoaked – *Chardonnay*.

℥ **Ch. Calon-Ségur** [kal-lon say-goor] (*St. Estèphe 3ème Cru Classé, Bordeaux*, France) Traditional *St. Estèphe* now surpassing its status. Fine in 2000.

℥ **Quinta de Camarate** (*Estremadura*, Portugal) Rich, supple red from the ever-reliable company of José Maria da Fonseca.

℥ **Ch Cambon la Pelouse** (*Bordeaux*, France) Excellent *Cru Bourgeois Médoc*. 2000 and 2001 are particularly good, and good value too.

℥ **Cambria** (*Santa Barbara*, California) Huge operation in the *Santa Maria Valley* belonging to the dynamic *Kendall Jackson* and producing fairly priced and good, if rarely complex, *Chardonnay, Pinot Noir, Syrah, Viognier,* and *Sangiovese*. ★★★★★ 1997 Julia's Vineyard £

℥ **Ch. Camensac** [kam-mon-sak] (*Haut-Médoc 5ème Cru Classé, Bordeaux*, France) Improving property following investment in 1994.

℥ **Cameron** (*Oregon*, US) John Paul makes terrific *Pinot Noir* in this Yamhill estate – plus some impressive *Pinot Blanc*.

Campania [kahm-pan-nyah] (Italy) Region surrounding Naples, known for *Taurasi, Lacryma Christi*, and *Greco di Tufo* and wines from *Mastroberadino*.

℥ **Campbells** (*Rutherglen*, Australia) Classic producer of fortified *Muscat* and rich, concentrated reds under the Bobbie Burns label. ★★★★★ NV Campbells Rutherglen Muscat £

℥ **Campillo** [kam-pee-yoh] (*Rioja*, Spain) A small estate producing *Rioja* made purely from *Tempranillo*, showing what this grape can do. The white is less impressive. ★★★ 1992 Gran Reserva ££

℥ **Bodegas Campo Viejo** [kam-poh vyay-hoh] (*Rioja*, Spain) A go-ahead, if underrated *bodega* whose *Reserva* and *Gran Reserva* are full of rich fruit. Albor, the unoaked red (pure *Tempranillo*) and white (*Viura*) are first-class examples of modern Spanish winemaking. ★★★ 1998 Crianza £

Canada Surprising friends and foes alike, British Columbia (Okanagan) and *Ontario* are producing good *Chardonnay, Riesling*, improving *Pinot Noirs* and intense *Icewines*, usually from the *Vidal* grape. Cave Springs; *Chateau des Charmes;* Henry of Pelham; *Hillebrand;* Inniskillin; Jackson-Triggs; Konzelmann; Magnotta; *Mission Hill;* Pelee Island; Peller Estates; *Pilliteri;* Reif Estate; Stoney Ridge; Sumac Ridge; Vineland Estates.

℥ **Bodegas Humberto Canale** (Argentina) Cool climate *Pinot Noir* and *Sauvignon Blanc* lead the field. *Malbec* and *Merlot* are improving very impressively too. ★★★★ 2000 Black River Reserve Malbec ££

I Canard Duchêne [kan-nah doo-shayn] (*Champagne,* France) Improving and often fairly priced subsidiary of *Veuve Clicquot.*

I Canberra District (*New South Wales,* Australia) Confounding the critics, a small group of producers led by Clonakilla *Doonkuna, Helm's,* and *Lark Hill* are making good *Rhône*-style reds and *Rieslings* in high-altitude vineyards here. ★★★★ **2000 Lark Hill Exultation £££**

I Candido [kan-dee doh] (*Apulia,* Italy) Top producer of deliciously chocolatey Salice Salentino. ★★★ **1998 Salice Salentino Riserva Candido £**

I Canépa [can-nay-pah] (Chile) Good rather than great winery, making progress with *Chardonnays* and *Rieslings* and oaky reds. ★★★ **1999 Finisimo Cabernet Sauvignon Reserva Especial ££**

Cannonau [kan-non-now] (*Sardinia,* Italy) A red *clone* of the *Grenache,* producing a variety of wine styles from sweet to dry, mostly in *Sardinia.*

I Cannonau di Sardegna [kan-non-now dee sahrden-yah] (*Sardinia,* Italy) Heady, robust, dry-tosweet, *DOC* red made from the *Cannonau.*

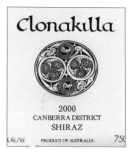

Clonakilla

2000
CANBERRA DISTRICT
SHIRAZ
% Alc/Vol   PRODUCT OF AUSTRALIA   750

I Ch. Canon [kan-non] (*St. Emilion Premier Grand Cru Classé, Bordeaux,* France) Back on track after a tricky patch in the 1990s. The keynote here is elegance rather than power.

I Ch. Canon de Brem [kan-non dur brem] (*Canon-Fronsac, Bordeaux,* France) A very good *Fronsac* property.

I Canon-Fronsac [kah-non fron-sak] (*Bordeaux,* France) Small *appellation* bordering on *Pomerol,* with attractive plummy, *Merlot*-based reds from increasingly good value, if rustic, petits *châteaux. Ch. Canon-Moueix;* Ch. Moulin Pey-Labrie.

I Ch. Canon-la-Gaffelière [kan-non lah gaf-fel-yehr] (*St. Emilion Grand Cru Classé, Bordeaux,* France) High-flying estate run by an innovative, qualityconscious German who, in 1996, created the instant superstar *la Mondotte.* Rich, ultra-concentrated wine.

I Ch. Canon-Moueix [kan-non mwex] (*Canon-Fronsac, Bordeaux,* France) A characteristically stylish addition to the *Moueix* empire in *Canon-Fronsac.* A wine to beat many a pricier *St. Emilion.*

I Ch. Cantemerle [kont-mehrl] (*Haut-Médoc 5ème Cru Classé, Bordeaux,* France) A *Cru Classé* situated outside the main villages of the *Médoc.* Classy, perfumed wine with bags of blackcurrant fruit.

I Ch. Cantenac-Brown [kont-nak brown] (*Margaux 3ème Cru Classé, Bordeaux,* France) Under the same ownership as Ch. Pichon Baron but less impressive.

Canterbury (New Zealand) Waipara, here in the South Island produces aromatic Riesling, Pinot Blanc, and Chablis-like Chardonnay. **Giesen; Pegasus Bay; Melness; Mark Rattray; St. Helena; Sherwood Estate; Waipara Springs.** ★★★ **2000 Waipara West Riesling ££; ★★★ 2000 Chancellor Estates Riesling £**

Cantina (Sociale) [kan-tee-nuh soh-chee-yah-lay] (Italy) Winery (cooperative).

I Capannelle Good producer of rich *Super-Tuscan* wine near Gaiole.

Cap Corse [kap-korss] (*Corsica,* France) 17 villages in the north of the island produce great, floral Muscat as well as some attractive herby dry Vermentino. **Antoine Arena; Dom de Catarelli; Clos Nicrosi.**

Cap Classique [kap-klas-seek] (South Africa) Now that the term *"Méthode Champenoise"* has unreasonably been outlawed, this is the phrase developed by the South Africans to describe their Champagne-method sparkling wine. ★★★ **1998 Bon Courage Cap Classique Jacques Bruère Brut Reserve ££**

I Ch. Cap-de-Mourlin [kap-dur-mer-lan] (*St. Emilion Grand Cru Classé, Bordeaux,* France) Good mid-range stuff.

I Caparzo [ka-pahrt-zoh] (*Tuscany,* Italy) Classy, *Brunello di Montalcino* estate producing wines that age brilliantly.

C

Cape (South Africa) The area that includes all of South Africa's vineyards. See *Stellenbosch, Paarl, Franschhoek, Walker Bay, Robertson, Tulbagh, Worcester,* etc.

⍨ **Cape Mentelle** [men-tel] (*Margaret River*, Western Australia) French-owned winery, founded, like *Cloudy Bay*, by David Hoehnen. Impressive *Semillon-Sauvignon, Shiraz, Cabernet* and a wild berryish *Zinfandel*, to shame many a Californian. ★★★★ 1999 Cabernet Merlot ££

⍨ **Capel Vale** [kay-puhl vayl] (Southwest coast, Western Australia) Just to the north of *Margaret River*. Good *Riesling, Gewürztraminer,* and *Shiraz*.

⍨ **Capezzana** [kap-pay-tzah-nah] (*Tuscany*, Italy) The early home of *Cabernet* and *Sangiovese* blends. ★★★★★ 1996 Vin Santo di Carignano Riserva £££

Capsule The sheath covering the cork. Once lead, now plastic or tin. In the case of "flanged" bottles, though, it is noticeable by its transparency or absence.

Carnuntum (Austria) Wine region east of Vienna and mostly south of the Danube. A relatively warmish climate means that reds are looking increasingly good, especially from the Zweigelt grape.

⍨ **Conde de Caralt** (*Penedes*, Spain) Good *cava* and attractive still wines. The company is owned by *Freixenet*.

⍨ **Caramany** [kah-ram-man-nee] (*Midi*, France) New *AC* for an old section of the *Côtes du Roussillon*-Villages, near the *Pyrénées*. *Vignerons Catalans.*

Carbonic Maceration See *Macération Carbonique.*

⍨ **Ch. Carbonnieux** [kar-bon-nyeuh] (*Graves Cru Classé, Bordeaux,* France) Since 1991, the whites have greatly improved and the raspberryish reds are among the most reliable in the region.

⍨ **Carcavelos** [kar-kah-veh-losh] (Portugal) *DO* region in the Lisbon suburbs producing usually disappointing fortified wines.

⍨ **Cardinale** (California) *Kendall-Jackson's* top line, produced by a former star Mondavi winemaker from grapes grown on mostly hillside vines. The Royale white is impressively *Bordeaux*-like. ★★★★★ 1996 Cardinale

⍨ **Ch. la Cardonne** [kar-don] (*Bordeaux*, France) *Cru Bourgeois* whose quality is improving since its sale by the Rothschilds of *Ch. Lafite*.

⍨ **Carema** [kah-ray-mah] (*Piedmont*, Italy) Wonderful perfumed *Nebbiolo* produced in limited quantities largely by Cantina dei Produttori Nebbiolo.

🍇 **Carignan** [kah-ree-nyon] Prolific red grape used in *Corbières, Minervois,* and *Fitou,* and making either dull, coarse wine or richer spicier stuff when vines are old and yields low. In Spain it is known as *Cariñena* and Mazuelo, while Italians call it Carignano. ★★★★ 2001 Terroir Club France Aude £

⍨ **Carignano del Sulcis** [ka-reen-yah-noh dehl sool-chees] (*Sardinia*, Italy) Dynamic *DOC* spearheaded by the Santadi cooperative.

⍨ **Louis Carillon & Fils** [ka-ree-yon] (*Burgundy,* France) Great modern *Puligny* estate. ★★★ 1999 Puligny-Montrachet £££

⍨ **Cariñena** [kah-ree-nyeh-nah] (Spain) Important *DO* of Aragon for rustic reds, high in alcohol and, confusingly, made not from the *Cariñena* (or *Carignan*) grape, but mostly from the *Garnacha Tinta*. Also some whites.

🍇 **Cariñena** [kah-ree-nyeh-nah] (Spain) The Spanish name for *Carignan*.

⍨ **Carmel** (Israel) Huge producer offering a wide range of pleasant but generally unremarkable wines.

⍨ **Viña Carmen** [veen-yah kahr-men] (*Maipo*, Chile) Quietly developing a reputation as one of the best red wine producers in Chile. Increasingly organic.

🍇 **Carmenère** [kahr-meh-nehr] (Chile) Smoky-spicily distinctive grape that although almost extinct in Bordeaux is still a permitted variety for claret. Widely planted in Chile where it has traditionally been sold as Merlot. Look for examples like the Santa Inès Carmenère, *Carmen* Grand Vidure, or *Veramonte Merlot*. ★★★★ 2001 Laura Hartwig Carmenère ££

⍨ **Carmenet Vineyard** [kahr-men-nay] (*Sonoma Valley*, California) Unusual winery tucked away in the hills and producing long-lived, very *Bordeaux*-like but approachable reds, fairly-priced *Chardonnay*, and also (even more unusually for California) good *Semillon-Sauvignon* and *Cabernet Franc*.

C

ⵉ **Les Carmes-Haut-Brion** [lay kahrm oh bree-yon] (*Bordeaux*, France)
Small property neighbouring *Ch. Haut-Brion* in *Pessac-Léognan*. Particularly
good in 1999.

ⵉ **Carmignano** [kahr-mee-nyah-noh] (*Tuscany*, Italy) Nearby alternative to
Chianti, with the traditional addition of more *Cabernet* grapes. See
Capezzana.

ⵉ **Quinta do Carmo** [Keen-tah doh Kar-moh] (*Alentejo*, Portugal) The
Ch. Lafite Rothschilds' best foreign venture to date. Rich, tastily modern
reds.

Carneros [kahr-neh-ros] (California) Small, fog-cooled, high-quality
region shared between the *Napa* and *Sonoma Valleys* and used by just
about everybody as a source for cool-climate grapes. Producing top-class
Chardonnay, Pinot Noir, and now, *Merlot.* Some of the best examples are
from from Hudson and Hyde vineyards. *Acacia; Carneros Creek; Cuvaison;
Domaine Carneros; Domaine Chandon; Kistler;* Macrostie; Marcassin; Mondavi;
Mumm Cuvée Napa; Patz & Hall; Pine Ridge; Ramey; Saintsbury; Shafer; Swanson;
Truchard.* ★★★★ 2000 Schug Carneros Pinot Noir ££

ⵉ **Domaine Carneros** (*Napa Valley,* California) *Champagne Taittinger's* US
sparkling wine – produced in a ludicrously incongruous replica of their
French HQ. The wine, however, is one of the best New World efforts by the
Champenois.

ⵉ **Carneros Creek** (*Carneros,* California) Produces ambitious *Pinot Noir* under
this name and somewhat better (and cheaper) berryish Fleur de Carneros.

ⵉ **Caronne-Ste-Gemme** [kah-ronn-sant jem] (*Bordeaux*, France) Reliable
Cru Bourgeois that delivers value – even in poorer vintages.

ⵉ **Carpineto** [Kah-pi-neh-toh] (*Tuscany*, Italy) High-quality producer of
Chianti, and *Chardonnay* and *Cabernet* that are sold under the Farnito label.

ⵉ **Carr Taylor** (*Sussex,* England) Sparkling wines are the best buys.

ⵉ **Ch. Carras** [kar-ras] (*Macedonia,* Greece) Greece's best-known estate, left
behind by more modern producers. Now in new hands.

ⵉ **Herdade de Cartuxa** [har-dah-day de car-too-shah] (*Alentejo*, Portugal)
Huge estate recently handed over to a charity by its owner. Pera-Manca is the
top red.Whites are creamily complex

ⵉ **Les Carruades de Lafite** [kah-roo-ahd dur la-feet]
(*Pauillac, Bordeaux,* France) The second label of *Ch.
Lafite.* Rarely (quite) as good as *les Forts de Latour,*
nor *Ch. Margaux's Pavillon Rouge.*

ⵉ **Ch. Carsin** [kahr-san] (*Premières Côtes de
Bordeaux,* France) Finnish-owned, Aussie-style estate
with particularly tasty whites from Sauvignon Gris.
★★★★ 1998 Chateau Carsin Cuvee Prestige ££

ⵉ **Carta Vieja** [kah-ta vee-yay-ha] (Chile) Family
winery making good reds, decent whites.

ⵉ **Quinta do Carvalhais** [keen-tah doh car-vay-
yash] (*Dão*, Portugal) Single estate which, under the
forward-looking ownership of *Sogrape,* is showing
how good *Dão* can be.

Casa [kah-sah] (Italy, Spain, Portugal) Firm or company.

Casablanca [kas-sab-lan-ka] (*Aconcagua*, Chile) Cool region in *Aconcagua*,
producing especially impressive *Sauvignons, Chardonnays,* and
*Gewürztraminers. Caliterra; Viña Casablanca; Concha y Toro; Errazuriz; Santa
Carolina; Santa Emiliana; Santa Rita; Veramonte; Villard.*

ⵉ **Viña Casablanca** [veen-yah kas-sab-lan-ka] (*Casablanca,* Chile)
Enterprising winery in the region of the same name. ★★★★ 2000 Santa
Isabel MerlotVina Casablanca ££; ★★★ 1999 White Label Merlot £

ⵉ **Casanova di Neri** [kah-sah-NOH-vah dee NAY-ree] (*Tuscany,* Italy) Fine
producer of *Brunello* and *Rosso di Montalcino.* ★★★ 1997 Brunello di
Montalcino ££

C

🍾 **Casse Basse** [kah-seh-bas-say] (*Tuscany,* Italy) Soldera's hard-to-find and pricy *Brunello di Montalcino* is developing a cult following in the US.

🍾 **Caslot-Galbrun** [kah-loh gal-bruhn] (*Loire,* France) Top-class producer of serious, long-lived red *Loires*.

🍾 **Cassegrain** [kas-grayn] (*New South Wales,* Australia) Variable, but often impressive.wines from the Hastings Valley on the east coast and elsewhere.

Cassis [ka-sees] (*Provence,* France) Coastal *appellation* producing (variable) red, (often dull) white and (good) rosé. **Clos Ste. Magdeleine; la Ferme Blanche.**

🍾 **Castel del Monte** [Ka-stel del mon-tay] (*Puglia,* Italy) Interesting southern region where Rivera makes excellent Il Falcone reds and Bianca di Svevia whites. Grapes grown include the local Aglianico, Pampanuto, Bombino Bianco and Nero, and Nero di Troia. ★★★ 1999 Cappellaccio Riserva ££

🍾 **Castelgiocondo** [kas-tel-jee-yah-kon-doh] (*Tuscany,* Italy) High-quality *Brunello* estate owned by *Frescobaldi.*

🍾 **Castellare** [kas-teh-LAH-ray] (*Tuscany,* Italy) Innovative small *Chianti Classico* estate whose *Sangiovese-Malvasia* blend, Nera I Sodi di San Niccoló, *Vino da Tavola,* is worth seeking out.

🍾 **Castellblanch** [kas-tel-blantch] (*Catalonia,* Spain) Producer of better-than-most *Cava* – but catch it young.

🍾 **Castell de Remei** [kas-te'y day reh-may-yee] (*Costers del Segre,* Spain) International grape varieties - *Merlot, Cabernet, Chardonnay, Sauvignon* - dominate at this property. Whites are good, reds better.

🍾 **Casteller** [kas-teh-ler] (*Trentino-Alto Adige,* Italy) Pale red, creamy-fruity wines for early drinking, made from *Schiava.* See *Ca'Vit.*

🍾 **Castello di Ama** [kas-tel-loh-dee-ah-mah] (*Tuscany,* Italy) Producer of great single-vineyard *Chianti Classico* (esp. the Bellavista Riserva) plus the stunning Vigna l'Apparita Merlot.

🍾 **Castell'sches, Fürstlich Domänenamt** [kas-tel-shs foorst-likh Doh-mehn-en-ahmt] (*Franken,* Germany) Good *Auslese Scheurebe* and Rieslaner and dry *Silvaner.* Dornfelder reds are interesting too.

🍾 **Castillo de Monjardin** [kas-tee-yoh deh mon-har-deen] (*Navarra,* Spain). Navarra rising star with good *Chardonnay, Pinot Noir,* and *Merlot.*

Cat's pee Describes the tangy smell frequently found in typical *Müller-Thurgau* and unripe *Sauvignon Blanc.*

Catalonia [kat-tal-loh-nee-yah] (Spain) Semi-autonomous region including *Penedés, Priorato, Conca de Barberá, Terra Alta,* and *Costers del Segre.*

🍾 **Catena Estate** [kat-tay-nah] (Argentina) Quality-focused part of the giant Catena-Esmeralda concern, helped by the expertise of ex-*Simi* Californian winemaker Paul Hobbs. ★★★★★ 2000 Alamos Chardonnay £

🍾 **Cattier** [Kat-ee-yay] (*Champagne,* France) Up-and-coming producer with good non-vintage wines.

🍾 **Dom. Cauhapé** [koh-ap-pay] (*Southwest,* France) Extraordinary *Jurançon* producer of excellent *Vendange Tardive* and dry wines from the *Manseng* grape.

🍾 **Cava** [kah-vah] (*Catalonia,* Spain) Sparkling wine produced in *Penedés* by the *Methode Champenoise* handicapped by dull local grapes. Avoid *vintage* versions and look instead for Anna de *Codorníu* and *Raimat* Cava – both made from *Chardonnay* – or such well-made exceptions to the earthy rule as *Juvé y Camps, Conde de Caralt, Cava Chandon,* and *Segura Viudas.* ★★★ 1999 Xenius Cava Brut Reserva £

Cava (Greece) Legal term for wood- and bottle-aged wine.

🍾 **Cavalleri** [kah-vah-yah-ree] (*Lombardy,* Italy) One of the top sparkling wines in Italy.

Cave [kahv] (France) Cellar.

🍾 **Cave Spring** (*Ontario,* Canada) One of Canada's most reliable producers, with especially good Chardonnay.

🍾 **Ca'Vit** [kah-veet] (*Trentino,* Italy) The umbrella name of a group of co-ops.

C

🍷 **Caymus Vineyards** [kay-muhs] (*Napa Valley*, California) Producer of concentrated Italianate reds (including a forceful *Zinfandel*) and a characterful *Cabernet Franc*. Liberty School is the *second label*.

🍷 **Dom. Cazes** [kahrs] (*Midi*, France) Producer of great *Muscat de Rivesaltes*, rich marmaladey stuff which makes most *Muscat de Beaumes de Venise* seem dull.

🍷 **Cellier le Brun** [sel-yay luh-bruhn] (*Marlborough*, New Zealand) Producer of *Méthode Champenoise* sparkling wine. ★★★ 2001 Terrace Road Sauvignon Blanc ££

🍇 **Cencibel** [sen-thee-bel] (*Valdepeñas*, Spain) Alternative name for *Tempranillo*.

Central Coast (California) Geographically varied set of regions south of San Francisco, including *Santa Barbara, Monterey, Santa Cruz,* and *San Luis Obispo*. Hardly surprisingly, the wines vary widely. ★★★ 1998 Alban Viognier

🍷 **Central Otago** [oh-tah-goh] (*South Island*, New Zealand) "New" region attracting a similar cult following to *Marlborough*. *Pinot Noir, Gewurztraminer,* and *Riesling* flourish. Black Ridge; Chard Farm; *Felton Road*; Gibbston Valley; Rippon Vineyards. ★★★★ 2000 Mt Difficulty Pinot Noir £££

Central Valley (California) Huge irrigated region controlled by giants which make three-quarters of the state's wines without, so far, matching the efforts of similar regions Down Under. New vineyards and a concentration on cooler parts of the region are paying off for the *Sauvignon Blanc* but I doubt the potential of the increasingly widely planted *Merlot*. Smaller-scale winemaking is beginning to help (this is wine-factory country), but good wines are still the exception to the rule. *Quady's* fortified and sweet wines are still by far the best wines here. ★★★★ 2001 Caliterra Merlot Reserva ££

Central Valley (Viticultural Region) (Chile) The region in which most of *Chile's* wines are made. It includes *Maipo, Rapel, Maule,* and *Curico,* but not *Casablanca*, which is in *Aconcagua*, further north.

Cépage [say-pahzh] (France) Grape variety.

🍷 **Cepparello** [chep-par-rel-loh] (*Tuscany*, Italy) Brilliant pure *Sangiovese IGT* made by Paolo de Marchi of *Isole e Olena*. Well worth laying down for a decade or more. ★★★★ 1999 Cepparello Isole e Olena Fattorie ££££

Cerasuolo [chay-rah-soo-woh-loh] (*Abruzzo*, Italy) Rosato wine made from the *Montepulciano* grape in *Abruzzo*.

🍷 **Ceretto** [cher-ret-toh] (*Piedmont*, Italy) Producer of good modern *Barolos* and increasingly impressive single-vineyard examples, plus excellent La Bernardina varietals (Syrah, Pinot Noir, etc.)

🍷 **Ch. de Cérons** [say-ron] (*Bordeaux*, France) One of the best properties in little known *appellation* of *Cérons*.

🍷 **Ch. Certan de May** [sehr-ton dur may] (*Pomerol, Bordeaux*, France) Top-class *Pomerol* estate with subtly plummy wine. Made a great 2000.

🍷 **Lagar de Cervara** [lah-gar day chair-vair-rah] (*Rías Baixas*, Spain) One of the best *Albariños*. The wine is elegant, peachy-apricoty and firm.

🍷 **LA Cetto** [chet-toh] (*Baja California*, Mexico) Producer of tasty *Cabernet* and spicy-soft *Petite Sirah* good enough to give wines on the US side of the border a run for their money. ★★★★★ 2000 L.A. Cetto Petite Sirah £

Chablais [shab-lay] (*Vaud*, Switzerland) A good place to find *Pinot Noir* rosé and young *Chasselas* (sold as *Dorin*).

🍷 **Chablis** [shab-lee] (*Burgundy*, France) When not over-priced, *Chablis* offers a steely European finesse that New World *Chardonnays* rarely capture. *Petits* and, more particularly *Grands Crus* should (but do not always) show extra complexity. A new Union, des Grands Crus de Chablis, founded in 2000, is already beginning to improve quality.. Bessin; Bichot; Billaud-Simon; Pascal Bouchard; J-M Brocard; La Chablisienne; D Dampt; René Dauvissat; D&E Defaix; J-P Droin; Joseph Drouhin; Durup; William Fèvre; Laroche; Louis Michel; Moreau-Naudin; S. Mosnier; Gilbert Picq; Raveneau; Servin; Tremblay; Verget; Vocoret.

C

☖ **La Chablisienne** [shab-lees-yen] (*Burgundy,* France) Cooperative making wines from *Petit Chablis* to *Grands Crus* under a host of labels. Rivals the best estates in the *appellation*. ★★★ **1999 Chablis Les Vieilles Vignes La ££**

Chacolí [shab-koh-lee] (*País Vasco,* Spain) Mostly white, light, acidic wine from the *Basque* country. Good with the local fish-and-red-peppers.

Chai [shay] (France) Cellar/winery.

☖ **Chain of Ponds** (*South Australia*) Enterprising Adelaide Hills winery with an impressive *Chardonnay*. ★★★★ **2000 Corkscrew Road Chardonnay ££**

☖ **Chalk Hill** (*Sonoma,* California) Producer of rich *Chardonnay,* stylish *Sauvignon Blanc,* lovely berryish *Cabernet* and great *Sauternes*-style whites. Chalk is ideal soil for Chardonnay. Here in California though, the only chalk you would find is in the name of the winery.

☖ **Chalone** [shal-lohn] (*Monterey,* California) Under the same ownership as *Acacia, Edna Valley,* and *Carmenet,* this 25-year old winery is one of the big names for *Pinot Noir* and *Chardonnay.* Unusually *Burgundian,* long-lived.

Chalonnais/Côte Chalonnaise [shal-lohn-nay] (*Burgundy,* France) Source of lesser-known, potentially good value but often rustic *Burgundies – Givry, Montagny, Rully,* and *Mercurey.* The Bourgogne Rouge can be a good buy.

☖ **Chambers** (*Rutherglen,* Australia) Competes with *Morris* for the crown of best *Liqueur Muscat* maker. The Rosewood is great.

☖ **Ch. Chambert-Marbuzet** [shom-behr mahr-boo-zay] (*St. Estèphe Cru Bourgeois, Bordeaux,* France) Characterful *Cabernet*-based *St. Estèphe.*

☖ **Chambertin** [shom-behr-tan] (*Burgundy,* France) Ultra-cherryish, damsony *Grand Cru* whose name was adopted by the village of Gevrey. Famous in the 14th century, and Napoleon's favourite. Chambertin Clos-de-Bèze, Charmes-Chambertin, Griottes-Chambertin, Latricières-Chambertin, Mazis-Chambertin, and Ruchottes-Chambertin are neighbouring *Grands Crus.*
 Pierre Amiot; Bachelet; Alain Burguet; Bruno Clair; Pierre Damoy; Drouhin; Dugat-Py; Dujac; Engel; Faiveley; Groffier; Raymond Launay; Leroy; Denis Mortet; Bernard Meaume; Jean Raphet; Roty; Henri Rebourseau; Armand Rousseau; Jean Trapet.

☖ **Chambolle-Musigny** [shom-bol moo-see-nyee] (*Burgundy,* France) *Côte de Nuits* village whose wines can be like perfumed examples from the *Côte de Beaune. Georges Roumier* is the local star, and *Drouhin, Dujac,* and *Ponsot* are all reliable, as are *Bertagna, Drouhin, Anne Gros, Ghislaine Barthod, Dominique Laurent Mugnier, de Vogüé,* and *Leroy.* ★★★★★ **2000 Domaine Michel Gros £££**

☖ **Champagne** [sham-payn] (France) Region producing what ought to be the greatest sparkling wines, from *Pinot Noir, Pinot Meunier,* and *Chardonnay.* See individual listings.

☖ **Didier Champalou** [dee-dee-yay shom-pah-loo] (*Loire,* France) Estate with serious sweet, dry and sparkling *Vouvray.*

☖ **Champy** [shom-pee] (*Burgundy,* France) Long-established, recently much-improved *Beaune négociant.* ★★★★ **2000 Côte de Beaune Villages ££**

☖ **Clos la Chance** (*Napa,* California) Up-and-coming producer of good-value *Chardonnay.*

☖ **Dom. Chandon** [doh-mayn shahn-dahn] (*Napa Valley,* California) *Moët & Chandon's* California winery now competes with its counterpart in Australia.

☖ **Dom. Chandon** [doh-mine shon-don] (*Yarra Valley,* Australia) Sold as *Green Point* and proving that Australian grapes, grown in a variety of cool climates, can compete with *Champagne.* Now joined by a creditable, *Chablis*-like, still Colonades *Chardonnay.*

☖ **Dom. Chandon de Briailles** [shon-don dur bree-iy] (*Burgundy,* France) Good *Savigny-lès-Beaune* estate. ★★★★ **1999 Corton Grand Cru Clos du Roi ££**

☖ **Chanson** [shon-son] (*Burgundy,* France) *Beaune* merchant now improving since its purchase by *Bollinger.*

☖ **Ch. de Chantegrive** [shont-greev] (*Graves, Bordeaux,* France) Large modern *Graves* estate with excellent modern reds and whites.

C

Chapel Down (*Kent,* England) Winery that also now owns Carr Taylor and Lamberhurst. Now known as Curious Grape wines.

Chapel Hill Winery (*McLaren Vale,* Australia) Pam Dunsford's impressively rich reds and whites are balanced by a leaner, unoaked *Chardonnay*. ★★★★ 1999 McLaren Vale Coonawarra Cabernet Sauvignon ££

Chapelle-Chambertin [shap-pell shom-behr-ta'n] (*Burgundy*, France) See *Chambertin*.

Chappellet (*Napa,* California) Innovative winery with the courage to make wines such as an oaked *Chenin Blanc*, Tocai Friulano, and "Moelleux" *late-harvest* wines rather than stick to mainstream *Chardonnay* and *Merlot*.

Chapoutier [shah-poo-tyay] (*Rhône,* France) Family-owned merchant using more or less organic methods. Not all wines live up to their early promise but credit is deserved for the initiative of printing labels in braille. Now making wine in Australia. ★★★★★ 2000 Crozes-Hermitage La Petite Ruche ££

Chaptalization [shap-tal-li-zay-shuhn] The legal (in some regions) addition of sugar during fermentation to boost a wine's *alcohol* content.

Charbono [shar-boh-noh] (California) Obscure grape variety producing spicy, full-bodied reds at *Inglenook, Duxoup,* and *Bonny Doon*.

Chardonnay [shar-don-nay] The great white grape of *Burgundy, Champagne,* and now just about everywhere else. See regions and producers.

Vin de Pays du Charentais [shar-ron-tay] (*Southwest,* France) Competing with its brandy-producing neighbour Gascogne, this region now makes pleasant light reds and whites. **Blanchard.**

Charmat [shar-mat] The inventor of the *Cuve Close* method of producing cheap sparkling wines. See *Cuve Close*.

Ch. des Charmes [day sharm] (*Ontario,* Canada) Good maker of *Pinot, Chardonnay,* and *Icewine*. ★★★★ 1997 Paul Bosc Estate Riesling Icewine £££

Charta [kahr-tah] (*Rheingau,* Germany) Syndicate formed in the *Rheingau* using an arch as a symbol to indicate (often searingly) dry (*Trocken*) styles designed to be suitable for ageing and drinking with food. Recently reborn with (thankfully) less rigorously dry aspirations, as part of the *VDP*.

Chartron & Trébuchet [shar-tron ay tray-boo-shay] (*Burgundy,* France) Good small merchant specialising in white *Burgundies*.

Chassagne-Montrachet [shah-san mon-rash-shay] (*Burgundy,* France) *Côte de Beaune* commune making grassy, *biscuity,* fresh yet rich whites and mid-weight, often rustic-tasting, wild fruit reds. Pricey but sometimes less so than neighbouring *Puligny* and as recommendable. *Carillon; Marc Colin;* Colin-Déleger; Jean-Noël Gagnard; Henri Germain; Ch. de Maltroye; M. Morey; Michel Niellon; J. Pillot; Roux; Ramonet.

Ch. Chasse-Spleen [shas spleen] (*Moulis Cru Bourgeois, Bordeaux,* France) *Cru Bourgeois château* whose wines can, in good years, rival those of a *Cru Classé*. A slightly dull patch in the 1990s but is now back on track.

Chasselas [shas-slah] Widely grown, prolific white grape making light often dull wine principally in Switzerland, eastern France, and Germany. Good examples are rare. *Pierre Sparr*.

Ch. du Chasseloir [shas-slwah] (*Loire,* France) Good *Muscadet domaine*

Château [sha-toh] (*Bordeaux,* France) Literally means "castle". Some châteaux are extremely grand, many are merely farmhouses. A building is not required; the term applies to a vineyard or wine estate. Château names cannot be invented, but there are plenty of defunct titles that are used unashamedly by large cooperative wineries to market their members' wines.

Château-Chalon [sha-toh sha-lo'n] (*Jura,* France) Like *Château Grillet*, this is, confusingly, an appellation. Unlike *Château Grillet*, however, here there isn't even a vinous château. The name applies to top-flight *Vin Jaune. Berthet-Bondet; Durand-Perron; Jean Macle*.

Chateau Hornsby (Alice Springs, Australia) Producer in Alice Springs where nature never intended vines to grow. Wines aren't wonderful but the winery is great for the Ayer's Rock tourist trade.

C

Chateau Ste. Michelle (*Washington State*) Dynamic winery, with commercial *Merlot, Syrah, Sauvignon,* and *Riesling*. Joint ventures with *Dr. Loosen* and *Antinori* are proving fruitful. Columbia Crest is a good associated brand.

Chateau Woltner (*Napa,* California) Producer of a range of unusually Burgundian single-vineyard *Chardonnays*, whose style owes much to the winemaker's experience in France.

Châteauneuf-du-Pape [shah-toh-nurf-doo-pap] (*Rhône,* France) Traditionally these are considered to be the best reds (rich and spicy) and whites (rich and floral) of the southern *Rhône*. There are 13 varieties that can be used for the red, though purists favour *Grenache*. Pierre André; *Ch. de Beaucastel;* Beaurenard; *Henri Bonneau; Bosquet des Papes; Lucien & André Brunel;* Cabrières; *Chapoutier; la Charbonnière; Clos des Mont-Olivet; Clos des Papes; Delas; Font de Michelle;* Fortia la Gardine; *Guigal; Jaboulet Aîné;* la Mordorée; *La Nerthe;* du Pegaü; *Rayas;* Réserve des Célestins; Tardieu-Laurent; Vieux Télégraphe.

Jean-Claude Chatelain [shat-lan] (*Loire,* France) Producer of classy individual *Pouilly-Fumés* and *Sancerre*.

Jean-Louis Chave [sharv] (*Rhône,* France) Gérard Chave and his son Jean-Louis run the best estate in *Hermitage*. These are great wines but they demand patience and are easily overlooked by those looking for richer, more instantly accessible fare. ★★★★★ 1999 Hermitage ££££

Ch. Chauvin [shoh-va'n] (*Bordeaux*, France) Improving *St-Emilion Grand Cru Classé* making wine of increasing complexity. A property to watch. ★★★★ 1999 ££

Dom Gérard Chavy [shah-vee] (*Burgundy,* France) High-quality estate. ★★★★★ 1998 Puligny-Montrachet Les Perrières ££££

Chehalem [sheh-hay-lem] (*Oregon*) Top class Yamhill producer of *Pinot Noir, Chardonnay,* and *Pinot Gris*, and benefitting from collaborating with the go-getting Patrice *Rion* from *Burgundy*.

Chenas [shay-nass] (*Burgundy,* France) Good but least well-known of the *Beaujolais Crus* – supposedly with a naturally woody flavour (Chêne = oak). Louis Champagnon; Daniel Robin, Hubert Lapierre, Bernard Santé, and *Duboeuf* make worthy examples.

Dom. du Chêne [doo-shehn] (*Rhône,* France) Small estate producing rich ripe *Condrieu* and top-class *St. Joseph*. The best *cuvée* is "Anais".

Chêne [shayn] (France) Oak, as in *Fûts de Chêne* (oak barrels).

Chenin Blanc [shur-nah-blo'n for France, shen nin blonk elsewhere] Honeyed white grape of the *Loire*. Wines vary from bone-dry to sweet and long-lived. High acidity makes it ideal for sparkling wine, while sweet versions benefit from *noble rot*. French examples are hugely improved, and are both riper than they used to be, and suffer less from an excess of *sulphur dioxide*. When they are good, they are very good indeed. Also grown in South Africa (where it is known as *Steen*), in New Zealand (where it is lovingly – and successfully – grown by *Millton*), and Australia (where it is skilfully oaked by *Moondah Brook Steen*). It is generally disappointing in California (but see *Chappellet*). See *Vouvray, Quarts de Chaumes, Bonnezeaux, Saumur.*

Ch. de Chenonceau [sheh-non-soh] (*Loire,* France) Tourist attraction château that also produces high quality still and sparkling *Chenin Blanc*.

Chéreau-Carré [shay-roh kah-ray] (*Loire Valley*, France) Producer of excellent single estate Muscadets including Ch. du Chasseloir, Ch. du Coing and Comte Leloup de Chasseloir. ★★★★ 2000 Muscadet de Sevre et Maine, Grand Fief de la Cormeraie $

Ch. Cheval Blanc [shuh-vahl blon] (*St. Emilion Premier Grand Cru Classé, Bordeaux,* France) Supreme *St. Emilion* property, unusual in using more *Cabernet Franc* than *Merlot*. A truly great 2000. ★★★★ 1995 ££££

Dom. de Chevalier [shuh-val-yay] (*Graves Cru Classé, Bordeaux*, France) Great *Pessac-Léognan* estate which proves itself in difficult years for both red and white. Very fine 1999s ★★★★★ 1998 Blanc, Pessac-Léognan ££££

C

Chevaliers de Tastevin [shuh-val-yay duh tast-van] (*Burgundy*, France) A brotherhood – *confrérie* – based in *Clos de Vougeot*. Wines approved at an annual tasting carry a special "tasteviné" label. (See the *Beaune* label).

Ⓧ **Cheverny** [shuh-vehr-nee] (*Loire*, France) Light floral whites from *Sauvignon* and *Chenin Blanc* and now, under the new "Cour Cheverny" *appellation*, wines made from the limey local *Romarantin* grape. 97 **Caves Bellier; François Cazin; Ch de la Gaudronnière.**

Ⓧ **Robert Chevillon** [roh-behr shuh-vee-yon] (*Burgundy*, France) Produces long-lived wines. ★★★★★ **1999 Nuits St-Georges Aux Chaignots £££**

Ⓧ **Chianti** [kee-an-tee] (*Tuscany*, Italy) (*Classico/Putto/Rufina*) *Sangiovese*-dominant, now often *Cabernet*-influenced, *DOCG*. Generally better than pre-1984, when it was usual to add wine from further south, and to put dull white grapes in with the black. Wines labelled with insignia of the *Classico*, *Putto*, or the *Rufina* areas are supposed to be better too, as are wines from *Colli Fiorentini* and *Colli Senesi*. Trusting good producers, however, is a far safer bet. **Castello di Ama; Antinori; Frescobaldi; Castellare; Castell'in Villa; Isole e Olena; Fonterutoli Felsina; Ruffino; Rocca di Castagnoli; Selvapiana; Castello dei Rampolla; Castello di Volpaia.**

Ⓧ **Chiaretto di Bardolino** [kee-ahr-reh-toh dee bahr-doh-lee-noh] (*Lombardy*, Italy) Berryish, light reds and rosés from around Lake Garda. **Corte Gardoni; Guerrieri Rizzardi; Nicolis e Figli; Santi.**

Ⓧ **Michele Chiarlo** [mee-Kayleh Kee-ahr-loh] (*Piedmont*, Italy) Increasingly impressive modern producer of *single-vineyard Barolo, Monferrato, Barbaresco* and *Barbera*. ★★★ **2000 Barbera d'Asti Superiore ££**

Ⓧ **Chignin** [sheen-ya'n] (*Savoie*, France) Fresh red (made from the *Mondeuse*) and white wines that go especially well with cheese. **A&M Quénard.**

Chile Rising source of juicy, blackcurranty *Cabernet* and (potentially even better) *Merlot, Carmenère*. See individual entries

Ⓧ **Chimney Rock** (*Stag's Leap District*, California) Producer of serious, fairly priced *Cabernet*. ★★★★ **1997 Cabernet Sauvignon Reserve £££**

Ⓧ **Chinon** [shee-non] (*Loire*, France) An *AC* within *Touraine* for (mostly) red wines from the *Cabernet Franc* grape. Excellent and long-lived from good producers in ripe years; otherwise potentially thin and green. *Olga Raffault* makes one of the best, Otherwise: **Philippe Alliet; Bernard Baudry; Couly-Dutheil; Delauney; Ch. de la Grille; Charles Joguet; Logis de la Bouchardière.**

Ⓧ **Chiroubles** [shee-roo-bl] (*Burgundy*, France) Fragrant and early-maturing *Beaujolais Cru*, best expressed by the likes of Bernard Méziat. **Emile Cheysson; Georges Duboeuf; Hubert Lapierre; Andrè Mètrat; Bernard Méziat; Alain Passot; Ch de Raousset.**

Ⓧ **Chivite** [shee-vee-tay] (*Navarra*, Spain) Highly innovative producer outclassing many big name *Rioja bodegas*. A new winery was opened recently by the King of Spain. ★★★ **1995 Gran Feudo Vinas Viejas Reserva ££**

Ⓧ **Chorey-lès-Beaune** [shaw-ray lay bohn] (*Burgundy*, France) Modest raspberry and damson reds once sold as *Côte de Beaune Villages* and now appreciated in their own right. **Allexant; Arnoux; Ch. de Chorey; Drouhin; Gay; Maillard; Tollot-Beaut.**

★★★ **2000 'Les Confrelins' Chorey-lès-Beaune Arnoux Père et Fils ££**

Ⓧ **JJ Christoffel** [kris-tof-fell] (*Mosel*, Germany) Fine Riesling producer in Erden and Ürzig. ★★★★★ **1992 Urziger Würzgarten Riesling Spätlese ££**

Ⓧ **Church Road** (*Hawkes Bay*, New Zealand) A Montana subsidiary that has established an identity for itself with a range of premium *Hawkes Bay* wines. Look out for the Tom red blend. ★★★★ **1999 Church Road Reserve Chardonnay ££**

C

☷ **Churchill** (*Douro*, Portugal) Dynamic young firm founded by Johnny Graham, whose family once owned a rather bigger *port* house. Good White Port. Red: ★★★★★ 2000 Quinta da Gricha £££

☷ **Chusclan** [shoos-klon] (*Rhône*, France) Named village of *Côtes du Rhône* with maybe the best rosé of the area. ★★★ 1999 Caves de Chusclan ££

☷ **Cinque Terre** [chin-kweh-TEH-reh] (*Liguria*, Italy) Traditionally dull but improving dry, and sweet holiday whites. Forlini e Cappellini; la Pollenza.

🌢 **Cinsaut/Cinsault** [san-soh] Fruity-spicy red grape with high acidity, often blended with *Grenache*. One of 13 permitted varieties of *Châteauneuf-du-Pape*, and also in the blend of *Ch. Musar* in the *Lebanon*.

☷ **Cirò** [chih-Roh] (*Calabria*, Italy) Thanks to the efforts of pioneering producer Librandi, these southern reds (made from Maglioppo) and whites (made from Greco) can be well worth buying. Caparra & Siciliani; Librandi.

☷ **Ch. Cissac** [see-sak] (*Haut-Médoc Cru Bourgeois, Bordeaux*, France) Traditional *Cru Bourgeois*, close to *St. Estèphe*, making tough wines that last. Those who dislike *tannin* should stick to ripe vintages like 2000. ★★★★ 1995 £££

☷ **Ch. Citran** [see-tron] (*Haut-Médoc Cru Bourgeois, Bordeaux*, France) Improving – though still not dazzling – *Cru Bourgeois*, thanks to major investment by the Japanese.

☷ **Bruno Clair** [klehr] (*Burgundy*, France) *Marsannay* estate with good *Fixin, Gevrey-Chambertin, Morey-St.-Denis* (inc. a rare white), and *Savigny*. ★★★★ 1999 Marsannay Les Longeroies ££.

Clairet [klehr-ray] (*Bordeaux*, France) The word from which we derived *claret* – originally a very pale-coloured red from *Bordeaux*. Seldom used.

🌢 **Clairette** [klehr-ret] (*Midi*, France) Dull white grape of southern France.

☷ **Clairette de Die** [klehr-rheht duh dee] (*Rhône*, France) The dry Crémant de Die is unexciting sparkling wine, but the "Méthode Dioise Traditionelle" (previously known as "Tradition") made with *Muscat* is invariably far better; grapey and fresh – like a top-class French *Asti*. Cave Diose; Jaillance.

☷ **Auguste Clape** [klap] (*Rhône*, France) The supreme master of *Cornas*. Great, intense, long-lived traditional wines. ★★★★★ 1998 Cornas ££££

☷ **La Clape** [la klap] (*Languedoc-Roussillon*, France) Little-known *cru* within the *Coteaux de Languedoc* with tasty *Carignan* reds and soft, creamy whites. Pech-Céleyran; Pech-Redon. ★★★ 2000 Chateau Bouisset Cuvee Eugenie £.

Clare Valley [klehr] (South Australia) Slatey soil region enjoying a renaissance with quality *Rieslings* that age well, and deep-flavoured *Shiraz, Cabernet*, and *Malbec*. Also the region that took the matter of corked wine into its own hands – by bottling over half of its 2000 *Riesling* with *Stelvin* screwcaps. *Tim Adams; Jim Barry; Leo Buring; Grosset; Knappstein; Leasingham; Penfolds; Petaluma; Mitchells; Mount Horrocks; Pike; Sevenhill; Wendouree.*

☷ **Clarendon Hills** (*Blewitt Springs*, South Australia) Over-praised by one US critic – to be the best winery in Australia. Sidestep the overpriced Australis and over-praised *Merlot*, and go for the old-vine *Grenache*. Whites are characterful too. ★★★★★ 1998 Hickinbotham Vineyard Shiraz ££££

Claret [klar-ret] English term for red *Bordeaux*.

Clarete [klah-reh-Tay] (Spain) Term for light red – frowned on by the EU.

☷ **Ch. Clarke** (*Bordeaux*, France) *Cru Bourgeois* Listrac château improving fast (especially in 2001) as more *Merlot* is introduced.

Classed Growth (France) Literal translation of *Cru Classé*, commonly used when referring to the status of *Bordeaux châteaux*.

Classico [kla-sih-koh] (Italy) A defined area within a *DOC* identifying the supposedly best vineyards, e.g., *Chianti* Classico, *Valpolicella* Classico.

☷ **Henri Clerc et fils** [klehr] (*Burgundy*, France) Top-class white *Burgundy* estate.

☷ **Ch. Clerc-Milon** [klehr mee-lon] (*Pauillac 5ème Cru Classé, Bordeaux*, France) Juicy member of the *Mouton-Rothschild* stable. ★★★★ 1998 £££

C

- **Domenico Clerico** [doh-meh-nee-koh Klay-ree-koh] (*Piedmont,* Italy) New-wave producers of a truly great *Barolo* and *Dolcetto*. Also of note is Arte, a delicious *Nebbiolo-Barbera* blend that could be described as a Piedmontese answer to all those hyped "*Super-Tuscans*". ★★★★ **Arte 1990 ££.**
Climat [klee-mah] (*Burgundy,* France) Individual named vineyard – not always a *Premier Cru.*
- **Ch. Climens** [klee-mons] (*Barsac Premier Cru Classé, Bordeaux,* France) Gorgeous, but delicate, *Barsac* that easily outlasts many heftier *Sauternes.* ★★★★★ **2001 £££.**
- **Cline** (*Carneros,* California) A winery to watch for innovative Rhône-style wines, including a delicious *Roussanne* and a bizarrely wonderful sweet *late-harvest Mourvèdre.* California needs mavericks like this. ★★★★ **1997 Big Break Vineyard Late Harvest Mourvèdre £££**
- **Ch. Clinet** [klee-nay] (*Pomerol, Bordeaux,* France) Starry property; lovely, complex, intense wines.
Clone [klohn] Specific strain of a given grape variety. For example, more than 300 clones of *Pinot Noir* have been identified.
Clos [kloh] (France) Literally, a walled vineyard.
- **Clos de Gamot** [kloh duh gah-moh] (*Southwest,* France) One of the most reliable producers in *Cahors.* ★★★★ **1998 Vignes Centenaires ££**
- **Clos de la Roche** [kloh duh lah rosh] (*Burgundy,* France) One of the most reliable *Côte d'Or Grands Crus. Drouhin; Dujac; Faivelay;* Lecheneault; *Leroy;* Perrot-Minot; Ponsot; Jean Raphet; Louis Rémy; *Rousseau.*
- **Clos Haut-Peyraguey** [kloh oh-pay-roh gay] (*Bordeaux,* France) A small *First Growth Sauternes* property now happily producing high quality once again.
- **Clos de Mesnil** [kloh duh may-neel] (*Champagne,* France) *Krug's* single vineyard *Champagne* made entirely from *Chardonnay* grown in the Clos de Mesnil vineyard. ★★★★★ **1989 ££££**
- **Clos de l'Oratoire** [kloh duh loh-rah-twar] (*Bordeaux,* France) *St Emilion* property under the same ownership as Canon-la-Gaffelière and La Mondotte. The wine is very good, but usually less flamboyant than its siblings.
- **Clos de Tart** [kloh duh tahr] (*Burgundy,* France) Fine *Grand Cru* vineyard in *Morey St.-Denis,* exclusive to Mommessin. Wines repay keeping. ★★★★ **1999 ££££**
- **Clos de Vougeot** [kloh duh voo-joh] (*Burgundy,* France) *Grand Cru* vineyard with more than 70 owners of mixed quality. Amiot-Servelle; Robert Arnoux; *Bertagna; Bouchard Père et Fils; Champy; Jean-Jacques Confuron; Joseph Drouhin; Engel; Jean Grivot; Anne Gros; Jean Gros; Faiveley; Leroy;* Méo Camuzet; *Mugneret-Gibourg; Jacques Prieur; Prieuré Roch; Jean Raphet;* Henri *Rebourseau; Dom. Rion;* Ch. de la Tour.

Mis au Domaine

CLOS DE VOUGEOT
GRAND CRU
Appellation Contrôlée
Domaine Méo-Camuzet
PROPRIÉTAIRE A VOSNE-ROMANÉE, CÔTE-D'OR, FRANCE
13% vol.   PRODUCE OF FRANCE   75 cl

- **Ch. Clos des Jacobins** [kloh day zha-koh-Ban] (*St. Emilion Grand Cru Classé, Bordeaux,* France) Rich long-lasting, if not always complex, wine.
Clos des Lambrays (*Burgundy,* France) *Grand Cru* in *Morey-St-Denis.*
Clos des Mouches (*Burgundy,* France) A *Premier Cru* vineyard in *Beaune. Drouhin* owns most of it, and makes flagship reds and whites.
- **Clos des Mont-Olivet** [kloh day mon-to-lee-vay] (*Rhône,* France) *Châteauneuf-du-Pape* estate with a rare mastery of white wine.
- **Clos des Papes** [kloh day pap] (*Rhône,* France) Producer of serious *Châteauneuf-du-Pape,* which – in top vintages – rewards cellaring.
- **Clos du Bois** [kloh doo bwah] (*Sonoma Valley,* California) Top-flight producer whose "Calcaire" *Chardonnay* and Marlstone *Cabernet Merlot* are particularly fine. ★★★★ **1998 Alexander Valley Reserve Cabernet £££**

C

Clos du Clocher [kloh doo klosh-shay] (*Pomerol, Bordeaux,* France) Reliably rich, plummy wine. ★★★★ 2000 £££

Clos du Marquis [kloh doo mahr-kee] (*St. Julien, Bordeaux,* France) The *second label* of *Léoville-Las-Cases.*

Clos du Roi [kloh doo rwah] (*Burgundy,* France) *Beaune Premier Cru* that is also part of *Corton Grand Cru.*

Clos du Val [kloh doo vahl] (*Napa Valley,* California) Bernard Portet, brother of Dominique who used to run *Taltarni* in Australia, makes stylish *Stags Leap* reds – including *Cabernet* and *Merlot.* They develop with time.

Clos l'Eglise [klos lay-gleez] (*Pomerol, Bordeaux,* France) Spicy wines from a consistent small *Pomerol* estate.

Clos Floridène [kloh floh-ree-dehn] (*Graves, Bordeaux,* France) Classy, oaked, white *Graves* made by superstar *Denis Dubourdieu.*

Clos Fourtet [kloh-for-tay] (*Bordeaux,* France) Shifting from one branch of the Lurton family to another, this long-time under-performer is now part of André Lurton's portfolio. Watch this space.

Clos Malverne (*Stellenbosch,* South Africa) Small, quality-conscious estate making particularly good *Pinotage* and a *Merlot-Pinotage* blend called Auret. ★★★★ 2000 Pinotage Reserve $$

Clos Mogador [klohs-moh-gah-dor] (*Priorato,* Spain) *René Barbier's* rich, modern, juicy red from Priorato. A wine whose quality, fame – and price – have all helped to revolutionize the Spanish wine scene.

Clos Pegase (*Napa,* California) The architectural masterpiece-cum-winery is worth a visit. The wines are less exciting.

Clos René [kloh ruh-nay] (*Pomerol, Bordeaux,* France) Estate making increasingly concentrated though approachable wines.

Clos St. Denis [kloh san dur-nee] (*Burgundy,* France) Top *Grand Cru* vineyard in *Morey St. Denis.* *Dujac; G Lignier; Ponsot.*

Clos St.-Landelin [kloh San lon-duhr-lan] (*Alsace,* France) Long-lived wines; the sister label to *Muré.* ★★★★★ 1999 Riesling Vorbourg ££

Clos Uroulat [oo-roo-lah] (*Southwest,* France) A standard-bearer for the Jurançon appellation, with limited quantities of impeccably made dry and sweet examples. ★★★★ 1999 Jurançon ££

Cloudy Bay (*Marlborough,* New Zealand) Under the same French ownership as *Cape Mentelle,* this cult winery has a waiting list for every vintage of its *Sauvignon.* The new Te Koko oaked, Bordeaux-like Sauvignon will be worth watching. *Chardonnay* and *Pelorus* sparkling wine are impressive, as are the rare *late-harvest* wines. The Pinot Noir is a recent success.

Clusel-Roch [kloo-se rosh] (*Rhône,* France) Good, traditional *Côte Rôtie* and *Condrieu* producer. ★★★★★ 1999 Côte Rôtie Grandes Places £££

la Clusière [kloo-see-yehr] (*Bordeaux,* France) Recent, tiny-production (250–300 case) *St. Emilion* microwine from the new owners of *Ch. Pavie.*

JF Coche-Dury [kosh doo-ree] (*Burgundy,* France) A superstar *Meursault* producer whose basic reds and whites outclass his neighbours' supposedly finer fare. ★★★★★ 1999 Meursault Perrières £££

Cockburn-Smithes [koh burn] (*Douro,* Portugal) Unexceptional Special Reserve but producer of great *vintage* and superlative *tawny port.* ★★★★ 10 Year Old Tawny £££. ★★★★ 1999 Quinta dos Canais Vintage Port ££

Codorníu [kod-dor-nyoo] (*Catalonia,* Spain) Huge sparkling winemaker whose Anna de Codorníu is good *Chardonnay*-based *Cava.* The Raventos wines are recommendable too, as are the efforts of the *Raimat* subsidiary. The California offshoot Codorníu Napa's sparkling wine is *Cava*-ish and dull despite using *Champagne* varieties. The *Pinot Noirs* are more impressive.

BR Cohn (*Sonoma,* California) A reliable source of Sonoma Valley *Cabernet Sauvignon.*

Colares [koh-lah-raish] (Portugal) Coastal wine region west of Lisbon famous for the ungrafted vines grown in its sandy soils. The wines are rare and getting rarer; the style is tannic and dark, and bottle age is needed.

C

Colchagua Valley [kohl-shah-gwah] (*Central Valley*, Chile) Up-and-coming sub-region. **Bisquertt; *Casa Lapostolle; Undurraga; Los Vascos*.**

꙰ **Coldstream Hills** (*Yarra Valley*, Australia) Founded by lawyer-turned winemaker and wine writer *James Halliday*, but now in the same stable as *Penfolds*. Stunning *Pinot Noir*, *Chardonnay*, fine *Cabernets*, and *Merlots*.
★★★★ **1999 Cabernet Sauvignon Merlot Cabernet Franc £££**
★★★★★ **2000 Pinot Noir £££**

Colheita [kol-yay-tah] (Portugal) Harvest or vintage – particularly used to describe *tawny port* of a specific year.

꙰ **Marc Colin** [mahrk koh-lan] (*Burgundy*, France) Family estate with affordable wines from St. Aubin and a small chunk of (rather pricier) *Le Montrachet* ★★★★ **2000 St.-Aubin Chateniere £££**

꙰ **Michel Colin-Deleger** [koh-lah day-lay-jay] (*Burgundy*, France) Up-and-coming *Chassagne-Montrachet* estate.

꙰ **Collards** [kol-lards] (*Auckland*, New Zealand) Small producer of lovely pineappley *Chardonnay* and appley *Chenin Blanc*.

꙰ **Collegiata** [koh-lay-jee jah-tah] (*Toro*, Spain) Rich, red wine from the *Tempranillo* produced in a little-known region.

Colle/colli [kol-lay/kol-lee] (Italy) Hill/hills.

꙰ **Colli Berici** [kol-lee bay-ree-chee] (*Veneto*, Italy) Red and white *DOC*.

꙰ **Colli Bolognesi** [kol lee bol lon yeh see] (*Emilia-Romagna*, Italy) Up-and-coming region for *Merlot* and *Cabernet Sauvignon* reds and fresh white *Sauvignon Blanc* and the local *Pinot Bianco* and Pignoletto. **Bonzara; Gaggioli; Sandoni; Tizzano; Vallona.**

꙰ **Colli Euganei** [kol lee yoo-gah-nay] (*Veneto*, Italy) Hills near Padova where Vignalta produces its Gemola *Cabernet-Merlot*. Other wines are less impressive.

꙰ **Colli Orientali del Friuli** [kol-lee oh-ree yehn-tah-lee del frec-yoo-lee] (*Friuli-Venezia Giulia*, Italy) Lively, single-variety whites and reds from near the Slovenian border. Subtle, honeyed, and very pricey *Picolit*, too.

꙰ **Colli Piacentini** [kol-lee pee-yah-chayn-tee-nee] (*Emiglia-Romagna*, Italy) A very varied *DOC*, covering characterful, off-dry Malvasia sparkling wine and the Bonarda-*Barbera*-based Guttiunio. **la Stoppa; la Tosa; il Pociarello.**

꙰ **Vin de Pays des Collines Rhodaniennes** [kol-leen roh-dah nee-enn] (*Rhône*, France) The *Vin de Pays* region of the northern *Rhône*, using *Rhône* varieties, *Gamay* and *Merlot*. **St. Désirat Cooperative; G Vernay.**

꙰ **Collio** [kol-lee-yoh] (*Friuli-Venezia Giulia*, Italy) High-altitude region with a basketful of white varieties, plus those of *Bordeaux* and red *Burgundy*. Refreshing and often restrained. **Borgo Conventi; Borgo del Tiglio; L. Felluga; Gravner; Jermann; Puiatti; Schiopetto; Venica & Venica; Villa Russiz.**

꙰ **Collioure** [kol-yoor] (*Midi*, France) Intense *Rhône*-style *Languedoc-Roussillon* red, often marked by the presence of *Mourvèdre* in the blend. A good group of producers here are beginning to attract attention. **Ch. de Jau; Dom du Mas Blanc; Clos de Paulilles; de la Rectorie; la Tour Vieille.**

🍇 **Colombard/French Colombard** [kol-om-bahrd] White grape grown in *Southwest* France for Armagnac and light, modern whites by *Yves Grassa* and *Plaimont*. Also planted in Australia (*Primo Estate* and *Best's*) and the US.

꙰ **Jean-Luc Colombo** [kol-lom-boh] (*Rhône*, France) Oenologist guru to an impressive number of *Rhône* estates – and producer of his own modern, oaky *Côtes du Rhône* and *Cornas*. ★★★★★ **1999 Cornas Les Ruchets £££**

꙰ **Columbia Crest** (*Washington State*) Winery associated with *Ch. Ste. Michelle*. ★★★★ **1999 Columbia Crest Grand Estates Merlot £££**

꙰ **Columbia Winery** (*Washington State*) Producer of good, fairly priced, *Chablis*-style *Chardonnay* and *Graves*-like *Semillon*, subtle single-vineyard *Cabernet*, especially good *Merlot*, *Syrah*, and *Burgundian Pinot Noir*.
★★★★ **1999 Columbia Winery Syrah ££**

Commandaria [com-man-dah-ree-yah] (Cyprus) Rare raisiny dessert wine.

Commune [kom-moon] (France) Small demarcated plot of land named after its principal town or village. Equivalent to an English parish.

C

⊻ **Vin de Pays des Comtés Rhodaniens** [kom-tay roh-dah nee-yen] (*Rhône/Savoie*, France) Fresh, aromatic whites are the stars here (*Sauvignon, Viognier*) plus some juicy *Rhône* reds (*Grenache, Syrah*).

⊻ **Vin de Pays des Comtés Tolosan** [kom-tay toh-loh-so'n] (*Southwest*, France) Fast-improving blends of *Bordeaux* and indigenous grapes.

⊻ **Bodegas Con Class** (*Rueda*, Spain) Good *Sauvignon Blanc* and Verdejo/Viura. **Conca de Barberá** [kon-kah deh bahr-beh-rah] (*Catalonia*, Spain) Cool source of *Torres's* impressive Milmanda *Chardonnay* and Grandes Murailles.

⊻ **Viña Concha y Toro** [veen-yah kon-chah ee tohr-roh] (*Maipo*, Chile) Steadily improving, thanks to and investment in *Casablanca*. Best wines are Don Melchior, Marques de Casa Concha, Trio, Casillero del Diablo, and *Almaviva*, its joint venture with *Mouton Rothschild*.

⊻ **Condado de Haza** [kon-dah-doh deh hah-thah] (*Ribera del Duero*, Spain) Impressive new venture from the owner of *Pesquera*.

⊻ **Conde de Caralt** [kon-day day kah-ralt] (*Catalonia*, Spain) One of the best names in *Cava*. Catch it young.

⊻ **Condrieu** [kon-dree-yuhh] (*Rhône*, France) One of the places where actor Gerard Dépardieu owns vines. Fabulous, pricey, pure *Viognier*: a cross between dry, white wine and perfume. Far better than the hyped and high-priced *Ch. Grillet* next door. Ch. d'Ampuis; Patrick & Christophe Bonneford; Louis Chèze; Gilbert Chirat; Yves Cuilleron; Pierre Dumazet; *Philippe Faury; Pierre Gaillard; Michel Gerin; Etienne Guigal;* de Monteillet; *Antoine Montez; Robert Niero;* Alain Parent (& Gerard Dépardieu); *André Perret;* Phillipe & Christophe Pichon; *Hervé Richard; Georges Vernay;* Francois Villand; Gerard Villano.

Confréries [kon-fray-ree] (France) Promotional brotherhoods linked to a particular wine or area. Many, however, are nowadays more about pomp and pageantry, kudos and backslapping, than active promotion.

⊻ **Jean-Jacques Confuron** [con-foor-ron] (*Burgundy*, France) Innovative producer with good *Nuits-St.-Georges, Vosne-Romanée,* and *Clos Vougeot*.

⊻ **Cono Sur** [kon-noh soor] (Chile) *Concha y Toro* subsidiary with a range of varietals, including a classy *Pinot Noir* from *Casablanca*. Back on form after the arrival of a new winemaker (in 1998). The Isla Negra wines are good too.
★★★★★ 2001 Cono Sur 20 Barrel Pinot Noir Limited Edition £££

⊻ **Ch. la Conseillante** [lah kon-say-yont] (*Pomerol, Bordeaux*, France) Brilliant property with lovely, complex, perfumed wines.

Consejo Regulador [kon-say-hoh ray-goo-lah-dohr] (Spain) Administrative body responsible for *DO* laws.

Consorzio [kon-sohr-zee-yoh] (Italy) Producers' syndicate.

Constantia [kon-stan-tee-yah] (South Africa) The first New World wine region. Until recently, the big name was *Groot Constantia*. Now *Constantia Uitsig, Klein Constantia, Buitenverwachting,* and *Steenberg* support the enduring reputation, but better wines are often easier to find elsewhere in the Cape. *Klein Constantia's* late-harvest Vin de Constance is the region's flagship, recalling the days when Constantia wines were talked of in the same breath as *Port* and *Bordeaux*.

⊻ **Aldo Conterno** [al-doh kon-tehr-noh] (*Piedmont*, Italy) Great, traditional producer of single-vineyard *Barolo* (esp. Gran Bussia) and similarly top-class *Barbera*. Other varieties are well handled too, particularly Grignolino and Freisa. Nobody does it better.

⊻ **Giacomo Conterno** [dja-ko-mo con-tehr-noh] (*Piedmont*, Italy) Aldo's (see above) older brother is even more traditional, and makes splendid Barolos of immense proportions and lifespan. His son Roberto is now taking over the winemaking.

C

❖ **Conterno Fantino** [kon-tehr-noh fan-tee-noh] (*Piedmont,* Italy) Another brilliant Conterno. ★★★★★ 1997 Barolo Vigna del Gris ££££

❖ **Viñedos del Contino** [veen-yay-dos del con-tee-no] (*Rioja,* Spain) CVNE-owned *Rioja* Alavesa estate whose wines can have more fruit and structure than most. ★★★★ 1989 Rioja Reserva ££

Controliran (Bulgaria) Bulgarian version of *Appellation Contrôlée*

Coonawarra [koon-nah-wah-rah] (*South* Australia) Internationally acknowledged top-class mini-region, stuck in the middle of nowhere, with a cool(ish) climate, terra rossa (red) soil, and a long-brewed controversy over where precisely its boundaries ought to be drawn. (There are nearby "islands" of red soil whose wines have been excluded from the Coonawarra designation). The best Coonawarra reds are great, blackcurranty-minty *Cabernet Sauvignons* and underrated *Shirazes*. Whites are less impressive; big *Chardonnays* and full-bodied *Rieslings*. *Bowen Estate; Hardy's; Katnook; Lindemans; Mildara; Orlando; Petaluma; Parker Estate; Penfolds; Penley Estate; Ravenswood (Hollick); Rosemount; Rouge Homme; Yalumba; Wynns.*

❖ **Coopers Creek** (*Auckland,* New Zealand) Individualistic whites including a *Chenin-Semillon* blend, *Chardonnay, Sauvignon,* and *Riesling.*

❖ **Copertino** [kop-per-tee-noh] (*Apulia,* Italy) Fascinating berryish wine made from the "bitter-black" *Negroamaro.* ★★★★ 1998 Riserva Piccini ££

❖ **Corbans** (*Henderson,* New Zealand) Big producer (encompassing *Cooks*) making wines in several regions. Good, rich, *Merlot* reds (even, occasionally, from *Marlborough*). ★★★★ 1998 Cottage Block Cabernet Sauvignon - Cabernet Franc - Merlot ££

❖ **Corbières** [kawr-byayr] (*Languedoc-Roussillon,* France) Region where a growing number of small estates are now making tasty red wines. Ch. d'Aguilhar; Aiguilloux; Caraguilhes; des Chandelles; Etang des Colombes; Grand Caumont; Hélène; de Lastours; *Mont Tauch;* Pech-Latt; Vignerons de la Méditerranée; Meunier St. Louis; d'Ornaisons; les Palais du Révérend; St. Auriol; St. Estève; Celliers St. Martin; Salvagnac; Villemajou; *la Voulte Gasparets.*

❖ **Ch Corbin** [cor-ba'n] (*Bordeaux,* France) *St-Emilion Grand Cru Classé* sometimes (but not consistently) making wine of richness and density.

❖ **Ch Corbin-Michotte** [cor-ba'n mee-shott] (*Bordeaux,* France) This *Grand Cru Classé St-Emilion* property often has the edge, quality-wise, on *Ch. Corbin.* The wines can be lusciously fruity, with good complexity.

❖ **Ch Cordeillan-Bages** [cor-day-yo'n Baj] (*Bordeaux,* France) A *Pauillac* château now an hotel under the same ownership as *Ch. Lynch-Bages.*

❖ **Cordier** [cor-dee-yay] (*Bordeaux,* France) Large shipper which also owns châteaux including Clos des Jacobins, Meyney and Cantemerle.

❖ **Cordoba** (*Stellenbosch,* South Africa) Producer of wines high on the *Helderberg,* (so far) over-enthusiastically described as a local *"First Growth".*

❖ **Cordon Negro** [kawr-don nay-groh] (*Catalonia,* Spain) Brand name for *Freixenet's* successful *Cava.* The matte-black bottle and generous marketing must account for sales. Not a sparkling wine I voluntarily drink.

❖ **Corino** [koh-ree-noh] (*Piedmont,* Italy) Up-and-coming winery, winning applause for the quality of its Barolo. ★★★★ 1997 Barolo Vecchie Vigne ££

❖ **Coriole** [koh-ree-ohl] (*McLaren Vale,* Australia) *Shiraz* specialist that has diversified into *Sangiovese.* The *Semillons* and *Rieslings* are pretty good, too.

❖ **Corison** [kaw-ree-son] (*Napa,* California) Winery specializing in juicy *Cabernet.*

Corked Unpleasant, musty smell and flavour, caused by (usually invisible) mould in the cork. At the International Wine Challenge, out of over 9,000 bottles, 4.6% were spoiled by bad corks. Visit: **www.corkwatch.com.**

❖ **Cornas** [kaw-re-nas] (*Rhône,* France) Smoky, spicy *Syrah;* tannic when young, but worth keeping. *Thierry Allemand; de Barjac; Chapoutier; Auguste Clape; Jean-Luc Colombo; Courbis; Eric & Joël Durand;* Durvieu; Jaboulet Aîné; *Juge; Jacques Lemercier; Jean Lionnet; Robert Michel; Michel Rochepertuis; de St. Pierre; Serette;* Tain Cooperative; *Tardieu-Laurent; Noël Verset; Alain Voge.*

C

Fattoria Coroncino [kawr-ron-chee-noh] (*Marche*, Italy) One of the best producers of *Verdicchio Castello dei Jesi Classico Superiore*.

Corsica (France) Mediterranean island making robust reds, whites, and rosés under a raft of *appellations* (doled out generously to assuage rebellious islanders). *Vins de Pays (de l'Ile de Beauté)* are often more interesting.

Dom. Corsin [kawr-san] (*Burgundy*, France) Reliable *Pouilly-Fuissé* and *St. Véran* estate. ★★★★ 1999 Pouilly Fuissé ££

Cortes de Cima [kawrtsh-day shee-mah] (*Alentejo*, Portugal) Estate making good reds from local grapes plus a *Syrah* called Incognito.

Cortese [kawr-tay-seh] (*Piedmont*, Italy) Herby white grape used in *Piedmont* and to make *Gavi*. Drink young.

Corton [kawr-ton] (*Burgundy*, France) *Grand Cru* hill potentially making great, intense, long-lived reds and – as *Corton-Charlemagne* – whites. White: 90 92 95 96 97 98 99 00 01 Red: 90 92 95 98 99 00 Bertrand Ambroise; *Bonneau du Martray; Chandon de Briailles; Dubreuil-Fontaine; Faiveley;* Laleur-Piot; *Louis Latour (white); Leroy;* Maillard; Nudant; *Jacques Prieur;Tollot-Beaut; Thomas Moillard.*

Corzano & Paterno [kawrt-zah-noh eh pah-tehr-noh] (*Tuscany*, Italy) Fine Chianti Colli Fiorentini and Vin Santo.

Corvo [kawr-voh] (*Sicily*, Italy) Brand used by Duca di Salaparuta for its recently repackaged pleasant reds and whites.

Ch. Cos d'Estournel [koss-des-tawr-nel] (*St. Estèphe 2ème Cru Classé Bordeaux*, France) Recently sold *estate* making top-class wines with *Pauillac* richness and fruit. Spice is the hallmark. 85 86 88 89 90 95 96 98 00 01

Ch. Cos Labory [koss la-baw-ree] (*St. Estèphe 5ème Cru Classé, Bordeaux*, France) Good, traditional, if tough, wines.

Cosecha [coh-seh-chah] (Spain) Harvest or *vintage*.

Cosentino (*Napa*, California) Producer of serious, long-lived reds.

Cossart Gordon (*Madeira*, Portugal) High-quality brand used by the *Madeira Wine Co.* ★★★★★ 10 year old Bual £££

Costanti (*Tuscany*, Italy) Serious *Brunello di Montalcino* producer with classy, long-lived wines. ★★★★★ 1988 Brunello di Montalcino ££££

Costers del Segre [kos-tehrs del say-greh] (*Catalonia*, Spain) *DO* created for the excellent *Raimat*, whose irrigated vineyards helped to persuade Spain's wine authorities to allow other producers to give thirsty vines a drink. ★★★★★ 1994 Raimat Cabernet Sauvignon Reserva £££

Costers de Siurana [kos-tehrs deh see-yoo-rah-nah] (*Priorato*, Spain) One of the stars of *Priorato*. Grape varieties for the Clos de l'Obac include *Syrah, Cabernet, Merlot*, plus local *Garnacha, Cariñena*, and *Tempranillo*.

Costières de Nîmes [kos-tee-yehr duh neem] (*Midi*, France) An up-and-coming region whose *Syrah*-based reds can match the best of the Northern Rhône. Ch. de l'Amarine; de Campuget; Dom. des Cantarelles; Mas de Bressades; Ch. Mourges du Grès; de Nages; Tuilerie de Pazac; Valcombe.

Cot [koh] (France) Red grape of *Cahors* and the *Loire* (aka *Malbec*).

Cotat Frères [koh-tah] (*Loire*, France) One of the few *Loire Sauvignon* producers to achieve superstar status in the US. The Cotats' *Sancerres* repay ageing and deserve their success. ★★★★★ 1999 les Monts Damnés £££

Côte Chalonnaise [koht shh-loh-nays] (*Burgundy*, France) Region south of the *Côte d'Or*, considerably bigger, and the source of much basic *Burgundy* as well as some rather better wines. Principal villages are Bouzeron, Mercurey (the region can also be called the Région de Mercurey), Montagny, Givry and Rully.

Côte d'Or [koht dor] (*Burgundy*, France) Geographical designation for the finest part of Burgundy, slopes encompassing the *Côte de Nuits* and *Côte de Beaune*.

C

⏣ **Côte de Beaune (Villages)** [koht duh bohn] (*Burgundy,* France) The southern half of the *Côte d'Or.* With the suffix *"Villages",* indicates red wines from one or more of the specified *communes.* Confusingly, wine labelled simply *"Côte de Beaune"* comes from a small area around *Beaune* itself and often tastes like wines of that *appellation.*

⏣ **Côte de Brouilly** [koht duh broo-yee] (*Burgundy,* France) *Beaujolais Cru*: distinct from *Brouilly* – often finer. Floral and ripely fruity; will keep for a few years. 97 98 99 00 *Duboeuf;* Pivot; Ch. Thivin.

⏣ **Côte de Nuits (Villages)** [koht duh nwee] (*Burgundy,* France) Northern, and principally "red" end of the *Côte d'Or.* The suffix *"Villages"* indicates wine from one or more specified *communes.*

⏣ **Côte Rôtie** [koh troh tee] (*Rhône,* France) Smoky yet refined *Syrah* (possibly with some white *Viognier*) from the northern *Rhône appellation* divided into "Brune" and "Blonde" hillsides. Most need at least six years. 89 90 95 96 98 99 00 01 Ch. d'Ampuis. *Barge;* Bonnefond; *Burgaud;* Champet; *Cuilleron;* Clusel-Roch; Gallet; *Gasse;* Gentaz-Dervieux; *Gerin; Guigal;* Jamet; Jasmin; Ogier; Rostaing; Saugère; L. de Vallouit; *Vernay;* Vidal Fleury; F. Villard.

Côte(s), Coteaux [koht] (France) Hillsides.

⏣ **Coteaux d'Aix-en-Provence** [koh-toh dayks on prov vons] (*Provence,* France) A recent *AC* region producing light floral whites, fruity reds, and dry rosés using *Bordeaux* and *Rhône* varieties. Château Calissanne; Ch. Revelette; Mas Ste.-Berthe; Ch. Vignelaure.

⏣ **Coteaux d'Ancenis** [koh-toh don-suh-nee] (*Loire,* France) So far, only *VDQS* status for this region near Nantes, producing light reds and deep pinks from the *Cabernet Franc* and *Gamay,* and also *Muscadet*-style whites.

⏣ **Coteaux de l'Ardèche** [koh-toh dahr-desh] (*Rhône,* France) Light country wines, mainly from the *Syrah* and *Chardonnay.* A popular place with *Burgundians* to produce affordable alternatives to their own white wine.

⏣ **Coteaux Champenois** [koh-toh shom-puh-nwah] (*Champagne,* France) Overpriced, mostly thin, acidic, still red or white wine. *Laurent Perrier's* is about the best.

⏣ **Coteaux du Languedoc** [koh-toh doo long-dok] (*Midi,* France) A big *appellation,* and a source of fast-improving rich reds such as *Pic St. Loup.*

⏣ **Coteaux du Layon** [koh-toh doo lay-yon] (*Loire,* France) *Chenin Blancs*; some dry wines; sweet *Bonnezeaux* and *Quarts de Chaume.* Sweet White: 88 89 90 94 95 96 97 98 Perre Aguilas; Patrick Baudoin; Dom. des Baumard; Ch. Pierre Bise; Ch. du Breuil; Cady; Delesvaux; des Forges; Godineau; Guimoniere; Ch. la Plaisance; Ch. des Rochettes; de la Roulerie; des Sablonettes; Ch. Soucherie; la Varière.

⏣ **Coteaux du Loir** [koh-toh doo lwahr] (*Loire,* France) Clean, vigorous whites from a *Loire* tributary. 96 97 98

⏣ **Coteaux du Lyonnais** [koh-toh doo lee-ohn-nay] (*Rhône,* France) Just to the south of *Beaujolais,* making some very acceptable good-value wines from the same grapes. Descottes; *Duboeuf;* Fayolle; Sain Bel Co-operative.

⏣ **Coteaux du Tricastin** [koh-toh doo tris-kass-tan] (*Rhône,* France) Southern *Rhône appellation,* emerging as a source of good-value, peppery-blackcurranty reds. Dom. de Grangeneuve; de Rozets; du Vieux Micoulier.

⏣ **Coteaux Varois** [koh-toh vahr-rwah] (*Provence,* France) Inexpensive, fruity reds, whites, and rosés. Deffends.

⏣ **Côtes de/Premières Côtes de Blaye** [koht duh/pruh-myerh koht duh blay] (*Bordeaux,* France) A ferryride across the river from *St. Julien.* Poor winemaking prevents many *estates* from living up to their potential. Premières are usually red; *Côtes,* white. 95 96 97 98 00 Ch. Bertinerie; Gigault; Haut-Sociondo; les Jonqueyres; Segonzac; des Tourtes.

⏣ **Côtes de Bourg** [koht duh boor] (*Bordeaux,* France) Clay-soil region just across the water from the *Médoc* and an increasingly reliable source of good-value, *Merlot*-dominated, plummy reds. Brulesécaille; Falfas; Fougas; Guerry; les Jonquières; Maldoror; Repimplet; Robin; Roc-de-Cambes; Rousset; Tayac.

C

❧ **Côtes de Castillon** [koht duh kass-tee-yon] (*Bordeaux*, France) Region where the *Merlot* is often a lot more lovingly handled than in nearby *St. Emilion*. Ch. d'Aiguilhe; de Belcier; Cap de Faugères; Champ de Mars; Côte Montpezat; Grande Maye; Lapeyronie; de Parenchère; Pitray; Poupille; Robin.

❧ **Côtes de Duras** [koht duh doo-rahs] (*Bordeaux*, France) Inexpensive *Sauvignons*, often better value than basic *Bordeaux* Blanc. Amblard; Duras Cooperative; Moulin des Groyes.

❧ **Côtes de Francs** [koht duh fron] (*Bordeaux*, France) Up-and-coming region close to *St. Emilion;* increasingly good reds. Charmes-Godard; de Francs; la Claverie; la Prade; *Puygeraud;*Vieux Chateau Champs de Mars.

❧ **Vin de Pays des Côtes de Gascogne** [koht duh gas-koñ] (*Southwest*, France) Armagnac-producing region where dynamic producers *Yves Grassa* and the *Plaimont* cooperative used modern winemaking techniques on grapes that would in the past have been used for brandy. *Ugni Blanc* and *Colombard* are giving way to *Sauvignon Blanc*. Grassa; Plaimont.

❧ **Côtes de Provence** [koht dur prov-vonss] (*Provence*, France) Improving, good-value, fruity whites and ripe, spicy reds. The famous rosés, however, are often carelessly made and stored, but vacationers rarely notice that the so-called pink wine is a deep shade of bronze and decidedly unrefreshing. A region with as much appeal to organic winemakers as to fans of Mr Mayle's rural tales. Dom. la Bernarde; la Courtade; d'Esclans; Commanderie e Peyrassol; Gavoty; de Mireille; Ott; Rabiega; Richeaume;Vanniéres.

❧ **Côtes de St. Mont** [koht duh san-mon] (*Southwest*, France) Large *VDQS* area encompassing the whole of the Armagnac region. *Plaimont* is the largest and best-known producer.

❧ **Vin de Pays des Côtes de Tarn** [koht duh tarn] (*Southwest*, France) Fresh, fruity, simple reds and whites, mostly for drinking in-situ rather than outside France. Labastide-de-Levis Cooperative.

❧ **Vin de Pays des Côtes de Thau** [koht duh toh] (*Languedoc-Roussillon*, France) Fresh whites to drink with seafood in the canalside restaurants of *Sète*. Les Vignerons des Garrigues.

❧ **Vin de Pays des Côtes de Thongue** [koht duh tong] (*Languedoc-Roussillon*, France) Up-and-coming region between Béziers and Toulouse. Domaines d'Arjolle, Condamine, l'Eveque,Teisserenc, and Deshenrys

❧ **Côtes du Frontonnais** [koht doo fron-ton-nay] (*Southwest*, France) Up-and-coming, inexpensive red (and some rosé); characterful wines. Ch. Baudare; Bellevue la Forêt; Cave de Fronton; le Roc;Viguerie de Beulaygue

❧ **Côtes du Jura** [koht duh joo-rah] (France) *Vin Jaune* and *Vin de Paille* are the styles to look for in this area close to Arbois, as well as sparkling wine and Poulsard and Trousseau reds. Ch. d'Arlay; Jean Bourdy; Couret; Delay.

Côtes du Luberon (*Provence*, France) A region that boasts starry properties: Val-Joanis,Vieille Ferme, Ch. de la Canorgue and Ch. de l'Isolette.

❧ **Côtes du Marmandais** [koht doo mahr-mon-day] (*Southwest*, France) Uses the *Bordeaux* red grapes plus *Gamay*, *Syrah*, and others to make pleasant, fruity, inexpensive wines. Ch. de Beaulieu; Les Vignerons de Beaupuy; Cave de Cocument.

❧ **Côtes du Rhône (Villages)** [koht doo rohn] (*Rhône*, France) Spicy reds mostly from the southern *Rhône* Valley. The best supposedly come from a set of better *Villages* (and are sold as *CdR Villages*), though some single *domaine* "simple" *Côtes du Rhônes* outclass many *Villages* wines. *Grenache* is the key grape, though recent years have seen a growing use of the *Syrah*. Whites, which can include new-wave *Viogniers*, are improving. Red: **95 96 97 98 99 00 01** Beaucastel (Coudoulet); Dom. de Beaurenard; Cabasse; les Goubert; *Grand Moulas; Guigal;* Richaud; la Soumade; Ste. Anne.

❧ **Côtes du Roussillon (Villages)** [koht doo roo-see-yon] (*Midi*, France) *Appellation* for red, white, and rosé of pretty variable quality. *Côtes du Roussillon Villages* is generally better. Brial; des Chênes; Fontanel; Força Réal; *Gauby*; de Jau;Vignerons Catalans.

C

Côtes du Ventoux [koht doo von-too] (*Rhône*, France) Steadily improving everyday country reds that are similar to *Côtes du Rhône*, but often a touch better value. 97 98 99 00 01 Brusset; Jaboulet Aîné; Pascal; Perrin; la Vieille Ferme.

Côtes du Vivarais [koht doo vee-vah-ray] (*Provence*, France) Light southern *Rhône*-like reds, fruity rosés, and fragrant light whites.

Cotesti [kot tesh-tee] (Romania) Easterly vineyards growing varieties such as *Pinots Noir, Blanc, Gris*, and *Merlot*.

Cotnari [kot nah-ree] (Romania) Traditional and now very rare white dessert wine. Has potential.

Bodegas el Coto [el kot-toh] (*Rioja*, Spain) Small *estate* producing classy, medium-bodied El Coto and Coto de Imaz reds.

Quinta do Côtto [keen-tah doh kot-toh] (*Douro*, Portugal) Ports and intense, tannic, berryish red table wines – labelled as Grande Escolha – produced in a more southerly part of the Douro River than most other vintage *ports*.

Covey Run (*Washington State*, USA) A *Yakima Valley* property making good *Merlot, Cabernet* and *Chardonnay*.

Coulée de Serrant [koo-lay duh seh-ron] (*Loire*, France) Great dry *Chenin* from a top property in *Savennières* run by *Nicolas Joly*, a leading champion of "biodynamique" winemaking. The Becherelle vineyard is fine too.

Paul Coulon et Fils [Koo-lon] (*Rhône*, France) Serious *Rhône* producer.

Coulure [koo-loor] Climate-related winegrowing disorder. The condition causes reduced yields (and possibly higher quality) as grapes shrivel and fall off the vine.

Couly-Dutheil [koo-lee doo-tay] (*Loire*, France) High-quality *Chinon* from vineyards just behind the *château* in which Henry II of England imprisoned his wife, Eleanor of Aquitaine. ★★★★ 1998 Clos de L'Echo £££

Viña Cousiño Macul [koo-sin-yoh mah-kool] (*Maipo*, Chile) The most traditional producer in Chile. Reds are more successful than whites. ★★★ 1995 Finis Terrae ££

Pierre Coursodon [koor-soh-don] (*Rhône*, France) Maker of superlative traditional *St. Josephs* that need time but develop layers of flavour and complexity that are lacking in many a pricier *Hermitage*.

Ch Couhins-Lurton [koo-ans loor-to'n] (*Bordeaux*, France) A *Graves Classed Growth* making notable *Sauvignon Blanc*.

Ch la Couspaude [koos-pohd] (*Bordeaux*, France) This *St-Emilion Grand Cru Classé* has started to make wines in the fashionably rich, extracted style, and has won much critical acclaim because of it. Oak is used in extravagant amounts.

Ch. Coutet [koo-tay] (*Barsac Premier Cru Classé, Bordeaux*, France) Delicate neighbour to *Ch. Climens*, often making comparable wines: Cuvée Madame is top flight. 90 95 96 97 98 99 00 01

Ch. Couvent-des-Jacobins [koo-von day zhah-koh-ban] (*St. Emilion Grand Cru Classé, Bordeaux*, France) Producer of juicy, plummy-spicy wines. 90 92 93 94 95 96 98 99 00 01 ★★★ 1998 £££

Cowra [kow-rah] (*New South Wales*, Australia) Up-and-coming region, making a name for itself with *Chardonnay*, for which it will one day eclipse its better known but less viticulturally ideal neighbour, the *Hunter Valley*.

Dom. de Coyeux [duh cwah-yuh] (*Rhône*, France) One of the best producers of *Côtes du Rhône* and *Muscat de Beaumes de Venise*.

Craggy Range (*Hawkes Bay*, New Zealand) New kid on the block, with lots of US money behind it. Good *Sauvignon Blanc* and promising *Pinot Noir*.

Cranswick Estate (*Riverina, NSW*, Australia) Successful producer making reliable, fairly-priced wines under its own and the Barramundi label and some great *late-harvest* whites.

C

QUINTA DO
CRASTO

DOURO
DENOMINAÇÃO DE ORIGEM CONTROLADA

1998
Vinho Tinto / Red Wine

℣ **Quinta do Crasto** [kin-tah doo crash-too] (*Douro,* Portugal) An up-and-coming small port producer with good red table wines too, slightly more international in style than some. ★★★★ 1998 Douro Reserva ££

℣ **Cream Sherry** (*Jerez,* Spain) Popular style (though not in Spain) produced by sweetening an *oloroso.* A visitor to *Harvey's* apparently preferred one of the company's *sherries* to the then popular "Bristol Milk". "If that's the milk," she joked, "this must be the cream".

Crémant [kray-mon] (France) Term previously used in *Champagne,* denoting a slightly sparkling style due to a lower pressure of gas in the bottle. Now used only elsewhere in France to indicate sparkling wine made by the traditional method, e.g., Crémant de *Bourgogne,* de *Loire,* and d'*Alsace.*

℣ **Crépy** [kray-pee] (*Savoie,* France) Crisp floral white from *Savoie.*

Criado y Embotellado (por) [kree-yah-doh ee em-bot-tay-yah-doh] (Spain) Grown and bottled (by).

Crianza [kree-yan-thah] (Spain) Literally keeping "con Crianza" means aged in wood – for less time than, and thus often preferable, to the *Reservas* and *Gran Reservas,* which are highly prized by Spaniards but can, to modern palates, taste dull and dried-out.

℣ **Crichton Hall** [kri-ton] (*Rutherford,* California) Small winery specializing in top-class *Chardonnay.*

℣ **Criots-Batard-Montrachet** [kree-yoh ba-tar mon rah-shay] (*Burgundy,* France) See *Montrachet.*

Crisp Fresh, with good *acidity.*

℣ **Lucien Crochet** [loo-see-yen kroh-shay] (*Loire,* France) Top maker of red and white *Sancerre.* The *Cuvée Prestige* wines in both colours are – unusually for this appellation – worth keeping.
★★★★★ 1997 Sancerre Prestige £££

℣ **Ch. le Crock** [lur krok] (*St. Estèphe Cru Bourgeois, Bordeaux,* France) Traditional property that, like *Léoville-Poyferré,* its stablemate, has shown great recent improvement but still tends towards toughness. 90 95 96 98 00 01

℣ **Croft** (Spain/Portugal) *Port* and *sherry* producer making highly commercial but rarely memorable wines. The *vintage port* is up to scratch. 82 85 94 97 00

℣ **Ch. La Croix** [la crwah] (*Pomerol, Bordeaux,* France) Producer of long-lasting traditional wines.

℣ **Ch. la Croix-de-Gay** [la crwah duh gay] (*Pomerol, Bordeaux,* France) Classy *estate* whose complex wines have good, blackcurranty-plummy fruit. 90 95 96 00 01

℣ **Ch. Croizet-Bages** [krwah-zay bahzh] (*Pauillac 5ème Cru Classé, Bordeaux,* France) Underperformer showing some signs of improvement. Successful in 2001.

℣ **Croser** [kroh-sur] (*Adelaide Hills,* Australia) Made by *Brian Croser* of *Petaluma* in the Piccadilly Valley, this is one of the New World's most *Champagne*-like sparkling wines. ★★★★ 1996 Brut £££

🍇 **Crouchen** [kroo-shen] (France) Obscure white grape known as Clare Riesling in Australia and Paarl Riesling in South Africa.

℣ **Crozes-Hermitage** [krohz ehr-mee-tahzh] (*Rhône,* France) Up-and-coming *appellation* in the hills behind supposedly greater *Hermitage.* Smoky, blackberryish reds are pure *Syrah.* Whites (made from *Marsanne* and *Roussanne*) are creamy but less impressive. And they rarely keep. Red: 90 95 96 00 01 *Dom Belle; Chapoutier;* Colombier; Combier; *Delas; Alain Graillot;* Dom. du Pavilion-Mercure; Pochon; *Sorrel; Tain l'Hermitage Cooperative.*

C

Cru Bourgeois [kroo boor-zhwah] (*Bordeaux,* France) Wines beneath the *Crus Classés,* supposedly satisfying certain requirements, which can be good value for money and, in certain cases, better than more prestigious *classed growths.* Since around half the wine in the *Médoc* comes from Crus Bourgeois (and a quarter from *Crus Classés*), don't expect the words to mean too much. A new classification of the Crus Bourgeois is in progress, and will tighten up various loopholes, but is unlikely to remove the accolade from many underachieving wines. It is due to be announced in 2003. In any case, the best Crus Bourgeois do not rely on their classification to attract customers. *d'Angludet; Beaumont; Chasse-Spleen; Citran; Fourcas-Hosten; Haut-Marbuzet; Gloria, la Gurgue; Labégorce; Labégorce-Zédé; Marbuzet; Meyney; Monbrison; de Pez; Phélan-Ségur; Pibran; Potensac; Poujeaux; Siran; Sociando-Mallet; la Tour Haut-Caussin.*

Cru Classé [kroo klas-say] (*Bordeaux,* France) The *Médoc* was split into five categories of crus classés, from first (top) to fifth growth (or *Cru*) for the 1855 Great Exhibition. The *Graves, St. Emilion,* and *Sauternes* have their own classifications. Some wines are better than others of the same classification.

⟁ **Weingut Hans Crusius** [hans skroos-yuhs] (*Nahe,* Germany) Family-run *estate* prized for the quality of its highly traditional wines.

Crusted Port (*Douro,* Portugal) An affordable alternative to *vintage* port – a blend of different years, bottled young, and allowed to throw a deposit. *Churchill's; Graham's; Dow's.*

⟁ **Yves Cuilleron** [Kwee-yehr-ron] (*Rhône,* France) Rising star producing great (red and white) *St. Joseph* and *Condrieu.* If you want to experience great late-harvest *Viognier,* this is the place.

⟁ **Cullen** (*Margaret River,* Australia) Brilliant pioneering *estate* showing off the sensitive winemaking skills of Australian Winemaker of the Year (2000), Vanya Cullen. Source of stunning *Sauvignon-Semillon* blends, *claret*-like reds, a highly individual *Pinot Noir,* and a *Burgundian*-style *Chardonnay.* ★★★★★ **1999 Sauvignon Blanc Semillon £££**

Cultivar [kul-tee-vahr] (South Africa) South African for grape variety.

⟁ **Ch. Curé-Bon-la-Madelaine** [koo-ray bon lah mad-layn] (*St. Emilion Grand Cru Classé, Bordeaux,* France) Very small *St. Emilion estate* next to *Ausone.* **90 94 95 96 97 98 00 01**

Curico [koo-ree-koh] (Chile) Region in which *Torres, San Pedro,* and *Caliterra* have vineyards. Now being eclipsed by *Casablanca* as a source for cool-climate whites, but still one of Chile's best wine areas for red and white. *Caliterra; Echeverria; la Fortuna; Montes; Miguel Torres; Valdivieso.*

⟁ **Cuvaison Winery** [koo-vay-san] (*Napa Valley,* California) Reliable Swiss-owned winery with high-quality *Carneros Chardonnay,* approachable *Merlot,* and now good *Pinot Noir.* Calistoga Vineyards is a *second label.*

Cuve close [koov klohs] The third-best way of making sparkling wine, in which the wine undergoes secondary fermentation in a tank and is then bottled. Also called the *Charmat* or *Tank method.*

Cuvée (de Prestige) [koo-vay] Most frequently a blend put together in a process called *assemblage.* Prestige *Cuvées* are (particularly in *Champagne*) supposed to be the best a producer has to offer.

⟁ **Cuvée Napa** (*Napa,* California) The well-established California venture launched by *Mumm Champagne,* and still offering significantly better quality and value for money than the parent company back in France.

⟁ **CVNE** [koo-nay] (*Rioja,* Spain) The Compania Vinicola del Norte de Espana (usually referred to as "koo-nay") is a large high-quality operation run by the owners of *Contino* and producing the excellent Viña Real in *Crianza, Reserva, Imperial,* or *Gran Reserva* forms in the best years, as well as a light *CVNE Tinto.* Some recent releases have been slightly less dazzling.

Cyprus Shifting its focus away from making ersatz "*sherry*". Even so, the best wine is still the fortified *Commandaria.*

D

Ⓨ **Didier Dagueneau** [dee-dee-yay dag-guhn-noh] (*Loire*, France) The iconoclastic producer of steely, oak-aged *Pouilly-Fumé*, and even *late-harvest* efforts that upsets the authorities. Look out for the "Pur Sang" (made from rare, ungrafted vines) and oak-fermented "Silex" bottlings.

Ⓨ **Romano dal Forno** [roh-mah-noh dal for-noh] (*Veneto*, Italy) Innovative estate for top-class Valpolicella (with some particularly good *Amarones*).

Ⓨ **Ch. Dalem** [dah-lem] (*Fronsac, Bordeaux,* France) Rich, full-bodied *Fronsac.*

Ⓨ **Dalla Valle** (*Napa*, California) One of the leading lights in the new trend toward Italian flavours, this small winery makes a delicious *Super-Tuscan* look-alike in the shape of the *Sangiovese-based* Pietre Rosso.

Ⓨ **Dallas Conte** [dah-lass con-tay] (Chile) Joint venture between Australian *Mildara Blass* and Chilean *Santa Carolina*, focusing on commercial *Chardonnay* (from Casablanca) and *Cabernet*.

Ⓨ **Dalwhinnie** [dal-win-nee] (*Pyrenees, Victoria,* Australia) Quietly classy producer close to *Taltarni,* whose reds and whites are made to last.
★★★★ 1998 Moonambel Shiraz £££

Ⓨ **Dão** [downg] (Portugal) Once Portugal's best-known region – despite the traditional dullness of its wines. Thanks to pioneering producers like *Sogrape* and *Aliança*, and the introduction of better grape varieties such as the *Touriga Nacional*, both reds and whites are improving. Sogrape's Quinta dos Carvalhais is particularly recommendable. Red: 96 97 98 00 01 Boas Quintas; Duque de Viseu; Porta dos Cavaleiros; Quinta dos Roques; Casa de Santar.

Grão Vasco
DÃO

Ⓨ **Darioush** [dah-ree-oosh] (*Napa*, California) Recently launched, Iranian-backed venture with high hopes – and a *Viognier* that is far more impressive than those of many of its neighbours.

Ⓨ **Kurt Darting** [koort dahr-ting] (*Pfalz,* Germany) New-wave producer who cares more about ripe flavour than making the tooth-scouringly dry wine favoured by some of his neighbours. *Rieslings* are terrific, but so are examples of other varieties. Great *late-harvest* wines.
★★★★ 1998 Dürkheimer Hochbenn Riesling Kabinett £££

Ⓨ **Ch. Dassault** [das-soh] (*St. Emilion Grand Cru Classé, Bordeaux,* France) Named after the producer of France's fighter planes, this is good, juicy *St. Emilion.* 90 94 95 96 98 00 01

Ⓨ **Ch. de la Dauphine** [duh lah doh-feen] (*Fronsac, Bordeaux,* France) Like *Ch. Dalem*, this is roof that *Fronsac* really can match *St. Emilion* whose reputation this region once rivaled..

Ⓨ **Domaine d'Auvenay** [Dohv-nay] (*Burgundy,* France) Estate belonging to Lalou Bize Leroy, former co-owner of the *Dom. de la Romanée-Conti*, and now at *Dom. Leroy*. Great, if pricey, long-lived, examples of *Auxey-Duresses, Meursault, Puligny-Montrachet*, and *Grands Crus of the Côtes de Nuits.*
★★★★★ 1997 Puligny-Montrachet Les Folatières £££

Ⓨ **René and Vincent Dauvissat** [doh-vee-sah] (*Burgundy,* France) One of the best *estates* in *Chablis*. Watch for other Dauvissats though, the name is also used by the *La Chablisienne* cooperative.

Ⓨ **Ch. Dauzac** [doh-zak] (*Margaux 5ème Cru Classé, Bordeaux,* France) Rejuvenated, following its purchase in 1993 by André Lurton of *Ch. la Louvière.* 90 95 96 98 00 01

Ⓨ **Dealul Mare** [day-al-ool mah-ray] (Romania) Carpathian region once known for whites, now producing surprisingly good *Pinot Noir.*

Ⓨ **Etienne & Daniel Defaix** [duh-fay] (*Burgundy,* France) Classy traditional *Chablis* producer, making long-lived wines with a steely bite. ★★★ 1997 Chablis Vieilles Vignes ££

D

𝗫 Grof Dégenfeld [dehg-en-feld] (*Tokaj*, Hungary) Large new Tokaji producer.
Dégorgée (dégorgement) [day-gor-jay] The removal of the deposit of inert
yeasts from *Champagne* after maturation.

𝗫 Dehlinger (*Sonoma*, California) *Russian River Pinot Noir* and *Chardonnay*
specialist (with some great single-vineyard examples) that is proving highly
successful with *Syrah* and *Cabernet Sauvignon.* ★★★★ **1997 Russian River
Valley Late Bottled ReserveChardonnay ££**

Deidesheim [di-dess-hime] (*Pfalz*, Germany) Distinguished wine town
noted for flavoursome *Rieslings.* QbA/Kab/Spät: 98 99 00 01
Aus/Beeren/Tba: 96 97 98 99 00 01 *Bassermann-Jordan; Josef Biffar; Reichsrat
von Buhl; JL Wolf.*

𝗫 Deinhard [dine-hard] (*Mosel*, Germany) See *Wegeler Deinhard.*

𝗫 Marcel Deiss [dise] (*Alsace*, France) Small property producing some of
the best wine in the region, including some unusually good *Pinot Noir.*
★★★★★ **1998 Riesling Altenberg de Bergheim ££££**

𝗫 Delaforce [del-lah-forss] (*Douro*, Portugal) Small *port* house with lightish
but good *vintage* and *tawny.* 75 77 85 94 97 00
★★★ **1995 Quinta da Corte Vintage Port £££**

𝗫 Delaire (South Africa) Quality-conscious winery with fruit grown at high
altitudes. Look for Merlot-Cabernet blend. ★★★★ **Botmaskop.**

𝗫 Delamotte [del-lah-mot] (*Champagne*, France) Established among the
Chardonnay vineyards of the Côte des Blancs in 1760, and now a subsidiary
of *Laurent-Perrier* (and thus in the same group as *Salon*), this can be one of
the best sources for *Blanc de Blancs Champagne.*

𝗫 Delas Frères [del-las] (*Rhône*, France) *Négociant* with great *Hermitage*
vineyards and now promising much since its purchase by *Louis Roederer.*
A name to watch. ★★★★★ **1997 Hermitage les Bessards ££££**

𝗫 Delatite [del-la-tite] (*Victoria*, Australia) Producer of lean structured,
long-lived wines. The *Riesling* and, more particularly the *Gewurztraminer*,
are the stars, but the Devil's River red is fine too.

𝗫 Delbeck [del-bek] (*Champagne*, France) Underrated little producer, whose
wines are strongly *Pinot*-influenced.

𝗫 Delegats [del-leg-gats] (*Auckland*, New Zealand) Family firm that has hit
its stride recently with impressively (for New Zealand) ripe reds, especially
plummy *Merlots.* Look for the "Reserve" wines. The *second label* is "*Oyster
Bay*". ★★★★ **1998 Reserve Hawkes Bay Merlot £££**

𝗫 Philippe Delesvaux [Dels-voh] (*Loire*, France) Quality-conscious *Coteaux
de Layon* estate with some good red too.

𝗫 Delgado Zuleta [dayl-gah-doh thoo-lay-tah] (Sanlucar, Spain) Old-
established Manzanilla producer ★★★★ La Goya Manzanilla Pasada.

𝗫 Delheim Wines [del-hime] (*Stellenbosch*, South Africa) A commercial
estate with lean, quite traditional reds and white.

𝗫 DeLille Cellars (*Washington State*) A small producer of very classy
Bordeaux-style reds and whites under this and the Chaleur Estate labels.

𝗫 DeLoach Vineyards (*Sonoma*, California) *Russian River* winery with rich
Chardonnay and huge single-vineyard *Zinfandels.*

𝗫 André Delorme [del-lorm] (*Burgundy*, France) Little-known *négociant*
based in the Côte Chalonnaise and specializing in sparkling wines.
Demi-sec [duh-mee sek] (France) Medium-dry.

𝗫 Demoiselle [duh-mwah-zel] (*Champagne*, France). A new *Champagne*
name to watch with attractive, light, creamy wines.

𝗫 Denbies Wine Estate [den-bees] (*Surrey*, England) Part tourist attraction,
part winery, the largest wine *estate* England has so far produced. Sweet
wines are the best of the batch so far. ★★★★ **Special Late Harvest £££**
Deutscher Tafelwein [doyt-shur tah-fuhl-vihn] (Germany) Table wine,
guaranteed German as opposed to Germanic-style EC *Tafelwein.* Can be
good value – and often no worse than *Qualitätswein*, the supposedly
"quality" wine designation that includes every bottle of *Liebfraumilch.*

D

Deutsches Weinsiegel [doyt-shus vine-see-gel] (Germany) Seals of various colours – usually neck labels – awarded (over-generously) to supposedly higher quality wines. Treat with circumspection.

� **Deutz** [duhtz] (*Champagne,* France, and also Spain, New Zealand, California) Reliable small but dynamic producer at home and abroad, now owned by *Roederer.* The *Montana Marlborough* Cuvée from New Zealand was created with the assistance of *Deutz,* as was the *Yalumba "D"* in Australia. Maison Deutz is a 150-acre cool-climate vineyard joint venture in California with Nestlé and *Deutz* where, unusually, a bit of *Pinot Blanc* goes into the – generally – excellent blend. The *Cuvée William Deutz* is the star wine.

� **Devaux** [duh-voh] (*Champagne,* France) Small producer with a knack of producing fairly-priced wine and unusually good rosé and *Blanc de Noirs.*

� **Devil's Lair** (*Margaret River,* Australia) Concentrated, rich, dense wines, especially *Pinot Noir, Cabernet-Merlot* and *Chardonnay.*

Dézaley [days-lay] (*Vaud,* Switzerland) One of the few places in the world where the Chasselas (here called the *Dorin*) makes decent wine. **Pinget.**

Diabetiker Wein [dee-ah-beh-tih-ker vine] (Germany) Very dry wine with most of the sugar fermented out (as in a Diat lager); suitable for diabetics, but daunting for others.

� **Diamond Creek** (*Napa Valley,* California) Big Name producer with a set of very good vineyards (Gravelly Meadow, Red Rock Terrace, and Volcanic Hill); toughly intense red wines which demand, and now – more than in the past – repay patience. ★★★★ 1995 Cabernet Sauvignon Volcanic Hill ££££

� **Diamond Valley** (*Victoria,* Australia) Producer of one of Australia's – and the New World's best examples of *Pinot Noir.*

Schlossgut Diel [shloss-goot deel] (*Nahe,* Germany) Wine writer Armin Diel makes sublime *Rieslings* and pioneering oaked *Rülander* and *Weissburgunder.*

🌲 **Dimiat** [deem-yaht] (Bulgaria) White grape said to be named after a town on the Nile Delta, but now producing simple, aromatic wine in Bulgaria.

� **Dieu Donné Vineyards** [dyur don-nay] (*Franschhoek,* South Africa) Variable producer of quality varietals in the Franschhoek valley.

� **Dom. Disznókó** [diss-noh-koh] (*Tokaji,* Hungary) Estate belonging, like *Quinta da Noval,* to *AXA.* Top-class modern *Tokaji* and dry lemony *Furmint.* ★★★★★ 1995 Tokaji Aszu 5 Puttonyos £££

DLG (*Deutsche Landwirtschaft Gesellschaft*) (Germany) Body awarding medals for excellence to German wines – far too generously.

DO (*Denominac/ion/ão de Origen*) (Spain, Portugal) Demarcated quality area, guaranteeing origin, grape varieties, and production standards (everything, in other words except the quality of the stuff in the bottle).

� **DOC (*Denominación de Origem Controlada*)** (Portugal) Replacing the old RD (Região Demarcada) as Portugal's equivalent of Italy's *DOCG.*

DOC (*Denominacion de Origen Calificada*) (Spain) Ludicrously, and confusingly, Spain's recently launched higher quality equivalent to Italy's *DOCG* shares the same initials as Italy's lower quality *DOC* wines. So far, restricted to *Rioja* – good, bad, and indifferent. In other words, this official designation should be treated – like Italy's *DOCs* and *DOCGs* and France's *Appellation Contrôlée* – with something less than total respect.

DOC(G) (*Denominazione di Origine Controllata [e Garantita]*) (Italy) Quality control designation based on grape variety and/or origin. "Garantita" is supposed to imply a higher quality level, but all too often it does no such thing and has more to do with regional politics than with tasty wines. The recently introduced IGT designation for quality wines previously sold as Vino da Tavola has helped to put DOC and DOCG into perspective as an indication of the region in which a wine was produced and its likely style.

� **Ch. Doisy-Daëne** [dwah-zee dai-yen] (*Barsac 2ème Cru Classé, Bordeaux,* France) Fine *Barsac* property whose wines are typically more restrained than many a *Sauternes.* The 2000 is a star. The top wine is L'Extravagance. 90 94 95 96 97 98 99 00 01

D

Ⓣ **Ch. Doisy-Dubroca** [dwah-zee doo-brohkah] (*Barsac 2ème Cru Classé, Bordeaux,* France) Underrated *estate* producing ultra-rich wines at often attractively low prices. **90 95 96 97 98 01**

Ⓣ **Ch. Doisy-Védrines** [dwah-zee vay-dreen] (*Barsac 2ème Cru Classé, Bordeaux,* France) Reliable *Barsac* property.

🍇 **Dolcetto (d'Alba, di Ovada)** [dohl-cheh-toh] (*Piedmont,* Italy) Grape producing anything from soft everyday red to very robust and long-lasting examples. Generally worth catching quite young though. *Bests* use it to good effect in Australia. **Altare; Bava; Elvo Cogno; Aldo Conterno; Cortese; Vajra.**

Dôle [Dohl] (Switzerland) *Appellation* of *Valais* producing attractive reds from *Pinot Noir* and/or *Gamay* grapes. **Germanier.**

Ⓣ **Dom Pérignon** [dom peh-reen-yon] (*Champagne,* France) *Moët et Chandon's Prestige Cuvée,* named after the cellarmaster who is erroneously said to have invented the *Champagne* method. Impeccable white and (rare) rosé. (*Moët* will disgorge older *vintages* to order). ★★★★ **1993 ££££**

Domaine (Dom.) [doh-mayn] (France) Wine estate.

Ⓣ **Domecq** [doh-mek] (*Jerez/Rioja,* Spain) Producer of (disappointing) *La Ina Fino* and the rare, wonderful *511A Amontillado* and Sibarita *Palo Cortado.*

Ⓣ **Ch. la Dominique** [lah doh-mee-neek] (*St. Emilion Grand Cru Classé, Bordeaux,* France) High-flying property; one of the finest in *St. Emilion.* **90 93 94 95 96 97 98 99 00 01**

Ⓣ **Dominus** [dahm-ih-nuhs] (*Napa Valley,* California) *Christian Moueix* of *Ch. Petrus's* concentrated wine that is built to last. ★★★★★ **1997 ££££**

Ⓣ **Domus** [doh-moos] (Chile) Star winemakers Ignacio Recabarren and Ricardo Peña's Maipo's estate makes good *Chardonnay* and better *Cabernet.*

Ⓣ **Donauland** [doh-now-lend] (Austria) Varied wine region associated with good *Grüner Veltliner* but without a specific style of its own.

Ⓣ **Hermann Dönnhoff** (*Nahe,* Germany) Brilliant winemaker who crafts great *late-harvest* wine and *Eiswein* from his Hermannshöhle vineyard.

Ⓣ **Donnafugata** [don-na-foo-gah-tah] (*Sicily,* Italy) Large, modern winery making balanced, reliable wines from both local and international varieties.

Ⓣ **Doonkuna** [doon-koo-nah] (*New South Wales,* Australia) Small winery making decent red wine. ★★★★ **1997 Cabernet Merlot ££**

Ⓣ **Dopff "Au Moulin"** [dop-foh-moo-lan] (*Alsace,* France) *Négociant* with fine *Grand Crus.* ★★★★ **1997 Riesling Schoenenbourg £££**

Ⓣ **Dopff & Irion** [dop-fay-ee-ree-yon] (*Alsace,* France) Not to be confused with Dopff "Au Moulin" this is also a name to watch.

Ⓣ **Vin de Pays de la Dordogne** [dor-doyn] (*Southwest,* France) To the east of *Bordeaux,* this improving region offers light *Bordeaux*-style wines.

Ⓣ **Girolamo Dorigo** [Jee-roh-lah-moh doh-ree-goh] (*Friuli-Venezia Giulia,* Italy) Classy Collio Orientali del Friuli producer with good reds (made from grapes such as the local Pignolo and *Refosco*) and even more impressive whites including a *Chardonnay, Verduzzo,* and *Picolit.*

🍇 **Dorin** [doh-ran] (*Vaud,* Switzerland) Name for the *Chasselas* in the *Vaud.*

🍇 **Dornfelder** [dorn-fel-duh] (Germany) Sadly underrated early-ripening, juicy, berryish grape that is beginning to attract some interest among pioneering winemakers in the southern part of Germany.

Dosage [doh-sazh] The addition of sweetening syrup to naturally dry *Champagne* after *dégorgement* to replace the wine lost with the yeast, and to set the sugar to the desired level (even *Brut Champagne* requires up to four grams per liter of sugar to make it palatable).

Douro [doo-roh] (Portugal) The port region and river whose only famous table wine was *Ferreira's* long-established *Barca Velha.* Now, however, thanks largely to *Quinta do Cotto,* port houses like *Ramos Pinto* and *Niepoort,* and firms like *Sogrape,* there's a growing range of other stars to choose from. **Alianca, Barca Velha; Quinta do Cotto; do Crasto; Duas Quintas; do Fojo; da Gaivosa; Redoma; de las Rosa; Vale Doña Maria; Vale da Raposa; Vallado.**

D

Dourthe [doort] (*Bordeaux*, France) Dynamic *négociant* whose Dourthe No.1 offers unusually reliable, good value (especially white) Bordeaux.

Doux [doo] (France) Sweet.

⌇ **Dow** [dow] (*Douro*, Portugal) One of the big two (with *Taylor's*) and under the same family ownership as *Warre*, *Smith Woodhouse*, and *Graham*. Great *vintage port* and similarly impressive *tawny*. The *single-quinta* Quinta do Bomfim wines offer a chance to taste the Dow's style affordably.

⌇ **Drappier** [drap-pee-yay] (*Champagne*, France) Small, reliably recommendable producer. ★★★★★ "Val des Demoiselles" Rosé £££

⌇ **Jean-Paul Droin** [drwan] (*Burgundy*, France) Good, small *Chablis* producer with approachable "modern" wines. ★★★★★ 1998 Chablis Grand Cru Valmur £££

⌇ **Dromana Estate** [droh-mah-nah] (*Mornington Peninsula*, Australia) Viticulturalist Gary Crittenden makes good, if light, *Chardonnay* and raspberryish *Pinot Noir*, as well as an impressive range of Italian varietals sold under the "I" label.

⌇ **Domaine Drouhin** [droo-an] (*Oregon*) Top *Burgundy* producer's highly expensive investment in the US that's increasingly producing world-class reds – thanks to Veronique Drouhin's skill and commitment and some of *Oregon's* best vineyards. ★★★★ Lauréne1997 Pinot Noir ££££

⌇ **Joseph Drouhin** [droo-an] (*Burgundy*, France) Probably *Burgundy's* best *négociant*, with first-class red and white wines that are unusually representative of their particular *appellations*. Also look out for the rare white *Beaune* from its own Clos des Mouches, top-class *Clos de Vougeot*, and unusually (for a *négociant*) high-quality *Chablis*. The Marquis de Laguiche *Montrachet* is sublime. ★★★★★ 1998 Beaune Clos des Mouches Rouge £££

⌇ **Pierre-Jacques Druet** [droo-ay] (*Loire*, France) Wonderfully reliable *Bourgueil* producer making characterful individual cuvées. ★★★★ 1996 Grand Mont £££

Dry Creek (*Sonoma*, California) A rare example of a California *AVA* region whose wines have an identifiable quality and style. Look out for *Sauvignon Blanc* and *Zinfandel*. *Beaulieu Vineyard; Collier Falls; Dry Creek; Duxoup; Gallo Sonoma; Nalle; Pezzi-King; Quivira; Rabbit Ridge; Rafanell; Turley.*

⌇ **Dry Creek Vineyard** (*Sonoma*, California) Eponymous vineyard within the *Dry Creek AVA* making well-known *Fumé Blanc*, great *Chenin Blanc*, and impressive reds.

⌇ **Dry River** (*Martinborough*, New Zealand) Small *estate* with particularly impressive *Pinot Noir* and *Pinot Gris* and delicious *late-harvest* wines.

⌇ **Duboeuf** [doo-burf] (*Burgundy*, France) The "King of *Beaujolais*", who introduced the world to the penny-candy flavour of young *Gamay*. Duboeuf offers good examples from individual growers, vineyards, and villages. These include reliable *nouveau*, good straightforward *Mâconnais* white, single *domaine Rhônes*, and now large amounts of commercial rather than fine Vin de Pays *Viognier*.

⌇ **Dubreuil-Fontaine** [doo-broy fon-tayn] (*Burgundy*, France) Quite traditional *estate*, producing full-flavoured red and white individual cuvées from the *Corton* hillsides.

Duca di Salaparuta [sah-la-pah-ROO-tah] (*Sicily*, Italy) Huge producer of good, reliable wines made to modern standards. The brand name is Corvo.

⌇ **Duckhorn** (*Napa Valley*, California) Once the producer of dauntingly tough *Merlot*, Duckhorn is now making far more approachable examples of this and other varieties. Decoy, the second label, offers an affordable, earlier-drinking taste of the house style, while the unusual Paraduxx *Cabernet-Zinfandel* is a delicious and immediately likeable novelty.

E

Ⓣ Ch. Ducru-Beaucaillou [doo-kroo boh-ki-yoo] (*St. Julien 2ème Cru Classé, Bordeaux,* France) *"Super Second"* with a decidedly less obvious style than peers such as *Léoville-Las-Cases* and *Pichon-Lalande.* Especially good in 1996, 1997, and (brilliantly in) 1998 and 1999 after a disappointing patch in the late 1980s and early 1990s. The 2000 and 2001 are fine too. Second wine is Croix-Beaucaillou.

Ⓣ Dom. Bernard Dugat-Py [doo-gah pee] (*Burgundy,* France) Superstar *Gevrey-Chambertin estate* with great vineyards, from which M. Dugat makes delicious and unusually fairly priced wines *Grand Cru.*
★★★★★ 1998 Gevrey-Chambertin Premier Cru ££££

Ⓣ Ch. Duhart-Milon-Rothschild [doo-ahr mee-lon rot-sheeld] (*Pauillac 4ème Cru Classé, Bordeaux,* France) Under the same management as *Lafite* and benefiting from heavy investment.

Ⓣ Dom. Dujac [doo-zhak] (*Burgundy,* France) Cult *Burgundy* producer Jacques Seysses makes fine, long-lived, and quite modern wines from *Morey-St.-Denis* (including a particularly good *Clos de la Roche*), which are packed with intense *Pinot Noir* flavour. Now helped by Gary Farr of the excellent *Bannockburn* in Australia, and investing in vineyards in southern France.

Ⓣ Dulong [doo-long] (*Bordeaux,* France) Reliable *négociant* that shocked some of its neighbours by producing *International Wine Challenge* medal-winning multi-regional *Vin de Table* blends under the "Rebelle" label.

Dumb As in dumb nose, meaning without smell.

Ⓣ Dunn Vineyards (*Napa Valley,* California) Randy Dunn makes tough, forbidding *Cabernets* from *Howell Mountain* for patient collectors. Give them time, though; eventually, they yield extraordinary spicy, berryish flavours.
★★★★★ 1997 Cabernet Sauvignon Howell Mountain ££££

Durbach [door-bahk] (*Baden,* Germany) Top vineyard area of this *Anbaugebiet.* Andreas Laible; Wolf-Metternich.

Ⓣ Ch. Durfort-Vivens [door-for vee-va'ns] (*Margaux 2ème Cru Classé, Bordeaux,* France) Never really starry, but sometimes very classic, elegant wine, now with a new generation in charge. Recent vintages show decided improvement. 95 96 98 99 00 01

🍇 Durif [dyoor-if] See *Petite Sirah.*

Ⓣ Jean Durup [doo-roop] (*Burgundy,* France) Modern *estate* whose owner believes in extending vineyards of *Chablis* into less distinguished soil. Wines are good rather than great. The best are sold as Ch. de Maligny.

Ⓣ Duval-Leroy [doo-val luh-rwah] (*Champagne,* France) Previously popular among retailers and restaurateurs to whom it supplied excellent own-label wines. Fleur de Champagne and Cuvée des Rois are worth looking out for.

Ⓣ Duxoup Wine Works [duk-soop] (*Sonoma Valley,* California) Inspired winery-in-a-shed, producing fine *Syrah* from bought-in grapes.

E

Ⓣ E&E (*Barossa,* South Australia) Top wine produced by *Barossa Valley Estate.*

Ⓣ Maurice Ecard [Ay-car] (*Burgundy,* France) Very recommendable *Savigny-lès-Beaune* estate with good *Premier Cru* vineyards.

Ⓣ Echeverria [eh-che-veh-ree-yah] (*Maule,* Chile) Impressive Curico producer with good *Cabernets, Chardonnays,* and *Sauvignon Blancs.*

Ⓣ Echézeaux [eh-shay-zoh] (*Burgundy,* France) *Grand Cru* between *Clos de Vougeot* and *Vosne-Romanée* and more or less an extension of the latter *commune. Flagey-Echézeaux,* a village on the relatively vineless side of the Route Nationale, takes its name from the "flagellation" used by the peasants to gather corn in the 6th century. Grands-Echézeaux should be finer. *Dujac; R Engel; Grivot; Henri Jayer; Jayer-Gilles; D. Laurent; Mongeard-Mugneret; Mugneret-Gibourg; de la Romanée-Conti; E. Rouget; F. Vigot.*

E

L' Ecole No. 41 [ay-kohl] (*Washington State*)
Superlative producer of classy *Chardonnay* and
Merlot, as well as some lovely rich *Semillon*.
★★★★ 1998 Fries Vineyard Semillon ££££

Edelfäule [ay-del-foy-luh] (Germany) *Botrytis
cinerea*, or "*noble rot*".

Edelzwicker [ay-del-zvick-kur] (*Alsace*, France)
Generic name for a blend of grapes. The idea of blends
is coming back – but not the name (see *Hugel*).

Eden Valley (Australia) Prime region for lean, limey
Riesling; but the complicated geography and geology
here means that the valley can also produce good reds.

Edes [ay-desh] (Hungary) Sweet.

Edmunds St. John (*Alameda*, California) Producer with his heart in the
Rhône – and a taste for rich, spicy *Syrah* and *Zinfandel* reds. ★★★★★ 1995
Durell Vineyard Syrah ££££

Edna Valley Vineyard (California) Long-standing maker of rich, buttery
Chardonnay in the *AVA* of the same name. In the same stable as *Chalone*,
Carmenet and *Acacia*, and now in a joint Californian venture with *Penfolds*.

Luís Felipé Edwards (Chile) High quality from an ex-pat Aussie winemaker.
Look out for the lemony *Chardonnay*.

Eger [eg-gur] (Hungary) Region of Hungary where *Bull's Blood* is made.

Dom. de l'Eglise [duh lay glees] (*Pomerol, Bordeaux*, France) Fairly
priced, mid-line, wines. 90 95 96 98 00 01

Ch. l'Eglise-Clinet [Lay gleez klee-nay] (*Pomerol, Bordeaux*, France)
Terrific small estate that has gained – and earned – recent superstar status.

Egri Bikaver [eh-grih bih-kah vehr] (*Eger*, Hungary) See *Bull's Blood*.

Cave Vinicole d'Eguisheim [Eh-gees-hime] (*Alsace*, France) Dynamic
cooperative with grand cru vineyards (including Hengst and Speigel) and
alternative brands: Wolfberger and Willm. Look for the Sigillé wines.

Eikendal Vineyards [ehk-ken-dahl] (*Stellenbosch,* South Africa)
Understated wines (esp. *Chardonnay*) from the *Helderberg*.

Eiswein/Eiswein [ice-vine] (Germany/Austria/Canada) Ultra-concentrated
late harvest wine, made from grapes naturally frozen on the vine and often
picked a long time after the rest of the crop. (Some German vintages are
harvested in the January of the following year!) Hard to make (and
consequently very pricey) in Germany but much easier and more affordable
in *Canada* where "Icewine" is a huge success. Unlike other top-quality
sweet wines, Eiswein does not rely on *noble rot*. In fact, this characteristic
is normally absent because winemakers need frozen grapes in a perfect state.

Eitelsbach [ih-tel-sbahk] (*Mosel*, Germany) One of the top two *Ruwer*
wine towns, and the site of the famed Karthäuserhofberg vineyard.

Elaborado y Anejado Por [ay-lah-boh-rah-doh ee anay-hahdo pohr]
(Spain) "Made and aged for".

Elbling [el-bling] (Germany) A popular grape in Medieval Germany,
nowadays this highly acidic white grape is found in the upper Mosel Valley
and in Luxembourg for (mostly) sparkling wine.

Elderton (*Barossa Valley*, Australia) Highly commercial maker of big, rich,
competition-winning wines, especially *Shiraz* and *Cabernet*.

Elever/éleveur [ay-lur-vay/ay-lur-vuhr] To mature or "nurture" wine,
especially in the cellars of the *Burgundy négociants*, who act as éleveurs
after traditionally buying in wine made by small estates.

Elgin [el-gin] (South Africa) Coolish – *Burgundy*-like – apple-growing
country which is increasingly attracting the interest of big wine producers.
Watch out for the *Paul Cluver* reds and whites from *Neil Ellis*. May
eventually overshadow all but the best parts of *Stellenbosch* and *Paarl*.

Elk Cove (*Oregon*, USA) Organic Willamette Valley winery with sound range
of whites.

E

🍷 **Neil Ellis** (*Stellenbosch*, South Africa) New-wave Cape winemaker – and a pioneer of the new region of *Elgin*. ★★★ **2000 Sauvignon Blanc ££**
Eltville [elt-vil] (*Rheingau*, Germany) Town housing the *Rheingau* state cellars and the German Wine Academy, producing good *Riesling* with backbone.

🍷 **Elyse Wine Cellars** (*Napa,* California) *Zinfandel* specialist with *Howell Mountain Vineyards*. Look out too for the fine Cabernet and a Nero Misto spicy *Zinfandel-Petite Sirah* blend. ★★★★★ **1997 Napa Syrah £££**
Emilia-Romagna [eh-mee-lee-yah roh-ma-nya] (Italy) Region around Bologna best known for *Lambrusco*; also the source of *Albana, Sangiovese* di Romagna, and *Pagadebit*.

Enate [eh-nah-tay] (*Somontano,* Spain) Dynamic modern winery specializing in varietals, including particularly successful Chardonnays.
En primeur [on pree-muh] New wine, usually *Bordeaux*. Producers and specialist merchants buy and offer wine *en primeur* before it has been released. In the US and Australia, where producers like *Mondavi* and *Petaluma* sell in this way, the process is known as buying "futures".

🍷 **Ch. l'Enclos** [lon kloh] (*Pomerol, Bordeaux,* France.) Gorgeously rich, fairly priced wines. **90 95 96 97 98 00 01**

🍷 **René Engel** [On-jel] (*Burgundy,* France) Producer of rich, long-lived wines in *Vosne-Romanée* and *Clos Vougeot*. ★★★★★ **1998 Vosne-Romanée ££££**
English wine Quality has improved in recent years as winemakers have moved from semi-sweet, mock-Germanic to dry mock-*Loire* and, increasingly, sparkling, aromatic-but-dry and *late harvest*. **Breaky Bottom; Thames Valley Vineyards; Nyetimber, Bruisyard; Three Choirs; Carr Taylor; Chiltern Valley.**
Enoteca [ee-noh-teh-kah] (Italy) Literally wine library or, now, wine shop.

🍷 **Entre-Deux-Mers** [on-truh duh mehr] (*Bordeaux*, France) Once a region of appalling sweet wine from vineyards between the Dordogne and Garonne rivers. Now a source of basic *Bordeaux* Blanc and principally dry *Sauvignon*. Reds are sold as *Bordeaux* Rouge. Both reds and whites suffer from the difficulty grapes have in ripening in cool years. **Ch. Bonnet; Fontenille; Sainte-Marie; Tour-de-Mirambeau; Turcaud.**

🍷 **Erath Vineyards** [ee-rath] (*Oregon*, US) One of Oregon's pioneering *Pinot Noir* producers, now better than ever.
Erbach [ayr-bahkh] (*Rheingau*, Germany) Town noted for fine full *Riesling*, particularly from the Marcobrunn vineyard.

🍇 **Erbaluce** [ehr-bah-loo-chay] (*Piedmont*, Italy) White grape responsible for the light dry wines of the *Caluso*, and the sweet sun-dried *Caluso Passito*.

🍷 **Erbaluce di Caluso** [ehr-bah-loo-chay dee kah-loo-soh] (*Piedmont*, Italy) Dry, quite herby white made from the *Erbaluce* grape. Also used to make sparkling wine. ★★★★ **1998 Cieck, Calliope £££**
Erden [ehr-durn] (*Mosel-Saar-Ruwer,* Germany) In the *Bernkastel Bereich,* this northerly village produces some of the finest, full crisp *Riesling* in the *Mosel*, and includes the famous Treppchen vineyard. *JJ Christoffel; Dr Loosen;* Mönchhof; Peter Nicolay.

🍇 **Ermitage** [ehr-mee-tahj] (Switzerland) The Swiss name for the *Marsanne*.

🍷 **Errazuriz** [ehr-raz-zoo-riz] (*Aconcagua Valley,* Chile) One of Chile's big name producers and owner of *Caliterra*. Wines have been improved by input from *Mondavi*. Look out for the "Wild Ferment" *Chardonnay* and recently launched *Syrah*. The top wine, Don Maximiano is one of Chile's very best reds. ★★★★ **1998 El Descanso Estate Merlot ££**
Erstes Gewächs [air-shtes geh-vex] (Germany) First Growth: a new (2000) classification of the (hopefully) top parts of the *Rheingau's* best vineyards, and part of Germany's drive to do better and be seen to be doing better. The classification seems to have been generous, and includes 35 per cent of the Rheingau's vineyards. The jury is still out on the wines.
Erzeugerabfüllung [ayr-tsoy-guhr-ap-few-loong] (Germany) Bottled by the grower/estate.

E

T **Esk Valley** (*Hawkes Bay,* New Zealand) Under the same ownership as *Vidal* and *Villa Maria*. Successful with *Bordeaux*-style reds and juicy rosé. ★★★★★ 1997 Reserve Merlot/Malbec/Cabernet Sauvignon ££

T **Esporão** [esp-per-row] (*Alentejo,* Portugal) Revolutionary wines (including some fascinating varietals) made with help from Australian-born, Portuguese-based *David Baverstock*.

Espum/oso/ante [es-poom-mo-soh/san-tay] (Spain/Portugal) Sparkling.

T **Est! Est!! Est!!!** [ehst-ehst-ehst] (*Lazio,* Italy) Red named after the repeated exclamation of a bishop's servant when he found a good wine. Apart from the ones made by *Falesco*, today's examples rarely offer much to exclaim about.

Esters Chemical components in wine responsible for all those extraordinary odours of fruits, vegetables, hamster cages, and trainers.

T **Estremadura** [ehst-reh-mah-doo-rah] (Portugal) Huge area producing mostly dull wine. Quintas da Pancas and Boavista show what can be done.

Estufa [esh-too-fah] (*Madeira,* Portugal) The vats in which *Madeira* is heated, speeding maturity and imparting its familiar "cooked" flavour.

Eszencia [es-sen-tsee-yah] (*Tokaji,* Hungary) Incredibly concentrated syrup made by piling around 22 kg of *late harvested, botrytised* grapes into *puttonyos* and letting as little as three litres of syrup dribble out of the bottom. This will only ferment up to about 4 per cent alcohol, over several weeks, before stopping completely. It is then stored and used to sweeten normal *Aszú* wines. The Czars of Russia discovered the joys of Eszencia, and it has been prized for its effects on the male libido. It is hard to find, even by those who can see the point in doing anything with the expensive syrup other than pouring it on ice cream. The easier-to-find *Aszú Essencia* (one step sweeter than *Aszú 6 puttonyos*) is far better value.

T **Arnaldo Etchart** [et-shaht] (*Cafayate,* Argentina) Dynamic producer, benefiting from advice by *Michel Rolland* of *Pomerol* fame, and also investment by its French owners Pernod Ricard. The key wine here, though, is the grapey white *Torrontes*.

T **l'Etoile** [eh-twah] (*Jura,* France) Theoretically the best *appellation* in the *Jura*. *Chardonnay* and *Savagnin* whites and sparkling wines can be good, and the *Vin Jaune* is of interest. Ch de l'Etoile; Michel Geneletti; Montbo

T **Etude** [ay-tewd] (*Napa,* California) Thoughtful superstar consultant Tony Soter experiments by marrying specific sites and clones of *Pinot Noir*. Apart from these wines, there are good rich *Napa Cabernets* and *Carneros Chardonnays*. ★★★★★ 1996 Heirloom Carneros Pinot Noir £££

T **Ch. l' Evangile** [lay-van-zheel] (*Pomerol, Bordeaux,* France) One of the top wines of 2000. A classy and increasingly sought-after property that can, in great *vintages* like 1988, 1989 and 1990, sometimes rival its neighbour *Pétrus*, but in a more *tannic* style.

T **Evans Family/Evans Wine Co** (*Hunter Valley,* Australia) Len Evans's (founder and ex-chairman of *Rothbury Vineyards*) own estate and company. Rich *Chardonnay* and *Semillon* as characterful and generous as their maker. See also *Tower Estates*.

T **Evans & Tate** (*Margaret River,* Australia) Much improved producer with good *Chardonnay* and *Shiraz* (including an impressive *International Wine Challenge* trophy winner).

T **Eventail de Vignerons Producteurs** [ay-van-tih] (*Burgundy,* France) Reliable source of *Beaujolais*.

T **Eyrie Vineyards** [ai-ree] (*Oregon*) Pioneering *Pinot Noir* producer in the *Willamette Valley,* whose memorable success in a blind tasting of *Burgundies* helped to attract *Joseph Drouhin* to invest his francs in a vineyard here.

F

Fabre Montmayou [fab-re mon-mey-yoo] (*Mendoza,* Argentina) Luján de Cuyo winery to watch for rich *Michel Rolland*-influenced reds.

Fairview Estate (*Paarl,* South Africa) Progressive estate where Charles Back – both under his own name and under that of Fairview makes wines such as the wittily named and labelled "Goats do Roam". See also *Spice Route.*

Joseph Faiveley [fay-vlay] (*Burgundy,* France) Impressive modern *négoçiant* with particular strength in vineyards in the *Côte de Nuits* and *Nuits-St.-Georges.* ★★★★ 1998 Nuits St Georges Clos de la Maréchale ££££

Falchini [fal kee-noh] (*Tuscany,* Italy) One of the key producers of *Vernacchia di San Gimignano.*

Falerno del Massico [fah-LEHR-noh del mah-see-koh] (*Campania,* Italy) Modern producers such as Villa Matilde are leading the renaissance of a region famous among Ancient Roman wine drinkers. Reds and whites from local varieties: *Falanghina (white) Piedirosso, Aglianico and Primitivo (red).*

Falesco [fah leh-skoh] (*Lazio,* Italy) Producer of fine *Montiano, Merlot, Grechetto,* and *Est Est Est.*

Ch. Falfas [fal-fas] (*Côtes de Bourg, Bordeaux,* France) One of the best estates in the *appellation* – and a fine example of biodynamic winemaking.

Théo Faller/Domaine Weinbach [tay-yoh fal-lehr vine-bach] (*Alsace,* France) Family domaine of quirky character and very high quality. The wine style is rich and concentrated, and the wines benefit from bottle age. Several are named after the family. The Cuvée Laurence is a regular success.

Bodegas Fariña [fah ree-nah] (*Toro,* Spain) Top producer in Toro, making cask-aged (Gran Colegiata) and fruitier, non-cask-aged Colegiata.

Far Niente [fah nee-yen-tay] (*Napa Valley,* California) Well regarded producer of sometimes over-showy *Chardonnay* and *Cabernet.*

Ch. de Fargues [duh-fahrg] (*Sauternes, Bordeaux,* France) Elegant wines made by the winemaker at *Ch. d'Yquem* – and a good alternative.

Farnese [fahr-nay-say] (*Abruzzo,* Italy) Dynamic producer with unusually good Trebbiano d'Abruzzo.

Gary Farrell (*Sonoma,* California) A Russian River *Pinot Noir* and *Merlot* maker to watch.

Fat Has a silky texture which fills the mouth. More fleshy than meaty.

Fattoria [fah-tor-ree-ah] (Italy) *Estate*, particularly in *Tuscany*.

Faugères [foh-zhehr] (*Midi,* France) With neighbouring *St. Chinian*, this gently hilly region is a major cut above the surrounding *Coteaux du Languedoc*, and potentially the source of really exciting red. For the moment, however, most still taste pretty rustic. Ch. des Adouzes; Gilbert Alquier; Ch. Chenaie; des Estanilles; Grézan; Cave Cooperative de Laurens; la Liquière; de Météore; Moulin Couderc; des Peyregran; du Rouge Gorge; St. Antonin.

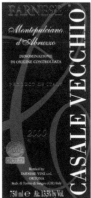

Bernard Faurie [fow-ree] (*Rhône,* France) Tournon-based producer who makes intense perfumed wines with great longevity.

Bodegas Faustino [fows-tee-noh] (*Rioja,* Spain) Dependable *Rioja* producer with excellent *(Gran) Reservas*, fair whites, and a decent *cava.* ★★★ 1995 Reserva £££

Favorita [fahvoh-ree-tah] (*Piedmont,* Italy) Traditional variety from *Piedmont* transformed by modern winemaking into delicate floral whites. Conterno; Villa Lanata; *Bava.*

Federspiel [fay-dur-shpeel] (*Wachau,* Austria) Local quality category (the middle one of three) for high quality dry wines. The rough equivalent of Kabinett. See also *Steinfeder* and *Smaragd.*

F

�>< **Weingut Feiler-Artinger** [fih-luh arh-ting-guh] (*Rust,* Austria) Superlative innovative producer of dry and, especially, *late-harvest* wines.
★★★★ 1999 Ruster Ausbruch Traminer £££

�>< **Fattoria di Felsina Berardenga** [fah-toh-ree-ah dee fehl-see-nah beh-rah-den-gah] (*Tuscany,* Italy) Very high-quality *Chianti* estate.

�>< **Livio Felluga** [feh-LOO-gah] (*Friuli,* Italy) Estate with terrific range of pure varietals and blends (e.g. *Terre Alte: Sauvignon, Tocai and Pinot Bianco*).

�>< **Felton Road** (*Central Otago,* New Zealand) This is an instant superstar, producing what may be New Zealand's top *Pinot Noir* as well as some very stylish *Riesling.* ★★★★★ 1998 Block 3 Pinot Noir £££

🍇 **Fendant** [fon-don] (Switzerland) See *Chasselas.*

🍇 **Fer** [fehr] (*South-West,* France) Grape used to make *Marcillac.*
Fermentazione naturale [fehr-men-tat-zee-oh-nay] (Italy) "Naturally sparkling" but, in fact, indicates the *cuve close* method.

🍇 **Fernão Pires** [fehr-now pee-rehsh] (Portugal) *Muscat*ty grape, used to great effect by *Peter Bright* of the João Pires winery.

�>< **Ch. Ferrand** [feh-ron] (*St. Emilion, Bordeaux,* France) Not to be confused with *Ferrand Lartigue,* this is a big estate, producing rather tough wines.

�>< **Ch. Ferrand Lartique** [feh-ron lah-teek] (*St. Emilion Grand Cru, Bordeaux,* France) Small five-acre estate producing full-bodied rich wines.

�>< **Luigi Ferrando** (*Piedmont* Italy) Producer in the Carema *DOC* of good *Nebbiolo*-based wines that are attractively light and elegant in style.

�>< **Antonio Ferrari** [feh-rah-ree] (*Piemonte,* Italy) Small family estate that still has (tiny) stocks of an astonishingly fine port-and-curry-spice 1978 Piemontese Salice Salentino

�>< **Ferrari** [feh-rah-ree] (*Trentino,* Italy) A sexy name for sexy *Champagne*-method sparkling wines. The Riserva del Fondatore is the star of the show.

�>< **Ferrari-Carano** (*Sonoma,* California) Improving winery best known for its oaky, crowd-pleasing *Chardonnay, Cabernet Sauvignon, Zinfandel,* and rich *Merlot*. All these are good in their unsubtle way, but Siena, the Italianate *Sangiovese*-Cabernet blend, and the *Syrah* are both more interesting.

�>< **AA Ferreira** [feh-ray-rah] (*Douro,* Portugal) Associated with *Sogrape,* this traditional Portuguese *port* producer is as famous for its excellent *tawnies* as for its *Barca Velha,* Portugal's best traditional unfortified red. ★★★★ Duque de Braganca 20 Year Old Tawny ££

�>< **Gloria Ferrer** (*Sonoma,* California) New World offshoot of *Freixenet* (the people behind *Cordon Negro*) making unmemorable sparkling wine and somewhat more interesting *Chardonnay* and *Pinot Noir* from its *Carneros* vineyards.

�>< **Ch. Ferrière** [feh-ree-yehr] (*Margaux 3ème Cru Classé, Bordeaux,* France) Once small, now rather bigger, thanks to the convenience of belonging to the same owners as the *Margaux Cru Bourgeois, Ch. la Gurgue* – and the legal right to swap land between estates in the same appellation.

�>< **Ch. de Fesles** [dur fel] (*Loire,* France) Classic *Bonnezeaux* has now been joined by *Anjou* and *Savennières.* ★★★★★ 1998 Bonnezeaux ££££

�>< **Sylvain Fessy** [seel-van fes-see] (*Burgundy,* France) Reliable small *Beaujolais* producer with wide range of *crus.*

�>< **Henry Fessy** [on-ree fes-see] (*Burgundy,* France) Consistent *négociant,* vineyard owner and producer of *Beaujolais.*

🍇 **Feteasca** [fay-tay-yas-cah] (Romania) White grape giving fair, peachy wine. F. Regala is slightly better than F. Alba. Red F. Neagra also exists.

�>< **Fetzer** [fet-zuh] (*Mendocino,* California) Confusingly, this big producer offers quite different lines of wines in the UK and US – which helps to explain why the name is more respected in the US. Fortunately, the whole world can buy the excellent "Bonterra" line which is among the best examples of commercial organic wine in the world. ★★★★★ 1998 Bonterra Chardonnay ££; ★★★★★ 1998 Bonterra Zinfandel ££

F

- **Feudi di San Gregorio** [foy-di dee san gray-gor-yoh] (*Campania*, Italy) The Fiano grape at its best, with sweetish ★★★★★ Privilegio £££ at the top of the tree. Other varieties are also excellent, including ★★★★★ Serpico ££££, a complex Aglianico-Merlot blend. Subtle, elegant wines right across the board.
- **Nicolas Feuillatte** [fuh-yet] (*Champagne*, France) Quietly rising star with good-value wine. ★★★★ **1992 Palmes d'Or £££**
- **William Fèvre** [weel-yum feh-vr] (*Burgundy*, France) Quality *Chablis* producer that is now under the same (Henriot) ownership as *Bouchard Père & Fils*, and showing similar improvements in quality: oak use, in particular, is more delicate. Fèvre's efforts in Chile (he still owns the Chilean operation) have got better with each vintage too. ★★★ **1998 Chablis Vaillons ££££**
- **Ch. Feytit-Clinet** [fay-tee klee-nay] (*Pomerol, Bordeaux*, France) A *Moueix* property with good, delicate wines. **90 95 96 98 00 01**
- **Fiano** [fee-yah-noh] (Italy) Herby white grape variety used to make Fiano di Avellino in the south.
- **Les Fiefs-de-Lagrange** [fee-ef duh lag-ronzh] (*St. Julien, Bordeaux*, France) Recommendable *second label* of *Ch. Lagrange*.
- **Fiefs Vendéens** [fee-ef von-day-yi'n] (*Loire*, France) Surviving VDQS region close to Muscadet and offering a wide range of grape varieties – and fresh, light wines that are well worth buying in ripe vintages.
- **Ch. de Fieuzal** [duh fyuh-zahl] (*Pessac-Léognan Grand Cru* Classé, *Bordeaux*, France) *Pessac-Léognan* property returning to form and producing great whites and lovely raspberryish reds Abeille de Fieuzal is *second label*.

GRAND VIN DE BORDEAUX

1995

Les Fiefs de Lagrange

SAINT-JULIEN
APPELLATION SAINT-JULIEN CONTROLEE

Alc 12,5% vol.   *Mis en Bouteille à la Propriété*   e 750 ml
CHATEAU LAGRANGE SA
PROPRIETAIRE A SAINT-JULIEN BEYCHEVELLE (GIRONDE) FRANCE
PRODUCE OF FRANCE

- **Ch. Figeac** [fee-zhak] (*St. Emilion Premier Grand Cru, Bordeaux*, France) Forever in the shadow of its neighbour, *Cheval Blanc*, and often unpredictable in its evolution. One of the most characterful *St. Emilions*.
- **Walter Filiputti** [feel-lee-put-tee] (*Friuli- Venezia Guilia*, Italy) Top-ranking winemaker with his own label since 1995. Filiputti's crusade is to prove Pignolo the greatest red grape in Friuli; he makes a range of others as well.
- **Granxa Fillaboa** [gran-shah fee-yah-boh-wah] (*Galicia*, Spain) One of the best *Albariño* producers in *Rias Baixas*.
- **Filliatreau** (*Loire*, France) Exemplary producer of Saumur Champigny which shows how tasty the *Cabernet* Franc can be – and how it can age.
- **Ch. Filhot** [fee-yoh] (*Sauternes*, France) Rarely among the most complex examples of Sauternes, this is nonetheless one of the most reliable sources of well-made, good value wine. ★★★★★ **1997 £££**
  Finger Lakes (*New York State*) Cold region whose producers struggle (sometimes effectively) to produce good *vinifera*, including *Pinot Noir* and *late-harvest Riesling*. *Hybrids* such as *Seyval Blanc* are more reliable. *Fox Run; Heron Hill; Lamaroux Landing; Wagner.*
  Fining The clarifying of young wine before bottling to remove impurities, using a number of agents including *isinglass* and *bentonite*.
  Finish What you can still taste after swallowing.
- **Fino** [fee-noh] (*Jerez*, Spain) Dry, delicate *sherry* which gains its distinctive flavour from the *flor* or yeast which grows on the surface of the wine during maturation. Drink chilled, with tapas, preferably within two weeks of opening. *Lustau; Barbadillo; Hidalgo; Gonzalez Byass.*
- **Firestone** (*Santa Ynez*, California) Good producer – particularly of good value *Chardonnay*, *Merlot* and *Sauvignon* and *late-harvest Riesling* – in southern California.
- **Fisher** (*Sonoma*, California) Top-class producer of limited-production, single-vineyard *Cabernets* and *Chardonnays* from hillside vineyards.

F

☷ **Fitou** [fee-too] (*Midi*, France) Long considered to be an upmarket *Corbières* but actually rather a basic southern *AC*, making reds largely from the *Carignan* grape. The wines here may have become more refined, with a woody warmth, but they never quite shake off their rustic air. **Ch. d'Espigne; Lepaumier; Lerys; de Nouvelles; *Mont Tauch; de Rolland; Val d'Orbieu*.**

☷ **Fixin** [fee-san] (*Burgundy*, France) Northerly village of *Côte de Nuits*, whose lean, tough, uncommercial reds can mature well. New-wave winemaking and later harvesting are thankfully introducing friendlier fare. **Dom Bart; Vincent Berthaut; *Bruno Clair*; Michel Defrance; Derey Frères; Fougeray de Beauclair; Pierre Gelin; André Geoffroy; J-P Guyard; *Louis Jadot*; Philippe Joliet; Denis Philibert.**

Flabby Lacking balancing acidity.

☷ **Ch. La Fleur** [flur] (*St. Emilion, Bordeaux,* France) Small *St. Emilion* property producing softly fruity wines.

☷ **Ch. la Fleur de Gay** [flur duh gay] (*Pomerol, Bordeaux,* France) *Ch. Croix de Gay*'s best wine and thus heavily sought after. Good in 2000 and 2001.

Fleur du Cap (South Africa) Reliable but dull wines. The new Unfiltered Collection has more personality.

☷ **Ch. la Fleur-Pétrus** [flur pay-trooss] (*Pomerol, Bordeaux*, France) For those who find *Pétrus* a touch unaffordable, this next-door neighbour offers gorgeously accessible *Pomerol* flavour for (in *Pétrus* terms) a bargain price.

☷ **Fleurie** [fluh-ree] (*Burgundy*, France) One of the 10 *Beaujolais Crus*, ideally fresh and fragrant, as its name suggests. Best vineyards include La Madonne and Pointe du Jour. Dom. Bachelard and Guy Depardon are names to watch. **90 95 96 97 98 J-M Aujoux; Berrod; P-M Chermette; M Chignard; Després; *Duboeuf*; Ch. Labourons; Dom de la Madone; A Métrat; Andre Vaisse.**

☷ **Finca Flichman** (Argentina) New ownership, by Portugal's *Sogrape*, should help this old-established company. Quality is interesting.

Flor [flawr] Yeast which grows naturally on the surface of some maturing *sherries*, making them potential *finos*.

🍇 **Flora** [flor-rah] A cross between *Semillon* and *Gewürztraminer*, best known in *Brown Brothers Orange Muscat* and Flora.

☷ **Flora Springs** (*Napa Valley*, California) One good, unusual *Sauvignon Blanc* (Soliloquy) and classy *Merlot, Cabernet Sauvignon & Cabernet Franc* blend (Trilogy). ★★★★ **1996 Rutherford Hillside Reserve Cabernet £££**

☷ **Emile Florentin** [floh-ron-tan] (*Rhône,* France) Maker of ultra-traditional, ultra-*tannic*, chewy *St. Joseph.* ★★★★ **St. Joseph Clos de l'Arbalestrier £££**

Flying winemakers Young winemakers contracted by overseas customers make better and more reliable wine than wineries' own teams can manage. Often, European co-operatives' wines are transformed by picking riper grapes and keeping tanks and pipes clean.

☷ **Vinha do Fojo** (*Douro*, Portugal) Critical acclaim for this table wine sent prices soaring. It's dense and good, but having to look to its laurels.

☷ **Ch. Fombrauge** [fom-brohzh] (*St. Emilion, Bordeaux,* France) *St. Emilion* that is improving since its purchase by the owners of *Malesan.*

☷ **Ch. Fonbadet** (*Bordeaux*, France) Reliable, good value *Pauillac* Cru Bourgeois. Made an attractive 2001.

☷ **Ch. Fonplégade** [fon-pleh-gahd] (*St. Emilion Grand Cru Classé, Bordeaux,* France) If you like your *St. Emilion* tough, this is for you.

☷ **Ch. Fonréaud** (*Bordeaux*, France) Unusually approachable *Listrac.*

☷ **Ch. Fonroque** [fon-rok] (*St. Emilion Grand Cru Classé, Bordeaux,* France) Property with concentrated wines, but not always one of *Moueix*'s very finest.

☷ **Fonseca Guimaraens** [fon-say-ka gih-mah-rans] (*Douro*, Portugal) A subsidiary of *Taylor*'s, but independently making great *port*. Often beats supposedly classier houses' supposedly finer vintages. ★★★★★ **1984**

☷ **JM da Fonseca Internacional** [fon-say-ka in-tuhr-nah-soh-nahl] (*Setúbal Peninsula*, Portugal) Highly commercial firm whose wines include Lancers, the *Mateus*-taste-alike sold in mock-crocks.

F

⊻ JM da Fonseca Successores [fon-say-ka suk-ses-saw-rays] (*Estremadura,* Portugal) Unrelated to the *port* house of the same name and no longer connected to *JM da Fonseca Internacional*. Family-run firm, which with *Aliança* and *Sogrape* is one of Portugal's big three dynamic wine companies. Top reds include Pasmados, *Periquita* (from the grape of the same name), *Quinta da Camarate*, Terras Altas Dão, and the *Cabernet*-influenced "TE" *Garrafeiras*. Dry whites are less impressive, but the sweet old *Moscatel de Setúbals* are luscious classics. ★★★★ **1997 Moscatel de Setúbal,Terras do Sado ££££**

⊻ Dom. Font de Michelle [fon-duh-mee-shel] (*Rhône,* France) Reliable producer of medium-bodied red *Châteauneuf-du-Pape* and small quantities of excellent, almost unobtainable, white.

⊻ Fontana Candida [fon-tah-nah kan-dee-dah] (*Lazio,* Italy) Good producer, especially for *Frascati*. The top wine is Colle Gaio.

⊻ Fontanafredda [fon-tah-nah-freh-dah] (*Piedmont,* Italy) Big producer with impressive *Asti* and very approachable (especially single-vineyard) *Barolo*.

⊻ Ch. Fontenil (*Bordeaux,* France) Michel Rolland is the name behind this *Fronsac* property. Predictably rich, oaky wines.

⊻ Domaine de Font Sane [fon-sen] (*Rhône,* France) Producer of fine *Gigondas*. Very traditional and full-bodied.

⊻ Castello di Fonterutoli (*Tuscany,* Italy) *Chianti* Classico producer of real class, which also produces great non-*DOC* blends: Concerto and Siepi.

⊻ Fontodi [Fon-toh-dee] (*Tuscany,* Italy) Classy Tuscan producer with Flaccianello, a truly top class *Vino da Tavola*.

⊻ Foradori [Foh-rah-doh-ree] (*Trentino,* Italy) Specialist producer of *Teroldego* (Granato is the reserve wine) plus an inventive *Chardonnay-Pinot Bianco-Sauvignon* white blend.

⊻ Forman (*Napa Valley,* California) Rick Forman makes good *Cabernet* and *Merlot* and refreshingly crisp *Chardonnay*.

Forst [fawrst] (*Pfalz,* Germany) Wine town producing great concentrated *Riesling*. Famous for the *Jesuitengarten* vineyard.

⊻ Fortant de France [faw-tan duh frons] (*Languedoc-Roussillon,* France) Good-quality revolutionary brand owned by *Skalli* and specializing in varietal *Vin de Pays d'Oc*.

⊻ Château Fortia (*Rhône,* France) Improving ultra-traditional *Châteauneuf-du-Pape* estate.

⊻ Les Forts de Latour [lay faw duh lah-toor] (*Pauillac, Bordeaux,* France) *Second label* of *Ch. Latour*. Like the *second labels* of other top châteaux; still often better than lesser *classed growth châteaux'* top wines. Very fine 2000.

⊻ Ch. Fourcas-Dupré [foor-kah doo-pray] (*Listrac Cru Bourgeois, Bordeaux,* France) Tough, very traditional *Listrac*.

⊻ Ch. Fourcas-Hosten [foor-kah hos-ten] (*Listrac Cru Bourgeois, Bordeaux,* France) Improving *Listrac* property.

⊻ Fox Run Vineyards (*New York*) Successful Finger Lakes producer, with good sparkling wine, *Riesling*, and *Chardonnay*.

⊻ Foxen (*Santa Ynez,* California) Successful producer of single-vineyard *Pinot* and *Chardonnay*, now moving into *Syrah*.

⊻ Ch. de France (*Bordeaux,* France) Pessac-Léognan property benefitting from tighter selection and later picking. One to watch.

⊻ Franciacorta [fran-chee yah-kor-tah] (*Lombardy,* Italy) *DOC* for good, light, French-influenced reds but better noted for – often Champagne-price – sparklers *Champagne*. *Bellavista; Ca' Del Bosco; Cavalleri; Monte Rossa;* Uberti.

F

Franciscan Vineyards [fran-sis-kan] (*Napa Valley*, California) Now part of the huge Canandaigua company, reliable *Napa* winery whose Chilean boss, Augustin Huneeus, has pioneered natural yeast wines with his *Burgundy*-like "Cuvée Sauvage" *Chardonnay* and has punctured the pretentious balloons of some of his neighbours. Now also making wine in Chile – at *Veramonte*.

Ch. Franc-Mayne [fron' mayn] (*Bordeaux*, France) *St-Emilion Grand Cru Classé* with improving quality and deep pockets for investment.

Ch. de Francs [duh fron] (*Côtes de Francs, Bordeaux*, France) Well-run estate which makes great-value crunchy, blackcurranty wine and, with *Ch. Puygeraud*, helps to prove the worth of this little-known region.

Franken [fran-ken] (Germany) *Anbaugebiet* making characterful, sometimes earthy, dry whites, traditionally presented in the squat, flagon-shaped "*Bocksbeutel*" on which the *Mateus* bottle was modelled. A key variety is the *Silvaner*, which explains the earthiness of many of the wines. Juliusspital; Horst Sauer; Reiss. ★★★★★ 2001 Silvaner Eiswein Horst Sauer ££££

Franschhoek [fran-shook] (South Africa) Valley leading into the mountains away from Paarl. The best producers are mostly clustered at the top of the valley, around the picturesque town. Dieu Donne; Veenwouden; Graham Beck.

Frascati [fras-kah-tee] (*Latium*, Italy) Clichéd dry or semi-dry white from *Latium*. At its best it is soft and clean with a fascinating "sour cream" flavour. Drink within 12 months of *vintage*. *Fontana Candida;* Pallavincini.

Ca' dei Frati [kah day-yee frah-tee] (*Lombardy*, Italy) Fine producers of *Lugana* and *Chardonnay*-based sparkling wine. ★★★ 2000 'Brolettino' ££

Freemark Abbey (*Napa Valley*, California) Well-regarded (in the US) producer of good *Cabernet*. The Bosche examples are the ones to look for. ★★★★★ 1995 Freemark Abbey Bosche Cabernet £££

Freie Weingärtner Wachau [fri-eh vine-gehrt-nur vah-kow] (*Wachau*, Austria) Fine co-operative with great vineyards, dry and sweet versions of the *Grüner Veltliner* and gloriously concentrated *Rieslings* that outclass the efforts of many a big-name estate in Germany.

Freisa [fray-ee-sah] (Italy) Perfumed red wine grape with lovely cherryish, raspberryish flavours, popular with Hemingway and grown in *Piedmont* by producers like Gilli and *Vajra*. Drink young. *Bava; Aldo Conterno.*

Freixenet [fresh-net] (*Catalonia*, Spain) Giant in the *cava* field and proponent of traditional *Catalonian* grapes in sparkling wine. Its dull, off-dry big-selling *Cordon Negro* made from traditional grapes is a perfect justification for adding *Chardonnay* to the blend. ★★★★★ 1998 Prior Terrae ££££

Marchesi de' Frescobaldi [mah-kay-see day fres-koh-bal-dee] (*Tuscany*, Italy) Family estate with classy wines: *Castelgiocondo*, Mormoreto (*Cabernet Sauvignon*-based wine), the rich white Pomino Il Benefizio *Chardonnay*, *Pomino Rosso* using *Merlot* and *Cabernet Sauvignon*, and Nippozano in *Chianti*. Now in joint venture to make *Luce* with *Mondavi*. ★★★★ 1999 Montesodi Chianti Rufina £; ★★★ 1999 Mormoreto Chianti Rufina ££££

Freycinet [fres-sih-net] (*Tasmania*, Australia) Small East Coast winery with some of Australia's best *Pinot Noir* and great *Chardonnay*.

Friuli-Venezia Giulia [free-yoo-lee veh-neht-zee-yah zhee-yoo-lee-yah] (Italy) Northerly region containing a number of *DOCs*: Colli Orientali, Collio, Friuli Grave and Aquileia and Isonzo, with single-variety wines like *Merlot*, *Cabernet Franc, Pinot Bianco, Pinot Grigio*, and *Tocai*. Some are dilute and over-cropped; others are complex masterpieces. Jermann; Bidoli; Puiatti; Feudi di Romans; Zof.

J Fritz (*Sonoma*, California) Serious producer of *Dry Creek Sauvignon Blanc* that actually does repay ageing.

Frizzante [freet-zan-tay] (Italy) Semi-sparkling, especially *Lambrusco*.

Frog's Leap (*Napa Valley*, California) Winery with a fine sense of humour (their slogan is "Time's fun when you're having flies".). Tasty *Zinfandel*, "wild yeast" *Chardonnay*, and unusually good *Sauvignon Blanc*. ★★★★ 1997 Frog's Leap Cabernet Sauvignon Blend £££

G

☗ **Fronsac/Canon Fronsac** [fron-sak] (*Bordeaux,* France) *Pomerol* neighbours, who regularly produce rich, intense, affordable wines. They are rarely subtle. However, with some good winemaking from men like *Christian Moueix* of *Ch. Pétrus,* they can often represent some of the best buys in *Bordeaux.* Canon Fronsac is thought by some to be the better of the pair. *Ch. Canon*; Cassagne; la Vieille; Arnauton; Mayne-Vieil; *Dalem*; Fontenil.

☗ **Frontignan** [fron-tin-yo'n] (France) Source of sweet, fortified Muscat Vin Doux Naturel. Usually lacks the finesse of Muscat de Beaumes des Venise.

☗ **Ch. de Fuissé** [duh fwee-say] (*Burgundy,* France) Jean-Jacques Vincent makes wines comparable to some of the best of the *Côte d'Or.* The *Vieilles Vignes* can last as long as a good *Chassagne-Montrachet,* the other *cuvées* run it a close race. ★★★ **2000** Château de Fuissé Pouilly-Fuissé

Fumé Blanc [fyoo-may blahnk] Name originally adapted from *Pouilly Blanc Fumé* by *Robert Mondavi* to describe his California oaked *Sauvignon.* Now widely used – though not exclusively – in the New World for this style.

☗ **Furmint** [foor-mint] (*Tokaji,* Hungary) Lemony white grape, used in Hungary for *Tokaji* and, given modern winemaking, good dry wines. See *Royal Tokaji Wine Co* and *Disznókö.*

☗ **Rudolf Fürst** [foorst] (*Franken,* Germany) One of Germany's best producers of ripe red *Pinot Noir Spätburgunder,* and lovely floral *Riesling.*

☗ **Fürstlich Castell'sches Domänenamt** [foorst-likh kas-tel-shes doh-mehnen-amt] (*Franken,* Germany) Prestigious producer of typically full-bodied dry whites from the German *Anbaugebiet* of *Franken.*

Fûts de Chêne (élévé en) [foo duh shayne] (France) Oak barrels (aged in).

Futures See *En Primeur.*

G

☗ **Ch. la Gaffelière** [gaf-fuh-lyehr] (*St. Emilion Premier Grand Cru, Bordeaux,* France) Lightish-bodied but well-made wines. Not to be confused with *Ch. Canon la Gaffelière.*

☗ **Dom. Jean-Noël Gagnard** [jon noh-wel gan-yahr] (*Burgundy,* France) A *domaine* with vineyards across *Chassagne-Montrachet.* There is also some *Santenay.* ★★★ **1999** Chassagne-Montrachet Les Caillerets 1er Cru £££

☗ **Jacques Gagnard-Delagrange** [gan-yahr duh lag-ronzh] (*Burgundy,* France) A top-class producer who favours a light touch with oak. *Blain-Gagnard* and *Fontaine-Gagnard* are good estates owned by his daughters.

☗ **Gaia** [gai-ee-yahr] (*Nemea,* Greece) Up-and-coming modern estate.

Gaillac [gai-yak] (*South-West* France) Light, fresh, good-value reds and (sweet, dry and slightly sparkling) whites, produced using *Gamay* and *Sauvignon* grapes, as well as the indigenous *Mauzac.* The reds can rival *Beaujolais. Ch.* Clement Ternes; Labastide de Levis; Domaine de Gineste.

☗ **Pierre Gaillard** [gai-yahr] (*Rhône,* France) A good producer of *Côte Rôtie, St. Joseph,* and *Condrieu.* ★★★★ **1997** Côtes Brune et Blonde Côte Rôtie £££

☗ **Gainey Vineyard** [gay-nee] (*Santa Barbara,* California) Classy *Merlot, Pinot* and *Chardonnay.*

☗ **Gaja** [gai-yah] (*Piedmont,* Italy) In 1999, Angelo Gaja, the man who proved that wines from *Barbaresco* could sell for higher prices than top-class *clarets,* let alone the supposedly classier neighbours *Barolo,* announced that his highly prized – and priced – individual vineyard *Barbaresco* would henceforth be sold under the *Langhe* denomination. This would, he argued, focus attention on his excellent blended *Barolo* and *Barbaresco.* Whatever their legal handle, questioning the price of these wines is like querying the cost of a Ferrari. ★★★★★ **1997** Barberesco ££££

Galestro [gah-less-troh] (*Tuscany,* Italy) The light white of the *Chianti* region. *Antinori; Frescobaldi.*

G

♔ **E & J Gallo** [gal-loh] (*Central Valley,* California) The world's biggest wine producer; with around 60 per cent of the total California harvest. The top end *Cabernet* and (particularly impressive) *Chardonnay* from individual "ranch" vineyards and Gallo's own "Northern *Sonoma* Estate", a piece of land which was physically recontoured by their bulldozers. The new Turning Leaf wines are good too, at their level. The rest of the basic range, though much improved and very widely stocked, is still pretty ordinary. ★★★★ 1998 Northern Sonoma Chardonnay £££; ★★★★ 1998 Sonoma Selection Cabernet Sauvignon ££

⚘ **Gamay** [ga-may] (*Beaujolais,* France) Light-skinned grape traditional to *Beaujolais* where it is used to make fresh and fruity reds for early drinking, usually by the *carbonic maceration* method, and more serious *cru* wines that resemble light *Burgundy.* Also successful in California (*J Lohr*), Australia (*Sorrenberg*) and South Africa (*Fairview*).

⚘ **Gamay** [ga-may] (California) Confusingly unrelated to the *Gamay.*
Gamey Smell or taste oddly reminiscent of hung game – associated with *Pinot Noir* and *Syrah.* Sometimes partly attributable to the combination of those grapes' natural characteristics with careless use of *sulphur dioxide.* Another explanation can be the presence of a vineyard infection called Brettanomyces, feared in California but often unnoticed in France where gamey wines are (sometimes approvingly) said to "renarder" – to smell of fox.

⚘ **Gamza** [gam-zah] (Bulgaria) Local name for the Kadarka grape of Hungary.

♔ **Gancia** [gan-chee-yah] (*Piedmont,* Italy) Reliable producer of *Asti* and good dry *Pinot* di *Pinot,* as well as *Pinot Blanc* sparkling wine.

♔ **Vin de Pays du Gard** [doo gahr'] (*Languedoc-Roussillon,* France) Fresh, undemanding red and rosé wines from the southern part of the *Rhône.* Drink young, and quite possibly chilled.

♔ **Garganega** [gahr-GAN-nay-gah] (Italy) White grape at its best – and worst – in *Soave* in the *Veneto.* In the right site and when not overcropped, it produces interesting almondy flavours. Otherwise the wines it makes are simply light and dull. Now being blended with *Chardonnay.*

⚘ **Garnacha** [gahr-na-cha] (Spain and France) See *Grenache.*
Garrafeira [gah-rah-fay-rah] (Portugal) Indicates a producer's *"reserve"* wine, which has been selected and given extra time in cask (minimum two years) and bottle (minimum one year).

♔ **Garvey** [gahr-vay] (*Jerez,* Spain) Old-established sherry producer, most famous for good San Patricio fino.

♔ **Vincent Gasse** [gass] (*Rhône,* France) Next to the La Landonne vineyard and producing superb, concentrated, inky black wines.

♔ **Gattinara** [Gat-tee-nah-rah] (*Piedmont,* Italy) Red *DOC* from the *Nebbiolo* – varying in quality but generally full-flavoured and dry. **Travaglini.**

♔ **Domaine Gauby** [Goh-Bee] (*Côtes de Roussillon,* France) Serious *Roussillon* reds and (*Muscat*) whites. The Muntada *Syrah* is the top *cuvée.*

♔ **Gavi** [gah-vee] (*Piedmont,* Italy) Often unexceptional white wine from the *Cortese* grape. Compared by Italians to white *Burgundy,* with which it and the creamily pleasant Gavi di Gavi share a propensity for high prices. ★★★★ 2001 Villa Lanata Gavi di Gavi ££

♔ **Ch. le Gay** [luh gay] (*Pomerol, Bordeaux,* France) Good *Moueix* property with intense complex wine.

♔ **Ch. Gazin** [Ga-zan] (*Pomerol, Bordeaux,* France) Increasingly polished since the mid-1980s.
Geelong [zhee-long] (*Victoria,* Australia) Cool region pioneered by Idyll Vineyards (makers of old-fashioned reds) and rapidly attracting notice with Clyde Park and with *Bannockburn's* and *Scotchman Hill's Pinot Noirs.* ★★★ 2000 Shadowfax Pinot Noir ££
Geisenheim [gi-zen-hime] (*Rheingau,* Germany) Home of the German Wine Institute wine school, once one of the best in the world, but now overtaken by more progressive seats of learning in France, California, and Australia.

G

Ch. de la Genaiserie [Jeh-nay-seh-Ree] (*Loire*, France) Classy, lusciously honeyed, single-vineyard wines from *Coteaux du Layon*.

Generoso [zheh-neh-roh-soh] (Spain) Fortified or dessert wine.

Genève [jer-nev] (Switzerland) Region best known for high quality, if often lightweight, *Gamay* and slightly sparkling "Perlan" *Chasselas*.

Gentilini [zhen-tee-lee-nee] (*Cephalonia*, Greece) One of Greece's best new wave producers, Nick Cosmetatos makes impressive modern white wines, using both classic Greek grapes and French varieties. ★★★★ **2001 Corelli's Ribola ££**

JM Gerin [ger-an] (*Rhône*, France) A producer of good modern *Côte Rôtie* and *Condrieu*; uses new oak to make powerful, long-lived wines.

Gerovassilou [jeh-roh-vah-see-loo] (*Cephalonia*, Greece) Producer of successful new wave whites, including impressive *Viognier.*

Gevrey-Chambertin [zheh-vray shom-behr-tan] (*Burgundy*, France) Best-known big red *Côte de Nuits commune*; very variable, but still capable of superb, plummy, cherryish wine. The top *Grand Cru* is *Le Chambertin* but, in the right hands, *Premiers Crus* like Les Cazetiers can beat this and the other *Grands Crus*. Denis Bachelet; Albert Bichot; Alain Burguet; Bourrée (Vallet); Champy, Charlopin; Bruno Clair; P. Damoy; Joseph Drouhin; Dugat-Py; Dujac; Leroy; Château de Marsannay; Denis Mortet; Henri Rebourseau; Roty; Rossignol-Trapet; Armand Rousseau; Marc Roy; Gérard Seguin.

🍇 **Gewürztraminer** [geh-voort-strah-mee-nehr] White (well, slightly pink) grape, making dry-to-sweet, full, oily-textured, spicy wine. Best in *Alsace* (where it is spelled Gewurztraminer, without the umlaut accent) but also grown in Australasia, Italy, the US, and Eastern Europe. Instantly recognisable by its parma-violets-and-lychees character. **Alsace; Casablanca.**

Geyser Peak [Gih-Suhr] (*Alexander Valley*, California) Australian winemaker Darryl Groom revolutionized Californian thinking in this once Australian-owned winery with his *Semillon-Chardonnay* blend, and with reds which show an Australian attitude toward ripe *tannin*. A name to watch. Canyon Road is the good-value *second label*. ★★★★★ **1999 Geyser Peak Reserve Sonoma County Cabernet Sauvignon £££**

Ghemme [gem-may] (*Piedmont*, Italy) Spicy *Nebbiolo* usually unfavourably compared to its neighbour *Gattinara*. Cantalupo is the star producer.

Ghiaie della Furba see *Capezzana*.

Giaconda [zhee-ya-kon-dah] (*Victoria*, Australia) Small winery hidden away high in the hills. Sells out of its impressive *Pinot Noir* and *Chardonnay en primeur*. The *Cabernet* is fine too.

Bruno Giacosa [zhee-yah-koh-sah] (*Piedmont*, Italy) Stunning winemaker with a large range, including *Barolos* (Vigna Rionda in best years) and *Barbarescos* (Santo Stefano, again, in best years). Recent success with whites, including a *Spumante*.

Gie les Rameaux [lay ram-moh] (*Corsica*, France) One of this island's top producers.

Giesen [gee-sen] (*Canterbury*, New Zealand) Small estate, with particularly appley *Riesling* (plus a late harvest version) from *Canterbury*, and *Sauvignon* from *Marlborough*. ★★★ **2001 Giesen Marlborough Blanc £**

Gigondas [zhee gon-dass] (*Rhône*, France) *Côtes du Rhône commune*, with good-value, spicy/peppery, blackcurrant reds which show the *Grenache* at its best. A good competitor for nearby Châteauneuf. **Dom des Bosquets; Brusset; de Cabasse; du Cayron; Delas; Font-Sane; Entrefaux; des Espiers; les Goubert; Guigal; Pochon; Sorrel; de Thalabert; Vidal-Fleury.**

Ch. Gilette [zheel-lette] (*Sauternes, Bordeaux*, France) Eccentric, unclassified but of classed-growth quality *Sauternes* kept in tank (rather than cask) for 20 or 30 years. Rare, expensive, worth it.

Gimblett Road (*Hawkes Bay*, New Zealand). New appellation for New Zealand – including the best land in Hawkes Bay. ★★★ **2000 Matariki Reserve Chardonnay ££;** ★★★ **1999 Gimblett Road Chardonnay Trinity Hill £££.**

Ginestet [jeen-nes-stay] (*Bordeaux*, France) Huge *Bordeaux* merchant

Gippsland [gip-sland] (*Victoria*, Australia) Up-and-coming coastal region where *Bass Philip* and *Nicholson River* are producing fascinating and quite European-style wines. Watch out for some of Australia's finest *Pinot Noirs*.

Vincent Girardin [van-son zhee-rahr-dan] (*Burgundy*, France) Dynamic *Santenay* producer and (since 1996) *négociant*, with vines in several other *communes*. ★★★ 2000 Rully 1er Cru Les Cloux ££

Giropalette [zhee-roh-pal-let] Large machine which automatically and highly efficiently replaces the human beings who used to perform the task of *remuage*. Used by most *Champagne* houses which, needless to say, prefer to conceal them from visiting tourists.

Camille Giroud [kah-mee zhee-roo] (*Burgundy*, France) Traditional *négociant* with small stocks of great mature wine that go a long way to prove that good *Burgundy* really doesn't need oak to taste good. A change of ownership in 2002 should – paradoxically – guarantee continuity.

Gisborne [giz-bawn] (New Zealand) North Island vine-growing area since the 1920s. Cool, wettish climate, giving New Zealand's best *Chardonnay*. An ideal partner for *Marlborough* in blends. *Corbans;* Kim Crawford; Matawhero; *Matua Valley; Millton; Montana; Revington;* Tohu Wines.

Ch. Giscours [zhees-koor] (*Margaux 3ème Cru Classé, Bordeaux*, France) Recently-bought *Margaux* property which is only (since 1999) beginning to offer the quality associated with the vintages of the late 1970s. A good 2001.

Louis Gisselbrecht [gees-sel-brekt] (*Alsace*, France) Recommendable grower and *negociant* which, like cousin Willy, has good vines in the Frankstein *Grand Cru*.

Givry [zheev-ree] (*Burgundy*, France) *Côte Chalonnaise commune*, making typical and affordable, if rather jammily rustic, reds and creamy whites. French wine snobs recall that this was one of King Henri IV's favourite wines, forgetting the fact that a) he had many such favourites dotted all over France and b) his mistress – of whom he also probably had several – happened to live here. Bourgeon; Derain; *Joblot;* Lumpp; Mouton; Ragot; Clos Salomon; Steinmaier; Thénard.

Glen Carlou [kah-loo] (*Paarl*, South Africa) Small-scale winery with rich, oily, oaky *Chardonnay*. ★★★★★ 2000 Glen Carlou Chardonnay Reserve ££; ★★★★★ 2001 Glen Carlou Shiraz ££.

Glen Ellen (*Sonoma Valley*, California) Dynamic firm producing large amounts of commercial tropical fruit juice-like *Chardonnay* under its "Proprietor's Reserve" label. Reds are better value.

Glenrowan [glen-roh-wan] (*Victoria*, Australia) Area near *Rutherglen* with a similar range of excellent *liqueur Muscats* and *Tokays*.

Ch. Gloria [glaw-ree-yah] (*St. Julien Cru Bourgeois, Bordeaux*, France) One of the first of the super *Crus Bourgeois*. Now back on form.

Golan [goh-lan] (Israel) One of the three principal labels used by the *Golan Heights Winery*.

Golan Heights Winery [goh-lan] (Israel) California expertise is used to produce good *Kosher Cabernet* and *Muscat*. Labels include Gamla, Golan, and Yarden (used for the top wines).

Goldwater Estate (*Auckland*, New Zealand) *Bordeaux*-like red wine specialist on *Waiheke Island* whose wines are expensive but every bit as good as many similarly-priced Californian offerings. The *Sauvignon Blanc* is fine too, if leaner than most New Zealand examples.

La Gomerie [lah goh'm-ree] (*Bordeaux*, France) 100 per cent Merlot garage wine produced by the owners of Ch. Beau-Séjour-Bécot.

G

Ⅼ **Gonzalez Byass** [gon-thah-leth bee-yass] (*Jerez*, Spain) If *sherry* is beginning to enjoy a long-awaited comeback, this is the company that should take much of the credit. Producer of the world's best-selling *fino*, *Tio Pepe* – and a supporting cast of the finest, most complex, traditional *sherries* available to mankind. ★★★★★ **Matusalem ££**

Ⅼ **Gordon Brothers** (*Washington State*) Grapegrowers-turned-winemakers, and now a name to look for when shopping for well-made *Washington State Merlot* and *Chardonnay*

Ⅼ **Gosset** [gos-say] (*Champagne*, France) The oldest house in *Champagne* producing some marvellous and very long-lived *cuvées*, particularly the Celebris. ★★★★ **1995 Celebris £££**

Ⅼ **Henri Gouges** [Gooj] (*Burgundy*, France) Long-established *Nuits St. Georges* estate, producing some truly classic, long-lived wines. ★★★★★ **1999 Nuits St. Georges les Porrets ££**

Ⅼ **Marquis de Goulaine** [goo-layn] (*Loire*, France) One of the best producers of *Muscadet* – and a butterfly museum to boot. **Goulburn Valley** [gohl-boorn] (*Victoria*, Australia) Small, long-established region, now known as Nagambic and reigned over by the respectively ancient and modern *Ch. Tahbilk* and *Mitchelton*, both of whom make great *Marsanne*, though in very different styles. Also **Osicka; Plunkett; David Traeger; McPherson.** ★★★★★ **1999 Chateau Tahbilk Shiraz ££**

Ⅼ **Gould Campbell** [goold] (*Douro*, Portugal) Underrated member of the same stable as *Dow's*, *Graham's* and *Warre's*. **Goumenissa** [goo-may-nee-sah] (Greece) Appellation for sturdy reds from Macedonia. ★★★ **2000 Goumenissa Boutari J. Boutari & Son £**

Ⅼ **Goundrey** [gown-dree] (*Western* Australia) Winery in the up-and-coming region of *Mount Barker*, bought by an American millionaire who has continued the founder's policy of making fruity but not overstated *Chardonnay* and *Cabernet*. **Graach** [grahkh] (*Mosel-Saar-Ruwer*, Germany) *Mittelmosel* village producing fine wines. Best known for its *Himmelreich* vineyard. **Deinhard; JJ Prüm; Max Ferd Richter; Von Kesselstadt.**

Ⅼ **Grace Family Vineyards** (*Napa*, California) Small quantities – occasionally fewer than 100 cases – of *Cabernet* whose rarity makes for prices of £300-400 per bottle. (If potatoes were harder to grow, they'd cost more, too.) **Viña Gracia** [veen-yah gra-see-yah] (Chile) Rapidly-improving venture. Good Cabernet Reserva; look out for *Syrah* and *Mourvèdre* in the future. ★★★★★ **2000 Gracia de Chile, Porquenó Reserva Lo Mejor Cabernet Sauvignon ££**

Ⅼ **Graham** [gray-yam] (*Douro*, Portugal) Sweetly delicate wines that can outclass the same stable's supposedly finer but heftier *Dow's*. Malvedos is erroneously thought of as the single *quinta*. ★★★★★ **NV Graham's Crusted Port Bottled 1999 W & J Graham ££**

Ⅼ **Alain Graillot** [al-lan grai-yoh] (*Rhône*, France) Progressive-minded producer who should be applauded for shaking up the sleepy, largely undistinguished *appellation* of *Crozes-Hermitage*, using grapes from rented vineyards. All the reds are excellent, and La Guiraude is the wine from the top vineyard. ★★★★ **1999 Crozes Hermitage ££** **Grampians** (*Victoria*, Australia) New name for *Great Western*.

Ch. Grand-Corbin-Despagne [gro'n cor-ba'n day-span'y] (*Bordeaux*, France) *St-Emilion Grand Cru* that used to be a *Grand Cru Classé* and is determined to be so again. Quality improving year by year; value is excellent.

Gran Reserva [gran rays-sehr-vah] (Spain) Quality wine aged for a designated number of years in wood and, in theory, only produced in the best *vintages*. However, Gran Reserva can on occasion be dried out and less worthwhile than *Crianza* or *Reserva*.

Grand Cru [gron kroo] (France) Prepare to be confused. Term referring to the finest vineyards and the – supposedly – equally fine wine made in them. It is an official designation in *Bordeaux, Burgundy, Champagne* and *Alsace,* but its use varies. In *Alsace* where there are 50 or so *Grand Cru* vineyards, some are more convincingly grand than others. In *Burgundy Grand Cru* vineyards with their own *AC*s, e.g., *Montrachet,* do not need to carry the name of the village (e.g., *Chassagne-Montrachet*) on their label. Where these regions apply the designation to pieces of soil, in *Bordeaux* it applies to châteaux whose vineyards can be bought and sold. More confusingly, still *St. Emilion* can be described as either *Grand Cru, Grand Cru Classé* – or both – or *Premier Grand Cru Classé.* Just remember that in St. Emilion, the words *Grand Cru* by themselves provide absolutely no indication of quality at all.

⏆ **Ch. Grand Mayne** [Gron-mayn] (*St. Emilion Grand Cru, Bordeaux,* France) Producer of rich, deeply flavoursome, modern *St. Emilion.* A candidate for promotion to *Premier Grand Cru* status.

⏆ **Ch. du Grand Moulas** [gron moo-lahs] (*Rhône,* France) Very classy *Côtes du Rhône* property with unusually complex red wines.

Grand Vin [gron van] (*Bordeaux,* France) The first (quality) wine of an estate – as opposed to its *second label.*

⏆ **Ch. Grand-Pontet** [gron pon-tay] (*St. Emilion Grand Cru Classé, Bordeaux,* France) Rising star with showy wines.

⏆ **Ch. Grand-Puy-Ducasse** [gron pwee doo-kass] (*Pauillac 5ème Cru Classé, Bordeaux,* France) Excellent wines from an over-performing fifth growth *Pauillac* property.

⏆ **Ch. Grand-Puy-Lacoste** [gron pwee lah-kost] (*Pauillac 5ème Cru Classé, Bordeaux,* France) Top-class fifth growth owned by the Borie family of *Ducru-Beaucaillou* and now right up there among the *Super Seconds.*

⏆ **Grande Rue** [grond-roo] (*Burgundy,* France) Recently promoted *Grand Cru* in Vosne-Romanée, across the way from Romanée-Conti (hence the promotion). Sadly, the Dom. Lamarche to which this *monopole* belongs is an improving but long-term underperformer.

Grandes Marques [grond mahrk] (*Champagne,* France) Once-official designation for "big name" *Champagne* houses, irrespective of the quality of their wines. Now, although the "Syndicat" of which they were members has been disbanded, the expression is still quite widely used.

⏆ **Grands-Echézeaux** [grons EH-shay-zoh] (*Burgundy,* France) One of the best *Grand Crus* in *Burgundy*; and supposedly better than *Echézeaux.* The *Domaine de la Romanée-Conti* is a famous producer here.

⏆ **Grange** [graynzh] (*South Australia*) *Penfolds'* and Australia's greatest wine – "The Southern Hemisphere's only first growth" – pioneered by Max Schubert in the early 1950s following a visit to Europe. Although Schubert was aiming to match top *Bordeaux,* he used *Shiraz* and American (rather than French) oak barrels and a blend of grapes from 70-year-old vines sited in several South Australian regions. Now very popular in the US. It needs time for its true complexity to become apparent.

⏆ **Dom de la Grange des Pères** [gronj day pehr] (*Languedoc,* France) A competitor for *Mas de Daumas Gassac.* Vin de Pays de l'Hérault that's better than many from a smart appellation.

⏆ **Grangehurst** [graynzh-huhrst] (*Stellenbosch,* South Africa) Concentrated modern reds from a small winery converted from the family squash court! Expanding. Good *Cabernet* and *Pinotage.*

Granite Belt (*Queensland,* Australia) High altitude vineyards but still not cool as cool goes. Best for reds and *Semillon.*

⏆ **Weingut Grans-Fassian** [grans-fass-yan] (*Mosel,* Germany) Improving estate with some really fine, classic wine – especially at a supposedly basic level.

G

Grão Vasco [grow vash-koo] (*Dão*, Portugal) Large volume, reliable brand of *Dão* from *Sogrape*.

ℑ **Yves Grassa** [gras-sah] (*Southwest*, France). Pioneering producer of *Vin de Pays des Côtes de Gascogne* – moving from *Colombard* and *Ugni Blanc* into *Sauvignon* and *late-harvest* styles.

ℑ **Elio Grasso** [eh-lee-yoh grah-so] (*Piedmont*, Italy) Producer of high quality, single-vineyard *Barolo* (Casa Maté and Chiniera), *Barbera*, *Dolcetto*, and *Chardonnay*.

ℑ **Alfred Gratien** [gras-see-yen] (*Champagne*, France) Good *Champagne* house, using traditional methods. Also owner of *Loire* sparkling winemaker Gratien et Meyer, based in *Saumur*.

❦ **Grauerburgunder** [grow-uh-buhr-goon-duhr] (Germany) Another name for *Pinot Gris*. *Müller-Catoir.*

ℑ **Dom. la Grave** [lah grahv] (*Graves, Bordeaux*, France) Small property in the *Graves* with a growing reputation for 100 per cent *Sémillon* whites.

ℑ **La Grave à Pomerol** [lah grahv ah pom-rohl] (*Pomerol, Bordeaux*, France) One of the excellent Christian *Mouiex's* characteristically stylish estates that shows off *Pomerol's* plummy-cherry fruit at its best.

ℑ **Grave del Friuli** [grah-veh del free-yoo lce] (*Friuli-Venezia Giulia*, Italy) DOC for young-drinking reds and whites. *Cabernet, Merlot*, and *Chardonnay* are increasingly successful.

ℑ **Graves** [grahv] (*Bordeaux*, France) Large region producing vast quantities of red and white, ranging from good to indifferent. The best whites come from *Pessac-Léognan* in the northern part of the region. Reds can have a lovely raspberryish character. **Ch. d'Archambeau; de Chantegrive; Clos Floridène; Lesparre; Rahoul; du Seuil; Villa Bel Air.**

ℑ **Josko Gravner** [grahv-nehr] (*Friuli-Venezia Giulia*, Italy) Innovative producer with brilliant oaked *Chardonnay* and *Sauvignon Blanc* produced in *Collio* but not under the rules of that denomination. The blended white Breg, which includes no fewer than six varieties, is good too, as is Rujino, a mixture of *Merlot* and *Cabernet Sauvignon*.

Great Western (*Victoria*, Australia) Old name for region noted for *Seppelt's* sparkling wines including the astonishing "Sparkling *Burgundy*" *Shirazes*, for *Best's* and for the wines of *Mount Langi Ghiran*. Now renamed *Grampians*, though I suspect it will take time for enthusiasts to get used to the new name.

❦ **Grechetto** [grek-keh-toh] (Italy) Subtly spicy white grape used to fine effect in *Umbria* by *Adanti, Falesco*, Goretti and Palazzone.

ℑ **Greco di Tufo** [greh-koh dee too-foh] (*Campania*, Italy) From *Campania*, best-known white from the ancient Greco grape; dry, characterfully herby southern wine. **Botromagno; Librandi; Mastroberardino; Feudi di San Gregorio.**

Greece This country is finally, if belatedly, beginning to exploit the potential of a set of grapes grown nowhere else. Unfortunately, as Greece begins to rid itself of its taste for the stewed, oxidized styles of the past, the modern wines are so popular in the stylish restaurants in Athens that they tend to be both expensive and hard to find overseas. **Amethystos; Antonopoulos; Boutari; Ch. Carras; Gaia; Gentilini; Gerovassilou; Hatzimichalis; Ktima; Lazarides; Papantonis; Skouras; Strofilia.**

ℑ **Green Point** (*Yarra Valley*, Australia) See *Dom. Chandon*.

ℑ **Green & Red** (*Napa Valley*, California) Rising star with good *Zinfandel*. ★★★★ **1998 Chiles Mill Vineyard Zinfandel**

❦ **Grenache** [greh-nash] Red grape of the *Rhône* (aka *Garnacha* in Spain) making spicy, peppery, full-bodied wine, provided yields are kept low. Also used to make rosés across Southern France, Australia, and California.

❦ **Grenache Blanc** [greh-nash blon] Widely grown in Southern France and Spain, where it is used to make mostly dull, slightly peppery, white wine. Treated with love and care, however, it can add welcome spice to a blend.

G

Ch. Gressier-Grand-Poujeaux [gress-yay gron' poo-joh] (Bordeaux, France) Moulis Cru Bourgeois making wine of good structure and fruit.

Marchesi de Gresy [mah-kay-see day greh-see] (*Piedmont*, Italy) Good producer of single-vineyard *Barbaresco*. ★★★★ 1997 Barberesco Camp Gros

Ch. Greysac [gray-sak] (*Bordeaux*, France) Médoc *Cru Bourgeois* with a good, if slightly rustic style.

Grgich Hills [guhr-gich] (*Napa Valley*, California) Pioneering producer of *Cabernet Sauvignon*, *Chardonnay*, and *Fumé Blanc*. The name is a concatenation of the two founders – Mike Grgich and Austin Hills, rather than a topographical feature. ★★★★ 1994 Cabernet Sauvignon Yountville

Miljenko Grgich [mell-yen-koh guhr-gich] (Croatia) The coast of Dalmatia gets the *Grgich Hills* treatment – and a Californian rediscovers his roots.

Grignolino [green-yoh-lee-noh] (*Piedmont,* Italy) Red grape and modest but refreshing cherryish wine, e.g. the *DOC* Grignolino d'Asti. Drink young.

Ch. Grillet [gree-yay] (*Rhône*, France) *Appellation* consisting of a single estate and producer of improving *Viognier* white. Neighbouring *Condrieu* is still better value.

Marqués de Griñon [green-yon] (*La Mancha, Rioja, Ribera del Duero,* Spain/Argentina) Dynamic exception to the dull *La Mancha* rule, making wines, with the help of **Michel Rolland**, which can outclass *Rioja*. The juicy *Cabernet Merlot* and fresh white *Rueda* have been joined by Durius, a blend from *Ribera del Duero*, an exceptional new *Syrah* and an extraordinary *Petit Verdot*. Look out too for new wines from Argentina.

Griotte-Chambertin [gree-yot] (*Burgundy*, France) see *Chambertin*.

Bernard Gripa [gree-pah] (*Rhône,* France) Maker of top-notch *St. Joseph* – ripe, thick, *tarry* wine that could age forever.

Jean-Louis Grippat [gree-pah] (*Rhône,* France) The domaine has been sold to Marcel Guigal, but Grippat was an unusually great white *Rhône* producer in *Hermitage* and *St. Joseph*. His reds in both appellations were less stunning, but worth buying in their subtler-than-most way. Look out for his Cuvée des Hospices. *St. Joseph* Rouge.

Gristina [gris-tee-nah] (*New York State*) Pioneering Long Island winery which has established a deserved local reputation for its *Merlot* and its *Chardonnay*. Both stand comparison with pricier California fare.

Dom. Jean Grivot [gree-voh] (*Burgundy*, France) Top-class *Vosne-Romanée* estate whose winemaker Etienne has one of the most sensitive touches in Burgundy. ★★★★★ 1999 Vosne-Romanée 1er Cru Les Beaux Monts

Robert Groffier [grof-fee-yay] (*Burgundy*, France) Up-and-coming estate with top-class wines from *Chambolle-Musigny*.

Groot Constantia [khroot-kon-stan-tee-yah] (*Constantia,* South Africa) Government-run, 300-year-old wine estate and national monument that is finally making worthwhile – if not great – wines. ★★★ 2001 Groot Constantia Sauvignon Blanc £

Groote Post [khroot-ter post] (*Darling*, South Africa) Blazing a trail in the "new" region of Darling in the West Coast a few miles from the Atlantic, this young estate is already producing one of the Cape's top *Sauvignon Blancs* and promising *Pinot Noir*. ★★★ 2001 Groote Post Sauvignon Blanc ££

Dom. Anne Gros [groh] (*Burgundy*, France) Unfortunately for one's wallet, the best wines from this *Vosne-Romanée domaine* are as expensive as they are delicious – but they are worth every cent. ★★★★★ 2000 Domaine Anne-Françoise Gros Vosne-Romanée aux Réas ££££

Jean Gros [groh] (*Burgundy*, France) Slightly less impressive *Vosne-Romanée* producer, but the *Clos Vougeots* are good.

Michel Gros [groh] (*Burgundy*, France) Least recommendable of the Gros clan – unless you love toasty new oak as much as some US critics do. ★★★★★ 2000 Vosne-Romanée 1er Cru Aux Brûlées £

G

🍇 **Gros Lot/Grolleau** [groh-loh] (*Loire*, France) The workhorse black grape of the *Loire*, particularly in *Anjou*, used to make white, rosé, and sparkling *Saumur*.

🍇 **Gros Plant (du Pays Nantais)** [groh-plon doo pay-yee non-tay] (*Loire*, France) Light, sharp white *VDQS* wine from the western *Loire*. In all but the best hands, serves to make even a poor *Muscadet* look good.

🍷 **Grosset** [gros-set] (*Clare Valley*, South Australia) White (*Chardonnay*, *Semillon*, and especially *Riesling*) specialist now making great reds (the Gaia red *Bordeaux*-blend and lovely *Pinot Noir*). Give all wines time to develop. (Mrs. Grosset is responsible for the similarly brilliant *Mount Horrocks* wines). Both are in the (wine) news this year for leading the move to putting Clare Riesling into "*Stelvin*" screwcaps.

Grosslage [gross-lah-guh] (Germany) Wine district, the third subdivision after *Anbaugebiet* (e.g., *Rheingau*) and *Bereich* (e.g., *Nierstein*). For example, *Michelsberg* is a *Grosslage* of the *Bereich Piesport*.

🍷 **Groth** [grahth] (*Napa Valley*, California) Serious producer of quality *Cabernet* and *Chardonnay*.

🍷 **Grove Mill** (New Zealand) Young *Marlborough* winery with good *Sauvignon Blanc*, *Chardonnay* and *Riesling*.

🍷 **Ch. Gruaud-Larose** [groo-oh lah-rohz] (*St. Julien 2ème Cru Classé*, *Bordeaux*, France) Now under the same ownership as Chasse-Spleen, and right on form in 2000. The second wine is "Le Sarget".

🍇 **Gruner Veltliner** [groo-nuhr felt-lee-nuhr] Spicy white grape of Austria and Eastern Europe, producing light, fresh, aromatic wine – and for *Willi Opitz* an extraordinary *late harvest* version. *Knoll; Kracher; Lang; Metternich-Sándor; Opitz; Pichler; Prager;* Schuster; Steininger; Johann Topf Strasser.

🍷 **Bodegas Guelbenzu** [guhl-bent-zoo] (*Navarra*, Spain) Starry new wave producer of rich red wines using local grapes and *Cabernet*. Has just left the Navarra DO, preferring to rely on the prestige of its brand to attract customers. ★★★★★ 2001 Vierlas Bodegas Guelbenzu Spain, Navarre £

🍷 **Guerrieri-Rizzardi** [gwer-reh-ree rit-zar-dee] (*Veneto*, Italy) Organic producer, with good rather than great *Amarone* and *Soave Classico*.

🍷 **Guffens-Heynen** [goof-fens ay-na(n)] (*Burgundy*, France) Rising star in *Pouilly-Fuissé* and the man behind the *Verget* empire. Look out for wines (from Burgundy and the Jura) from his partner Jean Rijckaert.

🍷 **E Guigal** [gee-gahl] (*Rhône*, France) Still the yardstick for *Rhône* reds, despite increased competition from *Chapoutier*. His extraordinarily pricey single-vineyard La Mouline, La Landonne and La Turque wines from *Côte Rôtie* and Château d'Ampuis wines are still ahead of the field and the "Brune et Blonde" blend of grapes from two hillsides remains a benchmark for this *appellation*. The basic red and white *Côtes du Rhône* are less exciting than they have been, but the *Condrieu* remains a great example of *Viognier*. ★★★★★ 1999 Crozes Hermitage ££

🍷 **Guimaraens** [gee-mah-rens] (*Douro*, Portugal) See *Fonseca*.

🍷 **Ch. Guiraud** [gee-roh] (*Sauternes Premier Cru Classé*, *Bordeaux*, France) *Sauternes* classed growth, recently restored to original quality. Good wines but rarely among the most complex sweet *Bordeaux*. An impressive 2001 (like most of its neighbours).

Gumpoldskirchen [goom-pohld-skeerk-ken] (Austria) Part of *Thermen* region noted for its spicy sweet wines made from *Rotgipfler* and *Zierfandler* grapes.

🍷 **Weingut Gunderloch** [goon-duhr-lokh] (*Rheinhessen*, Germany) One of the few estates to make *Rheinhessen* wines of truly reliable quality. ★★★★ 2000 Gunderloch Jean Baptiste Riesling Kabinett ££

🍷 **Gundlach-Bundschu** [guhnd-lakh buhnd-shoo] (*Sonoma Valley*, California) Good, well-made, juicy *Merlot* and spicy *Zinfandel*.

🍷 **Louis Guntrum** [goon-troom] (*Rheinhessen*, Germany) Family-run estate with a penchant for *Silvaner*.

Ⓨ **Ch. la Gurgue** [lah guhrg] (*Margaux Cru Bourgeois, Bordeaux,* France) *Cru Bourgeois* across the track from *Ch. Margaux*. Less impressive since the same owner's neighbouring *Ch. Ferrière* has both improved and increased its production, but the 1999 is a winner.

🍇 **Gutedel** [goot-edel] (Germany) German name for the *Chasselas* grape.

Ⓨ **Friedrich-Wilhelm Gymnasium** [free-drikh vil-helm-gim-nahz-yuhm] (*Mosel,* Germany) Big-name estate making good, rather than great wine.

H

Ⓨ **Weingut Fritz Haag** [hahg] (*Mosel-Saar-Ruwer,* Germany) Superlative small estate with classic *Rieslings.* ★★★ 1995 Brauneberger Juffer Sonnenuhr Riesling Auslese £££

Ⓨ **Weingut Reinhold Haart** [rine-hohld hahrt] (*Mosel,* Germany) *Piesport* star.

Ⓨ **Franz Haas** (*Alto Adige,* Italy) Very good producer getting still better. Highly scented Moscato Rosa is a speciality, *Merlot* is splendidly fruity and Pinot Nero is complex and supple. He's a great experimenter with new vines like Petit Verdot and Petit Manseng and novel blends such as his Manna Gewürztraminer/Chardonnay/ Sauvignon. ★★★★★ 1999 Manna £££

MANNA '98

Halbtrocken [hahlb-trok-en] (Germany) Off-dry. Usually a safer buy than *Trocken* in regions like the *Mosel, Rheingau* and *Rheinhessen,* but still often aggressively *acidic.* Look for *QbA* or *Auslese* versions.

Hallgarten [hal-gahr-ten] (*Rheingau,* Germany) Important town near *Hattenheim* producing robust wines including the (in Germany) well-regarded produce from *Schloss Vollrads.*

Ⓨ **Hamilton Russell Vineyards** (*Walker Bay,* South Africa) Pioneer of impressive *Pinot Noir* and *Chardonnay* at a winery in Hermanus at the southernmost tip of the *Cape*. Now expanded to include a *second label* – Southern Right – to produce a varietal *Pinot*age, and a *Chenin*-based white. Ashbourne, the top wine, is pricy but recommendable.

Ⓨ **Handley Cellars** (*Mendocino,* California) Fine sparkling wine producer with a particularly good pure *Chardonnay Blanc de Blanc*. The still *Chardonnay* is pretty impressive, too.

Ⓨ **Hanging Rock** (*Victoria,* Australia) This winery makes Australia's biggest, butteriest sparkling wine and some pretty good reds and whites.

Ⓨ **Hanzell** (*Sonoma,* California) One of the great old names of California wine, and a pioneer producer of *Chardonnay* and *Pinot Noir*. The former grape is still a major success story – in its traditional California style.

Ⓨ **Haras de Pirque** (Chile) New *Maipo* estate with characterful, serious wines.

Ⓨ **BRL Hardy** (*South* Australia) The second biggest wine producer in Australia, encompassing *Houghton* and *Moondah Brook* in *Western Australia, Leasingham* in the *Clare Valley, Redman* in *Coonawarra, E& E* in *Barossa,* Hardy's itself, and *Ch. Reynella. Hardy's* reliable range includes the commercial Nottage Hill, new Bankside, and Banrock Station, and multiregional blends, but the wines to look for are the top-of-the-line Eileen and Thomas Hardy. The *Ch. Reynella* wines from *McLaren Vale* fruit (and, in the case of the reds, using *basket presses*) are good, very lean examples of the region. Hardy's ventures in Italy (d'Istinto), France (la Baume) and Chile (Dallas Conte) are less impressive. ★★★★★ 1997 Eileen Hardy Shiraz ££££; ★★★★ 1999 Chateau Reynella Basket Pressed Shiraz ££

H

Hargrave Vineyard (*Long Island*, New York) This 30-year-old winery put the North Fork of Long Island – not to say the island as a whole – on the wine map with its Chardonnay and Merlot. And it so impressed the owner of *Ch. Pichon-Lalande* when she visited that she apparently briefly considered making wine here.

Harlan Estate (*Napa Valley*, California) Fiercely pricey, small quantities of *Bordeaux*-style reds, made with input from *Michel Rolland*, and using grapes from hillside vineyards. Join the waiting list.

Hárslevelü [harsh-leh-veh-loo] (Hungary) White grape used in *Tokaji* and for light table wines.

Hartenberg Estate [gree-yay] (*Stellenbosch*, South Africa) A name to watch, for rich, ripe reds (including an unusually good Shiraz) and the only example I've seen of Pontac, alias Teinturier du Cher, a seldom-grown red-fleshed French grape. Chardonnay and Riesling are fine, too.

Harveys (*Jerez*, Spain) Maker of the ubiquitous *Bristol Cream*. Other styles are unimpressive apart from the 1796 range and Club Classic.

Haskovo [hash-koh-voh] (Bulgaria) Along with the more frequently seen Stambolovo and Sakar, this is a name to look out for. All three are newly privatised cooperatives that can make good, rich, red wine.

Hattenheim [hat-ten-hime] (*Rheingau*, Germany) One of the finest villages in the *Rheingau*, with wines from producers such as *Balthasar Ress*, Von Simmern, *Schloss Rheinhartshausen*, and *Schloss Schönborn*.

Hatzimichalis [hat-zee-mikh-ahlis] (*Atalanti*, Greece) The face of future Greek winemaking? Hopefully. This self-taught producer's small estate makes variable but often top-notch *Cabernet Sauvignon*, *Merlot*, *Chardonnay*, and fresh dry Atalanti white. ★★★ **2000 Domaine Hatzimichalis Merlot £**

Ch. Haut-Bages-Averous [oh-bahj-aveh-roo] (*Pauillac Cru Bourgeois*, *Bordeaux*, France) *Second label* of *Ch. Lynch-Bages*. Good value black-curranty *Pauillac*.

Ch. Haut-Bages-Libéral [oh-bahj-lib-ay-ral] (*Pauillac 5ème Cru Classé*, *Bordeaux*, France) Classy small property in the same stable as *Chasse-Spleen*.

Ch. Haut-Bailly [oh bai-yee] (*Pessac-Léognan Cru Classé*, *Bordeaux*, France) Recently sold: brilliant *Pessac Léognan* property consistently making reliable, excellent-quality, long-lived red (unusually in this region, there are no whites) wines. A stunning 1998 and 2000.

Ch. Haut-Batailley [oh-ba-tai-yee] (*Pauillac 5ème Cru Classé*, *Bordeaux*, France) Subtly-styled wine from the same stable as *Ducru-Beaucaillou* and *Grand-Puy-Lacoste*

Ch. Haut-Brion [oh bree-yon] (*Pessac-Léognan Premier Cru Classé*, *Bordeaux*, France) Pepys' favourite wine and still the only non-*Médoc* first growth. Situated in the *Graves* on the outskirts of *Bordeaux* in the shadow of the gas company. Wines can be tough and hard to judge when young, but at their best they develop a rich, fruity, perfumed character which sets them apart from their peers. 1996, 1998, 1999, and 2000 were especially good, as – comparatively – were 1993, 1994, and 1995. Even so, competition is heating up from stablemate, la *Mission-Haut-Brion*. The white is rare and often sublime.

Ch. Haut-Marbuzet [oh-mahr-boo-zay] (*St. Estèphe Cru Bourgeois*, *Bordeaux*, France) *Cru bourgeois* which thinks it's a *cru classé*. Immediately imposing new-wave *St. Estèphe*. Decidedly new-wave *St. Estèphe*.

Haut-Médoc [oh-may-dok] (*Bordeaux*, France) Large *appellation* which includes nearly all of the well-known *crus classés*. Basic *Haut-Médoc* should be better than plain *Médoc*.

Haut-Montravel [oh-mo'n rah-vel] (*South-West*, France) A rare, but potentially good alternative to *Monbazillac* and even *Sauternes*.

H

☧ **Haut-Poitou** [oh-pwa-too] (*Loire*, France) A source of inexpensive *Sauvignon*.

☧ **Hautes Côtes de Beaune** [oht-coht-duh-bohn] (*Burgundy*, France) Rustic wines from the hills above the big-name *communes*. Worth buying in good *vintages*; in poorer ones the grapes have problems ripening. The Cave des Hautes Côtes co-operative makes good examples.

☧ **Hautes Côtes de Nuits** [oht-coht-duh-nwee] (*Burgundy*, France) This appellation produces mostly red wines that are slightly tougher than *Hautes Côtes de Beaune*.

Hawkes Bay (New Zealand) Major North Island vineyard area which is finally beginning to live up to the promise of producing top-class reds. Whites can be fine too, though rarely achieving the bite of *Marlborough*. *Babich; Brookfields; Church Road; Cleview; Craggy Range; Delegats; Esk Valley; Matua Valley, Mills Reef; Mission; Montana; Morton Estate; Ngatarawa; CJ Pask; Sacred Hill; Te Mata; Trinity Hill; Vidal; Villa Maria; Unison.*

☧ **Hedges** (*Washington State*) Producer of good, rich, berryish reds from a number of the best vineyards in Washington State.

☧ **Heemskerk** [heems-kuhrk] (*Tasmania*, Australia) Generally underperforming winery until its purchase by its neighbour *Pipers Brook*. The *Jansz* sparkling wine label (originally launched as a joint venture with *Roederer*) now belongs to *Yalumba*, while Heemskerk's own (excellent) sparkling wine has been renamed *Pirie*, after the owner of *Pipers Brook*.

☧ **Dr. Heger** [hay-gehr] (*Baden*, Germany) A brilliant exponent of the *Grauerburgunder* which ripens well in this warm region of Germany.

☧ **Heggies** [heg-gees] (*South* Australia) Impressive *Adelaide Hills* label in the same camp as *Yalumba*. Lovely *Riesling, Viognier, Merlot, Pinot Noir,* and sweet wines. ★★★ 1998 Heggies Merlot ££; ★★★ 1999 Heggies Chardonnay ££

✋ **Heida** [hi-da] (Switzerland) Spicy Swiss grape variety, thought to be related to *Gewürztraminer*. When carefully handled, produces refreshing wines.

☧ **Charles Heidsieck** [hide-seek] (*Champagne*, France) Innovative producer whose late winemaker Daniel Thibaut (*Bonnet, Piper Heidsieck*) introduced the clever notion of labelling non-*vintage* wine with a "mis en cave" bottling date. Wines are all recommendable. ★★★★★ 1990 Blanc des Millénaires ££££; ★★★★★ 1982 Blancs de Blancs ££££

☧ **Heidsieck Dry Monopole** [hide-seek] (*Champagne*, France) A subsidiary of *Mumm* and thus until 1999 controlled by Seagrams. Recent *vintages* have shown some improvement from previously unambitious levels. ★★★ Heidsieck & Co Monopole Extra Dry £££

☧ **Gernot Heinrich** (*Burgenland*, Austria) Go-ahead producer in Gols, with his sights firmly set on structured dry wines.

☧ **Heitz Cellars** [hites] (*Napa Valley,* California) One of the great names of California and the source of stunning Martha's Vineyard and Bella Oaks reds in the 1970s, but less impressive in more recent years. Post-1996 *vintages* of Martha's Vineyard are made from newly replanted (post-*phylloxera*) vines. Trailside Vineyard is a newish label for *Cabernet*.

☧ **Helderberg** (*Stellenbosch*, South Africa) The mountain on which are situated some of the best vineyards in Stellenbosch, including *Vergelegen, Yonder Hill, Avontuur,* and *Cordoba*. Competes with *Simonsberg*.

Hengst (*Alsace*, France) Top-flight *Grand Cru* vineyard, especially good for *Riesling* and *Gewurztraminer*. ★★★★ 2000 Hengst Riesling Grand Cru Domaine Barmes-Buecher ££££; ★★★ 2000 Gewurztraminer Hengst Grand Cru Domaine Zind Humbrecht ££££

☧ **Joseph Henriot** [on-ree-yoh] (*Champagne*, France) Modern *Champagne* house producing soft, rich wines. Now also shaking things up and improving wines at its recently purchased *Bouchard Père et Fils négociant* and at the William Fèvre Chablis estate in *Burgundy*.

☧ **Henriques & Henriques** [hen-reeks] (*Madeira*, Portugal) One of the few independent producers still active in *Madeira*. Top quality. ★★★★★ 15 Year Old Bual £££; ★★★★ Single Harvest 1995 ££

H

Henry of Pelham (*Ontario*, Canada) One of Canada's better producers of Chardonnay – plus a rare recommendable example of the Baco Noir grape.

Henschke [hench-kee] (*Adelaide Hills,* Australia) One of the world's best. From the long-established Hill of Grace with its 130-year-old vines and (slightly less intense) Mount Edelstone *Shirazes* to the Abbott's Prayer *Merlot-Cabernet* from *Lenswood*, the *Riesling*, Cranes Chardonnay and Tilly's Vineyard white blend, there's not a poor wine here. The reds last forever.
★★★★★ 2000 Cranes Chardonnay £££

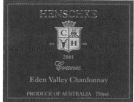

Vin de Pays de l'Hérault [Eh-roh] (*Languedoc-Roussillon*, France) Large region made famous by the Aimé Guibert's *Mas de Daumas Gassac*. Other producers such as *Grange-des-Pères* and Domaine Limbardie are following in his footsteps.

Hermitage [ayr-mee-tazh] (*Rhône*, France) Supreme Northern *Rhône appellation* for long-lived pure *Syrah*. Whites are less reliable. *Belle Père & Fils*; *Michel Bernard*; *Chapoutier*; *Chave*; *Dom.* Colombier; *Grippat*; *Guigal*; *Delas*; *Bernard Faurie*; *Jaboulet Aîné*; *Sorrel*; *Cave de Tain l'Hermitage*; *Tardieu-Laurent*. ★★★★★ 1998 Hermitage Bernard Faurie £££; ★★★ 1999 M Chapoutier La Sizeranne M ££££

James Herrick [heh-rick] (*Languedoc-Roussillon*, France) Dynamic Briton who brought an Australian philosophy to southern France, planting extensive *Chardonnay* vineyards and producing good-value varietal wine. Now part of Southcorp (*Penfolds* etc).

The Hess Collection (*Napa Valley,* California) High-class *Cabernet* producer high in the *Mount Veeder* hills named after the owner's art collection (see *Vinopolis*). The lower-priced Hess Select *Monterey* wines are worth buying, too.

Hessische Bergstrasse [hess-ishuh behrg-strah-suh] (Germany) Smallest *Anbaugebiet* capable of fine *Eisweins* and dry *Silvaners* which can surpass those of nearby *Franken*.

Heuriger [hoy-rig-gur] (*Austria*) Austria's equivalent of *Beaujolais* Nouveau – except that this newborn wine is white and sold by the carafe in cafés. Of interest if only as a taste of the way most wine used to be drunk.

Heyl zu Herrnsheim [highl zoo hehrn-sime] (*Rheinhessen*, Germany) Organic estate in *Nierstein* with good *Riesling* from the Plettenthal vineyard.

Heymann-Löwenstein [hay-mun lur-ven-shtine] (*Mosel-Saar-Ruwer,* Germany) A rising star with bone dry to lusciously sweet Rieslings.

Vinicola Hidalgo y Cia [hid-algoh ee-thia] (*Jerez*, Spain) Speciality producer of impeccable dry "La Gitana" *sherry* and a great many own-label offerings.
★★★ La Gitana Manzanilla £; ★★★ Emilio Hidalgo Pedro Ximenez ££

Cavas Hill [kah-vas heel] (*Penedés*, Spain) Best-known for its sparkling wine, but also producing rich, fruity *Tempranillo* reds. A name to watch as Spain's wine industry evolves. ★★★ 1999 Gran Civet Cavas Hill £

Hillebrand Estates (*Ontario*, Canada) Highly promising *Riesling* and Bordeaux-blend red. ★★★ 1999 Trius Grand Red ££; ★★★★ 1999 Trius Vidal Icewine ££

Hill-Smith (South Australia) Dynamic but still very classy firm, under the same family ownership as *Pewsey Vale*, *Yalumba*, and *Heggies* Vineyard, and now active in Tasmania (Jansz sparkling wine), New Zealand (*Nautilus*), and California (where its *Voss* wines are made). Also produces the Australian wine sold by E&J Gallo under its own Garnet Point label.
★★★★ 2001 Garnet Point Shiraz Cabernet £; ★★★★ NV Jansz ££; ★★★★ 1996 Voss Shiraz

Hillstowe [hil-stoh] (*South Australia*) Up-and-coming producer in the *McLaren Vale*, using grapes from various parts of the region to produce stylish *Chardonnay, Sauvignon Blanc,Shiraz* and *Cabernet-Merlot*. ★★★ 1999 Udy's Mill Lenswood Chardonnay ££; ★★★ 1999 Mary's Hundred Shiraz £££

H

♟ **Hilltops** (*New South Wales,* Australia) Exciting new coolish-climate area previously known as Young. The pioneers are McWilliams, which established its Barwang estate and label here. Stand by for classy *Cabernet Sauvignon, Merlot,* and *Shiraz.* **Demondrille; Barwang.**

Himmelreich [him-mel-raikh] (*Mosel,* Germany) One of the finest vineyards in *Graach.* See JJ Prum.

Franz Hitzberger [fruntz hits-ber-gur] (*Wachau,* Austria) A name to remember for reliable dry *Grüner Veltliner* and *Riesling.*

♟ **Paul Hobbs** (*Sonoma,* California) Former winemaker at *Simi,* and currently engaged as a consultant at *Catena* and *Valdivieso,* Paul Hobbs produces fine *Pinot Noir,* lean *Cabernet,* and rich *Chardonnay* from the memorably-named "Dinner Vineyard".

Hochfeinste [hokh-fine-stuh] (Germany) "Very finest".

Hochgewächs QbA [hokh-geh-fex] (Germany) Recent official designation for *Rieslings* which are as ripe as a *QmP* but can still only call themselves *QbA.* This from a nation supposedly dedicated to simplifying what are acknowledged to be the most complicated labels in the world.

Hochheim [hokh-hihm] (*Rheingau,* Germany) Village whose fine *Rieslings* gave the English the word *"Hock".* ★★★★★ **1999 Hochheimer Kirchenstuck Riesling Auslese Trocken Franz Kunstler £££**

♟ **Reichsgraf zu Hoensbroech** [rike-sgrahf tzoo hoh-ern sbroh-urch] (*Baden,* Germany) A large estate specializing in *Pinot Blanc* (Weissburgunder) and *Pinot Gris* (Grauburgunder).

♟ **Höffstatter** [Hurf-shtah-ter] (*Alto Adige,* Italy) Star new wave producer with unusually good *Pinot Noir* and *Gewurztraminer.*

♟ **Hogue Cellars** [hohg] (*Washington State*) Highly dynamic, family-owned *Yakima Valley* producer of good *Chardonnay, Riesling, Merlot,* and *Cabernet.*

♟ **Hollick** (*Coonawarra,* Australia) A good, traditional producer; the *Ravenswood* is particularly worth seeking out. ★★★★ **1998 Ravenswood £££;** ★★★ **2000 Hollick Riesling ££**

♟ **Ch. Hortevie** (*Bordeaux,* France) There aren't many *Crus Bourgeois* in *St-Julien,* and this one produces rich, dense, approachable wine.

♟ **Dom. de l'Hortus** [Or-Toos] (*Languedoc-Roussillon,* France) Exciting spicy *Syrah* reds from *Pic St. Loup* in the *Coteaux de Languedoc* that easily outclass many an effort from big-name producers in the *Rhône.*

♟ **Hosanna** [Oh-zah-nah] (*Pomerol, Bordeaux,* France) Christian Moueix's sleek new stablemate for *Pétrus* – produced from the best part of the *Certan-Guiraud* vineyard,

♟ **Hospices de Beaune** [os-peess duh bohn] (*Burgundy,* France) Hospital whose wines (often *cuvées* or blends of different vineyards) are sold at an annual charity auction, the prices of which are erroneously thought to set the tone for the *Côte d'Or* year. In the early 1990s, wines were generally substandard, improving instantly in 1994 with the welcome return of winemaker André Porcheret who, before leaving once again, proved controversial by (in 1997) making wines that struck some critics (not this one) as too big and rich. In any case, be aware that although price lists often merely indicate "Hospices de Beaune" as a producer, all of the wines bought at the auction are matured and bottled by local merchants, some of whom are a great deal more scrupulous than others.

♟ **Houghton** [haw-ton] (*Swan Valley,* Australia) Long-established subsidiary of *Hardy's.* Best known in Australia for its *Chenin*-based rich white blend traditionally sold down under as "White *Burgundy*" and in Europe as "HWB". The Wildflower Ridge commercial wines are good, as are the ones from *Moondah Brook.* Look out too for the more recently launched *Cabernet-Shiraz-Malbec* "Jack Mann", named after one of *Western Australia's* pioneering winemakers who was once quoted as saying that any wine that couldn't be enjoyed after being diluted 50–50 with water was too light-bodied. ★★★ **1998 Jack Mann Cabernet Sauvignon ££££**

Weingut von Hovel [fon huh-vel] (*Mosel-Saar-Ruwer*, Germany) A 200-year-old estate with fine *Rieslings* from great vineyards. These repay the patience that they demand.

Howard Park (*Western Australia*) John Wade is one of the best winemakers in *Western Australia*. He is also one of the finest *Riesling* producers in the whole of Australia. Madfish Bay is the *second label*. ★★★ 2000 Madfish Cabernet Sauvignon Merlot Cabernet Franc ££

Howell Mountain [how-wel] (*Napa Valley*, California) Increasingly well-respected hillside region in the north of the *Napa Valley*, capable of fine whites and reds that justify its *AVA*. *Beringer; Duckhorn; Dunn; la Jota; Liparita; Turley.*

Huadong Winery (*Shandong Province*, China) Joint venture producing the perfectly acceptable Tsing Tao brand of wines.

Bernard Huber (*Baden*, Germany) International oak-aged wines from the Pinot family: *Spätburgunder, Weissburgunder, Chardonnay.*

Alain Hudelot-Noëllat [ood-uh-loh noh-el-lah] (*Burgundy*, France) A great winemaker whose generosity with oak is matched, especially in his *Grand Cru Richebourg* and *Romanée St.Vivant*, by the intense fruit flavours of his wine.

Huelva [wel-vah] (*Extremadura*, Spain) *DO* of the *Extremadura* region, producing rather heavy whites and fortified wines.

Gaston Huët [oo-wet] (*Loire*, France) Organic winemaker Noël Pinguet produces top-quality individual vineyard examples of *Sec, Demi-Sec*, and *Moëlleux* wines. The non-*vintage* sparkling wine, though only made occasionally, is top class too.

Hugel et Fils [oo-gel] (*Alsace*, France) Reliable *négociant*. Best are the *late harvest* and Jubilee wines. The wine "Gentil" revives the tradition of blending different grape varieties. ★★★★ 1998 Riesling ££

Hungary Country too long known for its infamous *Bull's Blood* and *Olasz Rizling*, rather than *Tokaji.* *Disznókö; Egervin; Megyer; Kym Milne; Nagyrede; Neszmély; Pajsos; Royal Tokay; Hugh Ryman.*

Hunter Valley (*New South Wales*, Australia) The best-known wine region in Australia is one of the least suitable places to make wine. When the vines are not dying of heat and thirst they are drowning beneath torrential harvest-time rains. Even so, the *Shirazes* and *Semillons* – traditionally sold as "*Hermitage*", "*Claret*", "*Burgundy*", "*Chablis*" and "*Hunter Valley Riesling*" – develop remarkably. *Allandale; Allanmere; Brokenwood; Evans Family; Lake's Folly; Lindemans; McWilliams; Petersons; Reynolds; Rosemount; Rothbury Estate; Tyrrells; Wilderness Estate.* ★★★★★ 2000 Reynolds Handpicked Shiraz ££

Hunter's (*Marlborough*, New Zealand) One of *Marlborough's* most consistent producers of ripe fruity *Sauvignon Blancs* and now a quality sparkling wine. ★★★ 1999 Miru Miru Malborough Brut ££

Ch. de Hureau [oo-roh] (*Loire*, France) One of the few producers to excel in all styles of *Saumur*, from rich red to sparkling white.

Huxelrebe [huk-sel-ray-buh] Minor white grape, often grown in England but proving what it can do when harvested late in Germany. **Anselmann (Germany); Barkham Manor; Nutbourne Manor (England).**

Hybrid [high-brid] Crossbred grape *Vitis vinifera* (European) x *Vitis labrusca* (North American) – an example is *Seyval Blanc.*

Hydrogen sulphide Naturally occurring rotten egg-like gas produced by yeasts as a by-product of fermentation, or alternatively by *reductive* conditions. Before bottling, may be cured by *racking*. If left untreated, hydrogen sulphide will react with other components in the wine to form *mercaptans*. Stinky bottled wines may often be "cleaned up" by decanting or by the addition of a copper coin. Unfortunately, too many go unnoticed, especially in France where wines are still sometimes relaxedly described as smelling of foxes (*renarder*).

I

Iambol [yam-bohl] (*Southern Region,* Hungary) Large, former co-operative which now makes commercial *Merlot* and *Cabernet Sauvignon* reds, particularly for sale overseas under the Domaines Boyar label.

Icewine Increasingly popular Anglicization of the German term *Eiswein,* used particularly by Canadian producers making luscious, spicily exotic wines from grapes of varieties like *Vidal,* frozen on the vine. ★★★★★ 2000 Pillitteri Estates Vidal Icewine ££; ★★★★★ 2000 Strewn Icewine Riesling £££

IGT – Indicazione Geografiche Tipici (Italy) New designation designed to create a home for quality non-*DOC/DOCG* wines that were previously sold as *Vino da Tavola.* Originally derided by just about everyone, but now recognised as the masterstroke that allowed Italy's producers to play by Old and New World rules simultaneously.

Vin de Pays de l'Île de Beauté [eel-duh-bow-tay] (*Corsica,* France) Designation that includes varietal wines (including *Pinot Noir, Cabernet, Syrah,* and *Merlot* as well as local grapes). Often better than the island's *ACs.*

Imbottigliato nel'origine [im-bot-til-yah-toh neh-loh-ree-zhee-nay] (Italy) Estate-bottled.

Imperial(e) [am-pay-ray-ahl] (*Bordeaux,* France) Bottle containing almost six and a half litres of wine (eight and a half bottles). Such bottles are sought by collectors for their rarity and the extra longevity they give their contents.

India Source of generally execrable table wine and surprisingly reliable sparkling wine, labelled as Marquis de Pompadour or *Omar Khayam.*

Inferno [een-fehr-noh] (*Lombardy,* Italy) *Lombardy DOC. Nebbiolo* red that needs ageing for at least five years. ★★★ 1998 Caven "Al Carmine" ££

Inglenook Vineyards [ing-gel-nook] (*Napa Valley,* California) Once-great winery which, like *Beaulieu,* fell into the hands of the giant Grand Metropolitan. The Gothic building and vineyards now belong appropriately to Francis Ford Coppola. The now far-from-dazzling brand has been sold to the giant Canandaigua which has also recently bought *Franciscan* and *Simi.*

Inniskillin (*Ontario,* Canada) Pioneering winery which produces some good *Icewines* (from the Vidal grape), highly successful *Chardonnay,* improving *Pinot Noir,* and a rare example of a good *Maréchal Foch.* ★★★★★ 1999 Vidal Sparkling Ice Wine ££££; ★★★★★ 1999 Silver Riesling Ice Wine ££££

Institut National des Appellations d'Origine (INAO) (France) French official body which designates and (half-heartedly) polices quality, and outlaws a number of manifestly sensible techniques such as irrigation and the blending of *vintages,* which are permitted elsewhere. Which is why *Appellation Contrôlée* wines are often inferior to – and sell at lower prices than – the newer *Vins de Pays.*

International Wine Challenge (England) Wine competition, held in London by WINE Magazine and in China, Hong Kong, Vietnam and Singapore. (The author is founder-chairman).

International Wine & Spirit Competition (England) Wine competition, held in London.

Iphofen (*Franken,* Germany) One of the finest places to sample wines made from the *Silvaner.* Modern wine drinkers may, however, prefer the *Rieslings,* which are fruitier and less earthy in style.

IPR – Indicação de Proveniência Regulamentada (Portugal) Designation for wines that fall beneath the top – *DOC* – grade and above the basic Vinho Regional.

Irancy [ee-ron-see] (*Burgundy,* France) Little-known light reds and rosés made near *Chablis* from a blend of grapes including the *Pinot Noir* and the little-known *César.* Recently elevated to AC status. *Brocard;* Simonnet-Fèbvre.

Iron Horse Vineyards (*Sonoma* Valley, California) One of the most consistent and best sparkling-wine producers in the New World. Reds and still whites are increasingly impressive too.

Irouléguy [ee-roo-lay-gee] (*Southwest,* France) Earthy, spicy reds and rosés, and improving whites from Basque country where names seem to include an abundance of the letter "x". *Dom. Brana;* Etxegaraya; Irouléguy Cooperative.

🍷 **Isabel Estate** (*Marlborough,* New Zealand) Producer of reliably good, rather than great *Sauvignon,* but some rather more impressive Riesling, and a stunning late harvest wine. ★★★ 2001 Isabel Estate Riesling ££

Isinglass [Ih-sing-glahs] *Fining* agent derived from sturgeon bladders.

🍷 **Isole e Olena** [ee-soh-lay ay oh-lay-nah] (*Tuscany,* Italy) Brilliant pioneering small *Chianti* estate with a pure *Sangiovese Super-Tuscan, Cepparello,* and Italy's first *Syrah.* ★★★★ 1999 Cepparello Fattorie Isole e Olena ££££

🍷 **Isonzo** [Ih-son-zoh] (*Friuli-Venezia Giulia,* Italy) One of the best *DOCs* in this region, offering a wide range of varietal wines from some very progressive producers. Lis Neris-Pecorari; Ronco del Gelso; *Vic di Romans.* ★★★ 2001 Sauvignon I Feudi di Romans ££

Israel Once the source of appalling stuff, but the new-style varietal wines are increasingly impressive. *Golan Heights; Carmel.*

🍷 **Ch. d'Issan** [dee-son] (*Margaux 3ème Cru Classé, Bordeaux,* France) Recently revived *Margaux* third growth with lovely, recognizable blackcurranty *Cabernet Sauvignon* intensity. Good in 2000.

🍇 **Italian Riesling/Riesling Italico** [ee-tah-lee-koh] Not the great *Rhine Riesling,* but another name for an unrelated variety, which also goes by the names *Welschriesling, Riesling Italico,* and *Laski Rizling,* and is widely grown in Northern and Eastern Europe. At its best in Austria.

Italy Tantalizing, seductive, infuriating. In many ways the most exciting wine nation in the world, though, as ever, in a state of change as it reorganizes its wine laws. See individual regions.

J

🍷 **J** (Sonoma, California) Reliable California sparkling wine, launched by *Jordan* and now independently produced by Judy *Jordan.*

🍷 **JP Vinhos** (Portugal) See *Peter Bright.*

🍷 **Paul Jaboulet Aîné** [zha-boo-lay ay-nay] (*Rhône,* France) This once reliable firm is now a frequently disappointing producer of a wide range of Rhône wines. The Hermitage La Chapelle is the flagship wine.

🍷 **Jackson Estate** (*Marlborough,* New Zealand) Neighbour of *Cloudy Bay* and producer of *Sauvignon,* which doesn't quite have that winery's lustre at the moment. The sparkling wine is good though. ★★★ 2001 Sauvignon Blanc ££

🍷 **Jacob's Creek** (*South Australia*) Brilliantly commercial *South Australian* wines made by *Orlando* and taken up a major step by the recent introduction of a decent sparkling wine and classy trophy-winning "Limited Release" reds and whites. ★★★★ 1999 Reserve Shiraz Orlando Wyndham ££

🍷 **Jacquart** [zha-kahr] (*Champagne,* France) Large co-operative with some top-class wines. ★★★★ 1996 Jacquart Brut Mosaique Blanc de Blancs £££; ★★★★ NV Jacquart Brut Rose Mosaique £££

🍇 **Jacquère** [zha-kehr] The slightly citrusy grape of *Savoie.*

🍷 **Jacquesson et Fils** [jak-son] (*Champagne,* France) A small *Champagne* house that deserves to be better known, particularly for its delicately stylish *Blanc de Blancs.*

🍷 **Jade Mountain** (*Napa,* California) Rhône varieties are the speciality here, done with considerable stylishness.

J

☓ **Louis Jadot** [zha-doh] (*Burgundy,* France) Good, occasionally great, *Beaune négociant* with a growing number of its own top-class vineyards in *Beaune, Chassagne-,* and Puligny-Montrachet. Jadot has also been a pioneering producer of *Rully* in the *Côte Chalonnaise.* Whites are most impressive. ★★★★★ **1999 Pommard £££;** ★★★ **1999 Beaune Boucherottes £££**

☓ **Jaffelin** [zhaf-lan] (*Burgundy,* France) Small *négociant,* particularly good at supposedly "lesser" *appellations* – *Rully Blanc* and *Monthelie* are particularly good – but winemaker Bernard Repolt (who is now also responsible for the improving wines at *Bouchard Aîné*) is now showing his skills across the board.

☓ **Josef Jamek** (*Wachau,* Austria) Powerful, elegant dry whites that age well.

☓ **Joseph Jamet** [zha-may] (*Rhône,* France) Top-class *Côte Rôtie* estate, making wines that are more stylish than many in this *appellation.*

☓ **Jamieson's Run** (*Coonawarra,* Australia) *Mildara's* pair of prize-winning, good-value red and white wines. Just what commercial wines should be.

☓ **Dom. de la Janasse** [ja-nass] (*Rhône,* France) High-quality *Châteauneuf-du-Pape* estate, producing three individual wines under this *appellation,* plus a good *Côtes du Rhône* les Garrigues and unusually good whites, including a Viognier-based Vin de Pays. ★★★ **1999 Châteauneuf du Pape, Cuvée Vieilles Vignes £££**

☓ **Jansz** [yantz] (*Tasmania,* Australia) One if Australia's most successful sparkling wines. See *Yalumba* and *Pirie.*

☓ **Vin de Pays du Jardin de la France** [jar-da'n duh lah fronss] (*Loire,* France) Large *Loire* region that can produce alternatives to the region's *appellations,* but tends to offer light, unripe whites.

☓ **Robert Jasmin** [zhas-man] (*Rhône,* France) Traditionalist *Côte Rotie* estate, producing great wine despite (or thanks to) his dislike of new oak.

Jasnières [zhan-yehr] (*Loire,* France) Relatively seldom seen bone-dry and – even more seldom seen – *moelleux,* sweet *Chenin Blanc* wines from *Touraine.* Buy very carefully. ★★★★ **2000 Jasnières Cuvée les Rosiers £££**

☓ **Jasper Hill** (*Bendigo,* Australia) Winery in Heathcote with a cult following for both reds and whites – especially those from the Georgia's Paddock vineyard.

☓ **Jaume Serra** [how-may seh-rah] (*Penedès,* Spain) Privately owned company which recently relocated from *Alella* to *Penedès,* and is doing good things with *Xarel-lo.* ★★★ **1999 Tempranillo Roble £**

☓ **Patrick Javillier** [zha-vil-yay] (*Burgundy,* France) Reliable, small merchant making meticulous village *Meursault.* ★★★★ 2000 **Meursault Clos du Cromin £££;** ★★★★ 2000 **Meursault Les Clous £££**

☓ **Henri Jayer** [zha-yay] (*Burgundy,* France) Now retired cult winemaker who is still represented on labels referring to Georges et Henri. Also an influence on the wines of *Méo-Camuzet.*

☓ **Robert Jayer-Gilles** [zhah-yay-zheel] (*Burgundy,* France) *Henri Jayer's* cousin, whose top wines – including an *Echézeaux* – bear comparison with those of his more famous relative. (His *Hautes Côtes de Nuits* wines, including the *Aligoté* – are good too). ★★★★ 1999 **Nuits St Georges les Damodes £££**

Jerez (de la Frontera) [hay-reth] (Spain) Centre of the *sherry* trade, giving its name to entire *DO* area. *Gonzalez Byass; Lustau; Hidalgo; Barbadillo.*

☓ **Jermann** [zhehr-man] (*Friuli-Venezia Giulia,* Italy) Brilliant, if unashamedly showy, winemaker with a cult following who gets outrageous flavours – and prices – out of every white grape variety he touches. Look out for the *Vintage* Tunina blend of *Tocai, Picolit,* and *Malvasia,* and the "Dreams" white blend plus the Ribolla-based Vinnae and the single-vineyard Capo Martino. Also good at *Chardonnay, Pinot Gris, Pinot Blanc,* and the *Cabernets.* ★★★ **2001 Vinnae ££**

J

Jeroboam [dzhe-roh-bohm] Large bottle; in *Champagne* holding three litres (four bottles); in *Bordeaux,* four and a half (six bottles). Best to make sure before writing your cheque.

Jesuitengarten [yez-oo-witten-gahr-ten] (*Rheingau,* Germany) One of Germany's top vineyards – well handled by *Bassermann-Jordan.*

Jeunes Vignes [zhuhn veeñ] Denotes vines too young for their crop to be sold as an *Appellation Contrôlée* wine – in other words, vines that have not yet reached their fourth year.

☿ **Dom. François Jobard** [fron-swah joh-bahr] (*Burgundy,* France) Great white wine estate in *Meursault.*

☿ **Dom. Joblot** [zhob-loh] (*Burgundy,* France) One of the top *domaines* in *Givry.*

☿ **Charles Joguet** [zho-gay] (*Loire,* France) Recently-retired producer of single-vineyard *Chinon* wines that last. The more basic wines still produced by the estate are less impressive but Joguet's remains one of the names to remember in this region.

Johannisberg [zho-han-is-buhrg.] (*Rheingau,* Germany) Village making superb *Riesling,* which has lent its name to a *Bereich* covering all the *Rheingau.* ★★★ 2000 Riesling Schloss Johannisberger £

☙ **Johannisberg Riesling** [rees-ling] California name for *Rhine Riesling.*

☿ **Johannishof** [zhoh-hah-niss-hoff] (*Rheingau,* Germany) Exemplary family-owned estate with fine examples of wines from *Johannisberg* and *Rüdesheim.*

☿ **Weingut Karl-Heinz Johner** [karl-hihntz yoh-nuh] (*Baden,* Germany) Former winemaker at *Lamberhurst,* now making exceptional oaky *Pinot Noir* in southern Germany. Also makes wine in New Zealand.

☿ **Pascal Jolivet** [zhol-lee-vay] (*Loire,* France) Superstar producer of modern *Sancerre* and *Pouilly-Fumé.*

☿ **Nicolas Joly** [Zhoh-lee] (*Loire,* France) The biodynamic owner-winemaker behind the *Coulée de Serrant* in *Savennières* – and probably the most famous spokesman for biodynamic viticulture.

☿ **Jordan** (*Stellenbosch,* South Africa) Young winery whose California-trained winemakers first hit the mark with *Sauvignon* and *Chardonnay,* and are now doing as well with *Cabernet* and *Merlot.*
★★★★ 2001 Jordan Barrel Fermented Chenin Blanc £;
★★★★ 2000 Jordan Chardonnay ££

☿ **Jordan** (*Sonoma Valley,* California) *Sonoma* winery surrounded by the kind of hype more usually associated with *Napa.* Table wines – from the *Alexander Valley* – are mostly good rather than great.

☿ **Joseph** (*South Australia*) Primo Estate's label for its top wines (including the excellent sparkling *Shiraz*) and olive oils.
★★★ 1998 Joseph La Magia Botrytis Riesling Primo Estate ££

☿ **Josmeyer** [jos-mi-yur] (*Alsace,* France) Estate producing wines that are more delicate and restrained than those of some of its neighbours.
★★★★ 1999 Gewurztraminer les Folastries ££

☿ **Weingut Toni Jost** [toh-nee yohst] (*Mittelrhein,* Germany) A new-wave producer with (well-sited) vines in Bacharach, good reds, and a penchant for experimenting (often successfully) with new oak barrels.

☿ **La Jota** [lah hoh-tah] (*Napa Valley,* California) Small *Howell Mountain* producer with very stylish reds, including an unusually good *Cabernet Franc.*

☿ **Judd's Hill** (*Napa Valley,* California) Young winery making an impact with dazzling *Cabernets.*

Juffer [yoof-fuh] (*Mosel,* Germany) Famous vineyard in the village of *Brauneberg* and producing delicious, typically slatey wines.
★★★ 1995 Brauneberger Juffer Sonnenuhr Riesling Auslese Fritz Haag £££

Jug wine (California) American term for quaffable *Vin Ordinaire.*

☿ **Marcel Juge** [zhoozh] (*Rhône,* France) Producer of one of the subtlest, classiest examples of *Cornas.*

Ⲓ **Juliénas** [joo-lee-yay-nas] (*Burgundy*, France) One of 10 *Beaujolais Crus*, producing classic, vigorous wine which often benefits from a few years in bottle. E. Aujas; Jean Benon; Bernard Broyer; François Condemine; Georges Descombes; *Georges Duboeuf;* Eventail des Producteurs; Pierre Ferraud; Paul Granger; Ch. de Juliénas; Henri Lespinasse; Dom. Michel Tête; Raymond Trichard. ★★★ 2001 Julienas Les Envas Eventail de Vignerons Producteurs £

Ⲓ **Weingut Juliusspital** [yoo-lee-yoos-shpit-ahl] (Franken, Germany) Large estate whose profits benefit its hospital. Good *Riesling* and *Silvaner*. ★★★★★ 2000 Iphöfer Julius-Echter-Berg Silvaner Spätlese Trocken ££

Jumilla [hoo-mee-yah] (Spain) *DO* region in northern Murcia, traditionally known for high-alcohol wines but now making lighter *Beaujolais*-style ones. ★★★★ 2000 Altos de Finca Luzon ££

Ⲓ **Jurançon** [zhoo-ron-son] (*Southwest*, France) Rich, dry, apricoty white wines and excellent sweet wines that are made from the *Gros* and *Petit Manseng*. Bellegarde; Dom. J-P Bousquet; *Brana;* Bru-Baché; Castera; *Cauhapé;* Clos Guirouilh; Clos Lapeyre; Cru Lamouiroux; Clos Uroulat. ★★★ 1999 Domaine Larredya Juracon Moelleux Selection des Terrasses ££

Ⲓ **Justin** (*San Luis Obispo*, California) A winery to watch, with stunning reds, including a great *Cabernet Franc* and Isosceles, a *Bordeaux* blend. ★★★★ 1999 Isosceles ££££

Ⲓ **Juvé y Camps** [hoo-vay ee kamps] (*Catalonia*, Spain) The exception which proves the rule – by making and maturing decent cava from traditional grapes and excellent *vintage Brut*.

K

Ⲓ **Kaapzicht Estate** [kahp-tsikt] (South Africa) Steytler Pinotage is tops; the *Cabernet, Merlot, Pinotage, Shiraz* are good too. ★★★★★ 2000 Pinotage £££

Kabinett (Germany) Now unfashionable first step in German quality ladder, describes – usually off-dry – wines made from naturally ripened grapes.

🍇 **Kadarka** [kah-dar-ka] (Hungary) Red grape that used to be the mainstay of *Bull's Blood*. Handled well and not overcropped it makes good weighty wine.

Kaefferkopf [kay-fur-kopf] (*Alsace*, France) Excellent vineyard never made a *Grand Cru* because its forte is blends, not varietals. ★★★ 2000 Kaefferkopf Kuehn ££

Kaiserstuhl-Tuniberg [ki-sehr shtool too-nee-behrg] (*Baden*, Germany) Supposedly the finest *Baden* Bereich (actually, it covers a third of *Baden's* vineyards) with top villages producing rich, spicy *Riesling* and *Sylvaner* from volcanic slopes. Dr. Heger, Bercher, Karl-Heinz Johner.

Kallstadt [kahl-shtaht] (*Pfalz*, Germany) Village containing the best-known and finest vineyard of Annaberg, making luscious full *Riesling*.

Ⲓ **Kalin** (Sonoma County, California) Producer of unusually long-lived *Pinot Noirs* and *Chardonnays*.

Ⲓ **Kamptal** [kamp-tal] (*Niederösterreich*, Austria) Up-and-coming region for rich dry white *Grüner Veltliners* and *Rieslings*, thanks largely to the efforts of star producer *Bründlmayer*. ★★★ 2001 Weingut Allram Zöbinger Heiligenstein Riesling, Kamptal ££££

Ⲓ **Kanonkop Estate** [ka-non-kop] (*Stellenbosch*, South Africa) Famous for top-quality *Pinotage* but the *Bordeaux*-style "Paul Sauer" is better. The light red blend, "Kadette," is good too. ★★★★ 1998 Kanonkop Paul Sauer ££

Ⲓ **Karlsmühle** [kahl-smoo-lur] (*Mosel-Saar-Ruwer*, Germany) Very high-class estate producing good Riesling in the heart of the *Ruwer*.

Ⲓ **Karly** (Anmador County, California) A name to remember if you enjoy rich, dark *Zinfandels* with loads of character. Sadie Upton is the best of the single-vineyard examples. Try the *Syrah* and the Orange *Muscat* too.

K

I **Karthäuserhof** [kart-oy-ser-hof] (*Mosel-Saar-Ruwer*, Germany) *Ruwer* estate with great Eitelsbach Rieslings in naked bottles – apart from a stylish neck label. ★★★★★ 1997 Riesling Kabinett Eitelsbacher Karthäuserhofberg £££

I **Katnook Estate** (*Coonawarra*, Australia) Small estate making the highly commercial Deakin Estate wines as well as plenty of such innovative stuff as a *late harvest Coonawarra Chardonnay* and top-class *Coonawarra Merlot* and *Cabernet*. ★★★★★ 1999 Katnook Estate Shiraz ££

I **Katsaros** [kaht-sah-rohs] (Greece) One of the classiest new-wave *Cabernet Sauvignon* producers in Greece.

I **Ch. Kefraya** [keh-frah-ya] (Lebanon) *Ch. Musar* is not the only Lebanese winery; this is another one worth taking seriously.

🍇 **Kekfrankos** [kek-frenk-kosh] Another name for *Blaufränkisch*.
Kellerei/Kellerabfüllung [kel-luh-ri/kel-luh-rap few loong] (Germany) Cellar/producer/estate-bottled.

I **Kendall-Jackson** (*Clear Lake*, California) Extraordinarily dynamic, fast-growing producer at the centre of takeover rumours in 2001, making popular, consistent but somewhat off-dry "Vintner's Reserve" *Chardonnay* and *Sauvignon*, of which millions of cases are produced. Reds and "Grand Reserve" wines are better. Other associated brands include Cambria and (the more generally impressive) *Stonestreet*. ★★★★ 1999 Great Estates Pinot Noir £££

I **Ken Forrester Vineyards** (*Stellenbosch*, South Africa) Former restaurateur Ken Forrester makes serious *Chenin Blanc* and *Sauvignon*. Reds are good too.

I **Kenwood Vineyards** (*Sonoma Valley*, California) Classy *Sonoma* winery with good single-vineyard *Chardonnays* and impressive *Cabernets* (including one made from the author Jack London's vineyard). The other stars are the brilliant *Zinfandel* and *Sauvignon*.

🍇 **Kerner** [kehr-nuh] A white grape variety. A *Riesling*-cross that is grown in Germany and also widely in England. **Anselmann**.

I **Weingut August Kesseler** [kes-sel-lur] (*Rheingau*, Germany) Maker of good Assmannshausen Spätburgunder and elegant *Rieslings* too.

I **Weingut Reichsgraf von Kesselstatt** [rikh-sgraf fon kes-sel-shtat] (*Mosel-Saar-Ruwer*, Germany) Large, impressive collection of four *Riesling* estates spread between the *Mosel, Saar,* and *Ruwer*.

Kiedrich [kee-drich] (*Rheingau*, Germany) Hillside village vineyards that produce intense *Rieslings*.

Kientzheim [keents-him] (*Alsace*, France) Village noted for its *Riesling*.

I **André Kientzler** [keent-zluh] (*Alsace*, France) Classy producer with better-than-average *Pinot Blanc*.

I **JF Kimich** [kih-mikh] (*Pfalz*, Germany) Fast-rising star making rich, spicy wines typical of the *Pfalz. Gewürztraminers* are as good as *Rieslings*.

I **King Estate** (*Oregon*) Huge, glitzy new winery whose own vineyards are in part of the state that has yet to produce top-class wine. Decent *Pinot Gris Reserve* and *Zinfandel* and pleasant *Reserve Pinot Noir*.

King Valley (*Victoria*, Australia) Popular high altitude region.

I **Kingston Estate** (*Murray Valley*, South Australia) Controversial commercial producer in the Riverland. ★★★★ 1999 Kingston Reserve Shiraz ££

I **Kiona** [kih-yoh-nah] (*Washington State*) Small producer with a penchant for berryish reds and intensely flavoured *late harvest* wines.

Kir (*Burgundy*, France) A mixture of sweet fortified Burgundian *Crème de* with simple and often rather *acidic* local white wine (*Aligoté* or basic *Bourgogne Blanc*) to produce a delicious summertime drink.

I **Ch. Kirwan** [keer-wahn] (*Margaux 3ème Cru Classé, Bordeaux*, France) Coming out of the doldrums, but still doesn't warrant its third growth status.

I **Kistler** [kist-luh] (*Sonoma Valley*, California) Probably California's top *Chardonnay* producer, with uncompromising complex single-vineyard wines and fast-improving *Pinot Noirs. Burgundy* quality at *Burgundy* prices.

K

☶ **Klein Constantia** [kline kon-stan-tee-yah] (*Constantia,* South Africa) Small, dynamic estate on the site of the great 17th-century *Constantia* vineyard, and proving a credit to the *Constantia* region. The star wine is the sweet "Vin de Constance" which is sadly hard to find outside South Africa. ★★★★ 1998 Klein Constantia Marlbrook ££

☶ **Kloster Eberbach** [klos-tur ay-bur-bark] (*Rheingau,* Germany) 12th Century Cistercian abbey now the HQ of the German Wine Academy.
Klüsserath [kloo-seh-raht] (*Mosel-Saar-Ruwer,* Germany) Small village best known for *Sonnenuhr* and Königsberg vineyards.

☶ **Knappstein** [nap-steen] (*Clare Valley,* South Australia). No longer associated with founder Tim (see *Knappstein Lenswood*) but producing good *Clare* wines. ★★★★ 1998 Knappstein Enterprise Shiraz ££

☶ **Emerich Knoll** [knowl] (*Wachau,* Austria). Maker of stunning new-wave *Riesling* and *Grüner Veltliner* wines.

☶ **Weingut Freiherr zu Knyphausen** [fry-hair tzoo knip-how-sen] (*Rheingau,* Germany) Large, quality-conscious producer. Very fine *Rieslings.*
Koehler-Ruprecht [kurler-roop-recht] (*Pfalz,* Germany) Classy estate in Kallstadt, producing good *Riesling* and unusually fine *Spätburgunder.*

☶ **Kollwentz-Römerhof** [kohl-ventz roh-mair-hof] (*Burgenland,* Austria) Go-ahead producer with serious international-style reds and good *Chardonnay.*

☶ **Konnsgaard** [kons-gahd] (*Napa,* California) The former winemaker at *Newton,* and the unsung hero behind that winery's success, removes his light from under a bushel with his own top-class *Chardonnay.*

☶ **Konocti Cellars** [ko-nok-tih] (*Lake County,* California) Dynamic producer with good straightforward wines.
Kosher (mostly Israel) Wine made under complex rules. Every seventh vintage is left unpicked; non-Jews are barred from the winemaking process.

☶ **Korbel** [Kor-BEL] (*Sonoma,* California) Big producer of basic California sparkling wine. Better wines like Le Premier Reserve show what can be done.

☶ **Kourtakis** [koor-tah-kis] (Greece) One of Greece's growing number of dynamic wine companies with unusually recommendable whites and the characterful native *Mavrodaphnes.* ★★★ NV Samos Muscat Sweet White £

☶ **Weinlaubenhof Weingut Alois Kracher** [Ah-loys krah-kuh] (*Neusiedlersee,* Austria) Frequent trophy winner at the *International Wine Challenge,* and source of world-class, (very) *late harvest* wines including an unusual effort which blends the *Chardonnay* with the *Welschriesling.* ★★★★★ 1999 Nouvelle Vague Trockenbeerenauslese No. 2 £££
Krems/Kremstal [krems] (*Wachau,* Austria) Town and *Wachau* vineyard area producing Austria's most stylish *Rieslings* from terraced vineyards. ★★★ 1999 Sepp Moser Weissburgunder Beerenauslese, Kremstal ££
Kreuznach [kroyt-znahkh] (*Nahe,* Germany) Northern *Bereich,* boasting fine vineyards situated around the town of *Bad Kreuznach.*

☶ **Dom. Kreydenweiss** [cry-den-vice] (*Alsace,* France) Top-class organic producer with particularly good *Muscat, Pinot Gris,* and *Riesling.*

☶ **Krondorf** [kron-dorf] (*Barossa Valley,* Australia) Fosters-owned winery specializing in traditional, big *Barossa* style wines.

☶ **Krug** [kroog] (*Champagne,* France) The *Ch. Latour* of *Champagne.* Great vintage wine, extraordinary rosé, and pure *Chardonnay* from the *Clos de Mesnil* vineyard. The *Grande Cuvée* is theoretically the ultimate non-vintage, thanks to the greater proportions of aged *Reserve* wine, but recent releases have been a little variable. Let's see what the effect the recent assimilation into the *Moët/Mercier/Veuve Clicquot/Pommery/Ruinart* stable will have.

☶ **Kruger-Rumpf** [kroo-gur roompf] (*Nahe,* Germany) *Nahe* estate, demonstrating the potential of varieties like the *Scheurebe.*

☶ **Kuentz-Bas** [koontz bah] (*Alsace,* France) Reliable producer for *Pinot Gris* and *Gewurztraminer.* ★★★★ 1998 Gewurztraminer Grand Cru Pfersigberg £££

☶ **Kuhling-Gillot** [koo-ling gil-lot] (*Rheinhessen,* Germany) Producer who is now fast developing a reputation for rich and concentrated wines.

L

Kumeu River [koo-myoo] (*Auckland,* New Zealand) Michael Brajkovich is successful with a wide range of wines, including a very unusual dry *botrytis* *Sauvignon* which easily outclasses many a dry wine from *Sauternes*.

Kunde [koon-day] (*Sonoma,* California) Producer of good *Chardonnay* and *Zinfandel*. ★★★★ 1998 Sonoma Reserve Chardonnay £££

Weingut Franz Künstler [koonst-luh] (*Rheingau,* Germany) A new superstar producer with superlative *Riesling*. ★★★★★ 1999 Hochheimer Domdechaney Riesling Auslese Franz Kunstler £££

KWV (*Cape,* South Africa) Huge cooperative formed by the South African government at a time when surplus wine seemed set to flood the industry and, for a long time, maintained by the National Party when it needed to keep members of the big wine cooperatives, well, cooperative. Winemaking has improved recently – especially the wines sold under the Cathedral Cellars label. Perold is the name of a new, pricey, "super-premium" red. ★★★ 2001 Cathedral Cellar Sauvignon Blanc KWV £

L

Ch. Labégorce [la-bay-gors] (*Bordeaux,* France) Good traditional *Margaux.*

Ch. Labégorce-Zédé [la-bay-gors zay-day] (*Margaux Cru Bourgeois, Bordeaux,* France). An estate that belongs to the same Thienpont family as *Vieux Château Certan* and *le Pin*. A wine beyond its Bourgeois class.

Labouré-Roi [la-boo-ray rwah] (*Burgundy,* France) A highly successful and very commercial *négociant,* responsible for some quite impressive wines. See *Cottin Frères.* ★★★ 1996 Corton Grand Cru Vaucher Pere et Fils ££££

Labrusca [la-broo-skah] *Vitis labrusca,* the North American species of vine, making wine which is often referred to as "foxy". All *vinifera* vine stocks are grafted on to *phylloxera*-resistant *labrusca* roots, though the vine itself is banned in Europe and its wines, thankfully, are almost unfindable.

Ch. Lacoste-Borie [la-cost-bo-ree] (*Pauillac, Bordeaux,* France) The reliable *second label* of *Grand-Puy-Lacoste.*

Lacryma Christi [la-kree-mah kris-tee] (*Campania,* Italy) Literally, "tears of Christ," the melancholy name for some amiable, light, rather rustic reds and whites. Those from Vesuvio are *DOC*. Grotta del Sole; Mastroberardino.

Ladoix [la-dwah] (*Burgundy,* France) Village (sometimes also referred to as Ladoix-Serrigny) including parts of *Corton* and *Corton-Charlemagne*. The village wines are not well-known and because of this some bargains are still to be found. Capitain-Gagnerot; Chevalier Père et Fils; *Dubreuil-Fontaine;* Gay; Launay; Maréchale; André Nudant.

Patrick de Ladoucette [duh la-doo-set] (*Loire,* France) Intense *Pouilly-Fumé,* sold as "Baron de L". Other wines are greatly improved in recent years.

Michel Lafarge [la-farzh] (*Burgundy,* France) One of the very best producers in *Volnay* – and indeed *Burgundy*. Fine, long-lived, modern wine.

Ch. Lafaurie-Peyraguey [la-foh-ree pay-rah-gay] (*Sauternes Premier Cru Classé, Bordeaux,* France) Much-improved *Sauternes* estate that has produced creamy, long-lived wines in the 1980s and in the 1990s.

Ch. Lafite-Rothschild [la-feet roth-chihld] (*Pauillac Premier Cru Classé, Bordeaux,* France) Often almost impossible to taste young, this *Pauillac* first growth is still one of the monuments of the wine world – especially since the early 1980s. A brilliant 1998 and 2000, and arguably the wine of the vintage in 2001. The *second wine, Carruades,* is worth looking out for, too.

L

☙ **Ch. Lafleur** [la-flur] (*Pomerol, Bordeaux,* France) *Christian Moueix's* pet *Pomerol,* often on a par with the wine *Moueix* makes at *Pétrus* – though in a more understated way.

☙ **Ch. Lafleur-Gazin** [la-flur-ga-zan] (*Pomerol, Bordeaux,* France) Another good *Moueix* wine.

☙ **Dom. des Comtes Lafon** [day comt la-fon] (*Burgundy,* France) The best domaine in *Meursault* (and one of the very best in the whole of Burgundy) with great vineyards in *Volnay,* a small slice of *Montrachet,* and a new venture with more affordable wines in the Mâconnais. The Côte d'Or wines last forever. Now biodynamic.
　　★★★★★ 1999 Meursault Clos de la Barre

☙ **Ch. Lafon-Rochet** [la-fon-ro-shay] (*St. Estèphe 4ème Cru Classé, Bordeaux,* France) Very classy modern *St. Estèphe.* Impressive in 1998.

☙ **Alois Lageder** [la-gay-duh] (*Trentino-Alto Adige,* Italy) New-wave producer of the kind of wine the *Alto Adige* ought to make.
　　Lago di Caldaro [la-goh dih kahl-dah-roh] (*Trentino-Alto Adige,* Italy) Also known as the *Kalterersee,* using the local *Schiava* grape to make cool light reds with slightly unripe, though pleasant, fruit.

☙ **Ch. Lagrange** [la-gronzh] (*St. Julien 3ème Cru Classé, Bordeaux,* France) A once underperforming third growth rejuvenated by Japanese cash and local know-how (for a while from Michel Delon of *Léoville-las-Cases*). Look out for *Les Fiefs de Lagrange,* the impressive *second wine.*

☙ **Ch. Lagrange** [la-gronzh] (*Pomerol, Bordeaux,* France) Yet another *Moueix* property – and yet another good wine.

❧ **Lagrein** [la-grayn] (Italy) Cherryish red grape of northeast Italy.

☙ **Marquis de Laguiche** [lah-geesh] (*Burgundy,* France) Owner of the largest chunk of Le Montrachet. The wines are made and sold by J. Drouhin.

☙ **Ch. la Lagune** [la-goon] (*Haut-Médoc 3ème Cru Classé, Bordeaux,* France) Lovely accessible wines which last well and are worth buying even in poorer years. A great 2000.

☙ **Weingut Andreas Laible** [ahn-dray-yas ly-blay] (*Baden,* Germany) Complex, racy wines from Scheurebe, Riesling, *Gewürztraminer,* and others.
　　Lake County (California) Vineyard district salvaged by improved irrigation techniques and now capable of some fine wines as well as *Kendall Jackson's* highly commercial efforts. ★★★ 2001 Bonterra Vineyards Muscat £

☙ **Lake's Folly** (*Hunter Valley,* Australia) Max Lake, surgeon-turned-winemaker/writer/researcher has great theories about the sexual effects of sniffing various kinds of wine. He is also a leading Australian pioneer of *Chardonnay,* with an unusually successful *Hunter Valley Cabernet Sauvignon.* Wines now made by Max's son, Stephen.

☙ **Lalande de Pomerol** [la-lond duh po-meh-rol] (*Bordeaux,* France) Bordering on *Pomerol* with similar, but less fine wines. Still generally better than similarly priced *St. Emilions.* Some good-value *Petits-Châteaux.* **Ch. Garraud; Grand Ormeau.**
　　Ch. Lalande-Borie [la-lond bo-ree] (*St. Julien, Bordeaux,* France) In the same stable as *Ch. Ducru-Beaucaillou.* Reliable wines.

☙ **Ch. Lamarque** [la-mahrk] (*Haut-Médoc Cru Bourgeois, Bordeaux,* France) Spectacular *château* with good, quite modern, wines.

☙ **Lamborn Family** (*Napa Valley,* California) Small *Howell Mountain* producer, focusing on rich, concentrated, long-lived *Zinfandel.*

☙ **Dom. des Lambrays** [lom-bray] (*Burgundy,* California) Under new ownership and promising further improvements in quality. Already very worthwhile, though. ★★★★★ 2000 Clos des Lambrays Grand Cru £££

☙ **Lambrusco** [lam-broos-koh] (*Emilia-Romagna,* Italy) Famous/infamous low-strength (7.5 per cent) sweet, sparkling UK and North American version of the sparkling, dry, red wine favoured in Italy. The real thing is far more fascinating with its dry, unripe cherry flavour – comes with a cork rather than a screw-cap. **Barbolini; F Bellei; Cavicchioli; O Lini.**

L

ℑ Lamoureaux Landing [lam-moh-roh] (*New York State*) Impressive young *Chardonnay* specialist in the *Finger Lakes*.

ℑ Bodegas LAN (*Rioja*, Spain) [lahn] Modern bodega benefiting from a recent shake-up. Culmen de Lan is the top wine. ★★★★ 1998 Vina Lanciano £££

ℑ Landmark (*Sonoma*, California) Small *Chardonnay* specialist with rich, fruity, buttery wines from individual "Damaris" and "Overlook" vineyards, and blends of Chardonnay from Sonoma, Santa Barbara, and Monterey.

Landwein [land-vine] (Germany) The equivalent of a French *Vin de Pays* from one of 11 named regions. Often dry.

ℑ Ch. Lanessan [la-neh-son] (*Haut-Médoc Cru Bourgeois, Bordeaux*, France). Recommendable *Cru Bourgeois* now more influenced by new oak than it used to be, but still quite traditional fare.

Langelois [lung-ger-loyss] (*Kamptal*, Austria). One of the best wine communes in Austria – the place where you will find such producers as Hiedler and Bründlmayer.

Langhe [lang-gay] (*Piedmont*, Italy) A range of hills; when preceded by "*Nebbiolo* delle," indicates declassified *Barolo* and *Barbaresco*. Also, the denomination now used by Angelo *Gaja* for his single-vineyard wines.

ℑ Langlois-Château [long-lwah-sha-toh] (*Loire*, France) Very good still and sparkling Saumur.

ℑ Ch. Langoa-Barton [lon-goh-wah-bahr-ton] (*St. Julien 3ème Cru Classé, Bordeaux*, France) *Léoville-Barton*'s (slightly) less complex kid brother. Often one of the best bargain classed growths in *Bordeaux*. Well made in poor years.

Languedoc-Roussillon [long-dok roo-see-yon] (*Midi*, France) One of the world's largest wine regions (producing 10 per cent of the planet's wine) and, until recently, a major source of the wine lake. But a combination of government-sponsored uprooting and activity by *flying winemakers* and (a few) dynamic producers is beginning to turn this into a worrying competitor for the New World. The region includes appellations like *Fitou, Corbières and Minervois, Faugères, St. Chinian, Coteaux de Languedoc, Côtes de Roussillon*, and a torrent of *Vin de Pays d'Oc*. Sadly, many of the best, more ambitious, wines are hard to find outside France where they are developing a cult following among consumers who relish the value they often offer.
★★★★★ 2000 Saint Drezery Chateau Puech Haut Château Gerard Bru £££

ℑ Lanson [lon-son] (*Champagne*, France) Much-improved *Champagne* house with decent non-vintage "Black Label", good *Demi-sec*, and fine *vintage champagne*. ★★★★ NV Masse Brut Lanson France, Champagne ££

ℑ Casa Lapostolle [la-pos-tol] (*Colchagua Valley*, Chile) Instant superstar. Belongs to the owners of Grand Marnier and benefits from the expertise of *Michel Rolland*. Cuvée Alexandre *Merlot* reds have been a classy instant success, though the whites need more work. The 1997 Clos Apalta *Merlot*-Carmenère blend is one of the best of Chile's new-wave flagship reds.
★★★ 1998 Cuvée Alexandre Cabernet Sauvignon ££

ℑ Ch. Larcis-Ducasse [lahr-see doo-kass] (*St. Emilion Grand Cru Classé, Bordeaux*, France) Wines rarely live up to the potential of its hillside site.

ℑ Ch. Larmande [lahr-mond] (*St. Emilion Grand Cru Classé, Bordeaux*, France) A property to watch for well-made ripe-tasting wines.

ℑ Dom. Laroche [la-rosh] (*Burgundy*, France) Highly reliable *Chablis* négociant with some enviable vineyards of its own, including top-class *Premiers* and *Grands Crus*. At more affordable prices, there are also reliable southern French *Chardonnay Vin de Pays d'Oc* (including a tasty new super-premium red effort) and innovative wines from *Corsica*.
★★★★ 2000 Chablis Grand Cru Les Blanchots £££

ℑ Ch. Larrivet-Haut-Brion [lah-ri-vay oh-bree-yo'n] (*Bordeaux*, France) Graves property that is improving under the consultancy of Michel Rolland.

ℑ Viña de Larose [veen-ya day lah-rose] (Chile) *Bordeaux* estate Ch. Larose-Trintaudon's New World venture, producing *Chardonnay* and blended red.
★★★ 1999 Leyenda Chardonnay Viña de Larose ££

L

℥ **Ch. Lascombes** [las-komb] (*Margaux 2ème Cru Classé, Bordeaux,* France)
Subtle second growth *Margaux* which can exemplify the perfumed character
of this *appellation*, but has been underperforming until recently. A change of
owners improved matters in 2000 and 2001.

🌣 **Laski Riesling/Rizling** [lash-kee riz-ling] (Former Yugoslavia) Yugoslav
name for a white grape also known as the *Welsch, Olasz,* and *Italico* Riesling
and unrelated to the *Rhine Riesling.*

℥ **Ch. de Lastours** [duh las-toor] (*Languedoc-Roussillon,* France) Combined
winery and home for people with mental disabilities. Look out for the *cuvée*
Simone Descamps. ★★★★ 1997 La Grande Rompue Corbières £

Late harvest Made from (riper) grapes picked after the main vintage.
Should have at least some *botrytis.*

Late-bottled Vintage (Port) (LBV) (*Douro,* Portugal) Officially, bottled
four or six years after a specific (usually nondeclared) *vintage.* Until the late
1970s, this made for a *vintage port*-style wine that matured early, was light
and easy to drink, but needed to be decanted. Until recently, the only houses
to persevere with this style were *Warre's* and *Smith Woodhouse,* labelling
their efforts *"Traditional" LBV.* Almost every other LBV around was of the
filtered, "modern" style pioneered by *Taylors.* These taste like upmarket *ruby*
and *vintage character ports,* need no decanting, and bear little resemblance
to real *vintage* or even *crusted port.* Belatedly, a growing number of
producers are now confusingly offering "Traditional" as well as modern LBV.
For the moment, buyers can tell one style from the other by reading the
small print, but there are proposals from the port shippers to ban the use of
the word "Traditional". If they do, the same name will be used for these two
different styles of wine. As one very prominent retired *port* maker admitted,
he and his competitors have always done well out of confusing their clients.

Latium/Lazio [lah-tee-yoom] (Italy) The vineyard area surrounding
Rome, including *Frascati* and Marino. **Fontana Candida; Falesco.**

℥ **Louis Latour** [loo-wee lah-toor] (*Burgundy,* France) Underperforming
négociant who still pasteurizes his reds, treating them in a way no quality-
conscious New World producer would contemplate. Some whites, however,
including *Corton-Charlemagne,* can be sublime, and Latour deserves credit
for pioneering regions such as *Mâcon Lugny* and the *Ardèche.* ★★★ 1999
Nuits Saint Georges 1er Cru Les Crots £££

℥ **Ch. Latour** [lah-toor] (*Pauillac Premier Cru Classé, Bordeaux,* France)
Recently bought – from its British owners, Allied Domecq – by the same self-
made French millionaire who recently bought Christie's. First growth *Pauillac*
which can be very tricky to judge when young, but which develops
majestically. *Les Forts de Latour* is the – often worthwhile – second label. The
1999 and 2000 were both among the very top wines of the vintage.

℥ **Ch. Latour-à-Pomerol** [lah-toor ah po-meh-rol] (*Pomerol, Bordeaux,* France)
A great-value, small (3,500-case) *Pomerol* estate under the same ownership as
Ch. Pétrus and the same *Moueix* winemaking team. It is a little less
concentrated than its big brother, but then it is around a quarter of the price.

℥ **Ch. Latour-Martillac** [la-toor mah-tee-yak] (*Graves Cru Classé, Bordeaux,*
France) Good, sometimes overlooked reds and whites.

Laudun [loh-duhn] (*Rhône,* France) Named village of *Côtes du Rhône,* with
peppery reds and attractive rosés. ★★★ 1999 Chateau de Bord Laudun £

℥ **Laurel Glen** (*Sonoma Mountain,* California) Small hillside estate with *claret*-
style reds that are respected by true Californian wine lovers. Terra Rosa is the
accessible *second label.*

℥ **Dominique Laurent** [Loh-ron] (*Burgundy,* France) A young *négociant*
founded a few years ago by a former pastry chef who has rapidly shown
his skills at buying and maturing top-class wines from several *appellations.*

℥ **Laurent-Perrier** [law-ron pay-ree-yay] (*Champagne,* France) Historically
one of the more reliable larger houses, though some recent bottlings have
seemed variable. ★★★★★ 1990 Grand Siècle Lumière du Millénaire ££££

L

♈ **Lavaux** [la-voh] (Switzerland) A wine region in the Vaud, itself the second most important wine region in Switzerland. This is a good place to taste varied examples of *Chasselas* (known here as "*Fendant*") and Pinot Noir.

♈ **Ch. Laville Haut-Brion** [la-veel oh-bree-yon] (*Graves Cru Classé, Bordeaux,* France) Exquisite white *Graves* that lasts for 20 years or more.

♈ **Lawson's Dry Hills** (*Marlborough,* New Zealand) Producer of good *Sauvignon Blanc* and an unusually good *Gewürztraminer.*

♈ **Ch. Lazaridi** (Greece) One of Greece's best producers of red wines, making no use of the national appellation system. ★★★★ 2001 Amethystos Rosé £

♈ **Lazy Creek** (*Sonoma,* California) An Anderson Valley *Pinot Noir* producer to watch. ★★★★ 1998 Lazy Creek Gewürztraminer £££

♈ **Kostas Lazarides** (Greece) An up-and-coming producer of various styles of wine, including an unusually good rosé.

Lazio [lat-zee-yoh] (Italy) See *Latium.*

LBV (*Douro,* Portugal) See *Late-bottled Vintage.*

♈ **Leacock** (*Madeira,* Portual) Part of the *Madeira Wine Company.*

Lean Lacking body.

♈ **Leasingham** (*South Australia*) BRL Hardy subsidiary in the *Clare Valley* that makes top-flight reds and whites, including great *Shiraz, Cabernet,* and *Chardonnay.* ★★★★ 1999 Leasingham Classic Clare Shiraz £££

Lebanon Best known for the remarkable *Ch. Musar* from the *Bekaa Valley.*

♈ **Leconfield** [leh-kon-feeld] (*South Australia*) Reliable producer of intense *Coonawarra* reds. (Ralph Fowler, the man behind the award winning recent vintages, has his own wine now and works for *Chapoutier,* Australia).

Lees or lie(s) The sediment of dead yeasts that fall in the barrel or vat as a wine develops. *Muscadet* – like some other white wines – is aged *Sur Lie.* Producers of modern *Chardonnay* also leave their wine in its lees, stirring it occasionally to maximize richness – the rich flavour provided by the yeasts.

♈ **Leeuwin Estate** [loo-win] (*Margaret River,* Western Australia) Showcase winery (and concert venue) whose vineyards were originally picked out by *Robert Mondavi.* The genuinely world-class ("art label") *Chardonnay* is one of Australia's priciest and longest-lived. Other wines are less dazzling.

♈ **Dom. Leflaive** [luh-flev] (*Burgundy,* France) Anne-Claude Leflaive has taken the domaine made famous by her father Vincent to new heights, possibly, she might argue, with the help of biodynamic methods. The various Montrachets (Chevalier, Batard etc.) are the stars here. All wines are hard to find, and well worth leaving for a few years in the cellar. ★★★★★ 1998 Puligny-Montrachet Les Folatières 1er Cru Domaine Leflaive ££££

♈ **Olivier Leflaive** [luh-flev] (*Burgundy,* France) The *négociant* business launched by Vincent Leflaive's nephew in 1994. Mostly high-class white wines, with just the occasional red. (Wines can also be tasted in a bistro restaurant close to the cellars).

♈ **Peter Lehmann** [lee-man] (*Barossa Valley,* Australia) The grand old man of the *Barossa,* Peter Lehmann and his son Doug make intense *Shiraz, Cabernet, Semillon,* and *Chardonnay* which make up in character (and value) what they lack in subtlety. Stonewell is the best red. ★★★★ 1996 Stonewell Shiraz Peter Lehmann £££

♈ **J. Leitz** [lites] (*Rheingau,* Germany) Up-and-coming estate with rich *Riesling.* ★★★ 2001 Josef Leitz Rudesheimer Berg Schlossberg Riesling Spatlese ££

🍇 **Lemberger** [lem-burg-gur] (Gemany) German and Washington State name for *Blaufränkisch.* In Germany it's found mostly in Württemberg.

Lemnos [lem-nohs] (Greece) Island for *Muscat* – sweet, fortified, and dry.

Length How long the taste lingers in the mouth.

Lenswood (*South Australia*) New region near *Adelaide,* proving its potential with *Sauvignon, Chardonnay, Pinot Noir,* and even (in the case of *Henschke's* Abbott's Prayer) *Merlot* and *Cabernet Sauvignon.* Pioneers include *Stafford Ridge, Shaw & Smith, Knappstein Lenswood,* and *Nepenthe.*

L

℞ **Lenswood** (*Lenswood,* South Australia) Winery where Tim Knappstein produces brilliant *Sauvignon, Semillon, Chardonnay, Pinot Noir,* and *Cabernets.* ★★★★ 1998 Lenswood The Palatine Knappstein £££

℞ **Lenz Vineyards** [lentz] (*Long Island, New York*) One of the best wineries on Long Island, with particularly recommendable *Merlot* and *Chardonnay.* **León** [lay-on] (Spain) Northwestern region producing acceptable dry, fruity reds and whites.

℞ **Jean León** [zhon lay-ON] (*Catalonia,* Spain) American pioneer of Spanish *Chardonnay* and *Cabernet,* whose wines have greatly improved since its purchase by *Torres.* ★★★ 1999 Jean Léon Merlot Miguel Torres ££

℞ **Leone de Castris** [lay-oh-nay day kah-streess] (*Puglia,* Italy) A leading exponent of Salice Salentino, Copertino, Salento Chardonnay, and pink Salento rosato. A name to watch as this region gathers prestige. ★★★★ 1998 Salice Salentino Riserva "Donna Lisa" Leone De Castris £££

℞ **Leonetti Cellars** [lee-oh-net-tee] (*Washington State*) One of the best red wine producers in the US. Now showing its skills with *Sangiovese* and an innovative "American" (Washington State/Dry Creek) *Merlot.*

℞ **Ch. Léoville-Barton** [lay-oh-veel bahr-ton] (*St. Julien 2ème Cru Classé, Bordeaux,* France) Anthony Barton's daughter Liliane is now taking over here, and produces one of the most reliably classy wines in *Bordeaux,* without – unlike a great many of her neighbours – recourse to the machines that concentrate the juice to provide "bigger" flavours. Then, again, unlike them, she has the temerity to ask a reasonable rather than extortionate price for it. *Langoa Barton* is the sister property. Both made great 2000.

℞ **Ch. Léoville-las-Cases** [lay-oh-veel las-kahz] (*St. Julien 2ème Cru Classé, Bordeaux,* France) Impeccably made *St. Julien Super Second* whose quality now often matches its neighbour *Ch. Latour* – a fact that its owner Hubert Delon reflects in his prices. The *Clos du Marquis second label* is also good.

℞ **Ch. Léoville-Poyferré** [lay-pwah-feh-ray] (*St. Julien 2ème Cru Classé, Bordeaux,* France) Fast improving, thanks to the efforts of *Michel Rolland* here. The *second label* is Moulin Riche. ★★★★ 1998 ££££

℞ **Dom. Leroy** [luh-rwah] (*Burgundy,* France) Organic domaine in *Vosne-Romanée* founded by the former co-owner of the *Dom. de la Romanée-Conti* and making wines as good as those of that estate. Prices are stratospheric, but the humblest wines are much better than other producers' *Grands Crus.*
★★★★ 1998 Volnay 1er Cru Clos de Chêne Vosne-Romanée ££££

℞ **Maison Leroy** [luh-rwah] (*Burgundy*) If you want to buy a really great old bottle of *Burgundy,* no matter the cost, this is the place to come.

℞ **Ch. Lestage** [les-stahj] (*Bordeaux,* France) Cru Bourgeois making attractive, supple wines.

🍇 **Lexia** [lex-ee-yah] See *Muscat d'Alexandrie.*

℞ **Librandi** [lee-bran-dee] (*Calabria,* Italy) Another flagship winery from the fast-improving regions of southern Italy. There are terrific examples of the Cirò grape, as well as Gravello, a great blend of the local Gaglioppo and the *Cabernet Sauvignon.* ★★★ 1999 Magno Megonio Librandi £££
Lie(s) See *Lees/Sur Lie.*
Liebfraumilch [leeb-frow-mihlch] (Germany) Seditious exploitation of the *QbA* system. Good examples are pleasant; most are alcoholic sugar-water bought on price alone.

℞ **Lievland** [leev-land] (*Stellenbosch,* South Africa) Estate which has a reputation in South Africa as a high-quality speciality producer of *Shiraz* and *late harvest* wines.

℞ **Hubert Lignier** [Lee-nee-yay] (*Burgundy,* France) Producer of classic long-lived *Morey-St.-Denis.*
Limestone Coast (*South Australia,* Australia) Zone in the south-east of the state that includes *Padthaway* and *Coonawarra.* ★★★★ 1999 St. Mary's House Block Cabernet Sauvignon Barry Mulligan Limestone Coast ££

L

� **Limestone Ridge** (*South Australia*) *Lindemans'* often excellent *Coonawarra* red blend.
Limousin [lee-moo-zan] (*France*) Oak forest that provides barrels that are high in wood *tannin*. Better, therefore, for red wine than for white.
Limoux [lee-moo] (*Midi, France*) (Relatively) cool-climate, chalky soil *appellation* that was recently created for *Chardonnay* which was previously sold as *Vin de Pays d'Oc*. Stories of tankers of wine being driven north by night to *Burgundy* have been hotly denied in the latter region – and given credibility by several Burgundian scandals. Now the site of a venture by the owners of *Ch. Mouton Rothschild*. Also see *Blanquette*.

☐ **Lindauer** [lin-dowr] (*Marlborough*, New Zealand) Good-value Montana sparkling wine. ★★★ **NV Lindauer Special Reserve ££**

☐ **Lindemans** (*South Australia*) Once *Penfolds'* greatest rival, now (like so many other once-independent Australian producers) its subsidiary. Noted for long-lived *Hunter Valley Semillon* and *Shiraz, Coonawarra* reds, and good-value multi-region blends, such as the internationally successful *Bin 65 Chardonnay*, *Bin 45 Cabernet*, and Cawarra wines. ★★★ **1998 Pyrus £££**

☐ **Weingut Karl Lingenfelder** [lin-gen-fel-duh] (*Pfalz*, Germany) Great new-wave *Rheinpfalz* producer of a special *Riesling, Dornfelder, Scheurebe*, and an unusually successful *Pinot Noir*.

☐ **Jean Lionnet** [lee-oh-nay] (*Rhône, France*) Classy *Cornas* producer whose Rochepertius is a worthwhile buy. The *St. Péray* is an unusually good example of its *appellation* too.

☐ **Ch. Liot** [lee-yoh] (*Barsac, Bordeaux*, France) Good light and elegant *Barsac*.
Liqueur Muscat (*Rutherglen*, Australia) A wine style unique to Australia. Other countries make fortified *Muscats*, but none achieve the caramelized-marmalade and Christmas-pudding flavours that *Rutherglen* can achieve. **Campbell's; Mick Morris; Seppelt; Yalumba.**
Liqueur d'Expédition [lee-kuhr dex-pay-dees-see-yon] (*Champagne*, France) Sweetening syrup for *dosage*.
Liqueur de Tirage [lee-kuhr duh tee-rahzh] (*Champagne*, France) The yeast and sugar added to base wine to induce secondary fermentation (and hence the bubbles) in bottle.
Liquoreux [lee-koh-ruh] (France) Rich and sweet.
Liquoroso [lee-koh-roh-soh] (Italy) Rich and sweet.

☐ **Ch. Lilian Ladouys** [lahd-weess] (*Bordeaux*, France) St-Estèphe *Cru Bourgeois* resurrected in the 1980s. Well-regarded by plenty of other people, but I find it disappointing.

☐ **Lirac** [lee-rak] (*Rhône*, France) Peppery, *Tavel*-like rosés, and increasingly impressive, deep berry-fruit reds. **Ch. D'Aqueria; Bouchassy; Delorme; Ch. Mayne Lalande; André Méjan; Perrin.**

☐ **Listel** [lees-tel] (*Languedoc-Roussillon*, France) Slowly improving firm with vineyards on beaches close to Sète. Best wines: rosé ("Grain de Gris") and sparkling *Muscat* (Pétillant de Raisin). ★★★ **2000 Cuvée Pierre Julian Rouge £**
Listrac-Médoc [lees-trak] (*Bordeaux*, France) Small *Haut-Médoc commune* near *Moulis*, though quite different in style. Clay makes this *Merlot* country, though this isn't always reflected in the vineyards. Wines historically have tended to be toughly unripe and fun-free even in warm vintages but recent efforts show definite improvement. *Ch. Clarke*, (which benefits from newly planted Merlot vineyards) in particular, made a very good 2001. **Clarke; Fonréaud; Fourcas-Dupré; Fourcas-Hosten.**

☐ **Littorai** (*Sonoma*, California) Classy *Chardonnay* from *Russian River Valley* (Mais Canyon Vineyard) and *Sonoma Coast* (Occidental Vineyard) where the Hirsch vineyard produces some stylish *Pinot Noir*.
Livermore (Valley) [liv-uhr-mohr] (California) Warm-climate vineyard area with fertile soil producing full rounded whites, including increasingly fine *Chardonnay*.
★★★ **1997 Murrieta's Well Vendimia Red Livermore Valley £££**

L

Llano Estacado [yah-noh es-ta-kah-doh] (*Texas*, USA) Texan pioneer. Signature red blend is good and Italian and Rhône varietals could prove interesting.

Los Llanos [los yah-nos] (*Valdepeñas*, Spain) Commendable modern exception to the tradition of dull *Valdepeñas*, with quality mature reds.

De Loach [duh lohch] (*Sonoma*, California) Look for the letters OFS – Our Finest Selection – on the *Chardonnay* and *Cabernet* – and for the stunning individual vineyard *Zinfandels*. ★★★ 2000 Russian River Zinfandel £££

Locorotondo [loh-koh-roh-ton-doh] (Italy) A memorable name for perfectly acceptable white from the South.

Carl Loewen [lur-ven] (*Mosel-Saar-Ruwer*, Germany) Outstanding wines of classic proportions, with a particular name for sweet wines of Auslese level.

J Lohr [lohr] (*Santa Clara*, California) Affordable wines, particularly the Wildflower range, and now a selection of more classic noble styles. ★★★★ 2000 Riverstone Arroyo Seco Chardonnay £

Loire [lwahr] (France) Varied region producing inexpensive, traditional dry whites such as *Muscadet*, classier *Savennières, Sancerre*, and *Pouilly-Fumé*; grassy summery reds (Chinon and Bourgueil); buckets of rosé – some good, most dreadful; glorious sweet whites (*Vouvray* etc.); and decent sparkling wines (also *Vouvray* plus *Crémant de Loire*).

Lombardy [lom-bahr-dee] (Italy) Region (and vineyards) around Milan, known mostly for sparkling wine but also for increasingly interesting reds, such as Valcalepio and *Oltrepò Pavese*, and the whites of *Lugana*.

Long Island (*New York State*) A unique microclimate where fields once full of potatoes now yield classy *Merlot* and *Chardonnay*. Local wines are sadly under-appreciated by New Yorkers, but many are discovering them on vacation in the Hamptons. Bedell; Bridgehampton; Gristina; Hargrave; Lenz; Palmer; Peconic; Pindar.

Long Vineyards (*Napa*, California) High-quality producer of long-lived *Cabernet Sauvignon, Chardonnay*, and *late-harvest Riesling*.

Longridge (*Stellenbosch*, South Africa) Designer winery tailoring three lines (Longridge, Bay View, and Capelands) to export markets.

Lontue [lon-too-way] (Chile) Good Merlot region. Lurton; San Pedro; Santa Carolina. ★★★★★ 1999 Single Vineyard Cabernet Franc Valdivieso ££

Weingut Dr. Loosen [loh-sen] (*Mosel-Saar-Ruwer*, Germany) New-wave *Riesling* producer. One of the best and most reliable in the *Mosel*. ★★★ 2001 Dr L Riesling £

Lopez de Heredia [loh-peth day hay-ray-dee-yah] (*Rioja*, Spain) Ultra-traditional winery with Viña Tondonia white and *Gran Reserva* reds.

Ch. Loudenne [loo-denn] (Bordeaux, France) New owners are investing in this showpiece *Cru Bourgeois*, and wine quality started rising in 2000. Expect trendier, denser, fleshier reds.

Louisvale [loo-wis-vayl] (*Stellenbosch*, South Africa) Once avowed *Chardonnay* specialists, now making good *Cabernet*-based reds.

Loupiac [loo-peeyak] (*Bordeaux*, France) *Sauternes* styles, but lighter. Clos-Jean; Ch. du Cros; Loupiac-Gaudiet; Mazarin; du Noble; de Ricaud.

Ch. Loupiac-Gaudiet [loo-pee-yak goh-dee-yay] (*Loupiac, Bordeaux*, France) A reliable producer.

Loureiro [loh-ray-roh] (Portugal) *Vinho Verde* grape.

Ch. la Louvière [lah loo-vee-yehr] (*Graves, Bordeaux*, France) Reliable, rich, modern whites and reds. The second wine is called "L" de Louvière.

Fürst Löwenstein [foorst ler-ven-shtine] (*Franken*, Germany) One of the very top producers of *Silvaner*.

Van Loveren [van loh-veh-ren] (*Robertson*, South Africa) Good value-for-money wine, especially classic fresh whites and soft reds. ★★★ 2000 Van Loveren Shiraz Limited Release £

APPELLATION LOUPIAC CONTROLÉE

CHÂTEAU
DE RICAUD
LOUPIAC

ALAIN THIÉNOT, PROPRIÉTAIRE, HAUT LOUPIAC (GIRONDE)
MIS EN BOUTEILLES AU CHÂTEAU

Côtes du Lubéron [koht doo LOO-bay-ron] (*Rhône*, France) Light reds, pink and sparkling wines, and *Chardonnay*-influenced whites. ★★★★ 1999 Domaine Faverot Cuvée du Général Domaine Côtes du Luberon ££

Ⓨ **Luce** [loo-chay] (Tuscany, Italy) Co-production between *Mondavi* and *Frescobaldi*, who have combined forces to produce a good, if pricey, red. The cheaper *second label*, Lucente, can be a good buy for earlier drinking.

Ⓨ **Lugana** [loo-gah-nah] (*Lombardy*, Italy) Potentially appley, almondy whites made from the *Trebbiano*. ★★★ 2000 'Brolettino' Lugana Ca' dei Frati ££

Lugny [loo-ñee] (*Burgundy*, France) See *Mâcon*.

Ⓨ **Luna** (*Napa*, California) A name to remember for anyone looking for good Californian versions of Italian classics such as *Sangiovese*.

Ⓨ **Pierre Luneau** [loo-noh] (*Loire*, France) A rare beast: a top-class *Muscadet* producer. His experiments with new oak barrels have appealed to some US critics – I prefer the unwooded wines. Try the L d'Or.

Ⓨ **Cantine Lungarotti** [kan-tee-nah loon-gah-roh-tee] (*Umbria*, Italy) Highly innovative producer, and the man who single-handedly created the *Torgiano* denomination. ★★★ 1992 Torgiano Rosso Riserva Rubesco Vigna Monticchio £

Ⓨ **Jacques & François Lurton** [loor-ton] Having succeeded at his father's *Ch. la Louvière* and *Ch. Bonnet*, Jacques makes wine worldwide. Look out for Hermanos Lurton labels from Spain and Bodega Lurton wines from Argentina. ★★★ 2001 Hermanos Lurton Blanco, Rueda £

Ⓨ **Ch. de Lussac** [loo-sak] (*Lussac St. Emilion, Bordeaux,* France) A name to watch out for in *Lussac St. Emilion*.

Ⓨ **Lussac St. Emilion** [loo-sak sant-ay-mee-yon] (*Bordeaux*, France) *St. Emilion* satellite with potential. ★★★ 1998 Chateau Villadiere Vinyrama ££

Ⓨ **Emilio Lustau** [loos-tow] (*Jerez*, Spain) Top-class *sherry* producer with great *almacanista* wines. ★★★★★ Lustau Old East India ££

Lutomer [loo-toh-muh] (Slovenia) Area still known for its (very basic) Lutomer *Laski Rizling*, now doing better things with *Chardonnay*.

Luxembourg [luk-sahm-burg] This small principality makes pleasant, fresh, white wines from *Alsace*-like grape varieties, and generally dire fizz.

Ⓨ **Ch. Lynch-Bages** [lansh bazh] (*Pauillac 5ème Cru Classé, Bordeaux,* France) Reliably overperforming fifth-growth *Pauillac*. Haut-Bages Averous is the *second label*. The (very rare) white is worth seeking out too. ★★★★ 1997 Chateau Lynch Bages Pauillac ££££

Ⓨ **Ch. Lynch-Moussas** [lansh moo-sahs] (*Pauillac 5ème Cru Classé, Bordeaux,* France) Slowly improving.

M

Ⓨ *Macération carbonique* [ma-say-ra-see-yon kahr-bon-eek] Technique of *fermenting* uncrushed grapes under a blanket of carbon dioxide gas to produce fresh fruity wine. Used in *Beaujolais* and elsewhere.

Ⓨ **Machard de Gramont** [ma-shahr duh gra-mon] (*Burgundy*, France) Producer of fine *Nuits-St.-Georges, Vosne-Romanée,* and *Savigny-lès Beaune.*

Macedonia (Greece) Relatively cool wine region growing a lot of black *Xynomavro* for spicy, earthy wines.

Mâcon/Mâconnais [ma-kon/nay] (*Burgundy*, France) Look for the suffix *Villages, Superieur,* or Prissé, Viré, Lugny, or Clessé. The region contains *St.-Véran* and *Pouilly-Fuissé.* For straight Mâcon you could try *Jadot* or *Duboeuf,* but Jean Thévenet Dom. de la Bongran from Clessé is of *Côte d'Or* quality. Bonhomme; Deux Roches; Roger Lasserat; Manciat; Caves de Lugny; Cave de Prissé; Verget; J-J Vincent.

M

ℤ **Maculan** [mah-koo-lahn] (*Veneto*, Italy) A superstar producer of blackcurranty *Cabernet* Breganze, an oaked *Pinot Bianco-Pinot Grigio-Chardonnay* blend called Prato di Canzio, and the lusciously sweet *Torcolato*.

ℤ **Madeira** [ma-deer-ruh] (Portugal) Atlantic island producing fortified wines, usually identified by style: *Bual, Sercial, Verdelho*, or *Malmsey*. Most is ordinary; some is finer fare of unique marmalady character. *Blandy; Cossart-Gordon; Barros e Souza; Henriques & Henriques, Leacock.* ★★★★★ 1978 Blandy's Malmsey Vintage Madeira ££££

Maderization [mad-uhr-ih-zay-shon] Deliberate procedure in *Madeira*, produced by the warming of wine in *estufas*. Otherwise an undesired effect produced by high temperatures during transport and storage, resulting in a dull, flat flavour. A frequent problem in Asia – and unfortunately in the US, where wines are occasionally handled carelessly during the hot summer.

ℤ **Madiran** [ma-dee-ron] (*South-West*, France) Robust reds made from *Tannat*; tannic when young, but worth ageing. **Aydie; Barréjat; Berthoumieu; Bouscassé; Dom. du Crampilh; Ch. Montus; Producteurs de Plaimont.**

ℤ **Ch. Magdelaine** [Mag-duh-layn] (*St. Emilion Premier Grand Cru, Bordeaux*, France) Impeccable, perfumed wines.

ℤ **Duc de Magenta** (*Burgundy*, France) Large *Burgundy* estate run by *Louis Jadot* and on the up quality-wise.

ℤ **Maglieri** [mag-lee-yeh-ree] (*McLaren Vale*, South Australia) Dynamic *Shiraz* specialist recently taken over by *Mildara-Blass*. ★★★★★ 1999 Steve Maglieri Shiraz ££

Magnum Large bottle containing the equivalent of two bottles of wine (one and a half litres in capacity). Wines age slower in big bottles, and fewer are produced. For both reasons, magnums tend to sell for more at auction.

ℤ **Magrez-Fombrauge** [mah-grehz-fohm-broh'j] (*St Emilion, Bordeaux*, France) Successful – in 2000 – *garage wine* from the boss of *Malesan*.

Maipo [my-poh] (Chile) Historic region with many good producers. Reds are most successful, especially *Cabernet* and *Merlot*, and softer *Chardonnays* are also made. New varieties and enterprising organic vineyards are moving in, but vineyards close to Santiago, the capital, increasingly have to compete with the needs of housing developers. *Aquitania* (Paul Bruno); Canepa; Carmen; Concha y Toro; Cousino Macul; Peteroa; Santa Carolina; Santa Inés; Santa Rita; Undurraga; Viña Carmen.

Maître de Chai [may-tr duh chay] (France) Cellar master.

Malaga [ma-la-gah] (Spain) A semi-moribund Andalusian *DO* producing raisiny dessert wines of varying degrees of sweetness. Immensely popular in the 19th century; sadly very hard to find nowadays. **Lopez Hermanos.**

🍇 **Malagousia** [mah-lah-goo-shah] (Greece) Good quality peachy, aromatic, low-acid white grape.

ℤ **Ch. Malartic-Lagravière** [mah-lahr-teek lah-gra-vee-yehr] (*Pessac-Léognan Cru Classé, Bordeaux*, France) Previously slumbering estate, bought in 1994 by *Laurent Perrier*. Improving new-wave whites; reds need time.

🍇 **Malbec** [mal-bek] Red grape, now rare in *Bordeaux* but widely planted in Argentina, the *Loire* (where it is known as the *Côt*), *Cahors*, and also in Australia. Producing rich, plummy, silky wines. ★★★★ 2000 Black River Reserve Malbec Humberto Canale, Río Negro ££

ℤ **Malesan** [ma-les-son] (France) Dynamic brand (mostly) for *Bordeaux*, launched by the spirits group William Pitters. Can be good. ★★★ 2000 Malesan Eleve en Futs de Chene Magrez Pere et Fils

ℤ **Ch. Malescasse** [ma-les-kas] (*Haut-Médoc Cru Bourgeois, Bordeaux*, France) Since 1993, wines have benefitted from being made by the former cellarmaster of *Pichon-Lalande*.

ℤ **Ch. Malescot-St.-Exupéry** [ma-les-koh san tek-soo-peh-ree] (*Margaux 3ème Cru Classé, Bordeaux*, France) Rarely impressive wines.

ℤ **Ch. de Malle** [duh mal] (*Sauternes 2ème Cru Classé, Bordeaux*, France) Good *Sauternes* property near Preignac, famous for its beautiful *château*.

M

Malmsey [marlm-say] (*Madeira*, Portugal) The sweetest style of Madeira. ★★★★★ Henriques & Henriques 10 Year Old Malmsey £££

Malolactic fermentation [ma-loh-lak-tik] Secondary "fermentation" in which appley *malic acid* is converted into the "softer", creamier *lactic* acid by naturally present or added strains of bacteria. Almost all red wines undergo a malolactic fermentation. For whites, it is common practice in *Burgundy*. Malolactic fermentation is often used in New World countries, where natural acid levels are often low. An excess is recognizable as a buttermilky flavour.

♆ **Ch. de la Maltroye** [mal-trwah] (*Burgundy*, France) Classy modern *Chassagne*-based estate. All the wines are made by *Dom. Parent*. ★★★★ **2000 Chassagne-Montrachet 1er Cru Les Grandes Ruchottes**

☙ **Malvasia** [mal-vah-see-ah] *Muscatty* white grape vinified dry in Italy (as a component in *Frascati*), but far more successfully as good, sweet, traditional *Madeira*, in which country it is known as Malmsey. Not the same grape as Malvoisie.

La Mancha [lah man-cha] (Spain) Huge region of inland Spain south of Madrid, known for mostly dull and old-fashioned wines. However, it is currently producing increasingly clean, modern examples. Also the place where the *Marqués de Griñon* is succeeding in his experiments with new techniques and grapes, especially *Syrah*.

♆ **Albert Mann** (*Alsace*, France) Top grower who always manages to express true varietal character without overblown flavours and excessive alcohol. ★★★★ **2000 Gewurztraminer Grand Cru Steingrübler £££**

☙ **Manseng (Gros M. & Petit M.)** [man-seng] (*Southwest*, France) Two varieties of white grape grown in south-western France. Both are capable of apricot-and-cream concentration, and the latter is used in the great *vendange tardive* wines of Jurançon. *Dom. Cauhapé; Grassa.* ★★★ **2001 Les Vertus d'Antan Colombard Gros Manseng Producteurs Plaimont £**

♆ **Josef Mantler** [yoh-sef mant-lehr] (*Krems*, Austria) Reliable producer of both Grüner and Roter Veltliner as well as good *Riesling* and *Chardonnay*.

Manzanilla [man-zah-nee-yah] (*Jerez*, Spain) Dry tangy *sherry* – a *fino* style, widely (possibly mistakenly) thought to take on a salty tang from the coastal *bodegas* of Sanlucar de Barrameda. *Barbadillo; Don Zoilo; Hidalgo.* ★★★★ Lustau Almacenista Manzanilla Pasada ££

♆ **Maranges** [mah-ronzh] (*Burgundy*, France) A hillside *appellation* promising potentially affordable, if a little rustic, *Côte d'Or* wines. *Bachelet;* Pierre Bresson; Chevrot; *Drouhin;Vincent Girardin; Claude Nouveau.*

♆ **Ch. Marbuzet** [mar-boo-zay] (*Bordeaux*, France) St-Estèphe Cru Bourgeois that was formerly the second wine of Ch. Cos d'Estournel.

Marc [mahr] (France) Residue of seeds, stalks, and skins left after grapes are pressed. Often distilled into fiery brandy, e.g., Marc de Bourgogne.

♆ **Marcassin** (*Sonoma*, California) Helen Turley produces expressive – and, for some, sometimes a touch overblown – *Côte d'Or Grand Cru*-quality *Chardonnays* in tiny quantities from a trio of vineyards. ★★★★★ **1996 Marcassin Estate Chardonnay ££££**

Marches/Le Marche [lay Mahr-kay] (Italy) Region on the Adriatic coast, below Venice. Best known for *Rosso Conero* and good, dry, fruity *Verdicchio* whites. Boccadigabbia; *Fattoria Coroncino;* Fazi Battaglia; *Garofoli;* Gioacchino Garafolli; San Savino; Umani Ronchi; Vallerosa Bonci.

♆ **Marcillac** [mah-see-yak] (*Southwest*, France) Full-flavoured country reds, made principally from the *Fer*, possibly blended with some *Cabernet* and *Gamay*. Du Cros; Lacombe; Cave du Vallon-Valady.

☙ **Maréchal Foch** [mah-ray-shahl fohsh] A *hybrid* vine producing red grapes in Canada and Eastern North America. *Inniskillin* makes a good example.

Maremma [mah-rem-mah] (*Tuscany*, Italy) Southern part of *Tuscany*, somewhat warmer than *Chianti* and the site of much new planting.

M

Margaret River (*Western* Australia) Cool(ish) vineyard area on the coast, almost at Australia's southwestern tip, now gaining notice for *Cabernet Sauvignon* and *Chardonnay*. Also one of Australia's only *Zinfandels*. Brookland Valley; *Cape Mentelle; Cullen; Devil's Lair; Evans & Tate; Leeuwin; Moss Wood; Pierro; Vasse Felix;* Voyager Estate; *Ch. Xanadu.*

Ⓣ **Margaux** [mahr-goh] (*Bordeaux,* France) Large, very varied *commune* with a concentration of *crus classés* including *Ch. Margaux, Palmer,* and *Lascombes*. Sadly, other wines that should be deliciously blackberryish are variable, partly thanks to the diverse nature of the soil, and partly through the producers' readiness to sacrifice quality for the sake of yields. Matters improved in 2000, however, which was a good vintage here.

Ⓣ **Ch. Margaux** [mahr-goh] (*Margaux Premier Cru Classé, Bordeaux,* France) Intense wines with cedary perfume and velvet softness when mature. The top *second label* is Pavillon Rouge. ★★★★★ 1996 Pavillon Rouge de Château Margaux ££££

Ⓣ **Henry Marionet** [mah-ree-yoh-nay] (*Loire,* France) Top-class producer with great old-clone *Gamay* and distinctive whites made from the Romarantin.

Ⓣ **Markham** (*Napa Valley,* California) Unusually fairly priced reds and whites.

Marlborough [morl-buh-ruh] (New Zealand) Cool-climate South Island region at the north-western tip of the island, opposite Wellington: excellent *Sauvignon, Chardonnay,* improving *Merlot* and *Pinot Noir,* good sparkling wines. *Babich; Cellier le Brun; Cloudy Bay; Corbans Giesen; Grove Mill; Hunter's; Jackson Estate; Montana; Stoneleigh; Vavasour.*

Ⓣ **Marojallia** [mah-roh-jah-lee-yah] (*Bordeaux,* France) The first *garage wine* in *Margaux* – or the *Médoc* for that matter. Inevitably, from Jean-Luc Thunevin.

Ⓣ **Marne et Champagne** [mahr-nay-shom-pañ] (*Champagne,* France) Huge cooperative that owns the Besserat de Bellefon, *Lanson,* and Alfred Rothschild labels, and can provide good own-label wines. ★★★★★ 1995 Andre Simon Champagne Brut Vintage Marne et Champagne Diffusion £££

Ⓣ **Ch. Marquis-de-Terme** [mahr-kee duh tehrm] (*Margaux 4ème Cru Classé, Bordeaux,* France) Traditional property with quite tough wines.

Ⓣ **Marsala** [mahr-sah-lah] (*Sicily,* Italy) Rich, fortified wine from *Sicily* for use in recipes such as Zabaglione. *De Bartoli;* Cantine Florio; Pellegrino; Rallo. ★★★★★ 1991 Terre Arse Marsala Vergine Cantine Florio ££

Ⓣ **Marsannay** [mahr-sah-nay] (*Burgundy,* France) Northernmost village of the *Côte de Nuits* with a range of largely undistinguished but, for *Burgundy,* affordable *Chardonnay,* and *Pinot Noir* (red and rosé). Fougeray de Beauclair; Louis Jadot. ★★★★ 1999 Domaine Bruno Clair Marsannay Les Longeroies

🌱 **Marsanne** [mahr-san] (*Rhône,* France) Grape that is blended with *Roussanne* in northern *Rhône* whites. Also successful in the *Goulburn Valley* in *Victoria* for *Ch. Tahbilk* and *Mitchelton* and in California for *Bonny Doon*. Has a delicate, perfumed intensity when young, and fattens with age. Look for unoaked versions from Australia. *Bonny Doon; Guigal; Mitchelton;* Tahbilk.

Martinborough (New Zealand) Up-and-coming North Island region for *Pinot Noir* and *Chardonnay*. Alana Estate; *Ata Rangi; Dry River; Martinborough Vineyard; Palliser Estate.*

Ⓣ **Martinborough Vineyard** (*Martinborough,* New Zealand) Top Kiwi *Pinot Noir* and one of the best *Chardonnays*. ★★★★ 2000 Pinot Noir £££

Ⓣ **Martinelli** (*Sonoma,* California) Century-old *Zinfandel* specialists, making rich intense reds from this variety and juicy *Pinot Noirs*. ★★★★★ 1997 Martinelli Russian River Pinot Noir

Ⓣ **Bodegas Martinez Bujanda** [mahr-tee-neth boo-han-dah] (*Rioja,* Spain) New-wave producer of fruit-driven wines sold as *Conde de Valdemar*. Probably the most consistently recommendable producer in *Rioja*. ★★★★ 1997 Rioja Reserva ££

M

♈ Martini (*Piedmont,* Italy) Good *Asti* from the producer of the vermouth house that invented "lifestyle" advertising.

♈ Louis Martini (*Napa Valley,* California) Grand old family-owned winery, right on form at the moment. Superlative long-lived *Cabernet* from the Monte Rosso vineyard.

🍇 Marzemino [mahrt-zeh-mee-noh] (Italy) Grape that makes spicy-plummy wines. ★★★ 2000 Maso Romani Marzemino Ca'Vit, Trentino-Alto Adige ££

♈ Mas Amiel [mahs ah-mee-yel] (*Provence,* France) Wonderful rich *port*-like wine in the *appellation* of *Maury.*

♈ Mas Brugière [mas bro-gee-yehr] (*Languedoc-Roussillon,* France) Producer of top class, single-vineyard *Pic St. Loup.*

♈ Mas de Daumas Gassac [mas duh doh-mas gas-sac] (*Midi,* France) Groundbreaking *Vin de Pays* red from a blend including *Pinot Noir, Syrah, Mourvèdre,* and *Cabernet.* Good when young, but also lasts for ages. A white with *Viognier* is similarly impressive.

♈ Mas Jullien [mas joo-lye'n] (*Languedoc-Roussillon,* France) The most stylish wines in the *Coteaux du Languedoc* (or elsewhere in southern France). Classic individual reds and whites from classic traditional grapes.

♈ Mas Martinet [mas mahr-tee-neht] (*Priorato,* Spain) One of a pair of dazzling *Priorato* wines. The *second label* is Martinet Bru.

♈ Bartolo Mascarello [mas-kah-reh-loh] (*Piedmont,* Italy) Ultra-traditional *Barolo* specialist whose rose-petally wine proves that the old ways can compete with the new. But they do call for patience.

♈ Giuseppe Mascarello [mas-kah-reh-loh] (*Piedmont,* Italy) Top-class *Barolo* estate (unconnected with that of *Bartolo Mascarello*), producing characterful wine from individual vineyards. Succeeds in tricky vintages. Great *Dolcetto.*

♈ Gianni Masciarelli [mash-chee-yah-reh-lee] (*Abruzzo,* Italy) One of the starriest makers of Montepulciano d'Abruzzo.

♈ Masi [mah-see] (*Veneto,* Italy) Producer with reliable, affordable reds and whites and single-vineyard wines that serve as a justification for *Valpolicella's* denomination. ★★★★★ 1997 Vaio Amarone Serego Alighieri Masi £££

♈ La Massa [mah-sah] (*Tuscany,* Italy) Top class *Chianti* producer with a spectacularly good 1996 Chianti Classico.

♈ Massandra [mahsan-drah] (*Crimea,* Ukraine) Famous as the source of great, historic, dessert wines, now a place for okay *Cabernet Sauvignon.*

♈ Massaya [mas-sie-yah] (Lebanon) New venture by a group of French producers including Hubert de Bouard of Ch. l'Angélus. First results are promising.

Master of Wine **(MW)** One of a small number of people (around 260) internationally who have passed a gruelling set of wine exams.

♈ Mastroberadino [maas-tro-be-rah-dino] (*Campania,* Italy) Top producer of rich *Taurasi* in Italy's south as well as fine Fiano di Avellino.

♈ Matanzas Creek [muh-tan-zuhs] (*Sonoma Valley,* California) Top-class complex *Chardonnay* (one of California's best), good *Sauvignon,* and high-quality accessible *Merlot.* ★★★★ 1998 Matanzas Creek Merlot

🍇 Mataro [muh-tah-roh] See *Mourvèdre.*

♈ Mateus [ma-tay-oos] (Portugal) Pink and white off-dry *frizzante* wine sold in bottles that are traditional in Franken, Germany, and with a label depicting a palace with which the wine has no connection. A 50-year-old marketing masterpiece. The name is now also used for more serious reds.

♈ Thierry Matrot [tee-yer-ree ma-troh] (*Burgundy,* France) Top-class white producer with great white and recommendable red *Blagny.*

♈ Chateau Matsa [maht-sah] (*Attica,* Greece) Good Greek new-wave producer.

♈ Matteo Correggia [mah-tey-yoh coh-rey-djee-yah] (*Piedmont,* Italy) Producer excelling with Barbera d'Alba and Nebbiolo d'Alba.

♈ Matthew Cellars (*Washington State*) Up-and-coming maker of *Cabernet* and *Sémillon.*

M

Matua Valley [ma-tyoo-wah] (*Auckland*, New Zealand) Reliable maker of great (*Marlborough*) *Sauvignon*, (Judd Estate) *Chardonnay*, and *Merlot*. Also producer of the even better *Ararimu* red and white. Shingle Peak is the *second label*. ★★★★ 2001 Marlborough Sauvignon Blanc £

Yvon Mau [ee-von moh] (*Bordeaux & Southwest*, France) Highly commercial producer of *Bordeaux* and other, mostly white, wines from Southwest France. Occasionally good. ★★★ 1999 Château Grange Neuve, Pomerol ££

Ch. Maucaillou [mow-kai-yoo] (*Moulis Cru Bourgeois, Bordeaux*, France) *Cru Bourgeois* in the *commune* of *Moulis* regularly producing approachable wines to beat some *crus classés*.

Maule [mow-lay] (Chile) Up-and-coming *Central Valley* region; especially for white wines but warm enough for red. J Bouchon; *Santa Carolina*; Carta Vieja. ★★★★ 2000 Santa Carolina Barrica Syrah ££

Bernard Maume [mohm] (*Burgundy*, France) Small *Gevrey-Chambertin* estate making long-lived wines.

Bodegas Mauro [mow-roh] (Spain) Just outside the *Ribera del Duero DO*, but making very similar rich red wines.

Maury [moh-ree] (*Languedoc-Roussillon*, France) Potentially rich sweet wine to compete with *Banyuls* and *port*. Sadly, too many examples are light and feeble.

Mauzac [moh-zak] (France) White grape used in southern France for *Vin de Pays* and *Gaillac*. Can be characterful and floral or dull and earthy.

Mavrodaphne [mav-roh-daf-nee] (Greece) Characterful indigenous Greek red grape, and the wine made from it. Dark and strong, needs ageing to be worth drinking. **Kourtakis**.

Mavrud [mah-vrood] (Bulgaria) Rustic, characterful red grape and wine.

Maximin Grünhaus [mak-siee-min groon-hows] (*Mosel-Saar-Ruwer,* Germany) 1,000-year-old estate producing intense *Rieslings*.

Maxwell (*McLaren Vale*, Australia) Reliable producer of *Shiraz, Merlot*, and *Sémillon*, and good mead. ★★★ 1999 Maxwell Ellen Street Shiraz ££

Mayacamas [my-yah-kah-mas] (*Napa Valley*, California) Long-established winery on *Mount Veeder* with *tannic* but good old-fashioned *Cabernet*, and long-lived, rich *Chardonnay*.

Mazis-Chambertin [mah-zee shom-behr-tan] (*Burgundy*, France) Grand Cru vineyard in which some of Gevrey-Chambertin's best producers have land.

McGuigan Brothers (*Hunter Valley*, Australia) Commercial and occasionally impressive stuff from the former owners of *Wyndham Estate*. Too often, however, wines are too oaky and/or too sweet.

McLaren Vale (*South Australia*) Region renowned for European-style wines, but with varied topography, soil, and climate.*D'Arenberg; Hardy's*; Kays Amery, *Maglieri; Geoff Merrill; Ch. Reynella;Wirra Wirra*. ★★★★★ 2000 Tatachilla McLaren Vale Shiraz ££

McWilliams (*Hunter Valley*, Australia) Big, *Hunter Valley*-based, evidently non-republican firm with great traditional ("Elizabeth") *Semillon* and ("Philip") *Shiraz*. Fortified wines can be good, too, as are the pioneering *Barwang* and improved *Brand's* wines.

Médoc [may-dok] (*Bordeaux*, France) Area of *Bordeaux* immediately south of the *Gironde* and north of the town of *Bordeaux* in which the *Cru Classés* as well as far more ordinary fare are made. Should be better than basic *Bordeaux* and less good than *Haut-Médoc*. This is not always the case.

Meerlust Estate [meer-loost] (*Stellenbosch*, South Africa) Top *Cape* estate. Classy *Merlots* and a highly rated *Bordeaux*-blend called "Rubicon".

Gabriel Meffre [mef-fr] (*Rhône*, France) Sound *Rhône* and, now, southern France producer under the Galet Vineyards and Wild Pig labels. ★★★★★ 2000 Domaine De Longue Toque Gigondas Gabriel Meffre ££

Ch. Megyer [meg-yer] (*Tokaji*, Hungary) French-owned pioneer of *Tokaji* and *Furmint*.

Alphonse Mellot [mel-loh] (*Loire*, France) Dynamic, quality-driven producer. ★★★ 2001 Sancerre Blanc la Moussière Alphonse Mellot ££

M

🍇 **Melnik** [mehl-neek] (Bulgaria) Both a grape variety and a commune where rich reds are produced.

🍇 **Melon de Bourgogne** [muh-lon duh boor-goyn] (France) Grape originally imported from *Burgundy* (where it is no longer grown) to the *Loire* by Dutch brandy distillers who liked its resistance to frost. Now grown for *Muscadet*.

🍷 **Charles Melton** (*Barossa Valley,* Australia) Lovely still and sparkling *Shiraz* and world-class rosé called "Rose of Virginia", as well as Nine Popes, a wine based on *Châteauneuf-du-Pape*.

Mendocino [men-doh-see-noh] (California) Northern, coastal wine county known for unofficial marijuana farming and for its laid-back winemakers who successfully exploit cool microclimates to make "European-style" wines. *Fetzer; Handley Cellars;* Hidden Cellars; *Lazy Creek; Parducci; Roederer.*

Mendoza [men-doh-zah] (Argentina) Source of good rich reds, traditional but bright-fruited, from firms including **La Agricola;** Bianchi; *Catena; Etchart;* Finca Flichman; *Lurton; Morande; Norton; la Rural;* San Telmo; *Trapiche; Weinert.*

🍷 **Menetou-Salon** [men-too sah-lon] (*Loire,* France) Bordering on *Sancerre,* making similar if earthier, less pricey *Sauvignon,* as well as some decent *Pinot Noir.* Henri Pellé makes the best. **De Beaurepaire; R. Champault; Charet; Fournier; de Loye;** *Pellé;* **la Tour St Martin.**

🍷 **Dom. Méo-Camuzet** [may-oh-ka-moo-zay] (*Burgundy,* France) Brilliant *Côte de Nuits* estate with top-class vineyards and intense, oaky wines, made, until his retirement, by the great *Henri Jayer.* ★★★★★ **1999 Nuits St Georges 1er Cru Aux Boudots**

Mercaptans [mehr-kap-ton] See *Hydrogen sulphide.*

🍷 **Mer Soleil** [mehr soh-lay] (California) Producer of big, oaky, fruity, slightly old-fashioned Central Coast *Chardonnays.*

🍇 **Melnik** [mehl-neek] (Bulgaria) Both a grape variety and a commune where rich reds are produced.

🍷 **Mercier** [mehr-see-yay] (*Champagne,* France) Sister company of *Moët & Chandon,* and producer of improving but pretty commercial sparkling wine that, according to the advertisements, is the biggest seller in France. ★★★ **Champagne Mercier demi-sec £££**

🍷 **Mercouri** [mehr-koo-ree] (*Peloponnese,* Greece) Starry new-wave producer with good reds and very successful Roditis.

🍷 **Mercurey** [mehr-koo-ray] (*Burgundy,* France) *Côte Chalonnaise* village, where *Faiveley* makes high-quality wine. **Dom Brintet; Marguerite Carillon; Ch. de Chamirey;** *Dom. Faiveley;* **Genot-Boulanger; Michel Juillot;** *Olivier Leflaive;* **Meix-Foulot;** *Pillot.* ★★★ **2000 Mercurey 1er Cru Les Byots Domaine Menand ££**

Région de Mercurey [ray-jee-yo'n dur mehr-koo-ray] (*Burgundy,* France) Alternative name for the Côte Chalonnaise.

🍷 **Meridian** (*San Luis Obispo,* California) Unusually good-value *Pinot Noir* from *Santa Barbara.* The *Merlot* and *Chardonnay* are impressive too.

Meritage [may-rit-taj] (California) Term for red or white Bordeaux-style blends. ★★★ **1999 Jackson-Triggs Proprietors' Grand Reserve Meritage ££**

🍇 **Merlot** [mehr-loh] Red variety used to balance the more *tannic Cabernet Sauvignon* throughout the *Médoc,* where it is the most planted grape (as it is in *Pomerol* and *St. Emilion).* Increasingly, though not spectacularly, successful in the *Languedoc.* California's best include *Newton, Matanzas Creek,* and (recently) *Duckhorn.* Australia, South Africa, and New Zealand have had few real stars, but there are impressive efforts from *Washington State* and Chile. At best, appealing soft, honeyed, toffeeish wine.

🍷 **Merricks Estate** (*Mornington Peninsula,* Australia) Small *Shiraz* specialist..

🍷 **Geoff Merrill** (*McLaren Vale,* Australia) The ebullient moustachioed winemaker who has nicknamed himself "The Wizard of Oz". Impressive if restrained *Semillon, Chardonnay,* and *Cabernet* in *McLaren Vale* under his own label, plus easier-going Mount Hurtle wines (especially the rosé). ★★★★ **1997 Wickham Estate Shiraz Geoff Merrill ££**

M

℺ **Merry Edwards** (*California*, USA) Star consultant winemaker Edwards has established her own *Pinot Noir* vineyard, with (so far) excellent results.

℺ **Merryvale** (*Napa Valley*, California) Starry winery with especially good Reserve and Silhouette *Chardonnay* and Profile *Cabernet*.

℺ **Louis Métaireau** [meht-teh-roh] (*Loire*, France) The Cadillac of *Muscadet*, which comes here in the form of individual *cuvées*. Cuvée One is the star.

Méthode Champenoise [may-tohd shom-puh-nwahz] Term now outlawed by the EU but still used to describe the way all quality sparkling wines are made. Labour intensive because bubbles are made by secondary fermentation in bottle, rather than in a vat or by the introduction of gas. Bottles are given the "*dégorgement* process", more champagne is added, and they are recorked.

Methuselah Same size bottle as an *Imperiale* (six litres). Used in *Champagne*.

℺ **Meursault** [muhr-soh] (*Burgundy*, France) Superb *Chardonnay* with nutty, buttery richness. It has no *Grands Crus* but great *Premiers Crus* like Charmes, Perrières, and Genevrières. There is a little red, some sold as *Volnay-Santenots*. Ampeau; d'Auvenay; Coche-Dury; Drouhin; Henri Germain; Jobard; Comtes Lafon; Michelot; Pierre Morey; Jacques Prieur; Ch. de Puligny-Montrachet; Ropiteau; Roulot; Roux Père et Fils; Verget. ★★★★ 1999 Meursault Les Charmes Bouchard Aîné £££

℺ **Ch. de Meursault** [muhr-soh] (*Burgundy*, France) One of *Burgundy's* few *châteaux* and worth a visit. The wines – better than most produced by its owner, *Patriarche* – are good too. ★★★ 1999 Pommard Clos des Epenots £££

Mexico See *Baja California*.

℺ **Ch. Meyney** [may-nay] (*St. Estèphe Cru Bourgeois, Bordeaux*, France) Improving *St. Estèphe* property, with quite rich-flavoured wines.

℺ **Miani** [mee-yah-nee] (*Friuli-Venezia Giulia*, Italy) Good *Bordeaux*-style reds, *Riesling*, and *Chardonnay* from Enzo Pontoni.

℺ **Peter Michael** (*Sonoma*, California) UK-born Sir Peter Michael produces stunning *Sonoma, Burgundy*-like *Chardonnay*, *Sauvignon*, and *Cabernet*. ★★★★★ 1998 Les Pavots Knight's Valley £££

℺ **Louis Michel et Fils** [mee-shel] (*Burgundy*, France) Top-class *Chablis* producer. ★★★★★ 2000 Chablis 1er Cru Montmain ££££

℺ **Robert Michel** (*Rhône*, France) Produces softer *Cornas* than most from this sometimes tough *appellation*: beautiful, strong yet silky wines.

℺ **Alain Michelot** [mee-shloh] (*Burgundy*, France) Producer of perfumed, elegant *Nuits-St.-Georges* that can be enjoyed young – but is worth keeping.

℺ **Dom. Michelot-Buisson** [mee-shloh bwee-son] (*Burgundy*, France) Wines are rarely subtle, but they never lack *Meursault* flavour.

Micro-Wine/Micro-Vin Term used to describe limited-production wines such as *Le Pin* and *Screaming Eagle*.

℺ **Mildara Blass** [mil-dah-rah] (*South Australia*) Dynamic, market-driven company whose portfolio includes *Rothbury, Yarra Ridge, Yellowglen, Wolf Blass, Balgownia*, Mount Helen, *Stonyfell, Saltram*, and *Maglieri*. *Coonawarra* wines, including the very commercial *Jamieson's Run*, are best. ★★★★ 2001 The Rothbury Estate Verdelho Hunter Valley £

℺ **Millton Estate** (*Gisborne*, New Zealand) James Millton makes first-class organic *Chenin Blanc* and *Chardonnay* wine in *Gisborne*.

℺ **Milmanda** [mil-man-dah] (*Conca de Barbera*, Spain) *Torres'* top *Chardonnay*. ★★★ 2000 Milmanda Miguel Torres Catalonia £££

℺ **Kym Milne** Successful antipodean *flying winemaker* working with Vinfruco in South Africa, at Le Trulle in southern Italy, and at *Nagyrede* in Hungary.

℺ **Minervois** [mee-nehr-vwah] (*Southwest*, France) Improving reds. Old-vine *Carignan* can be richly intense; *maceration-carbonique* wines from younger *Carignan* can compete with *Beaujolais*; *Mourvèdre* can be perfumed, and *Syrah*, spicy. Look for the la Livinière sub-region, where Jean-Christophe Piccinini is based. Whites and rosés are considerably less interesting. Abbott's; Clos Centeilles; Gourgazaud; Ch. d'Oupia; Piccinini; Ste. Eulalie; la Tour Boisée; Villerambert-Julien.

M

Minöségi Bor [mee-ner-shay-gee bohr-] (Hungary) Quality wine; the local equivalent of AC.

Mis en Bouteille au Ch./Dom. [mee zon boo-tay] (France) Estate-bottled.

Misket (Bulgaria) Dullish, sometimes faintly herby white grape.

Mission (*Hawkes Bay,* New Zealand) Still run by monks nearly 150 years after its foundation, this estate is now one of the best in New Zealand.

Mission Hill (*British Columbia,* Canada) Dynamic producer of styles, ranging from *Riesling icewine* to *Merlot.* ★★★★ **2000 Chardonnay Icewine £££**

Ch. la Mission-Haut-Brion [lah mee-see-yon oh-bree-yon] (*Pessac-Léognan Cru Classé, Bordeaux,* France) Rich reds that rival and occasionally (in 1999) even overtake its supposedly classier neighbour *Haut-Brion.*

Mitchell (*Clare Valley,* Australia) Good producer of *Riesling* and of the Peppertree *Shiraz.* Also good for powerful *Grenache, Riesling, Semillon,* and sparkling *Shiraz.* ★★★ **2001 Auburn Hills Mitchell Riesling £**

Mitchelton (*Goulburn Valley,* Australia) Producer of good *Marsanne* and *Sémillon. Late harvest Rieslings* are also good, as is a *Beaujolais*-style red, "Cab Mac". The French-style Preece range – named after the former winemaker – is also worth seeking out. ★★★ **2000 Preece Cabernet Sauvignon £**

Mittelhaardt [mit-tel-hahrt] (*Pfalz,* Germany) Central and best *Bereich* of the *Rheinpfalz.*

Mittelmosel [mit-tel-moh-zul] (*Mosel-Saar-Ruwer,* Germany) Middle and best section of the *Mosel,* including the *Bernkastel Bereich.*

Mittelrhein [mit-tel-rine] (Germany) Small, northern section of the *Rhine.* Good *Rieslings* that sadly are rarely seen outside Germany. **Toni Jost.**

Mittnacht-Klack [mit-nakt-clack] (*Alsace,* France) Seriously high-quality wines with particular accent on *"vendange tardive"* and *late harvest* wines.

Moelleux [mwah-luh] (France) Sweet.

Moët & Chandon [moh-wet ay shon-don] (*Champagne,* France) The biggest producer in *Champagne. Dom Perignon,* the top wine, and *vintage* Moët are fine, and Brut Imperial NonVintage usually reliable. Watch out too for a good *Brut* rosé. ★★★★★ **1995 Dom Perignon ££££**

Clos Mogador [kloh MOH-gah-dor] (*Priorato,* Spain) Juicy, modern, and more importantly, stylish red wine from the once ultra-traditional and rustic region of *Priorat.* The shape of things to come.

Moillard [mwah-yar] (*Burgundy,* France) *Négociant* whose best wines are sold under the "Dom. Thomas Moillard" label.

Molino [moh-lee-noh] (*Piedmont,* Italy) Modern Barolo worth seeking out, and good Barbaresco. ★★★ **1997 Barolo Bricco Zuncai £££**

Monbazillac [mon-ba-zee-yak] (*Southwest,* France) *Bergerac AC* using the white grapes of *Bordeaux* – Sémillon and Sauvignon, plus some Muscadelle – to make alternatives to *Sauternes.* ★★★ **1999 Domaine du Haut-Rauly, Monbazillac Pierre Alard £**

Ch. Monbousquet [mon-boo-skay] (*St. Emilion Grand Cru Classé, Bordeaux,* France) Rich, concentrated wines. The 1995 was notable.

Ch. Monbrison [mon-bree-son] (*Margaux, Bordeaux,* France) *Cru Bourgeois* that has become a reliable, constant overperformer. A great 2001.

Mönchof [mern-chof] (*Mosel,* Germany) Top *Mosel* producer in *Ürzig.*

Ch. de Moncontour [mon-con-toor] (*Loire,* France) Recommendable source of *Vouvray.*

Robert Mondavi [mawn-dah-vee] (*Napa Valley,* California) Pioneering producer of great Reserve *Cabernet* and *Pinot Noir,* and *Chardonnay,* and inventor of *oaky Fumé Blanc Sauvignon.* Co-owner of *Opus One* and now in a joint venture with *Caliterra* in Chile and *Frescobaldi* in *Tuscany.*
★★★★ **2000 Sena ££££**

M

🍇 **Mondeuse** [mon-durz] (France) Red grape found in Savoie; Refosco in Italy.

🍷 **la Mondotte** [mon-dot] (*St. Emilion, Bordeaux,* France) Ultra-intense rich micro-wine produced by the owner of Canon la Gaffelière.

🍷 **Mongeard-Mugneret** [mon-zhahr moon-yeh-ray] (*Burgundy,* France) A reliable source of excellent and sometimes stunningly exotic red *Burgundy.*

🍇 **Monica (di Cagliari/Sardegna)** [moh-nee-kah] (*Sardinia,* Italy) Red grape and wine of *Sardinia* producing drily tasty and fortified spicy wine.

🍷 **Marqués de Monistrol** [moh-nee-strol] (*Catalonia,* Spain) Single-estate *Cava.* Also successfully producing noble varietals.

Monopole [mo-noh-pohl] (France) Literally, exclusive – single ownership of an entire vineyard. Romanée-Conti and Château Grillet are good examples.

🍷 **Mont Gras** [mon gra] (*Colchagua,* Chile) Fast-improving winery.
★★★★ 2000 Syrah Single Vineyard La Cruz ££

🍷 **Clos du Mont Olivet** [Mo(n)-toh-lee-vay] (*Rhône,* France) Good *Châteauneuf-du-Pape* producer. *Cuvée du Pape* is the top wine.

🍷 **Les Producteurs du Mont Tauch** [mon-tohsh] (*Midi,* France) Southern cooperative with surprisingly good, top-of-the-line wines.
★★★★ 2001 Fitou l'Exception ££

🍷 **Montagne St. Emilion** [mon-tan-yuh san tay-mee-yon] (*Bordeaux,* France) A "satellite" of *St. Emilion.* Often very good-value *Merlot-dominant* reds which can outclass supposedly finer fare from *St. Emilion* itself. Drink young. Ch. d'Arvouet; *Beauséjour;* Bonfort; *Calon;* Corbin; Faizeau; Fauconnière; Vieux Château Calon.

🍷 **Montagny** [mon-tan-yee] (*Burgundy,* France) Small hillside *Côte Chalonnaise* commune producing good, lean *Chardonnay* that can be a match for many *Pouilly-Fuissés.* Confusingly, unlike other parts of Burgundy, *Premier Crus* here are not from better vineyards; they're just made from riper grapes. Bertrand & Juillot; *J-M Boillot;* Cave de Buxy; *Ch. de Davenay; Joseph Faiveley; Louis Latour; Olivier Leflaive; Bernard Michel; Moillard; Antonin Rodet;* Ch. de la Saule; Jean Vachet.
★★★★ 2000 François d'Allaines Montagny Vignes Derrière 1er cru £££

🍷 **Montalcino** [mon-tal-chee-noh] (*Tuscany,* Italy) Village near Sienna known for *Brunello di Montalcino, Chianti's* big brother, whose reputation was largely created by *Biondi Santi,* whose wines no longer deserve the prices they command. *Rosso di Montalcino* is lighter. Altesino; Banfi; Costanti; Frescobaldi; Poggio Antico. ★★★★ 1997 Banfi Brunello di Montalcino Poggio Alle Juira ££££

🍷 **Montana** (*Marlborough,* New Zealand) Impressively consistent, huge firm with tremendous *Sauvignons,* improving *Chardonnays,* and good-value *Lindauer* and *Deutz Marlborough Cuvée* sparkling wine. Reds are improving but still tend to be on the green side. Look out for the Church Road wines and the smartly packaged single-estate wines such as the Brancott *Sauvignon.* ★★★★★ 2000 Stoneleigh Rapaura Series Pinot Noir Marlborough ££

🍷 **Domaine du Mont d'Or** [mon dohr] (Valais, Switzerland) Good quality across the board from this estate.

🍷 **Monte Real** [mon-tay ray-al] (*Rioja,* Spain) Made by Bodegas Riojanos; generally decent, richly flavoured, and *tannic Rioja.*

🍷 **Montecarlo** [mon-tay car-loh] (*Tuscany,* Italy) A wide variety of grapes are allowed here, including Rhône varieties such as the *Syrah* and *Roussanne* as well as the *Sangiovese* and the red and white *Bordeaux* varieties. Unsurprisingly, there are good *IGTs* too. Carmignani; Wandanna.

🍷 **Fattoria di Montechiari** [mon-tay-kee-yah-ree] (*Tuscany,* Italy) A fast-rising star in Montecarlo, producing rich, berryish, varietal reds under the Montechiari name using the *Cabernet Sauvignon, Sangiovese,* and *Pinot Noir.* The *Chardonnay* is worth looking out for too.

🍷 **Bodegas Montecillo** [mon-tay-thee-yoh] (*Rioja,* Spain) Classy wines including the oddly named Viña Monty. The Cumbrero Blanco white is good, too. ★★★★ 2000 Montecillo Blanco £

🍷 **Montée de Tonnerre** [mon-tay duh ton-nehr] (*Burgundy,* France) Excellent *Chablis Premier Cru.*

M

⚙ **Montefalco Sagrantino** [mon-teh-fal-koh sag-ran-tee-noh] (Umbria, Italy) Intense and very characterful, cherryish red made from the local Sagrantino grape. Rosso di Montefalco is a blend of Sagrantino with Sangiovese and Trebbiano.

⚙ **Ch. Montelena** [mon-teh-lay-nah] (*Napa Valley,* California) Its two long-lived *Chardonnays* (from Napa and the rather better Alexander Valley) make this one of the more impressive producers in the state. The vanilla-and-blackcurranty *Cabernet* can be impenetrable. I prefer the *Zinfandel.*

🍇 **Montepulciano** [mon-tay-pool-chee-yah-noh] (Italy) Very confusingly, this is both a grape used to make rich red wines in central and south-eastern Italy (Montepulciano *d'Abruzzi,* etc) and the name of a wine-producing town in *Tuscany* (see *Vino Nobile di Montepulciano*) which (yes, you guessed) uses a different grape altogether.

Monterey [mon-teh-ray] (California) Underrated region south of San Francisco, producing potentially good if sometimes rather grassy wines. Jekel; Sterling Redwood Trail; Estancia. ★★★★ 2000 Garys' Vineyard Pinot Noir ££££

⚙ **The Monterey Vineyard** (*Monterey,* California) Generally reliably inexpensive varietal wines now sold overseas under the Redwood Trail label.

⚙ **Monte Rossa** [mon-teh ros-sah] (*Lombardy,* Italy) A really top class Franciacorta producer with two key wines in the Satèn and Cabochon cuvées.

⚙ **Viña Montes** [mon-tehs] (*Curico,* Chile) Leading Chilean oenologist, Aurelio Montes' go-getting winery with good reds, including the flagship Alpha M and improved *Sauvignon.* Montes Folly is the new *Syrah*-based super-cuvée ★★★★★ 2001 Montes Folly ££££

⚙ **Fattoria di Montevertine** [mon-teh-ver-TEE-neh] (*Tuscany,* Italy) Less famous outside Italy than *Antinori* and *Frescobaldi* perhaps, but just as instrumental in the evolution of modern *Tuscan* wine, and of the rediscovery of the *Sangiovese* grape. Le Pergole Torte is the long-lived top wine. Il Sodaccio is fine too, however.

⚙ **Montevetrano** [mon-teh-veh-trah-noh] (*Campania,* Italy) Innovative producer applying skilled winemaking to a novel blend of the local Aglianico and the *Cabernet Sauvignon* and *Merlot* – and making a world-class red.

⚙ **Monteviña** [mon-tay-veen-yah] (*Amador County,* California) Sutter Home subsidiary, making exceptionally good *Zinfandel* from *Amador County* and reliable *Cabernet, Chardonnay,* and *Fumé Blanc.* ★★★★ 1997 Barbera ££

⚙ **Monthelie** [mon-tuh-lee] (*Burgundy,* France) Often overlooked *Côte de Beaune* village producing potentially stylish reds and whites. The appropriately named Dom. Monthelie-Douhairet is the most reliable estate. *Coche-Dury; Jaffelin; Comtes Lafon; Olivier Leflaive; Leroy; Monthelie-Douhairet; Ch. de Puligny-Montrachet; Roulot.* ★★★ 1997 Ch. de Monthélie Eric de Suremain £££

Montilla-Moriles [mon-tee-yah maw-ree-lehs] (Spain) *DO* region in which *sherry*-type wines are produced in *solera* systems. These are often so high in alcohol as to render fortification unnecessary. Good examples offer far better value than many sherries. Occasional successes achieve far more. **Pérez Barquero; Albalá.** ★★★ 1972 Don PX Dulce Gran Reserva Bodegas Toro ££

⚙ **Dom. de Montille** [duh mon-tee] (*Burgundy,* France) A lawyer-cum-winemaker whose *Volnays* and *Pommards,* if rather tough and astringent when young, are unusually fine and long-lived. Classy stuff.

⚙ **Montlouis** [mon-lwee] (*Loire,* France) Neighbour of *Vouvray* making similar, lighter-bodied, dry, sweet, and sparkling wines. **Berger; Delétang; Levasseur; Moyer; la Taille aux Loups.** ★★★ 1990 Domaine de la Taille aux Loups ££££

⚙ **Le Montrachet** [luh mon-ra-shay] (*Burgundy,* France) This *Grand Cru* vineyard (also known as plain Montrachet) is shared between *Chassagne*-and *Puligny-Montrachet,* with its neighbours Bâtard-M., Chevalier-M., Bienvenue-Bâtard-M,.and Criots-Bâtard-M. Potentially the greatest, biscuitiest white *Burgundy* – and thus dry white wine – in the world. *Marc Colin; Drouhin (Marquis de Laguiche); Comtes Lafon; Leflaive; Ramonet; Domaine de la Romanée-Conti; Sauzet.*

M

🍷 **Montravel** [mon'-ravel] (Southwest France) Region with four separate *appellations*: Montravel itself, for dry *Sémillon/Sauvignon* and now for Bordeaux-style red; and *Côtes de Montravel* and Haut-Montravel, both of which produce semi-sweet, medium-sweet, and *late-harvest* whites. **Ch du Bloy; Pique-Serre; Puy-Servain; la Roche-Marot.**

🍷 **Ch. de Mont-Redon** [mo'n-rur-do'n] (*Rhône*, France) Large and excellent Châteauneuf-du-Pape estate; white has finesse and weight, too.

🍷 **Ch. Montrose** [mon-rohz] (*St. Estèphe 2ème Cru Classé, Bordeaux,* France) Back-on-track *St. Estèphe* renowned for its longevity. More typical of the *appellation* than *Cos d'Estournel* but often less approachable in its youth. However, still maintains a rich, tarry, inky style.

🍷 **Ch. Montus** [mon-toos] (*Southwest,* France) Ambitious producer in *Madiran* with carefully oaked examples of *Tannat* and *Pacherenc de Vic Bilh. Bouscassé* is a cheaper, more approachable label.

🍷 **Moondah Brook** (*Swan Valley,* Australia) An atypically (for the baking *Swan Valley*) cool vineyard belonging to *Houghtons* (and thus *Hardys*). The stars are the wonderful tangy *Verdelho* and richly oaky *Chenin Blanc.* The *Chardonnay* and reds are less impressive.

🍷 **Moorilla Estate** [moo-rillah] (*Tasmania,* Australia) Long-established, recently reconstituted estate with particularly good *Riesling.*

🍷 **Mór** [moh-uhr] (Hungary) Region gaining a name for its dry whites.

🍷 **Moraga** (*Bel Air,* California) Multi-million dollar homes were demolished to create this steeply sloping seven-acre vineyard in the heart of Bel Air. So, the $50 price tag on its Bordeaux-like wine seems almost modest. The quality is good, too – thanks to the involvement of Tony Soter of *Etude.*

🍷 **Morande** [moh-ran-day] (Argentina/Chile) Impressive winemaker, producing wine often from pioneering varieties that are grown on both sides of the Andes. ★★★★ **2001 Morande Terrarum Pinot Noir £**

🍷 **Moreau-Naudet** [moh-roh noh-day] (*Burgundy,* France) Small, up-and-coming producer of *Chablis.* ★★★★ **2000 Chablis 1er Cru Montée de Tonnerre**

🍇 **Morellino di Scansano** [moh-ray-lee-noh dee skan-sah-noh] (*Tuscany,* Italy) Amazing cherry and raspberry, young-drinking red made from a clone of *Sangiovese.* **Cantina Cooperativa; Motta; le Pupile.**

🍷 **Dom. Marc Morey** [maw-ray] (*Burgundy,* France) Estate producing stylish white *Burgundy.* ★★★★ **2000 Chassagne-Montrachet 1er Cru Les Vergers £££**

🍷 **Dom. Pierre Morey** [maw-ray] (*Burgundy,* France) Top-class *Meursault* producer known for concentrated wines in good vintages. ★★★ 1999 Monthélie **£££**

🍷 **Bernard Morey et Fils** [maw-ray] (*Burgundy,* France) Top-class producer in *Chassagne-Montrachet* with good vineyards here and in *St. Aubin.* ★★★★ **2000 Chassagne-Montrachet 1er Cru Les Embrazées £££**

🍷 **Morey-St.-Denis** [maw-ray san duh-nee] (*Burgundy,* France) *Côtes de Nuits* village which produces richly smooth reds, especially the *Grand Cru* "Clos de la Roche". Best producer is *Domaine Dujac,* which virtually makes this *appellation* its own. *Bruno Clair; Dujac; Faiveley; Georges Lignier; Hubert Lignier; Ponsot.*

🍷 **Morgon** [mohr-gon] (*Burgundy,* France) One of the 10 *Beaujolais Crus.* Worth maturing, as it can take on a delightful chocolate/cherry character. **Dom. Calon;** *Georges Duboeuf (aka Marc Dudet);* Jean Descombes; *Sylvain Fessy;* Jean Foillard; Lapierre; Piron; Savoye. ★★★★ **2000 Morgon Les Charmes Cuvée Roche-Briday Bernard Collonge ££**

🍇 **Morio Muskat** [maw-ree-yoh moos-kat] White grape grown in Germany and Eastern Europe and making simple, grapey wine.

Moris Farms (Italy) Splendid *Morellino di Scansano* and even better Avvoltore, *Sangiovese/Cabernet/Syrah.*

M

Mornington Peninsula (*Victoria*, Australia) Some of Australia's newest and most southerly vineyards on a perpetual upward crescent. Close to Melbourne and under threat from housing developers. Good *Pinot Noir*, minty *Cabernet* and juicy *Chardonnay*, though other varieties are now proving successful. *Dromana; Paringa; Stonier;* T'Gallant.

🍷 **Morris of Rutherglen** (*Rutherglen*, Australia) Despite the takeover by *Orlando* and the retirement of local hero and champion winemaker Mick Morris, this is still an extraordinarily successful producer of delicious *Liqueur Muscat* and *Tokay* (seek out the Show Reserve). Also worth buying is a weird and wonderful *Shiraz-Durif* sparkling red.

🍷 **Denis Mortet** [mor-tay] (*Burgundy*, France) Fast up-and-coming producer with intense, rich, dark, straight *Gevrey-Chambertin*, every bit as good as some of his neighbours' *Grands Crus*. ★★★ 1998 Gevrey-Chambertin Au Vellé £££

🍷 **Morton Estate** (*Waikato*, New Zealand) Producer of fine *Sauvignon*, *Chardonnay*, and *Bordeaux* styles. ★★★ 2001 Colefield Sauvigon Blanc ££

🍷 **Mosbacher** [moss-bahk-kur] (*Pfalz*, Germany) High-quality estate producing spicy *Rieslings* in Forst.

Moscadello di Montalcino [moss-kah-del-loh dee mon-tal-chee noh] (*Tuscany*, Italy) Once common sweet white that's now being revived. It comes in fizzy and passito versions, too.

🍷 **Moscatel de Setúbal** [mos-kah-tel day say-too-bahl] (Portugal) See *Setúbal*.

🍇 **Moscato** [mos-kah-toh] (Italy) The Italian name for *Muscat*, widely used across Italy in all styles of white wine from *Moscato d'Asti*, through the more serious *Asti*, to dessert wines like *Moscato di Pantelleria*. ★★★ 2000 La Bella Estate Piemonte Moscato Passito Terre da Vino ££

🍷 **Moscato d'Asti** [mos-kah-toh das-tee] (Italy) Delightfully grapey, sweet, and fizzy, low-alcohol wine from the *Muscat*, or *Moscato*, grape. Far more flavoursome (and cheaper) than designer alcoholic lemonade. Drink young.

🍷 **Moscato Passito di Pantelleria** [pah-see-toh dee pan-teh-leh-ree-yah] (*Sicily*, Italy) Gloriously traditional sweet wine made on an island off *Sicily* from grapes that are dried out of doors until they have shrivelled into raisins. ★★★★ 2000 Ben Ryé Donnafugata Sicily, Moscato di Pantelleria £

🍇 **Moscofilero** [moss-koh-fee-leh-roh] (Greece) Aromatic, quite spicy white grape with good acidity. Good quality.

🍷 **Mosel/Moselle** [moh-zuhl] (Germany) River and term loosely used for wines made around the Mosel and nearby Saar and Ruwer rivers. Equivalent to the "*Hock*" of the Rhine. (Moselblümchen is the equivalent of Liebfraumilch.) Not to be confused with France's uninspiring *Vins de Moselle*. The wines tend to have flavours of green fruits when young but develop a wonderful ripeness as they fill out with age. *Dr. Loosen;* JJ Christobel; Jakoby-Mathy; Freiherr von Heddersdorff; Willi Haag; Heribert Kerpen; Weingut Karlsmuhle; Karp-Schreiber; *Immich Batterieberg*.

🍷 **Lenz Moser** [lents moh-zur] (Austria) Big producer with crisp, dry whites and luscious dessert wines. Best efforts come from the Klosterkeller Siegendorf. ★★★ 2000 Lenz Moser Selection Blauer Zweigelt £

🍷 **Moss Wood** (*Margaret River*, Australia) Pioneer producer of *Pinot Noir*, *Cabernet*, and *Semillon*. The wines have long cellaring potential and have a very French feel to them. The *Semillon* is reliably good in both its oaked and unoaked form; the *Chardonnay* is big and forward and the *Pinot Noir*, though improving, never quite lives up to the promise of the early 1980s.

🍷 **La Motte Estate** [la mot] (*Franschhoek*, South Africa) Best known for top *Shiraz*. ★★★ 1998 La Motte Cabernet Sauvignon £

🍷 **Herdade de Mouchão** [Hehr-dah-day dey moo sha-'oh] (*Alentejo*, Portugal) Estate producing high-quality reds in this up-and-coming region.

🍷 **J.P. Moueix** [mwex] (*Bordeaux*, France) Top-class *négociant*/producer, Christian *Moueix* specializes in stylishly traditional *Pomerol* and *St. Emilion* and is responsible for *Pétrus, La Fleur-Pétrus, Bel Air*, Richotey, and *Dominus* in California. (Do not confuse with any other Moueixs.)

M

✠ **Moulin Touchais** [moo-lan too-shay] (*Loire*, France) Producer of intensely honeyed, long-lasting, sweet white from *Coteaux du Layon*.

✠ **Moulin-à-Vent** [moo-lan-na-von] (*Burgundy*, France) One of the 10 *Beaujolais Crus* – big and rich at its best, like *Morgon*, it can benefit from ageing. Charvet; Degrange; *Duboeuf;* Paul Janin; Janodet; Lapierre; *Ch. du Moulin-à-Vent;* la Tour du Bief. ★★★ 2000 Domaine de Champ de Cour £

✠ **Ch. Moulin-à-Vent** [moo-lan-na-von] (*Moulis Cru Bourgeois, Bordeaux,* France) Leading *Moulis* property.

✠ **Ch. du Moulin-à-Vent** [moo-lan-na-von] (*Burgundy*, France) Reliable producer of *Moulin-à-Vent.*

✠ **Moulis** [moo-lees] (*Bordeaux*, France) Red wine village of the *Haut-Médoc*; often paired with *Listrac*, but making far more approachable good-value *Crus Bourgeois*. Ch. Anthonic; *Chasse-Spleen; Maucaillou;* Moulis; *Poujeaux.*

Mount Barker (Western Australia) Cooler-climate, southern region with great *Riesling, Verdelho*, impressive *Chardonnay*, and restrained *Shiraz.* Frankland Estate; *Goundrey; Howard Park; Plantagenet;* Wignalls.

✠ **Mount Horrocks** (*Clare Valley*, Australia) Inventive *Shiraz* and *Riesling* producer that has made a speciality out of reviving an old method of winemaking called "Cordon Cut", which concentrates the flavour of the *Riesling* juice by cutting the canes some time before picking the grapes.

✠ **Mount Hurtle** (*McLaren Vale*, South Australia) See *Geoff Merrill.*

✠ **Mount Langi Ghiran** [lan-gee gee-ran] (*Victoria*, Australia) A maker of excellent cool-climate *Riesling*, peppery *Shiraz*, and very good *Cabernet.* ★★★★ 1999 Cherry Tree Grenache Shiraz Cabernet ££

✠ **Mount Mary** (*Yarra Valley*, Australia) Dr. Middleton makes *Pinot Noir* and *Chardonnay* that are astonishingly and unpredictably *Burgundy*-like in the best and worst sense of the term. The Quintet red and Triolet white versions of Bordeaux are more reliable.

Mount Veeder (*Napa Valley*, California) Convincing hillside *appellation* producing impressive reds, especially from *Cabernet Sauvignon* and *Zinfandel.* Hess Collection; *Mayacamas; Mount Veeder Winery; Ch. Potelle.*

✠ **Mountadam** (*High Eden Ridge*, Australia) Recently purchased by the giant LVMH which owns *Moët & Chandon, Krug*, and *Cloudy Bay*, this hilltop winery makes classy Burgundian *Chardonnay* and *Pinot Noir* (both still and sparkling) and an impressive blend called "The Red". Also worth seeking out are the *Eden Ridge* organic wines, the fruity *David Wynn* line, and the "Samuel's Bay" *second label.*

🍇 **Mourvèdre** [mor-veh-dr] (*Rhône*, France) Floral-spicy *Rhône* grape usually found in blends. Increasingly popular in France and California where, as in Australia, it is called *Mataro.* Jade Mountain; Penfolds; *Ridge.*

Mousse [mooss] The bubbles in *Champagne* and sparkling wines.

Mousseux [moo-sur] (France) Cheap unremarkable sparkling wine.

✠ **Mouton-Cadet** [moo-ton ka-day] (*Bordeaux*, France) A brilliant commercial invention by Philippe de Rothschild who used it to profit from the name of *Mouton-Rothschild*, with which it has no discernible connection. Until recently the quality and the value for money offered by these wines has been poor, but there have been improvements. The "Réserve" is now better than the basic, and the recently launched white *Graves Réserve* creditable in its own right. Even so, there are better buys to be found on the shelves.

✠ **Ch. Mouton-Baronne-Philippe** [moo-ton ba-ron-fee-leep] (*Pauillac, 5ème Cru Classé, Bordeaux,* France) Known as Mouton d'Armailhac until 1933, then as Mouton-Baron-Philippe, then Mouton-Baronne-Philippe (in 1975) before becoming *Ch. d'Armailhac* in 1989.

✠ **Ch. Mouton-Rothschild** [moo-ton roth-child] (*Pauillac Premier Cru Classé, Bordeaux,* France) The only *château* to be elevated to a first growth from a second, Mouton can have gloriously rich, complex flavours of roast coffee and blackcurrant. Recent vintages were eclipsed by *Margaux, Lafite,* and *Latour,* but the 1998 and 1999 show a return to quality.

M

Mudgee [mud-zhee] (*New South Wales*, Australia) Australia's first *appellation* region, a coolish-climate area now being championed by *Rosemount* as well as by *Rothbury*. **Botobolar; Huntington Estate.** ★★★★ 2000 Rosemount Hill of Gold Cabernet Sauvignon ££

Ⅰ **Bodegas Muga** [moo-gah] (*Rioja*, Spain) Producer of good old-fashioned *Riojas*, of which Prado Enea is the best. ★★★★ 1998 Muga Rioja Reserva ££

Ⅰ **Mugneret/Mugneret Gibourg** [moon-yeh-ray jee-boor] (*Burgundy*, France) *Côte de Nuits* estate making outstanding quality.

Ⅰ **Jacques-Frederic Mugnier** [moo-nee-yay] (*Burgundy*, France) *Chambolle-Musigny* estate making long-lived wines from vineyards such as Bonnes-Mares and *Musigny*.

Ⅰ **Mulderbosch** [mool-duh-bosh] (*Stellenbosch*, South Africa) South Africa's answer to *Cloudy Bay*: exciting *Sauvignon* and *Meursault*-like *Chardonnay*, not to mention a red blend called Faithful Hound.

Ⅰ **Weingut Müller-Catoir** [moo-luh kah-twah] (*Pfalz*, Germany) Great new-wave producer using new-wave grapes as well as *Riesling*. Search out powerful Grauburgunder, Rieslaner, and *Scheurebe* wines.

Ⅰ **Egon Müller-Scharzhof** [moo-luh shahrtz-hof] (*Mosel-Saar-Ruwer*, Germany) Truly brilliant *Saar* producer.

🍇 **Müller-Thurgau** [moo-lur-toor-gow] (Germany) Workhorse white grape, which is a *Riesling* x *Sylvaner* cross. It is also known as *Rivaner*. Müller-Thurgau is used for making much unremarkable wine in Germany, but it also yields some gems for certain producers, such as *Müller-Catoir*. Very successful in England.

Ⅰ **Mumm/Mumm Napa** [murm] (*Champagne*, France/California) Maker of much improved Cordon Rouge *Champagne* and now slightly less good *Cuvée Napa* from California. Newly (1999) sold by its owners, Seagram. New owners have greater ambitions. ★★★ NV Mumm **Cuvée Napa Brut Prestige £££**

Ⅰ **René Muré** [moo-ray] (*Alsace*, France) Producer of full bodied wines, especially from the Clos St. Landelin vineyard.

Ⅰ **Klosterkellerei Muri Gries** [klos-ter-kel-lehr-rih moo-ree gree-ess] (*Alto Adige*, Italy) Lagrein specialist with seductive Kretzer pink, sturdy red Dunkel, and lovely Abtei Muri riserva.

Murfatlar [moor-fat-lah] (Romania) Major vineyard and research area that is currently having increasing success with *Chardonnay* (including some late-harvest sweet examples), and also with *Cabernet Sauvignon*.

Ⅰ **Murphy-Goode** (*Alexander Valley*, California) Classy producer of white wines that are quite Burgundian in style and sell at – considering this is California – affordable prices. Murphy-Goode also makes a high quality Cabernet Sauvignon.

Ⅰ **Bodegas Marqués de Murrieta** [mar-kays day moo-ree-eh-tah] (*Rioja*, Spain) Probably Spain's best old-style *oaky* white (sold as Castillo Ygay), and a traditional version of *Rioja* that is increasingly hard to find nowadays. The red, at its best, is one of the most long-lived, elegant example of this region's wines. You should definitely look out for the old Castillo Ygays from the 1960s with their distinctive old-style labels.

Ⅰ **Murrietta's Well** (*Livermore*, California) An innovative blend of *Zinfandel*, *Cabernet*, and *Merlot*. ★★★ 1997 Murrieta's Well Vendimia Red £££

Ⅰ **Ch. Musar** [moo-sahr] (*Ghazir*, Lebanon) Lebanon's leading winemaker *Serge Hochar* makes a different red every year, varying the blend of *Cabernet*, *Cinsault*, and *Syrah*. The style veers between *Bordeaux*, the *Rhône*, and Italy, but certainly with Château Musar there's never a risk of becoming bored. Good vintages easily keep for a decade. The *Chardonnay*-based whites are less than dazzling, though, and the Rosé can be very old fashioned. ★★★★★ 1999 ££

M

🍇 **Muscadelle** [mus-kah-del] Spicy ingredient in white *Bordeaux*. Confusingly used in the region of *Rutherglen* in Australia to produce fortified wine known there as *Tokay*.

🍷 **Muscadet des Coteaux de la Loire/Côtes de Grand Lieu/de Sèvre et Maine** [moos-kah-day day koh-toh dur lah lwar/koht dur gron lyur/dur say-vr' eh mayn] (*Loire*, France) Non-aromatic wines that are made from the *Melon de Bourgogne*. Worthwhile examples are matured for a brief period before being bottled ("*sur lie*") on their dead yeasts or *lees*. The Côtes de Grand Lieu and the rare Coteaux de la *Loire* can be good, but Sèvre et Maine is less reliable. *Dom. de Chasseloir;* Bossard; Chéreau-Carré; Couillaud; Guindon; *de Goulaine; Pierre Luneau;* Metaireau; Marcel Sautejeau; Sauvion.

🍇 **Muscat** [mus-kat] Generic name for a species of white grape (aka *Moscato* in Italy) of which there are a number of different subspecies.

🍇 **Muscat à Petits Grains** [moos-kah ah puh-tee gran] Aka *Frontignan*, the best variety of Muscat and the grape responsible for *Muscat de Beaumes de Venise, Muscat de Rivesaltes, Asti, Muscat of Samos,* and *Rutherglen* Muscats.

🍷 **Muscat de Cap Corse/Frontignan/Mireval/Rivesaltes/St. Jean de Minervois** (*Languedoc-Roussillon*, France) Potentially luscious fortified Muscats of which Rivesaltes is the most commonly encountered and St. Jean de Minervois is possibly the best.

🍇 **Muscat of Alexandria** [moos-kah] Grape responsible for *Moscatel de Setúbal, Moscatel de Valencia,* and sweet South Australians. Also known as *Lexia*. It is also grown in South Africa (where it is known by both names) and satisfies the Afrikaner sweet tooth as Hanepoot.

🍇 **Muscat Ottonel** [moos-kah ot-oh-nel] *Muscat* variety grown in Middle and Eastern Europe.

🍷 **Musigny** [moo-zee-nyee] (*Burgundy*, France) Potentially wonderful *Grand Cru* from which *Chambolle-Musigny* takes its name. A tiny amount of white is produced here. *De Vogüé; Groffier; Leroy; Mugnier; Prieur.* ★★★★★ 1999 Domaine Mugnier Musigny Grand Cru

Must Unfermented grape juice.

MW See *Master of Wine*.

N

Nackenheim [nahk-ehn-hime] (*Rheinhessen*, Germany) Village in the *Nierstein Bereich* that is unfortunately best known for its nowadays debased *Grosslage*, Gutes Domtal. *Gunderloch;* Kurfürstenhof; Heinrich Seip.

🍷 **Fiorenzo Nada** [fee-yor-ren-zoh nah-dah] (*Piedmont*, Italy) Look for *Barbaresco, Dolcetto d'Alba,* and the Seifile, barrique-aged *Barbera/Nebbiolo*.

Nahe [nah-huh] (Germany) *Anbaugebiet* producing wines which can in the right circumstances combine delicate flavour with full body and taut structure. *Crusius; Schlossgut Diel;* Hermann Donnhoff; Hehner Kiltz; *Kruger-Rumpf.*

🍷 **Ch. Nairac** [nay-rak] (*Barsac 2ème Cru Classé, Bordeaux,* France) Lush, long-lasting wine sometimes lacking a little complexity. Fine in 2001.

🍷 **Nalle** (*Sonoma*, California) Great *Dry Creek* producer of some of California's (and thus the world's) greatest *Zinfandel*.

Naoussa [nah-oosa] (Greece) Region producing dry red wines, often from the Xynomavro grape. ★★★ 2000 Naoussa J. Boutari & Sons, Imathia £

Napa [na-pa] (California) Named after the Native American word for "plenty", this is a region with plentiful wines ranging from ordinary to sublime. Too many are commercially hyped; and none is cheap. Another problem is that the region as a whole is far too varied in altitude and

N

winemaking conditions to make proper sense as a single *appellation*. On the other hand the 20 or so smaller *appellations* that are found within Napa, such as *Carneros, Stag's Leap, Howell Mountain,* and *Mt. Veeder* deserve greater prominence – as do nearby regions like *Sonoma. Atlas Peak; Beaulieu; Beringer; Cain; Cakebread; Caymus; Chimney Rock; Clos du Val; Crichton Hall; Cuvaison; Diamond Creek; Dom. Chandon; Duckhorn; Dunn; Flora Springs; Franciscan; Frog's Leap; Heitz; Hess Collection; Ch. Montelena; Monteviña; Mumm; Newton; Niebaum-Coppola; Opus One; Ch. Potelle; Phelps; Schramsberg; Screaming Eagle; Shafer; Stag's Leap; Sterling; Turley.*

Ï **Napa Ridge** (California) Highly successful brand, most of whose pleasant, commercial wines are made with juice from grapes that have been grown outside *Napa*. (Exports from this producer are less confusingly labelled as "Coastal Ridge".)

Ï **Nautilus Estate** [naw-tih-luhs] (*Marlborough,* New Zealand) *Yalumba's* New Zealand offshoot. Sparkling wine and *Sauvignon.* ★★★★ 2001 Nautilus Sauvignon Blanc ££

Ï **Navajas** [na-VA-khas] (*Rioja,* Spain) Small producer making impressive reds and *oaky* whites worth keeping. ★★★ 2000 Navajas Graciano Rioja £

Ï **Navarra** [na-VAH-rah] (Spain) Northern Spanish *DO*, located not far from Pamplona and the western Pyrenees, traditionally renowned for rosés and heavy reds but now producing wines to rival those from neighbouring *Rioja,* where prices are often higher. Look for innovative *Cabernet Sauvignon* and *Tempranillo* blends. *Chivite; Guelbenzu;* Castillo de Monjardin; Vinicola Murchantina; Nekeas; *Ochoa;* Palacio de la Vega; Senorio de Sarria. ★★★★ 1998 Palacio de la Vega Cabernet Sauvignon Reserva ££

Navarro Correas [na-vah-roh koh-ray-yas] (Argentina) Big, oaky wines with loads of personality. ★★★ 2000 Navarro Correas Colleccion Privada Malbec Viñas la Heredad Mendoza £

❦ **Nebbiolo** [neh-bee-oh-loh] (*Piedmont,* Italy) Grape of *Piedmont,* producing wines with tarry, cherryish, spicy flavours that are slow to mature but become richly complex – epitomized by *Barolo* and *Barbaresco.* Quality and style vary enormously depending on soil. Aka *Spanna.*

Ï **Nederburg** [neh-dur-burg] (*Paarl,* South Africa) Huge commercial producer. The Edelkeur *late harvest* wines are the gems of the cellar. Sadly, the best wines are only sold at the annual Nederburg Auction. ★★★★ 2000 Nederburg Auction Reserve Eminence £££

Ï **Neetlingshof** [neet-lings-hof] (South Africa) Large estate with decent quality and an abundance of labels. Lord Neethling Reserve and Lord Neethling Laurentius are Bordeaux blends.

Négociant [nay-goh-see-yon] (France) Merchant who buys, matures, and bottles wine. See also *Eléveur.*

Négociant-manipulant (NM) [ma-nih-pyoo-lon] (*Champagne,* France) Buyer and blender of wines for *Champagne,* identifiable by the NM number which is mandatory on the label.

Ï **Negroamaro** [nay-groh-ah-mah-roh] (*Puglia,* Italy) A Puglian grape whose name means "bitter-black" and produces fascinating, spicy-gamey reds. Found in *Salice Salentino* and *Copertino* and in a growing number of increasingly impressive *IGT* wines. ★★★ 2000 La Corte Negroamaro Masseria la Corte ££

Nelson (New Zealand) Small region, a glorious bus ride to the north-west of *Marlborough. Neudorf* and *Seifried/Redwood* Valley are the stars. ★★★★ 2001 Waimea Estates Sauvignon Blanc £

Ï **Nemea** [nur-may-yah] (Peloponnese, Greece) Improving cool(ish) climate region for reds made from Agiorgitiko. *Boutari; Semeli; Tsantalis.*

Ch. Nenin [neh-na'n] (*Bordeaux,* France) Large *Pomerol* estate now under the same ownership as *Léoville-Lascases* and making a great 2001.

Ï **Nepenthe** [neh-pen-thi] (*Adelaide Hills,* South Australia) Instant star with dazzling *Chardonnay, Semillon, Sauvignon, Pinot Noir, Cabernet-Merlot,* and *Zinfandel.* ★★★★ 2001 Nepenthe Pinot Gris ££

N

℞ **Ch. la Nerthe** [nehrt] (*Rhône*, France) One of the most exciting estates in *Châteauneuf-du-Pape*, producing rich wines with seductive dark fruit.

℞ **Neuburger** [noy-bur-gur] (Austria) A white grape that makes spicy, broad wines, sweet or dry, with more richness than finesse.

Neuchâtel [nur-sha-tel] (Switzerland) Lakeside region. Together with Les Trois Lacs, a source of good red and rosé, *Pinot Noir*, and *Chasselas* and *Chardonnay* whites. **Ch. d'Auvernier; Porret.**

℞ **Neudorf** [noy-dorf] (*Nelson*, New Zealand) Pioneering small-scale producer of beautifully made *Chardonnay*, *Semillon*, *Sauvignon*, *Riesling*, and *Pinot Noir*.

℞ **Neumayer** [noy-my-yer] (Traisental, Austria) Vigorous dry wines including *Grüner Veltliner* and *Riesling*, from a family estate.

Neusiedlersee [noy-zeed-lur-zay] (Austria) *Burgenland* region on the Hungarian border centred on the broad, shallow Neusiedl lake. Great *late-harvest* and improving whites and reds. **Fieler-Artinger; Kracher; Lang; Willi Opitz; Tschida. ★★★★★ 1998 Seewinkler Impressionen Chardonnay Trockenbeerenauslese Weinhaus Kaisergarten Neusiedlersee ££££**

Neusidlersee-Hügelland [noy-zeed-lur-zay hoo-gurl-lend] (Austria) Region on the western side of the Neusiedlersee, where sweet whites can be made in a narrow strip near the lake, and good dry wines, up in the hills.

Nevers [nur-vehr] (France) Subtlest oak – from a forest in *Burgundy*.

New South Wales (Australia) Major wine-producing state, which is home to the famous *Hunter Valley*, along with the increasingly impressive *Cowra*, *Mudgee, Orange,* and *Murrumbidgee* regions. **★★★★ 2000 The Mill Shiraz £**

New Zealand Instant superstar with proven *Sauvignon Blanc* and *Chardonnay* and – despite most expectations – increasingly successful *Merlots* and more particularly *Pinot Noirs*. Syrah can work well too occasionally, as can *Pinot Gris* and *Gewürztraminer*. *Cabernet Sauvignon*, however, rarely ripens properly. Vintages vary, however. See *Marlborough, Martinborough, Hawkes Bay, Nelson, Gisborne, Auckland.*

℞ **Newton Vineyards** (*Napa Valley,* California) High-altitude vineyards with top-class *Chardonnay*, *Merlot*, and *Cabernet*, now being made with help from *Michel Rolland.*

℞ **Neszmély** (Hungary) Progressive winery in Aszar-Neszmély producing good commercial white wines.

℞ **Ngatarawa** [na-TA-ra-wah] (*Hawkes Bay*, New Zealand) Small winery that can make impressive reds and even better *Chardonnays* and *late harvest* whites. **★★★ 2000 Alwyn Reserve Merlot Cabernet £££**

Niagara (*Ontario*, Canada) Area close to the falls of the same name, and to the shores of lakes Ontario and Erie, where the *Vidal* is used to make good *Icewine. Chardonnay, Riesling,* and – though generally less successfully – red varieties such as *Pinot Noir* and *Merlot* are now used too by some eager producers. Watch this space. **Ch. des Charmes; Henry of Pelham; Inniskillin; Magnotta; Reif; Southbrook. ★★★★★ 2000 Pillitteri Estates Vidal Icewine ££**

℞ **Nicholson River** (*Gippsland*, Australia) The temperamental *Gippsland* climate makes for a small production of stunning *Chardonnays*, some of which are of a very Burgundian style.

℞ **Niebaum-Coppola** [nee-bowm coh-po-la] (*Napa Valley,* California) You've seen the movie. Now taste the wine. The *Dracula* and *Godfather* director is very serious about the vineyards of an estate that now includes the appropriately Gothic *Inglenook* winery and has some of the oldest vines about. Inglenook makes intensely concentrated *Cabernets* that will definitely suit the patient. **★★★★ 1994 Rubicon ££££**

Niederösterreich [nee-dur-os-tur-rike] (Austria) Lower Austria: the region where over half of the country's vineyards are situated.

N

I **Niederhausen Schlossböckelheim** [nee-dur-how sen shlos-berk-ehl-hime] (*Nahe*, Germany) State-owned estate producing highly concentrated *Riesling* from great vineyards.

I **Dom. Michel Niellon** [nee-el-lon] (*Burgundy*, France) One of the top five white *Burgundy* producers, making highly concentrated wines. ★★★★ 2000 Chassagne-Montrachet 1er Cru Chenevottes

I **Niepoort** [nee-poort] (*Douro*, Portugal) Small, independent *port* house making subtle vintage and particularly impressive *colheita tawnies*. A name to watch. ★★★★ 1999 Quinta de Passadouro £££

Nierstein [neer-shtine] (*Rheinhessen*, Germany) The fine wines made here are obscured by the notoriety of the reliably dull Niersteiner Gutes Domtal. Balbach; Gunderloch; Heyl zu Herrnsheim. ★★★ 1999 Niersteiner Findling Auslese Weingut Eugen Wehrheim £

I **Nieto & Senetiner** [nee-yeh-toh eh seh-neh-tee-nehr] (*Mendoza*, Argentina) Reliable wines sold under Valle de Vistalba and Cadus labels. ★★★ 2001 Finca Las Marias Barbera £

I **Nigl** [nee-gel] (*Kremstal*, Austria) One of Austria's best producers of dry *Riesling* and *Grüner Veltliner*.

I **Weingut Nikolaihof** [nih-koh-li-hof] (*Niederösterreich*, Austria) Producers of top class *Grüner Veltliners* and *Rieslings*.

I **Nipozzano** [nip-ots-zano] (*Tuscany*, Italy) See *Frescobaldi*.

I **Nino Negri** [nee-noh neh-gree] (*Lombardy*, Italy) Casimiro Maule makes one of the best examples of Valtellina Sfursat.

I **Nobilo** [nob-ih-loh] (*Huapai*, New Zealand) Kiwi colony of the BRL Hardy empire making good *Chardonnay* from *Gisborne*, "*Icon*" wines from *Marlborough* including the commercial off-dry *White Cloud* blend. ★★★★ 2001 House of Nobilo Icon Series Sauvignon Blanc £

Noble rot Popular term for *botrytis cinerea*

I **Vino Nocetto** (*Shendoah Valley*, California) Winery that has been unusually successful with Italian style Sangiovese.

I **Normans** (*McLaren Vale*, Australia) Fast-improving *Cabernet* and *Shiraz* specialist. ★★★★ 1998 Normans Chais Clarendon Shiraz ££

North Fork (New York State, USA) Long Island *AVA*, with most of Long Island's wineries.

I **Bodegas Norton** [naw-ton] (*Argentina*) This is one of Argentina's most recommendable producers, producing a wide range of *varietal* wines. The "Privada" wines are the cream of the crop. ★★★★ 2000 Cabernet Sauvignon ££

Nouveau [noo-voh] New wine, most popularly used of *Beaujolais*.

I **Nova** [meg-yer] (*Tokaji*, Hungary) French-owned pioneer of wines including *Tokaji* and *Furmint*.

I **Quinta do Noval** (*Douro*, Portugal) Fine and potentially finer estate. The ultra-rare Nacional *vintage ports* are the jewel in the crown, made from ungrafted vines. Also of note are great *colheita tawny ports*. ★★★★ 1997 Noval Unfiltered Late Bottled Vintage ££

I **Albet i Noya** [al-bet-ee-noy-ya] (*Spain*) Innovative producer with red and white traditional and imported varieties. A superstar in the making. ★★★ NV Cava Vendrell Albet i Noya Brut Reserve ££

I **Nuits-St.-Georges** [noo-wee san zhawzh] (*Burgundy*, France) *Commune* producing the most *claret*-like of red *Burgundies*, properly tough and lean when young but glorious with age. Whites are good but ultra-rare. *Dom. de l'Arlot; Robert Chevillon; Jean-Jacques Confuron; Faiveley; Henri Gouges; Jean Grivot; Leroy; Alain Michelot; Patrice Rion; Henri & Gilles Remoriquet.*

I **Nuragus di Cagliari** [noo-rah-goos dee ka-lee-yah-ree] (*Sardinia*, Italy) Good-value, tangy, floral wine from the Nuragus grape.

NV Non-vintage, meaning a blend of wines from different years.

Nyetimber [nie-tim-bur] (England) Sussex vineyard exploiting England's potential for sparkling wine with promising efforts made from *Chardonnay*, *Pinot Noir* and *Pinot Meunier*.

O

☿ **Oakville Ranch** (*Napa Valley,* California) Potentially one of the *Napa's* most exciting red wine producers, but wines have so far been a little too tough. ★★★ 1999 Miner Family Vineyards Chardonnay Oakville Ranch

Oaky Flavour imparted by oak casks which varies depending on the source of the oak (American is sweeter than French). Woody is usually less flattering.

☿ **Vin de Pays d'Oc** [pay-doc] (*Languedoc-Roussillon,* France) The world's biggest wine region, encompassing *appellations* such as *Corbières* and *Minervois* and several smaller *Vins de Pays* regions. Pioneers here include *Mas de Daumas Gassac* and *Skalli.*

☿ **Bodegas Ochoa** [och-oh-wah] (*Navarra,* Spain) New-wave producer of creamy, fresh *Cabernet, Tempranillo,* and *Viura.* ★★★ 2001 Garnacha Rosado £

Ockfen [ok-fehn] (*Mosel-Saar-Ruwer,* Germany) Village producing some of the best, steeliest wines of the *Saar-Ruwer Bereich,* especially *Rieslings* from the *Bockstein* vineyard. ★★★ 1999 Ockfener Bockstein Riesling Auslese Weingut Sankt Urbans-Hof £

☿ **Oddero** [od-DEHR-roh] (Piedmont, Italy) Barolo producer with marvellous vineyards and fast-improving Barolo. ★★★★ 1997 Barolo Serralunga d'Alba 'Vigna Rionda'

Oechsle [urk-slur] (Germany) Indication of the sugar level in grapes or wine.

Oeste [wes-teh] (Portugal) Western region in which a growing number of fresh, light, commercial wines are being made, of which the most successful has undoubtedly been Arruda. ★★★ 1997 Arruda Tinto Adega Co-op £

Oestrich [ur-strihckh] (*Rheingau,* Germany) Source of good *Riesling. Wegeler Deinhard; Balthazar Ress.* ★★★ 2000 Oestricher Lenchen Riesling Kabinett Weingut Peter Jacob Kuhn ££

☿ **Michel Ogier** [ogee-yay] (*Rhône,* France) *Côte-Rôtie* producer, making less muscular wines than most of his neighbours.

Oïdium [oh-id-ee-yum] Fungal grape infection, shrivelling the berries and turning them grey.

☿ **Ojai Vineyard** [oh-high] (*Santa Barbara,* California) The specialities here are a *Sauvignon-Semillon* blend and – more interestingly – a *Rhône*-like *Syrah.*

Okanagan (*British Columbia,* Canada) This is the principal wine region in the west of Canada. Despite frosts, the *Pinot Noir* can produce good wine here. *Mission Hill.* ★★★★ 1999 Jackson-Triggs Grand Reserve Chardonnay ££

☙ **Olasz Rizling** [oh-lash-riz-ling] (Hungary) Name for the *Welschriesling.*

☿ **Ch. Olivier** [oh-liv-ee-yay] (*Pessac-Léognan Cru Classé, Bordeaux,* France) An underperformer which has yet to join the *Graves* revolution.

Oloroso [ol-oh-roh-soh] (*Jerez,* Spain) Style of full-bodied *sherry,* either dry or semi-sweet. ★★★★★ Royal Corregidor Sandeman £

☿ **Oltrepò Pavese** [ohl-tray-poh pa-vay-say] (*Lombardy,* Italy) Still and sparkling *DOC* made from grapes such as the spicy red Gutturnio and white Ortrugo. Ca' di Frara; *Tenuta il Bosco;* Cabanon; Fugazza; Mazzolina; Bruno Verdi.

☿ **Omar Khayyam (Champagne India)** [oh-mah-ki-yam] (*Maharashtra,* India) Pleasant *Champagne*-method wine. The producer's cheeky name, "*Champagne* India", annoys the Champenois, but they, in the shape of *Piper Heidsieck,* were happy enough to sell the Indians their expertise.

Ontario (Canada) The main wine region of eastern Canada, famous for Ice Wine and with increasingly good Chardonnay, Riesling, Cabernet Franc, Pinot Gris. Vineyards are in Lake Erie, Pelee Island, and Niagara Peninsula.

☿ **Willi Opitz** [oh-pitz] (*Neusiedlersee,* Austria) Oddball pet food-manufacturer-turned-producer of a magical mystery tour of *late-harvest* and straw-dried wines (Schilfwein), including an extraordinary *botrytis* red labelled – to the discomfort of some Californians – "Opitz One".

Oppenheim [op-en-hime] (*Rheinhessen,* Germany) Village in *Nierstein Bereich* best known – unfairly – for unexciting wines from the Krottenbrunnen. Elsewhere produces soft wines with concentrated flavour.

Opus One (*Napa Valley,* California) Twenty-year-old co-production between *Mouton-Rothschild* and *Robert Mondavi.* Opus one is a classy, *claret*-like, blackcurranty wine that sells at an appropriately classy, *claret*-like price.

Orange (*New South Wales,* Australia) Coolish region which, like *Cowra,* now competes with the *Hunter Valley.* Try the Orange *Shiraz* made by Philip Shaw of *Rosemount* from vineyards of which he is co-owner. Cabonne; Little Boomey; Logan; Reynolds; Rosemount. ★★★★★ 1999 Rosemount Orange Shiraz £££

Orange Muscat Another highly eccentric member of the *Muscat* family, best known for dessert wines in California by *Quady* and in Australia for the delicious *Brown Brothers Late Harvest Orange Muscat* and *Flora.*

Oregon Fashionable cool-climate state, whose winemakers make a speciality of growing *Pinot Noir.* The *Chardonnay, Riesling, Pinot Gris,* and sparkling wines show promise too. *Adelsheim; Amity; Argyle; Beaux Freres; Cameron; Chehalem; Dom Drouhin; Duck Pond; Erath; Eyrie; Henry Estate; King Estate; Ponzi; Rex Hill; Sokol Blosser.*

Oremus [oh-ray-mosh] (Tokaj, Hungary) 1: a Tokaji estate owned by Vega Sicilia and making outstanding quality; 2: a grape, a cross between Furmint and Bouvier, increasingly giving way to another Furmint x Bouvier called Zeta. ★★★★ 1995 Tokaji Aszú 5 Puttonyos Oremus £££

Oriachovitza [oh-ree-ak-hoh-vit-sah] (Bulgaria) Major source of reliable *Cabernet Sauvignon* and *Merlot.*

Orlando (South Australia) Huge, French-owned (Pernod-Ricard) producer of the reliable *Jacob's Creek* wines. Look for "Reserve" and "Limited Release" efforts. The RF range is good but the harder-to-find Gramps and Flaxmans wines are better. ★★★★ 1999 Jacob's Creek Reserve Shiraz Orlando ££

Orléanais [aw-lay-yo-nay] (*Loire,* France) A vineyard area around Orléans in the Central Vineyards region of the *Loire,* specializing in unusual white *Chardonnay/Pinot Gris* and red *Pinot Noir/Cabernet Franc* blends.

Ch. Olivier [oh-leev-ee-yay] (*Pessac-Léognan, Bordeaux,* France) Picturesque château that is beginning to improve after a long dull patch.

Ch. Les Ormes-de-Pez [awm dur-pay] (*St. Estèphe Cru Bourgeois, Bordeaux,* France) Stablemate of *Lynch-Bages* and made with similar skill.

Tenuta dell'Ornellaia [teh-noo-tah del-aw-nel-li-ya] (*Tuscany,* Italy) *Bordeaux*-blend *Bolgheri Super-Tuscan* from the brother of Piero Antinori. This is serious wine that is worth maturing. ★★★★★ 2000 Ornellaia ££££

Ortega [aw-tay-gah] This is a recently developed grape variety that is well used by *Biddenden* and *Denbies.* Can make good *late-harvest* wine.

Orvieto [ohr-vee-yet-toh] (*Umbria,* Italy) White Umbrian *DOC* responsible for a quantity of dull wine. Orvieto *Classico* is better. Look out for Secco if you like your white wine dry; *Amabile* if you have a sweet tooth. *Antinori; Bigi; La Carraia; Covio Cardetto; Palazzone.*

Osborne [os-sbaw-nay] (*Jerez,* Spain) Producer of a good range of *sherries* including a brilliant *Pedro Ximenez.* ★★★ NV Fino Quinta Pale Dry £

Dom. Ostertag [os-tur-tahg] (*Alsace,* France) Poet and philosopher André Ostertag's superb *Alsace domaine.*

Overgaauw [oh-ver-gow] (South Africa) Heavyweight reds which benefit from bottle age. Look out for *Cabernet Sauvignon* and *Merlot.* ★★★ 2000 Merlot ££

Oxidation The effect (usually detrimental, occasionally – as in *sherry* – intentional) of oxygen on wine.

Oxidative The opposite to reductive. Certain wines – most reds, and whites like *Chardonnay* – benefit from limited exposure to oxygen during their fermentation and maturation, such as barrel ageing.

Oyster Bay (*Marlborough,* New Zealand) See entry for *Delegats.* ★★★ 2001 Oyster Bay Chardonnay £

P

Paarl [pahl] (South Africa) Warm region in which *Backsberg* and *Boschendal* make appealing wines. Hotter and drier than neighbouring *Stellenbosch*. *Charles Back/Fairview; KWV; Backsberg; Glen Carlou;Villiera; Plaisir de Merle.*

⊺ **Pacherenc du Vic-Bilh** [pa-shur-renk doo veek beel] (*Southwest*, France) Rare, dry, or fairly sweet white wine made from the *Petit* and *Gros Manseng*. A speciality of *Madiran*. ★★★ 2000 Saint Albert Producteurs Plaimont ££

⊺ **Pacific Echo** Recommendable sparkling wine, once called *Scharffenberger.*

Padthaway [pad-thah-way] (South Australia) Vineyard area just north of *Coonawarra* specializing in *Chardonnay* and *Sauvignon*, though reds work well here too. *Angove's Hardys; Lindemans; Orlando; Penfolds.* ★★★★ 1999 Stonehaven Limited Vineyard Release Chardonnay ££

⊺ **Pagadebit di Romagna** [pah-gah-deh-bit dee roh-man-ya] (*Emilia-Romagna*, Italy) Dry, sweet, and sparkling whites from the Pagadebit grape.

⊺ **Pago de Carrovejas** [pah-goh deh kah-roh-vay-jash] (*Ribera del Duero*, Portugal) One of the best producers in Ribera del Duero.

⊺ **Pahlmeyer** (*Napa Valley*, California) One of California's most interesting winemakers, producing *Burgundian Chardonnay* and a *Bordeaux*-blend red.

⊺ **Paitin** [pie-teen] (*Piedmont*, Italy) The Sori Paitin vineyard in Barbaresco can offer Gaja quality at affordable prices.

⊺ **Ch. Pajzos** [pah-zhohs] (*Tokaj*, Hungary) Serious, French-owned producer of new-wave *Tokaji*.

⊺ **Bodegas Palacio** [pa-las-see-yoh] (*Rioja*, Spain) Underrated *bodega* with stylish, fruit-driven reds and distinctively oaky whites. Also helped by wine guru *Michel Rolland*. ★★★ 1998 Cosme Palacio y Hermanos Rioja £

⊺ **Palacio de Fefiñanes** [pah-las-see-yoh day fay-feen-yah-nays] (*Galicia*, Spain) Fine producer of *Rias Baixas Albariño*.

⊺ **Palacio de la Vega** [pah-lath-yo deh lah vay-gah] (*Navarra*, Spain) Good Tempranillo and international varieties. ★★★★ 1998 Cabernet Reserva ££

⊺ **Alvaro Palacios** [pah-las-see-yohs] (*Catalonia*, Spain) Superstar *Priorat* estate producing individual wines with rich, concentrated flavours. L'Ermita is the (very pricey) top wine. Finca Dofi and Les Terrasses are more affordable.

Palate Nebulous term describing the apparatus used for tasting (i.e., the tongue) as well as the skill of the taster (e.g., "he has a good palate").

⊺ **Podere Il Palazzino** [poh-day-ray eel pal-lat-zee-noh] (Tuscany, Italy) Ripe, juicy *Chianti* aged in barrique. Try the Reserva, Grossa Sanese.

⊺ **Palette** [pa-let] (*Provence*, France) Usually overpriced *AC* rosé and creamy white, well liked by holidayers in St. Tropez

⊺ **Palliser Estate** [pa-lih-sur] (*Martinborough*, New Zealand) Source of classy *Sauvignon Blanc*, *Chardonnay* and – increasingly – *Pinot Noir* from *Martinborough*. ★★★★★ 2000 Palliser Estate Pinot Noir ££

Palmela [pal-may-lah] (Terras do Sado, Portugal) Region making attractive reds from Periquita, among others. ★★★ 1992 Caves Vidigal Palmela £

⊺ **Ch. Palmer** [pahl-mur] (*Margaux 3ème Cru Classé, Bordeaux*, France) Third-growth *Margaux* stands alongside the best of the *Médoc* and often outclasses its more highly ranked neighbours. Wonderfully perfumed.

⊺ **Palo Cortado** [pah-loh kaw-tah doh] (*Jerez*, Spain) Rare *sherry* pitched between *amontillado* and *oloroso*. *Gonzalez Byass; Hidalgo; Lustau; Osborne; Valdespino.* ★★★★★ NV Barbadillo Obispo Gascon Palo Cortado £££

❀ **Palomino** [pa-loh-mee-noh] (*Jerez*, Spain) White grape responsible for virtually all fine *sherries* – and almost invariably dull white wine, when unfortified. Also widely grown in South Africa.

⊺ **Quinta das Pancas** [keen-tah dash-pan-kash] (Estremadura, Portugal) Modern estate with good Cabernet and Chardonnay and Touriga Nacional.

⊺ **Marchese Pancrazi** [mar-kay-say pan-crat-zee] (Tuscany, Italy) This property planted Pinot Noir thinking it to be Sangiovese – the nursery had sent the wrong vines. Now now it makes rather good Pinot Nero.

P

I **Panther Creek** (*Oregon*) Fine Pinot Noir producer in the Willamette Valley. The Shea Vineyard wines are worth cellaring for a while.

I **Ch. Pape-Clément** [pap klay-mon] (*Pessac-Léognan Cru Classé, Bordeaux, France*) Great source of rich reds since the mid-1980s and, more recently, small quantities of delicious, peach-oaky white. ★★★★ 1996 Ch. Pape-Clément £££

I **Paradigm** (California, USA) Good new estate in Oakville.

I **Parducci** [pah-doo-chee] (*Mendocino,* California) Steady producer whose *Petite Sirah* is a terrific bargain. ★★★ 2000 Parducci Chardonnay ££

I **Dom. Alain Paret** [pa-ray] (*Rhône,* France) Producer of a truly magnificent *St. Joseph* and *Condrieu*, in partnership with one of the world's best-known winemakers. (Though, to be fair, M Paret's associate, Gérard Depardieu does owe his fame to the movies rather than his efforts among the vines.) ★★★★ 2000 St Joseph Les Larmes Du Pere ££

I **Paringa Estate** (*Mornington, Victoria,* Australia) With *T'Galant, Dromana* and *Stoniers*, this is one of the stars of *Mornington Peninsula*. Fine *Shiraz*.

I **Parker Estate** (*Coonawarra,* Australia) Small producer sharing its name with the US guru, and calling its (very pricey) red "First Growth". Should be awarded good marks for chutzpah.

I **Parusso** [pah-roo-soh] (*Piedmont,* Italy) Very fine single-vineyard Barolos (Munie and Rocche) and wines sold under the Langhe designation. ★★★★ 1997 Barolo Castiglione Falletto Parusso 'Mariondino'

I **Parxet** [par-shet] (*Alella,* Spain) The only *cava* from *Alella*, and good dry white Marques de Alella, too. ★★★ NV Parxet Titiana ££

Pasado/Pasada [pa-sah-doh/dah] (Spain) Term applied to old or fine *fino* and *amontillado sherries*. ★★★ Hildago Manzanilla Pasada Pastrana ££

I **C.J. Pask** [pask] (*Hawkes Bay,* New Zealand) *Cabernet* pioneer with excellent *Chardonnay* and *Sauvignon*. One of New Zealand's very best. ★★★ 2000 CJ Pask Reserve Merlot ££

Paso Robles [pa-soh roh-blays] (*San Luis Obispo,* California) Warmish, long-established region, unaffected by coastal winds or marine fog, and good for *Zinfandel* (especially *Ridge*), *Rhône*, and Italian varieties. Plus increasingly successful *Chardonnays* and *Pinots*. ★★★★ 2000 EOS Cabernet Sauvignon ££

I **Pasqua** [pas-kwah] (*Veneto,* Italy) Producer of fairly priced, reliable wines.

Passetoutgrains [pas-stoo-gran] (*Burgundy,* France) Wine supposedly made from two-thirds *Gamay*, one-third *Pinot Noir*, though few producers respect these proportions. Once the Burgundians' daily red – until they decided to sell it and drink cheaper wine from other regions.

I **Passing Clouds** (*Bendigo,* Australia) "We get clouds, but it never rains ..." Despite a fairly hideous label, this is one of Australia's most serious red blends.

Passito [pa-see-toh] (Italy) Raisiny wine made from sun-dried *Erbaluce* grapes in Italy. This technique is now used in Australia by *Primo Estate*. ★★★ 1997 Gravisano Vino Passito Botromagno Puglia ££

I **Ch. Patache d'Aux** [pa-tash-doh] (*Médoc Cru Bourgeois, Bordeaux,* France) Château producing traditional, toughish stuff.

I **Frederico Paternina** [pa-tur-nee-na] (*Rioja,* Spain) Loved by Hemingway.

I **Luis Pato** [lweesh-pah-toh] (*Bairrada,* Portugal) One of Portugal's rare superstar winemakers, proving, among other things, that the *Baga* grape can make first-class spicy, berryish red wines. ★★★★★ 1999 Vinha Pan £££

Patras [pat-ras] (Greece) Appellation for white *Roditis*.

I **Patriarche** [pa-tree-arsh] (*Burgundy,* France) Improving merchant. Best wines are from the *Ch. de Meursault*. ★★★★ 1999 Volnay ££

I **Patrimonio** [pah-tree-moh-nee-yoh] (*Corsica,* France) One of the best appellations in Corsica. Grenache reds and rosés and Vermentino whites. **Aliso-Rossi; Arena; de Catarelli; Gentile; Leccia; Clos Marfisi; Orenga de Gaffory.**

I **Patz & Hall** (*Napa Valley,* California) Big, full-flavoured *Chardonnays*.

I **Pauillac** [poh-yak] (*Bordeaux,* France) One of the four famous "*communes*" of the *Médoc*, Pauillac is the home of *Châteaux Latour, Lafite*, and *Mouton-Rothschild*, as well as the two *Pichons* and *Lynch-Bages*.

P

- **Domaine Paul Bruno** (Chile) Joint venture in *Maipo* by Paul Pontallier of *Ch. Margaux* and Bruno Prats (formerly) of *Cos d'Estournel.* Now beginning to find its feet after an unconvincing start.
- **Paul Cluwer** (South Africa) Estate in *Elgin* with subtle Sauvignon, very good Pinot Noir, Chardonnay, and Gewurztraminer.
- **Clos de Paulilles** [poh-leey] (*Languedoc-Roussillon,* France) Top-class producer of *Banyuls* and *Collioure.*
- **Neil Paulett** [paw-let] (South Australia) Small, top-flight *Clare Valley Riesling* producer. ★★★ 1999 Pauletts Shiraz ££
- **Dr. Pauly-Bergweiler** [bur-gwi-lur] (*Mosel-Saar-Ruwer,* Germany) Ultra-modern winery with really stylish, modern, dry and late-harvest *Riesling.* ★★★ 2000 Bernkasteler Lay Riesling Beerenauslese £££

- **Ch. Pavie** [pa-vee] (*St. Emilion Premier Grand Cru Classé, Bordeaux,* France) Plummily rich, overblown, overpriced *St. Emilion* wines.
- **Ch. Pavie-Decesse** [pa-vee dur-ses] (*St. Emilion Grand Cru Classé, Bordeaux,* France) Neighbour to *Ch. Pavie,* but a shade less impressive.
- **Ch. Pavie-Macquin** [pa-vee ma-kan'] (*St. Emilion Grand Cru Classé, Bordeaux*) Returned to form since the late 1980s – and the producer of a startlingly good 1993.
- **Le Pavillon Blanc de Ch. Margaux** [pa-vee-yon blon] (*Bordeaux,* France) The (rare) all-*Sauvignon* white wine of *Ch. Margaux* which still acts as the yardstick for the growing number of *Médoc* white wines.
- **Pazo de Barrantes** [pa-thoh de bah-ran-tays] (*Galicia,* Spain) One of the newest names in *Rias Baixas,* producing lovely, spicy *Albariño.* Under the same ownership as *Marques de Murrieta.* ★★★ 2001 Albariño ££
- **Ca' del Pazzo** [kah-del-pat-soh] (*Tuscany,* Italy) Ultra-classy, *oaky Super-Tuscan* with loads of ripe fruit and oak.
  Pécharmant [pay-shar-mon] (*Southwest,* France) In the *Bergerac* area, producing light, *Bordeaux*-like reds. Worth trying.
- 🍇 **Pedro Ximénez** (PX) [peh-droh khee-MEH-nes] (*Jerez,* Spain) White grape, dried in the sun to create a sweet, curranty wine, which is used in the blending of the sweeter *sherry* styles, and in its own right by *Osborne,* and by *Gonzalez Byass* for its brilliant Noe. Also produces a very unusual wine at *De Bortoli* in Australia. ★★★★★ Pedro Ximenez El Candado Valdespino ££
- **Viña Pedrosa** [veen-ya pay-droh-sah] (*Ribera del Duero,* Spain) Modern blend of *Tempranillo* and classic *Bordelais* varieties. The Spanish equivalent of a *Super-Tuscan.*
- **Clos Pegase** [kloh-pay-gas] (*Napa Valley,* California) Showcase winery with improving but historically generally overpraised wines. ★★★ 1997 Graveyard Hill Cabernet Sauvignon £££
- **Pegasus Bay** (New Zealand) Well structured Riesling and supple Pinot Noir, plus elegant Chardonnay and good Cabernet blend.
- **Pelissero** [peh-lee-seh-roh] (*Piedmont,* Italy) Oaky Barberas, rich, dark Dolcetto, and lovely single-vineyard Barbaresco. ★★★★ 1997 Barberesco 'Vanotu' ££
- **Dom. Henry Pellé** [on-ree pel-lay] (*Loire,* France) Reliable producer of fruitier-than-usual *Menetou-Salon.*
- **Pellegrini** (*Long Island,* New York) Producer of fine *Merlot* on the North Fork of Long Island.
- **Pelorus** [pe-law-rus] (*Marlborough,* New Zealand) Showy, big, buttery, yeasty, almost Champagne-style New Zealand sparkling wine from *Cloudy Bay.*
  Pemberton (Western Australia) Up-and-coming cooler climate region for more restrained styles of *Chardonnay* and *Pinot Noir; Picardy, Plantagenet,* and *Smithbrook* are the names to look out for. ★★★ 2000 Smithbrook Merlot ££

P

☲ **Peñaflor** [pen-yah-flaw] (Argentina) Huge, dynamic firm producing increasingly good-value wines. ★★★ **2000 Elementos Red £**

Penedés [peh-neh-dehs] (*Catalonia*, Spain) Largest *DOC* of *Catalonia* with varying altitudes, climates, and styles ranging from *cava* to still wines pioneered by *Torres* and others, though some not as successfully. The current trend toward increasing use of *varietals* such as *Cabernet Sauvignon*, *Merlot*, and *Chardonnay* allows more French-style winemaking without losing any of the intrinsic Spanish character. Belatedly living up to some of its early promise. *Albet i Noya; Can Feixes; Can Ráfols dels Caus; Freixenet; Cavas Hill; Juvé y Camps;* Jean Leon*; Monistrol;* Puigi Roca*; Torres.*

☲ **Penfolds** (*South Australia*) Now associated with Rosemount. The world's biggest premium wine company with a high-quality line, from Bin 2 to *Grange*. Previously a red wine specialist but now rapidly becoming a skilful producer of still white wines such as the improving Yattarna (good but not yet living up to its supposed role as the "White *Grange*"). Under the same ownership as *Wynns, Seaview, Rouge Homme, Lindemans, Tullochs, Leo Buring, Seppelt*, and now James Halliday's *Coldstream Hills* and *Devil's Lair* in the *Margaret River*. ★★★★ **2001 Penfolds Rawsons Bin 202 £**

☲ **Penley Estate** (*Coonawarra*, Australia) High-quality *Coonawarra* estate with rich *Chardonnay* and very blackcurranty *Cabernet*.

☲ **Peppoli** [peh-poh-lee] (*Tuscany*, France) One of *Antinori's* most reliable *Chianti Classicos*.

☲ **Comte Peraldi** [peh-ral-dee] (*Corsica*, France) High-class *Corsican* wine producer, now also making good wine in Romania.

☲ **Perez Pascuas** [peh-reth Pas-scoo-was] (*Ribera del Duero*, Spain) Producer of Viña Pedrosa, one of the top examples of *Ribera del Duero*.

☲ **Le Pergole Torte** [pur-goh-leh taw-teh] (*Tuscany*, Italy) Long-established pure *Sangiovese*, oaky *Super-Tuscan*.

🥀 **Periquita** [peh-ree-kee-tah] (Portugal) Spicy, tobaccoey grape – and the wine *J.M. da Fonseca* makes from it. Its official name is Castelão Francês.

Perlé/Perlant [pehr-lay/lon] (France) Lightly sparkling.

Perlwein [pehrl-vine] (Germany) Sparkling wine.

Pernand-Vergelesses [pehr-non vehr-zhur-less] (*Burgundy*, France) *Commune* producing rather jammy reds but fine whites, including some *Côte d'Or* best buys. (Many producers here also make Corton) Arnoux; Champy; *Chandon de Briailles; Dubreuil-Fontaine; Germain (Château de Chorey); Jadot; Laleure-Piot; Pavelot; Rapet; Dom. Rollin.* ★★★★ **2000 Rémi Rollin (GV) Pernand-Vergelesses Blanc Sous Frétille 1er Cru**

☲ **André Perret** (*Rhône*, France) Producer of notable *Condrieu* and some unusually good examples of *St. Joseph*. ★★★ **1999 St Joseph £££**

☲ **Joseph Perrier** [payh-ree-yay] (*Champagne*, France) Family-run producer whose long-lasting elegant *Champagnes* have a heavy *Pinot Noir* influence. ★★★★ **NV Joseph Perrier Cuvee Royale Chalons £££**

☲ **Perrier-Jouët** [payh-ree-yay zhoo-way] (*Champagne*, France) Hitherto sadly underperforming *Champagne* house which, like *Mumm*, has now been sold by Canadian distillers, Seagram and is benefitting from greater attention from new owners. Sidestep the non-vintage for the genuinely worthwhile – and brilliantly packaged – Belle Epoque prestige cuvée white and rosé sparkling wine.

☲ **Elio Perrone** [eh-lee-yoh peh-roh-nay] (*Piedmont*, Italy) Good Barberas, Chardonnays and Dolcettos and truly spectacular Moscato.

☲ **Pesquera** [peh-SKEH-ra] (*Ribera del Duero*, Spain) Robert Parker dubbed this the *Ch. Pétrus* of Spain. Recent vintages have been less impressive.

Pessac-Léognan [peh-sak lay-on-yon] (*Bordeaux*, France) *Graves commune* containing most of the finest *châteaux*. Unusually in Bordeaux, most estates here make both red and white wine. *Ch. Bouscaut; Carbonnieux; Fieuzal; Domaine de Chevalier; Haut-Bailly; Haut-Brion; Larrivet-Haut-Brion; Laville-Haut-Brion; La Louvière; Malartic-Lagravière; la Mission-Haut-Brion; Smith-Haut-Laffite; la Tour-Haut-Brion.* ★★★★ **1999 Château Smith-Haut-Lafitte £££**

P

Petaluma [peh-ta-loo-ma] (*Adelaide Hills*, Australia) Recently purchased by a bif brewery, this high-tech creation of *Brian Croser* is a role model for other producers in the New World who are interested in combining innovative winemaking with the fruit of individually characterful vineyards. Classy *Chardonnays* and *Viogniers* from Piccadilly in the *Adelaide Hills, Clare Rieslings* (particularly good *late harvest*), and *Coonawarra* reds. Also owns *Smithbrook* and *Mitchelton*. ★★★★ 2000 Petaluma Chardonnay ££

PETALUMA
TIERS
PICCADILLY VALLEY
1999 CHARDONNAY

Pétavin [peht-tah-va'n] (*Catillon/Côtes de St Bernard*, France) Venture doggedly promoted by the Pet-Rus Corp., both as a means of applying the benefits of the *French Parrotdox* to our four-legged and feathered friends – and of disposing of unwanted wine. *Gout de Terrier* was developed by Alsatian producers *Cattin* and *Whinebark*, using *Rkatstelli, Cataratto,* and *Muscat* grapes grown on the Dalmatian coast. Burgundy superstar *Miaow-Camuzet* sells a *Beaune-Dry* Cuvée through Yapp Bros (see page 386), Loire producer *Yves Dogueneau* has launched *Mousecadet* and *Oh-Puss-One* for cats and *Bonn'zeau* for dogs, while *Woof Blass, Babitch* and *Katnip* are jointly selling *Grape Dane* in *Scandinavia*.

Pétillant [pay-tee-yon] Lightly sparkling.

Petit Chablis [pur-tee shab-lee] (*Burgundy*, France) Theoretically, this is a less fine wine than plain *Chablis* – though plenty of vineyards that were previously designated as Petit Chablis are now allowed to produce wines sold as *Chablis*. Hardly surprisingly, the ones that are left as Petit Chablis are often poor value. *La Chablisienne; Jean-Paul Droin; William Fèvre*; Dom des Malandes.

Petit Verdot [pur-tee vehr-doh] (*Bordeaux*, France) Highly trendy and excitingly spicy, if *tannic* variety traditionally used in small proportions in red *Bordeaux*, in California (rarely) and now (increasingly often) as a pure varietal in Australia (*Kingston Estate, Leconfield, Pirramimma*), Italy, and Spain (*Marqués de Griñon*). ★★★★ 1998 Pirramimma Petit Verdot ££

Ch. Petit Village [pur-tee vee-lahzh] (*Pomerol, Bordeaux*, France) Classy, intense, blackcurranty-plummy *Pomerol* now under the same ownership as *Ch. Pichon-Longueville*. Worth keeping.

Petite Sirah [peh-teet sih-rah] Spicy, rustic red grape grown in California and Mexico and as *Durif* in the *Midi* and Australia. *LA Cetto; Carmen; Fetzer; Morris; Parducci; Ridge; Turley*. ★★★ 1998 Concannon Petite Sirah £££

Petrolly A not unpleasant overtone often found in mature *Riesling*. Arrives faster in Australia than in Germany.

Ch. Pétrus [pay-trooss] (*Pomerol, Bordeaux*, France) Until *Le Pin* came along, this was the priciest of all *clarets*. Voluptuous *Pomerol* hits the target especially well in the US, and is finding a growing market in the Far East. Beware of fakes (especially big bottles) which crop up increasingly often.

Pewsey Vale [pyoo-zee vayl] (*Adelaide Hills*, Australia) Classy, cool-climate wines. Under the same ownership as *Yalumba, Hill-Smith,* and *Heggies*. ★★★ 2001 Pewsey Vale Riesling ££

Peyre Rose [pehr rohz] (*Languedoc-Roussillon*, France) Truly stylish producer of *Coteaux du Languedoc Syrah* that competes with examples from the Northern *Rhône* – and sells at similar prices.

Ch. de Pez [dur pez] (*St. Estèphe Cru Bourgeois, Bordeaux*, France) Fast-improving *St. Estèphe*, especially since its recent purchase by *Louis Roederer*. In good vintages, well worth ageing.

Pfalz [Pfaltz] (Germany) Formerly known as the *Rheinpfalz*, and before that as the *Palatinate*. Warm, southerly *Anbaugebiet* noted for riper, spicier *Riesling*. Currently competing with the *Mosel* for the prize of best of Germany's wine regions. *Kurt Darting; Lingenfelder; Müller-Cattoir*. ★★★★★ 1998 Dürkenheimer Steinberg Vier Jahreszeiten Eiswein £££

Weingut Pfeffingen [Pfef-fing-gen] (Pfalz, Germany) Look out for excellent Riesling and Scheurebe from well-sited vineyards.

P

Ch. Phélan-Ségur [fay-lon say-goor] (*St. Estèphe Cru Bourgeois, Bordeaux,* France) Good-value property since the late-1980s, with ripe, well-made wines.

Joseph Phelps (*Napa Valley,* California) Pioneer *Napa* user of *Rhône* varieties (*Syrah* and *Viognier*), and a rare source of *late-harvest Riesling.* *Cabernet* is a strength and the *Bordeaux*-like Insignia is a star wine. ★★★★ 1997 Insignia £££££

Philipponnat [fee-lee-poh-nah] (*Champagne,* France) Small producer famous for Clos des Goisses. Other wines are currently disappointing.

RH Phillips (*California*) Producer whose great value California wines deserve to be better known.

Phylloxera vastatrix [fih-lok-seh-rah] Root-eating louse that wiped out Europe's vines in the 19th century. Foiled by grafting *vinifera* vines onto resistant American *labrusca* rootstock. Pockets of pre-phylloxera and/or ungrafted vines still exist in France (in a *Bollinger* vineyard and on the south coast – the louse hates sand), Portugal (in *Quinta do Noval's* "Nacional" vineyard), Australia, and Chile. Elsewhere, phylloxera recently devastated *Napa Valley* vines.

Piave [pee-yah-vay] (*Veneto,* Italy) *DOC* in *Veneto* region, including reds made from a *Bordeaux*-like mix of grapes.

Ch. Pibarnon [pee-bah-non] (*Bandol,* France) Top-class producer of modern *Bandol*. ★★★ 1999 Chateau de Pibarnon £££

Ch. Pibran [pee-bron] (*Pauillac Cru Bourgeois, Bordeaux,* France) Small but high-quality and classically *Pauillac* property. ★★★ 1999 Ch. Tour Pibran £££

Picardy (*Pemberton,* Western Australia) Impressive new *Pinot Noir* and *Shiraz* specialist by the former winemaker of *Moss Wood.*

Pic St. Loup [peek-sa'-loo] (*Languedoc-Roussillon,* France) Up-and-coming region within the *Coteaux du Languedoc* for *Syrah*-based, *Rhône*-style reds, and whites. *Dom. l'Hortus; Mas Bruguière.* ★★★★ 2000 Ermitage du Pic St Loup Anderson £

FX Pichler [peek-lehr] (*Wachau Cru,* Austria) Arguably the best dry ("*Trocken*") winemaker in Austria – and certainly a great exponent of the *Grüner Veltliner* and *Riesling* at their richly dry best.

Ch. Pichon-Lalande [pee-shon la-lond] (*Pauillac 2ème Cru Classé, Bordeaux,* France) The new name for Pichon-Longueville-Lalande. Famed *super second* and tremendous success story, thanks to top-class winemaking and the immediate appeal of its unusually high *Merlot* content. A great 1996, but surprisingly a slightly less exciting 1998.

Ch. Pichon-Longueville [pee-shon long-veel] (*Pauillac 2ème Cru Classé, Bordeaux,* France) New name for Pichon-Longueville-Baron. An under-performing second growth *Pauillac* until its purchase by *AXA* in 1988. Now level with, and sometimes ahead of, *Ch. Pichon-Lalande,* once the other half of the estate. Wines are intense and complex. Les Tourelles, the *second label,* is a good-value alternative.

Picolit [pee-koh-leet] (*Friuli,* Italy) Grape used to make both sweet and dry white wine. *Jermann* makes a good one.

Picpoul de Pinet [peek-pool duh pee-nay] (South-West France) Underrated herby white that is particularly well made by Dom. St. Martin de la Garrigue.

Piedmont/Piemonte [pee-yed-mont/pee-yeh-mon-tay] (Italy) Ancient and modern north-western region producing old-fashioned, tough *Barolo* and *Barbaresco* and brilliant, modern, fruit-packed wines. Also makes *Oltrepò Pavese, Asti,* and *Dolcetto d'Alba.* See *Nebbiolo.*

Bodegas Piedmonte [pee-yehd-mohn-teh] (*Navarra,* Spain) Confusingly named (see above) cooperative producing good *Tempranillo, Cabernet,* and *Merlot* reds.

P

Pieropan [pee-yehr-oh-pan] (*Veneto,* Italy) *Soave's* top producer, which more or less invented single-vineyard wines here and is still a great exception to the dull *Soave* rule. Lovely, almondy wine.

Pieroth [pee-roth] Huge company whose salesmen visit clients' homes offering wines that are rarely recommendable.

Pierro [pee-yehr-roh] (*Margaret River,* Australia) Small estate producing rich, buttery, *Meursault*-like *Chardonnay.*

Piesport [pees-sport] (*Mosel-Saar-Ruwer,* Germany) Produced in the *Grosslage Michelsberg,* a region infamous for dull German wine, and bought by people who think themselves above *Liebfraumilch.* Try a single-vineyard – Günterslay or Goldtröpchen – for something more memorable. ★★★★ 1996 Piesporter Goldtropfchen Kabinett Weller-Lehnert £

Pieve di Santa Restituta [pee-yeh-vay dee san-tah res-tit-too-tah] (Tuscany, Italy) Angelo Gaja's Tuscan venture, with harmonious, balanced Brunello *crus* Rennina and Sugarille. Promis is from young vines.

Pighin [pee-gheen] (*Friuli,* Italy) Good, rather than great, Collio producer, with creditable examples of most of the styles produced here.

Pikes (*Clare Valley,* South Australia) Top-class estate with great *Riesling, Shiraz, Sangiovese,* and *Sauvignon.*

Jean Pillot [pee-yoh] (*Burgundy,* France) There are three estates called Pillot in *Chassagne-Montrachet.* This one is the best – and produces by far the finest red. ★★★★★ 2000 Chassagne Montrachet 1er Cru Chenevottes

Le Pin [lur pan] (*Pomerol, Bordeaux,* France) Ultra-hyped, small, recently formed estate whose – admittedly delicious – wines sell at silly prices in the US and the Far East. The forerunner of a string of other similar honey-traps (see *Ch. Valandraud* and *la Mondotte*).

Pindar Vineyards (New York State, USA) Good commercial quality from Long Island, especially Mythology, a *Bordeaux* blend.

Pine Ridge (*Napa Valley,* California) Greatly improved *Stags Leap* producer that is now also making good quality reds on *Howell Mountain.* The Oregon *Archery Summit* wines are also worth seeking out.★★★★ 1998 Merlot

Pineau de Charentes [pee-noh dur sha-ront] (*Southwest,* France) Fortified wine from the Cognac region.

Pingus [pin-goos] (*Ribeiro del Duero,* Spain) Probably the finest wine now being made in this region. Expect cleaner, richer, more modern wines than those from many of the neighbours.

Pinot Blanc/Bianco [pee-noh blon] Like *Chardonnay* without the fruit, and rarely as classy. Fresh, creamy, and adaptable. At its best in *Alsace* (Pinot d'Alsace), the Alto Adige in Italy (as *Pinot Bianco*), Germany and Austria (as *Weissburgunder*). In California it is a synonym for *Melon de Bourgogne.*

Pinot Chardonnay (Australia) Misleading name for *Chardonnay,* still used by *Tyrrells.* Don't confuse with *Pinot Noir/Chardonnay* sparkling wine blends such as the excellent *Seaview* and *Yalumba.*

Pinot Gris/Grigio [pee-noh gree] (*Alsace,* France) Spicy white grape of uncertain origins. Best in *Alsace* (also known as *Tokay d'Alsace*), Italy (as *Pinot Grigio*), and Germany (as *Ruländer* or *Grauburgunder*). Ernst Brun; Bott-Geyl; Dopff & Irion; Kreydenweiss; Ostertag; Piper's Brook; Schleret; Sorg; Cave de Turckheim; Weinbach (Faller).★★★★★ 1998 Pinot Gris Rangen SGN Zind Humbrecht ££££

Pinot Meunier [pee-noh-mur-nee-yay] (*Champagne,* France) Dark, pink-skinned grape. Plays an unsung but major role in *Champagne.* Can also be used to produce a still varietal wine. Best's; Bonny Doon; William Wheeler.

Pinot Noir [pee-noh nwahr] Black grape responsible for all red *Burgundy* and in part for white *Champagne.* Also successfully grown in the New World in with sites whose climate is neither too warm nor too cold. See *Oregon, Carneros, Yarra, Santa Barbara, Martinborough, Tasmania, Burgundy.*

P

🌱 **Pinotage** [pee-noh-tazh] (South Africa) *Pinot Noir* x *Cinsault* cross with a spicy, plummy character, used in South Africa and (now very rarely) New Zealand. Good old examples are brilliant but rare; most taste muddy and rubbery. New winemaking and international demand are making for more exciting wines. *Beyerskloof; Clos Malverne; Fairview; Grangehurst; Kanonkop; Saxenberg; Simonsig; Warwick.* ★★★★★ 2000 Spice Route Flagship Pinotage £££

🍷 **Pio Cesare** [pee-yoh CHAY-ser-ray] (Piedmont, Italy) Slightly mixed quality, but the modern cru Barolos and Barbarescos are tops.

🍷 **Piper Heidsieck** [pi-pur hide-seek] (*Champagne,* France) Greatly improved *Champagne* made by the late Daniel Thibault of *Charles Heidsieck.* The "Rare" is worth looking out for. ★★★★★ 1995 Vintage Champagne £££

🍷 **Pipers Brook Vineyards** (*Tasmania,* Australia) Dr. Andrew Pirie, who recently bought *Heemskerk,* is a pioneering producer of fine *Burgundian Chardonnay, Pinot Noir,* and *Pinot Gris.* Ninth Island, the *second label,* includes an excellent unoaked *Chablis*-like *Chardonnay.* The new Pirie sparkling wine is good too. ★★★★ 1999 The Lyre Single Site Pinot Noir £££

🍷 **E. Pira** [pee-rah] (*Piedmont,* Italy) Chiara Boschis's impressive small *Barolo* estate makes long-lived wines. ★★★★ 1997 Barolo 'Cannubi'

🍷 **Pirramimma** (Australia) McLaren Vale winery with especially good Petit Verdot. ★★★★ 1999 Shiraz ££

🍷 **Producteurs Plaimont** [play-mon] (*Southwest,* France) Reliable *Côtes de St. Mont* cooperative, with *Bordeaux*-lookalike reds and good whites made from local grapes. See also *Pacherenc du Vic-Bilh* and *Madiran.*

🍷 **Plaisir de Merle** [play-zeer dur mehrl] (*Paarl,* South Africa) Paul Pontallier of *Ch. Margaux* helps to make ripe, soft reds and rich whites for *Stellenbosch Farmers' Winery* in this new showcase operation. ★★★ 2000 Chardonnay ££

🍷 **Planeta** [plah-nay-tah] (Sicily, Italy) A name to watch among the growing number of starry producers in Sicily. Wines are well made and very fairly priced ★★★★★ 2001 Cometa £££

🍷 **Plantagenet** (*Mount Barker,* Western Australia) This is a good producer of *Chardonnay, Riesling, Cabernet,* and lean *Shiraz* in the southwest corner of Australia. ★★★★ 1998 Mount Barker Cabernet Sauvignon ££

🍷 **Plumpjack** (*Napa,* California) Small Cabernet specialist that hit the headlines by having the courage to bottle some of its Reserve *Cabernet* in screwtop bottles (to avoid cork taint). Bidders at the 2000 Napa Valley Charity Auction were undeterred and paid a record sum for the wine.

🍷 **Il Podere dell'Olivos** [eel poh-deh-reh del-oh-lee-vohs] (California) Pioneering producer of Italian varietals.

🍷 **Poggio Antico** [pod-zhee-yoh an-tee-koh] (*Tuscany,* Italy) Ultra-reliable *Brunello* producer.

🍷 **Pojer & Sandri** [poh-zhehr eh san-dree] (*Trentino,* Italy) Good red and white and, especially, sparkling wines.

🍷 **Pol Roger** [pol rod-zhay] (*Champagne,* France) Fine non-vintage that improves with keeping. The Cuvée Winston Churchill (named in honour of a faithful fan) is spectacular, and the *Demi-sec* is a rare treat.

🍷 **Erich & Walter Polz** [poltz] (*Styria,* Austria) Fine dry wines, including Pinot Blanc and Gris, and good Sauvignon Blancs. ★★★ 2001 Polz Hochgrassnitzberg Sauvignon Blanc ££

🍷 **Poliziano** [poh-leet-zee-yah-noh] (*Tuscany,* Italy) Apart from a pack-leading *Vino Nobile di Montepulciano,* this is the place to find the delicious Elegia and Le Stanze *Vini da Tavola.* ★★★★★ 2001 Rosso di Montepulciano ££

🍷 **Pomerol** [pom-meh-rohl] (*Bordeaux,* France) With *St. Emilion,* the *Bordeaux* for lovers of the *Merlot,* which predominates in its rich, plummy wines. None are cheap because production is often limited to a few thousand cases (in the *Médoc,* 20,000 is more common). Quality is more consistent than in *St. Emilion.* See *Pétrus, Moueix,* and individual châteaux.

P

I **Pomino** [poh-mee-noh] (*Tuscany*, Italy) Small *DOC* within *Chianti Rufina*; virtually a monopoly for *Frescobaldi* which makes a delicious, buttery, unwooded, white *Pinot Bianco/Chardonnay*, the oaky-rich Il Benefizio, and a tasty *Sangiovese/Cabernet*. ★★★ 2000 Pomino Benefizio ££

I **Pommard** [pom-mahr] (*Burgundy*, France) Variable quality *commune*, that can make slow-to-mature, then solid and complex reds. *Comte Armand; Jean-Marc Boillot; Girardin; Dominique Laurent; Leroy; Château de Meursault; de Montille; Mussy; Dom. de Pousse d'Or.* ★★★★ 2000 Pommard Doudet Naudin £

I **Ch de Pommard** [pom-mahr] (*Burgundy*, France) Estate just purchased by the dynamic owners of Ch. Smith-Haut-Lafitte. Watch this space.

I **Pommery** [pom-meh-ree] (*Champagne*, France) Back-on-track big-name with rich full-flavoured style. The top-label *Louise Pommery* white and rosé are tremendous. ★★★★★ 1992 Louise Pommery Rose ££££

I **Pongràcz** [pon-gratz] (South Africa) Brand name for the *Bergkelder's* (excellent) *Cap Classique* sparkling wine.

I **Dom. Ponsot** [pon-soh] (*Burgundy*, France) Top-class estate noted for *Clos de la Roche*, *Chambertin*, and (rare) white *Morey-St.-Denis*. More affordable is the excellent *Gevrey*.

I **Ch. Pontet-Canet** [pon-tay ka-nay] (*Pauillac 5ème Cru Classé, Bordeaux*, France) Rich, concentrated, up-and-coming *Pauillac*. The same family owns the similarly fine *Lafon-Rochet*.

I **Ponzi** [pon-zee] (*Oregon*) The ideal combination: a maker of good *Pinot Noir, Chardonnay*, and even better beer.

Port (*Douro*, Portugal) Fortified wine made in the upper *Douro* valley. Comes in several styles; see *Tawny, Ruby, LBV, Vintage, Crusted*, and *White port*.

I **Viña Porta** [veen-yah por-ta] (*Rapel*, Chile) Dynamic winery that specializes in juicy *Cabernet* and *Merlot*. The *Chardonnay* is good too. ★★★★ 2000 Porta Select Reserve Cabernet Sauvignon ££

Quinta do Portal [keentah doo por-tahl] (*Douro*, Portugal) Pricey table wine and port estate. ★★★★ 2000 Tinta Roriz £££

I **Ch. Potelle** (*Napa Valley*, California) French-owned *Mount Veeder* winery whose stylish wines have been served at the White House.

I **Ch. Potensac** [po-ton-sak] (*Médoc Cru Bourgeois, Bordeaux*, France) Under the same ownership as the great *Léoville-las-Cases*, and offering a more affordable taste of the winemaking that goes into that wine.

Pouilly-Fuissé [poo-yee fwee-say] (*Burgundy*, France) Variable white often sold at vastly inflated prices. Pouilly-Vinzelles, Pouilly-Loché, and other *Mâconnais* wines are often better value, though top-class Pouilly-Fuissé from producers like *Ch. Fuissé*, Dom. Noblet, or Dom. Ferret can compete with the best of the *Côte d'Or*. *Barraud; Corsin; Ferret; Ch. Fuissé; Lapierre; Noblet; Philibert; Verget.* ★★★ 2000 Domaine Vessigaud Cru de Bourgogne Pouilly-Fuissé ££

I **Pouilly-Fumé** [poo-yee foo-may] (*Loire*, France) Potentially ultra-elegant *Sauvignon Blanc* with classic gooseberry fruit and "smoky" overtones derived from flint ("silex") subsoil. Like *Sancerre*, rarely repays cellaring. See *Ladoucette* and *Didier Dagueneau*. ★★★★ 2000 Pouilly-Fumé Cuvée du Troncsec Joseph Mellot ££

I **Ch. Poujeaux** [poo-joh] (*Moulis Cru Bourgeois, Bordeaux*, France) Up-and-coming, reliable, plummy-blackcurranty wine.

Pourriture noble [poo-ree-toor nohbl] (France) See *Botrytis cinerea* or *noble rot*.

I **Dom. de la Pousse d'Or** [poos-daw] (*Burgundy*, France) One of the top estates in *Volnay*. (The *Pommard* and *Santenay* wines are good too.)

Prädikat [pray-dee-ket] (Germany) As in Qualitätswein mit Prädikat (*QmP*), the (supposedly) higher quality level for German and Austrian wines, indicating a greater degree of natural ripeness.

☿ **Franz Prager** [prah-gur] (*Wachau,* Austria) Top-class producer of a wide range of impressive *Grüner-Veltliners* and now *Rieslings*.

Precipitation The creation of a harmless deposit, usually of *tartrate* crystals, in white wine, which the Germans romantically call "diamonds."

Premier Cru [prur-mee-yay kroo] In *Burgundy,* indicates wines that fall between *village* and *Grand Cru* quality. Some major *communes* such as *Beaune* and *Nuits-St.-Georges* have no *Grand Cru*. Meursault Premier Cru, for example, is probably a blend from two or more vineyards.

☿ **Premières Côtes de Blaye** See *Côtes de Blaye*

☿ **Premières Côtes de Bordeaux** [prur-mee-yehr koht dur bohr-doh] (*Bordeaux,* France) Up-and-coming riverside *appellation* for reds and (often less interestingly) sweet whites. *Carsin;* Grand-Mouëys; *Reynon*.

Prestige Cuvée [koo-vay] (*Champagne,* France) The top wine of a *Champagne* house. Expensive and elaborately packaged. Some, like *Dom Pérignon,* are excellent; others less so. Other best-known examples include *Veuve Clicquot's* Grand Dame and *Roederer's* Cristal.

☿ **Preston Vineyards** (*Sonoma,* California) Winery making the most of *Dry Creek Zinfandel* and *Syrah*. A white Meritage blend is pretty good too, and there is an improving *Viognier*.

☿ **Pride Mountain** (*Napa,* California) Small Napa label whose Merlot is worth seeking out.

☿ **Dom. Jacques Prieur** [pree-yur] (*Burgundy,* France) Estate with fine vineyards. Increasingly impressive since takeover by *Antonin Rodet*.
★★★★ **2000 Clos de Vougeot Grand Cru**

☿ **Ch. Prieuré-Lichine** [pree-yur-ray lih-sheen] (*Margaux 4ème Cru Classé, Bordeaux,* France) Recently (1999) sold and – in 2000 – much improved *château* making good if rarely subtle blackcurrant wine that benefits from input by *Michel Rolland*. One of the very few *châteaux* with a gift shop, and a helicopter landing pad on its roof. The 2001 vintage was controversial, striking some – including the editor of this guide – as too rich and dark for a Margaux.

Primeur [prue-mur] (France) New wine, e.g., *Beaujolais* Primeur (a.k.a. *Beaujolais Nouveau*) or, as in *en primeur,* wine which sold in the barrel. Known in the US as futures.

☿ **Primitivo** [pree-mih-tee-voh] (*Puglia,* Italy) Italian name for the *Zinfandel*.
★★★★★ **2000 Canaletto Primitivo di Puglia Girelli £**

☿ **Primo Estate** [pree-moh] (*South Australia*) Imaginative venture among the fruit farms of the Adelaide Plains. Passion-fruity *Colombard,* sparkling *Shiraz,* and *Merlot* made *Amarone*-style, using grapes partially dried in the sun. The olive oil is good too. ★★★★ **2000 Il Briccone Primo Estate ££**

☿ **Principe de Viana** [preen-chee-pay de vee-yah-nah] (*Navarra,* Spain) Highly commercial winery producing large amounts of good value red and white wine. The Agramont label is particularly worthwhile. ★★★★ **2000 Agramont Cosecha Tempranillo £**

☿ **Prinz zu Salm-Dalberg** [zoo sahlm dal-burg] (*Nahe,* Germany) Innovative producer with good red *Spätburgunder* and (especially) *Scheurebe*.

☿ **Priorato/Priorat** [pree-yaw-rah-toh/raht] (*Catalonia,* Spain) Highly prized/priced, sexy new-wave wines from a region once known for hefty alcoholic reds from *Cariñena* and *Garnacha* grapes. *Rene Barbier (Clos Mogador); Costers del Siurana; Mas Martinet;* Clos i Terrasses; J.M. Fuentes; Daphne Glorian; *Alvaro Palacios;* Pasanau Germans; Scala Dei; Vilella de la Cartoixa. ★★★★★ **1998 Prior Terrae Freixenet ££££**

Propriétaire (Récoltant) [pro-pree-yeh-tehr ray-kohl-ton] (France) Vineyard owner-manager.

☿ **Prosecco di Conegliano-Valdobbiàdene** [proh-sek-koh dee coh-nay-lee-anoh val-doh-bee-yah-day-nay] (*Veneto,* Italy) Soft, slightly earthy, dry and sweet sparkling wine made from the *Prosecco* grape. Less boisterous and fruity than *Asti*. Drink young. Bisol; Bortolin; Canevel; Produttori; Ruggeri; Zardetto. ★★★ NV Villa Sandi Prosecco di Valdobbiadene Brut £

Provence [proh-vons] (France) Southern region producing fast-improving wine with a number of minor *ACs*. Rosé de Provence should be dry and fruity with a hint of peppery spice. See *Bandol, Coteaux d'Aix-en-Provence, Palette.*

Provins [proh-vah'] (*Valais*, Switzerland) Dynamic cooperative, making the most of *Chasselas* and more interesting varieties such as the *Arvine*.

J.J. Prüm [proom] (*Mosel-Saar-Ruwer*, Germany) *Riesling* producer with fine *Wehlener* vineyards. ★★★★★ 1995 Wehlener Sonnenuhr Riesling Auslese £££

Dom. Michel Prunier [proo-nee-yay] (*Burgundy*, France) Best estate in *Auxey-Duresses*. ★★★★ 2000 Auxey-Duresses Vieilles Vignes 1er Cru £££

Alfredo Prunotto [proo-not-toh] (*Piedmont*, Italy) Good *Barolo* producer recently bought by *Antinori*. ★★★★★ 1997 Barolo Monforte D'Alba Bussia £££

Puerto de Santa María [pwehr-toh day san-tah mah-ree-yah] (Spain) Sherry town. Fino here can be softer and lighter than that from Jerez.

Puglia [poo-lee-yah] (Italy) Hot region, now making cool wines, thanks to *flying winemakers* like *Kym Milne*. Also see *Salice Salentino* and *Copertino*.

Puiatti [pwee-yah-tee] (*Friuli-Venezia Giulia*, Italy) Producer of some of Italy's best *Chardonnay, Pinot Bianco, Pinot Grigio*, and *Tocai Friulano*. The Archetipi are the cream of the crop. ★★★★ 2001 Pinot Grigio Le Zuccole ££

Puisseguin St. Emilion [pwees-gan san tay-mee-lee-yon] (*Bordeaux*, France) Satellite of *St. Emilion* making similar, *Merlot*-dominant wines which are often far better value.

Puligny-Montrachet [poo-lee-nee mon-ra-shay] (*Burgundy*, France) Aristocratic white *Côte d'Or commune* that shares the *Montrachet* vineyard with *Chassagne*. Should be complex buttery *Chardonnay*. *Carillon, Sauzet, Ramonet, Drouhin*, and *Dom. Leflaive* are all worth their money. *D'Auvenay; Carillon; Chavy; Drouhin; Leflaive (Olivier & Domaine);* Marquis de Laguiche; *Ch de Puligny-Montrachet; Ramonet.* ★★★★★ *1998 Puligny-Montrachet Les Perrières 1er Cru Etienne Sauzet £££*

Putto [poot-toh] (Italy) See *Chianti*.

Puttonyos [poot-toh-nyos] (*Tokaji*, Hungary) The measure of sweetness (from 1 to 6) of *Tokaji*. The number indicates the number of puttonyos (baskets) of sweet *aszú* paste added to the base wine.

Ch. Puygeraud [Pwee-gay-roh] (*Bordeaux*, France) Perhaps the best property on the *Côtes de Francs*.

Pyrenees (*Victoria*, Australia) One of the classiest regions in *Victoria*, thanks to the efforts of *Taltarni* and *Dalwhinnie*. ★★★ 2000 Blue Pyrenees Shiraz ££

Pyrus [pi-rus] (Australia) *Lindemans Coonawarra* wine that's right back on form. ★★★ 1998 Pyrus £££

Q

QbA Qualitätswein bestimmter Anbaugebiet: [kvah-lih-tayts-vine behr-shtihmt-tuhr ahn-bow-geh-beet] (Germany) Basic-quality German wine from one of the 13 *Anbaugebiete*, e.g. *Rheinhessen*.

QmP Qualitätswein mit Prädikat: [pray-dee-kaht] (Germany) *QbA* wine (supposedly) with "special qualities." The QmP blanket designation is broken into five quality rungs, from *Kabinett* to *Trockenbeerenauslese* plus *Eiswein*.

Quady [kway-dee] (*Central Valley*, California) Makes "Starboard" (served in a decanter), *Orange Muscat* Essencia (great with chocolate), *Black Muscat* Elysium, low-alcohol Electra, and Vya Sweet Vermouth.
★★★★ NV Vya Sweet Vermouth £££

Quarles Harris [kwahrls] (*Douro*, Portugal) Underrated *port* producer with a fine 1980 and 1983.

Quarts de Chaume [kahr dur shohm] (*Loire*, France) Luscious but light sweet wines, ageing beautifully, from the *Coteaux du Layon*. The *Dom. des Baumard* is exceptional. Sweet white: *Dom des Baumard; Pierre Soulez.*

Ꙩ **Querciabella** [kehr-chee-yah-BEH-lah] (*Tuscany*, Italy) Top class *Chianti Classico* estate with a great *Sangiovese-Cabernet* blend called Camartina.

Ꙩ **Quilceda Creek** [kwil-see-dah] (*Washington State*) Producer of one of the best, most blackcurranty *Cabernets* in the American Northwest.

Ꙩ **Quincy** [kan-see] (*Loire*, France) Dry *Sauvignon*, lesser-known and sometimes good alternative to *Sancerre* or *Pouilly-Fumé*. ★★★ 2001 Joseph Mellot Quincy Le Rimonet £

Ꙩ **Quinault l'Enclos** [kee-noh lon-kloh] (*St. Emilion*, Bordeaux, France) Recently – 1997 – created, tiny-production wine from the same stable as la Croix de Gay and la Fleur de Gay, and produced from previously unvaunted land close to both *Pomerol* and the town of Libourne. Like most such wines, it's rich, dark, and concentrated.

Quinta [keen-ta] (Portugal) Vineyard or estate, particularly in the *Douro*, where "single Quinta" *vintage ports* are increasingly being taken as seriously as the big-name blends. See *Crasto*, *Vesuvio*, and *de la Rosa*. ★★★★★ 1999 Quinta do Crasto Vintage Port £££

Ꙩ **Quintessa** (*Napa*, California) Exciting venture from Agustin Huneeus, the man behind *Franciscan* and *Veramonte*. ★★★★ 1997 Cabernet Sauvignon

Ꙩ **Guiseppe Quintarelli** [keen-ta-reh-lee] (*Veneto*, Italy) Old-fashioned *Recioto*-maker producing quirky, sublime *Valpolicella*, recognizable by the apparently handwritten labels. Try the more affordable Molinara.

Ꙩ **Quivira** (*Sonoma*, California) Great *Dry Creek* producer of intense *Zinfandel* and *Syrah* and a deliciously clever *Rhône*-meets-California blend that includes both varieties.

Ꙩ **Qupé** [kyoo-pay] (*Central Coast*, California) Run by one of the founders of *Au Bon Climat*, this *Santa Barbara* winery produces brilliant *Syrah* and *Rhône*-style whites. ★★★★ 1998 Syrah Bien Nacido £££

R

Ꙩ **Ch. Rabaud-Promis** [rrah boh prraw-mee] (*Sauternes Premier Cru Classé*, *Bordeaux*, France) Underperforming until 1986; now making top-class wines.

Ꙩ **Rabbit Ridge** (*Sonoma*, California) Small producer with a fairly priced, very starry, Russian River Zinfandel

Racking The drawing off of wine from its *lees* into a clean cask or vat.

Ꙩ **Rafael Estate** [raf-fay-yel] (*Mendoza*, Argentina) Dynamic producer of great value *Malbec*-based reds with the assistance of *flying winemaker* Hugh Ryman.

Ꙩ **A Rafanelli** [ra-fur-nel-lee] (*Sonoma*, California) Great *Dry Creek* winery with great *Cabernet* Sauvignon. The *Zinfandel* is the jewel in the crown though.

Ꙩ **Olga Raffault** [ra-foh] (*Loire*, France) There are several Raffaults in *Chinon*; this is the best – and the best source of some of the longest-lived wines.

Ꙩ **Le Ragose** [lay-rah-goh-say] (*Veneto*, Italy) A name to look out for in *Valpolicella* – for great *Amarone*, *Recioto*, and Valpolicella Classico (le Sassine).

Ꙩ **Raïmat** [ri-mat] (*Catalonia*, Spain) Innovative *Codorníu*-owned winery in the *Costers del Segre* region. *Merlot*, a *Cabernet/Merlot* blend called Abadia, and *Tempranillo* are interesting though less impressive than in the past, and *Chardonnay* – both still and sparkling – is good. ★★★★★ 1998 Tempranillo ££

Rainwater (*Madeira*, Portugal) Light, dry style of *Madeira* popular in the US.

Ꙩ **Ch. Ramage-la-Batisse** [ra-mazh la ba-teess] (*Haut-Médoc Cru Bourgeois*, *Bordeaux*, France) Good-value wine from the commune of St. Laurent.

Ꙩ **Ramitello** [ra-mee-tel-loh] (*Molise*, Italy) Spicy-fruity reds and creamy citrus whites produced by di Majo Norante in Biferno on the Adriatic coast.

Ꙩ **Adriano Ramos Pinto** [rah-mosh pin-toh] (*Douro*, Portugal) Dynamic family-run winery that belongs to *Roederer*. *Colheita tawnies* are a delicious speciality, but the *vintage* wines and *single quintas* are good too. ★★★★★ 1997 LBV ££

R

☨ **Dom. Ramonet** [ra-moh-nay] (*Burgundy*, France) Supreme *Chassagne-Montrachet* estate with top-flight *Montrachet*, *Bâtard*, and *Bienvenues-Bâtard-Montrachet* and fine complex *Premiers Crus*. Pure class; worth waiting for, too.
★★★★★ 2000 Chassagne-Montrachet 1er Cru Les Ruchottes ££££

☨ **João Portugal Ramos** [jwow por-too-gahl ramosh] (Portugal) One of this conservative country's best new-wave winemakers. ★★★ 2000 Trincadeira £

☨ **Castello dei Rampolla** [kas-teh-loh day-ee ram-poh-la] (*Tuscany*, Italy) Good *Chianti*-producer whose wines need time to soften. The berryish Sammarco *Vino da Tavola* is also impressive.

Rancio [ran-see-yoh] Term for the peculiarly tangy, and yet highly prized, *oxidized* flavour of certain fortified wines, particularly in France (e.g., *Banyuls*) and Spain.

Randersacker [ran-dehr-sak-kur] (*Franken*, Germany) One of the most successful homes of the *Silvaner*, especially when made by Weingut *Juliusspital*. ★★★ 2000 Randersackerer Teutels Spätlese Weingut Erust Gebhardt ££

Rangen [rang-gen] (*Alsace*, France) *Grand Cru* vineyard especially good for *Riesling*, but also *Gewurztraminer, Pinot Gris*. ★★★★ 2000 Clos Saint Urbain Rangen de Thann Riesling Domaine Zind Humbrecht ££££

Rapel [ra-pel] (Central Valley, Chile) Important sub-region of the *Central Valley*, especially for reds. Includes *Colchagua* and *Cachapoal*. ★★★★★ 2001 La Palmeria Merlot Gran Reserva ££

☨ **Rapitalà** [ra-pih-tah-la] (*Sicily*, Italy) Estate producing a fresh, peary white wine from a blend of local grapes.

☨ **Kent Rasmussen** (*Carneros*, California) One of California's too-small band of truly inventive winemakers, producing great *Burgundy*-like *Pinot Noir* and *Chardonnay* and Italianate *Sangiovese* and *Dolcetto*. Ramsey is a second label. ★★★ 1999 Pinot Noir £££

Rasteau [ras-stoh] (*Rhône*, France) Southern village producing peppery reds with rich, berry fruit. The fortified *Muscat* can be good, too. Red: Bressy-Masson; des Coteaux des Travers; Dom des Girasols; de la Grangeneuve; Marie-France Masson; Rabasse-Charavin; La Soumade; François Vache. ★★★ 2000 Perrin L'Andeol Rasteau ££

☨ **Renato Ratti** [rah-tee] (*Piedmont*, Italy) One of the finest, oldest producers of *Barolo*. ★★★★ 1997 Barolo la Morra 'Marcenasco' £££

Rauenthal [row-en-tahl] (*Rheingau*, Germany) *Georg Breuer* is the most interesting producer in this beautiful village. Other names to look for include *Schloss Schönborn* and *Schloss Rheinhartshausen*.

☨ **Ch. Rauzan-Gassies** [roh-zon ga-sees] (*Margaux 2ème Cru Classé, Bordeaux*, France) Compared to *Rauzan-Ségla* its neighbour, this property is still underperforming magnificently. Better in 2001.

☨ **Ch. Rauzan-Ségla** [roh-zon say-glah] (*Margaux 2ème Cru Classé, Bordeaux*, France) For a long time this used to be an underperforming *Margaux*. Now, since its purchase by Chanel in 1994, it has become one of the best buys in *Bordeaux*. ★★★★★ 1997 Chateau Rauzan-Ségla ££££

☨ **Jean-Marie Raveneau** [rav-noh] (*Burgundy*, France) The long-established king of *Chablis*, with impeccably made *Grand* and *Premier Cru* wines that last wonderfully well. ★★★★ 1999 Chablis Blanchot Grand Cru £££

☨ **Ravenswood** (*Sonoma Valley*, California) Brilliant *Zinfandel*-maker whose individual-vineyard wines are wonderful examples of this variety. The *Merlots* and *Cabernet* are fine, too. ★★★★ 1999 Lodi Zinfandel ££

☨ **Ravenswood** (South Australia) Label confusingly adopted by *Hollick* for its top *Coonawarra* reds (no relation to the above entry). ★★★★ 1999 Starvedog Lane Shiraz ££

R

⚱ Raventos i Blanc [ra-vayn-tos ee blank] (*Catalonia*, Spain) Josep Raventos' ambition is to produce the best sparkling wine in Spain, adding *Chardonnay* to local varieties. ★★★★ 2001 Heretat Vall-Ventós Chardonnay £

⚱ Ch. Rayas [rye-yas] (*Rhône*, France) The only chance to taste *Châteauneuf-du-Pape* made solely from the *Grenache*. Pricey but good.

⚱ Raymond (*Napa Valley*, California) Maker of tasty, intense *Cabernets* and *Chardonnays*.

⚱ Ch. Raymond-Lafon [ray-mon la-fon] (*Sauternes, Bordeaux*, France) Very good small producer whose wines deserve keeping.

⚱ Ch. de Rayne-Vigneau [rayn veen-yoh] (*Sauternes Premier Cru Classé, Bordeaux*, France) *Sauternes* estate, located at *Bommes*, producing a deliciously rich complex wine.

RD **(*Récemment Dégorgée*)** (*Champagne*, France) A term invented by *Bollinger* for their delicious vintage *Champagne*, which has been allowed a longer-than-usual period (as much as 15 years) on its *lees*.

⚱ Real Companhia Vinicola do Norte de Portugal [ray-yahl com-pah-nee-yah vee-nee-koh-lah doh nor-tay day por-too-gahl] (*Douro*, Portugal) The full name of the firm that is better known as the *Royal Oporto Wine Co*. The best wines are the *tawny* ports; these are sold under the Quinta dos Carvalhas label. The whole company is being revived by a new generation.

Rebholz [reb-holtz] (Pfalz, Germany) High quality estate making superb *Spätburgunder, Gewürztraminer, Chardonnay* and *Muskateller*.

Ignacio Recabarren [ig-na-see-yoh reh-ka-ba-ren] (Chile) Superstar winemaker and Casablanca pioneer.

Recioto [ray-chee-yo-toh] (*Veneto*, Italy) Sweet or dry alcoholic wine made from semi-dried, ripe grapes. Usually associated with *Valpolicella* and *Soave*. ★★★★★ 1996 Casal dei Ronchi Recioto Classico Serego Alighieri / Masi £££

Récoltant-manipulant **(RM)** [ray-kohl-ton ma-nee-poo-lon] (*Champagne*, France) Term for an individual winegrower and blender, identified by what is known as the RM number on the label.

Récolte [ray-kohlt] (France) Vintage, literally "harvest."

⚱ Dom. de la Rectorie [rehc-toh-ree] (*Languedoc-Roussillon*, France) One of top names in *Banyuls*, and producer of fine *Collioure*.

⚱ Redman (South Australia) Improved *Coonawarra* estate with intense reds.

⚱ Redoma [ray-doh-mah] (*Douro*, Portugal) New-wave red and white table wines from the dynamic, yet reliable port producer Dirk *Niepoort*.

⚱ Redwood Valley Estate See *Seifried*.

🍇 Refosco [re-fos-koh] (*Friuli-Venezia Giulia*, Italy) Red grape and its dry and full-bodied *DOC* wine. Benefits from ageing. ★★★ 1997 Refosco Giovanni Dri £££

⚱ Regaleali [ray-ga-lay-ah-lee] (*Sicily*, Italy) Ambitious aristocratic estate, using local varieties to produce some of *Sicily's* most serious wines.

Régisseur [rey-jee-sur] (*Bordeaux*, France) In *Bordeaux* (only), the cellar-master.

⚱ Régnié [ray-nyay] (*Burgundy*, France) Once sold as *Beaujolais Villages*, Régnié now has to compete with *Chiroubles, Chénas*, and the other *crus*. It is mostly like an amateur competing against professionals. Fortunately enough for Régnié, these particular professionals often aren't great. *Duboeuf* makes a typical example. *Duboeuf; Dubost; Piron; Sapin; Trichard.*

⚱ Reguengos (*Alentejo*, Portugal) Richly flavoursome reds pioneered by Esporão and the Reguengos de Monsaraz cooperative. ★★★ 2001 Reguengos Cooperativa Agricola de Reguengos de Monsaraz £

🍇 Reichensteiner [rike-en-sti-ner] Recently developed white grape, popular in England (and Wales).

⚱ Reif Estate Winery [reef] (*Ontario*, Canada) Impressive *icewine* specialist. ★★★★ 2000 Vidal Icewine £££

⚱ Remelluri [ray-may-yoo-ree] (*Rioja*, Spain) For most modernists, this is the nearest *Rioja* has got to a top-class, small-scale organic estate. Wines are more serious (and *tannic*) than most, but they're fuller in flavour, and built to last.

R

Remuage [reh-moo-wazh] (*Champagne,* France) Part of the *méthode champenoise,* the gradual turning and tilting of bottles so that the yeast deposit collects in the neck ready for *dégorgement.*

☿ **Renaissance** (*California,* USA) Idealistic estate run on almost religious philosophical lines. Very good *Riesling* and *Roussanne*; subtle, elegant flavours across the board. ★★★ 1999 Renaissance Le Provencal £££

Reserva [ray-sehr-vah] (Spain) Wine aged for a period specified by the relevant *DO*: usually one year for reds and six months for whites and pinks.

Réserve [reh-surv] (France) Legally meaningless, as in "Réserve Personelle," but implying a wine selected and given more age.

Residual sugar Term for wines that have retained grape sugar not converted to *alcohol* by yeasts during fermentation. Bone-dry wines have less than 2 grams per litre of residual sugar. In the US, many so-called "dry" white wines contain as much as 10, and some supposedly dry red *Zinfandels* definitely have more than a trace of sweetness. New Zealand Sauvignons are rarely bone dry, but their *acidity* balances and conceals any residual sugar.

☿ **Weingut Balthasar Ress** [bahl-ta-zah rress] (*Rheingau,* Germany) Good producer in *Hattenheim,* blending delicacy with concentration. ★★★★ 1999 Hattenheimer Nussbrunnen Riesling Auslese £££

Retsina [ret-see-nah] (Greece) Wine made the way the ancient Greeks used to make it – resinating it with pine to keep it from spoiling. Today, it's an acquired taste for non-holidaying, non-Greeks. Pick the freshest examples you can find (though this isn't easy when labels mention no vintage).

Reuilly [rur-yee] (*Loire,* France) (Mostly) white *AC* for dry *Sauvignons,* good-value, if sometimes rather earthy alternatives to nearby *Sancerre* and *Pouilly-Fumé* and spicy *Pinot* rosé. *Henri Beurdin;* Bigonneau; *Lafond.*

☿ **Rex Hill Vineyards** (*Oregon*) Greatly improved *Pinot* specialist.

☿ **Chateau Reynella** [ray-nel-la] (*McLaren Vale,* Australia) BRL Hardy subsidiary, mastering both reds and whites. ★★★★ 1999 Chateau Reynella Basket-Press Shiraz ££

☿ **Ch. Reynon** [ray-non] (*Premier Côtes de Bordeaux,* France) Fine red and especially recommendable white wines from *Denis Dubourdieu.*

Rheingau [rine-gow] (Germany) Traditional home of the finest *Rieslings* of the 13 *Anbaugebiete*; now overshadowed by *Pfalz* and *Mosel.* QbA/Kab/Spät: *Künstler; Balthasar Ress; Domdechant Werner'sches; HH Eser.*

Rheinhessen [rine-hehs-sen] (Germany) Largest of the 13 *Anbaugebiete,* now well known for *Liebfraumilch* and *Niersteiner.* Fewer than one vine in 20 is now *Riesling*; sadly, easier-to-grow varieties, and lazy cooperative wineries, generally prevail. There are a few stars, however. *Balbach;* Keller; *Gunderloch.* ★★★★★ 1999 Keller Hubacker Riesling Eiswein ££££

☿ **Rhône** [rohn] (France) Fast-improving, exciting, packed with increasingly sexy *Grenache, Syrah,* and *Viognier* wines. See *St. Joseph, Crozes-Hermitage, Hermitage, Condrieu, Côtes du Rhône, Châteauneuf-du-Pape, Tavel, Lirac, Gigondas, Ch. Grillet, Beaumes de Venise.*

☿ **Rias Baixas** [ree-yahs bi-shahs] (*Galicia,* Spain) The place to find spicy *Albariño.* Lagar de Cervera; *Pazo de Barrantes; Santiago Ruiz;* Valdamor. ★★★★ 2001 Burgáns Albariño Martín Codáx £

☿ **Ribatejo** [ree-bah-tay-joh] (Portugal) *DO* area north of Lisbon where *Peter Bright* and the cooperatives are beginning to make highly commercial white and red wine, but traditional *Garrafeiras* are worth watching out for, too.

☿ **Ribera del Duero** [ree-bay-rah del doo-way-roh] (Spain) One of the regions to watch in Spain for good reds. Unfortunately, despite the established success of *Vega Sicilia* and of producers like *Pesquera, Pingus, Arroyo,* and *Alion,* there is still far too much poor winemaking. *Pesquera; Pedrosa; Pingus; Hermanos Sastre;* Valtravieso; *Vega Sicilia.* ★★★★ 1999 Viña Solorca Crianza ££; ★★★★ 1998 Valduero Reserva £

🍇 **Ribolla** [rib-bol-lah] (Italy) White grape from the Northeast with nuttiness and good acidity but not a lot else. It becomes Robola in Greece.

R

Dom. Richeaume [ree-shohm] (*Provence*, France) Dynamic producer of good, earthy, long-lived, organic *Cabernet* and *Syrah*. Sadly, as with many other smaller organic wineries, quality can vary from bottle to bottle. Recommendable, nonetheless.

Richebourg [reesh-boor] (*Burgundy*, France) Top-class *Grand Cru* vineyard just outside *Vosne-Romanée* with a recognizable floral-plummy style.*Grivot; Anne Gros; Leroy; Méo-Camuzet; D&D Mugneret; Noëllat; Romanée-Conti.* ★★★★★ 1999 Richebourg Grand Cru Domaine A F Gros ££££

Richou [ree-shoo] (*Loire*, France) Fine *Anjou* producer with reliable reds and whites and fine, affordable, sweet whites from Coteaux de l'Aubance.

Weingut Max Ferd Richter [rikh-tur] (*Mosel-Saar-Ruwer*, Germany) Excellent producer of long-lived, concentrated-yet-elegant *Mosel Rieslings* from high-quality vineyards. The *cuvée* Constantin is the unusually successful dry wine, while at the other end of the scale, the *Eisweins* are sublime. ★★★★ 2001 Brauneberg Juffer Sonnenuhr Riesling Auslese 2001 £££

John Riddoch (South Australia) Classic *Wynn's Coonawarra* red. One of Australia's best and longest-lasting wines. (Not to be confused with the wines that *Katnook Estate* sells under its own "Riddoch" label.) ★★★ 2000 Shiraz ££

Ridge Vineyards (*Santa Cruz*, California) Paul Draper, and Ridge's hilltop *Santa Cruz* and *Sonoma* vineyards, consistently produce some of California's very finest *Zinfandel*, *Cabernet*, *Mataro*, and *Chardonnay*.

Riecine [ree-eh-chee-nay] (*Tuscany*, Italy) Modern estate with fine *Chianti* and an even more impressive la Gioia *Vino da Tavola*.

Rieslaner [rees-lah-nur] (Germany) A decent modern grape crossing, *Silvaner x Riesling* with a good curranty flavour when ripe. ★★★★★ 2000 Monsheimer Silberberg TBA Weingut Keller ££££

Riesling [reez-ling] The noble grape responsible for Germany's finest offerings, ranging from light, floral, everyday wines, to the delights of *botrytis* affected sweet wines, which retain their freshness for decades. Reaching its zenith in the superbly balanced, racy wines of the *Mosel*, and the richer offerings from the *Rheingau*, it also performs well in *Alsace*, California, South Africa, and Australia. Watch out for the emergence of the *Wachau* region as a leader of the Austrian *Riesling* pack.

Riesling Italico See *Italian Riesling*, etc.

Ch. Rieussec [ree-yur-sek] (*Sauternes Premier Cru Classé, Bordeaux*, France) Fantastically rich and concentrated *Sauternes*, often deep in colour and generally at the head of the pack chasing d'*Yquem*. Owned by the Rothschilds of *Lafite*. R de Rieussec is the unexceptional dry white wine.

Rioja [ree-ok-hah] (Spain) Spain's best-known wine region, split into three parts. The Alta produces the best wines, followed by the Alavesa, while the Baja is the largest. Most Riojas are blends by large *bodegas*: small *Bordeaux*- and *Burgundy*-style estates are rare. New-wave Riojas are abjuring the tradition of long oak ageing and producing fruitier, modern wines, and "experimental" *Cabernet* is being planted alongside the traditional *Tempranillo* and lesser-quality *Garnacha*. Allende; Amézola de la Mora; Ardanza; Artadi; Baron de Ley; Berberana; Breton; Campillo; Campo Viejo; Contino; El Coto; Lopez de Heredia; Marqués de Griñon; Marqués de Murrieta; Marqués de Riscal; Marqués de Vargas; Martinez Bujanda; Montecillo; Ondarre; Palacio; Remelluri; La Rioja Alta; Riojanos.

La Rioja Alta [ree-ok-hah ahl-ta] (*Rioja*, Spain) Of all the big companies in *Rioja*, this is the most important name to remember. Its Viña Ardanza, Reserva 904, and (rarely produced) Reserva 890 are all among the most reliable and recommendable wines in the region. ★★★ 1994 Vina Ardanza ££

Dom. Daniel Rion [ree-yon] (*Burgundy*, France) Patrice Rion produces impeccably made modern Nuits-St.-Georges and Vosne-Romanées. ★★★★ 2000 Nuits St Georges Grandes Vignes £££

R

Ripasso [ree-pas-soh] (*Veneto,* Italy) Winemaking method whereby newly made *Valpolicella* is partially refermented in vessels that have recently been vacated by *Recioto* and *Amarone*. Ripasso wines made in this way are richer, alcoholic, and raisiny. Increases the *alcohol* and *body* of the wine. *Tedeschi; Quintarelli; Masi.* ★★★★★ 1999 Zenato Valpolicella Ripasso ££

⟁ **Marqués de Riscal** [ris-kahl] (*Rioja,* Spain) Historic *Rioja* name now back on course thanks to more modern winemaking for both reds and whites. The Baron de Chirel is the recently launched top wine. ★★★★★ 1998 Marqués de Riscal Reserva ££

Riserva [ree-zEHr-vah] (Italy) *DOC* wines aged for a specified number of years – often an unwelcome term on labels of wines like *Bardolino*, which are usually far better drunk young.

⟁ **Ritchie Creek** (*Napa,* California) Small producer with dazzling Cabernet from the region of Spring Mountain.

🍇 **Rivaner** [rih-vah-nur] (Germany) The name used for *Müller-Thurgau* (a cross between *Riesling* and *Silvaner*) in parts of Germany and Luxembourg.

⟁ **Rivera** [ree-vay-ra] (*Puglia,* Italy) One of the new wave of producers who are turning the southern region of *Puglia* into a source of interesting wines. The red Riserva il Falcone is the star wine here. ★★★ 1999 Il Falcone Riserva Castel del Monte ££

Riverina [rih-vur-ee-na] (*New South Wales,* Australia) Irrigated *New South Wales* region which produces basic-to-good wine, much of which ends up in *"Southeast Australian"* blends. Late-harvest *Semillons* can, however, be surprisingly spectacular. *Cranswick Estate, McWilliams.*

⟁ **Rivesaltes** [reev-zalt] (*Languedoc-Roussillon,* France) Fortified dessert wine of both colours. The white made from the *Muscat* is lighter and more lemony than *Beaumes de Venise*, while the *Grenache* red is like liquid Christmas pudding and ages wonderfully. *Cazes; Ch. de Corneilla; Força Réal; Ch. de Jau; Sarda-Malet.* ★★★ 1982 Rivesaltes Ambré Hors D'Age Arnaud de Villeneuve ££

⟁ **Giorgio Rivetti** [ree-VAY-tee] (*Piedmont,* Italy) Superstar producer of wonderfully aromatic Moscato d'Asti, *Barbaresco*, and *Barbera*. ★★★ 1999 Pin La Spinetta Rivetti £££

Riviera Ligure di Ponente [reev-ee-yeh-ra lee-goo-ray dee poh-nen-tay] (*Liguria,* Italy) Little-known northwestern region, close to Genoa, where local grapes like the *Vermentino* produce light aromatic reds and whites.

🍇 **Rkatsiteli** [r'kat-sit-tel-lee] (Russia, Eastern Europe) Widely grown neutral white grape with enough acidity to stand up to poor winemaking.

🍇 **Robola** [roh-boh-lah] (Greece) The *Ribolla* of Italy.

Robertson (South Africa) Warm area where *Chardonnays* and *Sauvignons* are taking over from the *Muscats* that used to be the region's pride. *Graham Beck; Springfield; Robertson Winery; Van Loveren;* Weltevrede.

⟁ **Rocche dei Manzoni** [rok-keh day-yee mant-zoh-nee] (*Piedmont,* Italy) The Nebbiolo-Barbera Bricco Manzoni is the top wine here, but the single-vineyard *Barolo* is good too and there's some lovely *Chardonnay*.

⟁ **Rocca delle Macie** [ro-ka del leh mah-chee-yay] (*Tuscany,* Italy) Reliable if unspectacular *Chianti* producer.

⟁ **La Roche aux Moines** [rosh oh mwahn] See *Nicolas Joly*.

⟁ **Joe Rochioli** [roh-kee-yoh-lee] (*Sonoma,* California) Brilliant *Russian River Pinot Noir* and *Chardonnay* producer whose name also appears on single-vineyard wines from *Williams Selyem*.

⟁ **Rockford** (*Barossa Valley,* Australia) Robert "Rocky" O'Callaghan makes a great intense *Barossa Shiraz* using 100-year-old vines and 50-year-old equipment. There's a mouthfilling *Semillon*, a wonderful Black *Shiraz* sparkling wine, and a magical *Alicante Bouschet* rosé, which is sadly only to be found at the winery.

⟁ **Antonin Rodet** [on-toh-nan roh-day] (*Burgundy,* France) Very impressive *Mercurey*-based *négociant*, which has also improved the wines of the *Jacques Prieur domaine* in *Meursault*. *Ch. de Chamery; de Rully.*

R

🍇 **Roditis** [roh-dee-tiss] (Greece) A pink-skinned grape with good acidity much used for retsina. It can, however, make interesting unresinated wine.

🍷 **Louis Roederer** [roh-dur-rehr] (*Champagne,* France) This is still a family-owned *Champagne* house, and still one of the most reliable of these; its delicious non-vintage wine benefits from being cellared for a few years. Roederer's prestige Cristal remains a most deliciously "wine-like" *Champagne.*

Roederer Estate [roh-dur-rehr] (*Mendocino,* California) No longer involved with the *Jansz* sparkling wine in *Tasmania* but making top-class wine in California, which is sold in the US as Roederer Estate and in the UK as Quartet. ★★★★ **NV Quartet Estate Bottled Roederer £££**

🍷 **Roero** [roh-weh-roh] (*Piedmont,* Italy) *Nebbiolo* red and *Arneis* white (sold as Roero Arneis) which are now among Italy's most interesting wines. *Ceretto; Bruno Giacosa; Prunotto;* Serafino; Vietti. ★★★ **2001 Contea di Castiglione Roero Arneis Araldica Vini Piemontesi ££**

Michel Rolland [roh-lon] Based in *Pomerol* and *St. Emilion,* Rolland is now an increasingly international guru-oenologist, whose taste for ripe fruit flavours is influencing wines from *Ch. Ausone* to Argentina and beyond.

🍷 **Rol Valentin** [rohl-vah-lo'n-ta'n] (*Bordeaux,* France) *St-Emilion* garage wine with the expected concentration and price.

🍷 **Rolly-Gassmann** [rroh-lee gas-sman] (*Alsace,* France) Fine producer of subtle, long-lasting wines.

🍷 **Dom. de la Romanée-Conti** [rroh-ma-nay kon-tee] (*Burgundy,* France) Aka "DRC". Small *Grand Cru* estate. The jewel in the crown is the Romanée-Conti vineyard itself, though *La Tâche* runs it a close second. Both can be extraordinary, ultraconcentrated spicy wine, as can the *Romanée-St.-Vivant.* The *Richebourg, Echézeaux,* and *Grands Echézeaux* and *Montrachet* are comparable to those produced by other estates – and sold by them for less kingly ransoms.

Romania Traditional source of sweet reds and whites, now developing drier styles from classic European varieties. Unreliability is a constant problem, though *flying winemakers* are helping, as is the owner of the *Comte Peraldi* estate in *Corsica.* Note that Romania's well-praised *Pinot Noirs* are generally made from a different variety, mistaken for the *Pinot.* ★★★ **1999 La Cetate Merlot £**

🍇 **Romarantin** [roh-ma-ron-tan] (*Loire,* France) Interesting, limey grape found in obscure white blends in the *Loire.* See *Cheverny.*

Römerlay [rrur-mehr-lay] (*Mosel,* Germany) One of the *Grosslagen* in the *Ruwer* river valley.

🍷 **Ronchi di Manzano** [ron-kee dee mant-zah-noh] (*Friuli-Venezia Giulia,* Italy) Famed in Italy for its *Merlot* (Ronc di Subule), this producer's most interesting wine may well be its rich white *Picolit.*

🍷 **Ronco del Gnemiz** [ron-koh del gneh-meez] (*Friuli-Venezia Giulia,* Italy) One of the world's few producers of great *Müller-Thurgau,* and some pretty good *Chardonnay* in the *Colli Orientali.*

🍷 **Ronco delle Betulle** [ron-koh deh-leh beh-too-leh] (*Friuli-Venezia Giulia,* Italy) Try the *Bordeaux*-blend Narciso here – or the *Tocai Friulano, Sauvignon, Pinot Bianco,* or *Grigio.* You won't be disappointed.

🍷 **Rongopai** [ron-goh-pi] (*Te Kauwhata,* New Zealand) Estate in a region of the North Island pioneered by *Cooks,* but which has fallen out of favour with that company and with other producers. The speciality here is *botrytis* wines, but the *Chardonnay* is good, too.

🍷 **La Rosa** (Chile) One of the fastest-growing wineries in Chile, with new vineyards and great winemaking from *Ignacio Recabarren.* Las Palmeras is a highly reliable *second label.* ★★★★★ **2001 Las Palmeras Merlot Gran Reserva ££**

🍷 **Quinta de la Rosa** (*Douro,* Portugal) Recently established estate producing excellent port and exemplary dry red wine, under guidance from David Baverstock, Australian-born former winemaker at *Dow's* and responsible for the wines of *Esporão.* ★★★★ **2000 Quinta de la Rosa ££**

R

Rosato (Italy) Rosé.

Ⓘ **Rosé d'Anjou** [roh-zay don-joo] (*Loire,* France) Usually dull, semi-sweet pink from the *Malbec, Groslot,* and (less usually) *Cabernet Franc.*

Ⓘ **Rosé de Loire** [roh-zay duh-lwahr] (*Loire,* France) The wine *Rosé d'Anjou* ought to be. Dry, fruity stuff. *Richou;* **Cave des Vignerons de Saumur.**

Ⓘ **Rosé de Riceys** [roh-zay dur ree-say] (*Champagne,* France) Rare and occasionally delicious still rosé from *Pinot Noir.* Pricey. **Alexandre Bonnet.**

Ⓘ **Rosemount Estate** (*Hunter Valley,* Australia) Dynamic company now merged with Southcorp (*Penfolds, Lindemans* etc.). Famous for its Show Reserve and Roxburgh *Hunter Chardonnay.* Now makes impressive *Syrah*s and *Chardonnay*s Orange and Mountain Blue from *Mudgee.*

Ⓘ **Rosenblum** (*Alameda,* California) Great *Zinfandel*s from *Napa, Sonoma, Contra Costa,* and *Paso Robles* vineyards, plus great multi-regional blends.

Ⓘ **Rossese di Dolceaqua** [ros-seh-seh di dohl-chay-ah-kwah] (*Liguria,* Italy) Attractive, generally early-drinking wines made from the Rossese. Single-vineyard examples like Terre Bianche's Bricco Arcagna are more serious.

Ⓘ **Dom. Rossignol-Trapet** [ros-seen-yol tra-pay] (*Burgundy,* France) Once old-fashioned, now more recommendable estate in *Gevrey-Chambertin.*

Ⓘ **Rosso Conero** [ros-soh kon-neh-roh] (*Marches,* Italy) Big, *Montepulciano* and *Sangiovese* red, with rich, herby flavour. Good-value, characterful stuff. ★★★★ 1999 Vigneto San Lorenzo Rosso Conero Umani Ronchi ££

Ⓘ **Rosso di Montalcino** [ros-soh dee mon-tal-chee-noh] (*Tuscany,* Italy) *DO* for lighter, earlier-drinking versions of the more famous *Brunello di Montalcino.* Often better – and better value – than that wine. *Altesino; Caparzo;* Fattoria dei Barbi; Talenti. ★★★ 2000 Castello di Monastero ££

Ⓘ **Rosso Piceno** [ros-soh pee-chay-noh] (*Marches,* Italy) Traditionally rustic red made from a blend of the *Montepulciano* and *Sangiovese.* ★★★★ 1998 Il Grifone Superiore Tenuta Cocci £

Ⓘ **René Rostaing** [ros-tang] (*Rhône,* France) Producer of serious northern *Rhône* reds, including a more affordable alternative to *Guigal's* la Landonne.

Ⓘ **Rothbury Estate** (*Hunter Valley,* Australia) Founded by Len Evans, Svengali of Australian wine; the company is now a subsidiary of *Mildara*–Blass and Fosters. Rothbury is a great source of *Shiraz, Semillon,* and *Chardonnay* from the *Hunter Valley, Cowra Chardonnay* and *Marlborough Sauvignon.*

Ⓘ **Rotllan Torra** [rot-lahn tor-rah] (*Priorato,* Spain) Concentrated, weighty red wines made in the current mode, especially Amadis, Balandra. ★★★ Rotllan I Torra Moscatel ££

Ⓘ **Joseph Roty** [roh-tee] (*Burgundy,* France) Superstar producer of a range of intensely concentrated but unsubtle wines in *Gevrey-Chambertin.* One of the first "new-wave" winemakers in Burgundy.

Ⓘ **Rouge Homme** (*Coonawarra,* Australia) Reliable *Coonawarra* producer. founded by Mr. *Redman;* now under the same ownership as *Penfolds.*

Ⓘ **Emmanuel Rouget** [roo-jay] (*Burgundy,* France) Rouget inherited *Henri Jayer's* superb vineyards. Top quality.

Ⓘ **Dom. Guy Roulot** [roo-loh] (*Burgundy,* France) One of the greatest *domaines* in *Meursault.* ★★★★ 2000 Meursault Les Vireuils £££

Ⓘ **Georges Roumier** [roo-me-yay] (*Burgundy,* France) Blue-chip winery with great quality at every level, from village *Chambolle-Musigny* to the *Grand Cru,* Bonnes Mares, and (more rarely seen) white *Corton-Charlemagne.* ★★★★★ 1999 Bonnes Mares Grand Cru ££££

Ⓘ **Round Hill** (*Napa,* California) A rare source of Californian bargains. Large-production, inexpensive *Merlot*s and *Chardonnay*s.

🍇 **Roussanne** [roos-sahn] (*Rhône,* France) With the *Marsanne,* one of the key white grapes of the northern *Rhône.* In the US, has been mistaken for *Viognier.* ★★★★ 2001 Bonterra Vineyards Roussanne ££

R

Ⓣ Armand Rousseau [roos-soh] (*Burgundy,* France) *Gevrey-Chambertin* top-class estate with a line of *Premiers* and *Grands Crus.* Well-made, long-lasting wines. ★★★★ 1999 Gevrey-Chambertin ££££

Ⓖ Roussette de Savoie [roo-sette] (*Savoie,* France) The local name for the equally local Altesse grape. Fresh, easy-drinking fare. ★★★ 2001 Roussette de Savoie Pierre Boniface Domaine de Rocailles £

Roussillon [roos-see-yon] (*Languedoc-Roussillon,* France) Vibrant up-and-coming region, redefining traditional varieties, especially *Muscat.*

Ⓣ Ch. Routas [roo-tahs] (*Provence,* France) Impressive producer of intense reds and whites in the *Coteaux Varois.*

Ⓣ Royal Oporto Wine Co. (*Douro,* Portugal) Large and now improving producer of occasionally high-quality wines, including very good table wines.

Ⓣ The Royal Tokaji Wine Co. (*Tokaji,* Hungary) Pioneering part-foreign-owned company which – with other foreign investors – has helped to drag *Tokaji* into the late 20th (and early 21st) century with a succession of great single-vineyard wines.

Ⓣ Rozendal Farm [rooh-zen-dahl] (*Stellenbosch,* South Africa) Impeccably made, organic, Bordeaux-style reds from a producer whose quality consciousness made him decide not to release the 1997 vintage.

Ⓣ Rubesco di Torgiano [roo-bes-koh dee taw-jee-yah-noh] (*Umbria,* Italy) Modern red *DOCG;* more or less the exclusive creation of *Lungarotti.*

Ⓣ Rubino [roo-bee-noh] (*Umbria,* Italy) Rich "Super-Umbrian" red from the la Pazzola estate. Matches many a *Super-Tuscan.*

Ruby (*Douro,* Portugal) Cheapest, basic *port*; young, blended, sweetly fruity. ★★★ Dow's Fine Ruby Port ££

Ⓖ Ruby Cabernet [roo-bee ka-behr-nay] (California) A *Cabernet Sauvignon/ Carignan* cross making basic wines in California, Australia, and South Africa.

Ⓖ Ruche [roo-kay] (*Piedmont,* Italy) Raspberryish red grape from northern Italy producing early-drinking wines. Best from *Bava.*

Rüdesheim [rroo-des-hime] (*Rheingau,* Germany) Tourist town producing powerful *Rieslings. Georg Breuer;* August Kesseler; Schloss Schönborn; Staatsweingüter Kloster Eberbach. ★★★ 2001 Josef Leitz Rudesheimer Berg Schlossberg Riesling Spatlese ££

Ⓣ Rueda [roo way-dah] (Spain) *DO* in north-west Spain for clean, dry whites from the local *Verdejo.* Progress is being led most particularly by the *Lurtons, Marqués de Riscal,* and *Marqués de Griñon.*

Ⓣ Ruffino [roof-fee-noh] (*Tuscany,* Italy) Big *Chianti* producer with impressive top-of-the-line wines, including the reliable *Cabreo Vino da Tavola.* ★★★ 1999 Romitorio di Santedame ££££

Rufina [roo-fee-na] (*Tuscany,* Italy) A sub-region within *Chianti,* producing supposedly classier wine. ★★★★ 1999 Montesodi Frescobaldi £

Ⓣ Ruinart [roo-wee-nahr] (*Champagne,* France) High-quality sister to *Moët & Chandon,* with superlative *Blanc de Blancs.* ★★★★★ 1988 Dom Ruinart Rosé ££££

Ⓖ Ruländer [roo-len-dur] (Germany) German name for *Pinot Gris.*

Ⓣ Rully [roo-yee] (*Burgundy,* France) *Côte Chalonnaise commune* producing rich white and a red that's been called the "poor man's" *Volnay.* See *Antonin Rodet, Jadot,* and *Olivier Leflaive. Faiveley;* Jacqueson; *Jadot; Olivier Leflaive; Antonin Rodet.* ★★★ 2000 Rully 1er Cru Les Cloux Vincent Girardin ££

Ruppertsberg [roo-pehrt-sbehrg] (*Pfalz,* Germany) Top-ranking village with a number of excellent vineyards making vigorous fruity *Riesling. Bürklin-Wolf;* Kimich; Werlé. ★★★ 2001 Ruppertsberg Eiswein Winzerverein ££

Ⓣ la Rural [lah roo-rahl] (*Mendoza,* Argentina) Old-established producer, now making good, commercial wines. The Malbec is the strongest card.

Ⓣ Rusden (*Barossa,* South Australia) Small, new estate gaining instant recognition in the US for its rich Barossa Cabernets and Grenaches.

Russe [rooss] (Bulgaria) Danube town best known in Britain for its reliable red blends but vaunted in *Bulgaria* as a source of modern whites.

R

Russian River Valley (California) Cult, cool-climate area to the north of *Sonoma* and west of *Napa*. Ideal for apples and good sparkling wine, as is proven by the excellent *Iron Horse*, which also makes impressive table wines. Great *Pinot Noir* country. *Dehlinger; de Loach; Iron Horse; Kistler; Rochioli; Sonoma-Cutrer;* Joseph Swann; *Marimar Torres;Williams Selyem.* ★★★★★ 1997 Martinelli Pinot Noir £££

Rust [roost] (*Burgenland,* Austria) Wine centre of *Burgenland,* famous for Ruster *Ausbruch* sweet white wine. ★★★★ 1999 Ruster Ausbruch Essenz Weingut Feiler-Artinger ££££

Ⓨ Rust-en-Vrede (*Stellenbosch,* South Africa) Vastly improved estate, thanks to the efforts of a new generation.

Ⓨ Rustenberg (*Stellenbosch,* South Africa) On a roll since 1996 with investment in the cellars (which put an end to musty flavours encountered in previous vintages), this now a leading light in the Cape. The lower-priced Brampton efforts are quite good, too. ★★★★ 2000 Chardonnay ££

Rutherford (California) *Napa* region in which some producers believe sufficiently to propose it – and its geological "bench" – as an *appellation.*

Rutherglen (*Victoria,* Australia) Hot area on the *Murray River* pioneered by gold miners. Today noted for rich *Muscat* and *Tokay* dessert and *port*-style wines.The reds are often tough and the *Chardonnays* are used by cool-region winemakers to demonstrate why *port* and light, dry whites are hard to make in the same climate. *All Saints; Chambers; Morris; Pfeiffer; Seppelt; Stanton & Killeen.* ★★★★★ NV Campbells Rutherglen Muscat £

Ⓨ Rutz Cellars (*Sonoma,* California) Competing with Kistler to produce superlative Russian River Chardonnay, Rutz offers the chance to taste a different Chardonnay from the Dutton Ranch vineyard.

Ruwer [roo-vur] (*Mosel-Saar-Ruwer,* Germany) *Mosel* tributary alongside which is to be found the *Römerlay Grosslage,* and includes Kasel, *Eitelsbach* and the great *Maximin Grünhaus* estate.

Hugh Ryman [ri-man] *Flying winemaker* whose team turns grapes into wine under contract in *Bordeaux, Burgundy,* southern France, Spain, Germany, Moldova, Chile, California, South Africa, and Hungary. Wines tend to bear the initials HDR at the foot of the label – or one of Ryman's own brands: Santara, Kirkwood, Richemont, Rafael Estate.

Ⓨ Rymill [ri-mil] (South Australia) One of several *Coonawarra* wineries to mention *Riddoch* on its label (in its Riddoch Run) and a rising star. Rymill at least has the legitimacy of a family link to *John Riddoch,* the region's founder. The *Shiraz* and *Cabernet* are first class, as are the whites and the sparkling wine. ★★★★ 1998 Cabernet Sauvignon ££

S

Saale-Unstrut [zah-leh oon-shtruht] (Germany) Remember East Germany? Well, this is where poor wines used to be made there in the bad old days. Today, good ones are being produced, by producers like Lützkendorf.

Saar [zahr] (*Mosel-Saar-Ruwer,* Germany) The other *Mosel* tributary associated with lean, slatey *Riesling.* Villages include *Ayl, Ockfen,* Saarburg, Serrig, *Wiltingen.*

Sablet [sa-blay] (*Rhône,* France) Good *Côtes du Rhône* village.

Ⓨ Sachsen [zak-zen] (Germany) Revived former East German region where Klaus Seifert is producing good *Riesling.*

Ⓨ St. Amour [san ta-moor] (*Burgundy,* France) One of the 10 *Beaujolais Crus* – usually light and fruity. Billards; la Cave Lamartine; *Duboeuf;* Patissier; Revillon.

S

Weingut St Antony (*Rheinhessen*, Germany) First class *Riesling*: this is as good as Nierstein gets.

St. Aubin [san toh-ban] (*Burgundy*, France) Underrated *Côte d'Or* village for (jammily rustic) reds and rich, nutty, rather classier white; affordable alternatives to *Meursault*. *Jean-Claude Bachelet; Champy; Marc Colin;* Hubert Lamy-Monnot; *Olivier Leflaive;* Henri Prudhon; *Ch de Puligny-Montrachet;* Roux Père et Fils; Gérard Thomas. ★★★ 2000 Domaine Chartron Père et Fils (GV) St Aubin 1er Cru Murgers des Dents de Chien

St. Bris [san bree] (*Burgundy*, France) Best known for its VDQS *Sauvignon de St. Bris,* this village close to *Chablis* can also make good examples of the *Aligoté* grape. *Jean-Marc Brocard; la Chablisienne;* Joel et David Griffe; Sorin Defrance.

St. Chinian [san shee-nee-yon] (*Southwest*, France) Neighbour of *Faugères* in the *Coteaux du Languedoc*, producing midweight wines from *Carignan* and other *Rhône* grapes. **Ch. des Albières; de Astide Rousse; Babeau;** Mas Champart; Clos Bagatelle; Canet-Valette; Cazel-Viel; Coujan; Cooperative de Roquebrun; Mas de la Tour; Maurel Fonsalade; Ch. Quartironi de Sars.

St. Clement (*Napa Valley,* California) Japanese-owned winery whose best wine is the Oroppas red blend. In case you were wondering, the name isn't a Native American word, but that of the owner spelled backward.

St. Emilion [san tay-mee-lee-yon] (*Bordeaux*, France) Large *commune* with varied soils and wines. At best, sublime *Merlot*-dominated *claret*; at worst dull, earthy and fruitless. Some 170 or so *"Grand cru"* St. Emilions are made in better-sited vineyards and have to undergo a tasting every vintage to be able to use these words on their labels, and too few fail. *Grand Cru Classé* refers to 68 *châteaux*, of which two – *Ausone* and *Cheval-Blanc* – are rated as *"Premier Grands Crus Classés"* and 11 are *"Premiers Grands Crus Classés B."* These ratings are reviewed every decade. Supposedly "lesser" satellite neighbours – *Lussac, Puisseguin, St. Georges,* etc. – often make better value wine than basic St. Emilion. *Angélus; Ausone;* Beau-Séjour-Bécot; *Beauséjour; Belair; Canon; Canon la Gaffelière; Cheval Blanc; Clos des Jacobins; Clos Fourtet; Figeac; Franc Mayne; Grand Mayne; Larcis Ducasse; Magdelaine; la Mondotte; Pavie;* Tertre Rôteboeuf; *Troplong-Mondot; Trottevieille; Valandraud.*

St. Estèphe [san teh-stef] (*Bordeaux*, France) Northernmost *Médoc commune* with clay soil and wines which can be a shade more rustic than those of neighbouring *Pauillac* and *St. Julien,* but which are often longer-lived and more structured than some of the juicy, easy-to-drink *St. Emilions* and *Pomerols* that tend to win approval from critics. **Calon-Ségur;** *Cos d'Estournel; Haut-Marbuzet; Lafon-Rochet; Marbuzet; Montrose; de Pez; Ormes de Pez; Phélan-Ségur.*

St. Francis (*Sonoma,* California) Innovative winery with great *Zinfandels,* and Reserve *Chardonnays* and *Cabernets.* The first Californian to introduce artificial corks to protect wine drinkers from faulty bottles. ★★★★★ 1998 Nuns Canyon Cabernet Sauvignon Reserve £££

St. Georges-St.Emilion [san jorrzh san tay-mee-lee-yon] (*Bordeaux,* France) Satellite of *St. Emilion* with good *Merlot*-dominant reds, often better value than *St. Emilion* itself. **Ch. Maquin St. Georges;** St. Georges.

St. Hallett (*Barossa Valley,* Australia) Superstar *Barossa* winery specializing in wines from old ("old block") *Shiraz* vines. Whites (especially *Semillon* and *Riesling*) are good too. ★★★★★ 1999 Barossa Shiraz ££

St. Hubert's (*Victoria,* Australia) Pioneering *Yarra* winery with ultra-fruity *Cabernet* and mouth-filling *Roussanne* whites.

Chateau St. Jean [jeen] (*Sonoma,* California) Named after the founder's wife; now Japanese-owned and a source of good single-vineyard *Chardonnays, late-harvest Rieslings* and *Bordeaux*-style reds.

St. Joseph [san joh-sef] (*Rhône,* France) Potentially vigorous, fruity *Syrah* from the northern *Rhône.* Whites range from flabby to fragrant *Marsannes. Chapoutier; Chave;* Courbis; Coursodon; *Cuilleron; Delas;* de Fauturie; Gacho-Pascal; *Gaillard; Graillot; Gripa; Grippat;* Perret; *Pichon;* St.-Désirat; Trollo; *Vernay.* ★★★★ 2000 Alain Paret St Joseph Les Larmes Du Pere ££

S

✠ **St. Julien** [san-joo-lee-yen] (*Bordeaux,* France) Aristocratic *Médoc commune* producing classic rich wines, full of cedar and deep, ripe fruit. *Beychevelle; Branaire; Ducru-Beaucaillou; Gruaud-Larose; Lagrange; Langoa-Barton; Léoville-Barton; Léoville-Las-Cases; Léoville-Poyferré; Talbot.*

🍇 **St. Laurent** [sant loh-rent] (Austria) *Pinot Noir*-like berryish red grape, mastered, in particular, by *Umathum*. ★★★ 2000 Steindorfer St Laurent Reserve Weingut Ernst und Rosa Steindorfer Burgenland ££

✠ **St. Nicolas de Bourgueil** [san nee-koh-lah duh boor-goy] (*Loire,* France) Lightly fruity *Cabernet Franc*; needs a warm year to ripen its raspberry fruit, but then can last for up to a decade. Pretty similar to Bourgueil. Yannick Amirault; *Caslot; Max* Cognard; Delauney; *Druet; Jamet;* Mabileau; Vallée.

✠ **St. Péray** [san pay-reh] (*Rhône,* France) *AC* near *Lyon* for full-bodied white and *traditional method* sparkling wine, at risk from encroaching housing. J-F Chapoud; *Auguste Clape; Bernard Gripa; Marcel Juge; Jean Lionnet; Alain Voge.*

✠ **Ch. St. Pierre** [san pee-yehr] (*St. Julien 4ème Cru Classé, Bordeaux,* France) Reliable *St. Julien* under the same ownership as *Ch. Gloria.*

✠ **St. Romain** [san roh-man] (*Burgundy,* France) *Hautes Côtes de Beaune* village producing undervalued fine whites and rustic reds. Christophe Buisson; Chassorney; Germain et Fils; Iain Gras; *Jaffelin;* Thévenin-Monthelie.

✠ **St. Véran** [san vay-ron] (*Burgundy,* France) Once sold as *Beaujolais Blanc;* affordable alternative to *Pouilly-Fuissé;* better than most *Mâconnais* whites. Ch. Fuissé is first class. *Barraud; Corsin;* Dom des Deux Roches; *Duboeuf; Ch. Fuissé;* Luquet; Pacquet. ★★★ 2000 Les Grandes Bruyeres Domaine Roger ££

✠ **Ste. Croix-du-Mont** [sant crwah doo mon] (*Bordeaux,* France) Never as luscious, rich, and complex as the better efforts of its neighbour *Sauternes –* but often a far more worthwhile buy than wines unashamedly sold under that name.

✠ **Saintsbury** (*Carneros,* California) Superstar *Carneros* producer of unfiltered *Chardonnay* and – more specially – *Pinot Noir.* The slogan: "Beaune in the USA" refers to the winery's Burgundian aspirations. The Reserve *Pinot* is a world-beater, while the easy-going Garnet is the good *second label.* ★★★★ 1999 Pinot Noir Reserve £££

Sakar [sa-kah] (Bulgaria) Long-time source of much of the best *Cabernet Sauvignon* to come from *Bulgaria.*

✠ **Castello della Sala** [kas-tel-loh del-la sah-lah] (*Umbria,* Italy) *Antinori's* overpriced but sound *Chardonnay, Sauvignon.* Also good *Sauvignon/Procanico* blend. ★★★ 2000 Castello della Sala Antinori £££

✠ **Ch de Sales** [duh sahl] (*Pomerol, Bordeaux*) Good but generally unexciting wine for relatively early drinking. Also worth looking out for is Stonyfell, which matches rich Shiraz flavours with an appealingly "retro" label.

✠ **Salice Salentino** [sa-lee-chay sah-len-tee-noh] (*Puglia,* Italy) Spicy, intense red made from the characterful *Negroamaro.* Great value, especially when mature. *Candido; Leone de Castris;* Taurino; Vallone. ★★★★★ 1998 Selvarossa Salice Salentino Riserva Cantine Due Palme £

✠ **Salomon-Undhof** [sah-loh-mon oond-hohf] (*Kremstal,* Austria) Top-class producer, with especially notable *Riesling.*

✠ **Salon le Mesnil** [sah-lon lur may-neel] (*Champagne,* France) Small, traditional subsidiary of *Laurent-Perrier* with cult following for pure long-lived *Chardonnay Champagne.* Only sold as a single-vintage cuvée.

Salta (Argentina) The world's highest vineyards.

✠ **Saltram** [sawl-tram] (South Australia) Fast-improving part of the *Mildara-Blass* empire. Rich, fairly priced *Barossa* reds and whites (also under the Mamre Brook label) and top-flight *"ports".* ★★★★★ 1999 Saltram No. I Shiraz £££

✠ **Samos** [sah-mos] (Greece) Aegean island producing sweet, fragrant, golden *Muscat* once called "the wine of the gods". ★★★ Muscat D. Kourtakis £

✠ **Cellier des Samsons** [sel-yay day som-son] (*Burgundy,* France) Source of better-than-average *Beaujolais.*

S

☓ **San Giusto a Rentennano** [san-jus-toh ah ren-ten-nah-noh] (*Tuscany*, Italy) Modern, international-style *Super-Tuscan* Percalo *Sangiovese* and *Merlot* La Ricolma, plus excellent *Chianti Classico*.

☓ **San Leonardo** [san lay-yoh-nar-doh] (*Trentino*, Italy) Look especially for the outstanding Bordeaux blend.

San Luis Obispo [san loo-wis oh-bis-poh] (California) Californian region gaining a reputation for *Chardonnay* and *Pinot Noir*. Try *Edna Valley*. ★★★★ 2000 Avila Pinot Noir ££

☓ **Viña San Pedro** [veen-ya san-pay-droh] (*Curico*, Chile) Huge firm whose wines are quietly and steadily improving thanks to the efforts of French consultant *Jacques Lurton*. ★★★★ 1999 Cabo de Hornos Cabernet Sauvignon £££

☓ **Sancerre** [son-sehr] (*Loire*, France) At its best, the epitome of elegant, steely dry *Sauvignon*; at its worst, oversulphured and fruitless. Reds and rosés, though well regarded and highly priced by French restaurants, are often little better than quaffable *Pinot Noir*. Bailly-Reverdy; Jean-Paul Balland; *Henri Bourgeois; Cotat*; Lucien Crochet; Vincent Delaporte; Pierre Dézat; Fouassier; de la Garenne; Gitton; les Grands Groux; *Pascal Jolivet; de Ladoucette*; Serge Laporte; Mellot; Thierry Merlin-Cherrier; Paul Millerioux; Natter; Vincent Pinard; Jean-Max Roger; *Vacheron*; André Vatan. ★★★★★ 2001 Domaine Michel Sancerre ££

☓ **Sanchez Romate** (*Jerez*, Spain) Top quality sherry producer with delicious NPU (Non Plus Ultra) Amontillado. ★★★★★ La Sacristia de Romate ££

☓ **Sandeman** (Spain/Portugal) Generally under-performing, but occasionally dazzling *port* and *sherry* producer. ★★★ NV Original Dry Don Medium Dry Amontillado Sherry £

☓ **Sanford Winery** (*Santa Barbara*, California) *Santa Barbara* superstar producer of *Chardonnay* and especially distinctive, slightly horseradishy *Pinot Noir*. ★★★★ 1999 Pinot Noir Sanford & Benedict £££

☙ **Sangiovese** [san-jee-yoh vay-seh] (Italy) The tobaccoey, herby-flavoured red grape of *Chianti* and *Montepulciano*, now being used increasingly in *Vino da Tavola* and – though rarely impressively – in California. *Antinori; Atlas Peak; Bonny Doon; Isole e Olena*. ★★★★ 1999 Brancaia Sangiovese Merlot £££

☓ **Castello di San Polo in Rosso** [san-poh-loh in -ros-soh] (*Tuscany*, Italy) Reliable, quite traditional *Chianti Classico* estate.

☓ **Luciano Sandrone** [loo-chee-yah-noh sahn-droh-nay] (*Piedmont*, Italy) With fellow revolutionaries *Clerico, Roberto Voerzio*, and *Altare*, Luciano Sandrone has spearheaded the move to modern *Barolo*. Great *Dolcetto* too. ★★★★ 1997 Barolo 'Cannubi Boschis'

Sanlúcar de Barrameda [san loo-kar- day bar-rah-may-dah] (Spain) One of the three sherry towns, and the source of Manzanilla.

Santa Barbara (California) Successful southern, cool-climate region for *Pinot Noir* and *Chardonnay*. *Au Bon Climat; Byron; Ojai; Qupé; Sanford*.

☓ **Viña Santa Carolina** [ka-roh-lee-na] (Chile) Greatly improved producer, thanks to *Ignacio Recabarren* and vineyards in *Casablanca*. Good reds. ★★★★ 2000 Santa Carolina Barrica Selection Pinot Noir ££

Santa Cruz Mountains [krooz] (California) Exciting region to the south of San Francisco. See *Ridge* and *Bonny Doon*.

☓ **Santa Emiliana** (*Aconcagua*, Chile) Large producer with good Andes Peak offerings from *Casablanca*, and wines from the new southern region of Mulchen.

☓ **Santadi** [san-tah-dee] (*Sardinia*, Italy) A co-op noted for good quality especially Terre Brune Carignano del Sulcis. ★★★ 2000 Latinia Santadi ££

☓ **Santa Maddalena** [san-tah mah-dah-LAY-nah] (*Alto Adige*, Italy) Light, spicy-fruity red made from the Schiava. Rarely found outside the region, but well worth seeeking out. Cantina Produttori Sta. Maddalena; Gojer.

S

☨ **Santa Rita** [ree-ta] (*Maipo*, Chile) The Casa Real is not only one of Chile's best and most fairly priced reds; it is also truly world class and the Carmenère-Cabernets "Triple C" a great value new arrival on the scene. ★★★ 2000 Santa Rita Merlot Syrah Reserva £

☨ **Santenay** [sont-nay] (*Burgundy*, France) Southern *Côte d'Or* village, producing pretty whites and good, though occasionally rather rustic, reds. Look for *Girardin* and *Pousse d'Or*. Roger Belland; *Fernand* Chevrot; *Marc Colin*; Colin-Deléger; *Girardin*; *Olivier Leflaive*; *Bernard Morey*; Lucien Muzet; Claude Nouveau; *Pousse d'Or*; Prieur Brunet. ★★★ 1999 Château de la Charrière Santenay 1er Cru Clos Rousseau Yves Girardin ££

☨ **Caves São João** [sow-jwow] (*Bairrada*, Portugal) Small company which can produce high-quality *Bairrada*.

Sardinia (Italy) Traditionally the source of powerful reds (try *Santadi*) and whites, increasingly interesting *DOC* fortified wines, and new-wave modern reds to match the best *Super-Tuscans*. *Sella e Mosca*.

☨ **Paolo Saracco** [pow-loh sah-rak-koh] (*Piedmont*, Italy) Competitor for the role of top *Moscato*-maker. Bianch del Luv *Chardonnay* is impressive too.

☨ **Sarget de Gruaud-Larose** [sahr-jay dur groowoh lah-rohs] (*St. Julien*, Bordeaux, France) Reliable *second label* of *Ch. Gruaud-Larose*.

☨ **Sassicaia** [sas-see-kai-ya] (*Tuscany*, Italy) World-class *Cabernet*-based *Super-Tuscan* with more of an Italian than a *claret* taste. No longer a mere *Vino da Tavola* since the *DOC* Bolgheri was introduced in 1994.

☨ **Saumur** [soh-moor] (*Loire*, France) Heartland of variable *Chenin*-based sparkling and still wine, and potentially more interesting *Saumur-Champigny*. Langlois-Château; Roches Neuves; Vatin; Cave des Vignerons de Saumur; Villeneuve. ★★★ 2001 Les Nivires Saumur Rouge Saumur des Caves £

☨ **Saumur-Champigny** [soh-moor shom-pee-nyee] (*Loire*, France) Crisp *Cabernet Franc* red; best served slightly chilled. Good examples are worth cellaring. *Bouvet-Ladubay; Couly-Dutheil; Filliatreau*; Foucault; *Ch. du Hureau*; Langlois-Château; Targé; Vatan; de Villeneuve. ★★★ 2001 Saumur Champigny 'Les Poyeux' Cave des Vignerons de Saumur ££

☨ **Saussignac** [soh-sin-yak] (*Southwest*, France) Historically in the shadow both of *Sauternes* and nearby Monbazillac, this sweet-wine region is enjoying a minor boom at the moment and putting many a Sauternes to shame. Ch la Chabrier; des Eyssards; Ch Grinou; Dom. Léonce Cuisset; Dom de Richard, Ch. les Miaudoux, Tourmentine; le Payral; Clos d'Yvigne. ★★★ 1998 Chateau Le Payral Cuvée Marie Jeanne ££

☨ **Sauternes** [soh-turn] (*Bordeaux*, France) Rich, potentially sublime, honeyed dessert wines from *Sauvignon* and *Sémillon* (and possibly *Muscadelle*) blends. Should be affected by *botrytis* but the climate does not always allow this. *Bastor-Lamontagne; Doisy-Daëne; Fargues; Filhot; Guiraud; Rieussec; Suduiraut; Yquem*. ★★★★ 1996 Chateau Filhot £££

🏆 **Sauvignon Blanc** [soh-vin-yon-blon] "Grassy", "catty", "asparagussy", "gooseberryish" grape widely grown but rarely really loved, so often blended, oaked, or made sweet. In France, at home in the *Loire* and *Bordeaux*. New Zealand gets it right – especially in *Marlborough*. In Australia, *Knappstein*, *Cullens*, *Stafford Ridge*, and *Shaw & Smith* are right on target. *Mondavi's* oaked *Fumé Blanc* and *Kendall Jackson's* sweet versions are successful but *Monteviña*, *Quivira, Dry Creek, Simi*, and – in blends with the *Semillon – Carmenet* are the stars. Chile makes better versions every year, despite starting out with a lesser variety. See *Caliterra, Casablanca, Canepa, Sta. Carolina*, and *Villard*. In South Africa, see *Thelema, Klein Constantia*, and *Neil Ellis*.

☨ **Sauvignon de St. Bris** [soh-veen-yon-duh san bree] (*Burgundy*, France) An affordable and often worthwhile alternative to *Sancerre*, produced in vineyards near *Chablis*. Jean-Marc Brocard; Moreau.

☨ **Etienne Sauzet** [soh-zay] (*Burgundy*, France) First-rank estate whose white wines are almost unfindable outside collectors' cellars and Michelin-starred restaurants. ★★★★★ 1998 Puligny-Montrachet Les Perrières 1er Cru £££

S

- **Savagnin** [sa-van-yan] (*Jura*, France) Unrelated to *Sauvignon*; a white *Jura* variety used for *Vin Jaune* and blended with *Chardonnay* for *Arbois*. Thought to be identical to Traminer, the non-aromatic form of *Gewürztraminer*.
- **Savanha** [sa-vah-nah] (South Africa) Great Bordeaux-like Naledi Cabernet and Sejana Merlot; both concentrated but subtle and made by joint venture with producers from *Pomerol*.
- **Savennières** [sa-ven-yehr] (*Loire*, France) Fine, if sometimes aggressively dry, *Chenin Blanc* whites. Very long-lived. des Baumard; Bise; du Closel; Coulée de Serrant; d'Epiré; La Roche aux Moines; de Plaisance; Soulez.

CLOS
DE LA
Coulée de Serrant
APPELLATION SAVENNIÈRES - COULÉE DE SERRANT CONTROLÉE

Mme A. JOLY, Propriétaire Viticulteur
au Château de la Roche-aux-Moines - 49170 SAVENNIÈRES

PRODUCT OF FRANCE   NET CONTENTS : 750 ML   ESTATE BOTTLED

- **Savigny-lès-Beaune** [sa-veen-yee lay bohn] (*Burgundy*, France) Distinctive whites (sometimes made from *Pinot Blanc*) and raspberry reds. At their best can compare with *Beaune*. Simon Bize; Chandon de Briailles; Ecard; Girard-Voillot; Girardin; Pavelot; Tollot-Beaut. ★★★ 2000 Signature Les Peuillets Bouchard Aîné ££
- **Savoie** [sav-wah] (Eastern France) Mountainous region near Geneva producing crisp, floral whites such as Abymes, *Apremont, Seyssel*, and *Crépy*. ★★★ 2001 Roussette de Savoie Pierre Boniface Domaine de Rocailles £
- **Saxenburg** (*Stellenbosch*, South Africa) Reliable producer of ripely flavoursome wines. Particularly good *Pinotage* and *Sauvignon Blanc*.
- **Cellers de Scala Dei** [sel-lehrs day skah-la day-yee] (*Priorat*, Spain) Long-established *bodega* currently making less exciting wine than the newcomers.
- **Scavino** [ska-vee-noh] (*Piedmont*, Italy) Terrific juicy reds, including single-vineyard *Barolos, Barberas* and *Dolcettos*.
- **Willi Schaefer** [shay-fur] (*Mosel-Saar-Ruwer*, Germany) Excellent grower in the Mosel vineyard of Himmelreich in the village of Graach (Grosslage Münzelay).
- **Scharffenberger** [shah-fen-bur-gur] (*Mendocino*, California) Pommery-owned, independently-run producer of top-class, top-value sparkling wine.
- **Scharzhofberg** [sharts-hof-behrg] (*Mosel-Saar-Ruwer*, Germany) Top-class *Saar* vineyard, producing great *Riesling*. Reichsgraf von Kesselstadt.
- **Schaumwein** [showm-vine] (Germany) Low-priced sparkling wine.
- **Scheurebe** [shoy-ray-bur] (Germany) Grapefruit-like *Riesling* x *Silvaner* cross, grown in Germany and England. In Austria, it is called Samling 88. Kurt Darting; Hafner; Alois Kracher; Lingenfelder. ★★★★ 1999 LYSS Doux Scheurebe TBA Riedenhof Kadlec Austria, ££££
- **Schiava** [skee yah-vah] (*Alto Adige*, Italy) Grape used in *Lago di Caldaro* and *Santa Maddalena* to make light reds.
- **Schilfwein** [shilf-vine] (Austria) Luscious "reed wine" – Austrian *vin de paille* pioneered by *Willi Opitz*. ★★★★ 2000 Weingut Hans Tschida Traminer Schilfwein Burgenland £££
- **Schiopetto** [skee yoh-peh-toh] (*Friuli-Venezia Giulia*, Italy) Gloriously intense, perfumed *Collio* white varietals to rival those of *Jermann*.
- **Schloss** [shloss] (Germany) Literally "castle"; in practice, vineyard or estate.
- **Schist** [shist] Type of slaty soil very suitable for growing vines.
- **Schloss Böckelheim** [shloss ber-kell-hime] (*Nahe*, Germany) Varied southern part of the Nahe. Wines from the Kupfergrube vineyard and the State Wine Domaine are worth buying.
- **Schloss Johannisberg** [shloss yo-hah-nis-behrg] (*Rheingau*, Germany) Beautiful princely estate, now back on track. ★★★ 2000 Riesling £
- **Schloss Lieser** [shloss lee-zuh] (*Mosel*, Germany) Excellent small estate related to *Fritz Haag*.
- **Schloss Reinhartshausen** [shloss rine-harts-how-zehn] (*Rheingau*, Germany) Successful with *Pinot Blanc* and *Chardonnay* (introduced following a suggestion by *Robert Mondavi*). The *Rieslings* are good too.

S

✶ **Schloss Saarstein** [shloss sahr-shtine] (*Mosel-Saar-Ruwer,* Germany) High-quality *Riesling* specialist in *Serrig.* ★★★★ 2001 Riesling Auslese ££

✶ **Schloss Schönborn** [shloss shern-born] (*Mosel-Saar-Ruwer,* Germany) Unreliable but sometimes brilliant estate.

✶ **Schloss Vollrads** [shloss fol-rahts] (*Rheingau,* Germany) Old-established estate enjoying a renaissance under new ownership and management. ★★★ **2000 Riesling Eiswein Gold ££££**

✶ **Schloss Wallhausen** [shloss val-how-zen] (*Nahe,* Germany) Prinz zu Salm-Dalberg's estate is one of the best in the Nahe, with fine dry Riesling. **Schlossböckelheim** [shloss berk-el-hime] (*Nahe,* Germany) Village giving its name to a large *Nahe Bereich,* producing elegant *Riesling.* Staatsweingut Niederhausen.

✶ **Schlossgut Diel** [deel] (*Nahe,* Germany) Armin Diel is both wine writer and winemaker. Co-author of the excellent *German Wine Guide,* his Dorsheimer Goldloch wines are worth seeking out.

✶ **Dom. Schlumberger** [shloom-behr-jay] (*Alsace,* France) Great, sizeable estate whose subtle top-level wines can often rival those of the somewhat more showy *Zind-Humbrecht.*

✶ **Schramsberg** [shram-sberg] (*Napa Valley,* California) The winery that single-handedly put California sparkling wine on the quality trail. Wines used to be too big for their boots, possibly because too many of the grapes were from warm vineyards in *Napa.* The J. Schram is aimed at *Dom Pérignon* and gets pretty close to the target.

✶ **Scotchman's Hill** (Victoria, Australia) *Pinot Noir* specialist in *Geelong. Sauvignons* and *Chardonnays* have been less exciting.

✶ **Screaming Eagle** (*Napa Valley,* California) Minuscule winery the size of many people's living room, which has been producing around 200 bottles of intense *Cabernet* per year since 1992 – and selling them at $100 a bottle. The owners are avowedly trying to make California's greatest wine. Sadly, most people will only ever read about it. ★★★★★ 1992 Screaming Eagle ££££

✶ **Seaview** (South Australia) *Penfold's* brand for brilliantly reliable sparkling wine and (less frequently) *McLaren Vale* red table wines. Look out for the Edwards & Chaffey label, too. ★★★ 1997 Seaview Pinot Noir Chardonnay ££

✶ **Sebastiani/Cecchetti Sebastiani** [seh-bas-tee-yan-nee] (*Sonoma Valley,* California) Sebastiani makes unexceptional wine from *Central Valley* grapes. The associated but separate Cecchetti Sebastiani, however, like the top end of *Gallo,* makes really good stuff in *Sonoma.* The Pepperwood Grove wines are good too. ★★★ 1999 Pepperwood Grove Zinfandel £

Sec/secco/seco [se-koh] (France/Italy/Spain) Dry.

Second label (*Bordeaux,* France) Wine from a producer's (generally a *Bordeaux château*) lesser vineyards, younger vines, and/or lesser *cuvées* of wine. Especially worth buying in good vintages. See *Les Forts de Latour.*

✶ **Seghesio** [seh-gay-see-yoh] (California, USA) An estate to seek out for old-vine *Zinfandel* of great density and depth. ★★★★ 1999 Seghesio Pinot Noir Keyhole Ranch ££

✶ **Segura Viudas** [say-goo-rah vee-yoo-dass] (*Catalonia,* Spain) The quality end of the Freixenet Cava giant.

✶ **Seifried Estate** [see-freed] (*Nelson,* New Zealand) Also known as *Redwood Valley Estate.* Superb *Riesling,* especially *late-harvest* style, and very creditable *Sauvignon* and *Chardonnay.* ★★★★ 2001 Sauvignon Blanc £

Sekt [zekt] (Germany) Very basic sparkling wine. Watch out for anything that does not state that it is made from *Riesling* – other grape varieties almost invariably make highly unpleasant wines. Only the prefix "Deutscher" guarantees German origin.

✶ **Selaks** [see-lax] (*Auckland,* New Zealand) Large company in Kumeu best known for the piercingly fruity *Sauvignon* originally made by a young man called Kevin Judd, who went on to produce *Cloudy Bay.* ★★★★ 2001 Selaks Premium Selection Sauvignon Blanc £

S

Ⓨ **Weingut Selbach-Oster** [zel-bahkh os-tehr] (*Mosel-Saar-Ruwer,* Germany) Archetypical *Mosel Riesling* of great finesse and balance. One of the region's best producers.

Sélection de Grains Nobles (SGN) [say-lek-see-yon duh gran nohbl] (Alsace, France) Equivalent to German *Beerenauslese*; rich, sweet *botrytized* wine from specially selected grapes. These wines are rare, expensive, and long-lived.

Ⓨ **Sella e Mosca** [seh-la eh mos-kah] (*Sardinia,* Italy) Dynamic firm with a good *Cabernet* called Villamarina, the rich *Anghelu Ruju*, and traditional *Cannonau* which is also blended with *Cabernet* to produce the highly impressive *Tanca Farra*.

Ⓨ **Ch. de Selle** (*Provence*, France) Serious wines, unflashy and rather expensive.

Ⓨ **Fattoria Selvapiana** [fah-taw-ree-ya sel-va-pee-yah-nah] (*Tuscany,* Italy) Great *Chianti Rufina, vin santo,* and olive oil. ★★★ 1999 Chianti Rufina Riserva 'Vigneto Bucerchiale' £££

Ⓨ **Château Semeli** [seh-meh-lee] (*Attica,* Greece) Producer of classy Cabernet and Nemea reds.

🍇 **Sémillon** [in France: say-mee-yon; in Australia: seh-mil-lon and even seh-mih-lee-yon] Peachy grape generally blended with *Sauvignon* to make sweet and dry *Bordeaux*, and vinified separately in Australia, where it is also sometimes blended with *Chardonnay*. Rarely as successful in other New World countries, where many versions taste more like *Sauvignon*. **Carmenet; Geyser Peak; McWilliams; Rothbury; Tyrrell; Xanadu.**

Ⓨ **Seña** [sen-ya] (Chile) A *Mondavi* and *Caliterra* co-production. A Mercedes of a wine: impeccably put together, and improving with every vintage. ★★★★★ 2000 Seña ££££

Ⓨ **Ch. Sénéjac** [say-nay-jak] (*Bordeaux*, France) *Cru Bourgeois* making wines to age.

Ⓨ **Sepp Moser** [sep moh-zur] (*Kremstal,* Austria) Serious producer of – especially – good *Grüner Veltiner* and late-harvest *Chardonnay* and *Riesling*. ★★★ 2000 Grüner Veltiner Breiter Rain ££

Ⓨ **Seppelt** (South Australia) Pioneer of great fortified wines and of the *Great Western* region where it makes still and sparkling *Shiraz* and Dorrien *Cabernet*. Other sparkling wines are recommendable too, though Salinger is less good than it was. ★★★★ NV Seppelt DP63 Show Muscat ££

Ⓨ **Sequioa Grove** [sek-koy-yah] (California, USA) Well structured wines, reliably good.

Ⓨ **Serafini & Vidotto** [seh-rah-fee-noh eh vee-dot-toh] (*Veneto,* Italy) Francesco Serafini and Antonello Vidotto make great Pinot Nero.

Ⓨ **Sercial** [sehr-see-yal] (Madeira) The driest style of Madeira. ★★★★ Henriques & Henriques 10 Year Old Sercial £££

Ⓨ **Seresin** [seh-ra-sin] (*Marlborough*, New Zealand) New venture launched by a British movie cameraman. Impeccable vineyards and really impressive *Chardonnay*, *Sauvignon*, and a promising *Pinot Noir*.

Servir frais (France) Serve chilled.

Ⓨ **Setúbal** [shtoo-bal] (Portugal) *DOC* on the *Setúbal Peninsula*. ★★★★★ 1991 Moscatel Roxo J.P. Vinhos £

Setúbal Peninsula [shtoo-bul] (Portugal) Home of the *Setúbal DOC*, but now notable for the rise of two new wine regions, Arrabida and Palmela, where *JM Fonseca Succs* and *JP Vinhos* are making excellent wines from local and international grape varieties. The lusciously rich *Moscatel de Setúbal*, however, is still the star of the show.

Ⓨ **Seyssel** [say-sehl] (*Savoie*, France) *AC* region near Geneva producing light white wines that are usually enjoyed in après-ski mood when no one is overly concerned about value for money. **Maison Mollex;** *Varichon et Clerc*.

S

🍇 **Seyval Blanc** [say-vahl blon] *Hybrid* grape – a cross between French and US vines – unpopular with EU authorities but successful in eastern US, Canada, and England, especially at *Breaky Bottom*. ★★★ 1997 Seyval Breaky Bottom £

🍷 **Shafer** [shay-fur] (*Napa Valley*, California) Top *Cabernet* producer in the *Stag's Leap* district, and maker of classy *Carneros Chardonnay* and *Merlot*. ★★★★★ 1997 Shafer Vineyards Hillside Select Cabernet Sauvignon £££

🍷 **Shaw & Smith** (*Adelaide Hills*, Australia) Winery producing fine *Sauvignon* and *Merlot* and *Burgundian Chardonnays* that demonstrate how good wines from this variety can taste with and without oak. ★★★ 2000 'M3 Vineyard' Chardonnay £££

🍷 **Sherry** (*Jerez*, Spain) The fortified wine made in the area surrounding *Jerez*. Wines made elsewhere – Australia, England, South Africa, etc. – may no longer use the name. See also *Almacenista; Fino; Amontillado; Manzanilla; Cream Sherry. Barbadillo; Gonzalez Byass; Hidalgo; Lustau.*

🍇 **Shiraz** [shee-raz] (Australia, South Africa) The *Syrah* grape in Australia and South Africa, named after its (erroneously) supposed birthplace in Iran. South African versions are lighter (and generally greener) than the Australians, while the Australians are usually riper and oakier than efforts from the *Rhône*. The move to cooler sites is broadening the range of Australian *Shiraz*, however. *Hardy's; Henschke; Maglieri; Lindemans; Rockford; Rothbury; Penfolds; Picardy; Plantagenet; St. Hallett; Saxenburg; Wolf Blass.*

🍷 **Shooting Star** (Lake County, California) One of California's avid proponents of Cabernet Franc. The Zinfandel and Cabernet Sauvignon are good too.

🍷 **Sichel & Co** [see-shel] ((Bordeaux, France) Merchant and owner or part-owner of châteaux including *Palmer, Angludet*, and with good Sirius brand. ★★★ 2000 Sirius £

Sicily (Italy) Historically best known for *Marsala* and sturdy "southern" table wines. Now, however, there is an array of other unusual fortified wines and a fast-growing range of new-wave reds and whites, many made from grapes grown nowhere else. *De Bartoli; Corvo; Planeta; Regaleali; Terre di Ginestra.*

🍷 **Sierra Vista** (California, USA) Subtle (for California) high quality Rhône varieties from this estate.

🍷 **Sieur d'Arques** [see-uhr dark] (*Languedoc-Roussillon*, France) High-tech *Limoux* cooperative with good *Blanquette de Limoux* sparkling wine and *Chardonnays* sold under the Toques et Clochers label. Now in joint venture with the owners of *Ch. Mouton Rothschild*.

🍷 **Ch. Sigalas-Rabaud** [see-gah-lah rah-boh] (*Bordeaux*, France) Fine Sauternes estate, producing rich, but delicate, wines.

🍷 **Siglo** [seeg-loh] (*Rioja*, Spain) Good brand of modern red (traditionally sold in a burlap "sack") and old-fashioned whites. ★★★ 2000 Siglo Bodegas & Bebidas £

🍷 **Signorello** (*Napa Valley*, California) Small winery making *Burgundian Chardonnay* with yeasty richness, *Bordeaux*-style *Semillon* and *Sauvignon* as well as *Cabernets* that are blackcurranty and stylish. ★★★ 1998 Cabernet Sauvignon

🍷 **Sileni** [sil-lay-nee] (*Hawkes Bay*, New Zealand) Large new venture with very promising *Chardonnay, Semillon, Merlot/Cabernet*.

Silex [see-lex] (France) Term describing flinty soil, used by *Didier Dagueneau* for his oak-fermented *Pouilly-Fumé*.

🍇 **Silvaner** German spelling for *Sylvaner*.

🍷 **Silver Oak Cellars** (*Napa Valley*, California) Superb specialized *Cabernet* producers favouring fruitily accessible, but still classy, wines which benefit from long ageing in (American oak) barrels and bottled before release. ★★★★★ 1995 Napa Valley Cabernet £££

🍷 **Silverado** [sil-veh-rah-doh] (*Napa Valley*, California) Reliable *Cabernet*, *Chardonnay*, and *Sangiovese* winery that belongs to Walt Disney's widow.

🍷 **Simi Winery** [see-mee] (*Sonoma Valley*, California) Winery made famous by the thoughtful Zelma Long and her complex, long-lived Burgundian *Chardonnay*, archetypical *Sauvignon*, and lovely, blackcurranty *Alexander Valley Cabernet*. A New Zealand-born winemaker maintains the tradition.

S

☶ **Langwerth von Simmern** [lang-vehrt fon sim-mehrn] (*Rheingau*, Germany) A famous estate that is now showing signs of a revival.

☶ **Bert Simon** (*Mosel-Saar-Ruwer*, Germany) Newish estate in the *Saar* river valley with supersoft *Rieslings* and unusually elegant *Weissburgunder*.

☶ **Simonsberg** (*Stellenbosch*, South Africa) The mountain on which *Thelema's* vineyards are situated. ★★★★★ 1999 Warwick Estate Trilogy Simonsberg ££

☶ **Simonsig Estate** [see-mon-sikh] (*Stellenbosch*, South Africa) Big estate with a very impressive commercial range, and the occasional gem – try the *Shiraz, Cabernet, Pinotage, Chardonnay* the Kaapse Vonkel sparkler. ★★★ 1999 Simonsig Merindol Syrah £££

Sin Crianza [sin cree-an-tha] (Spain) Not aged in wood.

☶ **Sion** [see-yo'n] (*Valais*, Switzerland) One of the proud homes of the grape the Swiss call the Fendant and outsiders know as *Chasselas*. Dull elsewhere, it can produce creditable (and even occasionally ageworthy) wines.

☶ **Ch. Siran** [see-ron] (*Margaux Cru Bourgeois, Bordeaux*, France) Beautiful *château* outperforming its classification and producing increasingly impressive and generally fairly priced wines.

☶ **Skalli** [skal-lee] (Languedoc-Roussillon France) Pioneering producer of quality *Vins de Pays* under the Fortant label. ★★★ 1999 Merlot Edition Limitée ££

☶ **Skillogalee** [skil-log-gah-lee] (*Clare Valley*, Australia) Well-respected *Clare* producer, specializing in *Riesling*, but also showing his skill with reds. ★★★ 2001 Skillogalee Riesling ££

Skin contact The longer the skins of black grapes are left in with the juice after the grapes have been crushed, the greater the *tannin* and the deeper the colour. Some non-aromatic white varieties (*Chardonnay* and *Semillon* in particular) can also benefit from extended skin contact (usually between six and 24 hours) to increase flavour.

☶ **Skouras** (*Peloponnese*, Greece) Eager producer, making good Nemea reds and Viognier whites.

Sliven [slee-ven] Bulgarian region offering good-value, simple reds and better-than-average whites. ★★★ 2001 Blueridge Chardonnay Boyar Estates £

Slovakia Up-and-coming source of wines from grapes little seen elsewhere, such as the *Muscat*ty Irsay Oliver.

Slovenia Former Yugoslavian region in which *Laski Rizling* is king. Other grapes show greater promise. ★★★ 2001 Traminec Holeumuos Jeruzalem Ormoz, Podravje, Ljutomer-Ormoz

Smaragd [shmah-ragd] ((Austria) Highest quality category in *Wachau* for dry wines. See also Federspiel and Steinfeder.

☶ **Smith & Hook** (*Mendocino*, California) Winery with a cult following for its zippy, blackcurranty *Cabernet Sauvignon*. These lack the ripe richness sought by most US critics, however.

☶ **Smith-Madrone** (*Napa*, California) Long-established winery that bucks the trend by using the *Riesling* (which is being uprooted elsewhere) to make good wine. *Chardonnay* is good too.

☶ **Smith Woodhouse** (*Douro*, Portugal) Part of the same empire as *Dow's, Graham's,* and *Warre's* but often overlooked. *Vintage ports* can be good, as is the house speciality *Traditional Late Bottled Vintage*. ★★★★★ 1990 LBV ££

☶ **Ch. Smith-Haut-Lafitte** [oh-lah-feet] (*Pessac-Léognan Cru Classé, Bordeaux*, France) Estate flying high under its new ownership. Increasingly classy reds and (specially) pure *Sauvignon* whites. Grape seeds from the estate are also used to make an anti-ageing skin cream called Caudalie. ★★★★ 1999 Château Smith-Haut-Lafitte £

☶ **Smithbrook** (Western Australia) *Petaluma* subsidiary in the southerly region of *Pemberton*. ★★★ 2000 Smithbrook Merlot ££

☶ **Soave** [swah-veh] (*Veneto*, Italy) Mostly dull stuff, but *Soave Classico* is better, single-vineyard versions are best. Sweet *Recioto* di Soave is delicious. *Pieropan* is almost uniformly excellent. *Anselmi; La Cappuccina; Inama; Masi; Pieropan; Pra; Tedeschi; Zenato.* ★★★ 2001 Tufaie Soave Classico Fratelli Bolla £

S

♁ **Ch. Sociando-Mallet** [soh-see-yon-doh ma-lay] (*Haut-Médoc Cru Bourgeois, Bordeaux,* France) A *Cru Bourgeois* whose oaked, fruity red wines are way above its status.

♁ **Sogrape** [soh-grap] (Portugal) Having invented *Mateus* Rosé half a century ago, this large firm is now modernizing the wines of *Dão* (with the new Quinta dos Carvalhais), *Douro* and *Bairrada*, and *Alentejo* (Vinha do Monte) bringing out flavours these once-dull wines never seemed to possess. *Sogrape* also owns the *port* houses of *Sandeman* and *Ferreira* and is thus also responsible for *Barca Velha*, Portugal's top red table wine.

♁ **Sokol Blosser** (*Oregon*) Highly successful makers of rich *Chardonnay*. The *Pinot* is good too.

♁ **Solaia** [soh-lie-yah] (*Tuscany,* Italy) Yet another *Antinori Super-Tuscan*. A phenomenal blend of *Cabernet Sauvignon* and *Franc*, with a little *Sangiovese*. Italy's top red?

Solera [soh-leh-rah] (*Jerez,* Spain) Ageing system involving older wine being continually "refreshed" by slightly younger wine of the same style.

♁ **Bodegas Felix Solís** [fay-leex soh-lees] (*Valdepeñas,* Spain) By far the biggest, most progressive winery in *Valdepeñas*. ★★★ 2000 Caliza £

Somontano [soh-mon-tah-noh] (Spain) *DO* region in the foothills of the Pyrenees in Aragon, now experimenting with international grape varieties. COVISA; *Enate;* Pirineos; *Viñas del Vero*.

Sonoma Valley [so-noh-ma] (California) Despite the *Napa* hype, this lesser-known region not only contains some of the state's top wineries, it is also home to *E&J Gallo's* superpremium vineyard and *Dry Creek*, home of some of California's best *Zinfandels*. The region is subdivided into the *Sonoma, Alexander,* and *Russian River Valleys* and *Dry Creek*. Adler Fels; Arrowood; Carmenet; Ch. St Jean Clos du Bois; Dry Creek; Duxoup; E&J Gallo; Geyser Peak; Gundlach Bundschu; Cecchetti Sebastiani; Iron Horse; Jordan; Kenwood; Kistler; Laurel Glen; Matanzas Creek; Peter Michael; Quivira; Ravenswood; Ridge; St. Francis; Sonoma-Cutrer; Simi; Marimar Torres; Joseph Swan.

♁ **Sonoma-Cutrer** [soh-noh-ma koo-trehr] (*Sonoma Valley*, California) Recently sold producer of world-class single-vineyard *Chardonnay* that can rival *Puligny-Montrachet*. The "Les Pierres" is the tops.

♁ **Bruno Sorg** (*Alsace*, France) Excellent quality from this small estate.

♁ **Marc Sorrel** [sor-rel] (*Rhône*, France) *Hermitage* producer who is – unusually – as successful in white as red. The "le Gréal" single-vineyard red is the wine to buy, though the "les Roccoules" white ages well.

♁ **Pierre Soulez** [soo-layz] (*Loire*, France) Producer of *Savennières*, especially Clos du Papillon and Roche-aux-Moines *late harvest* wines.

♁ **Ch. Soutard** [soo-tahr] (*St. Emilion, Bordeaux,* France) Traditional *St. Emilion* estate with long-lived wines that rely on far less oak than many.

South Africa Quality is patchy but improving, with riper, more characterful wine that apes neither France nor Australia. Below the top level, look for inexpensive, simple, dry and off-dry *Chenins*, lovely *late-harvest* and fortified wines, and surprisingly good *Pinotages*; otherwise very patchy. Fairview; Grangehurst; Klein Constantia; Jordan; Kanonkop; Mulderbosch; Plaisir de Merle; Saxenburg; Simonsig; Thelema; Vergelegen.

South Australia Home of almost all the biggest wine companies, and still producing over half of Australia's wine. The *Barossa Valley* is one of the country's oldest wine regions, but like its neighbours *Clare* and *McLaren Vale*, faces competition from cooler areas like *Adelaide Hills, Padthaway,* and *Coonawarra*.

Southeast Australia A cleverly meaningless regional description. Technically, it covers around 85 per cent of Australia's vineyards.

Southwest France An unofficial umbrella term covering the areas between *Bordeaux* and the Pyrenees, *Bergerac, Madiran, Cahors, Jurançon*, and the *Vins de Pays* of the Côtes de Gascogne.

⚘ **Spanna** [spah-nah] (*Piedmont,* Italy) The *Piedmontese* name for the *Nebbiolo* grape and the more humble wines made from it.

S

Y **Pierre Sparr** (*Alsace,* France) Big producer offering a rare chance to taste traditional *Chasselas.*

Y **Spätburgunder** [shpayt-bur-goon-dur](Germany) Alias of *Pinot Noir.*
Spätlese [shpayt-lay-zeh] (Germany) Second step in the QmP scale, *late-harvest*ed grapes making wine a notch drier than *Auslese.*

Y **Fratelli Speri** [speh-ree] (*Veneto,* Italy) A fast-rising star with delicious Monte Sant'Urbano Amarone della Valpolicella Classico.

Y **Spice Route** (South Africa) Label showing the skills of Charles Back of Fairview. Good value, reliable wines from Malmesbury. Top wines are labelled "Flagship". ★★★★★ 2000 Spice Route Flagship Pinotage £££

Y **Domaine Spiropoulos** [spee ro-poo-los] (*Peloponnese,* Greece) Fine producer of organic wine, including Porfyros, one of Greece's best modern reds.

Y **Spottswoode** (*Napa Valley,* California) Excellent small producer of complex *Cabernet* and unusually good *Sauvignon Blanc.* Deserves greater recognition.

Y **Spring Mountain** (*Napa Valley,* California) Revived old winery with great vineyards and classy, berryish *Cabernet.* ★★★★★ 1997 Cain Five £££

Y **Springfield Estate** (*Robertson,* South Africa) Fast improving producer, with crisp dry *Sauvignons,* and a good "methode ancienne" *Chardonnay*
★★★ 2001 Life from Stone Sauvignon Blanc ££

Spritz/ig [shpritz/ich] Slight sparkle/sparkling. Also *pétillant.*
Spumante [spoo-man-tay] (Italy) Sparkling.

Y **Squinzano** [skeen-tzah-noh] (*Puglia,* Italy) Traditional, often rustic reds from the warm South. The *Santa Barbara* cooperative makes the best wines.
Staatsweingut [staht-svine-goot] (Germany) A state-owned wine estate such as Staatsweingüter Eltville (*Rheingau*), a major cellar in *Eltville.*

Y **Standing Stones** (*New York State*) Recommendable Finger Lakes producer with an especially good Riesling.

Y **Stafford Ridge** (*Adelaide Hills,* Australia) Fine *Chardonnay* and especially *Sauvignon* from *Lenswood* by Geoff Weaver, former winemaker of *Hardys.*
Stags Leap District (*Napa Valley,* California) Established hillside region, specializing in blackcurranty *Cabernet Sauvignon.* S.Anderson; *Clos du Val;* Cronin; Hartwell; *Pine Ridge; Shafer; Silverado Vineyards; Stag's Leap;* Steltzner.

Y **Stag's Leap Wine Cellars** (*Napa* Valley, California) Pioneering supporter of the *Stag's Leap appellation,* and one of the finest wineries in California. The best wines are the Faye Vineyard, SLV, and Cask 23 *Cabernets.* Don't confuse with the not nearly as good Stags' Leap Winery. ★★★★★ 1997 Cask 23 £££

Y **Staglin** (*Napa Valley,* California) Classy producer of Bordeaux-like *Cabernet* and pioneering *Sangiovese.*
Stalky or stemmy Flavour of the stem rather than of the juice.

Y **Stanton & Killeen** (*Rutherglen,* Australia) Reliable producer of *Liqueur Muscat.* ★★★★ NV Muscat ££

Y **Steele** (*Lake County,* California) The former winemaker of *Kendall Jackson;* a master when it comes to producing fruitily crowd-pleasing *Chardonnays* from various regions and more complex *Zinfandel.*
Steely Refers to young wine with evident *acidity.* A compliment when paid to *Chablis* and dry *Sauvignons.*

🍇 **Steen** [steen] (South Africa) Local name for (and possibly odd *clone* of) *Chenin Blanc.* Widely planted (over 30 per cent of the vineyard area). The best come from *Boschendal* and *Fairview.*

Y **Steiermark/Styria** (Austria) Sunny southern region where the *Chardonnay* is now being used (under the name of "Morillon") to produce rich, buttery, but often quite Burgundian wines. ★★★ 2000 Der Chardonnay Domäne Müller ££

Y **Steinfeder** [shtine-fay-dur] (*Wachau,* Austria) Category for the lightest dry wines. See also *Federspiel, Smaragd.*

S

Stellenbosch [stel-len-bosh] (South Africa) Centre of the *Cape* wine industry, and a climatically and topographically diverse region that, like the *Napa Valley*, is taken far too seriously as a regional *appellation*. Hillside sub-regions like Helderberg make more sense. *Bergkelder; Delheim; Neil Ellis; Grangehurst; Hartenburg; Jordan; Kanonkop; Meerlust; Mulderbosch; Rustenberg; Saxenburg; Stellenzicht; Thelema; Warwick.* ★★★★★ 2000 Kaapzicht Pinotage £££

☛ **Stellenbosch Farmers' Winery** (*Stellenbosch*, South Africa) South Africa's biggest producer, with Sable View, Libertas, *Nederburg*, Plaisir de Merle.

☛ **Stellenzicht Vineyards** [stel-len-zikht] (*Stellenbosch*, South Africa) Sister estate of Neethlingshof, with a good *Sauvignon* and a *Shiraz* good enough to beat *Penfolds Grange* in a blind tasting. ★★★ 1999 Syrah £££

Stelvin Brand of screwcap, specifically designed for wine bottled by its French manufacturer. Long respected by open-minded professionals, Stelvins have had a new boost following the decision by top producers to use them.

☛ **Sterling Vineyards** (*Napa Valley*, California) Founded by Peter Newton (now at *Newton* vineyards) and once the plaything of Coca-Cola, this showcase estate now belongs to Canadian liquor giant Seagram. Among the current successes are the Reserve *Cabernet*, *Pinot Noir*, and fairly priced Redwood Trail wines. ★★★★ 1999 Merlot £££

☛ **Weingut Georg Stiegelmar** [stee-gel-mahr] (*Burgenland*, Austria) Producer of pricey, highly acclaimed, dry *Chardonnay* and *Pinot Blanc*, *late-harvest* wines, and some particularly good *Pinot Noir* and *St. Laurent*.

☛ **Stoneleigh** (*Marlborough*, New Zealand) Reliable *Marlborough* label, now part of *Montana*. ★★★★★ 2000 Stoneleigh Rapaura Series Pinot Noir ££

☛ **Stonestreet** (*Sonoma*, California) Highly commercial wines from the *Kendall-Jackson* stable.

☛ **Stonier's** [stoh-nee-yurs] (*Mornington Peninsula*, Australia) Small *Mornington* winery, successful with impressive *Pinot Noir*, *Chardonnay*, and *Merlot*. (Previously known as Stoniers-Merrick; and now a subsidiary of *Petaluma*.)

☛ **Stony Hill** (*Napa Valley*, California) Unfashionable old winery with the guts to produce long-lived, complex *Chardonnay* that tastes like unoaked *Grand Cru Chablis*, rather than follow the herd in aping buttery-rich *Meursault*.

☛ **Stonyridge** (*Auckland*, New Zealand) Rapidly rising star on fashionable Waiheke Island, making impressive, if pricey, *Bordeaux*-style reds.

☛ **Storybook Mountain** (*Napa Valley*, California) Great individual-vineyard *Zinfandels* that taste good young but are built for the long haul. The *Howell Mountain* vines were replanted with *Cabernet Sauvignon*.

Structure The "structural" components of a wine include *tannin, acidity*, and *alcohol*. They provide the skeleton or backbone that supports the "flesh" of the fruit. A young wine with good structure should age well.

☛ **Ch. de Suduiraut** [soo-dee-rroh] (*Sauternes Premier Cru Classé, Bordeaux*, France) Producing great things since its purchase by French insurance giant, AXA. Top wines: "*Cuvée* Madame", "*Crème de Tête*". The 2001 was the Sauternes of the vintage. ★★★★ 1997 Ch. de Suduiraut £££

Suhindol [soo-win-dol] (Bulgaria) One of *Bulgaria*'s best-known regions, the source of widely available, fairly-priced *Cabernet Sauvignon*.

Sulphites US labelling requirement alerting those suffering from an (extremely rare) allergy to the presence of *sulphur dioxide*. Curiously, no such requirement is made of cans of baked beans and dried apricots, which contain twice as much of the chemical.

Sulphur dioxide/SO$_2$ Antiseptic routinely used by food packagers and winemakers to protect their produce from bacteria and *oxidation*.

☛ **Sumac Ridge** (*British Columbia*, Canada) Decent quality, especially *Sauvignon* and *Gewurztraminer*.

☛ **Super Second** (*Bordeaux*, France) *Médoc* second growths: *Pichon-Lalande, Pichon-Longueville, Léoville-las-Cases, Ducru-Beaucaillou, Cos d'Estournel*; whose wines can rival the first growths. Other overperformers include: *Rauzan-Ségla* and *Léoville-Barton, Lynch-Bages, Palmer, La Lagune, Montrose*.

Super-Tuscan (Italy) New-wave *Vino da Tavola/IGT* (usually red) wines, pioneered by producers like *Antinori*, which stand outside *DOC* rules. Generally *Bordeaux*-style blends or *Sangiovese* or a mixture of both.

Supérieur/Superiore [soo-pay-ree-ur/soo-pay-ree-ohr-ray] (France/Italy) Often relatively meaningless in terms of discernible quality. Denotes wine (well or badly) made from riper grapes.

Sur lie [soor-lee] (France) The ageing "on its *lees*" – or dead yeasts – most commonly associated with *Muscadet*.

Süssreserve [soos-sreh-zurv] (Germany) Unfermented grape juice used to bolster sweetness and fruit in German and English wines.

☤ **Sutter Home Winery** (*Napa Valley*, California) Home of robust red *Zinfandel* in the 1970s, and responsible for the invention of successful sweet "white" (or, as the non-colour-blind might say, pink) *Zinfandel*. *Amador County Zinfandels* are still good, but rarely exceptional. The M. Trinchero Founders Estate *Cabernet* and *Chardonnay* are worth looking out for.

☤ **Joseph Swan** (*Sonoma*, California) Small Burgundian-scale winery whose enthusiastic winemaker, Rod Berglund, produces great single-vineyard, often attractively quirky, *Pinot Noir* and *Zinfandel*.

Swan Valley (*Western Australia*) Hot old vineyard area; good for fortified wines and a source of fruit for *Houghton's* successful *HWB*. *Houghton* also produces cooler-climate wines in the microclimate of *Moondah Brook*.

☤ **Swanson** [swon-son] (*Napa Valley*, California) Top flight, innovative producer of *Cabernet, Chardonnay, Sangiovese, Syrah,* and *late-harvest Semillon*. ★★★★★ 1999 Alexis £££

Switzerland Produces increasingly enjoyable wines from grapes ranging from the *Chasselas, Marsanne, Syrah*, and *Pinot Noir* to the local *Cornallin* and *Petite Arvine*. See *Dôle, Fendant, Chablais*. Also the only country to use screwcaps for much of its wine, thus facilitating recycling and avoiding the problems of faulty corks. Clever people, the Swiss.

🍇 **Sylvaner/Silvaner** [sill-vah-nur] Non-aromatic white grape, originally from *Austria* but found particularly in *Alsace* and *Franken*. Elsewhere, wines are often dry and earthy, though there are promising efforts in South Africa.

🍇 **Syrah** [see-rah] (*Rhône*, France) The red *Rhône* grape, an exotic mix of ripe fruit and spicy, smoky, gamey, leathery flavours. In Australia and S. Africa, it is called *Shiraz*. Increasingly popular in California, thanks to "*Rhône* Rangers" like *Bonny Doon* and *Phelps*. See *Qupé, Marqués de Griñon* in Spain and *Isole e Olena* in Italy, plus *Côte Rôtie, Hermitage, Shiraz*.

☤ **Szamorodni** [jam-moh-rod-nee] ((*Tokaj*, Hungary) Means 'as it comes' and denotes wine that is usually dry to sweetish. Makes a good aperitif. ★★★ 1999 Disznókö Tokaji Édes Szamorodni ££

T

TBA (Germany) Abbreviation for Trockenbeeren Auslese (qv).

☤ **La Tâche** [la tash] (*Burgundy*, France) Wine from the La Tâche vineyard, exclusively owned by the *Dom. de la Romanée Conti*. Frequently as good as the rarer and more expensive "La Romanée Conti".

Tafelwein [tah-fel-vine] (Germany) Table wine. Only the prefix "Deutscher" guarantees German origin.

☤ **Ch. Tahbilk** [tah-bilk] (*Victoria*, Australia) Old-fashioned winemaking in the *Goulbourn Valley/Nagambie*. Great long-lived *Shiraz* from 130-year-old vines, surprisingly good *Chardonnay*, and lemony *Marsanne* which needs a decade. The second wine is Dalfarras. ★★★ 2000 Marsanne £

☤ **Cave de Tain L'Hermitage** (*Rhône*, France) Reliable cooperative for *Crozes-Hermitage* and *Hermitage*.

T

☲ **Taittinger** [tat-tan-jehr] (*Champagne*, France) Producer of reliable non-vintage, and fine Comtes de *Champagne Blanc de Blancs* and Rosé. ★★★★ 1995 Taittinger Comtes de Champagne Blanc de Blancs ££££

☲ **Ch. Talbot** [tal-boh] (*St. Julien 4ème Cru Classé, Bordeaux,* France) Reliable, if sometimes slightly jammy, wine. In the same stable as Ch. Gruaud Larose. Connétable Talbot is the *second label.*

☲ **Talbott** (*Monterey,* California) Serious small producer of elegant *Chardonnay* and *Pinot Noir* that lasts.

☲ **Talley** (*San Luis Obispo,* California) Serious small producer of elegant *Chardonnay* and *Pinot Noir* that lasts.

☲ **Taltarni** [tal-tahr-nee] (*Victoria,* Australia) Until his recent departure, Dominique Portet made great European-style *Shiraz Cabernets* in this beautiful *Pyrenees* vineyard. ★★★ 1998 Taltarni Shiraz ££

🍇 **Tamîîoasa Romaneasca** [tem-yo-asha roh-mah-nay-yas-ka] (Romania) Local name for *Muscat Blanc à Petits Grains.* Other Tamîîoasas are different sorts of Muscat.

🍇 **Tannat** [ta-na] (France) Rustic French grape variety, traditionally used in the blend of *Cahors* and in South America, principally in *Uruguay.*

☲ **Lane Tanner** (*California,* USA) *Santa Barbara* estate with fine *Pinot Noir.*
Tannic See *Tannin.*
Tannin Astringent component of red wine that comes from the skins, seeds, and stalks, and helps the wine to age.

☲ **Jean Tardy** (*Burgundy,* France) Excellent domaine based in *Vosne-Romanée.*

☲ **Tardy & Ange** [tahr-dee ay onzh] (*Rhône,* France) Partnership producing classy *Crozes-Hermitage* at the Dom. de Entrefaux.

☲ **Tarragona** [ta-ra-go-nah] (*Catalonia,* Spain) *DO* region south of *Penedés* and home to many cooperatives. Contains the better-quality *Terra Alta.*

☲ **Tarrawarra** [ta-ra-wa-ra] (*Yarra Valley,* Australia) Increasingly successful *Pinot* pioneer in the cool-climate region of the *Yarra Valley. Second label* is Tunnel Hill. ★★★★★ 1999 Tarrawarra Pinot Noir £££

Tarry Red wines from hot countries often have an aroma and flavour reminiscent of tar. The *Syrah* and *Nebbiolo* exhibit this characteristic.

Tartaric Type of acid found in grapes. Also the form in which acid is added to wine in hot countries whose legislation allows this.

Tartrates [tar-trayts] Harmless white crystals often deposited by white wines in the bottle. In Germany, these are called "diamonds".

Tasmania (Australia) Cool-climate island, showing potential for sparkling wine, *Chardonnay, Riesling,* and *Pinot Noir.* Freycinet; Heemskerk; Jansz; Moorilla; Piper's Brook; Pirie; Tamar Ridge. ★★★★ NV Jansz ££

Tastevin [tat-van] Silver *Burgundy* tasting cup used as an insignia by vinous brotherhoods (*confréries*), as a badge of office by sommeliers, and as an ashtray by others. The *Chevaliers de Tastevin* organize tastings, awarding a mock-medieval Tastevinage label to the best wines. *Chevaliers de Tastevin* attend banquets, often wearing similarly mock-medieval gowns.

☲ **Taurasi** [tow-rah-see] (*Campania,* Italy) Big, old-fashioned *Aglianico.* Needs years to soften and develop a burned, cherry taste. Mastroberardino.

☲ **Cosimo Taurino** [tow-ree-noh] (*Puglia,* Italy) The name to look for when buying Salice Salentino. The red Patrigliono and Notapanaro and the Chardonnay are worth looking for, too. ★★★ 1995 Patriglione £

☲ **Tavel** [ta-vehl] (*Rhône,* France) Dry rosé. Often disappointing. Seek out young versions and avoid the bronze colour revered by traditionalists. Ch. d'Aquéria; Dom. de la Forcadière; de la Mordorée; du Prieuré; Ch. de Trinquevedel; de Valéry.

Tawny (*Douro,* Portugal) In theory, pale browny-red *port* that acquires its mature appearance and nutty flavour from long ageing in oak casks. *Port* houses, however, legally produce cheap "tawny" by mixing basic *ruby* with *white port* and skipping the tiresome business of barrel-ageing altogether. The real stuff comes with an indication of age, such as 10-

or 20-year-old, but these figures are approximate. A 10-year-old *port* only has to "taste as though it is that old". *Colheita ports* are tawnies of a specific vintage. *Noval; Taylor's; Graham's; Cockburn's; Dow's; Niepoort; Ramos Pinto; Calem.*

⊥ **Taylor (Fladgate & Yeatman)** (*Douro*, Portugal) With *Dow's*, one of the "first growths" of the *Douro*. Outstanding *vintage port*, "modern" *Late Bottled Vintage*. Also owns *Fonseca* and *Guimaraens*, and produces the excellent *Quinta de Vargellas* Single-*Quinta* port. ★★★★★ 1985 Vintage Port ££££

⊥ **Te Mata** [tay mah-tah] (*Hawkes Bay*, New Zealand) Pioneer John Buck proves what *New Zealand* can do with *Chardonnay* (in the Elston Vineyard) and pioneered reds with his Coleraine and (lighter) Awatea.

⊥ **Te Motu** [tay moh-too] ((New Zealand) Dense reds from *Waiheke Island*.

⊥ **Fratelli Tedeschi** [tay-dehs-kee] (*Veneto,* Italy) Reliable producer of rich and concentrated *Valpolicellas* and good *Soaves*. The *Amarones* are particularly impressive. ★★★★ 1999 Capitel San Rocco £

⊥ **Tement** [teh-ment] (*Steiermark*, Austria) Producer of a truly world-class barrel-fermented *Sauvignon Blanc* which competes directly with top *Pessac-Léognan* whites. *Chardonnays* are impressive, too.

⊥ **Dom. Tempier** [tom-pee-yay] (*Provence,* France) Provence superstar estate, producing single-vineyard red and rosé *Bandols* that support the claim that the *Mourvèdre* (from which they are largely made) ages well. The rosé is also one of the best in the region.

🍇 **Tempranillo** [tem-prah-nee-yoh] (Spain) The red grape of *Rioja* – and just about everywhere else in Spain, thanks to the way in which its strawberry fruit suits the vanilla/oak flavours of barrel-ageing. In *Navarra*, it is called *Cencibel*; in *Ribera del Duero,* Tinto Fino; in the *Penedés, Ull de Llebre*; in *Toro*, Tinto de Toro, and in Portugal – where it is used for *port* – it's known as *Tinto Roriz*. Now being planted outside Spain, especially in Australia. ★★★★ 2000 Agramont Tempranillo £

Tenuta [teh-noo-tah] (Italy) Estate or vineyard.

⊥ **Terlano/Terlaner** [tehr-LAH-noh/tehr-LAH-nehr] (*Trentino-Alto Adige,* Italy) Northern Italian village and its wine: usually fresh, crisp, and carrying the name of the grape from which it was made.

🍇 **Teroldego Rotaliano** [teh-rol-deh-goh roh-tah-lee-AH-noh] (*Trentino-Alto Adige,* Italy) Dry reds, quite full-bodied, with lean, slightly bitter berry flavours which make them better accompaniments to food. *Foradori.*

Terra Alta [tay ruh al-ta] (*Catalonia,* Spain) Small *DO* within the much larger *Tarragona DO*, producing wines of higher quality due to the difficult climate and resulting low yields. **Pedro Rovira.**

⊥ **Terrazas** [teh-rah-zas] (*Mendoza,* Argentina) The brand name of Moët & Chandon's recently launched impressive red and white Argentinian wines.

⊥ **Terre Rosse** [teh-reh roh-seh] (*Liguria,* Italy) One of the best estates in Liguria, with good examples of *Vermentino* and Pigato.

⊥ **Ch. Terrey-Gros-Caillou** [teh-ray groh kih-yoo] ((*Bordeaux*, France) Well made *Cru Bourgeois St-Julien.*

⊥ **Ch. du Tertre** [doo tehr-tr] (*Margaux 5ème Cru Classé, Bordeaux,* France) Recently restored to former glory by the owners of *Calon-Ségur.*

⊥ **Ch. Tertre-Daugay** [tehr-tr-doh-jay] (*St. Emilion, Grand Cru, Bordeaux,* France) Steadily improving property whose wines are cast in a classic mould and do not always have the immediate appeal of bigger, oakier neighbours.

⊥ **Ch. Tertre-Rôteboeuf** [Tehr-tr roht-burf] (*St. Emilion Grand Cru Classé, Bordeaux,* France) Good, rich, concentrated, crowd-pleasing wines.

⊥ **Teruzzi & Puthod** (Tuscany, Italy) Go-ahead producer based in San Gimignano. Very good whites.

Tête de Cuvée [teht dur coo-vay] (France) An old expression still used by traditionalists to describe their finest wine.

T

℧ **Thackrey** (*Marin County*, California) Rich, impressively concentrated wines that seek to emulate the *Rhône*, but actually come closer to Australia in style.

℧ **Thames Valley Vineyard** (*Reading*, England) England's most reliable and dynamic winery – and consultancy.

℧ **Dr. H Thanisch** [tah-nish] (*Mosel-Saar-Ruwer*, Germany) Two estates with confusingly similar labels. The best of the pair which has a *VDP* logo offers improved examples of *Bernkasteler* Doctor.

℧ **Thelema Mountain Vineyards** [thur-lee-ma] (*Stellenbosch*, South Africa) One of the very best wineries in South Africa, thanks to Gyles Webb's skill and to stunning hillside vineyards. *Chardonnay* and *Sauvignon* are the stars, though Webb is coming to terms with his reds, too.

Thermenregion [thehr -men-ray-gee-yon] (Austria) Big region close to Vienna, producing good reds and sweet and dry whites.

℧ **Jean Thevenet** [tev-nay] ((*Burgundy*, France) *Macon* producer who makes sweet white when he can. The domaine is called Domaine de la Bongran.

℧ **Ch. Thieuley** [tee-yur-lay] (*Entre-Deux-Mers, Bordeaux*, France) With *Château Bonnet*, this is one of the leading lights of this region. ★★★ 2001 Francis Courselle £

℧ **Michel Thomas** [toh-mah] (Loire, France) Producer of reliable modern Sancerre with rich flavours. ★★★★★ 2001 Sancerre ££

℧ **Paul Thomas** (*Washington State*) Dynamic brand now under the same ownership as Columbia Winery, and producing a broad range of wines, including good *Chardonnay* and *Semillon* whites and *Cabernet-Merlot* reds.

℧ **Three Choirs Vineyard** (*Gloucestershire*, England) Reliable estate, named for the three cathedrals of Gloucester, Hereford, and Worcester. Try the "Barrique-matured" whites and the "New Release" *Nouveau*.

℧ **Jean-Luc Thunevin** (*Bordeaux*, France) Producer of tiny-production, rich, concentrated "garage wines" such as *Valandraud* and *Marojallia*.

℧ **Thurston Wolfe** (*Washington State*) Enthusiastic supporter of the local speciality, the mulberryish red Lemberger – and producer, too, of good fortified "port" and Black Muscat.

℧ **Ticino** [tee-chee-noh] (Switzerland) One of the best parts of Switzerland to go looking for easy-drinking and (relatively) affordable reds, the best of which are made from *Merlot*. Interestingly, this region has also quietly pioneered White Merlot, a style of wine we will be encountering quite frequently in the next few years, as California grape growers and winemakers struggle to find ways of disposing of the surplus of this grape. ★★★ 2000 Castello di Marcote Tamboruni Carlo Eved £££

℧ **Tiefenbrunner** [tee-fen-broon-nehr] (*Trentino-Alto Adige*, Italy) Consistent producer of fair-to-good varietal whites, most particularly *Chardonnay* and *Gewürztraminer*.

℧ **Tignanello** [teen-yah-neh-loh] (*Tuscany*, Italy) *Antinori's Sangiovese-Cabernet Super-Tuscan* is one of Italy's original superstars. Should last for a decade.

🍇 **Tinta Roriz** [teen-tah roh-reesh] (Portugal) See *Tempranillo*

℧ **Tio Pepe** [tee-yoh peh-peh] (*Jerez*, Spain) *Gonzalez Byass's* Ultra-reliable fino.

🍇 **Tocai** [toh-kay] (Italy) Lightly herby Venetian white grape, confusingly unrelated to others of similar name. Drink young.

℧ **Philip Togni** (*Napa*, California) Producer of big, hefty *Cabernet Sauvignons* that take a long while to soften, but are well worth the wait.

℧ **Tokaji** [toh-ka-yee] (Hungary) Not to be confused with Australian *liqueur Tokay*, Tocai Friulano, or *Tokay d'Alsace*, Tokaji Aszú is a dessert wine made in a specific region of Eastern *Hungary* (and a small corner of *Slovakia*) by adding measured amounts (*puttonyos*) of *eszencia* (a paste made from individually-picked, overripe, and/or *botrytis*-affected grapes) to dry wine made from the local *Furmint* and *Hárslevelu* grapes. Sweetness levels, which depend on the amount of *eszencia* added, range from one to six *puttonyos*, anything beyond which is labelled *Aszú Eszencia*. This last is often confused with the pure syrup which is sold – at vast prices – as *Eszencia*. Wines are fresher (less *oxidized*) since the arrival of outside investment, which has also revived interest in making individual-vineyard wines from the best sites. Disznókö; *Royal Tokaji Wine Co; Ch. Megyer; Oremus; Pajzos;* Tokajkovago. ★★★★ 2000 Ch. Dereszla Tokaji Muskotaly ££

Tokaj Trading House (*Tokaj*, Hungary) The state-owned wine producing company, now modernising.

Tokay [in France: to-kay; in Australia: toh-kye] A number of wine regions use Tokay as a local name for various grape varieties. In Australia it is the name of a fortified wine made by *Rutherglen* from the *Muscadelle*. In *Alsace* it is the local name for *Pinot Gris*. The Italian *Tocai* is not related to either of these. Hungary's Tokay (renamed *Tokaji*) is largely made from the *Furmint*.

Tokay d'Alsace [to-kay dal-sas] (Alsace, France) See *Pinot Gris*.

Tollana [to-lah-nah] (South Australia) Another part of the Southcorp (*Penfolds, Lindeman,* etc.) empire – and a source of great value.

Dom. Tollot-Beaut [to-loh-boh] (*Burgundy,* France) *Burgundy* domaine in *Chorey-lès-Beaune,* with top-class *Corton* vineyards and a mastery over modern techniques and new oak. Wines have lots of rich fruit flavour. Some find them overly showy. ★★★★★ 1998 Corton Bressandes Grand Cru £££

Torbreck (*Barossa,* Australia) Producer of Rhône-like reds that blend *Shiraz* with *Viognier.* Look for Runrig, Descendent and Juveniles, originally produced for one of the best bar-restaurants in Paris.

Torcolato [taw-ko-lah-toh] (*Veneto,* Italy) See *Maculan.*

Torgiano [taw-jee-yah-noh] (*Umbria,* Italy) Zone in *Umbria* and modern red wine made famous by *Lungarotti.* See *Rubesco.* ★★★ 1992 Torgiano Rubesco

Michel Torino [Toh-ree-noh] (*Cafayate,* Argentina) Reliable producer of various wine styles from Salta – and a leading light in the move toward organic wine in Argentina. ★★★ 2001 Coleccion Michel Torino Malbec £

Toro [to-roh] (Spain) Up-and-coming region on the *Douro,* close to Portugal, producing intense reds such as Fariña's *Collegiata* from *Tempranillo,* confusingly known here as Tinta de Toro. **Bajoz;** *Fariña;* **Vega Saúco.** ★★★★ 1998 Toro Crianza Bajoz Bodega Vina Bajoz ££

Torre de Gall [to-ray day-gahl] (*Catalonia,* Spain) *Moët & Chandon's* Spanish sparkling wine – now better known as Cava Chandon. As good as it gets using traditional cava varieties.

Torres [TO-rehs] (*Catalonia,* Spain) *Miguel Torres* revolutionized Spain's wines with its Viña Sol, Gran Sangre de Toro, Esmeralda, and Gran Coronas, before doing the same for Chile. Today, while these all face heavier competition, efforts at the top end of the scale, like the *Milmanda Chardonnay,* Fransola *Sauvignon Blanc,* and Mas Borras ("Black Label") *Cabernet Sauvignon,* still look good. ★★★★★ 1998 Grans Muralles £££

Marimar Torres [TO-rehs] (*Sonoma,* California) *Miguel Torres'* sister is producing impressive *Pinot Noir* and *Chardonnay* from a spectacular little vineyard in *Russian River.* ★★★ 1999 Marimar Pinot Noir £££

Miguel Torres [TO-rehs] (*Curico,* Chile) Improving offshoot of the Spanish giant. Manso de Velasco is the star wine. ★★★ 2001 Santa Digna Merlot £££

Torreón de Paredes [tor-ray-yon day pah-ray-days] ((Chile) Erratic *Rapel* estate. Good Cabernet. ★★★ 2000 Torreon de Paredes Merlot Reserve £

Michel Torino (Argentina) Organic estate currently on a roll.

Torrontes [to-ron-tehs] (Argentina) Aromatic cousin of *Muscat.* Smells sweet even when the wine is bone dry. **Etchart; la Agricola.**

Toscana [tos-KAH-nah] (Italy) See *Tuscany.*

Ch. la Tour Blanche [lah toor blonsh] (*Sauternes Premier Cru Classé, Bordeaux,* France) Wine school, producing fine, long-lasting *Sauternes.*

T

Ch. la Tour-Carnet [lah toor kahr-nay] (*Haut-Médoc 4ème Cru Classé, Bordeaux,* France) Picturesque but only *Cru Bourgeois*-level fourth growth.

Ch. la Tour-de-By [lah toor dur bee] (*Médoc Cru Bourgeois, Bordeaux,* France) Reliable, in a traditional sort of way.

Ch. La Tour Figeac [lah toor fee-jak] (*Bordeaux*, France) A St Emilion *Grand Cru Classé* to watch, with careful winemaking and good terroir.

Ch. La Tour Haut Brion [lah toor oh-bree-yo'n] (*Bordeaux*, France) Until 1983 this was the second wine of Ch. La Mission Haut-Brion. Now it is an entirely separate wine, and is lighter, but still with great depth and style.

Ch. Tour-du-Haut-Caussan [toor doo oh koh-sa'n] (*Haut-Médoc, Bordeaux*, France) Highly reliable modern estate.

Ch. Tour-du-Haut-Moulin [toor doo oh moo-lan] (*Haut-Médoc Cru Bourgeois, Bordeaux,* France) Producer of what can be *cru classé* quality wine.

Ch. la Tour-Martillac [lah toor mah-tee-yak] (*Pessac Léognan, Bordeaux,* France) Organic *Pessac-Léognan* estate with juicy reds and good whites.

Touraine [too-rayn] (*Loire*, France) Area encompassing the *ACs Chinon, Vouvray,* and *Bourgueil*. Also an increasing source of quaffable *varietal* wines – *Sauvignon*, *Gamay* de Touraine, etc. Bellevue; de la Besnerie; Briare; Paul Buisse; Charmoise; de la Gabillière; Henry Marionet; Octavie; Oisly & Thésée; Oudin Frères. ★★★★ 2001 Domaine de l'Aumonier Sauvignon £

Les Tourelles de Longueville [lay too-rel dur long-ur-veel] (*Pauillac, Bordeaux*, France) The *second label* of *Pichon-Longueville*.

Touriga (Nacional/Franca) [too-ree-ga nah-see-yoh-nahl/fran-ka] (Portugal) Red *port* grapes, also (though rarely) seen in the New World. Now being used for good *varietal* wines in many parts of Portugal.

Tower Estates (Australia) Dynamic new venture led by Len Evans, founder of Rothbury Estate and Emperor of Australia's wine competitions Wines are produced in limited quantities in several different regions.

Traditional Generally meaningless term, except in sparkling wines where the "méthode traditionelle" is the new way to say "*méthode champenoise*" and in Portugal where "Traditional *Late Bottled Vintage*" refers to *port* that unlike non-traditional LBV, hasn't been filtered. ("Tradition" in some parts of France can also refer to – often unappealingly – old-fashioned winemaking).

Traisen [trih-sen] (Nahe, Germany) Star village of the Nahe, with Bastei and Rotenfels vineyards, and brilliant, fiery Rieslings.

Traminer [tra-mee-nur; in Australia: trah-MEE-nah] A less aromatic variant of the *Gewürztraminer* grape widely grown in Eastern Europe and Italy, although the term is confusingly also used as a pronounceable, alternative name for the latter grape – particularly in Australia.

Transfer Method A way of making sparkling wine, involving a second fermentation in the bottle, but unlike the *méthode champenoise* in that the wine is separated from the lees by pumping it out of the bottle into a pressurized tank for clarification before returning it to another bottle.

Bodegas Trapiche [tra-pee-chay] (Argentina) Huge, go-getting producer with noteworthy barrel-fermented *Chardonnay* and *Cabernet/Malbec*. ★★★★ 2000 Trapiche Oak Cask Pinot Noir £

Tras-os-Montes [tras-ohsh-montsh] (*Douro*, Portugal) Up-and-coming wine region of the *Upper Douro*, right up by the Spanish border. It's the source of *Barca Velha*. ★★★ 1999 Grantom Reserva Real Companhia Velha £

Trebbiano [treh-bee-yah-noh] (Italy) Ubiquitous white grape, known in France as *Ugni Blanc*.

Trebbiano d'Abruzzo [treh-bee-yah-noh dab-root-zoh] (*Abruzzo*, Italy) A *DOC* region where they grow a clone of *Trebbiano*, confusingly called Trebbiano di Toscana, and use it to make unexceptional dry whites.

Trefethen [treh-feh-then] (*Napa Valley,* California) Pioneering estate whose *Chardonnay* and *Cabernet* now taste oddly old-fashioned. The Eshcol wines, though cheaper, are curiously often a better buy.

Trentino [trehn-tee-noh] (Italy) Northern *DOC* in Italy. *Trentino* specialities include crunchy red *Marzemino*, nutty white Nosiola, and excellent *Vin Santo*. Winemaking here often suffers from overproduction, but less greedy winemakers can offer lovely, soft, easy-drinking wines. **Càvit; Ferrari; Foradori; Pojer & Sandri; San Leonardo;Vallarom; Roberto Zeni.**

Trentino-Alto Adige [trehn-tee-noh al-toh ah-dee-jay] (Italy) Northern region confusingly combining the two *DOC* areas *Trentino* and *Alto Adige*.

☨ **Dom. de Trévallon** [treh-vah-lon] (*Provence*, France) Superstar long-lived blend of *Cabernet Sauvignon* and *Syrah* that was sold under the *Les Baux de Provence appellation* but has now (because of crazily restrictive rules regarding grape varieties) been demoted to *Vin de Pays des Bouches du Rhône*.

☨ **Triebaumer** [tree-bow-mehr] (*Burgenland*, Austria) Fine producer of late-harvest wines (including good Sauvignon) and well-made reds, including some unusually good examples of the *Blaufränkisch*.

☨ **Dom. Frédéric-Emile Trimbach** [tram-bahkh] (*Alsace*, France) Distinguished grower and merchant with subtle, complex wines. Top *cuvées* are the Frédéric Emile, Clos St. Hune, and Seigneurs de Ribeaupierre.
★★★ 1999 Trimbach Pinot Gris Reserve £

Trittenheim [trit-ten-hime] (*Mosel-Saar-Ruwer*, Germany) Village whose vineyards are said to have been the first in Germany planted with *Riesling*, making honeyed wine.

Trocken [trok-ken] (Germany) Dry, often aggressively so. Avoid Trocken *Kabinett* from such northern areas as the *Mosel*, *Rheingau*, and *Rheinhessen*. *QbA* (*chaptalized*) and *Spätlese* Trocken wines (the latter made, by definition, from riper grapes) are better. See also *Halbtrocken*.

Trockenbeerenauslese [trok-ken-beh-ren-ows-lay-zeh] (Austria/Germany) Fifth rung of the *QmP* ladder, wine from selected dried grapes which are usually *botrytis*-affected and full of natural sugar. Only made in the best years, rare and expensive, though less so in Austria than Germany.

🍇 **Trollinger** [trroh-ling-gur] (Germany) The German name for the Black Hamburg grape, used in *Württemberg* to make light red wines.

Tronçais [tron-say] (France) Forest producing some of the best oak for barrels.

☨ **Ch. Tronquoy-Lalande** [trron-kwah-lah-lond] (*St. Estèphe Cru Bourgeois*, *Bordeaux*, France) Tough, traditional wines to buy in ripe years. Better than usual in 2000.

☨ **Ch. Troplong-Mondot** [trroh-lon mondoh] (*St. Emilion Grand Cru Classé*, *Bordeaux*, France) Excellently-sited, top-class property whose wines now sell for top-class prices. However, 1999 and 2000 have seemed a little less impressive than previous years.

☨ **Ch. Trotanoy** [trrot-teh-nwah] (*Pomerol*, *Bordeaux*, France) Never less than fine, and back on especially roaring form since the beginning of the 1990s to compete with *Pétrus*. Some may, however, prefer the lighter style of some of the 1980s than the denser wines on offer today.

☨ **Ch. Trottevieille** [trrott-vee-yay] (*St. Emilion Premier Grand Cru*, *Bordeaux*, France) Steadily improving property.

🍇 **Trousseau** [troo-soh] (Eastern France) Grape variety found in *Arbois*.

☨ **Tsantalis** [tsan-tah-lis] (*Nemea*, Greece) Increasingly impressive producer, redefining traditional varieties.

Tselepos [too-ree-ga nah-see-yoh-nahl/fran-ka] (Greece) Adventurous producer trying out *Gewurztraminer*, among other grapes. Good *Chardonnay* and *Cabernet-Merlot*.

Tualitin Vineyards [too-all-lit-tin] (*Oregon*, USA) Well-established property with good *Pinot Noir*.

☨ **Tua Rita** [too-wah ree-tah] (*Tuscany*, Italy) Young estate making tiny quantities of wines using grapes from vines that previously went into *Sassicaia*. Giusto dei Notri is the *Bordeaux* blend; Redigaffi is the pure *Merlot*.

☨ **Tulloch** [tul-lurk] (*Hunter Valley*, Australia) Underperforming backwater of the *Penfolds* empire.

T

Tunisia [too-nee-shuh] Best known for dessert *Muscat* wines.

☒ **Cave Vinicole de Turckheim** [turk-hime] (*Alsace,* France) Cooperative whose top wines can often rival those of some the region's best estates.
★★★★ 1999 Riesling Grand Cru Brand ££

☒ **Turkey Flat** (South Australia) Small maker of intensely rich *Barossa, Shiraz,* and *Grenache.*

☒ **Turley Cellars** (*Napa Valley,* California) Helen Turley, US guru Robert Parker's favourite winemaker, was here until 1995, and the wines still show all her hallmark qualities of intensity and ripeness. This is a source of concentrated *Petite Sirahs* and *Zinfandels,* including small quantities from very old vines.

☒ **Tursan** [toor-son] (Southwest France) Traditional region, producing fairly tough, old-fashioned reds.

Tuscany (Italy) Major region, the famous home of *Chianti* and reds such as *Brunello di Montalcino* and the new wave of *Super-Tuscan Vini da Tavola* and *IG* wines.

☒ **Tyrrell's** (*Hunter Valley,* Australia) *Chardonnay* (confusingly sold as *Pinot Chardonnay*) pioneer, and producer of old-fashioned *Shiraz* and (probably most impressively), long-lived, unoaked, lemony *Semillon* and even older-fashioned *Pinot Noir,* which tastes curiously like old-fashioned *Burgundy.*
★★★ 2001 Lost Block Semillon Hunter Valley ££

U

❧ **Ugni Blanc** [oo-ñee blon] (France) Undistinguished white grape whose neutrality makes it ideal for distillation. It needs modern winemaking to produce a wine with flavour. In Italy, where it is known as the *Trebbiano,* it takes on a mantle of (spurious) nobility. Try *Vin de Pays des Côtes de Gascogne.*

❧ **Ull de Llebre** [ool dur yay-bray] (Spain) Literally "hare's eye". See *Tempranillo.*

Ullage Space between surface of wine and top of cask or, in a bottle, the cork. The wider the gap, the greater the danger of oxidation. Older wines almost always have some degree of ullage; the less the better.

☒ **Umani Ronchi** [oo-mah-nee ron-kee] (*Marches,* Italy) Innovative producer whose wines, like the extraordinary new Pelago, prove that *Tuscany* and *Piedmont* are no longer the only exciting wine regions in Italy.
★★★★ 1999 Cumaro Rosso Conero Montepulciano £££

Umathum [oo-ma-toom] (*Neusiedlersee,* Austria) Producer of unusually good red wines including a wonderful *St. Laurent.* ★★★ 2000 Zweigelt £££

Umbria [uhm-bree-ah] (Italy) Central wine region, best known for white *Orvieto* and *Torgiano,* but also producing the excellent red *Rubesco.*

☒ **Viña Undurraga** [oon-dur-rah-ga] (*Central Valley,* Chile) Family-owned estate with a range of single varietal wines, including good *Carmenère.*

Unfiltered Filtering a wine can remove flavour – as can *fining* it with egg white or bentonite (clay). Most winemakers traditionally argue that both practices are necessary if the finished wine is going to be crystal-clear and free from bacteria that could turn it to vinegar. Many quality-conscious new-wave producers, however, are now cutting back on *fining* and/or filtering.

Ürzig [oort-zig] (*Mosel-Saar-Ruwer,* Germany) Village on the *Mosel* with steeply sloping vineyards and some of the very best producers, including *Christoffel, Mönchhof,* and *Dr. Loosen.* ★★★★ 1992 Urziger Wurzgarten Riesling Spatlese Christoffel Prum £

☒ **Utiel-Requena** [oo-tee-yel reh-kay-nah] (*Valencia,* Spain) DO of *Valencia,* producing heavy red and good fresh rosé from the Bobal grape. ★★★★ 2001 Portal Bobal Tempranillo £

V

℣ **Dom. Vacheron** [va-shur-ron] (*Loire*, France) Reliably classy producer of *Sancerre* – including a better-than-average and ageworthy red.

℣ **Vacqueyras** [va-kay-ras] (*Rhône*, France) *Côtes du Rhône* village with full-bodied, peppery reds which compete with (pricier) *Gigondas*. Cazaux; Combe; Couroulu; Fourmone; *Jaboulet Aîné*; Dom. de Mont Vac; Montmirail; de la Soleïade; Tardieu-Laurent; Ch. des Tours; *Cave de Vacqueyras*; Vidal-Fleury. ★★★ 1999 Vacqueyras Cuvée Doucinello le Sang des Cailloux Serge Ferigoule ££

℣ **Aldo Vajra** [vi-rah] (*Piedmont*, Italy) Producer of rich, complex *Barolo* and the deliciously different, *gamey* Freisa delle Langhe. ★★★ 1997 Barolo 'Bricco delle Viole' £££

Valais [va-lay] (Switzerland) Vineyard area on the upper *Rhône*, making good *Fendant* (*Chasselas*) which surmounts the usual innate dullness of that grape. There are also some reasonable – in all but price – light reds made from the *Pinot Noir*. Bonvin; Imesch; Provins.

Val/Valle d'Aosta [val-day-yos-tah] (Italy) Small, spectacularly beautiful area between *Piedmont* and the French/Swiss border. Better for tourism than wine.

℣ **Vignerons du Val d'Orbieu** [val-dor-byu] (*Languedoc-Roussillon*, France) Huge, would-be innovative association of over 200 cooperatives and growers that now also owns Cordier in *Bordeaux*, which it is turning into a good brand of generic styles from that region. Examples of Val d'Orbieu's Corbières and Minervois can also be very reliable but, apart from the generally excellent Cuvée Mythique, too many of the other wines leave room for improvement. Reds are far better than whites.

℣ **Valbuena** [val-boo-way-nah] (*Ribera del Duero*, France) The – relatively – younger version of *Vega Sicilia* hits the streets when it is around five years old.

℣ **Ch. Valandraud** [va-lon-droh] (*St. Emilion*, *Bordeaux*, France) The original garage wine; an instant superstar created in 1991 by former bank teller Jean-Luc Thunevin in his garage as competition for *Le Pin*. Production is tiny (of *Pomerol* proportions), quality meticulous, and the price astronomical. Values quintupled following demand from the US and Asia, where buyers seem uninterested in the fact that these wines are – however delicious – actually no finer than *Médoc* classics costing far less. Now joined by l'Interdit de Valandraud, Virginie de Valandraud, and Axelle de Valandraud.

℣ **Valdeorras** [bahl-day-ohr-ras] (*Galicia*, Spain) A barren and mountainous *DO* in *Galicia* beginning to exploit the *Cabernet Franc*-like local grape Mencia and the indigenous white Godello.

℣ **Valdepeñas** [bahl-deh-pay-nyass] (*La Mancha*, Spain) *La Mancha DO* striving to refine its rather hefty strong reds and whites. Progress is being made, particularly with reds. Miguel Calatayud; Los Llanos; Felix Solis. ★★★★ 1995 Vina Albali Tinto Gran Reserva Valdepeñas £

℣ **Valdespino** [bahl-deh-spee-noh] (*Jerez*, Spain) Old-fashioned *sherry* company that uses wooden casks to ferment most of its wines. Makes a classic *fino* Innocente and an excellent *Pedro Ximénez*. New ownership may change many things. ★★★★★ Amontillado Tio Diego Valdespino

℣ **Valdivieso** [val-deh-vee-yay-soh] (*Curico*, Chile) Dynamic winery with a range of good commercial wines, high-quality *Chardonnay* and (particularly) *Pinot Noir* and an award-winning blend of grapes, regions, and years called Caballo Loco whose heretical philosophical approach gives Gallic traditionalists apoplexy. ★★★★★ 1999 Single Vineyard Cabernet Franc ££

℣ **Abazzia di Vallechiara** [ah-bat-zee-yah dee val-leh-kee-yah-rah] (*Piedmont*, Italy) Following the lead of fellow actor Gérard Dépardieu, Ornella Muti now has her own wine estate, with some first class *Dolcetto*.

℣ **Valençay** [va-lon-say] (*Loire*, France) *AC* within Touraine, near *Cheverny*, making comparable whites: light and clean, if rather sharp.

℣ **Valencia** [bah-len-thee-yah] (Spain) Produces quite alcoholic red wines from the Monastrell and also deliciously sweet, grapey *Moscatel de Valencia*.

V

♀ **Edoardo Valentini** [vah-len-tee-nee] (*Abruzzo*, Italy) Good, old-fashioned Montepulciano d'Abruzzo and unusually good Trebbiano d'Abruzzo.

♀ **Vallet Frères** [va-lay frehr] (*Burgundy*, France) Small, traditional – not to say old-fashioned – merchant based in *Gevrey-Chambertin*. Also known as Pierre Bourrée. ★★★ 2000 Bourgogne Blanc Vallet Freres ££

♀ **Valpolicella** [val-poh-lee-cheh-lah] (*Veneto,* Italy) Overcommercialized, light, red wine, which should be drunk young to catch its interestingly bitter-cherryish flavour. *Classico* is better; best is *Ripasso*, made by refermenting the wine on the *lees* of an earlier vat. For a different taste, buy *Amarone* or *Recioto*. *Allegrini; Berta*. Only these, and Ripasso wines, should be aged. *Masi, Allegrini; Bolla; Boscaini;* Brunelli; *dal Forno; Guerrieri-Rizzardi; Masi;* Mazzi; *Quintarelli; Le Ragose;* Serego Alighieri; *Tedeschi;* Villa Spinosa; *Zenato;* Fratelli Zeni.

♀ **Valréas** [val-ray-yas] (*Rhône*, France) Peppery, inexpensive red wine from a *Côtes du Rhône* village. *Clos Petite Bellane; Earl Gaia.* ★★★ 2001 Domaine Grande Bellane Côtes du Rhône, Valréas £

♀ **Valtellina** [val-teh-lee-na] (*Lombardy,* Italy) Red DOC mostly from the *Nebbiolo* grape, of variable quality. Improves with age. The raisiny Sfursat, made from dried grapes, is more interesting. ★★★ 1997 Valtellina Sforzato Casa Vinicola Pietro Nera ££

♀ **Varichon et Clerc** [va-ree-shon ay klayr] (*Savoie,* France) Good producer of sparkling wine.

Varietal A wine made from and named after one or more grape varieties, e.g., California *Chardonnay*. The French authorities are trying to outlaw such references from the labels of most of their *appellation contrôlée* wines.

♀ **Viña los Vascos** [los vas-kos] (*Colchagua Valley,* Chile) Estate belonging to Eric de *Rothschild* of *Ch. Lafite*, and shamelessly sold with a *Lafite*-like label. The *Cabernet* Grande Reserve has improved, but the standard *Cabernet* is uninspiring and the white disappointing, not to say downright poor.

♀ **Vasse Felix** [vas-fee-liks] (*Margaret River,* Australia) Very classy *Margaret River* winery belonging to the widow of millionaire Rupert Holmes à Court, specializing in juicy, high-quality (multi-regional) *Cabernet, Shiraz, Semillon,* and *Riesling*. ★★★★ 2000 Vasse Felix Cabernet Sauvignon Merlot ££

♀ **Vaucluse** [voh-klooz] (*Rhône*, France) *Côtes du Rhône* region with good *Vin de Pays* and peppery reds and rosés. ★★★ 2000 Montirius Gigondas E. Saurel ££

Vaud [voh] (Switzerland) Swiss wine area on the shores of Lake Geneva, famous for unusually tangy *Chasselas* (Dorin) and light reds.

♀ **Vaudésir** [voh-day-zeer] (*Burgundy,* France) Possibly the best of the seven *Chablis Grands Crus*. ★★★ 1999 Chablis Grand Cru Vaudesir J-M Brocard £££

♀ **Vavasour** [va-va-soor] (*Marlborough,* New Zealand) Pioneers of the Awatere Valley sub-region of *Marlborough*, with *Bordeaux*-style reds, and impressive *Sauvignons* and *Chardonnays*. Dashwood is the *second label*.

VDP (Germany) Association of high-quality producers. Look for the eagle.

VDQS (*Vin Délimité de Qualité Supérieur*) (France) Official, neither-fish-nor-fowl designation for wines above *Vin de Pays* but humbler than *AC*.

♀ **Veenwouden** [fehn-foh-den] (*Paarl,* South Africa) A chance to taste what happens when Michel Rolland of Bordeaux gets his hands on vineyards in South Africa. Hardly surprisingly, riper and richer-tasting Merlot than is traditionally associated with South Africa. ★★★★ 1999 Merlot £££

Vecchio [veh-kee-yoh] (Italy) Old.

♀ **Vecchio Samperi** [veh-kee-yoh sam-peh-ree] (*Sicily,* Italy) Fine *De Bartoli Marsala* estate, making a dry aperitif similar to an *amontillado sherry*.

♀ **Vega Sicilia** [bay-gah sih-sih-lyah] (*Ribera del Duero,* Spain) Spain's top wine is a long (10 years) barrel-matured, eccentric *Tempranillo-Bordeaux* blend called Unico, sold for extravagant prices. For a cheaper, slightly fresher taste of the Vega Sicilia-style, try the supposedly lesser Valbuena.

Vegetal Often used of *Sauvignon Blanc*, like "grassy". Can be complimentary – though not in California or Australia, where it is held to mean "unripe".

☦ **Velich** [veh-likh] (*Burgenland*, Austria) High-quality producers of a wide range of wines including recommendable Chardonnay.

☦ **Caves Velhas** [kah-vash vay-yash] (Portugal) Large improving merchants who blend wine from all over the country, and saved the *Bucelas DO* from extinction. ★★★★★ **1999 Caves Velhas Romeira 3 Carvalhos £**

Velho/velhas [vay-yoh/vay-yash] (Portugal) Old, as in red wine.

Velletri [veh-leh-tree] (Italy) Town in the Alban hills (*Colli Albani*), producing mainly *Trebbiano* and *Malvasia*-based whites, similar to *Frascati*.

❦ **Veltliner** See *Grüner Veltliner*.

Vendange [von-donzh] (France) Harvest or vintage.

Vendange tardive [von-donzh tahr-deev] (France) Particularly in *Alsace*, wine from *late-harvested* grapes, usually lusciously sweet.

Vendemmia/Vendimia [ven-deh-mee-yah/ven-dee-mee-yah] (Italy, Spain) Harvest or vintage.

☦ **Venegazzú** [veh-neh-gaht-zoo] (*Veneto,* Italy) Fine, understated *claret*-like *Cabernet Sauvignon Vino da Tavola* "Super-Veneto" to compete with those *Super-Tuscans*. Needs five years. The black label is better.

Veneto [veh-neh-toh] (Italy) North-eastern wine region, the home of *Soave, Valpolicella*, and *Bardolino.*

Venica e Venica [veh-ni-ca] (*Friuli-Venezia Giulia*, Italy) Two brothers who make some of the most flavoursome whites in Collio, including Sauvignon, Pinot Bianco, and Chardonnay.

☦ **Veramonte** [vay-rah-mon-tay] (*Casablanca*, Chile) Venture by Augustin Huneeus of *Franciscan Vineyards*, producing impressive reds, especially the *Merlot* (which, like many others, is actually *Carmenère*). Now under the same ownership as Simi and Sonoma-Cutrer. ★★★★★ **1999 Primus ££**

❦ **Verdejo** [vehr-de-khoh] (Spain) Interestingly herby white grape; confusingly not the *Verdelho* of *Madeira* and Australia, but the variety used for new-wave *Rueda*. ★★★★ **2001 Aura ARS Vinum Verdejo £**

❦ **Verdelho** [in *Madeira*: vehr-deh-yoh; in *Australia*: vur-del-loh] (Madeira/Australia) White grape used for fortified *Madeira* and *white port* and for limey, dry table wine in Australia, especially in the Hunter Valley. **Capel Vale; Chapel Hill; Moondah Brook; Sandalford.** ★★★★ **2001 Temple Bruer Verdelho Langhorne Creek, South Australia ££**

❦ **Verdicchio** [vehr-dee-kee-yoh] (*Marches*, Italy) Spicy white grape seen in a number of *DOCs* in its own right, the best of which is *Verdicchio dei Castelli di Jesi*. In *Umbria* this grape is a major component of *Orvieto*.

☦ **Verdicchio dei Castelli di Jesi** [vehr-dee-kee-yoh day-ee kas-tay-lee dee yay-zee] (*Marches*, Italy) Light, clean, and crisp wines to drink with seafood. **Bucci; Garofoli; Monacesca; Umani Ronchi.**

❦ **Verduzzo** [vehr-doot-soh] (*Friuli-Venezia Giulia,* Italy) Flavoursome white grape making a dry and a fine *amabile-style* wine in the *Colli Orientale.*

☦ **Vergelegen** [vehr-kur-lek-hen] (*Somerset West,* South Africa) Hi-tech winery producing some of the Cape's more reliable wines. ★★★★★ **1998 Vergelegen Cabernet Sauvignon Stellenbosch £**

☦ **Verget** [vehr-jay] (*Burgundy,* France) Young Mâconnais *négociant* producing impeccable white wines, from *Mâcon Villages* to *Meursault* and *Chablis*.

❦ **Vermentino** [vayr-men-tee-noh] (*Liguria,* Italy) The spicy, dry white grape of the Adriatic and, increasingly, in modern southern French *Vin de Table*.

❦ **Vernaccia** [vayr-naht-chah] (*Tuscany*, Italy) White grape making the Tuscan *DOCG* Vernaccia di San Gimignano (where it's helped by a dash of *Chardonnay*) and *Sardinian* Vernaccia di Oristano. At its best has a distinctive nut and spice flavour. **Casale-Falchini; Teruzzi & Puthod.** ★★★ **2001 Vernaccia di San Gimignano Vigna A Solatio Casale-Falchini £**

☦ **Georges Vernay** [vayr-nay] (*Rhône*, France) The great master of *Condrieu* who can do things with *Viognier* that few seem able to match.

V

☿ **Noël Verset** [vehr-say] (*Cornas, Rhône*) Top-class *Cornas* producer.

☿ **Quinta do Vesuvio** [veh-soo-vee-yoh] (*Douro*, Portugal) Single *quinta port* from the family that owns *Dow's*, *Graham's*, *Warre's*, etc. ★★★ 1999 Symington's Quinta do Vesuvio £££

☿ **Veuve Clicquot-Ponsardin** [vurv klee-koh pon-sahr-dan] (*Champagne,* France) The distinctive orange label is the mark of reliable non-vintage *Brut*. The *prestige cuvée* is called Grande Dame after the famous Widow Clicquot; the *demi-sec* is a lovely, honeyed wine; and the vintage rosé is now one of the best pink wines in the region. ★★★★ 1995 Veuve Clicquot Rose Reserve ££££

Victoria (Australia) Wines range from the *Liqueur Muscats* of *Rutherglen* to the peppery *Shirazes* of *Bendigo* and the elegant *Pinot Noirs* of the *Yarra Valley*.

☿ **Vidal** [vee-dahl] (*Hawkes Bay*, New Zealand) One of New Zealand's top four red wine producers. Associated with *Villa Maria* and *Esk Valley*. *Chardonnays* are the strongest suit. ★★★★ 2000 Vidal Estate Reserve Chardonnay ££

🍇 **Vidal** [vi-dal] (Canada) A *hybrid* and highly frost-resistant variety looked down on by European authorities but widely and successfully grown in *Canada* for spicily exotic *icewine*. *Iniskillin; Rief Estate*. ★★★★★ 1999 Reif Vidal Icewine £££

☿ **J. Vidal-Fleury** [vee-dahl flur-ree] (*Rhône*, France) High-quality grower and shipper that belongs to *Guigal*.

VIDE [vee-day] (Italy) Syndicate supposedly denoting finer estate wines.

☿ **Vie di Romans** [vee dee roh-mans] (*Friuli-Venezia Giulia,* Italy) If you thought the only winemaking Gallos were in California, meet Gianfranco Gallo's delicious *Tocai Friulano*, *Pinot Grigio*, and *Sauvignon Blanc*.

☿ **la Vieille Ferme** [vee-yay fairm] (*Rhône*, France) Organic red and white *Côtes du Rhône* from the Perrin family of *Château de Beaucastel*. ★★★ 2000 La Vieille Ferme Côtes du Ventoux Domaines Perrin £

Vieilles Vignes [vee-yay veeñ] (France) Wine (supposedly) made from a producer's oldest vines. (In reality, while real vine maturity begins at 25, Vieilles Vignes can mean anything between 15 and 90 years of age.)

☿ **Vietti** [vee-yet-tee] (*Piedmont,* Italy) Impeccable single-vineyard *Barolo* (Rocche di Castiglione; Brunate; and Villero), *Barbaresco*, and *Barbera*. The white *Arneis* is pretty impressive, too.

☿ **Vieux Château Certan** [vee-yur-cha-toh-sehr-tan] (*Pomerol, Bordeaux,* France) Ultra-classy, small *Pomerol* property, known as "VCC'" to its fans, using a lot of Cabernet Franc to produce stylish complex wine. One of the stars of 2001.

☿ **Dom. du Vieux-Télégraphe** [vee-yuhr tay-lay-grahf] (*Rhône*, France) Modern *Châteauneuf-du-Pape* domaine now back on track after a dull patch. Great whites too.

☿ **Vignalta** [veen-yal-tah] (*Veneto,* Italy) Colli Eugeanei producer brewing up a storm with its Gemola (*Merlot-Cabernet Franc*) and Sirio (*Muscat*). ★★★ 2000 Agno Tinto ££

☿ **Vignamaggio** [veen-yah-maj-yo] (*Tuscany*, Italy) Chianti Classico estate, also producing "Obsession" a *Bordeaux* blend, and a *Cabernet Franc*.

☿ **Ch. Vignelaure** [veen-yah-lawrr] (*Provence,* France) Pioneering estate, now owned by David O'Brien, son of Vincent, the Irish racehorse trainer.

Vignoble [veen-yohbl] (France) Vineyard; vineyard area.

☿ **Villa Maria** (*Auckland,* New Zealand) One of New Zealand's biggest producers, and one which is unusual in coming close to hitting the target with its reds as well as its whites. *Riesling* is a particular success. ★★★★★ 2001 Villa Maria Reserve Chardonnay ££

☿ **Villa Mathilde** [mah-til-day] (*Campania*, Italy) Good DOC Falerno del Massico white and red.

☿ **Villa Sachsen** [zak-zen] (*Rheinhessen*, Germany) Estate with good-rather-than-great, low-yielding vineyards in *Bingen*.

V

Villa Russiz [roos-sitz] (*Friuli-Venezia Guilia*, Italy) Very good Sauvignon and *Pinot Bianco*, even better Chardonnay Gräfin and Merlot Graf de la Tour.
Villages (France) The suffix "villages" e.g., *Côtes du Rhône* or *Mâcon* generally – like *Classico* in Italy – indicates a slightly superior wine from a smaller delimited area encompassing certain villages.
Villany [vee-lah-nyee] (Hungary) Warm area of Hungary with a promising future for soft, young-drinking reds. ★★★ 1999 Vylyan Zweigelt £
Villard [vee-yarr] (Chile) Improving wines from French-born Thierry Villard, especially *Chardonnays* from *Casablanca*. ★★★★ 1999 Chardonnay Reserve Esencia ££
Ch. Villemaurine [veel-maw-reen] (*St. Emilion Grand Cru Classé, Bordeaux*, France) Often hard wines with overgenerous oak.
Ch de Villeneuve [veel-nurv] (*Loire*, France) Outstanding *Saumur* and *Saumur Champigny*.
Villiera Estate [vil-lee-yeh-rah] (*Paarl*, South Africa) Reliable range of affordable sparkling and still wines from the energetic Grier family. The *Sauvignons* and Cru Monro red and *Merlot* are the wines to buy.
Viñas del Vero [veen-yas del veh-roh] (*Somontano*, Spain) Modern producer of new-wave varietal wines, including recommendable Cabernet Sauvignon.
Vin de Corse [van dur kaws] (*Corsica*, France) *Appellation* within *Corsica*. Good sweet *Muscats* too. Gentile; Peraldi; Skalli; Toraccia.
Vin de garde [van dur gahrd] (France) Wine to keep.
Vin de l'Orléanais [van dur low-lay-yon-nay] (*Loire*, France) Small *VDQS* in the Central Vineyards of the *Loire*. See *Orléanais*.
Vin de Paille [van dur pie] (*Jura*, France) Traditional, now quite rare regional speciality; sweet, golden wine from grapes dried on straw mats.
Vin de Pays [van dur pay-yee] (France) Lowest/broadest geographical designation. In theory, simple country wines with regional characteristics. In fact, the producers of some of France's most exciting wines – such as *Dom. de Trévallon* and *Mas de Daumas Gassac* – prefer this designation and the freedom it offers. See *Côtes de Gascogne* and *Vin de Pays d'Oc*.
Vin de Savoie [van dur sav-wah] (Eastern France) Umbrella appellation encompassing mountainous sub-appellations such as *Aprément* and Chignon
Vin de table [van dur tahbl] (France) Table wine from no particular area.
Vin de Thouarsais [twar-say] (*Loire*, France) *VDQS* for a soft, light red from the *Cabernet Franc*; whites from the *Chenin Blanc*.
Vin doux naturel [doo nah-too-rrel] (France) Fortified – so not really "naturel" at all – dessert wines, particularly the sweet, liquorous *Muscats* of the South, such as Muscat de Beaumes-de-Venise, *Mireval*, and *Rivesaltes*.
Vinea Wachau [vee-nay-hay vak-cow] (*Wachau*, Austria) Top Wachau growers' organisation whose quality designations – *Steinfeder, Federspiel* and *Smaragd* – apply to wines that meet the organisation's criteria.
Vin Gris [van gree] (France) Chiefly from *Alsace* and the *Jura*, pale rosé from red grapes pressed after crushing or following a few hours of skin contact.
Vin Jaune [van john] (*Jura*, France) Golden-coloured *Arbois* speciality; slightly *oxidized* – like *fino sherry*. See *Ch. Chalon*.
Vin ordinaire (France) A simple local wine, usually served in carafes.
Vin Santo [veen sahn-toh] (Italy) Traditional white dessert wine made from bunches of grapes hung to dry in barns for up six months, especially in *Tuscany* and *Trentino*. Can compete with top medium *sherry*. Best with sweet almond ("Cantuccine") biscuits. Altesino; Avignonesi; Badia a Coltibuono; Berardenga; Felsina; Isole e Olena; Poliseano; Selvapiana. ★★★★ Antinori ££
Vin vert [van vehrr] (*Languedoc-Roussillon*, France) Light *acidic* white wine.
Vinsobres [van sohb-rruh] (*Rhône*, France) A weird name for a Côtes du Rhône Village. Dom. des Aussellons; Haume-Arnaud; Dom du Coriançon; du Moulin.
Vine Cliff (*Napa*, California) Estate with flavoursome, oaky *Cabernet* and Chardonnay. ★★★★ 1999 Proprietor's Reserve Chardonnay ££
Viña de Mesa [vee-ñah day may-sah] (Spain) Spanish for table wine.

V

☤ **Vinho Verde** [vee-ñoh vehrr-day] (Portugal) Literally "green" wine, meaning young; can be red or white. At worst, dull and sweet. At best delicious, refreshing, and slightly sparkling. Drink young.

☤ **Vinícola Navarra** [vee-nee-koh-lah na-vah-rah] (*Navarra*, Spain) Ultra-modern winemaking and newly-planted vineyards beginning to come on stream. Owned by *Bodegas y Bebida*. ★★★ 1998 Las Campanas Crianza £

Vinifera [vih-nih-feh-ra] Properly *Vitis vinifera*: species of all European vines: the ones used globally for quality wine.

Vino da Tavola [vee-noh dah tah-voh-lah] (Italy) Table wine, but the *DOC* quality designation net is so riddled with holes that producers of many superb – and pricey – wines have contented themselves with this "modest" *appellation*. Now replaced by *IGT*.

Vino de la Tierra [bee-noh day la tyay rah] (Spain) Spanish wine designation that can offer interesting, affordable, regional wines.

☤ **Vino Nobile di Montepulciano** [vee-noh noh-bee-lay dee mon-tay-pool-chee-ah-noh] (*Tuscany*, Italy) Potentially (though not often) truly noble, and made from the same grapes as Chianti. Can age well. Rosso di Monte-pulciano is the lighter, more accessible version. The *Montepulciano* of the title is the *Tuscan* town, not the grape variety. *Avignonesi; Boscarelli; Carpineto; Casale; del Cerro; Poliziano;* Tenuta Trerose. ★★★★★ 1999 Vino Nobile di Montepulciano Vigna Asinone Poliziano £££

Vino novello [vee-noh noh-vay-loh] (Italy) New wine; equivalent to French *nouveau*.

Vinopolis London wine museum/theme park.

Vintage Year of production.

Vintage Champagne (*Champagne*, France) Wine from a single "declared" year.

Vintage Character (port) (*Douro*, Portugal) Stylishly packaged upmarket *ruby* made by blending various years' wines.

Vintage (port) (*Douro*, Portugal) Produced only in "declared" years, aged in wood then in the bottle for many years. In "off" years, *port* houses release wines from their top estates as single-*quinta ports*. This style of *port* must be decanted, as it throws a sediment.

Vintners Quality Alliance / VQA (Canada) Quality symbol in Ontario and British Columbia. Treat Canadian non-VQA wine with suspicion.

🍇 **Viognier** [vee-YON-ñee-yay] (*Rhône*, France) Infuriating white variety which, at its best, produces floral, peachy wines. Once limited to the *Rhône* – *Condrieu* and *Ch. Grillet* – but now increasingly planted in southern France, California, and Australia. Benefits from a little – but not too much – contact with new oak. Some of the the Viognier grown in California is in fact *Roussanne*. *Calera; Duboeuf; Guigal; Heggies;* Andre Perret; Georges Vernay. ★★★★ 2001 The Last Ditch Viognier d'Arenberg McLaren Vale £

Viré-Clessé [vee-ray cles-say] (*Burgundy*, France) Newish *AC* centred on the two best white wine communes in *Mâcon*. New rules here have restricted the ability of *Thevenet* to make his sweet wine.

☤ **Virgin Hills** [*Victoria*, Australia] A single red blend that is unusually lean in style for Australia and repays keeping.

Visan [vee-so'n] (*Rhône*, France) *Rhône* village; decent reds, poor whites.

Viticulteur (-Propriétaire) (France) Vine grower (-vineyard owner).

🍇 **Viura** [vee-yoo-ra] (Spain) Dull white grape of the *Rioja* region and elsewhere, now being used to greater effect. ★★★ 2001 Alteza Viura Villa Malea £

☤ **Dom. Michel Voarick** [vwah-rik] (*Burgundy*, France) Old-fashioned wines that avoid the use of new oak. Fine *Corton-Charlemagne*.

☤ **Dom. Vocoret** [vok-ko-ray] (*Burgundy*, France) Classy *Chablis* producer whose wines age well. ★★★★★ 1998 Chablis Mont de Milieu £££

☤ **Gianni Voerzio** [vwayrt-zee-yoh] (*Piedmont*, Italy) Not quite as impressive as *Roberto* (see below), but a fine source of *Barbera, Freisa, Arneis,* and *Dolcetto*.

Ⅰ Roberto Voerzio [vwayrt-zee-yoh] (*Piedmont,* Italy) New-wave producer of juicy, spicy reds, with a first-rate *Barolo*. ★★★★★ 1997 Barolo 'Cerequio' £££

Ⅰ Alain Voge [vohzh] (*Rhône,* France) Traditional *Cornas* producer who also makes good *St. Péray.*

Ⅰ De Vogüé [dur voh-gway] (*Burgundy,* France) *Chambolle-Musigny* estate whose brilliant red wines deserve to be kept – for ages.

Volatile acidity (VA) Vinegary character in wine; caused by bacteria.

Ⅰ Volnay [vohl-nay] (*Burgundy,* France) Red wine village in the *Côte de Beaune* (the Caillerets vineyard, now a *Premier Cru,* was once ranked equal to *le Chambertin*). This is the home of fascinating, plummy, violety reds. Ampeau; d'Angerville; J-M Boillot; Bouchard Père et Fils; Joseph Drouhin; Vincent Girardin; Camille Giroud; Francois Buffet; Michel Lafarge; Comtes Lafon; Leroy; Dom de Montille; Pousse d'Or; Régis Rossignol-Changarnier, Vaudoisey; Voillot.

Ⅰ Castello di Volpaia [vol-pi-yah] (*Tuscany,* Italy) Top *Chianti* estate with *Super-Tuscans* Coltassala and Balifico.

Ⅰ Vosne-Romanée [vohn roh-ma-nay] (*Burgundy,* France) *Côte de Nuits* red wine village with *Romanée-Conti* among its many grand names, and other potentially gorgeous, plummy, rich wines, from many different producers. Arnoux; Cacheux; Confuron-Cotetidot; Engel; Anne Gros; Faiveley; Grivot; Hudelot-Noëllat; Jayer-Gilles; Laurent; Leroy; Méo-Camuzet; Mongeard-Mugneret; Mugneret-Gibourg; Rion; Romanée-Conti; Rouget; Jean Tardy; Thomas-Moillard.

Ⅰ Voss (*Sonoma,* California) Californian venture by *Yalumba,* producing lovely, intense *Zinfandel.* ★★★★ 1996 Voss Shiraz

Vougeot [voo-joh] (*Burgundy,* France) *Côte de Nuits commune* comprising the famous *Grand Cru Clos de Vougeot* and numerous growers of varying skill. Amiot-Servelle; Bertagna; Bouchard Père et Fils; Chopin-Groffier; J-J Confuron; Joseph Drouhin; Engel; Faiveley; Anne & François Gros; Louis Jadot; Leroy; Denis Mortet; Mugneret-Gibourg; Jacques Prieur; Prieuré Roch; Henri Rebourseau; Rion; Ch. de la Tour. ★★★★★ 1999 Domaine Méo-Camuzet Clos de Vougeot

Ⅰ la Voulte Gasparets [voot gas-pah-ray] (*Languedoc-Roussillon,* France) Unusually ambitious estate with single-vineyard bottlings (Romain Pauc is the best) that show just how good *Corbières* can be from the best sites.

Vouvray [voov-ray] (*Loire,* France) Whites from *Chenin Blanc,* ranging from clean dry whites and refreshing sparkling wines to *demi-secs* and honeyed, very long-lived, sweet *moelleux* wines. Des Aubuisières; Champalou; Huët; Foreau; Fouquet; Gaudrelle; Jarry; Mabille; Clos de Nouys; Pichot; Vaugondy.

Ⅰ Voyager Estate (*Margaret River,* Australia) Intense, concentrated wines, especially *Semillon, Chardonnay, Cabernet/Merlot.* ★★★★ 1999 Chardonnay ££

Ⅰ Champagne Vranken (*Champagne,* France) Group making good wine that also just bought *Pommery.* ★★★★ 1989 Charles Lafitte £££

Ⅰ Vriesenhof [free-zen-hof] (*Stellenbosch,* South Africa) Tough, occasionally classic reds and *Chardonnay.* ★★★ 1999 Vriesenhof Kallista ££

W

Wachau [vak-kow] (Austria) Major wine region producing some superlative *Riesling* from steep, terraced vineyards. Alzinger; Pichler; Hirtzberger; Jamek; Nikolaihof; Prager; Freie Weingärtner Wachau.

Wachenheim [vahkh-en-hime] (*Pfalz,* Germany) Superior *Mittelhaardt* village which should produce full, rich, unctuous *Riesling.* ★★★★ 2001 J L Wolf Wachenheimer ££

Ⅰ Dr Wagner [vahg-nehr] (Mosel-Saar-Ruwer, Germany) Outstanding, concentrated, taut Riesling.

Waiheke Island (*Auckland,* New Zealand) Tiny vacation island off Auckland producing some of New Zealand's best – and priciest – reds. *Goldwater Estate; Stonyridge; Te Motu.* ★★★ 1998 Obsidian Cabernet Merlot £££

Ⅰ **Waipara Springs** [wi-pah-rah] (*Canterbury*, New Zealand) Tiny producer offering the opportunity to taste wines from this southern region at their best.

Ⅰ **Wairau River** [wi-row] (*Marlborough*, New Zealand) Classic Kiwi *Chardonnays* and *Sauvignons* with piercing fruit character.

Wairarapa [why-rah-rah-pah] (New Zealand) Area in the south of the North Island that includes the better-known region of *Martinborough*.
★★★★★ 2000 Palliser Estate Pinot Noir Wairarapa, Martinborough ££

Walker Bay (South Africa) Promising region for *Pinot Noir* and *Chardonnay*. Established vineyards include *Hamilton Russell* and *Bouchard-Finlayson*.

Ⅰ **Warre's** [waw] (*Douro*, Portugal) Oldest of the big seven *port* houses and a stablemate to *Dow's*, *Graham's*, and *Smith Woodhouse*. Traditional *port*, which is both rather sweeter and more *tannic* than most. The old-fashioned *Late-bottled Vintage* is particularly worth seeking out too. Quinta da Cavadinha is the recommendable *single-quinta*.
★★★★ 1992 Warre's Late Bottled Vintage £££

Ⅰ **Warwick Estate** [wo-rik] (*Stellenbosch*, South Africa) Source of some of South Africa's best reds, including a good *Bordeaux*-blend called Trilogy. The *Cabernet Franc* grows extremely well here. ★★★★★ 1999 Trilogy ££

Washington State Underrated (especially in the US) state whose dusty irrigated vineyards produce classy *Riesling, Sauvignon*, and *Merlot. Col Solare; Columbia; Columbia Crest; L'Ecole No. 41; Hedges; Hogue; Kiona; Leonetti Cellars; Quilceda Creek;* Staton Hills; Ch. Ste. Michelle; *Paul Thomas;* Walla Walla Vintners; *Waterbrook;* Andrew Will; *Woodward Canyon.*

Ⅰ **Waterbrook** (*Washington State*) High-quality winery with stylish *Sauvignon Blanc, Viognier,* and *Chardonnay,* as well as berryish reds.

Jimmy Watson Trophy (*Victoria*, Australia) Coveted trophy given annually to the best young (still-in-barrel) red at the Melbourne Wine Show. Often criticized for hyping stuff that is not necessarily representative of what you'll be drinking when the wine gets in the bottle.

Ⅰ **Geheimrat J. Wegeler Deinhard** [vayg-lur dine-hard] (Germany) Once family-owned producer, now part of Henkell Söhnlein. Wines include top *Mosels* such as *Bernkasteler Doctor* and Wehlener Sonnenuhr.

Wehlen [vay-lehn] (*Mosel-Saar-Ruwer*, Germany) *Mittelmosel village* making fresh, sweet, honeyed wines; look for the *Sonnenuhr* vineyard. JJ Prüm; SA Prüm; *Richter; Selbach-Oster; Wegeler Deinhard.*

Ⅰ **Weingut Dr. Robert Weil** [vile] (*Rheingau*, Germany) Suntory-owned, family-run winery with stunning dry and *late-harvest* wines.

Ⅰ **Bodegas y Cavas de Weinert** [vine-nurt] (Argentina) Excellent *Cabernet Sauvignon* specialist, whose soft, ripe wines last extraordinarily well.

Weingut [vine-goot] (Germany) Wine estate.

Weinkellerei [vine-keh-lur-ri] (Germany) Cellar or winery.

Ⅰ **Dr Weins-Prüm** [vines-proom] (*Mosel-Saar-Ruwer*, Germany) Fine *Riesling* from top sites. ★★★★★ 1995 Wehlener Sonnenuhr Riesling Auslese £££

Weinviertel [vine-vehr-tel] (Austria) The largest Austrian wine region of all, seldom thrilling but often good for light whites.

🍇 **Weissburgunder** [vice-bur-goon-dur] (Germany/Austria) The *Pinot Blanc* in Germany and Austria. Relatively rare, so often made with care.

Ⅰ **Weissherbst** [vice-hairbst] (*Baden,* Germany) Spicy, berryish dry rosé made from various different grape varieties.

🍇 **Welschriesling** [velsh-reez-ling] Aka *Riesling Italico, Lutomer, Olasz, Laski Rizling.* Often dull grape, unrelated to the *Rhine Riesling.* Can make good dry wine in Austria; at its best when affected by *botrytis.*

Ⅰ **Wendouree** (*Clare,* Australia) Small winery with a cult following for its often *Malbec*-influenced reds. Wines are very hard to find outside Australia but are well worth seeking out.

W

- **Wente Brothers** (*Livermore,* California) Gradually improving family company in the up-and-coming region of Livermore that, despite – or perhaps because of – such distracting enterprises as producing cigars and joint ventures in Mexico, Israel, and Eastern Europe, is still trailing in quality and value behind firms like *Fetzer.* The Canoe Ridge and Reliz Creek wines can be worthwhile, but *Murrieta's Well* is still the strongest card in the Wente pack. ★★★ 1999 Duetto Wente Vineyards ££££

- **Weingut Domdechant Werner'sches** [vine-goot dom-dekh-ahnt vayr-nehr-ches] (*Rheingau,* Germany) Excellent vineyard sites at *Hochheim* and *Riesling* grapes combine to produce a number of traditional wines that age beautifully. ★★★ 1997 Hochheimer Kirchenstück Riesling Spätlese ££

Western Australia Very separate from the rest of the continent – some of the people here seriously dream of secession – this state has a very separate wine industry. Growing steadily southwards from their origins in the warm Swan Valley, close to Perth, the vineyards now include *Margaret River* – focus of Western Australian winemaking and fine for *Cabernet* and *Chardonnay*, Pemberton (a good area for *Pinot Noir*), and Great Southern.

- **De Wetshof Estate** [vets-hof] (*Robertson,* South Africa) *Chardonnay* pioneer, Danie de Wet makes up to seven different styles of wine for different markets. The "Sur Lie" produced in the same way as *Muscadet* is probably the most interesting. ★★★ 2001 Lesca Chardonnay £

- **William Wheeler Winery** (*Sonoma,* California) Inventive producer whose Quintet brings together such diverse grapes as the *Pinot Meunier,* the *Pinot Noir, Grenache,* and *Cabernet Sauvignon.*

- **White Cloud** (New Zealand) Commercial white made by *Nobilo.* **White port** (*Douro,* Portugal) Semi-dry aperitif, drunk by its makers with tonic water and ice, which shows what they think of it. *Churchill's* make a worthwhile version. ★★★★ 1952 Presidential Porto Reserve Golden White Da Silva £

- **Whitehall Lane** (*Napa Valley,* California) Producer of an impressive range of *Merlots* and *Cabernets.*

- **Wien** [veen] (Austria) Region close to the city of Vienna, producing ripe-tasting whites and reds. Mayer; Wieninger.

- **Fritz Wieninger** [vee-nin-gur] (Wien, Austria) Characterful wines with depth and elegance.

- **Wignall's** (*Western Australia,* Australia) *Pinot Noir* of originality and conviction.

- **Wild Horse** (*San Luis Obispo,* California) *Chardonnays, Pinot Blancs,* and *Pinot Noirs* are all good, but the perfumed *Malvasia Bianca* is the star.

- **Willakenzie Estate** (*Oregon,* USA) Newish, modern property with elegant wines of great promise. **Willamette Valley** [wil-AM-et] (*Oregon*) The heart of Oregon's *Pinot Noir* vineyards, on slopes that drain into the Willamette River.

- **William & Humbert** (*Jerez,* Spain) Very good Pando fino and Dos Cortados Palo Cortado, reliable Dry Sack medium amontillado.

- **Williams Selyem** [sel-yem] (*Sonoma,* California) Recently dissolved partnership producing fine *Burgundian*-style *Chardonnay* and *Pinot Noir.* **Wiltingen** [vill-ting-gehn] (*Mosel-Saar-Ruwer,* Germany) *Saar* village, making elegant, slatey wines. Well known for the *Scharzhofberg* vineyard.

- **Wing Canyon** (*Mount Veeder,* California) Small *Cabernet Sauvignon* specialist with vineyards high in the hills of *Mount Veeder.* Great, intense, blackcurranty wines. **Winkel** [vin-kel] (*Rheingau,* Germany) Village with a reputation for complex delicious wine, housing *Schloss Vollrads* estate. *Winzerverein/Winzergenossenschaft* [vint-zur-veh-rine/vint-zur-geh-noss-en-shaft] (Germany) Co-operative.

- **Wirra Wirra Vineyards** (*McLaren Vale,* Australia) First-class *Riesling* and *Cabernet* that, in best vintages, is sold as The Angelus. ★★★★★ 1998 Wirra Wirra RSW Shiraz ££; ★★★★ 1999 The Angelus Cabernet Sauvignon £££

T **Hans Wirsching** [veer-shing] (*Franken*, Germany) Large estate with very good vineyards, producing structured, elegant wines. One of the more go-ahead producers in Franken.

T **Wither Hills** (*Marlborough*, New Zealand) Instantly successful new venture from Brent Marris – former winemaker at *Delegat's*. The concentrated Pinot Noir is especially good. ★★★★ 2001 Sauvignon Blanc ££; ★★★ 2000 Pinot Noir ££

T **WO (Wine of Origin)** (South Africa) Official European-style certification system that is taken seriously in South Africa.

T **J.L. Wolf** [volf] (*Pfalz*, Germany) Classy estate, recently reconstituted by *Dr. Loosen*. ★★★★ 2001 Wachenheimer Goldbachel Spätlese Trocken £££

T **Wolfberger** [volf-behr-gur] (*Alsace*, France) Brand used by the dynamic Eguisheim cooperative for highly commercial wines.

T **Wolffer Estate** (*New York*) Long Island winery gaining a local following for its *Merlot* and *Chardonnay*.

T **Wolff-Metternich** [volf met-tur-nikh] (*Baden*, Germany) Good, rich *Riesling* from the granite slopes of *Baden*.

T **Woodward Canyon** (*Washington State*) Small producer of characterful but subtle *Chardonnay* and *Bordeaux*-style reds that compete with some of the over-hyped efforts from California. *Semillons* are pretty impressive too.

Württemberg [voor-thm-behrg] (Germany) *Anbaugebiet* surrounding the Neckar area, producing more red than any other German region.

T **Würzburg** [foor-ts-burg] (*Franken*, Germany) Great *Silvaner* country, though there are some fine *Rieslings* too. Some excellent steep vineyards. Bürgerspital; *Juliusspital*.

T **Wyken** (*Suffolk*, UK) Producer of one of England's most successful red wines (everything's relative) and rather better *Bacchus* white.

T **Wyndham Estate** (*Hunter Valley*, Australia) Ultracommercial *Hunter/Mudgee* producer that, like *Orlando*, now belongs to Pernod-Ricard. Wines are distinctly drier than they used to be, but they are still recognizably juicy in style. Quite what that firm's French customers would think of these often rather jammy blockbusters is anybody's guess. ★★★★ 2000 Wyndham Estate Bin 555 Shiraz £; ★★★★ 2001 Bin 777 Semillon £

T **Wynns** (*Coonawarra*, Australia) Subsidiary of *Penfolds*, based in *Coonawarra* and producer of the *John Riddoch Cabernet* and Michael *Shiraz*, both of which are only produced in good vintages and sell fast at high prices. There is also a big buttery *Chardonnay* and a commercial *Riesling*. ★★★★ 2001 Wynns Coonawarra Estate Riesling £

X

T **Xanadu** [za-na-doo] (*Margaret River*, Australia) The reputation here was built on *Semillon*, but the *Cabernet* and *Chardonnay* are both good, too. A takeover by venture capitalists who are eager to buy more wineries is helping to catapult Xanadu into the ranks of Australia's most dynamic producers. ★★★★ 2001 Xanadu Secession Shiraz Cabernet Sauvignon £

❦ **Xarel-lo** [sha-rehl-loh] (*Catalonia*, Spain) Fairly basic grape exclusive to *Catalonia*. Used for *Cava*; best in the hands of *Jaume Serra*. ★★★ NV Jaume Serra Cava Brut Reserva £

❦ **Xynasteri** [ksee-nahs-teh-ree] (Cyprus) Indigenous white grape.

Y

"Y" d'Yquem [ee-grek dee-kem] (*Bordeaux*, France) Hideously expensive dry wine of *Ch. d'Yquem*, which, like other such efforts by *Sauternes châteaux*, is of greater academic than hedonistic interest. (Under ludicrous Appellation Contrôlée rules, dry white wine from Sauternes properties has to be labelled as "Bordeaux Blanc" – like the region's very cheapest dry white wine.)

Yakima Valley [yak-ih-mah] (*Washington State*) Principal winegrowing region of *Washington State*. Particularly good for *Merlot, Riesling,* and *Sauvignon*. Blackwood Canyon; Chinook; *Columbia Crest; Columbia Winery; Hogue; Kiona;* Ch. Ste. Michelle; Staton Hills; Stewart; Tucker; Yakima River.

Yalumba [ya-lum-ba] (*Barossa Valley*, Australia) Associated with *Hill-Smith, Heggies, Pewsey-Vale,* and *Jansz* in Australia, *Nautilus* in New Zealand, and *Voss* in California. Producers of good-value reds and whites under the Oxford Landing label. Also produces more serious vineyard-designated reds, dry and sweet whites, and appealing sparkling wine, including *Angas Brut* and the excellent Cuvée One *Pinot Noir-Chardonnay.* ★★★★ 1998 The Menzies £££

Yarra Ridge [ya-ra] (Australia) *Mildara-Blass* label that might lead buyers to imagine that its wines all come from vineyards in the *Yarra Valley*. In fact, like *Napa Ridge,* this is a brand that is used for wine from vineyards in other regions. European laws, which are quite strict on this kind of thing, also apply to imported non-European wines, so bottles labelled "Yarra" and sold in the EU will be from Yarra.

Yarra Valley [ya-ra] (*Victoria*, Australia) Historic wine district whose "boutiques" make top-class *Burgundy*-like *Pinot Noir* and *Chardonnay* (*Coldstream Hills* and *Tarrawarra*), some stylish *Bordeaux*-style reds and, at *Yarra Yering*, a brilliant *Shiraz. De Bortoli; Dom. Chandon (Green Point); Coldstream Hills;* Diamond Valley; *Long Gully; Mount Mary;* Oakridge; St. Huberts; Seville Estate; *Tarrawarra; Yarra Yering; Yering Station.*

Yarra Yering [ya-ra yeh-ring] (*Yarra Valley*, Australia) Bailey Carrodus proves that the *Yarra Valley* is not just *Pinot Noir* country by producing a complex *Cabernet* blend, including a little *Petit Verdot* (Dry Red No.1) and a *Shiraz* (Dry Red No.2), in which he puts a bit of *Viognier.* Underhill is the *second label.*

Yecla [yeh-klah] (Spain) Generally uninspiring red wine region.

Yellowglen (South Australia) Producer of uninspiring basic sparkling wine and some really fine top-end fare, including the "Y", which looks oddly reminiscent of a sparkling wine called "J" from Judy Jordan in California.

Yering Station (*Victoria*, Australia) High quality young *Yarra Valley* estate, with rich, but stylish, *Chardonnay* and *Pinot Noir.* ★★★★ 1999 Reserve Chardonnay £££; ★★★★ 1998 Yarrabank Cuvee ££

Yeringberg (*Victoria*, Australia) Imposing old *Yarra Valley* estate making *Rhône* style reds and whites that are worth looking out for.

Yonder Hill (*Stellenbosch*, South Africa) New winery making waves with well-oaked reds. ★★★★ 2000 Merlot ££

Ch. Yon-Figeac [yo'n fee-jak] (*Bordeaux*, France) Not as fine as Château Figeac itself, but this Grand Cru Classé's wines are supple and fruity; very attractive, but not immensely long-lived.

Yonne [yon] (*Burgundy*, France) Northern *Burgundy* département in which *Chablis* is to be found.

Young's (California, USA) *Barbera* and *Zinfandel* are the ones to look for.

Ch. d'Yquem [dee-kem] (*Sauternes Premier Cru Supérieur, Bordeaux,* France) Sublime *Sauternes.* The grape pickers are sent out several times to select the best grapes. Not produced every year.

Z

℗ **Zaca Mesa** [za-ka may-sa] (*Santa Barbara,* California) Fast-improving winery with a focus on spicy *Rhône* varietals.

℗ **Zandvliet** [zand-fleet] (*Robertson,* South Africa) Estate well-thought-of in South Africa for its *Merlot.*

℗ **ZD** [zee-dee] (*Napa,* California) Long-established producer of very traditional, Californian, oaky, tropically fruity *Chardonnay* and plummy *Pinot Noir.* Also the producer of the highly acclaimed *Abacus.*

Zell [tzell] (*Mosel-Saar-Ruwer,* Germany) Bereich of lower *Mosel* and village, making pleasant, flowery *Riesling.* Famous for the *Schwarze Katz* (black cat) *Grosslage.*

Zema Estate [zee-mah] (*South Australia*) High-quality *Coonawarra* estate with characteristically rich, berryish reds.

℗ **Zenato** [zay-NAH-toh] (*Veneto,* Italy) Successful producer of modern *Valpolicella* (particularly *Amarone*), *Soave,* and *Lugana.* ★★★★★ 1999 Zenato Valpolicella Ripasso ££

Zentralkellerei [tzen-trahl-keh-lur-ri] (Germany) Massive central cellars for groups of co-operatives in six of the *Anbaugebiete* – the *Mosel-Saar-Ruwer* Zentralkellerei is Europe's largest cooperative.

℗ **Fattoria Zerbina** [zehr-bee-nah] (*Emilia-Romagna,* Italy) The eye-catching wine here is the Marzeno di Marzeno *Sangiovese-Cabernet,* but this producer deserves credit for making one of the only examples of Albana di Romagna to warrant the region's *DOCG* status.

℗ **Zevenwacht** [zeh-fen-fakht] (*Stellenbosch,* South Africa) One of South Africa's better producers of both *Shiraz* and *Pinotage.* Has also been successful with *Sauvignon Blanc* and *Pinot Noir.*

℗ **Zibibbo** [zee-BEE-boh] (*Sicily,* Italy) This is a good, light *Muscat* for easy summer drinking.

🍇 **Zierfandler** [zeer-fan-dlur] (Austria) Indigenous grape used in Thermenregion to make lightly spicy white wines. ★★★ 2000 Zierfandler Rutgipfler Die Creation Weinbau Hasenöhrl Thermenregion ££££

℗ **Zilliken** [tsi-li-ken] (*Saar,* Germany) Great *late-harvest Riesling* producer.

Zimbabwe An industry started by growing grapes in ex-tobacco fields is beginning to attain a level of international adequacy.

℗ **Dom. Zind-Humbrecht** [zind-hoom-brekht] (*Alsace,* France) Extraordinarily consistent producer of ultraconcentrated, single-vineyard wines and good *varietals* that have won numerous awards from the *International Wine Challenge* and drawn *Alsace* to the attention of a new generation of wine drinkers. ★★★★ 2000 Clos Saint Urbain Rangen Riesling ££££

🍇 **Zinfandel** [zin-fan-del] (California, Australia, South Africa) Versatile red grape, producing everything from dark, jammy, leathery reds in California, to (with a little help from sweet *Muscat*) pale pink "blush" wines, and even a little fortified wine that bears comparison with *port.* Also grown by *Cape Mentelle* and *Nepenthe* in Australia, and *Blauwklippen* in South Africa and, as *Primitivo,* by many producers in southern Italy. *Cline; Clos la Chance; De Loach; Edmeades; Elyse; Gary Farrell; Green & Red; Lamborn Family Vineyards; Ch. Potelle; Quivira; Rafanelli; Ravenswood; Ridge; Rocking Horse; Rosenblum; St. Francis; Steele; Storybook Mountain; Joseph Swan; Turley; Wellington.* ★★★★ 1999 St Francis Old Vines Zinfandel ££

℗ **Don Zoilo** [don zoy-loh] (*Jerez,* Spain) Classy *sherry* producer.

℗ **Zonin** [zoh-neen] (*Veneto,* Italy) Dynamic company producing good wines in the *Veneto, Piedmont,* and *Tuscany.*

🍇 **Zweigelt** [tzvi-gelt] (Austria) Berryish red wine grape, more or less restricted to Austria and Hungary. **Angerer; Hafner; Kracher; Müller; Umathum.** ★★★★ 2000 Zweigelt Barrique Weingut Skoff Styria £££

WINE
CHALLENGE
AWARDS
2002

International Wine Challenge

THE WORLD'S BIGGEST CONTEST

From tiny acorns... Way back in 1984, the wine writer and broadcaster Charles Metcalfe and I thought it might be interesting to compare a few English white wines with examples from other countries for a feature in *Wine*, the magazine we had launched a few months earlier. So, we set out a representative collection of some 50 carefully camouflaged bottles, in the basement of a London restaurant, and invited a group of experts to mark them out of 20. We never imagined that the home team would surprise everyone by beating well-known bottles from Burgundy, the Loire, and Germany – or that the modest enterprise we had immodestly called "The International Wine Challenge" would develop into the world's biggest, most respected wine competition.

The following year's Challenge attracted around 200 entries, while the third and fourth competitions saw numbers rise to 500 and 1,000 respectively. This annual doubling thankfully slowed down eventually, but by the end of the century we were within spitting distance of 10,000 entries, produced in countries ranging from France and Australia to Thailand and Uruguay. In May 2002 there were no fewer than 9,880 individual wines.

Origins in London

It is no accident that the International Wine Challenge was born in London. For centuries, British wine drinkers have enjoyed the luxury of being able to enjoy wines from a wide variety of countries. Samuel Pepys may have been a fan of Château Haut-Brion from Bordeaux, but plenty of other 18th-century sophisticates in London (and elsewhere in Britain) were just as excited about the sweet, late-harvest

Above: every wine's identity is hidden within specially-produced bags. Below: just some of the nearly 40,000 samples.

whites that were being produced at that time by early settlers in South Africa. More recently, as wine became steadily more popular, wines from California, Australia, New Zealand, and South America all found their way to these shores. Other arrivals were wines from regions, like Languedoc-Roussillon in France and Southern Italy, that had often been overlooked. As the 21st century dawned, Britain's biggest supermarket chains boasted daunting ranges of 700–800 different wines. A well-run competition provided an invaluable means of sorting the best and most interesting of these bottles from the rest.

The Tasting Panels

If the diversity of the wines on offer in Britain created a need for the International Wine Challenge, the calibre of this country's wine experts provided the means with which to run the competition. The nation that spawned the Institute of Masters of Wine – the trade body whose members have to pass the world's toughest wine exam – is also home to some of the most respected wine critics and merchants on the planet. These are the men and women – some 350 of them – who, along with winemakers and experts from overseas, make up the tasting panels for the Challenge. So, a set of wines might well have been judged by a group that included a traditional merchant, the buyer from a super-

Above: One cork was pulled every 20 seconds over nine days of tasting. Below: Robert Joseph and competition Co-Chairman Charles Metcalfe are surrounded by just some of the 350 tasters.

market chain, an Australian winemaker, a French sommelier, and a Portuguese wine critic. Argument between these diverse palates is surprisingly rare; when agreement is impossible, Co-Chairmen Robert Joseph, Charles Metcalfe, and Derek Smedley MW are called in to adjudicate.

Two-round format

During the first of the two rounds of the competition, wines are assessed to decide whether or not they are worthy of an award – be it a medal or a seal of approval. At this stage, typicality is taken into account, and tasters are informed that they are dealing, for example, with Chablis, Chianti, or South African Chenin Blanc. Around 36 per cent of the wines will leave the competition with no award. A further 30 per cent will receive Seals of Approval; the remainder will be given Gold, Silver, or Bronze medals.

The entries that have been thought to be medal-worthy in the first round, and the "seeded" entries that have already won recognition in the previous year's competition, then pass directly on to the second round. Now, the judges face the trickier task of deciding on the specific award each wine should receive – if any (they can still demote or throw wines out completely). At this stage, the wines are still grouped by grape and region, but now the wine's origins remain secret – there is no place for prejudices on behalf of or against a region or country.

Super-Jurors

As a final check, after it has been open for an hour or so, every wine goes before a team of "Super-Jurors". These are mostly Masters of Wine (including 39 of the just over 225 who have passed the gruelling exam since it was first set nearly half a century ago), and professional buyers from leading merchants and retailers whose daily work involves the accurately asses-

Helen McGinn, senior buyer for Tesco, Britain's biggest wine retailer, is a regular Super-Juror for the International Wine Challenge.

sment of hundreds of wines. The vital role of the Super-Jurors is both to ensure that tasters have not been overly harsh on wines that were reticent when first poured, or on wines with subtle cork taint that was initially unnoticed – and to watch out for entries that may have been over-estimated because of the immediate attraction of oakiness, for example. If two Super-Jurors agree, they can jointly up- or down-grade a wine.

TROPHY WINNERS

The Super-Jurors also decide which Gold medal winners deserve the additional recognition of a Trophy. These supreme awards can be given for any style, region, or nationality of wine. The judges are free to withhold trophies and to create them as they see appropriate (this year's Marsanne Trophy is a good example). The 2002 Trophy winners were as follows:

Cabernet/Merlot d'Arenberg The Coppermine Road Cabernet Sauvignon 2000
Shiraz Eileen Hardy Shiraz 1997
Bordeaux (the Edmond Penning Rowsell Trophy) Pavillon Rouge 1996
Italian Red Scrimaglio, Monferrato Rosso Tantra 1999
Pinot Noir Tarrawarra 1999
Pinotage Rijks Private Cellar 2000
Portuguese Red Caves Velhas Romeira 3 Carvalhos 1999
Spanish Red Freixenet, Prior Terrae 1998
Tempranillo Raimat 1998
Chardonnay Bodega Catena Zapata, Chardonnay 2000
Gewurztraminer Domaine Weinbach, Cuvée Laurence 1998
Pinot Gris Jechtinger Eichert, Grauer Burgunder Spätlese Trocken, Burg Sponeck Selecktion 2000

Riesling Weingut Fries, Wehlener Sonnenuhr Riesling Spätlese
Trocken 2001
Joh Joh Prüm, Wehlener Sonnenuhr Riesling Auslese 1995
Rousanne Château Puech-Haut, Tête de Cuvée Blanc 2000
Late Harvest Horst Sauer, Escherndorfer Lump Riesling
Trockenbeerenauslese 2000
Zind Humbrecht, Pinot Gris Rangen, Sélection Grains Nobles 1998
Icewine / Finest German Vier Jahreszeiten, Dürkenheimer Steinberg
Eiswein 1998
Fortified Muscat Campbells Rutherglen Muscat
Madeira Henriques & Henriques 15 Year Old Bual
Marsala Cantine Florio, Terre Arse Marsala Vergine 1991
Port Churchill's Vintage Port 1985
Sherry Barbadillo Obispo Gascon Palo Cortado

Top Trophy winners
Finest Red Freixenet Prior Terrae 1998
Finest White Vier Jahreszeiten Dürkenheimer Steinberg Eiswein 1998
Finest Sparkling (The Daniel Thibault Trophy) Piper Heidsieck 1995
Finest Fortified Churchill's Vintage Port 1985

GOOD VALUE AWARDS

We are often asked if we take account of the price of the wines we are
tasting. How can one judge a £3.99 Bulgarian red in the same way as a £39
Bordeaux? In fact, knowing how much a wine costs is
actually a hindrance: we all have our own notion of
value and prestige, and prices can go up or down after
the competition. So, all of the medals listed on the
following pages were earned irrespective of price.

But that's not to say that we're not interested in
value for money. Once the competition is over and the
medals and Seals of Approval have been distributed,
we carefully compare awards with prices (*see chart on
page 269)*. Entries that cost significantly less than the average for their level
of medal get their own Good Value awards, over 750 of which are listed in
the following pages, along with Gold medal winners available in the UK.

Following a separate blind-tasting by the super-jurors of the most
highly-rated and widely-available Good Value wines, the very best buys
of all are named *Great* Value Wines of the Year. Look out for these; they
tend to fly out of the shops very quickly and, of course, once a vintage
or cuvée has sold out, it can never be replaced.

THE GREAT VALUE WINES OF THE YEAR

Red
Merlot Reserva de Gras, Viña Montgras 2000, Chile
Tatachilla McLaren Vale Shiraz 2000, Australia
Chianti Cantine Leonardo 2001, Italy
J. St Honoré Vin de Pays Syrah 2001, France

White
Hardys Nottage Hill Chardonnay 2001, Australia
Winter Hill White, Foncalieu 2001, France
Alamos Chardonnay, Catena Zapata 2000, Argentina

Rosé
Fetzer Vineyards Valley Oaks Syrah Rosé 2001, California

Sparkling
Deutz Marlborough Cuvée, New Zealand
Jansz, Australia
Andre Simon Champagne Brut 1995, France

Fortified
Graham's Crusted Port Bottled 1999, Portugal
Waitrose Solera Jerezana Dry Amontillado Sherry, Spain
Campbells of Rutherglen Muscat, Australia

CATEGORY		STILL REDS AND WHITES	SPARKLING, PORT, AND MADEIRA	SWEET, FORTIFIED, MUSCAT, AND SHERRY
Gold medal	Ⓖ	*Less than* **£12.51**	*Less than* **£20.01**	*Less than* **£15.01**
Silver medal	Ⓢ	*Less than* **£7.51**	*Less than* **£15.01**	*Less than* **£10.01**
Bronze medal	Ⓑ	*Less than* **£5.01**	*Less than* **£10.01**	*Less than* **£7.51**
Seal of Approval	A	*Less than* **£4.01**	*Less than* **£7.51**	*Less than* **£5.01**

HOW TO USE THE AWARDS LIST

Every wine in this list gained an award at the 2002 International WINE Challenge. The wines are listed by country and style, with up to six headings: red, white, sweet, rosé, sparkling, and fortified.

Under each heading the wines are listed in price order, from the least to the most expensive. Wines of the same price are listed in medal order: Gold, Silver, and Bronze.

All Silver and Bronze medal winners and Seal of Approval wines listed are entries that were also given Good Value awards, following comparison of their retail price and the average price for the award they received in the International Wine Challenge. Following consultation with leading off-licences, appropriate price limits were established for particular styles of wine. A Good Value sparkling wine or port, for example, might sell at a higher price than a red table wine with the same medal.

This list does not include the Silver and Bronze medal winners and Seal of Approval wines that did not win Good Value awards (for these, visit internationalwinechallenge.com). All of the 230 Gold medal winners and Trophy winners – the finest wines in the competition – that are available in the UK, do appear. For full details of the price limits that were used to allocate Good Value awards, turn to page 269.

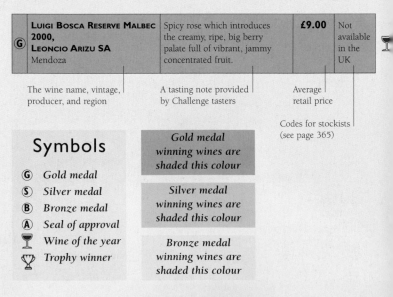

Ⓖ	**LUIGI BOSCA RESERVE MALBEC 2000,** **LEONCIO ARIZU SA** Mendoza	Spicy rose which introduces the creamy, ripe, big berry palate full of vibrant, jammy concentrated fruit.	**£9.00**	Not available in the UK

The wine name, vintage, producer, and region

A tasting note provided by Challenge tasters

Average retail price

Codes for stockists (see page 365)

Symbols

Ⓖ *Gold medal*
Ⓢ *Silver medal*
Ⓑ *Bronze medal*
Ⓐ *Seal of approval*
🍷 *Wine of the year*
🏆 *Trophy winner*

Gold medal winning wines are shaded this colour

Silver medal winning wines are shaded this colour

Bronze medal winning wines are shaded this colour

ARGENTINA

A few years ago, Australia was the undisputed champion of the New World when it came to offering value for money. Then Chile arrived to give the Aussies some competition, and now it's the turn of the Argentines. There are – inevitably – plenty of Cabernets, Merlots, and Chardonnays (including the dazzling Gold Medal winning Alamos from Catena), but there are also some styles that are uniquely Argentine, such as the grapey Torrontes whites, the peppery reds made from the Malbec, and the refreshingly juicy ones made from the Bonarda.

ARGENTINA • WHITE

(A)	**ASDA ARGENTINIAN TORRONTES 2001, LA RIOJANA** La Rioja	Prominent apricot scents and flavours.	**£3.50**	BGL
(A)	**SANTA FLORENTINA FAMATINA VALLEY TORRONTES 2001, LA RIOJANA** La Rioja	Generous and balanced. Lengthy finish.	**£3.50**	TOS ASD SAF
(B)	**MALAMBO CHENIN CHARDONNAY 2001, BODEGAS ESMERALDA** Mendoza	A user-friendly wine with good citrus fruit flavours and some weight. Clean and refreshing.	**£4.00**	BWL JSM
(A)	**SANTA JULIA CHENIN BLANC CHARDONNAY 2001, FAMILIA ZUCCARDI** Mendoza	Tropical green fruit aromas. Ripe.	**£4.00**	THI
(B)	**SAFEWAY ARGENTINIAN CHARDONNAY 2001, SANTA ANA** Mendoza	Taut lemon zest and butterscotch on the nose and palate. A fine example of measured oak use.	**£4.00**	SAF
(A)	**NAVARRO CORREAS CHARDONNAY 2001, VIÑAS LA HEREDAD** Mendoza	Pears and green apples. Full-bodied.	**£4.00**	MOR
(B)	**LA NATURE ORGANIC TORRONTES 2001, LA RIOJANA** La Rioja	Soft, peachy nose. Fresh acidity leads the attack on the light-bodied palate of good fruit concentration.	**£4.50**	JSM CWS ASD SAF
(S)	**ETCHART RIO DE PLATA TORRONTES 2001, BODEGAS ETCHART** Salta	A pronounced nose of peaches, flowers and vanilla. Good weight and depth of flavour on the palate.	**£5.00**	BAB COE PEA CAX

(S) **INTI CHARDONNAY 2001,** **LA RIOJANA** La Rioja	Refreshingly simple with rich fruit, excellent acidity and balance. Refined finish with mineral depth and complexity.	**£5.00**	VER
(G) **ALAMOS CHARDONNAY 2000,** **BODEGA CATENA ZAPATA** Mendoza	Concentrated citrus nose with notes of melons and nuttiness. Harmonious oak balance with a touch of vanilla.	**£6.00**	BWL MWW ODD UNS

ARGENTINA • RED

(A) **TESCO ARGENTINIAN RED NV,** **LA RIOJANA** Famatina Valley	Soft, light, and fruity style.	**£3.00**	TOS
(A) **LLAS LLANURAS ARGENTINE** **MALBEC 2001, LES GRANDS** **CHAIS DE FRANCE** Mendoza	Soft and spicy berry-driven style.	**£3.00**	ALD
(A) **VALLE ALTO MERLOT 2000,** **VALLE ALTO WINERY** Mendoza	Soft damson fruit palate. Ripe.	**£4.00**	BAB CHC
(A) **CASATERRA BONARDA 2001,** **MEDRANO** Mendoza	Powerful, ripe hedgerow fruit flavours.	**£4.00**	MOR OWC WWT
(A) **ASDA ARGENTINIAN** **TEMPRANILLO 2001,** **LA AGRICOLA** Mendoza	Good concentration of straightforward fruit.	**£4.00**	THI
(A) **STOWELLS OF CHELSEA** **MALBEC TEMPRANILLO NV,** **MATTHEW CLARK** Mendoza	Pleasant, uncomplicated everyday drinking.	**£4.00**	SAF MRN
(A) **BODEGAS ROSARIO** **BONARDA 2001,** **JFL ARGENTINA** Mendoza	Ripe red bramble fruit character.	**£4.00**	NTD
(B) **BODEGAS ROSARIO** **MALBEC 2000,** **JFL ARGENTINA** Mendoza	Fragrant and floral, this shows good depth and balance. Spicy, medium length finish.	**£4.00**	NTD
(B) **BODEGAS ROSARIO** **SHIRAZ 2001,** **JFL ARGENTINA** Mendoza	Rich, round and gently spicy. Some light green pepper character. Well coloured and long.	**£4.00**	NTD

(A)	**TESCO PICAJUAN PEAK MALBEC 2001, LA AGRICOLA** Mendoza	Inky fruit with supple tannins.	**£4.00**	TOS
(B)	**SOMERFIELD ARGENTINE TEMPRANILLO 2001, LA AGRÍCOLA** Mendoza	Jammy wine with heady, baked berry fruit aromas. The palate is soft and spicy with decent tannic structure.	**£4.00**	SMF
(A)	**CO-OP ARGENTINE MALBEC 2001, LA RIOJANA** La Rioja	Smoky with blackberry depth.	**£4.00**	CWS
(A)	**SAFEWAY ARGENTINIAN CABERNET SAUVIGNON 2001, LA RIOJANA** Famatina Valley	Fruit-driven with a soft heart.	**£4.00**	SAF
(A)	**NAVARRO CORREAS COLLECCION PRIVADA MALBEC 2000, VIÑAS LA HEREDAD** Mendoza	Good balance and spicy fruit.	**£4.00**	MOR
(B)	**SAFEWAY ARGENTINIAN SHIRAZ 2001, LA RIOJANA** Famatina Valley	Plummy fruit aromas and a jammy fruit palate. Very good lingering smoky finish.	**£4.30**	SAF
(B)	**ETCHART CAFAYATE MALBEC 1999, BODEGAS ETCHART** Mendoza	Drinking well now, this wine shows a touch of maturity in its ripe tannic structure.	**£4.50**	NTD WCR LON CAX
(B)	**ETCHART RIO DE PLATA MALBEC 2001, BODEGAS ETCHART** Mendoza	Earthy and meaty on the palate with a good touch of pepper. Well-made.	**£4.50**	CAX
(S)	**TERRA ORGANICA SANTA JULIA BONARDA SANGIOVESE 2001, FAMILIA ZUCCARDI** Mendoza	Sweet leather aromas. Cinnammon spice and unctuous raspberry and blackberry fruit. Earthy, with good length.	**£4.50**	PUR THI
(B)	**GRAFFIGNA SYRAH CABERNET NV, SANTIAGO GRAFFIGNA** San Juan	A restrained, elegant nose of mineral elements and notes of violets and scrub. Mouthwatering red fruit.	**£5.00**	HVB
(B)	**GRAFFIGNA MALBEC SELECCIÓN ESPECIAL 2000, SANTIAGO GRAFFIGNA** San Juan	A light and fresh example, showing spicy, white-pepper character on the nose and palate.	**£5.00**	HVB
(S)	**ARGENTO MALBEC 2001, BODEGAS ESMERALDA** Mendoza	Violet nose. Red fruit flavours with just a touch of animal aroma.	**£5.00**	BWL ASD SMF TOS

(B)	**FINCA LAS MARIAS BARBERA 2001, SA NIETO CARBO Y A SENETINER** Mendoza	A wine made from a Piedmont variety rapidly gaining popularity on the world stage.	**£5.00**	CPR
(S)	**SANTA JULIA BONARDA SANGIOVESE 2001, FAMILIA ZUCCARDI** Mendoza	Bags of meaty, savoury, dark fruit with minerally undertones. Ripe blackcurrant fruit with chocolatey oak.	**£5.00**	WTS MRN
(B)	**SANTA JULIA CABERNET SAUVIGNON 2001, FAMILIA ZUCCARDI** Mendoza	Good simple fruit and warm alcohol. A comforting wine that does not require too much thought.	**£5.00**	THI
(B)	**MONSTER SPICY RED 2001, PEÑAFLOR** San Juan	The palate bursts with fresh red raspberries. The nose is aromatic yet refined. Attractive garnet red.	**£5.00**	TOS
(B)	**ELEMENTOS RED 2000, PEÑAFLOR** San Juan	Cherry, redcurrant and subtle, toasty vanilla oak aromas. A touch of spice on the silky palate.	**£5.00**	JSM EHL
(B)	**BRIGHT BROTHERS RESERVE SHIRAZ 2001, PEÑAFLOR** San Juan	Bright and clean. A well balanced, fruity wine with a delicious peppery character and lifted aromas.	**£5.00**	JSM EHL CWS
(B)	**LA CONSULTA MALBEC 2000, FINCA LA CELIA** Mendoza	An intriguing nose of tar and petrol is followed by a mouthful of juicy black olives and liquorice.	**£5.00**	RWM MRN
(B)	**INTI CABERNET SAUVIGNON 2001, LA RIOJANA** La Rioja	Attractively-made wine with sweet currant aromas and a supple palate showing good black fruit intensity.	**£5.00**	VER
(S)	**ALAMOS CABERNET SAUVIGNON 1999, NICHOLAS CATENA** Mendoza	Cigar box and oak character show on the nose. Ripe tannins and intense spicy fruit dominate the palate.	**£6.00**	BWL JSM MWW WSO
(S)	**TERRAZAS ALTO MALBEC 2000, BODEGA TERRAZAS** Mendoza	Deep bramble and blackcurrant aromas. Good depth of ripe berry fruit and a rounded opulent texture.	**£6.00**	UNS MAK WBR
(S)	**ADISENO RESERVE SHIRAZ 1999, ORFILA** Mendoza	Peppery blackberry and spice perfume. The palate has good richness and impeccable harmony of fruit and oak.	**£6.00**	IWS
(S)	**MALBEC 1999, LUIS CORREAS** Mendoz	Violets, grilled meats and dark ripe fruit flavours. Superb floral nose. Rich and satisfying.	**£6.50**	PAT

Oak Cask Pinot Noir 2000, Bodegas Trapiche Mendoza	Leather, vanilla, and attractive cherries and redcurrants are given added interest by a hint of vegetation.	**£7.00**	HBJ

AUSTRALIA

A quarter of a century ago, Australian wine was the subject of a Monty Python sketch. Today, we have enough confidence in the Aussies to spend more per bottle on their wine than we do on efforts from the other side of the Channel. Australian prices have admittedly gone up recently, and cheaper reds in particular are less impressive than they used to be, but there is a steady trend towards making subtler, more stylish, less obviously oaky wine – and a growing number of interesting reds and whites from recently-developed cooler regions.

AUSTRALIA • SPARKLING

B **Stamp of Australia Sparkling Chardonnay Pinot Noir NV, BRL Hardy** South Eastern Australia	Pretty Pinot colour and rich, nutty Chardonnay fruit. Pleasant fresh grass and creamy vanilla flavours. Long finish.	**£6.00**	TOS SAF JSM
A **Nottage Hill Sparkling Brut 1999, BRL Hardy** South Eastern Australia	Bright golden yellow with fresh acidity.	**£7.00**	SAF JSM
A **Omni Brut NV, BRL Hardy** South Eastern Australia	Brisk mousse. A creamy, seamless texture with fresh, bright citrus fruit and some yeasty brioche overtones.	**£7.00**	JSM
A **Jacob's Creek Chardonnay Pinot Noir NV, Orlando Wyndham** South Eastern Australia	Fresh, floral, lemony, and lovely.	**£7.00**	ASD TOS SAF WRC
B **Seaview Brut NV, Seaview Wines** South Eastern Australia	A gorgeous nose of freshly baked apple pie. Creamy texture smooths out the green apple palate.	**£7.00**	PEF
B **Deakin Estate Brut NV, Wingara** Victoria	Bright, clear, fresh fruit. A refreshing, zippy acidity races through the very crisp palate.	**£7.00**	LLW

(S)	**BANROCK STATION SPARKLING SHIRAZ NV, BRL HARDY** South Australia	Deep, spicy and rich. Aromas of coconut and toast add depth to the palate of red summer fruits.	**£8.00**	JSM TOS WTS
(B)	**YELLOWGLEN NV, BERINGER BLASS** South Eastern Australia	Yeasty richness. Green apple fruit with just a touch of mandarin oranges on the palate.	**£8.50**	ODD MWW
(S)	**BRUT NV, JANSZ** Tasmania	Light, lively fruit. A hint of toastiness adds weight to the bright, ripe, attractive palate.	**£10.00**	ODD SEL COC VGN
(B)	**YELLOWGLEN VINTAGE 1998, BERINGER BLASS** South Eastern Australia	Ripe, forward fruit with an elegant flowery touch. Nutty aromas rise from the broad, apple-infused palate.	**£10.00**	ODD MWW
(S)	**YARRA BURN SPARKLING 1999, BRL HARDY** Victoria	Well-balanced and packed with fruit. Crisp acidity and excellent ripeness. An attractive fizz with good length.	**£13.00**	MHW
(S)	**YARRABANK CUVEE 1998, YERING STATION** Victoria	Rich dry fruit complements a gently chalky texture and fine mousse for a tidy balance and yeasty finish.	**£13.50**	SCK
(S)	**YALUMBA 'D' BLACK 1996, YALUMBA** South Australia	The blackberry palate is ripe yet balanced, with a backbone of acidity. A distinctive, original red sparkler.	**£14.00**	NYW NWG

AUSTRALIA • WHITE

(B)	**AUSTRALIAN SEMILLON CHARDONNAY NV, PAUL SAPIN** South Eastern Australia	Full bodied and rich with fat tropical fruit flavours, this is well made and balanced.	**£2.30**	ROG SAF
(B)	**MHV SCENIC RIDGE SEMILLON CHARDONNAY NV, REDELLO WINES** New South Wales	Full, round and oily textured, this combines lime fruit with balanced oak.	**£3.70**	MHV
(A)	**NINE PINES VINEYARD MARSANNE 1999, CRANSWICK** New South Wales	Stone fruits and white flowers.	**£3.70**	MHV
(A)	**KALGOORIE SEMILLON CHARDONNAY 2001, SOUTHCORP** South Eastern Australia	Lemon scents. Pineapple fruit palate.	**£3.80**	NTD

	Wine	Description	Price	Stockists
(S)	**MHV AUSTRALIAN SEMILLON NV, REDELLO WINES** New South Wales	Ripe and zesty with a lemon and lime bouquet. Clean, fresh palate with a pleasant waxy character.	**£3.80**	MHV
(A)	**BANROCK STATION COLOMBARD CHARDONNAY 2001, BRL HARDY** South Eastern Australia	Smooth, seductive white fruit palate.	**£4.00**	TOS SAF SMF JSM
(A)	**WOODBURY CHARDONNAY VERDELHO 2001, WOODBURY CELLARS** South Eastern Australia	Golden in colour with a round, ripe fruit palate.	**£4.00**	ALD
(A)	**WEERI SEMILLION CHARDONNAY NV, CDL** New South Wales	White flowers and apple fruit.	**£4.00**	ALD
(A)	**MHV SCENIC RIDGE AUSTRALIAN CHARDONNAY NV, REDELLO WINES** New South Wales	Medium-bodied lemons, pineapples and cream.	**£4.00**	MHV
(B)	**KIDMAN WAY CHARDONNAY 2001, CRANSWICK** South Eastern Australia	Touches of honey and mango make this a very pleasing Chardonnay. Good finish.	**£4.00**	ASD MRN
(A)	**HAIR OF THE DINGO SEMILLON CHARDONNAY NV, KINGSLAND WINES & SPIRITS** South Eastern Australia	Honeyed citrus and mineral style.	**£4.00**	SPR BFD CFN CWS
(A)	**VINFIVE SEMILLON CHARDONNAY 2001, NXG** South Eastern Australia	Ripe melon balanced with lemon zest.	**£4.00**	RCH
(A)	**MASTERPEACE SEMILLON COLOMBARD CHARDONNAY 2001, ANDREW PEACE** Victoria	Ripe with good mouth-watering acidity.	**£4.00**	VER
(A)	**MIGHTY MURRAY WHITE 2001, ANDREW PEACE** Victoria	Well-balanced with a clean finish.	**£4.00**	ASD
(A)	**CO-OP AUSTRALIAN CHARDONNAY 2001, ANGOVE'S** South Australia	Fresh melon and citrus-driven style.	**£4.00**	CWS
(A)	**CO-OP JACARANDA HILL SEMILLON 2001, ANGOVE'S** South Eastern Australia	Citrus-driven with a waxy finish.	**£4.00**	CWS

(A) WALLABY CREEK CHARDONNAY 2000, D'AQUINO South Eastern Australia	Rich and ripe citrus style.	**£4.00**	ROD
(B) MIGHTY MURRAY CHARDONNAY 2001, ANDREW PEACE Victoria	Rich melon and tropical fruit balanced by piercing acidity. The finish is clean with decent persistence.	**£4.50**	ASD
(B) BANROCK STATION CHARDONNAY 2001, BRL HARDY South Eastern Australia	Bright, ripe lemon palate. A nose of white peaches displays restrained vanilla oak. Crisp and delicious.	**£4.50**	TOS SAF SMF WTS
(B) MARSANNE 2001, CRANSWICK South Eastern Australia	Vanilla and ripe tropical fruit. Well-structured, with good texture in the mouth and fresh acidity.	**£4.50**	ASD
(G) HARDYS NOTTAGE HILL CHARDONNAY 2001, BRL HARDY South Eastern Australia	Scented with toasty oak, which carries through onto the smooth, buttery palate. Beautiful integration of oak and fruit.	**£5.00**	JSM TOS SAF WTS
(B) JACOB'S CREEK CHARDONNAY 2001, ORLANDO WYNDHAM South Eastern Australia	Pure, fresh peaches on the palate are given a lift by a lick of vanilla spice.	**£5.00**	ASD JSM TOS WRC
(S) THOMAS MITCHELL MARSANNE 2000, MITCHELTON South Eastern Australia	Ripe, with touches of spice and pineapple on the palate. Greenish yellow colour. Quite heady.	**£5.00**	ODD WRC
(S) OXFORD LANDING CHARDONNAY 2001, YALUMBA South Australia	Clean and fresh with ripe tropical fruit aromas and canteloupe flavours. Zingy acidity and a decent finish.	**£5.00**	TOS ASD SBS SAF ODD
(B) EAGLEHAWK CHARDONNAY 2001, BERINGER BLASS South Eastern Australia	Peachy fruit and gentle creamy oak character, with enough acidity to lift the palate.	**£5.00**	SAF ASD
(S) PENFOLDS RAWSONS BIN 202 2001, SOUTHCORP South Australia	Floral and apricot aromas. A fresh palate with citrus and sherbet flavours. Elegant and long.	**£5.00**	WTS
(B) BAROSSA VALLEY SEMILLON 2000, BASEDOW South Australia	Fresh with a good weighty mouthfilling texture. Golden green colour and a smoky oak nose.	**£5.00**	WTS
(B) JINDALEE CHARDONNAY 2001, JINDALEE ESTATE South Eastern Australia	Typical Australian Chardonnay flavours; tropical fruit and oak. Faultlessly made. A crowd pleaser.	**£5.00**	SAF SMF JSM MRN

(B) **TESCO FINEST AUSTRALIAN CHARDONNAY RESERVE 2001, SIMEON WINES** South Eastern Australia	Attractive lemon crush flavours attack the mouth. Deep, creamy overtones.	**£5.00**	TOS
(B) **MASTERPEACE CHARDONNAY 2001, ANDREW PEACE**	Creme caramel nose. A palate of ripe tropical fruit. Big, soft and buttery. Fresh lime acidity.	**£5.00**	SAF
(B) **DEAKIN ESTATE SAUVIGNON BLANC 2001, WINGARA** Victoria	Fresh with herbaceous aromas. Balanced palate of ripe gooseberry and citrus fruit intensity.	**£5.00**	ODD
(S) **FAMILY RESERVE RIESLING 2001, DE BORTOLI WINES** South Eastern Australia	Apples and limes on the concentrated mouthful of flowers and fruit. A bright, refreshing lime juice finish.	**£5.80**	LAI
(S) **CHARDONNAY 2001, ST HALLETT WINERY** South Australia	Rich, yet fresh with ripe tropical fruit nuances balanced by citrus tones and lively acidity.	**£6.00**	TOS
(S) **LITTLE BOOMEY LIMITED RELEASE CHARDONNAY 2001, CABONNE CELLARS** New South Wales	Flowers, fruit and toasted cashews. Powerful palate of expressive white fruit. Fresh acidity. Long finish.	**£6.00**	TOS
(S) **RIDDOCH SAUVIGNON BLANC 2001, KATNOOK ESTATE** South Australia	Fat, buttery style with luscious tropical fruit flavours on the nose and palate. Good concentration and depth.	**£6.30**	BWL
(S) **THE OLIVE GROVE CHARDONNAY 2001, D'ARENBERG** South Australia	Rich style with intense tropical fruit on the nose and a harmonious palate showing well-judged oak..	**£6.50**	BWL ODD
(S) **THE HERMIT CRAB MARSANNE VIOGNIER 2001, D'ARENBERG** South Australia	A spiced apricot and peach nose and some honeyed fruit flavours on the palate.	**£6.50**	BWL ODD
(S) **TWO VINES VERDELHO CHARDONNAY 2001, RIVERINA ESTATE** South Eastern Australia	Ripe, fruity nose of tangerines and lemons. Creamy soft stone fruit on the palate, with balanced acidity.	**£6.50**	LAI
(S) **TAPESTRY CHARDONNAY 2001, TAPESTRY VINEYARDS** South Australia	Intense citrus and peach aromas on the nose. Opulent tropical fruit and layered oak toast.	**£6.90**	VKW
(S) **ANNIE'S LANE CHARDONNAY 2001, BERINGER BLASS** South Australia	Elegant wine with greengage and pineapple aromas and a lively citrus palate with fresh acidity.	**£7.00**	ODD

(S)	**THE ROTHBURY ESTATE HUNTER VALLEY VERDELHO 2001, BERINGER BLASS** New South Wales	Refreshing and aromatic with melon and a touch of spice. Long and harmonious with a touch of sweetness.	**£7.00**	ODD MRN
(S)	**REYNOLDS ORANGE LANDSCAPE CHARDONNAY 2001, CABONNE CELLARS** New South Wales	Smoke and vanilla on the nose. The palate is opulent and packed with ripe tropical fruit.	**£7.00**	D&D
(S)	**OMRAH UNOAKED CHARDONNAY 2001, PLANTAGANET** Western Australia	A lifted nose redolent of peach and tropical fruit leads to a mouthfilling palate showing amazing concentration.	**£7.00**	SMF
(S)	**SEMILLON SAUVIGNON BLANC 2001, ST HALLETT WINERY** South Australia	Waxy, unctuous Semillon and tart Sauvignon with crisp green fruit flavours. Balanced, with rich yet youthful citrus fruit.	**£7.00**	NEG
(S)	**VERDELHO 2001, TEMPLE BRUER** South Australia	Overt, vivacious nose of green and yellow fruits. Round, almost creamy mouthfeel; zingy yet ripe grapefruit.	**£7.50**	JEF

AUSTRALIA • RED

(A)	**BADGERS CREEK SHIRAZ CABERNET 2000, LES GRANDS CHAIS DE FRANCE** South Eastern Australia	Lively acidity. Bright red fruit.	**£3.00**	ALD
(A)	**CARRAMAR ESTATE MERLOT 2001, CASELLA WINES** South Eastern Australia	Spicy, ripe, vivid red plums.	**£4.00**	TOS
(B)	**TORTOISESHELL BAY MOURVEDRE SHIRAZ 2001, CASELLA WINES** South Eastern Australia	Light tannins and soft ripe strawberry fruit character. A pleasingly complex hint of leather.	**£4.00**	SWS SMF MRN
(A)	**MHV SCENIC RIDGE SHIRAZ MERLOT NV, REDELLO WINES** New South Wales	Peppery black fruit. Soft palate.	**£4.00**	MHV
(A)	**HAIR OF THE DINGO CABERNET SHIRAZ NV, KINGSLAND WINES & SPIRITS** South Eastern Australia	Spicy with blueberry pie character.	**£4.00**	SPR CFN CWS BFD
(B)	**JACARANDA HILL SHIRAZ 2001, ANGOVE'S** South Australia	Packed full of fresh and fruity plum and smoky oak character. This is an elegant wine.	**£4.00**	CWS

(A) SAFEWAY SHIRAZ CABERNET SAUVIGNON 2001, BRL HARDY South Eastern Australia	Some age. Soft, characterful fruit.	**£4.00**	SAF
(A) DE BORTOLI SHIRAZ CABERNET 2000, SPAR UK South Australia	Smokey with intense blackberry flavours.	**£4.00**	SPR
(A) WALLABY CREEK SHIRAZ 1999, D'AQUINO South Eastern Australia	Mature, silky red plum palate.	**£4.00**	ROD
(B) CO-OP AUSTRALIAN GRENACHE 2001, KINGSTON South Eastern Australia	An attractive nose and palate of singing red berry fruit. Smooth, velvety palate. Very attractive.	**£4.30**	CWS
(S) STONERIDGE SHIRAZ CABERNET SAUVIGNON NV, ANGOVES South Eastern Australia	Smoky capsicum and plum aromas over a lightly textured but flavour packed palate. Multilayered and complex.	**£4.50**	WRT
(B) SACRED HILL SHIRAZ CABERNET 2001, DE BORTOLI New South Wales	Well made, clean and appealing. Very attractive ripe fruit and a perfectly balanced palate.	**£4.50**	BOR
(B) BARRAMUNDI MERLOT 2000, CRANSWICK South Eastern Australia	This mouthful of damson fruit is etched with notes of spice box. Soft structure. Round and appealing.	**£4.50**	ASD
(B) CO-OP AUSTRALIAN MERLOT 2001, SIMEON South Eastern Australia	Soft and plummy wine with well integrated oak and supple tannins. The finish is warm and juicy.	**£4.80**	CWS
(B) MHV SCENIC RIDGE AUSTRALIAN MERLOT NV, REDELLO WINES New South Wales	Soft and plummy wine with good blackberry fruit intensity and supple, well-integrated tannins.	**£4.90**	MHV
(B) BANROCK STATION SHIRAZ 2001, BRL HARDY South Eastern Australia	Simple and easy. Just enough complexity to make it interesting but in no way hard work.	**£5.00**	JSM SMF TOS SAF
(B) HARDYS STAMP OF AUSTRALIA CABERNET SAUVIGNON MERLOT 2001, BRL HARDY South Australia	Vanilla oak and plum fruit. Well balanced, it has soft tannins and fruity acidity.	**£5.00**	LON JSM TOS
(B) JACOB'S CREEK GRENACHE SHIRAZ 2001, ORLANDO WYNDHAM South Eastern Australia	Pleasing redcurrant aromas and good spicy fruit on the palate. Very easy to appreciate.	**£5.00**	ASD TOS SAF WRC

(B) **YELLOW TAIL SHIRAZ 2001, CASELLA WINES** South Eastern Australia	Warm and smoky with peppery raspberry fruit flavours to the fore. Very deeply coloured.	**£5.00**	SWS MRN ODD CRS
(B) **JINDALEE MERLOT 2001, JINDALEE ESTATE** South Eastern Australia	Fresh and easy, light red fruit. Quite spicy with good length and pleasing balance.	**£5.00**	SAF
(B) **JINDALEE SHIRAZ 2001, JINDALEE ESTATE** South Eastern Australia	With its developed colour and pleasant herbal character this is a chewy but finely textured wine.	**£5.00**	MRN WTS UNS
(B) **KANARIE CREEK CABERNET SAUVIGNON 2001, ANGOVES** South Eastern Australia	The rich berry fruit is matched and supported by the careful use of wood. Easy drinking.	**£5.00**	WRT
(B) **CABERNET MERLOT 2000, ANDREW GARRETT VINEYARD ESTATES** South Eastern Australia	Rich and full bodied. Rounded but firm tannins and juicy dark ripe fruit.	**£5.00**	THI
(S) **GARNET POINT SHIRAZ CABERNET 2001, GARNET POINT VINEYARDS** South Eastern Australia	Intense fruit and vanilla oak aromas. This wine is complex, complete and has a delicious smoky finish.	**£5.00**	ASD BGN TOS MAK
(B) **WOOLPUNDA MERLOT 2000, THOMPSON VINTNERS** South Australia	Soft, ripe damson fruit palate. The nose has a whiff of vanilla oak. Very attractive. Clean and velvety.	**£5.00**	BBZ
(B) **SOUTHERN STAR AUSTRALIA MERLOT PETIT VERDOT 2001, KINGSLAND WINES & SPIRITS**	The plummy merlot and sharp, tannic petit verdot blend beautifully in this ripe, rich offering of power and structure.	**£5.00**	MAC BFD
(B) **GRENACHE 2001, PETER LEHMANN** South Australia	Ripe and fleshy, a typical Grenache. Warm and spicy baked fruit flavours to spare.	**£5.00**	ODD UNS JSM ASD
(B) **DEAKIN ESTATE CABERNET SAUVIGNON 2001, WINGARA** Victoria	This wine shows currant and vanilla essence on the nose. The palate is soft with blackberry richness.	**£5.00**	ODD
(S) **HARDYS NOTTAGE HILL SHIRAZ 2000, BRL HARDY** South Australia	Supple wine with lashings of smoky oak on the nose and a palate strewn with super-ripe blackberries.	**£5.30**	BGN JSM SPR
(S) **TATACHILLA BREAKNECKCREEK CABERNET SAUVIGNON 2001,** South Australia	This wine has deep, spicy fruit and a touch of chocolate on the nose.	**£5.50**	MWW JSM SAF

(S) **XANADU SECESSION SHIRAZ CABERNET SAUVIGNON 2001,** **XANADU WINES** Western Australia	Intense black ruby colour. The concentration continues on the palate with copious black fruit and spice flavours.	**£6.00**	ASD ODD
(S) **NOVELLO NERO 2001,** **CHAIN OF PONDS** South Australia	Spring meadow flowers, spices, and savoury notes. Ripe, rich fruit dosed with nutmeg and cinnamon.	**£6.00**	BWL
(S) **THE MILL SHIRAZ COWRA ESTATE 2000,** **WINDOWRIE ESTATE** New South Wales	Powerful wine with suede and smoke aromas. Concentrated blackberry flavours allied to firm tannins and sweet vanilla oak.	**£6.00**	CPR
(S) **SHIRAZ 2001,** **ST HALLETT WINERY** South Australia	A generous wine with lovely smoky, tarry fruit. A refined and balanced wine of medium weight.	**£6.00**	TOS
(S) **DEAKIN ESTATE MERLOT 2001,** **WINGARA** Victoria	This wine is packed with sweet, plummy fruit supported by attractive tannins and well-integrated oak.	**£6.00**	WTS ODD
(S) **BETHANY GRENACHE 2001,** **BETHANY WINES** South Australia	The nose is warm with sweet raspberry fruit. The palate is attractive, creamy, and succulent.	**£6.50**	D&D MWW
(S) **DEEN VAT 1 DURIF 2001,** **DE BORTOLI** New South Wales	A blackberry-scented wine with a significant but very well placed tannic structure.	**£6.50**	BOR
(S) **BIN 2000 SHIRAZ 2001,** **McGUIGAN** South Eastern Australia	A nose of cherries and spice. Medium-bodied this wine has an appealing, open character and a long finish.	**£6.50**	WER VNO CER
(S) **WYNDHAM ESTATE BIN 555 SHIRAZ 2000,** **ORLANDO WYNDHAM** South Eastern Australia	Soft and round with cranberry and ripe blackberry aromas. A supple structured wine with integrated tannins.	**£7.00**	SAF MRN NTD BAB
(S) **Y MERLOT 2000,** **YALUMBA** South Australia	Juicy ripe plum and black soft fruit. Fuit-driven yet sufficiently complex and robust to maintain interest.	**£7.00**	SAF TOS
(S) **WAKEFIELD ESTATE CABERNET SAUVIGNON 2001,** **WAKEFIELD ESTATE** South Australia	Very satisfying mint, berry fruit and cigar box character lead into this full and robust wine.	**£7.00**	SWS UNS
(S) **WAKEFIELD CLARE VALLEY MERLOT 2001,** **WAKEFIELD ESTATE** South Australia	This wine is a veritable tapestry of succulent berry fruit intermingled with supple tannin and creamy oak.	**£7.00**	SWS

(S) **YANGARRA PARK MERLOT 2001,** **YANGARRA PARK** South Eastern Australia	Classy Merlot scented with ripe, dark plums and a sprinkle of cinnamon. The palate offers ripe blackcurrant fruit.	**£7.00**	KJW WTS
(S) **SARANTOS MERLOT 1999,** **KINGSTON ESTATE WINES** South Australia	Refined and elegant, this Merlot offers aromas of raspberry leaves and dark ripe plums.	**£7.00**	EOO CER CMB P&R
(S) **HASELGROVE PICTURE SHIRAZ 2000, BARRINGTON ESTATES** South Australia	Very showy. The nose is filled with aromas of plum and roasted meat. The palate is mouthfilling and rich.	**£7.00**	SAF
(S) **THE COCOPARRA VINEYARD SHIRAZ 1999,** **CRANSWICK** New South Wales	This blackberry-infused beauty is generously laced with vanilla, leather, and smoke. Rich, round, and velvety.	**£7.00**	GAR
(S) **BLEWITT SPRINGS SHIRAZ 1999,** **HILLSVIEW VINEYARDS** South Australia	Enormous. A rich concoction of fruit, spice, and leather. There are meaty notes and a lovely creamy oak element.	**£7.50**	ALL
(G) **ELLEN LANDING SHIRAZ 2000,** **SALENA ESTATE** South Australia	A lovely aromatic flavour of strawberries and redcurrants. Crisp acidity and a good grip of tannin.	**£8.00**	PAT
(G) **HANDPICKED SHIRAZ 2000,** **CABONNE CELLARS** New South Wales	An intense mint and spice nose. Strong berry flavours are balanced by smooth oak and velvety tannins.	**£8.00**	L&W EVW
(G) **TAPESTRY SHIRAZ 1998,** **TAPESTRY VINEYARDS** South Australia	Tightly-knit fruit, oak and tannins create a structured wine of weight, length and creamy texture.	**£9.00**	VKW
(G) **YALDARA ESTATE FARMS SHIRAZ RESERVE 1999,** **SIMEON WINES** South Eastern Australia	Massively complex this wine has layer upon layer of mature fruit, leather and spice. Hugely tannic yet round.	**£9.00**	IWS
(G) **MAMRE BROOK SHIRAZ 2000,** **SALTRAM WINE ESTATE** South Australia	Replete with lush, concentrated blackcurrant and raspberry fruit. Hints of chocolate and leather add interest.	**£9.00**	LAI
(G) **BAROSSA SHIRAZ 1999,** **ST. HALLETT** South Australia	Full and complex this wine is packed full of good stuff. It is wonderfully deep and well balanced.	**£9.00**	WRC EVW
(G) **McLAREN VALE SHIRAZ 2000,** **TATACHILLA** South Australia	The powerful palate of red and black fruit is structured, balanced and permeated by elegant oak notes.	**£9.00**	SAF

(G) **THE WILLOWS VINEYARD SHIRAZ 1999, WILLOWS** South Australia	Very big, very rich, very ripe, forward fruit, concentrated, deep and long. All of this plus finesse.	**£10.00**	ODD AUC
(G) **MARGARET RIVER SHIRAZ 2000, EVANS & TATE** Western Australia	This beautiful wine seems to swing between vibrant, youthful fruit and dark, mysterious aromas. Very well made.	**£10.00**	ODD
(G) **PINOT NOIR 2000, COLDSTREAM HILLS** Victoria	Plenty of ripe, brambly fruit rubbing shoulders with complex, toffee oak flavours.	**£11.00**	ODD
(G) **MOUNT IDA SHIRAZ 1999, BERINGER BLASS** Victoria	Massive. This Shiraz boasts a powerful, lifted nose of cassis laced with violets and vanilla.	**£11.00**	ODD
(G) **PINOT NOIR 2000, OAKRIDGE ESTATE** Victoria	Packed with rich summer fruit flavours and toasty vanilla oak. Underlying farmyard notes; earth and vegetation.	**£11.50**	SWS
(G) **THE HARVEY MCLAREN VALE SHIRAZ 1999, BRIGHT BROTHERS** South Australia	An attractive nose of pepper, spice, and blackcurrant. The palate has a pencil-shaving finesse about it.	**£13.00**	EHL
(G) **SHIRAZ BY SORBY 1999, TIM ADAMS WINES** South Australia	Heaps of plummy, blackberry and spice flavours which balance the friendly oak very well. Well structured.	**£13.00**	AUC
(G) **ELDERTON BAROSSA SHIRAZ 2000, ELDERTON WINES** South Australia	Wonderfully concentrated, rich and powerful. Elegantly integrated oak, excellent structure and palate weight.	**£13.00**	BBR ODF
(G) **KATNOOK ESTATE SHIRAZ 1999, WINGARA WINE GROUP** South Australia	Intense purple black colour. The high extract provides enormous fruit and supple tannins. Well knit oak .	**£13.00**	WST
(G) **RSW SHIRAZ 1998, WIRRA WIRRA** South Australia	Not only complex tobacco, mint and chocolate characters, gamey notes and a silky palate too.	**£13.00**	MGN
(G) **BLACKWELL SHIRAZ 1998, ST HALLETT** South Australia	Full, spicy and cedary with lots of fruit and a tannic spike of chocolate on the finish. Delicious.	**£14.00**	WRC EVW
(G) **STEVE MAGLIERI SHIRAZ 1999, BERINGER BLASS** South Australia	A big bruiser of a wine with potent cassis and bramble fruit. Lashings of liquid chocolate.	**£15.00**	ELD

(G) **RESERVE PINOT NOIR 2000, STONIER WINES** Victoria	Farmyardy, leathery aromas contrast with the rich strawberry fruit on the palate.	**£16.00**	WIM GHL MSF
(G) **PINOT NOIR 1999, TARRAWARRA** Victoria	Raspberry and strawbery fruit with more developed leathery, gamey flavours. Really high class stuff.	**£18.00**	HVB MSF SEL VGN
(G) **ROSEMOUNT ORANGE SHIRAZ 1999, ROSEMOUNT ESTATE** New South Wales	Delicious spice, burnt rubber, meat, and complex fruit flavours. Everything that you expect in a world class Shiraz.	**£18.00**	PEF
(G) **THE COPPERMINE ROAD CABERNET SAUVIGNON 2000, D'ARENBERG** South Australia	Integrated, well-crafted, and long, this is a wine of great finesse and elegance.	**£18.00**	BWL ODD
(G) **WOODSTOCK THE STOCKS SHIRAZ 1998, COLLETT WINES** South Australia	Profound dense blackberry and wood smoke aromas. The palate is dripping with lush fruit and creamy oak.	**£19.00**	FWC BLU WRW
(G) **WAKEFIELD ST. ANDREWS SHIRAZ 1999, WAKEFIELD ESTATE** South Australia	A wine with a magnificent track record. A top quality Shiraz from the relatively cool Clare Valley.	**£20.00**	SWS LAI
(G) **SALTRAM NO. 1 SHIRAZ 1999, BERINGER BLASS** South Australia	Inky and concentrated. A perfumed nose of blackberry, vanilla, and leather character. The palate is rich and ripe.	**£20.00**	LAI
(G) **ASHMEAD SINGLE VINEYARD CABERNET SAUVIGNON 1999, ELDERTON** South Australia	Flavours range from mint and chocolate to pepper, plums and spice. Balanced tannic structure and good length.	**£27.00**	BBR ODF
(G) **WOLF BLASS PLATINUM LABEL SHIRAZ 1998, BERINGER BLASS** South Australia	A nose of damson fruit, eucalyptus, and truffles. The palate is massive with incredible blackberry concentration.	**£30.00**	TOS
(G) **WOLF BLASS PLATINUM LABEL CABERNET SAUVIGNON 1998, BERINGER BLASS** South Australia	Massive cassis and vanilla-oak nose and a rich full palate laden with ripe berry fruit.	**£30.00**	ODD
(G) **HICKINBOTHAM VINEYARD SHIRAZ 1998, CLARENDON HILLS** South Australia	Stunning aromatics on the nose: wild herbs, tobacco, wet earth after a summer thunderstorm. Rich, ripe blackberry fruit.	**£35.00**	J&B
(G) **EILEEN HARDY SHIRAZ 1997, BRL HARDY** South Australia	Unctuous and powerful with a complex nose of blueberry, bramble and suede. The palate shows ripe fruit concentration.	**£38.00**	WTS

(G)	**JIM BARRY THE ARMAGH 1999, JIM BARRY** South Australia	Dense and deep. A hugely complex wine with dark fruit and smokey vanilla oak flavours.	**£40.00**	HAR L&W F&M RWM

AUSTRALIA • SWEET

(A)	**BROWN BROTHERS DRY MUSCAT 2001, BROWN BROTHERS WINES** Victoria	Pale lemon. Fresh and zingy.	**£5.00**	TOS MWW BTH LON
(B)	**PETER LEHMANN BOTRYTIS SEMILLON 2000, PETER LEHMANN WINES** South Australia	A very attractive clover and honey nose. Fabulous structure; excellent balance between sweetness and acidity.	**£6.00**	PLE
(S)	**BOTRYTIS SEMILLON 1999, CRANSWICK** New South Wales	A palate of waxy, honeyed orange fruit. Rich and concentrated, yet possessing a firm backbone of crisp acidity.	**£6.00**	SBS
(S)	**ZIRILLI BOTRYTIS SEMILLON 1997, CRANSWICK** New South Wales	A very appealing wine with many layers of toasty, honeyed fruit.	**£8.00**	CPW GHL HAY ALE
(S)	**RARE DRY BOTRYTIS SEMILLON 1996, DE BORTOLI** New South Wales	Evident botrytis is displayed on the honeyed, floral, complex nose. The very attractive palate is waxy and rich, yet dry.	**£8.50**	BOR
(S)	**MIRANDA GOLDEN BOTRYTIS 2000, MIRANDA WINES** Victoria	The powerfully scented nose and textured palate are laden with apricots and orange marmalade. Extremely luscious.	**£10.00**	AVB WIM RWM
(G)	**BLACK NOBLE NV, DE BORTOLI** New South Wales	The nose offers caramel, roasted coffee beans and honey. The palate has layers of grilled peaches and dried figs.	**£15.00**	BOR

AUSTRALIA • FORTIFIED

(G)	**CAMPBELLS RUTHERGLEN MUSCAT NV, CAMPBELLS OF RUTHERGLEN** Victoria	The concentration is astounding. Intensely citric. Richly sweet, powerful palate. Seville orange flavours and racy acidity.	**£6.50**	ODD P&S RBS CPW
(S)	**SEPPELT DP63 RUTHERGLEN SHOW MUSCAT NV, SEPPELT** Victoria	A bouquet of prunes and toffee and a powerful palate showing great length. Clean and harmonious.	**£7.50**	WTS

(S)	**CARLYLE MUSCAT NV, PFEIFFER WINES** Victoria	Mandarin orange fruit lines the palate of this magnificent dessert wine. Unctuous and rich, yet balanced.	**£7.50**	FOL
(S)	**YALUMBA MUSEUM RELEASE VICTORIA MUSCAT NV, YALUMBA**	Sweet and unctuous, the complex palate is full of raisined fruit, nuts and caramel. Beautifully balanced.	**£8.00**	BEN SOM WIM
(S)	**STANTON & KILLEEN RUTHERGLEN MUSCAT NV,** Victoria	Beautifully textured, raisined, and rich, with aromas of marmalade and honey. Luscious, balanced and vivid.	**£10.00**	WSG

BULGARIA

While the years of collective farming and winemaking did as few favours for Bulgaria as they did for any other country on the wrong side of the Iron Curtain, the Bulgarians did manage to build an international market for good value inexpensive reds and whites. Today, the now-privatised wine industry is still reliably producing plenty of those wines – as this year's International Wine Challenge results prove – but as yet there are no top medals. The potential to make finer and more exciting wine in Bulgaria certainly exists, however. Watch this space.

BULGARIA • WHITE

(A)	**MAGENTA BAY WHITE 2001, BOYAR ESTATES** Eastern Region	Stylish and perfumed. Sherbet hints.	**£2.80**	MRN
(A)	**COPPER CROSSING BULGARIAN MEDIUM DRY WHITE NV, SUHINDOL ESTATE**	Aromatic white with balanced sweetness.	**£3.00**	WRC
(A)	**DOMAINE BOYAR SHUMEN CHARDONNAY 2001, BOYAR ESTATES** Eastern Region	Clear, unadulterated pineapple flavour.	**£3.70**	DBO
(A)	**BLUERIDGE CHARDONNAY 2001, BOYAR ESTATES** Sub-Balkan Region	White peaches and citrus fruit.	**£4.00**	SMF WRC

(B) **DOMAINE BOYAR BARRIQUE CHARDONNAY 2001, BOYAR ESTATES** Eastern Region	Toasty wine with melon and sweet oak aromas. A rich palate balanced by good acidity.	**£4.00**	DBO BGN
(B) **TUK TAM SAUVIGNON BLANC 2000, LVK VINPROM** Sub-Balkan Region	Pleasingly aromatic with a hint of underlying oak and ripe boxy, peachy fruit.	**£4.00**	NTD BAB CHC

BULGARIA • ROSÉ

(B) **VALLEY OF THE ROSES CABERNET SAUVIGNON ROSÉ 2001, VINPROM SCHVISCHTOV** Northern Region	A deep ruby rosé colour with fresh strawberry fruit on the nose and palate.	**£3.80**	SAF CWS
(A) **BLUERIDGE BLACK ROSÉ 2001, BOYAR ESTATES** Sub-Balkan Region	A clean, fresh and crisp pink wine.	**£4.00**	SMF TOS

BULGARIA • RED

(A) **MHV BULGARIAN MERLOT CABERNET SAUVIGNON NV, VINIPROM SVISCHTOV** Northern Region	Round, layered red fruit palate.	**£3.00**	MHV
(A) **COPPER CROSSING BULGARIAN RED WINE NV, SUHINDOL ESTATE**	Soft, with ripe cherry flavours.	**£3.00**	WRC
(A) **MHV BULGARIAN CABERNET SAUVIGNON NV, VINPROM SVISCHTOV** Northern Region	Blackcurrants laced with cedar notes.	**£3.20**	MHV
(A) **SOMERFIELD BULGARIAN MERLOT 2000, VINPROM ROUSSE AD** Rousse	Juicy with good tannic structure.	**£3.50**	SMF
(A) **ROCKY VALLEY MERLOT 2001, BOYAR ESTATES** Northern Region	Fresh, youthful damson fruit flavours.	**£3.80**	DBO HDY
(A) **BLUERIDGE MERLOT 2001, BOYAR ESTATES** Sub-Balkan Region	Plums tinged with grassy undergrowth.	**£4.00**	TOS WRC

(A) **BULGARIAN CABERNET SAUVIGNON MERLOT RESERVE 2000, SUHINDOL ESTATE**	Blackberry and currant focused wine.	**£4.00**	SAF

CHILE

The Chilean wine industry has developed extraordinarily over the last 20 years. At the beginning of the 1980s, a small number of big producers were making generally old-fashioned wines. Then came the move into producing good, if often rather soulless, modern varietals at the lower end of the price scale. Now, we're into the third, most interesting phase, with recently-developed regions such as Casablanca, small wineries, and foreign investment galore. There are still plenty of bargains to be found – and a fair few top-flight wines to match the best in the world.

CHILE • WHITE

(A) **MHV SAN ANDRES CHILEAN SAUVIGNON CHARDONNAY NV, VIÑA CARTA VIEJA** Central Valley	Fresh tropical fruit. Green notes.	**£3.90**	MHV
(A) **SAINSBURY'S CHILEAN SAUVIGNON BLANC NV, VIÑA SAN PEDRO** Central Valley	Ripe gooseberries and green grass.	**£4.00**	JSM
(A) **LOS CAMACHOS SAUVIGNON BLANC 2001, VIÑA SAN PEDRO** Central Valley	Crisp yet ripe gooseberry fruit.	**£4.00**	WRT
(S) **LOS CAMACHOS CHARDONNAY 2001, VINA SAN PEDRO** Central Valley	Ripe and ready with tropical and melon nuances on the nose. The palate is buttery with pineapple intensity.	**£4.00**	WRT
(S) **SOMERFIELD CHILEAN SAUVIGNON BLANC 2001, JOSÉ CANEPA** Curicó	Grass and nettle aromas. The palate shows ripe citrus and gooseberry fruit allied to dancing acidity.	**£4.00**	SMF
(B) **ANTU MAPU SAUVIGNON BLANC 2002, CAV CAUQUENES** Maule	Very refreshing flavours of green apples and gooseberries. The palate is lifted by a brisk, mouthwatering acidity.	**£4.50**	MRN BAB CHC

(B)	**TIERRA ARENA SAUVIGNON BLANC 2001, VIÑA FRANCISCO AGUIRRE** Pisco	This delightfully crisp, green, elegant Sauvignon hails from the most northerly wine-producing region of Chile.	**£4.80**	AVB
(B)	**35 SOUTH SAUVIGNON BLANC 2001, VIÑA SAN PEDRO** Central Valley	Very attractive aromas of freshly cut grass. Flavours of lemons, limes and gooseberries. Crisp and refreshing.	**£4.80**	SBS JSM
(B)	**CASABLANCA WHITE LABEL CHARDONNAY 2001, VINA CASABLANCA** Aconcagua	Very attractive flavours and aromas of white peaches, green apples and lemons.	**£5.00**	MOR ODD POR
(S)	**CASABLANCA WHITE LABEL SAUVIGNON BLANC 2001, VINA CASABLANCA** Maipo	Aromatic, crisp and fresh with intense herbaceous and tropical fruit character. Harmonious fruit, weight and acidity.	**£5.00**	ODD MOR HVN JSM
(B)	**LA PALMERIA CHARDONNAY 2001, VINA LA ROSA** Central Valley	Ripe palate of pears, apples, and peaches, with hints of lime that lend the wine a fresh acidity.	**£5.00**	ODD UNS
(B)	**MORANDE CHARDONNAY 2001, MORANDE** Central Valley	This bright, lemony white is bursting with tropical fruit. The nose is fresh and penetrating, with floral notes.	**£5.00**	THI
(B)	**CHARDONNAY 2001, TERRAMATER** Central Valley	Ripe and refined with melon and peach aromas and a fresh, fruit palate showing good weight and balance.	**£5.00**	TOS
(S)	**SPAR CHILEAN CHARDONNAY 1999, CANEPA**	Ripe and quaffable with ripe melon and honey aromas. Light minerality, fine acidity and a spicy finish.	**£5.30**	SPR
(S)	**SANTA ISABEL ESTATE CHARDONNAY 2001, VIÑA CASABLANCA** Aconcagua	Rich and warm this wine is packed with ripe, juicy tropical and melon fruits.	**£7.00**	MOR DBY HAY
(S)	**GRAN ARAUCANO CHARDONNAY 2000, J&F LURTON** Rapel	Bright and zesty wine with sweet toasty notes on the nose and nutty richness on the palate.	**£7.00**	C&B

CHILE • ROSÉ

(A)	**CABERNET SAUVIGNON ROSÉ 2001, TERRAMATER** Central Valley	Attractive colour with strawberry palate.	**£4.00**	VER

CHILE • RED

(A)	**CASA ALVARES CHILEAN CABERNET SAUVIGNON NV, LOURDES SA** Central Valley	Beguiling, soft, ripe cassis flavours.	**£3.00** ALD
(A)	**SAN ANDRÉS CHILEAN VINO TINTO NV, VINA CARTA VIEJA** Central Valley	Clear, ripe hedgerow fruit flavours.	**£3.70** MHV
(B)	**LOS CAMACHOS MERLOT 2001, VINA SAN PEDRO** Central Valley	The charms of Merlot are apparent here. Ripe damson fruit, floral touches and a hint of minerality.	**£4.00** WRT
(B)	**SIERRA GRANDE MERLOT 2000, PAUL BOUTINOT** Central Valley	This wine is both warm and supple with ripe berry fruit. Good weight and silky tannins.	**£4.00** CPR
(B)	**TESCO CHILEAN CARMENERE NV, TERRAMATER** Central Valley	A very ripe nose reminiscent of cranberry and plums. Quite broad and perfumed, with good length.	**£4.00** TOS
(A)	**SCORPIUS SYRAH 2000, VINA SIEGEL** Rapel	Meaty, herbaceous nose. Cassis palate.	**£4.00** STN
(B)	**GRAN VERANO 2001, SAN JOSE DE APALTA** Central Valley	Quite herbal on the nose; the wine blossoms in the mouth with chocolate, tobacco, and dried fruit.	**£4.50** SAF
(S)	**CASA MAYOR CABERNET SAUVIGNON 2001, BODEGAS SANTO DOMINGO** Rapel	This wine has delicious fruit and real intensity. The tannins are smooth and the finish satisfying.	**£4.50** JKN
(B)	**ANTU MAPU MERLOT 2001, CAV CAUQUENES** Maule	Soft and warm berry fruit. An elegant, refined wine with a good clean and long finish.	**£4.50** MRN BAB CHC
(B)	**SOMERFIELD CHILEAN MERLOT 2001, VIÑA MORANDE S.A.** Central Valley	Ripe bramble and plum fruit aromas. A soft and juicy wine with a subtle spice edge.	**£4.50** SMF
(B)	**GRAN VERANO CARMENÈRE 2001, SAN JOSE DE APALTA** Rapel	Sweet, upfront fruit of blackberry and plum with furry tannins and a balanced structure.	**£4.50** SAF

(B) TIERRA ARENA CABERNET SAUVIGNON 2001, VIÑA FRANCISCO DE AGUIRRE Pisco	Clean and aromatic, with pronounced berry aromas and smoky blackcurrant fruit in the mouth.	**£4.80**	AVB
(B) 35 SOUTH CABERNET SAUVIGNON 2001, VINA SAN PEDRO Central Valley	Deep ruby. Green pepper and spice on the palate with well integrated tannins.	**£4.80**	SBS JSM
(B) VIÑA ALAMOSA CABERNET SAUVIGNON 2001, VIÑA DE LAROSE Rapel	Bright cherry fruit with a good smoky complexity and a good finish.	**£5.00**	GRT
(S) LA PALMERIA MERLOT 2001, VINA LA ROSA Central Valley	This wine is beautifully crafted with luscious blueberry fruit hung on silky tannins. Excellent length to finish.	**£5.00**	ODD
(B) SANTA INES CABERNET SAUVIGNON MERLOT 2001, SANTA INES Maipo	Good, rich bramble and cassis notes on a round, soft palate with a chocolatey finish.	**£5.00**	TOS WRC
(B) CABERNET SAUVIGNON 2001, VALDIVIESO Curicó	Deep, rich red colour. Attractive notes of blackcurrant on a medium bodied palate.	**£5.00**	BWL JSM TOS WRC
(B) MERLOT 2001, VALDIVIESO Central Valley	This wine has good cherry and berry fruit and supple tannins. Obvious but well used oak.	**£5.00**	BWL ASD WRC UNS
(B) CANEPA ZINFANDEL 2000, VIÑA CANEPA Maipo	Purple-hued red. Youthful strawberries on the nose. Dry, with good structure. Ripe and fleshy. Moderately long finish.	**£5.00**	UWM
(B) MERLOT 2001, MORANDE Central Valley	Intense berry and cherry fruit. Warm and juicy it has real but gentle power.	**£5.00**	HME
(S) SYRAH 2001, MORANDE Central Valley	Blackberry and wood smoke aromas. The palate shows layers of rich fruit, tannin and toasty oak.	**£5.00**	THI
(S) PORTA CABERNET SAUVIGNON 2000, VIÑA PORTA Rapel	The palate is full of soft, red fruit with a savoury touch. The finish is long and lush.	**£5.00**	UWM ADS ODD
(B) PORTA MERLOT 2000, VIÑA PORTA Rapel	Rich and ripe berry fruit. A warm, alcoholic and upbeat wine. Skillfully made and well balanced.	**£5.00**	UWM ADS

(B) **RESERVA CARMENÈRE 2001, VIÑA SEGÚ** Maule	Black and red fruit dominate this wine's personality, overlayed by coconutty oak.	**£5.00**	HWL
(S) **CASILLERO DEL DIABLO MERLOT 2001, CONCHA Y TORO** Rapel	Deep, lushly fruited damson palate spiked with nutmeg and cinnamon. Velvety texture.	**£5.00**	WRC ODD
(S) **CASILLERO DEL DIABLO SYRAH 2001, CONCHA Y TORO** Rapel	The nose is a multi-dimensional offering of flowers, minerals and punchy, ripe hedgerow fruits. Spices add interest.	**£5.00**	WRC ODD
(B) **ANTU MAPU CARMÈNERE 2001, CAV CAUQUENES** Maule	Good level of fruit; raspberries and redcurrants with a touch of mint and tobacco.	**£5.00**	MRN BAB CHC
(B) **TESCO FINEST CHILEAN MERLOT RESERVE 2001, VALDIVIESO** Curicó	A medium bodied soft and supple wine with pleasant ripe fruit character. Undemanding.	**£5.00**	TOS
(B) **CONO SUR MERLOT 2001, VINA CONO SUR** Rapel	Richly fruited wine with excellent plum and morello cherry depth. Well made with fine balance and structure.	**£5.00**	ASD MHV MWW UWM
(B) **CASA LA JOYA MERLOT 2000, VIÑAS BISQUERTT** Rapel	Light and delicate soft ripe fruit. Good velvety tannins and very juicy undemanding acidity.	**£5.00**	MCT
(B) **CARMENÈRE 2001, VIÑA FALERNIA** Pisco	Inky deep colour. Quite herbaceous and smoky on the palate with bags of fruit.	**£5.00**	LAI
(S) **MHV PASEO CHILEAN PINOT NOIR 2000, VINA CARTA VIEJA** Rapel	A slightly vegetal nose of undergrowth. The soft, understated palate features a hint of earthiness.	**£5.40**	MHV
(S) **PALO ALTO MERLOT 2001, VIÑA FRANCISCO AGUIRRE** Pisco	Gentle vanilla and soft but intense ripe plum fruit. Deeply coloured and spicy this is a complex wine.	**£5.40**	AVB
(S) **ISLA NEGRA SYRAH 2001, VINA CONO SUR** Rapel	Inviting aromas of blackcurrant and menthol precede the ripe, berry fruit and well-integrated creamy oak.	**£5.50**	TOS JSM
(S) **SAN ESTEBAN RESERVE MERLOT 2000, SAN ESTEBAN** Aconcagua	Supple wine with intense cherry and plum nuances. Fair depth and concentration to finish.	**£5.50**	AWS MHW

(S)	**SANTA ISABEL MERLOT 2000, VIÑA CASABLANCA** Aconcagua	Big and rich, yet refined. Mineral notes add grace and distinction to the nose of soft, luscious fruit.	**£6.00**	MOR BUT POR
(S)	**MERLOT RESERVA 2000, MONTGRAS** Rapel	Rich and round, deep plum fruit and a smoky charred oak nose. Complex, serious and upfront.	**£6.00**	JSM
(S)	**CABERNET SAUVIGNON RESERVA 2000, VIÑA MONTGRAS** Rapel	Intense blackcurrant and floral notes on the nose. Loaded with clean berry fruit and a certain minerality.	**£6.00**	SWG
(S)	**CALITERRA SYRAH 2000, CALITERRA** Rapel	Inky wine with a delicious smoke and bacon tinged nose. The palate is intense with rich mulberry fruit.	**£6.00**	TOS VGN WIM EVW
(S)	**CALITERRA SYRAH 2001, CALITERRA** Rapel	A brooding monster. An intriguing medley of smoky oak, fruit, and chocolate. Ripe, juicy tannins.	**£6.00**	TOS VGN WIM EVW
(S)	**TERRARUM PINOT NOIR 2001, MORANDE** Aconcagua	Scented with mint, cedar and tobacco. Laden with fresh, ripe summer berries.	**£6.00**	THI
(S)	**TRIO MERLOT 2000, CONCHA Y TORO** Rapel	Gorgeous, dense, silky Merlot. The nose is redolent of vanilla spice. Richness carries through onto the chocolatey palate.	**£6.00**	ODD WRC
(S)	**RESERVA MERLOT 2000, TERRAMATER** Central Valley	This wine has lovely berry perfume. The palate is ripe with creamy vanilla oak and supple tannins.	**£6.00**	TOS
(S)	**MAPA MERLOT 2000, BARON PHILIPPE DE ROTHSCHILD** Rapel	The nose shows rich plum fruit. The palate is well-made with rich fruit allied to velvety tannins.	**£6.50**	UNS PLA EUR
(G)	**VERAMONTE CABERNET SAUVIGNON 2000, FRANCISCAN ESTATES** Maipo	The deep cherry nose is laced with vanilla spice. The palate is ripe and round, juicy black cherry fruit.	**£7.00**	WRC MCT
(G)	**MERLOT RESERVA DE GRAS 2000, VIÑA MONTGRAS** Rapel	This Reserva is a powerful beast. Herbs, grass and tobacco on the nose. Voluptuously rich, dense.	**£8.00**	SWG
(G)	**LA PALMERIA MERLOT GRAN RESERVA 2001, VINA LA ROSA** Central Valley	Dark and rich flavour profile, lushly fruited, with soft acidity and good weight. Firm tannins underpin the fruit.	**£8.00**	WRC

(G) PRIMUS VERAMONTE 1999, FRANCISCAN ESTATES Aconcagua	Cassis and raspberry notes spiked with nutmeg. Green notes add interest to the ripe flavour profile.	**£10.00**	MCT WRC
(G) SINGLE VINEYARD RESERVE CABERNET FRANC 1999, VALDIVIESO Curicó	Dense and lush. Scented cigar box and a hint of undergrowth show on the seductively fruited nose.	**£10.00**	BWL SAF TOS
(G) 20 BARREL PINOT NOIR LIMITED EDITION 2000, VINA CONO SUR Rapel	Vibrant red berry fruit over voluptuous soft tannins. A year in French oak prior to bottling.	**£18.00**	WST
(G) 20 BARREL PINOT NOIR LIMITED EDITION 2001, VINA CONO SUR Rapel	Intensely concentrated and complex wine with masses of forward fruit and a finely balanced structure.	**£18.00**	MWW MYL HZW

FRANCE

France's soccer team may have had a disappointing year in 2002, but its winemakers did better in the International Wine Challenge than ever before. For the first time, there are more French Gold Medals than Australian ones – and the largest ever haul of awards across the board. You still have to tread carefully when buying wine here – the words "appellation contrôlée" often mean very little, and there is plenty of poor wine on offer in famous regions – but pick up a bottle of any of the wines we've listed here and you should be sure of satisfaction.

FRANCE • SPARKLING

(A) MHV SPARKLING CHARDONNAY BRUT NV, VARICHON & CLERC	Dry with a fresh, creamy mouthfeel.	**£5.00**	MHV
(A) BLANC DE BLANCS BRUT NV, FRANÇOIS MONTAND	Green apple palate with good length.	**£5.00**	GCF
(A) PHILLIPE MICHEL CRÉMANT DU JURA CHARDONNAY 1998, COMPAGNIE DES GRANDS VINS DU JURA Jura	Dry, fresh, appley and light-bodied.	**£5.00**	ALD

(A)	**VEUVE DU VERNAY BRUT NV, MARIE BRIZZARD** Bordeaux	Possesses a refreshing, moreish quality.	**£6.00**	JSM ASD MHV BGN
(A)	**WAITROSE SAUMUR BRUT NV, ACKERMANN** Loire	Rich, nutty and biscuity with real verve.	**£6.00**	WTS
(A)	**MHV SPARKLING SAUMUR BRUT NV, CFGV** Loire	Apricots and apples and a lively mousse.	**£6.00**	MHV
(B)	**BLANC FOUSSY NV, BLANC FOUSSY** Loire	Brisk and uplifting, with fresh, delicate flavours. Good concentration of fruit. A very long finish.	**£6.50**	EVW
(A)	**CLAIRETTE DE DIE JAILLANCE NV, JAILLANCE**	Pink grapefruit and guava confection.	**£7.00**	WTS
(S)	**BREDON BRUT N V, P & C HEIDSIECK** Champagne	A wonderful mixture of peas, fresh bread and apples. The brioche palate has excellent weight and ripeness.	**£10.00**	WTS
(S)	**MASSE BRUT NV, LANSON** Champagne	This is full of ripe berry fruit and a bready, toasty background to make an expressive, rounded wine.	**£15.00**	MCD
(G)	**ANDRÉ SIMON CHAMPAGNE BRUT VINTAGE 1995, MARNE ET CHAMPAGNE DIFFUSION** Champagne	An intense nose of ripe peaches with roast cashews and butter. A rich and round, yet delicate, palate.	**£17.00**	WRT
(G)	**VINTAGE BRUT 1996, CHAMPAGNE H. BLIN & CO** Champagne	Ripe, elegant citrus and green apples with toasty notes. Creamy texture. Complexity builds layer upon layer.	**£19.00**	ODD
(G)	**CHAMPAGNE MILLÉSIMÉ 1992, ESTERLIN** Champagne	Marvellous, mature vintage Champagne. A complex array of smoky aromas lead into a mature, autolytic, yeasty palate.	**£19.00**	CHS
(G)	**PIPER HEIDSIECK VINTAGE 1995, P&C HEIDSIECK** Champagne	Warm brioche and white blossom aromas. A luscious palate of delicate stone fruit, marzipan and ginger biscuits.	**£26.00**	MAX
(G)	**CHAMPAGNE MICHEL GONET CUVÉE SPÉCIAL PRESTIGE 1996, MICHEL GONET** Champagne	Vinified in the Champagne village of Avize it comes from one of the best vintages of recent times.	**£27.00**	BMG

(G)	**CHARLES HEIDSIECK BRUT RESERVE 1995, P&C HEIDSIECK** Champagne	The yeasty nose gives way to a creamy, delicate style showing both evolution and freshness. Deliciously rich.	**£27.50**	JSM ODD
(G)	**CHARLES HEIDSIECK BLANC DES MILLÉNAIRES 1990, P&C HEIDSIECK** Champagne	Silky texture, exquisite perfume and great delicacy. Roast nuts and ripe golden apples.	**£37.00**	MAX
(G)	**DOM PÉRIGNON 1995, MOET & CHANDON** Champagne	Toffee apples and cashew aromas. Fine, lemony acidity on the palate. Rapidly maturing, yet finely-knit and elegant.	**£65.00**	SAF WRC UNS TOS
(G)	**GRAND SIÈCLE LUMIÈRE DU MILLÉNAIRE 1990, LAURENT-PERRIER** Champagne	Green apple fruit and delicate aromas of toast. The creamy palate is saturated with crisp apple fruit.	**£65.00**	ODD SEL
(G)	**DOM RUINART ROSÉ 1988, RUINART** Champagne	Elegant nose of toast, black cherry, and almonds. Flavours of grilled strawberries are punctuated by white pepper.	**£67.00**	RUK
(G)	**CHARLES HEIDSIECK BLANCS DE BLANCS 1982, P&C HEIDSIECK** Champagne	Undulating, persistent mousse. Aromas of brioche, spring blossom and ripe apples and rich, mature fruit.	**£90.00**	WTS

FRANCE • WHITE

(A)	**PAUL SAPIN FRENCH CHARDONNAY NV, PAUL SAPIN SA** Languedoc-Roussillon	Refreshing citrus and pineapple style.	**£2.00**	ROG SAF
(A)	**LA CLEMENCIÈRE MUSCADET NV, JEAN BEAUQUIN** Loire	Zesty wine with flinty freshness.	**£3.00**	SMF
(A)	**MHV MAISON BLANC MEDIUM DRY NV, DOMINIQUE BAUD**	Crisp and refreshing. Floral notes.	**£3.00**	MHV
(A)	**MHV MAISON BLANC DRY NV, DOMINIQUE BAUD**	Aromatic, lively, youthful, and grassy.	**£3.00**	MHV
(A)	**MHV VIN DE PAYS DU GERS NV, PRODIS** South West	Almond nose. Crisp and structured.	**£3.00**	MHV

(A)	**MANDEVILLE CHARDONNAY 2001, PAUL SAPIN SA** Languedoc-Roussillon	Clean with melon and apple notes.	**£3.00** M&S
(A)	**BARON D'ARIGNAC BLANC DE BLANCS 2001, LES GRANDS CHAIS DE FRANCE** South West	Fresh, crisp, attractive stone fruit.	**£3.00** UNS
(S)	**HENRI VALLON MUSCADET DE SÈVRE ET MAINE 2001, JEAN BEAUQUIN** Loire	Fragrant fruit on the restrained nose. Light, elegant, sherberty palate. Youthful attack and brisk, marked acidity.	**£3.40** WRT
(A)	**ASDA CHARDONNAY PRESTIGE 2001, RHODANIENNE** Languedoc-Roussillon	Melon and peach, crisp acidity.	**£3.50** ASD
(A)	**CÔTES DE BERGERAC SWEET NV, MHV** South West	Floral nose and honeyed mandarin oranges.	**£3.50** MHV
(S)	**MARKS & SPENCER GOLD LABEL CHARDONNAY 2001, DOMAINES VIRGINIE** Languedoc-Roussillon	Restrained aromas of ripe peaches. An alluring, refined palate of zesty lemons and stone fruit.	**£3.50** M&S
(A)	**MARKS & SPENCER GOLD LABEL SAUVIGNON 2001, DOMAINES VIRGINIE** Languedoc-Roussillon	Ripe, tropical gooseberry fruit palate.	**£3.50** M&S
(A)	**JP CHENET COLOMBARD CHARDONNAY 2001, LES CAVES DE LANDIRAS** South West	Apples, lemons, and raspberry hints.	**£3.50** MHV MRN UNS
(A)	**VAN BLANC 2001, VIGNOBLES DU PELOUX** Rhône	Light, citrus and mineral-infused.	**£3.50** JSM
(A)	**CO-OP VIN DE PAYS DU JARDIN DE LA FRANCE SAUVIGNON BLANC NV, VINIVAL** Loire	Fresh gooseberry and nettle nuances.	**£3.50** CWS
(A)	**JEAN ST HONORE VIN DE PAYS CHARDONNAY 2001, VINIVAL** Loire	Steely pineapple fruit flavours. Attractive.	**£3.70** NTD
(A)	**SAINSBURYS MUSCADET DE SÈVRE-ET-MAINE 2001, VIGNERONS DE LA NOELLE** Loire	Clean, light-bodied, full, and attractive.	**£3.70** JSM

(A)	**BERGERAC BLANC 2001, YVON MAU** South West	Fresh, zesty with lively acidity.	**£3.70**	UNS WTS MAK
(A)	**SOMERFIELD MUSCADET 2001, JEAN BEAUQUIN** Loire	Perfumed, with a refreshing spritz.	**£3.80**	SMF
(A)	**ASDA PREMIUM FRENCH VIN DE PAYS CHARDONNAY 2001, GROUPE FONCALIEU** Languedoc-Roussillon	Vivacious, full palate of peaches.	**£4.00**	ASD
(A)	**LA LANDE VDP DES CÔTES DE GASCOGNE 2001, RIGAL** South West	Lime fruit nose and palate.	**£4.00**	SWG
(A)	**VIN DE PAYS DES CÔTES DU TARN 2001, DOMAINE VIGNE LOURAC** South West	Round flavours of crisp apple.	**£4.00**	GRT
(A)	**SAUVIGNON BLANC VIN DE PAYS DU JARDIN DE LA FRANCE 2001, ACKERMAN** Loire	Crisp, light, gooseberry-infused delight.	**£4.00**	JSM
(A)	**RIVERS MEET WHITE 2001, GINESTET** Bordeaux	Fresh, and perfumed with flowers.	**£4.00**	WRC
(A)	**PIAT D'OR COLOMBARD CHARDONNAY NV, PIAT PÉRE ET FILS**	Apples and sweet melons. Attractive.	**£4.00**	SAF SMF TOS NTD
(A)	**PIAT D'OR MEDIUM WHITE VIN DE PAYS DU GERS NV, PIAT PÉRE ET FILS**	Delicately scented with white flowers.	**£4.00**	SBS NTD PFC TRI
(A)	**RESERVE ST MARC SAUVIGNON 2001, GROUPE FONCALIEU** Languedoc-Roussillon	Ripe, green fruit flavours. Crisp.	**£4.00**	SBS
(A)	**DONJON DE LA TOUR WHITE NV, DEVEREAUX** Languedoc-Roussillon	Fresh, clear, zingy sherbet tones.	**£4.00**	MEW
(A)	**OLD TART TERRET SAUVIGNON 2001, PAUL BOUTINOT** Languedoc-Roussillon	Smoky ripe green fruit flavours.	**£4.00**	TOS JSM SMF BGN

(A)	**FRUITS OF FRANCE VIOGNIER 2001, PAUL BOUTINOT** Languedoc-Roussillon	Peachy, approachable, and well-balanced.	**£4.00**	PBA
(A)	**MARKS & SPENCER DOMAINE MANDEVILLE VIOGNIER 2001, DOMAINE MANDEVILLE** Languedoc-Roussillon	Nutmeg, lime blossom and apricots.	**£4.00**	M&S
(A)	**PELLEHAUT BLANC 2001, PETER A SICHEL** South West	Floral nose. Mouthfilling and minerally.	**£4.00**	BWC FTH BTH
(A)	**LA CHARME COLOMBARD NV, PRODUCTEURS PLAIMONT** South West	Herbaceous, grassy bouquet. Dry and light.	**£4.00**	HOT
(A)	**MARKS & SPENCER GOLD LABEL VIOGNIER 2001, PAUL SAPIN** Languedoc-Roussillon	Pear and citrus. Mineral elements.	**£4.00**	M&S
(A)	**MAUREGARD BORDEAUX BLANC 2001, YVON MAU** Bordeaux	Good structure, may improve.	**£4.00**	UNS
(A)	**VIN BIOLOGIQUE VERMENTINO BLANC 2001, LES GRANDS CHAIS DE FRANCE** Provence	Subtle orange and lime hints.	**£4.00**	ALD
(A)	**LOUIS ESCHENAUER CHARDONNAY 2000, LES CAVES DE LANDIRAS** Languedoc-Roussillon	Structured. Evolved. Pale green-hued yellow.	**£4.00**	UNS WIE
(A)	**CHÂTEAU PIERROUSSELLE BLANC 2001, GINESTET** Bordeaux	Zesty gooseberry-driven refresher.	**£4.00**	CWS
(A)	**CO-OP VIN DE PAYS D'OC CHARDONNAY NV, GROUPE FONCALIEU** Languedoc-Roussillon	Clean citrus and canteloupe style.	**£4.00**	CWS
(B)	**KIWI CUVEE CHARDONNAY VIOGNIER 2001, LES DOMAINES DE FONTCAUDE** Languedoc-Roussillon	The Viognier lends this wine an exotic feel. Good weight of tropical fruit and decent length.	**£4.00**	SMF
(A)	**KIWI CUVÉE SAUVIGNON BLANC 2001, LECHATEAU** Loire	Fresh with zingy gooseberry fruit.	**£4.00**	TOS ODD SMF BGN

(S)	**WINTER HILL WHITE 2001,** **GROUPE FONCALIEU** Languedoc-Roussillon	Fragrant citrus fruit nose. The palate is saturated with ripe melons. Well-balanced, with a fresh backbone of acidity.	**£4.00**	WTS MRN SMF CWS
(B)	**CÔTES DE SAINT MONT** **ANDRÉ DAGUIN BLANC 2001,** **PRODUCTEURS PLAIMONT** South West	A nose of talc, fresh flowers and minerals. Medium-bodied fruit on the light, attractive palate.	**£4.40**	ABY
(B)	**DOMAINE DU BOIS** **VIOGNIER 2000,** **MAUREL-VEDEAU** Languedoc-Roussillon	Intense floral nose. Honeyed, ripe, waxy, and structured palate. Expressive grass and stone fruit character.	**£4.50**	SMF
(S)	**LES MARIONETTES** **MARSANNE 2001,** **TERROIR CLUB** Languedoc-Roussillon	Understated melon and stone fruit on the nose. Soft vanilla rounds out the tropical fruit on the palate.	**£4.50**	SMF
(S)	**MUSCADET DE SÈVRE ET MAINE** **DOMAINE DU HAUT** **BANCHEREAU 2001,** **AUGUSTE BONHOMME**	Soft, ripe fruit. Delicate, light flavours and very fresh acidity. Youthful and appealing.	**£5.00**	ABY
(B)	**TERRASSES D'AZUR** **SAUVIGNON BLANC 2001,** **CASTEL FRÈRES** Languedoc-Roussillon	Lively citrus and passion fruit character dominates this pale yellow wine. Well balanced fruit and acidity.	**£5.00**	CLA
(B)	**CUVÉE DES ANGLAIS 2000,** **RICHARD SPEIRS AND PIERRE** **ROGRE** Languedoc-Roussillon	Perfumed and aromatic with ripe apricot and peach aromas. The palate is fresh with a spicy finish.	**£5.00**	JSM
(B)	**LA BAUME VIOGNIER 2001,** **BRL HARDY** Languedoc-Roussillon	A creamy nose complements the soft, integrated palate of ripe fruit. Mouth-coating texture, good balance and length.	**£5.00**	WTS
(B)	**MARKS & SPENCER GOLD** **LABEL RESERVE CHARDONNAY** **2000, DOMAINES VIRGINIE** Languedoc-Roussillon	Elegant, honeyed grapefruit palate.	**£5.00**	M&S
(B)	**TESCO FINEST** **CHARDONNAY 1999,** **MAUREL-VEDEAU** Languedoc-Roussillon	Honeyed, lengthy green plum palate.	**£5.00**	TOS
(S)	**LOUXOR CHARDONNAY** **VIN DE PAYS D'OC 2001,** **COMPAGNIE RHODANIENNE** Languedoc-Roussillon	Nectarines, yellow plums and butter. Clear palate of peaches and pineapple laced oak. Crisp, zingy acidity.	**£5.00**	JSM
(B)	**JEAN BERTEAU CÔTES DU** **RHÔNE BLANC 2001,** **COMPAGNIE RHODANIENNE** Rhône	Green-hued, with honeysuckle and herbs on the nose. Citrus flavours abound on the fresh palate.	**£5.00**	LAI

(G)	**CHÂTEAU CHANTELOUP BORDEAUX BLANC SEC 2001, VIGNOBLES MICHEL PION** Bordeaux	Scented with acacia blossom, cape gooseberries and lemons. Bags of citrus, Bramley apples and a satisfying mouthfeel.	**£5.00**	FRW THO
(B)	**PREMIUS BORDEAUX BLANC 2001, YVON MAU** Bordeaux	Concentrated and succulent with good palate weight and pleasing herbaceous fruit flavours. Good acidity.	**£5.00**	MAK
(B)	**MAS DU NOVI CHARDONNAY 2000, DOMAINE SAINT JEAN DU NOVICIAT** Languedoc-Roussillon	Soft, balanced, concentrated, and long.	**£5.00**	FCA
(S)	**CHÂTEAU DE LA ROCHE TOURAINE SAUVIGNON 2001, DONATIEN BAHUAUD** Loire	Fresh and herbaceous with grass and cat's pee nuances and lush gooseberry fruit on the palate.	**£5.30**	CLW
(S)	**DOMAINE DE L'AUMONIER TOURAINE SAUVIGNON 2001, DOMAINE DE L'AUMONIER** Loire	Graceful peapod and cut grass aromas. The palate boasts gooseberry, lemon, and apple flavours with a weighty texture.	**£5.50**	FRW JAS THO GRH
(S)	**DOMAINE LALANDE L'ECLUSE CHARDONNAY 2001, LAITHWAITE'S** Languedoc-Roussillon	Elegant with ripe citrus and butter nuances on the nose. The palate has a creamy mouthfeel and balancing acidity.	**£6.20**	LAI
(S)	**DOMAINE DU SEUIL BORDEAUX BLANC 2000, CHÂTEAU DU SEUIL** Bordeaux	Bright and fresh with lovely peach aromas. Apple and spice on the palate. Balanced, fine acidity.	**£6.50**	MCT MNH
(S)	**GEWURZTRAMINER BARON DE TURCKHEIM 2000, CAVE DE TURCKHEIM** Alsace	A delicious lychee nose. Very well balanced. Pale colour.	**£7.50**	VGN
(G)	**DOMAINE MICHEL THOMAS 2001, DOMAINE MICHEL THOMAS** Loire	The restrained grassy, lemon nose is classically Sancerre and delicious. Lively acidity and a hint of bottle development.	**£10.00**	LAI
(G)	**GEWURZTRAMINER ROSENBERG DE WETTOLSHEIM 2000, DOMAINE BARMES-BUECHER** Alsace	A soft, spicy style with fragrant lychee. Plenty of weight on the palate with a powerfully long finish.	**£18.00**	GON
(G)	**TÊTE DE CUVÉE BLANC 2000, CHÂTEAU PUECH-HAUT** Languedoc-Roussillon	Ripe tropical fruits, nuts, and vanilla all perfectly intermingle to produce a very impressive tasting experience.	**£20.00**	VLW VTH
(G)	**POUILLY-FUISSÉ VIEILLES VIGNES 1999, CHÂTEAU FUISSÉ** Burgundy	The nose shows gooseberry and passionfruit aromas and the integrated oak gives the palate some balanced weight.	**£20.00**	J&B

(G)	**DOMAINE WEINBACH CUVÉE LAURENCE GEWÜRZTRAMINER 1998, DOMAINE WEINBACH** Alsace	Notes of roses and lychees. Rich and concentrated with sweet, ripe fruit.	**£22.00**	J&B
(G)	**PULIGNY-MONTRACHET LES PERRIÈRES 1ER CRU 1998, ETIENNE SAUZET** Burgundy	Ripe, creamy fruit with nuts and peaches on the nose and a concentrated lemony palate.	**£37.00**	J&B
(G)	**PULIGNY-MONTRACHET LES FOLATIÈRES 1ER CRU 1998, DOMAINE LEFLAIVE** Burgundy	Big, long, intense and concentrated. It has peachy, citric flavours balanced with classy oak and a long finish.	**£58.00**	J&B

FRANCE • ROSÉ

(A)	**CABERNET FRANC ROSE 2001, ACKERMAN** Loire	Rustic yet refreshing, spicy rosé.	**£4.00**	JSM
(A)	**DEEP PINK 2001, BIG FRANK** Languedoc-Roussillon	Strawberry and almond on the palate.	**£4.00**	SBS
(A)	**CÔTES DU RHÔNE ROSÉ 2001, VIGNOBLES DU PELOUX** Rhône	Salmon pink with good freshness.	**£4.00**	TOS

FRANCE • RED

(A)	**CDL GRENACHE MERLOT NV, LES CAVES DE LANDIRAS** Languedoc-Roussillon	Cherry pie laced with mint.	**£1.50** (25cl)	WTS
(A)	**ASDA CLARET NV, ANDRÉ QUANCARD** Bordeaux	Round, attractive, and decidedly moreish.	**£3.00**	ASD
(A)	**PONT NEUF CÔTES DU RHÔNE 2001, PRINCES DE FRANCE** Rhône	Soft, spicy, juicy loganberry fruit.	**£3.00**	NTD
(A)	**PORTAN CARIGNAN 2001, DEVEREAUX** Languedoc-Roussillon	Youthful black fruit. Rustic style.	**£3.00**	JSM

(A)	**MHV MAISON ROUGE MEDIUM DRY NV, DOMINIQUE BAUD**	Spicy, characterful red. Ripe. Powerful.	**£3.00**	MHV
(A)	**MHV VIN DE PAYS DU GARD NV, PRODIS** Languedoc-Roussillon	Lifted, perfumed, juicy black cherries.	**£3.00**	MHV
(B)	**RESPLANDY CABERNET SAUVIGNON NV, VAL D'ORBIEU** Languedoc-Roussillon	Simple, yet well-made with good blackcurrant fruit intensity and spice on the nose and palate.	**£3.00**	SMF
(A)	**VAL D'ORBIEU CORBIÈRES NV, VAL D'ORBIEU** Languedoc-Roussillon	Spicy black fruit with herbal notes.	**£3.00**	SMF
(A)	**CÔTES DU RHÔNE 2001, VIGNOBLES DU PELOUX** Rhône	Supple with spicy blackberry fruit.	**£3.00**	TOS
(A)	**SAFEWAY MINERVOIS 2000, GEORGES BADRIOU** Languedoc-Roussillon	Youthful, spiced black cherry flavours.	**£3.10**	SAF
(B)	**SOMERFIELD CABERNET SAUVIGNON VIN DE PAYS D'OC NV, VAL D'ORBIEU** Languedoc-Roussillon	Chunky and full. This wine is full of typical Cabernet, herbaceous and blackcurrant fruit character.	**£3.30**	SMF
(A)	**SOMERFIELD CLARET NV, GVG** Bordeaux	Smooth mint and cassis appeal.	**£3.30**	SMF
(A)	**BEAUJOLAIS 2001, JEAN-PAUL SELLES** Beaujolais	Light style with bubblegum appeal.	**£3.50**	SMF
(S)	**MARKS & SPENCER GOLD LABEL CABERNET 2001, DOMAINES VIRGINIE** Languedoc-Roussillon	This Cabernet sports lifted scents of heather and cedar. The palate drips with powerful blackberry fruit.	**£3.50**	M&S
(A)	**PRINCE DE LA GARDE VIN DE PAYS DE TOLOSAN 2001, YVON MAU** Languedoc-Roussillon	Ripe with blackcurrant depth.	**£3.50**	ADD CHA
(A)	**SOMERFIELD MERLOT VIN DE PAYS DE L'ARDÈCHE NV, UVICA** Rhône	Plummy with lovely soft mouthfeel.	**£3.50**	SMF

(A) SOMERFIELD VIN DE PAYS DE L'ARDÈCHE RED NV, UVICA Rhône	Smoky with supple berry fruit.	**£3.50**	SMF
(B) RENARDS HILL GRENACHE MERLOT 2001, LES CAVES DE LANDIRAS Languedoc-Roussillon	Balanced, clean, straightforward and well-made.	**£3.50**	RCH
(A) CÔTES DU LUBERON RHÔNE VALLEY RED 2001, VIGNOBLES DU PELOUX Rhône	Pepper and plum fruit. Fresh.	**£3.50**	TOS MRN CRS
(B) CO-OP VIN DE PAYS D'OC CABERNET SAUVIGNON NV, GROUPE FONCALIEU Languedoc-Roussillon	Deep wine with blackcurrant and spice aromas. The palate is soft with jammy fruit and ripe tannins.	**£3.50**	CWS
(A) CO-OP VIN DE PAYS D'OC SYRAH NV, GROUPE FONCALIEU Languedoc-Roussillon	Spicy wine with herbal notes.	**£3.50**	CWS
(A) MHV CÔTES DU RHÔNE NV, GRANDS VINS SELECTION Rhône	Spiked with pepper on a ripe palate.	**£3.60**	MHV
(A) MHV CLARET 2001, YVON MAU Bordeaux	Soft yet structured. Youthful. Leafy.	**£3.60**	MHV
(B) DAVY'S FRENCH RED NV, E LORON ET FILS	Seductive aromas and flavours of freshly picked red berries. A kick of pepper on the nose.	**£3.60**	DVY
(A) JEAN ST HONORE VIN DE PAYS CABERNET SAUVIGNON 2001, VINIVAL Languedoc-Roussillon	Pure, ripe blackberries. Maquis scents.	**£3.70**	NTD
(S) J ST HONORE VIN DE PAYS SYRAH 2001, VINIVAL Languedoc-Roussillon	Full and round. The supple tannins and gorgeous acidity do a splendid job of holding it all together.	**£3.70**	NTD
(A) MHV MINERVOIS ROUGE NV, TRESCH Languedoc-Roussillon	Light raspberry palate and a long finish.	**£3.70**	MHV
(A) MHV BERGERAC ROUGE 2001, CAVES LEONARD South West	Spice-tinged with ripe red vine fruits.	**£3.70**	MHV

(A)	**MHV Vin de Pays d'Oc Merlot NV, Prodis** Languedoc-Roussillon	Round, juicy red fruit. Delightful.	**£3.80**	MHV
(S)	**Princes de France Côtes du Ventoux 2001, Vignobles du Peloux** Rhône	Raspberry and bramble fruit on the nose. Plenty of berry and spice intensity. Long and peppery.	**£3.80**	WTS
(A)	**Asda Merlot Premium 2000, Rhodanienne** Languedoc-Roussillon	Ripe plums scented with cedar.	**£4.00**	ASD
(A)	**Foncalieu Vin de Pays d'Oc Syrah 2001, Groupe Foncalieu** Languedoc-Roussillon	Soft red and black cherries.	**£4.00**	ASD
(A)	**Donjon de la Tour Red NV, Devereaux** Languedoc-Roussillon	Somewhat herbaceous black fruit palate.	**£4.00**	MEW
(B)	**Old Git Red Cotes du Ventoux 2001, Paul Boutinot** Rhône	Plum nose and sweet peppery fruit on the palate. Rich inky red and a dusty tannic mouthfeel.	**£4.00**	TOS JSM SAF ASD
(S)	**Fruits of France Cabernet Sauvignon 2001, Ets Paul Boutinot Sarl** Languedoc-Roussillon	Supple and fruity with good depth and fair persistence.	**£4.00**	TOS
(A)	**MHV Fitou NV, Charles de Roche** Languedoc-Roussillon	Balanced, structured, and lushly fruity.	**£4.00**	MHV
(S)	**Château de Valombré Costières de Nîmes 2000, Costières et Soleil** Languedoc-Roussillon	Opulent bramble aromas and velvety mouthfeel, supple tannins and blackberry fruit. The finish shows complexity.	**£4.00**	ALD
(A)	**Organic Rouge 2001, Bassac** South West	Bitter cherries and almonds. Long.	**£4.00**	VRT
(A)	**Cellier des Dauphins 2001, Cellier des Dauphins** Rhône	Peppery with a sweet mid-palate.	**£4.00**	JSM SAF MRN NTD
(A)	**Pic St Loup Vin d'Une Nuit 2001, SCA Les Coteaux du Pic** Languedoc-Roussillon	Herb tinged with smokey blueberries.	**£4.00**	MRN JBR WAV

(B) **FOLENVIE CABERNET MERLOT VIN DE PAYS DE L'AUDE 2001, YVON MAU** Languedoc-Roussillon	A smooth and soft wine with bright red fruit character. Well balanced and vibrant.	**£4.00**	MAK
(A) **TESCO FINEST CORBIÈRES RESERVE 2001, MONT TAUCH** Languedoc-Roussillon	Herb-strewn with berry depth.	**£4.00**	TOS
(A) **DOMAINE DE DISERTO CORSE 2000, LES GRANDS CHAIS DE FRANCE** Corsica	Ripe perfume with lush fruit.	**£4.00**	GCF
(A) **LOUIS ESCHENAUER SYRAH 2001, LES CAVES DE LANDIRAS** Languedoc-Roussillon	Blackberry-scented with earthy depth.	**£4.00**	UNS WIE
(A) **PRESTIGE GRENACHE 2001, FREDERIC ROGER** Languedoc-Roussillon	Clean, dry, fresh, and ripe.	**£4.00**	TOS
(A) **LES SIRIANES OAKED CÔTES DU RHÔNE 2001, VIGNOBLES DU PELOUX** Rhône	Spicy wine with 'bouquet garrigues'.	**£4.00**	TOS
(A) **LE FAUVE SYRAH 2001, TERROIR CLUB** Languedoc-Roussillon	Supple, with juicy hedgerow fruits.	**£4.00**	MWW
(A) **CO-OP CÔTES DU RHÔNE RESERVE NV, DU PELOUX** Rhône	Herbs tinged with supple fruit.	**£4.00**	CWS
(B) **SAFEWAY FITOU 2001, MONT TAUCH** Languedoc-Roussillon	Concentrated, with good length and balance. Soft and open. Approachable and ripe.	**£4.00**	SAF
(A) **DOMAINE DE LA COMBE GRANDE 2000, SPAR UK** Languedoc-Roussillon	Liquorice and hedgerow fruits. Structured.	**£4.00**	SPR
(S) **MAS DU NOVI CABERNET SAUVIGNON 1999, DOMAINE SAINT JEAN DU NOVICIAT** Languedoc-Roussillon	Sweet-fruited and rich with an expressive cassis nose and a lush palate of concentrated black fruit.	**£4.00**	FCA
(B) **CHATEAU ST BENOIT MINERVOIS 1999, MAUREL-VEDEAU** Languedoc-Roussillon	A deeply coloured wine that is warm and chunky and has a charming rustic feel.	**£4.30**	SMF

(B) GALLERIE TEMPRANILLO SYRAH 2001, DOMAINES VIRGINIE Languedoc-Roussillon	A somewhat unorthodox blend from the Languedoc, but a cracking wine. Rich, ripe, spicy, firm, and rustic.	**£4.50**	JSM
(B) LES MARIONETTES MERLOT 2001, TERROIR CLUB Languedoc-Roussillon	Robust and dark with juicy red fruit and acidity. The firm tannins yield beautifully in the mouth.	**£4.50**	HOT
(B) DOMAINE DU BOIS DES DAMES CÔTES DU RHÔNE VILLAGES 2000, LES CHAIS BEAUCAIROIS Rhône	Tobacco and spice nose. The palate has subtle and interresting leather, fruit and spice character.	**£4.80**	THI SMF
(B) TERRASSES D'AZUR MERLOT 2001, CASTEL FRÈRES Languedoc-Roussillon	Ample round and long in the mouth. Ripe forest fruit flavours dominate.	**£5.00**	CLA
(B) TERRASSES D'AZUR CABERNET SAUVIGNON 2001, CASTEL FRÈRES Languedoc-Roussillon	Green pepper and blackcurrant fruit on the palate. A well made straightforward and honest wine.	**£5.00**	CLA
(B) MONTPLAISIR CABERNET FRANC 2001, DOMAINE DE PEYRAT Languedoc-Roussillon	Very firm tannins support the deep, ripe red fruit palate. Rich, spicy aromas. Highly individual.	**£5.00**	BGL
(B) ROBERT SKALLI CABERNET SAUVIGNON 2000, LES VINS SKALLI Languedoc-Roussillon	Attractive sweet fruit and youthful tannins. Not very complicated but competently made and easy to appreciate.	**£5.00**	MCT
(B) WINTER HILL SHIRAZ 2001, GROUPE FONCALIEU Languedoc-Roussillon	Complex and rich with a touch of gaminess. Firm and full, with the faintest herbaceous nuance.	**£5.00**	WTS
(B) MICHEL LAROCHE SOUTH OF FRANCE SYRAH 2001, MICHEL LAROCHE SOUTH OF FRANCE Languedoc-Roussillon	Big and firm with a very pleasant and complex fruit nose. Elegant rather than 'knockout' fruit.	**£5.00**	BWL
(B) CORBIERES TERRA VITIS NV, MONT TAUCH Languedoc-Roussillon	Deep plum red with a purple rim. Very satisfying juicy cherry fruit and liquorice flavours.	**£5.00**	MWW WRC
(B) FRENCH KISS CORBIERES 2001, MONT TAUCH Languedoc-Roussillon	A solid wine displaying ripe blackberry fruit on the palate with good structure and medium length.	**£5.00**	JSM
(S) BLUE PRINT VIN DE PAYS D'OC CABERNET FRANC 2000, MAUREL-VEDEAU Languedoc-Roussillon	Ripe wine with deep cherry and plum aromas on the nose. The palate shows rich blackcurrant fruit intensity.	**£5.00**	TOS

(S)	**BEAUMES DE VENISE 2000, LES VIGNERONS DE BEAUMES DE VENISE** Rhône	Complex red berry and leather aromas and an opulent, jammy palate. Concentration and power on the spicy finish.	**£5.00**	SMF
(S)	**VIRGINIE CABERNET SAUVIGNON 2001, DOMAINES VIRGINIE** Languedoc-Roussillon	Ripe and dry, with aromas of wild herbs and summer flowers. Bramble fruits line the balanced palate.	**£5.00**	FOL BSE
(B)	**CABERNET SAUVIGNON VIN DE PAYS D'OC 2000, BARON PHILIPPE DE ROTHSCHILD** Languedoc-Roussillon	Rich and full. Complex fruit, leather, and spice dominate. Good attack and lingering finish.	**£5.00**	TOS LON MAK
(B)	**LOUXOR MERLOT VIN DE PAYS D'OC 2001, COMPAGNIE RHODANIENNE** Languedoc-Roussillon	Supple wine with rich plum fruit aromas. A balanced palate of ripe tannin and good currant intensity.	**£5.00**	JSM
(S)	**AMMONITE 2000, ABBOTT SNEYD ANDERSON** Languedoc-Roussillon	Complex wine with a highly perfumed nose showing violet and girolle nuances. The palate is thick and juicy.	**£5.00**	WRC YWL WBC
(B)	**TESCO FINEST BEAUJOLAIS VILLAGES 2001, VAUCHER PERE ET FILS** Beaujolais	Classic aromas of banana and bubblegum. Sweet red fruits and pleasing acidity.	**£5.00**	TOS
(B)	**TERRES D'AUTAN NEGRETTE CABERNET FRANC 2001, CAVE DE FRONTON** South West	Deeply coloured with an excellent fruit richness with a hint of leather. Complex and multilayered.	**£5.00**	LAI
(B)	**LA NATURE ORGANIC CABERNET SAUVIGNON 2001, AGENCE CLVD** Languedoc-Roussillon	Rather young, in time the tannins will melt into the herbaceous fruit and the oak will integrate.	**£5.00**	FUL
(S)	**CARIGNAN ANCIENNES VIGNES 2001, TERROIR CLUB** Languedoc-Roussillon	A young wine packed with sweet, spicy fruit. Rich and chunky. Perfectly balanced.	**£5.00**	SAF
(S)	**CHÂTEAU MONTBRUN DE GAUTHERIUS 2001, TERROIR CLUB** Languedoc-Roussillon	Rich and dense with glowing raspberry fruit, herb and rose. The smoke character is in abundance.	**£5.00**	SAF
(B)	**LA CHASSE DU PAPE RESERVE 2001, GABRIEL MEFFRE** Rhône	Concentrated and rich dark berry aromas. Vanilla oak and raspberry fruit on the palate.	**£5.00**	CWS WRC MRN
(B)	**BLUE PRINT MALBEC VIN DE PAYS D'OC 2000, MAUREL-VEDEAU** Languedoc-Roussillon	Sweet fruit, firm tannins, and a lifted violet nose. Deeply coloured, full bodied, and complex.	**£5.00**	THI

(G) **GRANDE ESTUDE SELECTION SALINAS GRENACHE MERLOT 2001, LAITHWAITE'S** Languedoc-Roussillon	Restrained nose with black fruit, liquorice, and coffee-oak notes.	**£5.20**	LAI
(G) **VIN DE PAYS SYRAH 2001, HUBERT DE BOUVEY** Languedoc-Roussillon	A perfumed nose of sweet blackberry and thyme. Dripping with ripe bramble fruit and a pleasing savoury character.	**£5.50**	TON
(S) **ERMITAGE DU PIC ST LOUP 2000, ANDERSON** Languedoc-Roussillon	Rich, smoky wine with bramble and herb aromas and leather and spice on the palate. Tannins are supple.	**£5.50**	WTS
(S) **MARKS AND SPENCER BEAUJOLAIS 2001, PAUL SAPIN SA** Beaujolais	Scented with violets and raspberries. The light-bodied palate is fresh and youthful, yet concentrated.	**£5.50**	M&S
(S) **ABBOTTS CUMULUS 2000, ABBOTT SNEYD ANDERSON** Languedoc-Roussillon	Pure, unadulterated Syrah at its aromatic best. Wildflowers, tar and wet stones scent the nose.	**£6.00**	WTS
(S) **LA CUVÉE MYTHIQUE 2000, VAL D'ORBIEU** Languedoc-Roussillon	Rich and full with mint aromas and a concentrated palate of ripe fruit. Balanced with fine tannins.	**£6.50**	SAF WTS JSM
(S) **MORGON LES CHARMES 1999, GERARD BRISSON** Beaujolais	Lush, with ripe cherry aromas. The palate shows structure and balance with raspberry fruit intensity.	**£6.50**	CWS
(S) **DOMAINE DES LAURIERS FAUGÈRES 1998, JEAN JEAN** Languedoc-Roussillon	Ripe, smoky and brooding. This sunny southerner is well-integrated, richly fruited and elegant.	**£6.50**	SAF
(S) **RESERVE MOMMESSIN 2000, MOMMESSIN** Beaujolais	Elegant and dainty wine. Delicate flowers, and cherry and redcurrant fruit.	**£7.00**	AVB
(S) **BARTON & GUESTIER CABERNET PREMIUM 2000, BARTON & GUESTIER** Languedoc-Roussillon	Concentrated with ripe currant and leaf aromas. The palate is well structured with supple tannins. Good length.	**£7.00**	PFC
(S) **LA GRANDE ROMPUE 1997, CHATEAU DE LASTOURS** Languedoc-Roussillon	Rustic yet complex wine with attractive gamey nuances on the nose. Peppery black fruit, herbs and farmyard elements.	**£7.00**	PBA
(S) **JACQUES ET FRANCK VIN DE PAYS D'OC OLD BUSH VINE SYRAH 2001, M GOUNDREY** Languedoc-Roussillon	Spicy notes and a powerful palate of damsons. The grower reckons his vines are more than 75 years old.	**£7.00**	VGN

(S) CHÂTEAU LAURET PIC-ST-LOUP 2000, SCA LES COTEAUX DU PIC Languedoc-Roussillon	Rich and powerful wine with a highly perfumed nose showing violet nuances. The palate is dense and spicy.	**£7.00**	EOR
(S) LOUIS BERNARD GRANDE RESERVE CÔTES DU RHÔNE 2000, LOUIS BERNARD Rhône	Rich bramble and fig notes on the nose. The palate is opulent with good black fruit persistence.	**£7.50**	D&D
(S) CUVÉE DU GÉNÉRAL 1999, DOMAINE FAVEROT Rhône	Rich wine showing bramble and herb nuances on the nose. The palate is rounded with well-integrated tannins.	**£7.50**	DIK
(G) DOMAINE DE LONGUE TOQUE GIGONDAS 2000, GABRIEL MEFFRE Rhône	Deeply coloured, and spiked with pepper spice. Wild thyme, rosemary, griotte and warm wet stones.	**£10.90**	GYW
(G) CHÂTEAU CÔTES DU ROL ST-EMILION GRAND CRU 2000, ROBERT GIRAUD Bordeaux	Wonderful violet and red berry fruit with earthy, leathery notes. Long and complex finish.	**£11.00**	AVB
(G) CROZES-HERMITAGE 1999, E GUIGAL Rhône	Intense red with tarry, spicy smoke and notes of terroir. Very complex and full.	**£11.00**	JEF
(G) SAVIGNY-LÈS-BEAUNE 2000, ARNOUX PÈRE ET FILS Burgundy	Light, forward berry fruit flavours and a zippy acidity that gives it a bright lively character.	**£12.80**	ABY
(G) CHÂTEAU DE PEZ 1998, CHÂTEAU DE PEZ Bordeaux	Very elegant and refined with classic cassis fruit and pencil lead notes. The finish is long and concentrated	**£18.00**	WIM SEL F&M
(G) SAVIGNY 1ER CRU LA BATAILLÈRE AUX VERGELESSES 1999, DME ALBERT MOROT Burgundy	Meaty savoury nose followed rapidly by an immense powerful mouthful of violets and mulberries.	**£19.00**	AVB
(G) RESERVE DE LA COMTESSE 1997, CHÂTEAU PICHON LONGUEVILLE LALANDE Bordeaux	Ripe berry fruit on the nose and classic grassy notes on the palate. Pauillac at its best.	**£20.00**	TOS
(G) HERMITAGE 1998, BERNARD FAURIE Rhône	Black cherries, gun smoke and minerals. The substantial tannins work well with the complex fruit, wood, and acidity.	**£21.00**	J&B
(G) POMMARD 1999, LOUIS JADOT Burgundy	Restrained but lively with firm yet unaggressive tannin. Oh, and lots of berry fruit flavour.	**£23.00**	WTS

(G)	**NUITS ST-GEORGES AUX CHAIGNOTS 1ER CRU 1999, DOMAINE ROBERT CHEVILLON** Burgundy	Ripe raspberry and strawberry fruit integrate well with the subtle oak and firm long-lived tannins.	**£23.00**	J&B
(G)	**VOLNAY 1999, COMTE LAFON** Burgundy	Beautifully balanced and harmonious. The rich strawberry fruit sits nicely on the tannic framework.	**£27.00**	J&B
(G)	**NSG PREMIER CRU CLOS DES FORETS ST GEORGES 1999, DOMAINE D'ARLOT** Burgundy	Great spicy ripeness in their fruit. Their subtle use of oak is exemplary and the perfumed style runs though to the finish.	**£28.00**	WTS
(G)	**CHATEAU RAUZAN-SÉGLA 2ÉME CRU CLASSÉ MARGAUX 1997, CH. RAUZAN-SÉGLA** Bordeaux	Stylish spice, roses, and violets on the nose. Fine tannins give backbone to the plummy cherry palate.	**£28.00**	J&B
(G)	**PAVILLON ROUGE 1996, CHÂTEAU MARGAUX** Bordeaux	Lots of cassis and plummy fruit and hints of black cherries and violets. Light elegance and freshness.	**£29.00**	J&B
(G)	**CORTON BRESSANDES GRAND CRU 1998, TOLLOT-BEAUT** Burgundy	Made in tiny quantities it shows a rare intensity and concentration of perfumed fruit. Absolutely at its peak.	**£36.00**	J&B
(G)	**1997 CHATEAU DUCRU-BEAUCAILLOU 2ÉME CRU CLASSÉ ST-JULIEN,** Bordeaux	This is perfumed and spicy with notes of tobacco and cigars. Fine tannins and bracing acidity.	**£41.00**	J&B
(G)	**1996 1ER GRAND CRU CLASSE ST-EMILION, CHÂTEAU L'ANGELUS** Bordeaux	Taking on some bottle aged complexity, the herbal fruit is supported beautifully by sheer weight and structure.	**£50.00**	J&B
(G)	**1996 POMEROL, CHÂTEAU L'EVANGILE** Bordeaux	Savoury, brambly aromas and a dusty tannic texture that is lifted by rich fruitcake and chocolate flavours.	**£70.00**	J&B
(G)	**GRAND CRU 1999, CLOS DE TART** Burgundy	Intense red fruit flavours supported by rich oak and firm tannins. A wine with a glorious future.	**£75.00**	J&B
(G)	**RICHEBOURG GRAND CRU 1999, DOMAINE A F GROS** Burgundy	Redcurrant fruit with hints of spice battle for supremacy with the plum and cherry notes.	**£85.00**	ESL MAF ROD

Pinpoint who sells the wine you wish to buy by turning to the stockist codes. If you know the name of the wine you want to buy, use the alphabetical index. If the price is your motivation, look out for the "Great Value Wine of the Year" symbol; the best red and white wines under £10, sparkling wines under £12 and champagne under £17.50. Happy hunting!

FRANCE • SWEET

(B)	**DOMAINE DU HAUT-RAULY MONBAZILLAC 1999, PIERRE ALARD** South West	Roast nuts on the nose. An inviting, waxy texture pairs well with a racy lemon peel acidity.	**£4.30**	CWS
(B)	**MUSCAT DE BEAUMES-DE-VENISE NV, VIGNERONS DE BEAUMES DE VENISE** Rhône	Warm stone fruit and spice character. Good acidity and a long finish.	**£5.00**	WTS
(B)	**LA FLEUR D'OR 1999, SICA** Bordeaux	Delicate golden colour. Subtle apricot and orange peel aromatics. Medium-weight fruit on the warming palate.	**£6.00**	SAF
(B)	**MUSCAT DE BEAUMES DE VENISE CUVÉE LES TROIS FONTS 2000, DOMAINE DE COYEAUX** Rhône	Lemon in colour. A very fresh, zesty style with spicy, honeyed fruit and a very long finish.	**£7.00**	AVB
(G)	**CLOS DADY 2000, CLOS DADY** Bordeaux	Deep gold with an unctuous palate showing botrytis and orange peel fruit cut by a neat, racy acidity.	**£20.00**	SWG

GERMANY

This year, a record number of top class German wines turned up to compete in the International Wine Challenge – and were rewarded with a record number of awards, including no fewer than four trophies. The heartening success of both dry and sweet wines, and of wines made from grapes such as the Pinot Gris and Silvaner as well as the Riesling, will come as no surprise to wine enthusiasts and professionals. It will, however, encourage many other wine drinkers to cast off their prejudice that Germany has little to offer beyond Liebfraumilch.

GERMANY • SPARKLING

(A)	**DEINHARD LILA NV, DEINHARD** Mosel-Saar-Ruwer	Soft. White and green fruit character.	**£6.00**	AVB

GERMANY • DRY & OFF-DRY WHITE

	Wine	Tasting Note	Price	Stockists
(A)	**LANGENBACH DRY RIESLING 2001, REH KENDERMANN** Pfalz	A restrained, mid-weight palate.	**£3.50**	MCT
(A)	**FIRE MOUNTAIN RIESLING 2001, ZIMMERMANN, GRAEFF & MULLER** Pfalz	Good balance and apple character.	**£4.00**	BTH SAF SMF TOS
(A)	**MOSELLAND RIESLING CLASSIC 2001, WEINKELLEREI NAHETAL** Nahe	Good fruit, persistence, and mouthfeel.	**£4.00**	WTS
(A)	**KENDERMANN DRY RIESLING 2001, REH KENDERMANN** Pfalz	Attractive palate of crisp fruit.	**£4.00**	JSM TOS ODD MRN
(A)	**KENDERMANN CLASSIC RIESLING 2001, REH KENDERMANN** Pfalz	Floral and apple aromas.	**£4.00**	RHC
(A)	**KENDERMANNS RIESLING KABINETT 2001, REH KENDERMANN** Mosel-Saar-Ruwer	Boiled sweet fruit. Good acidity.	**£4.00**	ASD
(B)	**F.W. LANGGUTH ERBEN RIESLING CLASSIC 2001, F.W. LANGGUTH** Mosel-Saar-Ruwer	A clean and delicate nose is supported by a fresh, balanced, and sweet palate.	**£4.50**	EHL
(S)	**CARL REH CLASSIC RIESLING 2001, REH KENDERMANN** Mosel-Saar-Ruwer	The rich, concentrated lime flavour on the palate is backed up by vibrant acidity.	**£4.50**	RHC
(S)	**PIESPORTER GOLDTROPFCHEN KABINETT 1996, WELLER-LEHNERT** Mosel-Saar-Ruwer	Perfumed wine with honeysuckle aromas. Mouthwatering citrus fruit and fresh acidity. Balanced, with a long finish.	**£5.00**	MWW
(B)	**VINEYARD SELECTION RIESLING GEWÜRZTRAMINER 2001, REH KENDERMANN** Pfalz	Pale gold colour. Aromatic pineapple and petrol. Quite round and fat on the palate.	**£5.00**	RHC
(G)	**ESCHERNDORFER LUMP RIESLING SPÄTLESE TROCKEN 2001, HORST SAUER** Franken	The palate boasts layer upon layer of ripe, delicate crystalline citrus fruit crowned with aristocratic minerality.	**£13.90**	J&B NYW

GERMANY • LATE HARVEST

(S)	**URZIGER WURZGARTEN RIESLING SPATLESE 1992, CHRISTOFFEL PRUM** Mosel-Saar-Ruwer	Refined and elegant with a cool slatey tang. The nose is restrained, yet perfumed with petrol. Excellent minerality.	**£5.00**	MWW
(G)	**WEHLENER SONNENUHR RIESLING SPATLESE 1992, WEINGUT JJ PRUM** Mosel-Saar-Ruwer	A perfect example of a mature Mosel Riesling. Intense lime and grapefruit flavours and kerosene and petrol notes.	**£10.00**	WTS
(G)	**JOH JOH PRÜM WEHLENER SONNENUHR RIESLING AUSLESE 1995, J J PRUM** Mosel-Saar-Ruwer	Classic petrolly Riesling nose develops into a honeyed lemon palate which shows wonderful length and elegance	**£19.50**	J&B
(G)	**ESCHERNDORFER LUMP RIESLING TROCKENBEERENAUSLESE 2000, HORST SAUER** Franken	A rich and complex wine with intense honey, quince, and saffron aromas on the nose.	**£53.00**	J&B NYW
(G)	**ESCHERNDORFER LUMP SILVANER EISWEIN 2001, HORST SAUER** Franken	Subtle honeyed fruit. Rich and smooth, it has good supporting acidity and a certain liveliness.	**£55.00**	J&B NYW

HUNGARY

The only country in Eastern Europe to produce top class wines as well as bottles that offer good value daily drinking, Hungary has benefited from extensive foreign investment in Tokaji and renewed local efforts to revive the fortunes of Eger Bikaver (Bull's Blood). Sadly, these wines have been slow to find buyers in the UK, which may explain why a disappointingly small number were entered into this year's International Wine Challenge. We were, however, pleased to see winners that included grapes such as the Irsay Oliver and Cserszegi Fuszeres, which are found nowhere else.

HUNGARY • SPARKLING

(A)	**CHAPEL HILL SPARKLING CHARDONNAY N/V, BALATONBOGLAR** South Transdanubia	Green apple fruit. Lively mousse.	**£5.00**	TOS

HUNGARY • WHITE

(A) **BUDAVAR CHARDONNAY 2001, DANUBIANA** Hungary	An attractive, understated Chardonnay.	**£2.80**	ALD
(A) **HILLTOP IRSAI OLIVER 2001, HILLTOP NESZMÉZLY** Duna	Aromatic nuances of freshly-mown hay.	**£3.00**	SAF
(A) **MATRA MOUNTAIN UNOAKED PINOT GRIGIO 2001, NAGYREDE** Nagyrede	Well balanced. A delicate nose.	**£3.70**	SAF
(A) **JON JOSH CHARDONNAY 2001, DANUBIANA** Hungary	Restrained nose and fruit-driven palate.	**£3.80**	CWS
(A) **ESTATE PINOT GRIS OAKED RESERVE 2001, NAGYREDE** Nagyrede	White pepper and green fruit.	**£4.00**	ODD
(A) **SPICE TRAIL WHITE 2001, SZOLOSKERT CO-OP** Nagyrede	Bold, assertive, and richly flavoured.	**£4.00**	SAF NTD WCR
(G) **BUDAI SAUVIGNON BLANC 2001, VINARIUM** North Transdanubia	Aromatic, peachy apricot aromas and honeyed gooseberry notes. Deliciously nettley, with overtones of lemons and elderflower.	**£4.00**	WOW
(A) **BUDAI CHARDONNAY 2001, VINARIUM** North Transdanubia	Fresh and lemon-infused. Crisp acidity.	**£4.00**	WOW
(A) **RIVERVIEW CHARDONNAY PINOT GRIGIO 2000, HILLTOP NESZMELY** Tolna	Rounded citrus and melon style.	**£4.00**	TOS ASD SAF WTS
(A) **THE UNPRONOUNCEABLE GRAPE CSERSZEGI FUSZERES 2001, HILLTOP NESZMELY** Duna	Vibrant grapefruit and lime palate.	**£4.00**	WRC
(A) **RIVERVIEW SAUVIGNON BLANC 2001, HILLTOP NESZMELY** North Transdanubia	Zesty lime and gooseberry style.	**£4.00**	TOS WTS

HUNGARY • RED

(A)	**MAGYAR CABERNET SAUVIGNON 2001, EGERVIN** Northern Massif	Youthful, brooding black fruit profile.	**£3.50**	NTD
(A)	**EGRI BULL'S BLOOD 2001, DANUBIANA** Northern Massif	Meaty wine with sanguine depth.	**£3.50**	ALD
(A)	**SZEKSZÁRDI CABERNET FRANC 2000, VINARIUM** South Transdanubia	Gently spiced, vivid cassis fruit.	**£4.00**	WOW
(B)	**RIVERVIEW CABERNET SAUVIGNON 2000, HILLTOP NESZMELY** North Transdanubia	A delightfully straightforward, fruit driven wine that requires no great thought or special foods to enjoy.	**£4.50**	BGN

ITALY

The most exciting wine-producing country in the world, Italy not only boasts a bewildering array of grape varieties and climates, but also a gloriously experimental band of winemakers who are far less hampered by obstructive rules than their neighbours in France, and – surprisingly perhaps – more open-minded than many of their counterparts in the New World. There were 24 Italian Gold Medals this year, representing a wide range of styles, from classics such as Chianti and Amarone to new wave Primitivos from the up-and-coming vineyards of the south.

ITALY • SPARKLING

(A)	**SOMERFIELD LAMBRUSCO BIANCO LIGHT NV, DONELLI VINI** Emilia Romagna	Pale yet lively. Lime scented.	**£1.50**	SMF
(A)	**MARANELLO MOSCATO FIZZ NV, GIACOBAZZI** Piemonte	Delicate fruit and fine mousse.	**£2.00**	SMF

(A)	**SOMERFIELD MOSCATO FIZZ 2001, GIACOBAZZI** Piemonte	Perfumed with lovely frothy mouthfeel.	**£2.00**	SMF
(A)	**SOMERFIELD LAMBRUSCO BIANCO NV, DONELLI VINI** Emilia Romagna	Aromas of apples and lemons. Fresh and crisp.	**£2.30**	SMF
(A)	**DOMANI LAMBRUSCO BIANCO NV, FRATELLI MARTINI** Emilia Romagna	Light, attractive guava fruit flavours.	**£3.00**	NTD
(A)	**VILLA JOLANDA MOSCATO D'ASTI NV, SANTERO** Piemonte	Attractive, rich, biscuity mature aromas.	**£3.50**	TOS
(B)	**MOMBELLO ASTI SPUMANTE 2000, CAPETTA** Piemonte	Aromas of turkish delight. Delicious.	**£4.00**	SMF
(A)	**CO-OP SWEET ASTI NV, FRATELLI MARTINI** Piemonte	Rich yet delicate. Lively mousse.	**£4.00**	CWS
(A)	**SAFEWAY ASTI SPUMANTE NV, ARIONE** Piemonte	Fine mousse. Yeasty aromas. Crisp.	**£4.00**	SAF
(A)	**DOMANI ASTI NV, FRATELLI MARTINI** Piemonte	Greenish tint. Attractive. Fine mousse.	**£4.50**	NTD
(S)	**MHV ASTI NV, SANTERO** Piemonte	This sparkler is everything Asti should be: fresh, fine, forward, and flowery. Opulent.	**£4.70**	MHV
(B)	**SAN SILVESTRO ASTI NV, SAN SILVESTRO** Piemonte	Delicate colour. Frothy, fine mousse. Aromatic nose of exquisitely perfumed flowers. Fresh, attractive fizz.	**£5.00**	AVB
(B)	**SOMERFIELD ASTI 2000, CAPETTA** Piemonte	A delectable Asti. Seductive aromas of rose petals and wild mint. Flavours of fresh apples.	**£5.00**	SMF
(A)	**TOSTI SPARKLING PINOT GRIGIO NV, BOSCA TOSTI** Lombardia	Restrained, soft, pear-like fruit character.	**£6.00**	TOS

(B)	**FRANCIACORTA BRUT MILLESIMATO 1996, IL MOSNEL** Lombardy	Bright, clean and fresh with lemon-lime hints and a crisp, zingy acidity and a razor clear finish.	**£8.50**	MON
(B)	**PROSECCO SANTO STEFANO NV, RUGGERI** Veneto	Fresh and balanced. Compelling toasty notes add interest to apples on the nose. Full, expressive, grapey palate.	**£9.50**	SWG

ITALY • WHITE

(A)	**LE CONTRADE FRASCATI 2001, MGM MONDO DEL VINO** Lazio	Good length and melon fruit.	**£3.00**	SMF
(A)	**CHARDONNAY DELLE VENEZIE 2001, CONCILIO** Veneto	Pure, fresh, crisp apple fruit.	**£4.00**	SAF
(A)	**ZAGARA CATARRATTO CHARDONNAY 2001, FIRRIATO** Sicily	Good golden colour. Quite sharp.	**£4.00**	CWS WTS
(A)	**MHV SOAVE OAK AGED NV, SARTORI** Veneto	Toast-tinged crisp apple fruit.	**£4.00**	MHV
(A)	**MHV SICILIAN ORGANIC INZOLIA 2001, CANTINE VOLPI** Sicily	Well made, balanced and fresh.	**£4.00**	MHV
(B)	**MOSCATO CARDINALE 2001, VILLA LANATA** Piemonte	Well-balanced and fresh. A very pleasant, clean wine with loads of charm.	**£4.00**	D&D
(A)	**GAVIOLI CHARDONNAY DEL VENETO 2001, DONELLI VINI** Veneto	Attractive lemon fruit flavour profile.	**£4.00**	SMF
(A)	**TERRA VIVA BIANCO 2001, PERLAGE** Marche	Refreshing, light, crisp green fruit.	**£4.00**	TOS
(B)	**CO-OP ORVIETO CLASSICO 2001, BARBI** Umbria	Fresh, creamy nose with citrus and almond nuances. Clean and balanced, with fine acidity.	**£4.00**	CWS

(A)	**CO-OP PUGLIA CHARDONNAY BOMBINO 2001, CANTELE** Puglia	Ripe citrus and melon style.	**£4.00**	CWS
(A)	**MEZZOMONDO CHARDONNAY VALLAGARINA 2001, MGM MONDO DEL VINO** Trentino-Alto Adige	Soft, clear apples and peaches.	**£4.00**	WTS CWS
(B)	**INYCON CHARDONNAY 2001, INYCON** Sicily	Flowers and honeyed tropical fruit aromas. Well-concentrated citrus and apricot fruit palate. Good structure and length.	**£5.00**	SMF TOS
(B)	**PODIUM 2000, GAROFOLI** Marche	This glinting green wine boasts minerals, ripe kiwi fruit, and scents of flowers.	**£5.00**	AVB
(B)	**TREBBIANO 2001, FARNESE VINI** Abruzzi	Restrained and crisp. The often maligned Trebbiano is a winner on this occasion.	**£5.00**	LAI
(S)	**VIGNA NOVALI VERDICCHIO CLASSICO RISERVA 1999, TERRE CORTESI MONCARO** Marche	Aromatic green fruit on the nose and a creamy intensity on the palate. Well balanced, with zippy acidity.	**£7.40**	EUW MHW EVW
(G)	**PINOT GRIGIO 'ISARGUS' 2000, LOACKER** Trentino-Alto Adige	Intensely floral, with just a hint of spice. Racy acidity and vibrant fruit.	**£9.00**	GRT
(G)	**COMETA 2001, PLANETA** Sicily	Rich, concentrated wine with intense floral and green apple aromas. Minerally, zesty lemon flavours.	**£17.00**	SWG

ITALY • RED

(A)	**CANTI ROSSO 2001, FRATELLI MARTINI**	Fresh, fragrant red summer fruits.	**£3.00**	TOS
(A)	**MHV VINO DA TAVOLA ROSSO NV, SARTORI** Veneto	Nutmeg aromas. Ripe and ready.	**£3.20**	MHV
(A)	**VINO DA TAVOLA ROSSO NV, RIVA**	Ripe with succulent berry fruit.	**£3.30**	SPR

(A) **MERLOT DELLE VENEZIE 2000, DONELLI VINI** Veneto	Soft with plum-duff richness.	**£3.50**	SMF
(A) **MHV VALPOLICELLA NV, SARTORI** Veneto	Straightforward, juicy, cherry fruit.	**£3.60**	MHV
(A) **SOMERFIELD BARDOLINO NV, PASQUA** Veneto	Light and fresh cherry fruit.	**£3.80**	SMF
(A) **MHV MONTEPULCIANNO D'ABRUZZO 2000, CASTELLANI SPA** Abruzzi	Fleshy red fruit. Fresh acidity.	**£3.90**	MHV
(B) **STOWELLS OF CHELSEA MOLISE MONTEPULCIANO 2000, MATTHEW CLARK**	Very supple, soft, and ripe. A complex tar nose and good length.	**£4.00**	SAF SMF MCT
(B) **ZAGARA NERO D'AVOLA CABERNET SAUVIGNON 2001, FIRRIATO** Sicily	The dark, inky colour is a good indicator of the wine's extraction and power. Needs time.	**£4.00**	CWS
(A) **VIGNALI BASILICATA ROSSO 2001, SARTORI** Veneto	Leafy, light fruit. Refreshing. Attractive.	**£4.00**	WTS
(A) **SAINSBURY'S SANGIOVESE DI SICILIA NV, SETTESOLI** Sicily	Crisp, crunchy redcurrants. Well-balanced.	**£4.00**	JSM
(A) **MHV SICILIAN NERO D'AVOLA 2001, CANTINE VOLPI** Sicily	Deliciously developed, savoury fruit character.	**£4.00**	MHV
(A) **NURACADA RED 2001, CANTINA DI DOLIANOVA** Sardinia	Very youthful. Cherries and spice.	**£4.00**	MAE
(B) **TERRA VIVA MARCHE SANGIOVESE 2001, PERLAGE** Marche	Balanced and fresh with a very attractive, light, fruity style similar to a good Beaujolais.	**£4.00**	TOS
(A) **CO-OP MONTEPULCIANO D'ABRUZZO 2001, MGM MONDO DEL VINO** Abruzzi	Well balanced. A touch green.	**£4.00**	CWS

B	**CO-OP PRIMITIVO SANGIOVESE 2001, MGM MONDO DEL VINO** Puglia	Cherry fruits, a lifted nose, and a full-bodied palate are the hallmarks of this southern red.	**£4.00**	CWS
A	**IL PADRINO FRAPPATO NERO D'AVOLA 2001, MGM MONDO DEL VINO** Sicily	Lively acidity. Bitter cherry fruit.	**£4.00**	TOS
A	**IL PADRINO SANGIOVESE 2001, MGM MONDO DEL VINO** Sicily	A full nose. Firm tannins.	**£4.00**	WTS BGN
A	**IL PADRINO SYRAH 2001, MGM MONDO DEL VINO** Sicily	Inky wine with blackberry depth.	**£4.00**	SMF UWM
A	**MEZZOMONDO MONTEPULCIANO 2001, MGM MONDO DEL VINO** Abruzzi	Mocha, plums, and zippy acidity.	**£4.00**	ODD
A	**MEZZOMONDO NEGROAMARO 2001, MGM MONDO DEL VINO** Puglia	Bursting with black fruit.	**£4.00**	WTS
B	**LA BROCCA PRIMITIVO 2001, BASILIUM** Basilicata	A real character of a wine, that is packed full of rich, ripe, and spicy fruit.	**£4.00**	AVB
B	**TERRALE PRIMITIVO 2001, CASA VINICOLA CALATRASI** Puglia	Soft and weighty, with well-defined fruit flavours. Very dark, deep and long. Fresh, lifted acidity.	**£4.50**	BWL SMF
B	**ALBERA BARBERA D'ASTI 2000, ARALDICA VINI PIEMONTESI** Piemonte	Gently firm with clean, pure, cherry fruit character. Finely textured, with a very fresh acidity and mouthfeel.	**£4.50**	WTS SAF JSM
B	**SOMERFIELD CABERNET SAUVIGNON DELLE VENEZIE NV, GRUPPO ITALIANO VINI** Veneto	Attractively light. This is a well balanced wine with simple berry fruit character.	**£4.50**	SMF
S	**TERRANTO PRIMITIVO 1999, CONTINE DUE PALME** Puglia	Full-bodied and complex. A firmly tannic wine that is starting to show signs of maturity.	**£4.50**	CTL
B	**AGLIANICO 2001, INYCON** Sicily	Juicy fragrant cherry fruit and rose aromas. Clean and fresh, with good balance.	**£5.00**	SWG

(B) ROCCA DI ACQUAVIVA ROSSO PICENO SUPERIORE 1999, TERRE CORTESI MONCARO Marche	Sweet, spicy, black-cherry nose. The palate has enough grippy fruit to make for an interesting sip.	**£5.00**	EVW
(B) CASTELLANI MONTEREGIO RESERVA 1998, CEVIN Tuscany	Intoxicating fruit and wood on the nose follow through onto the palate.	**£5.00**	AVB
(B) TRULLI PRIMITIVO DEL SALENTO 2000, CANTELE Puglia	Weight, intensity, and concentration. Pleasing cherry fruit character. Good mouthfeel.	**£5.00**	TOS CWS ASD
(B) TRULLI SALICE SALENTINO 1998, CANTELE Puglia	Sweet raspberry and ripe black cherry fruit with supple tannins. Well balanced.	**£5.00**	CWS
(G) CANALETTO PRIMITIVO DI PUGLIA 2000, GIRELLI Puglia	Peppery, liquorice, spicy aromas give way to complex fruit and a firm structure that runs on and on.	**£5.00**	WTS
(B) MEZZO GIORNO NERO D'AVOLA CABERNET SAUVIGNON 2000, PASQUA Sicily	Elegant and subtle, displaying rich redcurrant fruit and a soft, attractive finish. Very appealing.	**£5.00**	EOR
(B) DI NOTTE VALPOLICELLA 2000, PASQUA Veneto	Simple, soft and fleshy with a delightfully perfumed, plummy nose. Attractive and easy to appreciate.	**£5.00**	TOS
(S) 35TH PARALLEL PRIMITIVO MANDURIA 2001, FRATELLI MARTINI Puglia	Firm yet supple. Fruity yet serious. Fine and complex. Perfectly balanced and extremely long.	**£5.00**	D&D
(B) NERO D'AVOLA 2001, VILLA TONINO Sicily	Rich, gentle and long, with soft crushed fruit and a peach and black fruit nose.	**£5.00**	LIB
(B) VALPOLICELLA CLASSICO 1999, ZENATO Veneto	Spice box and almond nose. Luminous cherry fruit on the textured, mouthwatering palate.	**£5.00**	WRC
(B) CHIARO DI LUNA MONTEPULCIANO D'ABRUZZO 2001, MGM MONDO DEL VINO Abruzzi	Rich purple in colour. Strong aromas of cherries and woodland fruits. Long and firm.	**£5.00**	WSO

Pinpoint who sells the wine you wish to buy by turning to the stockist codes. If you know the name of the wine you want to buy, use the alphabetical index. If the price is your motivation, look out for the "Great Value Wine of the Year" symbol; the best red and white wines under £10, sparkling wines under £12 and champagne under £17.50. Happy hunting!

(B)	**NATURAL STATE MONTEPULCIANO 2001, MGM MONDO DEL VINO** Abruzzi	Candied fruit peel and spice on the nose. Good fruit and soft tannins.	**£5.00**	WTS
(B)	**NOLITA MONTEPULCIANO 2001, MGM MONDO DEL VINO** Abruzzi	Balanced. Cherry fruit nose, spicy flavours, and a touch of bitter chocolate.	**£5.00**	ODD
(S)	**POTENZA PRIMITIVO 2001, MGM MONDO DEL VINO** Puglia	Very big and toasty with a perfume of violets. High in acid and tannins. Good length.	**£5.00**	DIW
(S)	**COL DI SASSO 2000, BANFI** Tuscany	Well-structured wine with sweet berry and herb perfume. The palate has rich fruit intensity and a decent finish.	**£5.00**	MWW
(G)	**VELUTO PRIMITIVO 2000, CASA GIRELLI** Puglia	Dense plummy fruit, silky tannins, and lots of colour. Enough character and structure to evolve.	**£5.50**	LAI
(S)	**AMATIVO SALENTO IGT 2000, CANTELE** Puglia	Silky red fruit. Round and structured, with smoky oak and hints of vegetation.	**£6.00**	WFS
(S)	**TRULLI PREMIUM SELECTION OLD VINE ZINFANDEL DEL SALENTO 1999, CANTELE** Puglia	The nose of violets and red berries is tinged with cracked black pepper. Spices, depth, complexity, and intensity.	**£6.00**	ASD
(S)	**CHIANTI CANTINE LEONARDO 2001, CANTINE LEONARDO** Tuscany	Impeccably clean, bursting with black cherries, and laced with cinnamon and nutmeg spices.	**£6.00**	LIB
(S)	**PILLASTRO SALENTO OAKED AGED 2000, CANTINE DUE PALME** Puglia	Richly coloured, with a marvelous texture. Firm but yields superb fuit and juice flavours.	**£6.00**	LAI
(S)	**TERRAGNOLO PRIMITIVO 1998, VINICOLA DI APOLLONIO** Puglia	Intensely coloured. Big, rich and ready to drink. Good length and enough substance to last a few years.	**£6.50**	ALL
(S)	**SALENTO ROSSO VALLE CUPA 1998, VINICOLA DI APOLLONIO** Puglia	Complex herb and tar overtones. Rich. Superbly firm yet yielding tannins and extremely juicy acidity.	**£6.50**	ALL SWG
(S)	**LUCCARELLI PRIMITIVO 2001, LAITHWAITE'S PRIVATE CELLARS** Puglia	Deeply coloured, with good body, an elegant nose, and a lengthy finish.	**£6.70**	LAI

(G) **CASALE VECCHIO MONTEPULCIANO 2001, FARNESE VINI** Abruzzi	Warm liquorice, gamey notes, and ripe fruit. Well-structured and balanced. A well made wine.	**£6.80**	LAI
(S) **CAPITEL SAN ROCCO 1999, TEDESCHI** Veneto	Swooningly seductive nose of spices and ripe fruit. Complex, fresh, mouth-coating plum fruit.	**£7.00**	AVB
(S) **PARPAN BARBERA D'ALBA 2000, FONTANAFREDDA** Piemonte	Deep rich ruby colour. Spicy oak layered with ripe cassis, cherry, and raisin fruit flavours.	**£7.50**	SWG
(S) **VIGNETO SAN LORENZO ROSSO CONERO 1999, UMANI RONCHI** The Marches	Made entirely from Montepulciano grapes. Warm, spicy and extremely well-balanced.	**£7.50**	SWG
(S) **LA SEGRETA ROSSO 2001, PLANETA** Sicily	A full bodied, rich, spicy Sicilian. Blended from Merlot and Nero d'Avola.	**£7.50**	SWG
(S) **LA CASETTA DI ETTORE VALPOLICELLA RIPASSO 1999, DININI VENETI** Veneto	Scented with undergrowth and spices. Warm, ripe, mouthwatering cherry fruit.	**£7.50**	MWW
(S) **KALURA NERO D'AVOLA MERLOT SICILIA 2001, CS BIRGI** Sicily	Powerful and deep, the aromas of cassis are followed by chewy almond flavours and a long finish.	**£7.50**	ALI
(G) **VALPOLICELLA RIPASSO 1999, ZENATO** Veneto	Tarry, savoury, nose with a little new oak. Rich and concentrated, with power, complexity and a long finish.	**£8.00**	WRC
(G) **ROSSO DI MONTEPULCIANO 2001, POLIZIANO** Tuscany	Juicy, rich and full-bodied, with plenty of ripe fruit. Mature, with complexity building on the long finish.	**£10.00**	SWG
(G) **LIANO 1998, UMBERTO CESARI** Emilia Romagna	Herbal, minty, complex fruit aromas which merge well with the vanilla oak and the grippy texture.	**£10.00**	AVB
(G) **INFERI 1998, AZIENDA MARRAMIERO** Abruzzi	A big, beautiful wine with sweet cherries, black fruit, and tarry notes. Masses of concentrated style. Amazing stuff.	**£11.00**	ODD
(G) **RECIOTO DELLA VALPOLICELLA TESAURO 1999, CANTINE VALPANTENA** Veneto	Hint of sweetness lifts the palate. Racy acidity and vibrant youthful fruit flavours. Fine and delicate.	**£15.00**	SWG

(G) **HARMONIUM NERO D'AVOLA 1999, FIRRIATO** Sicily	Gently peppery, spicy, tobacco leaf complexity on the nose. A big mouthful of weight and complexity.	**£15.00**	IWS
(G) **CASAL DEI RONCHI RECIOTO CLASSICO SEREGO ALIGHIERI 1996, MASI** Veneto	Another cracking wine from Sergio Alghieri. Intense, ripe, raisined fruit over a blast of alcohol.	**£18.50**	BWC
(G) **SANTO IPPOLITO CANTINE LEONARDO 2000, CANTINE LEONARDO** Tuscany	A seriously impressive wine packed with masses of juicy fruit. Nuts and wildflowers. Dense and lush. Intense fruit.	**£19.00**	LIB
(G) **RECIOTO DELLA VALPOLICELLA CLASSICO 1999, CORTEFORTE** Veneto	A big wine: rich and concentrated. Floral, lightly spiced, raisined fruit and a supple, complex concentration.	**£19.80**	LIB
(G) **CHIANTI CLASSICO 2000, BRANCAIA** Tuscany	Restrained, youthful, vibrant fruit nose. Big, gutsy, dry fruit with good depth and complexity of pepper and spice.	**£20.00**	SWG
(G) **MONFERRATO ROSSO TANTRA 1999, SCRIMAGLIO** Piemonte	Youth, intenstiy and complexity. Incredibly deep colour and a nose of blackberries, raspberries and spice.	**£20.00**	FRI
(G) **VAIO AMARON AMARONE SEREGO ALIGHIERI 1997, MASI** Veneto	Classic style with prunes and damsons and typically herbal, savoury undertones. Crisp, dry balance.	**£23.00**	BWC
(G) **AMARONE DELLA VALPOLICELLA CLASSICO 1998, BRIGALDARA** Veneto	Brigaldara displays its class with this luscious Amarone. Masses of rich, ripe, sweet fruit with coffee notes.	**£25.00**	VIN BEL
(G) **VINO NOBILE DI MONTEPULCIANO VIGNA ASINONE 1999, POLIZIANO** Tuscany	A brooding monster. Velvety smooth. Immense cassis fruit with warmth, weight and a terrifically long finish.	**£28.00**	SWG
(G) **AMARONE VIGNETI DI JAGO 1997, CANTINA SOCIALE VALPOLICELLA** Veneto	Lots of berry fruit with complex vegetal undertones and a dry finish.	**£30.00**	BRA
(G) **AMARONE DELLA VALPOLICELLA CLASSICO 1998, ALLEGRINI** Veneto	Savoury, spicy, gamey aromas. Intense prune and cherry palate. Velvety tannins smooth out the finish.	**£32.00**	LIB
(G) **LA POJA 1998, ALLEGRINI** Veneto	Silky, structured mouthfeel. Concentrated and packed full of ripe cherry flavours and dark, mysterious scents.	**£37.00**	LIB

ITALY • SWEET

(A)	**ALASIA 2001,** **ARALDICA VINI PIEMONTESI** Piemonte	Lifted nose. Lush marmalade palate.	**£5.00**	VGN
(S)	**VINO SANTO NV,** **ANTINORI** Tuscany	Clean and vibrant, with toffee apple flavours. Very long and extremely well balanced.	**£9.00**	WTS
(G)	**VIN SANTO DI CARIMIGNANO** **RISERVA 1996, TENUTA DI** **CAPEZZANA** Tuscany	Superb applewood and almond aromas. Banana, toffee, apples, and spice. The finish seems to last forever.	**£16.00**	LIB

ITALY • FORTIFIED

(S)	**SAINSBURY'S VERMOUTH** **EXTRA DRY,** **KINGSLAND**	Bone dry wine with clove and orange zest aromas. Tangy palate with myriad botanical flavours. Long and zesty.	**£3.00**	JSM
(B)	**SAINSBURY'S** **VERMOUTH ROSSO,** **KINGSLAND**	Herbs infused with orange peel and cinnamon on the nose. Fresh palate with good botanical flavours.	**£3.00**	JSM
(A)	**MHV BARONA** **EXTRA DRY VERMOUTH NV,** **WINE SERVICES EUROPE**	Spicy with botanical nuances.	**£3.20**	MHV
(A)	**MHV BARONA** **BIANCO VERMOUTH NV,** **WINE SERVICES EUROPE**	Herbal and spicy. Sweet finish.	**£3.20**	MHV
(A)	**MHV BARONA** **ROSSO VERMOUTH NV,** **WINE SERVICES EUROPE**	Sweet with a medicinal character.	**£3.20**	MHV
(A)	**MARTINI FIERO,** **MARTINI**	Crisp, clear, appley, and refreshing.	**£4.70**	JSM
(G)	**TERRE ARSE MARSALA** **VERGINE 1991,** **CANTINE FLORIO** Sicily	Burnt toffee vies with marmalade and wildflowers on the nose. Developed smokey notes. Exquisite and refined.	**£11.00**	SWG

NEW ZEALAND

2002 was not a great International Wine Challenge year for New Zealand: some people might have expected that it would carry home more Gold Medals. The interesting thing about these results, however, is not the number of awards, but the style of wine to which they were given. A quartet of Pinot Noir Golds is an impressive tally by any standards, and an especially notable one for a country that only began to master this notoriously difficult variety a few years ago. Don't be surprised to see even greater Pinot success for the Kiwis next year.

NEW ZEALAND • SPARKLING

(B)	**LINDAUER SPECIAL RESERVE NV, MONTANA WINES** Marlborough	Light gold. Fine mousse, and flavours of strawberries and raspberries. A fruit-driven, highly enjoyable bubbly.	**£9.00**	TOS WRC ODD MWW
(S)	**DEUTZ MARLBOROUGH CUVEE NV, MONTANA WINES** Marlborough	Warm bread and biscuit aromas, with well-defined apple fruit flavours. This has depth, complexity and a long finish.	**£11.00**	WRC WTS ODD

NEW ZEALAND • WHITE

(S)	**CO-OP EXPLORERS VINEYARD SAUVIGNON BLANC 2001, ST CLAIR ESTATE** Marlborough	Zingy with herbaceous aromas. The palate is full of gooseberry and citrus fruit supported by mouthwatering acidity.	**£6.00**	CWS
(S)	**SELAKS PREMIUM SELECTION SAUVIGNON BLANC 2001, NOBILO WINE GROUP** Marlborough	Capsicum and green grass elements. The palate is lush and ripe, yet balanced. A stylish, focused wine.	**£7.00**	ODD SCA ALE SGL
(S)	**HOUSE OF NOBILO ICON SERIES SAUVIGNON BLANC 2001, NOBILO WINE GROUP** Marlborough	Gooseberry and blackberry leaf aromas and a ripe, almost sweet palate cut with a bright acidity.	**£7.00**	SMF ABY WTL
(S)	**MATUA VALLEY MARLBOROUGH SAUVIGNON BLANC 2001, BERINGER BLASS** Marlborough	Clean and fresh with a herbaceous nose and zesty gooseberry fruit. The finish shows persistence and harmony.	**£7.00**	TOS
(S)	**SEIFRIED SAUVIGNON BLANC 2001, SEIFRIED ESTATE** Nelson	Melon fruit character and an attractive breadth on the palate give a soft, accessible style.	**£7.00**	RAV POR BAB CLA

(G) **VILLA MARIA RESERVE CHARDONNAY 2001, VILLA MARIA** Marlborough	Complex aromas of guava, melon, and pineapple. Creamy notes carry through onto the buttery palate. Very complex.	**£10.00**	ODD
(G) **VILLA MARIA RESERVE CLIFFORD BAY SAUVIGON BLANC 2001, VILLA MARIA** Marlborough	Deliciously zingy, clean and fresh with grassy aromas. Lemony notes lift the palate, whilst pepper adds complexity.	**£11.00**	ODD MCT

NEW ZEALAND • RED

(B) **MATUA VALLEY NORTH ISLAND RED 2001, MATUA VALLEY WINES** North Island	A supple wine with berry and herbaceous aromas. The palate is balanced with sweet oak and soft tannins.	**£5.00**	TOS
(B) **TERRACE VIEW CABERNET MERLOT 2000, KEMBLEFIELD ESTATE** Hawke's Bay	Restrained with blackberry and leafy aromas. The palate shows good black fruit depth and friendly tannins.	**£5.00**	CWS
(G) **STONELEIGH RAPAURA SERIES PINOT NOIR 2000, MONTANA WINES LTD** Marlborough	A rich and complex wine with a highly perfumed nose showing ripe berry aromas. The palate is supple with silk tannins.	**£10.00**	MTW
(G) **PINOT NOIR 2000, PALLISER ESTATE** Wairarapa	An elegant nose introduces the forward, focussed fruit. Splendid balance. Restrained oak and velvety tannins.	**£12.00**	J&B
(G) **SEVENTEEN VALLEY PINOT NOIR 2000, MOUNT RILEY** Marlborough	Appealing wine with a rich nose offering berry, vanilla and leather aromas. The palate has balance and intensity.	**£22.30**	ALI
(G) **RESERVE PINOT NOIR 2001, GIBBSTON VALLEY WINES** Central Otago	Rich and concentrated with a fantastically complex palate wich defies description. The style is fruit-driven.	**£30.00**	NWG

Pinpoint who sells the wine you wish to buy by turning to the stockist codes. If you know the name of the wine you want to buy, use the alphabetical index. If the price is your motivation, look out for the "Great Value Wine of the Year" symbol; the best red and white wines under £10, sparkling wines under £12 and champagne under £17.50. Happy hunting!

PORTUGAL

One of the late developers of the wine world (or should that be re-developers), until now Portugal has had relatively few successes with its non-fortified wines. Its large tally of medals was always heavily dependent on port and Madeira. This year, however, its winemakers at last began to exploit the potential of traditional Portuguese grapes for producing good, individual table wines. Reds are still generally more successful than whites, but anyone with a taste for an unusual bargain should try the Gold Medal winning Alverinho-Chardonnay.

PORTUGAL • WHITE

(A)	**ALTA MESA WHITE 2001, DFJ VINHOS** Estremadura	Plump peaches. Elegant and soft.	**£3.00**	CWS BGN D&F
(A)	**JP BRANCO NV, JP VINHOS** Terras do Sado	Elegant, delicate, soft, and attractive.	**£3.50**	EHL
(B)	**SEGADA WHITE 2001, DFJ VINHOS** Ribatejo	Vivid, exotic nose. Grapefruit dominates the clean, light, refreshing palate. Herbaceous notes add interest. Long finish.	**£4.00**	ODD CWS BGN UNS
(A)	**FIUZA & BRIGHT SAUVIGNON BLANC 2001, FIUZA & BRIGHT** Ribatejo	Ripe yet youthful green flavours.	**£4.00**	EHL
(B)	**MONTE VELHO BRANCO 2001, ESPORÃO** Alentejo	Palest green-tinged yellow. The nose and palate display exotic fruit of good depth and length.	**£5.00**	IRV NYW
(G)	**GRAND'ARTE ALVERINHO CHARDONNAY 2000, DFJ VINHOS** Estremadura	An expressive melon and ripe peach nose. Full-bodied, opulent fruit on the palate with lemon and grapefruit flavours.	**£6.00**	TOS

PORTUGAL • RED

(A)	**RAMADA 2001, DFJ VINHOS** Estremadura	Pure, characterful, lush, and aromatic.	**£3.50**	JSM SAF SMF WRC CWS

(A) **TÂMARA 2000, FALUA** Ribatejo	Spicy with blackberry intensity.	**£3.50**	MRN SAF
(B) **PORTADA CASTELAO TINTA RORIZ 2001, DFJ VINHOS** Estremadura	Sweetly aromatic with berry and resinous notes. The palate has fruit richness, good structure, and fair intensity.	**£4.00**	BTH UNS SMF CWS
(B) **TERRA DE LOBOS 2001, CASAL BRANCO** Ribatejo	Fresh and light with jammy aromas. Fruit-filled palate with moderate tannins and a lingering finish.	**£4.00**	WTS
(A) **BRIGHT BROTHERS BAGA 2001, BRIGHT BROTHERS** Beiras	Spiced red plum flavour profile.	**£4.00**	SMF
(A) **FALUA DUAS CASTAS RED 1999, FALUA** Ribatejo	Ripe plum and damson fruit.	**£4.00**	WRC MRN
(B) **REGIONAL RIBATEJANO RED 1999, QUINTA DA ALORNA** Ribatejo	Cedar and blackcurrant fruit character that are so typical of well vinified, good quality Cabernet Sauvignon.	**£4.00**	L&S
(B) **SEGADA RED 2001, DFJ VINHOS** Ribatejo	This ruby red wine is brimming with spicy raspberry and other forest fruits. Gentle smoky oak.	**£4.50**	ODD JSM UNS WRC
(S) **DUQUE DE VISEU 1999, SOGRAPE** Beiras	A sweet-fruited wine with a good berry and spice perfume. The finish is long with tarry depth.	**£5.00**	MWW RWM GNW SGL
(S) **PEDRAS DO MONTE 2000, DFJ VINHOS** Terras do Sado	Fine, dusty tannins and an unusual apricot fruit nose. Ripe, succulent and great value for money.	**£5.00**	D&F WRC UNS SMF
(B) **VEGA DOURO 1999, DFJ VINHOS** Douro	An inky wine with intense baked fruit aromas and spicy depth. The finish has muscle and weight.	**£5.00**	CWS ADW WAW JOV
(B) **ALTANO 2000, SILVA & COSENS LDA** Douro	Vibrant wine with intense berry aromas. The palate is structured with sweet vanilla oak and good weight.	**£5.00**	WTS WIE LOH BCW
(B) **FIUZA CABERNET SAUVIGNON 2000, FIUZA & BRIGHT** Ribatejo	Red fruits and spice. A rich and full bodied wine with real weight and depth.	**£5.00**	EHL

(S) **FIUZA TOURIGA NACIONAL CABERNET SAUVIGNON 2001, FIUZA & BRIGHT** Ribatejo	A sun-drenched wine with succulent berry aromas. Laden with ripe cherry fruit and supple tannins.	**£5.00**	EHL
(S) **GRAND'ARTE TOURIGA FRANCA 2000, DFJ VINHOS** Estremadura	Rich with a layered palate of bilberries and blackcurrants. Balanced acidity, supple tannins and decent length.	**£6.00**	JSM
(S) **DFJ TOURIGA FRANCA & TOURIGA NACIONAL 2000, DFJ VINHOS** Estremadura	A powerful wine with baked berry fruit aromas and a concentrated black fruit palate. Underpinned by firm tannins.	**£6.00**	D&F TOS
(S) **CASA SANTOS LIMA MERLOT TINTA MIÚDA RED 2000, QUINTA DA BOAVISTA** Estremadura	Intensely plummy wine. The palate is rich and ripe with supple tannins and decent length and complexity.	**£6.00**	SWG
(S) **CASA SANTOS LIMA SYRAH CASTELAO RED 2000, QUINTA DA BOAVISTA** Estremadura	A concentrated and complex wine. It is big, full, and packed with wonderfully dark and enchanting spicy fruit flavours.	**£6.00**	SWG
(S) **PIORNOS TRINCADEIRA 2001, ADEGA COOPERATIVA DA COVILHA** Beiras	Fruits of the forest aromas and black fruit with gentle wood-smoke nuances on the palate.	**£6.00**	REY
(S) **QUINTA DE ALORNA CABERNET SAUVIGNON 1998, QUINTA DE ALORNA** Ribatejo	The palate is unctuous with a fresh mint character. Tannin, oak and fruit are all well-judged giving harmony.	**£7.00**	L&S
(S) **VALLADO DOURO RED 2000, MARIA ANTÓNIA FERREIRA** Douro	The nose is perfumed with baked fruit and spice. The palate is concentrated and supported by leathery tannins.	**£7.00**	I EA
(S) **QUINTA DE LA ROSA DOURO 2000, QUINTA DE LA ROSA** Douro	A concentrated wine with prune and fig aromas. The palate has good balance, firm tannins and admirable persistence.	**£7.40**	M&V TAN
(S) **QUINTA DO CRASTO DOURO 2000, QUINTA DO CRASTO** Douro	Full, rich, and flavoursome. Concentrated, soft and deep. Laden with over-ripe berry fruit. Excellent supporting wood.	**£7.50**	SWG
(G) **QUINTA DAS VERDELHAS 2000, CASA AGRICOLA ROBOREDO MADEIRA** Douro	This heavyweight is bursting with complex clove, spice, and ripe fruit flavours. Great concentration and long finish.	**£8.00**	REY
(G) **CORTES DE CIMA RESERVA 1998, HANS KRISTIAN JORGENSEN** Alentejo	Rich, deep, briary fruit. The oak is well-knit with the fruit and set off by the dry tannins.	**£9.00**	ADN

Ⓖ	**VINHA PAN 1999, LUIS PATO** Beiras	A complex wine. Heady leather and spice aromas. The palate has layers of rich berry and damson fruit.	**£16.80**	CSH FSW

PORTUGAL • FORTIFIED

Ⓐ	**ESCUDEIRO RUBY PORT NV, UNIAO** Douro	Lush red fruit. Rich. Glossy.	**£4.00**	CDC
Ⓐ	**NAVIGATORS RUBY PORT NV, REAL COMPANHIA VELHA** Douro	Sweet with lush briar fruit.	**£5.00**	SMF
Ⓐ	**CO-OP RUBY PORT NV, SMITH WOODHOUSE** Douro	Lush with sweet berry fruit.	**£5.40**	CWS
Ⓑ	**MHV REGIMENTAL FINE RUBY PORT NV, SILVA + COSENS** Douro	Sweet and lush with blackberry intensity, fine balance, and decent weight. Complex finish.	**£5.70**	MHV
Ⓐ	**REGIMENTAL FINE TAWNY PORT NV, SILVA + COSENS** Douro	Nuts and honey. Amber nectar.	**£5.70**	MHV
Ⓐ	**CO-OP TAWNY PORT NV, SMITH WOODHOUSE** Douro	Nutty with caramel notes.	**£5.90**	CWS
Ⓐ	**NAVIGATORS TAWNY PORT NV, REAL COMPANHIA VELHA** Douro	Caramelized style with nutty aromas.	**£5.90**	SMF
Ⓑ	**JP MOSCATEL DE SETÚBAL NV, JP VINHOS** Terras do Sado	Heady perfume of honey, wildflowers, and orange marmalade. Luscious and rich, yet refreshing.	**£6.00**	EHL
Ⓐ	**SPAR OLD CELLAR RUBY PORT NV, SPAR UK LTD** Douro	Rich and sweet with good balance.	**£6.30**	SPR
Ⓐ	**MONTE SECO NA, HENRIQUES & HENRIQUES** Madeira	Attractive, ripe red summer fruits.	**£6.50**	DIW ELD POR WTS

(B)	**NAVIGATORS VINTAGE CHARACTER PORT NV, REAL COMPANHIA VELHA** Douro	Velvety wine with intense blackberry and spice flavours. The sweetness is well judged. Decent length.	**£6.50**	SMF
(S)	**ASDA FINEST RESERVE PORT NV, SMITH WOODHOUSE & CA LDA** Douro	Mouthfilling wine with plenty of juicy damson and blackberry fruit on the palate. Pleasing soft tannins and wood.	**£7.00**	JEF ASD
(B)	**SAINSBURY'S FINEST RESERVE PORT, TAYLOR'S** Douro	A Plummy wine with a velvety mouthfeel. The nose is rich and the palate laced with brooding fruit.	**£7.00**	JSM
(A)	**ASDA LBV PORT 1995, SMITH WOODHOUSE & CA** Douro	Velvety with rich bramble fruit.	**£7.00**	ASD
(B)	**CO-OP VINTAGE CHARACTER PORT NV, SMITH WOODHOUSE** Douro	An intense, expressive berry and baked fruit nose. Thick and sweet with good concentration to finish.	**£7.10**	CWS
(A)	**SAINSBURY'S LATE BOTTLED VINTAGE PORT 1995, SILVA & COSENS** Douro	Intense with sweet blackberry fruit.	**£7.40**	JSM
(B)	**MHV REGIMENTAL SPECIAL RESERVE NV, SILVA + COSENS** Douro	Rich and supple with lovely mouthfeel. Concentrated damson fruit and good persistence on the finish	**£7.40**	MHV
(B)	**NAVIGATORS LATE BOTTLED VINTAGE PORT 1996, REAL COMPANHIA VELHA** Douro	Rich and unctuous with bramble aromas and a spicy character. The finish shows depth and concentration.	**£7.40**	SMF
(B)	**DOW'S FINE RUBY PORT NV, SILVA & COSENS** Douro	Rich wine with cherry, damson, and spice on the nose. A dundee cake palate of good length.	**£7.50**	JMC WAV MRN ELD
(B)	**CO-OP LATE BOTTLED VINTAGE PORT 1995, SMITH WOODHOUSE** Douro	Ripe and unctuous with lovely soft mouthfeel and delicious black cherry fruit. The finish is long and harmonious.	**£7.70**	CWS
(G)	**VISTA ALEGRE 10 YEAR OLD TAWNY PORT NV, VALLEGRE VINHOS DO PORTO** Douro	A rich Tawny with a pronounced nose of marmalade, pistachio, and walnut. The palate is light and beautifully balanced.	**£8.00**	HWA
(B)	**WAITROSE LBV PORT 1996, SMITH WOODHOUSE** Douro	As fine as many a proper Vintage Port. Textured, rich, and aromatic, it should age well.	**£8.20**	WTS

(B) OLD CELLAR LBV PORT 1995, SPAR UK Douro	A lush palate showing deep damson and plum fruit and a lick of spice to finish.	**£8.40**	SPR
(B) DOW'S TRADEMARK RESERVE PORT NV, SILVA & COSENS Douro	Ready for drinking now. A relatively simple wine that has an easy, mellow character.	**£9.00**	ROD ADN BAB G&M
(B) BURMESTER SOTTO VOCE PORTO RESERVE NV, J.W. BURMESTER Douro	Unctuous and rich with sweet berry and damson fruit. The palate is harmonious. Fair persistence.	**£9.00**	HBJ
(S) DOW'S LATE BOTTLED VINTAGE 1996, SILVA & COSENS Douro	Soft and fruity with amazing blackberry richness on the nose and palate. The oak is well-integrated.	**£9.50**	SAF JSM TOS ASD WTS
(B) BLANDY'S DUKE OF CLARENCE RICH MADEIRA NV, MADEIRA WINE COMPANY Madeira	Lemons and raisins dance on the nose. Rich and sweet, with nuts and dried fruit.	**£9.50**	JSM SAF WTS MRN MHV
(G) CÁLEM LATE BOTTLED VINTAGE 1997, A.A. CÁLEM & FILHO Douro	The ripe black fruits, spice, and brown sugar aromas lead to a much greater intensity on the palate.	**£9.50**	UWM
(S) HENRIQUES & HENRIQUES SINGLE HARVEST, HENRIQUES & HENRIQUES Madeira	Caramel and candied orange rind. The palate is sweet, yet impeccably balanced. Very long finish.	**£10.00**	BTH LEA CPW POR
(S) DOW'S CHRISTMAS RESERVE PORT NV, SILVA & COSENS Douro	Plump wine with rich damson fruit and clove aromas. The palate has depth, complexity and a velvety finish.	**£10.00**	TOS ASD JSM MAK
(B) TAYLORS LATE BOTTLE VINTAGE 1996, TAYLOR'S Douro	Succulent deep blackberry fruit aromas and a damson flavoured palate. Shows good persistence.	**£10.00**	JSM WTS WRC MWW
(B) CROFT LATE BOTTLE VINTAGE PORT 1995, CROFT Douro	Plump plum and berry fruit. Well structured it has firm supporting tannins. Good finish.	**£10.00**	CWS
(B) SOCIEDADE DOS VINHOS BORGES 1995, SOCIEDADE DOS VINHOS BORGES Douro	A complex wine showing excellent damson and blackberry fruit intensity. Rich with a long and harmonious finish.	**£10.00**	D&D
(S) QUINTA DO VALE DA MINA LBV 1997, LEMOS & VAN ZELLER Douro	A very dark and powerful damson nose. The palate is amazing with great intensity and depth of fruit.	**£10.00**	DIW

(G) **MOSCATEL ROXO 1991, JP VINHOS** Terras do Sado	Complex aromas of roast nuts, candied orange peel and toffee. Rich and long. Well made and beautifully balanced.	**£10.00**	EHL
(B) **QUINTA DO TEDO PORTO FINEST RESERVE BARRIQUE NO.31 NV, QUINTA DO TEDO** Douro	Classic style with a perfumed nose and rich damson fruit palate. The finish is long and sweet.	**£10.00**	MKV
(B) **KROHN LBV 1997, WIESE & KROHN** Douro	Rich wine with a concentrated and sweet palate showing ripe blackberry fruit. Balanced with good length.	**£10.00**	MER
(S) **FERREIRA LBV 1997, FERREIRA** Douro	Velvety wine with rich damson and cinnamon aromas. Balanced sweetness. Shows well on the finish.	**£10.00**	BWC
(S) **NOVAL UNFILTERED LATE BOTTLED VINTAGE 1997, QUINTA DO NOVAL** Douro	A very elegant rich fruitcake nose and unctuous blueberry palate. Long and harmonious with a lick of spice.	**£11.00**	GWI IVY LEA TAN
(S) **BLANDY'S FIVE YEAR OLD VERDELHO MADEIRA NV, MADEIRA WINE COMPANY** Madeira	Rich and honeyed wine with pronounced apple and floral nuances on the nose.	**£12.00**	ODD G&M VHW C&B
(S) **BLANDY'S FIVE YEAR OLD BUAL NV, MADEIRA WINE COMPANY** Madeira	Raisins, toffee, and nuts. A complex medium-weight wine with a superb tangy finish.	**£12.00**	ODD G&M GHL RIL
(G) **RAMOS PINTO LBV 1997, RAMOS PINTO** Douro	Crimson wine with complex smoke and earth aromas. The palate is dense with sultana and damson flavours.	**£12.00**	HMC WIM
(S) **COSSART GORDON'S FIVE YEAR OLD MALMSEY NV, MADEIRA WINE COMPANY** Madeira	Rich, weighty, aromatic, and nutty. The alcohol imparts smoothness and warmth without aggression.	**£12.50**	WIE DIW C&B HVN
(G) **CAZAL DOS JORDOES VINTAGE CHARACTER PORT 2001, ARLINDO PINTO E CRUZ** Douro	The nose is enticing with a rich complexity of prunes and medicinal overtones. Warm, intense and succulent.	**£12.50**	VRT
(S) **MAJARA VINTAGE CHARACTER PORT 2001, ARLINDO PINTO E CRUZ** Douro	This well-crafted wine has rich berry fruit aromas and a super-sweet plummy palate balanced by velvety tannins.	**£12.50**	VRT
(S) **DALVA PORTO RESERVE 1995, C. DA SILVA** Douro	Sweet and concentrated with berry and damson aromas. The jammy palate is rich with spice and vanilla oak.	**£12.70**	VSE

(S) **DOW'S CRUSTED PORT BOTTLED 1997, SILVA & COSENS** Douro	Rich and opulent with thick bramble fruit on the nose and palate. A concentrated, spicy finish.	**£13.00**	WTS JSM ODD BTH	
(G) **SILVA & COSENS CRUSTED PORT BOTTLED 1998, SILVA & COSENS** Douro	Rich berry and spice aromas. The palate is balanced with lush blackberry fruit, supple tannins and rich sweetness.	**£13.00**	WTS JSM ODD BTH	
(G) **GRAHAM'S CRUSTED PORT BOTTLED 1999, W & J GRAHAM** Douro	A supple wine with a perfumed nose showing fig and chocolate nuances. The palate is well balanced and jammy.	**£13.00**	MWW HAR CST MHV	
(S) **DOW'S CRUSTED PORT 1997, DOW'S** Douro	A blend of wines from different years vinified in a similar way to a Vintage Port. Needs decanting.	**£13.00**	JSM	
(S) **ROZÈS INFANTA ISABEL 10 YEAR OLD PORT NV, ROZES** Douro	Vibrant bouquet of dried apricots, figs and bitter oranges. The palate is finely textured. Nut and raisin notes.	**£14.00**	VRA	
(G) **SMITH WOODHOUSE LATE BOTTLED VINTAGE 1990, SMITH WOODHOUSE & CO** Douro	Good intense aromas. The velvety palate is packed with rich black fruit flavours. Admirable depth and complexity	**£15.00**	C&B AVB MYN MBW	
(S) **SMITH WOODHOUSE LATE BOTTLED VINTAGE 1992, SMITH WOODHOUSE & CO** Douro	Refined and powerful spicy berry aromas. Super-sweet fruit allied to a supple tannic frame. Long and concentrated.	**£15.00**	JEF	
(S) **BLANDY'S TEN YEAR OLD MALMSEY NV, MADEIRA WINE COMPANY** Madeira	This Malmsey is massively complex, deliciously aromatic and very well-balanced.	**£15.00**	ODD BBR G&M FEN	
(S) **WARRE'S TRADITIONAL LATE BOTTLED VINTAGE PORT 1992, WARRE'S** Douro	The nose is full of toasty, spiced blackberry and chocolate nuances. The palate shows lovely balance.	**£15.00**	JSM	
(G) **HENRIQUES & HENRIQUES 10 YEAR OLD VERDELHO, HENRIQUES & HENRIQUES** Madeira	A complex range of marmalade and bitter orange aromas with caramelised, nutty, orange flavours.	**£17.00**	SEL F&M HDS CPW	
(G) **HENRIQUES & HENRIQUES 10 YEAR OLD BUAL, HENRIQUES & HENRIQUES** Madeira	Big, rich fruitcake and figgy, orangey flavours. Zippy acidity provides balance and length.	**£17.00**	DBY PGW HOU	
(G) **HENRIQUES & HENRIQUES 10 YEAR OLD MALMSEY, HENRIQUES & HENRIQUES** Madeira	The nutty Malmsey has an intense toffee nose and plenty of dried fruit and hazelnut flavours.	**£17.00**	MFS HAR LEA TAN	

(G) **BLANDY'S FIFTEEN YEAR OLD MALMSEY NV, MADEIRA WINE COMPANY** Madeira	Christmas pudding with rich sherry-ish aromas. Caramel and coffee. Sheer heaven.	**£20.00**	BBR WSO BTH C&B
(G) **QUINTA DO VALE DONA MARIA VINTAGE PORT 1999, LEMOS & VAN ZELLER** Douro	Concentrated and aromatic. The palate is voluptuous with super-ripe morello cherry fruit allied to a supple tannic frame.	**£20.00**	BWL TAN DIW AVB
(G) **QUINTA DO CRASTO VINTAGE PORT 1999, QUINTA DO CRASTO** Douro	Inky black. The nose is an entrancing mix of griotte and spice box. An intriguing floral quality.	**£24.60**	SWG
(G) **HENRIQUES & HENRIQUES 15 YEAR OLD VERDELHO, HENRIQUES & HENRIQUES** Madeira	Smoky yet tangy, with a creme brulee richness. Racy candied citrus fruit flavours, caramel and toffee.	**£25.00**	DBY PGW HDS JNW
(G) **HENRIQUES & HENRIQUES 15 YEAR OLD BUAL, HENRIQUES & HENRIQUES** Madeira	Caramel, fruitcake and Seville oranges. Honeyed nuttiness. An amazingly long and well-structured finish.	**£25.00**	DBY ELD HDS L&W
(G) **HENRIQUES & HENRIQUES 15 YEAR OLD MALMSEY, HENRIQUES & HENRIQUES** Madeira	Full-bodied, plump juicy raisin and delicate fig flavour profile. Touches of butter. Long finish.	**£25.00**	F&M HDS LEA WTS
(G) **QUINTA DA GRICHA VINTAGE PORT 2000, CHURCHILL GRAHAM** Douro	Amazing extraction. The palate is super-sweet with rich perfumed damson fruit flavours and toasty notes.	**£25.00**	TAN CPW H&H
(G) **QUINTA DE LA ROSA VINTAGE PORT 1999, QUINTA DE LA ROSA** Douro	Very perfumed nose showing tar and rich berry fruit aromas. The palate is thick with rich damson fruit.	**£25.00**	M&V
(G) **CHURCHILL'S VINTAGE PORT 1991, CHURCHILL GRAHAM** Douro	Full and mellow with a lovely smoky nose. The palate is deep and has excellent bramble fruit intensity.	**£32.90**	TAN CPW H&H
(G) **CHURCHILL'S VINTAGE PORT 1985, CHURCHILL GRAHAM** Douro	A mellow nose showing complex fruitcake spice and raisiny aromas. Balanced with lots of depth and elegance to finish.	**£35.00**	TAN CPW H&H
(G) **BLANDY'S MALMSEY VINTAGE MADEIRA 1978, MADEIRA WINE COMPANY** Madeira	Tea and oranges. Crisp acidity defies the years. Luscious and complex. This is an amazing wine.	**£50.00**	RWM PGR
(G) **TAYLOR'S VINTAGE PORT 1985, TAYLOR'S** Douro	Extraordinary finesse, this Port has evolved and developed superbly well over the years. A truly great wine.	**£60.00**	JSM

SOUTH AFRICA

South Africa's wines were over-praised by far too many well-meaning critics when this country held its first representative elections, but the International Wine Challenge results told a different story. In simple terms, isolation had left the Cape winemakers unready to compete with the rest of the world. A decade later, there's no question that they are catching up very quickly and can now field a wide range of styles at a wide range of prices. Many of this year's award winners come from young vineyards in new regions, so stand by for even more successes in 2003.

SOUTH AFRICA • SPARKLING

(B) **INANDA BRUT NV, VREDENDAL WINERY** Olifantsriver	Full, clean, and appley with a frivolous, frothy mousse for a lively mouthful. Clean, fresh and well made.	**£5.00**	TOS JSM WEP MRN
(B) **GRAHAM BECK BRUT NV, GRAHAM BECK WINES** Robertson	Delicate and lightly perfumed on the nose. Surprisingly full fruit flavour and depth on the palate.	**£8.00**	BWL SAF
(B) **CAP CLASSIQUE JACQUES BRUÈRE BRUT RESERVE 1998, BON COURAGE ESTATE** Robertson	Aromatic key lime aromas. Masses of ripe fruit and racy lime notes on the palate. Long finish.	**£9.40**	GPA

SOUTH AFRICA • WHITE

(A) **ASDA CAPE CHARDONNAY 2001, WINECORP** Western Cape	Packed with ripe citrus fruit.	**£3.00**	ASD
(A) **CULLINAN VIEW CHENIN BLANC 2001, MATTHEW CLARK** Robertson	Light with ripe pear fruit.	**£3.50**	MCT
(A) **CAPE CREEK CHENIN BLANC 2001, LES GRANDS CHAIS DE FRANCE** Breede River Valley	Rounded wine with peachy fruit.	**£3.50**	GCF
(B) **KAYA CHENIN BLANC 2001, COPPOOLSE AND FINLAYSON** Western Cape	Fresh and fruity with pear and apple aromas. The palate is ripe and round with decent acidity.	**£3.50**	PIM WWT

(B) **KATHENBERG CHENIN BLANC 2001, WINECORP** Western Cape	A dry and delicate Chenin with a delicious floral character. Refreshing and well balanced.	**£3.70**	WRT
(A) **KAROO VELDT PREMIUM WHITE NV, OVERHEX VINEYARDS** Western Cape	Acacia-scented fresh pineapple fruit.	**£3.80**	NTD
(A) **SOMERFIELD SOUTH AFRICAN COLOMBARD 2001, AFRICAN TERROIR** Stellenbosch	Clean and aromatic. Waxy mouthfeel.	**£3.80**	SMF
(B) **LYNGROVE COLLECTION SAUVIGNON BLANC 2001, BAARSMA** Western Cape	Notes of asparagus and capsicum, medium bodied and with good length.	**£4.00**	CWS
(A) **COLOMBARD 2001, LUTZVILLE VINEYARDS** Olifantsriver	Lively citrus with a spritz.	**£4.00**	SWS
(B) **DUMISANI CHENIN CHARDONNAY 2001, WINECORP** Western Cape	The richness of the Chardonnay complements the racy acidity and fruit of the Chenin.	**£4.00**	ASD
(A) **MHV ROURKES DRIFT SOUTH AFRICAN CHARDONNAY 2001, AFRICAN TERROIR** Western Cape	Peppery palate of light-bodied fruit.	**£4.00**	MHV
(A) **VAN LOVEREN SAUVIGNON BLANC 2002, VAN LOVEREN** Robertson	Gooseberry and blackcurrant leaf aromas.	**£4.00**	SMF WRC WEP MRN
(A) **VAN LOVEREN SEMILLON 2002, VAN LOVEREN** Robertson	Grapefruit and elderflower cordial flavours.	**£4.00**	MRN WEP WRC
(A) **GÔIYA CHARDONNAY SAUVIGNON BLANC 2002, VREDENDAL WINERY** Olifantsriver	Fresh, lively citrus style.	**£4.00**	TOS JSM WEP MRN
(B) **RYLANDS GROVE BARREL FERMENTED CHENIN BLANC 2001, STELLENBOSCH VINEYARDS** Stellenbosch	Apricot, peach and a touch of honey. A skillfully crafted wine that is well balanced and long.	**£4.00**	TOS
(A) **CO-OP CAPE CHENIN BLANC OAK-AGED 2001, STELLENBOSCH VINEYARDS** Stellenbosch	Apple fruit on toasty oak.	**£4.00**	CWS

(A) **BARREL FERMENTED SEMILLON 2001, FRANSCHHOEK VALLEY CO-OP** Paarl	Waxy with good zesty fruit.	**£4.00**	CWS
(A) **NOT TOO DRY CHARDONNAY 2001, AFRICAN TERROIR** Western Cape	Full-bodied. Balanced. Attractive and well made.	**£4.00**	JSM CWS TOS MHV
(A) **COLOMBARD CHARDONNAY 2001, DOUGLAS GREEN BELLINGHAM** Western Cape	Round, soft, somewhat floral nose.	**£4.00**	TOS
(A) **KUMALA COLOMBARD CHARDONNAY 2001, WESTERN WINES** Western Cape	Buttery wine with ripe fruit.	**£4.00**	TOS ODD WTS VGN
(B) **NITIDA SAUVIGNON BLANC 2001, NITIDA** Durbanville	Tart yet lush exotic fruit. A fine example of the beautifully-crafted Sauvignons now emerging from South Africa.	**£4.00**	AVB
(A) **DEETLEFS ESTATE CHENIN BLANC 2000, DEETLEFS ESTATE** Breede River Valley	Fresh white flowers. Pineapple fruit.	**£4.00**	FOL
(A) **SEMILLON 2000, DEETLEFS ESTATE** Breede River Valley	Fresh, floral and quite elegant.	**£4.00**	FOL
(B) **EXCELSIOR ESTATE SAUVIGNON BLANC 2001, EXCELSIOR ESTATE** Robertson	Restrained on the nose, with just a whiff of gooseberry. Clean mineral palate.	**£4.50**	WTS
(B) **AFRICAN LEGEND CHARDONNAY 2001, AFRICAN TERROIR** Western Cape	Ripe wine with melon and pineapple aromas on the nose. The toasty palate is balanced by fresh acidity.	**£5.00**	WST
(S) **STONECROSS CHENIN BLANC CHARDONNAY 2001, DEETLEFS ESTATE** Breede River Valley	Rounded with intense pear and citrus aromas. Balanced palate with good fruit depth and piercing acidity.	**£5.00**	MYL
(B) **PORCUPINE RIDGE SAUVIGNON BLANC 2001, BOEKENHOUTSKLOOF** Western Cape	A distinctive nose of herbs and elderflower followed by a refreshing grassy, flinty palate.	**£5.00**	ASD
(B) **WELTEVREDE GEWÜRZTRAMINER 2001, WELTEVREDE** Robertson	Fresh, young, and lively. This wine has a greenish hue and well balanced fruit and acidity.	**£5.00**	AVB

(S)	**OUDE WELTEVREDEN CHARDONNAY 2000, WELTEVREDE LANDGOEDWYN** Robertson	Rich and buttery with a restrained nose of creamy fruit. The palate is ripe, well-structured, and elegant.	**£5.00**	AVB
(B)	**CHARDONNAY 2000, HOOPENBURG** Stellenbosch	Rich, ripe and toasty. Good weight and balance. Concentrated and long. Deep and creamy yet restrained.	**£5.00**	WTS
(S)	**SAUVIGNON BLANC 2001, BUITENVERWACHTING** Constantia	Ripe gooseberry and flint aromas. The palate is steely with excellent finesse and concentration.	**£6.00**	BWC
(S)	**BARREL FERMENTED CHENIN BLANC 2001, JORDAN WINERY** Stellenbosch	Candied fruit, honey and oak on the nose. Excellent balance, length and fruit flavours.	**£7.00**	WWT CNL FSW ALE
(S)	**SINCERELY SAUVIGNON BLANC 2001, NEIL ELLIS WINES** Coastal	A full, flavoursome wine with tropical fruit aromas and a rich gooseberry palate. Fine acidity and a decent finish.	**£7.00**	JSM
(S)	**FAIRVIEW LA BERYL BLANC 2000, WINES OF CHARLES BACK** Paarl	Classic lanolin nose with caramel and figs and a richly textured palate of ripe honeyed apples.	**£9.00**	CHN
(G)	**GLEN CARLOU CHARDONNAY RESERVE 2000, GLEN CARLOU VINEYARDS** Paarl	Full of rich toasty oak, over-ripe, creamy fruit and a hint of sweetness balancing the tingling acidity.	**£10.00**	ODD CPW FSW SWG

SOUTH AFRICA • ROSÉ

(B)	**VAN LOVEREN BLANC DE NOIR 2002, VAN LOVEREN** Robertson	Bubblegum and strawberry on the nose with a fruity palate and a pleasant, soft finish.	**£4.00**	TOS JSM WEP MRN

SOUTH AFRICA • RED

(A)	**CABERNET SAUVIGNON 1998, LA MOTTE** Paarl	Ripe, rich, and herbaceous cassis.	**£3.20**	PFC

Pinpoint who sells the wine you wish to buy by turning to the stockist codes. If you know the name of the wine you want to buy, use the alphabetical index. If the price is your motivation, look out for the "Great Value Wine of the Year" symbol; the best red and white wines under £10, sparkling wines under £12 and champagne under £17.50. Happy hunting!

(A)	**SHIRAZ 1999, LA MOTTE** Paarl	Violets and ripe tarry fruit.	**£3.70**	MHV
(A)	**SOUTH AFRICAN CAPE RED NV, AFRICAN TERROIR** Western Cape	Aromas of leather and redcurrants.	**£3.70**	MHV
(A)	**PEAKS VIEW SHIRAZ 2001, BOVLEI WINERY** Paarl	Ripe, warm, fragrant black fruit.	**£4.00**	MYL
(A)	**CULLINAN VIEW SHIRAZ 2001, W O ROBERTSON** Robertson	Inky brambles 'n' cream style.	**£4.00**	MCT
(A)	**KAROO VELDT PREMIUM CAPE RED NV, OVERHEX VINEYARDS** Western Cape	Leather-scented. Packed with blackberries.	**£4.00**	NTD
(A)	**DUMISANI CINSAULT MERLOT 2001, WINECORP** Western Cape	Spiced ripe red fruit palate.	**£4.00**	ASD
(A)	**SWARTLAND PINOTAGE 2001, SWARTLAND WINERY** Swartland	Ripe with rich damson fruit.	**£4.00**	MWW WEP
(A)	**OH SO SMOOTH MERLOT 2001, AFRICAN TERROIR** Western Cape	Plummy with silky mouthfeel.	**£4.00**	CWS
(A)	**CINSAULT PINOTAGE 2001, DOUGLAS GREEN BELLINGHAM** Western Cape	Spicy wine with jammy depth.	**£4.00**	TOS
(B)	**PINOTAGE 2000, CULEMBORG** Western Cape	Perfumed wine with baked plum and violet nuances. The palate is ripe and supple. A fair tannic structure.	**£4.60**	WTS
(B)	**SHIRAZ CABERNET SAUVIGNON 2001, LONG MOUNTAIN WINE COMPANY** Western Cape	A wine full of juicy redcurrants and a hint of pencil shavings. Good structure.	**£5.00**	CAX
(S)	**DUMISANI PINOTAGE 2001, WINECORP** Western Cape	Blackberry and pepper aromas. The palate has lots of fruit extract hung around a frame of supple tannins.	**£5.00**	PLB

(S) **Winds Of Change Merlot Pinotage 2001, African Terroir** Western Cape	Juicy wine with plum and blackberry aromas, a lush black fruit palate and balanced tannins.	**£5.00**	WST
(B) **Winds of Change Pinotage Cabernet Sauvignon 2001, African Terroir** Western Cape	A supple wine with plum and cassis fruit aromas. The palate shows ripe fruit character and well-integrated tannins.	**£5.00**	WST
(B) **Pinotage 2000, Deetlefs Estate** Breede River Valley	A fruity wine with blackberry and tar nuances. Elegant tannins and acidity on a ripe palate.	**£5.00**	FOL
(B) **Shiraz 2000, Boland Kelder** Paarl	Intense wine with bramble and smoke on the nose. The palate has juicy blackberry fruit and supple tannin.	**£5.00**	BWL
(S) **Pinotage 1999, Boland Kelder** Paarl	A well-rounded red with blackberry and tar aromas. The palate is soft-hearted with gooey fruit and unobtrusive tannins.	**£5.00**	BWL
(S) **Indaba Merlot 2001, Cape Classics** Coastal	Rich and ripe with plum and damson aromas. The palate has good depth and is well oaked.	**£5.00**	WSG VGN
(B) **Winds of Change Pinotage Cabernet Sauvignon 2001, African Terroir** Western Cape	Powerful flavours and aromas of ripe red fruit tinged with tar and smoke.	**£5.00**	SAF TOS SMF CWS
(B) **Southern Star Pinotage Cinsault 2001, Kingsland Wines & Spirits** Western Cape	A fine blend of two long established South African varieties.	**£5.00**	MAC BFD UWM
(B) **Goats do Roam Red 2001, Wines of Charles Back** Paarl	Good open fruit and an approachable structure make this wine a sure-fire crowd-pleaser.	**£5.00**	TOS MWW ODD BTH
(B) **Tesco Finest Beyers Truter Pinotage NV, Beyerskloof** Coastal	Pronounced berry aromas and a balanced palate showing black fruit intensity and supple tannins.	**£5.00**	TOS
(B) **Cape Soleil Pinotage 2001, African Terroir** Western Cape	A warm climate red with jammy aromas and a succulent baked blackberry palate. Shows some spice.	**£5.00**	SAF
(S) **Fairview Pinotage 2001, Wines of Charles Back** Paarl	Redcurrants and loganberries feature on the palate. A whiff of smoke graces the nose. Firm tannins add structure.	**£6.00**	JSM

(S) **FAIRVIEW SHIRAZ 2000, WINES OF CHARLES BACK** Coastal	Creamy new oak, spicy red fruit and a satisfying burst of tannin on the finish.	**£6.00**	TOS MRN WRC UNS
(S) **PINOTAGE 1999, MIDDELVLEI ESTATE** Stellenbosch	Vivid flavours of ripe black fruits and aromas of tar and rubber. Powerful structure; firm tannins.	**£7.00**	JSM WEP
(S) **CABERNET SAUVIGNON 1999, MIDDELVLEI ESTATE** Stellenbosch	The palate drips with ripe cassis underpinned by very firm tannins. Well-integrated and balanced with a long finish.	**£7.00**	ASD WEP
(G) **TRILOGY 1999, WARWICK ESTATE** Stellenbosch	Structured wine made in an elegant style. Cherry fruit runs throughout with a dash of oak for support.	**£10.00**	SAF
(G) **FAIRVIEW SOLITUDE SHIRAZ 2001, WINES OF CHARLES BACK** Paarl	Aromas of smoke, leather, liquorice and ripe black fruits over a palate of spices and black cherry fruit.	**£10.00**	GRT
(G) **GLEN CARLOU SHIRAZ 2001, GLEN CARLOU VINEYARDS** Paarl	Rich, ripe blackberry flavours laced liberally with smoke and cracked pepper. Excellent balance, structure and freshness.	**£11.00**	ODD
(G) **CABERNET SAUVIGNON 1999, BEYERSKLOOF** Stellenbosch	Rich wine with loads of cassis fruit. Coffee and chocolate notes are enhanced by sweet oak.	**£12.00**	ODD WEP SWG
(G) **CABERNET SAUVIGNON 1998, VERGELEGEN** Stellenbosch	Ripe and elegant, with a gentle maturity and fine integration of fruit, oak and structure.	**£13.00**	ODD SBS SWG
(G) **PINOTAGE 2000, KAAPZICHT ESTATE** Stellenbosch	Thick and tarry wine with complex savoury notes. The palate is very rich. Lashings of sweet toasty oak.	**£18.00**	SCK
(G) **SPICE ROUTE FLAGSHIP PINOTAGE 2000, SPICE ROUTE WINE COMPANY** Swartland	Good concentration of berry fruits, tobacco and chocolatey oak notes. A robust wine with well balanced fruit and tannins.	**£19.50**	SWG

SOUTH AFRICA • SWEET

(B) **WEISSER RIESLING 2001, BON COURAGE ESTATE** Robertson	Zesty and refreshing. Ripe citrus fruit married to fine acidity. Good length and depth of flavour.	**£6.50**	GPA

SPAIN

Spanish wine fans who have followed the International Wine Challenge over the last decade or so will recall years in which this country was lucky to carry home a couple of Gold Medals. Indeed, on occasion, the judges were so unimpressed that they declined even to award a trophy. This year, the set of red Golds was so impressive that, for the first time, it was decided to give Spain a *pair* of trophies. Do try these exciting new wave Spanish table wines – but don't forget to explore some of the award-winning sherries; they remain some of the undiscovered treasures of the wine world.

SPAIN • SPARKLING

(A)	**ASDA CAVA BRUT NV,** **CODORNIU** Catalonia	Soft, ripe and creamy with developed flavours.	**£4.00**	ASD
(A)	**MHV CAVA BRUT NV,** **COVIDES** Catalonia	Attractive, restrained sparkler. Berry palate.	**£4.70**	MHV
(A)	**BRUT CAVA NV,** **CODORNIU** Catalonia	Pale lemon yellow. Balanced and elegant.	**£5.00**	ASD TOS
(A)	**CUVEE 21 BRUT NV,** **PARXET** Catalonia	Racy apples and baking bread.	**£6.00**	MOR VGN ALE OWC
(A)	**ASDA VINTAGE CAVA 1998,** **CODORNIU** Catalonia	Delicate. Delicious Granny Smith apples.	**£6.50**	ASD
(A)	**TESCO FINEST** **VINTAGE CAVA 1998,** **MARQUES DE MONISTROL** Catalonia	Restrained mousse. Nutty, fruit-driven palate.	**£6.50**	TOS
(A)	**CHANDON SPAIN,** **CHANDON ESTATES** Catalonia	Stylish melon fruit palate; well-balanced.	**£7.00**	UNS ASD
(B)	**SOMERFIELD** **VINTAGE CAVA 1998,** **GONZALEZ BYASS** San Sadurni d'Anoia	Very clean and crisp with rhubarb and gooseberry fruit. Lightly fragrant and brightly crisp.	**£7.00**	SMF

(A)	**ONDARRE CAVA BRUT NV, BODEGAS ONDARRE** Rioja	Substantial weight; fresh, zippy acidity.	**£7.00**	AVB
(A)	**CORDON NEGRO BRUT NV, FREIXENET** Catalonia	Good chalky, lemony fruit.	**£7.50**	TOS WTS

SPAIN • WHITE

(A)	**MHV PENEDÈS MEDIUM DRY WHITE NV, COVIDES** Catalonia	Acacia blossoms and white peaches.	**£3.50**	MHV
(A)	**ALTEZA VIURA 2001, VILLA MALEA** Castilla-La Mancha	Round, ripe and floral. Refreshing.	**£4.00**	JSM MRN
(A)	**MARKS & SPENCER LUNARAN 2001, TELMO RODRIGUEZ** Castilla y León	Peapods and freshly cut grass.	**£4.00**	M&S
(A)	**HOMENAJE BLANCO 2001, BODEGAS MARCO REAL** Navarre	Almonds and apples. Light and fresh.	**£4.00**	WCR
(A)	**BLANCO OTOÑAL 2001, BODEGAS OLARRA** Rioja	Lifted guava and citrus nose.	**£4.50**	C&D
(S)	**AURA ARS VINUM VERDEJO 2001, BODEGAS & BEBIDAS** Castilla y León	An aromatic nose and refreshing green fruit palate showing melon and honey nuances.	**£6.00**	MER
(S)	**LA VAL ALBARIÑO 2001, BODEGAS LA VAL** Galicia	Lots of ripe fruit flavours with a hint of asparagus and lemon, and a pleasing weight and fruit concentration.	**£7.00**	RAM

SPAIN • ROSÉ

(A)	**MIRADOR DE LA SIERRA ROSADO 2001, BODEGAS MARCO REAL** Navarre	Crisp, with ripe cranberry fruit.	**£4.00**	TOS

SPAIN • RED

(A)	**PIEDEMONTE MERLOT TEMPRANILLO 2001, PIEDEMONTE** Navarre	Sweet oak and ripe raspberries.	**£3.00**	TOS
(A)	**DON HUGO SMOOTH RED NV, BODEGAS VICTORIANOS** Rioja	A mature, dry palate with hints of caramel on the nose.	**£3.30**	WTS
(A)	**VIÑA ALBALI TEMPRANILLO 2001, FELIX SOLIS BODEGAS** Castilla-La Mancha	Weighty, yet youthful with a lengthy finish.	**£3.50**	MRN
(B)	**GRAN LOPEZ TEMPRANILLO GARNACHA 2001, SANTO CRISTO** Aragón	Medium-bodied redcurrant fruit with touches of tobacco on the nose. Fresh, spicy, and smooth.	**£3.50**	WTS
(A)	**MHV PENEDES RED NV, COVIDES** Catalonia	Lifted nose and a powerful red palate.	**£3.50**	MHV
(A)	**TEMPRANILLO 2001, GRANDUC** Castilla-La Mancha	Freshly baked cherry pie aromas.	**£3.70**	SAF
(A)	**TEMPRANILLO GARNACHA 2001, GRANDUC** Castilla-La Mancha	Creamy cherry pie nose. Youthful.	**£3.70**	MYL
(A)	**MARINADA TINTO 2001, CAPEL VINOS** Castilla-La Mancha	Smooth, suave customer. Ripe. Attractive.	**£3.90**	BSS
(A)	**UCENDA BULLAS MONASTRELL 2001, BULLAS** Murcia	Spicy nose and packed with fabulous blackberry fruit.	**£4.00**	IWS
(B)	**VIÑA AZABACHE TEMPRANILLO 2001, ALDEANUEVA** Rioja	Powerful, lifted nose. Structured. Long.	**£4.00**	PLB
(S)	**TINTO AÑARES CRIANZA 1999, BODEGAS OLARRA** Rioja	Coconut oak, nutmeg, and cinnamon aromas. The palate has blackberries and raspberries underpinned by firm tannins.	**£4.00**	C&D

(A) **POEMA GARNACHA 2001, PAMELA GEDDES - EL JALON** Aragón	Spice-laden, soft and vivacious.	**£4.00**	MRN MOR GAR ALE
(A) **CAMINO MONASTRELL 2000, COOP DE SAN DIONISO** Murcia	Ripe, unfettered summer fruit palate.	**£4.00**	MOR OWC PHR
(A) **GARNACHA 2000, CRUZ DE PIEDRA** Aragón	White pepper and redcurrant fruit.	**£4.00**	GRT
(B) **VIÑA FUERTE GARNACHA 2001, SAN GREGORIO** Aragón	This powerfully flavoured, peppery red offers satisfyingly complex, saturated red berry flavours and aromas. Attractive.	**£4.00**	WTS
(S) **VIÑA ARMANTES GARNACHA 2001, SAN GREGORIO** Aragón	An excellent demonstration of a well made Garnacha. Fresh, yet brimming with super-ripe, peppery fruit.	**£4.00**	MWW
(B) **VENTUROSO TEMPRANILLO GARNACHA 2001, COVINCA** Aragón	Warm and robust chunky red fruit. Lots of body, depth and juicy acidity. Very satisfying.	**£4.00**	JSM
(A) **CAMPO LAGAZA TINTO 2001, VIRGEN BLANCA** Navarre	Elegant, soft, vanilla-scented fruit.	**£4.00**	SAF
(A) **VIÑA BORGIA GARNACHA 2001, BODEGAS BORSAO** Aragón	Soft, ripe loganberries. Pepper notes.	**£4.00**	BWL BTH
(A) **ALBOR BODEGAS ARTESANAS 2001, BODEGAS & BEBIDAS** Castilla y León	Aromatic, with firm, ripe red fruit.	**£4.00**	ODD WRC
(A) **INFIERNO 2000, BODEGAS CASTAÑO** Murcia	Jammy with a spiced fruit core.	**£4.00**	EHL
(A) **HOMENAJE TINTO 2001, BODEGAS MARCO REAL** Navarre	Dark, concentrated, and leathery. Firm.	**£4.00**	WCR
(B) **MIRADOR DE LA SIERRA TINTO 2001, BODEGAS MARCO REAL** Navarre	Elegant, spicy nose. Deep fruit and a strong backbone of tannin. Fresh acidity.	**£4.00**	TOS

(B)	**FOUR WINDS TINTO 2001, BODEGAS MARCO REAL** Navarre	Saturated deep red colour. A dark, plummy palate of soft, approachable ripe fruit. Very attractive.	**£4.00**	SAF
(S)	**BOBAL TEMPRANILLO 2001, PORTAL** Valencia	Soft red fruit and leather aromas. The palate is soft with supple tannins and a lengthy finish.	**£4.00**	LIB
(A)	**MARQUÉS DE NOMBREVILLA GARNACHA SELECCION 2001, SAN ALEJANDRO** Aragón	Sweet-fruited with brambly aromas.	**£4.00**	VER
(A)	**CO-OP TIERRA SANA TEMPRANILLO ORGANIC 2000, PARRA JIMENEZ** Castilla-La Mancha	Sweet oak, cherries and violets.	**£4.00**	CWS
(A)	**ED'S RED TEMPRANILLO 2001, BODEGAS CENTRO ESPAÑOLAS** Castilla-La Mancha	Ripe with juicy berry flavours.	**£4.00**	WRC
(A)	**THE WILDERNESS MONASTRELL 2001, FINCA LUZON** Murcia	Jammy with a spicy finish.	**£4.00**	MWW
(A)	**THE WILDERNESS TEMPRANILLO 2001, FINCA LUZON** Murcia	Very youthful, with juicy black fruit.	**£4.00**	SPR
(B)	**ESPIRAL CABERNET SAUVIGNON TEMPRANILLO 2001, PIRINEOS** Aragón	Soft tannins, ripe fruit and sweet vanilla oak. Well made and warm. Quite complex.	**£4.50**	WTS
(S)	**AGRAMONT COSECHA TEMPRANILLO 2000, PRINCIPE DE VIANA** Navarre	Intense, primary aromas of ripe plums lightly graced with spiced oak. Sweet ripe black fruit on the palate.	**£4.50**	VER
(S)	**BAJOZ TORO TINTO JOVEN 2000, BODEGA VIÑA BAJOZ** Castilla y León	An excellent product from a young and dynamic winery. Shows how good the wines from Toro can be.	**£4.70**	BWL
(B)	**SIERRA DE CODÉS CRIANZA TEMPRANILLO CABERNET 1998, BODEGAS VALCARLOS** Navarre	Mature colour and blackcurrant aromas.	**£5.00**	PLB
(B)	**DURERO CRIANZA TEMPRANILLO 1998, BODEGAS LEGANZA** Castilla-La Mancha	Aromatic, juicy black cherry fruit unifies beautifully with fine-grained tannins. Crisp acidity and creamy oak.	**£5.00**	PLB

(S) RIOJA PRIMI 2001, **LUIS GURPEGUI MUGA** Rioja	A huge wine filled with masses of spicy, peppery fruit, to make a big, balanced bruiser.	**£5.00**	BWL SAF
(B) SIGLO 1881 TINTO 2000, **BODEGAS & BEBIDAS** Rioja	A perfumed wine with lovely berry and vanilla aromas. The palate is harmonious with good depth and length.	**£5.00**	MER
(B) VIÑA IZADI CRIANZA 1999, **VIÑA VILLABUENA** Rioja	Rich, dark cherry palate. Concentrated.	**£5.00**	ALB
(S) TINTO AÑARES RESERVA 1998, **BODEGAS OLARRA** Rioja	This Rioja offers a smooth, vanilla palate. Structured tannins are well-integrated into the ripe redcurrant fruit.	**£5.60**	C&D
(G) GUELBENZU VIERLAS 2001, **BODEGAS GUELBENZU** Navarre	The palate shows some serious concentration and complexity with spicy, peppery ripeness and gutsy ripe red vine fruits.	**£6.00**	BUT MOR MFS P&R
(S) TINTO GRAN RESERVA 1995, **VIÑA ALBALI** Castilla-La Mancha	Straightforward berry fruit, but a subtle smokiness adds complexity to the palate.	**£6.00**	ASD JSM MRN WCR
(S) VIÑA ALCORTA TEMPRANILLO **RIOJA CRIANZA 1999,** **BODEGAS & BEBIDAS** Rioja	The nose features fine, ripe fruit and a dash of spice. The palate offers attractive, redcurrant fruit.	**£6.00**	MER
(S) SOMERFIELD VIÑA CANA RIOJA **CRIANZA 1999,** **GONZALEZ BYASS** Rioja	Ripe berry fruit and toast aromas. Refined palate with spicy red fruit and silky tannins.	**£6.00**	SMF
(S) CRIANZA 1998, **MARQUES DE VITORIA** Rioja	A rich bouquet of berries and spice. The palate is intense with a nice lick of creamy oak.	**£7.00**	WRC
(S) VALLOBERA CRIANZA 1998, **BODEGAS SAN PEDRO** Rioja	Lush redcurrants and raspberries on the nose. Complex, with very firm tannins underpinning the fruit.	**£7.00**	GRT
(S) CABERNET SAUVIGNON 1997, **RAIMAT** Catalonia	Expressive wine with blackcurrant and pepper aromas on the nose and thick cassis fruit on the palate.	**£7.00**	WRC
(S) BAJOZ TORO CRIANZA 1998, **BODEGA VIÑA BAJOZ** Castilla y León	Inky wine with concentrated berry and toast nose. The palate is warm and spicy with sweet oak undertones.	**£7.00**	BWL SWG

(G)	**TEMPRANILLO 1998, RAIMAT** Aragón	Smoky nose with delicate spiced flavours and chocolate and vanilla. Coconut-scented oak offsets the fruit.	**£8.00**	WTS
(G)	**RIOJA 1998, ALLENDE** Rioja	This has masses of plum and spice fruit with warm, earthy flavours pulled together by firm, smooth tannins.	**£9.40**	M&V HVN P&rS
(G)	**MARQUÉS DE RISCAL RESERVA 1998, MARQUÉS DE RISCAL** Rioja	Rich berry fruit and sweet oak nose. The palate has good red fruit concentration and smoky depth.	**£10.00**	WSO MWW
(G)	**PRIOR TERRAE 1998, FREIXENET** Catalonia	Rich damson, blueberry and violet perfume. Layers of rich fruit, supple tannin and expensive oak.	**£40.00**	WIM
(G)	**MIGUEL TORRES RESERVA REAL 1998, MIGUEL TORRES** Catalonia	The palate is powerful with intense black fruit, cocoa and clove. Lovely tannic structure and a harmonious finish.	**£70.00**	JEF

SPAIN • SWEET

(A)	**SAINSBURY'S MOSCATEL DE VALENCIA NV, SCHENK** Valencia	Roses. Marzipan. Oranges and lemons.	**£3.80**	JSM
(S)	**MOSCATEL ORO NV, DE MULLER**	Superb bitter orange marmelade on the nose and palate. Rich but fresh and very, very long.	**£4.00**	FSW L&S

SPAIN • FORTIFIED

(A)	**PORTMANS FINE RUBY NV, CDC WINES & SPIRITS**	Rich strawberry fruit and spice box.	**£3.50**	BGN SMF
(A)	**ASDA MANZANILLA SHERRY, REAL TESORO** Andalucia	Roast nuts and seaside tang.	**£3.90**	PLB
(A)	**SAINSBURY'S MANZANILLA , LUIS PAEZ** Andalucia	Nutty, fresh, floral, and yeasty.	**£4.00**	JSM

(B) **SAINSBURY'S PALE AMONTILLADO , LUSTAU** Andalucia	A rich, nutty wine with raisined aromas and a sweet caramelised palate. Decent finish.	**£4.00**	JSM
(A) **SAINSBURY'S MEDIUM AMONTILLADO , FRANCISCO GONZALEZ FERNANDEZ** Andalucia	Rich roast nut aromas. Luscious.	**£4.00**	JSM
(A) **SOMERFIELD FINO SHERRY, GONZALEZ BYASS** Andalucia	Fresh with a lively yeasty bite.	**£4.00**	SMF
(G) **SOMERFIELD AMONTILLADO NV, GONZALEZ BYASS** Andalucia	Compelling aromas of walnuts, raisins, and figs. The palate has rich, luscious dried fruits lifted by fresh acidity.	**£4.00**	SMF
(S) **CASERA FINO, BODEGAS DON JESUS** Andalucia	Fresh and zesty with distinctive flor yeast aromas. Nutty palate with a salty tang. Long and elegant.	**£4.00**	NTD
(A) **REGENCY CREAM, MATTHEW CLARK** Andalucia	Rich and nutty with a creamy finish.	**£4.10**	MCT
(A) **MHV GRAN CAPATAZ PALE CREAM SHERRY, ANTONIO BARBADILLO** Andalucia	Sweet with good depth and a long finish.	**£4.40**	MHV
(G) **CABRERA FINE PALE CREAM, GONAZALES BYASS** Andalucia	Pale in colour this wine has zingy Fino freshness and sweet nose. Served chilled with pate.	**£4.50**	WRT
(B) **CABRERA FULL RICH CREAM, GONZALES BYASS** Andalucia	Rich with caramel and nut aromas. Good depth and balance on the palate.	**£4.50**	WRT
(A) **CABRERA MEDIUM DRY AMONTILLADO, GONZALES BYASS** Andalucia	Roast cashew and flor aromas.	**£4.50**	WRT
(A) **CABRERA PALE DRY FINO, GONZALES BYASS** Andalucia	Crisp, clear, chalky white fruit.	**£4.50**	WRT
(B) **CABRERA MANZANILLA, GONZALES BYASS** Andalucia	Fresh and fruity with yeasty notes on the nose and a sea-fresh salty tang on the palate.	**£4.50**	WRT

(S)	**WAITROSE AMONTILLADO SHERRY NV, ESTEVEZ** Andalucia	Pronounced nut and raisin notes on the nose. Well made with good depth, complexity, and balance.	**£4.90**	WTS
(A)	**WAITROSE CREAM SHERRY, LUSTAU** Andalucia	Luscious palate of yeasty fruit.	**£4.90**	WTS
(B)	**FINO QUINTA PALE DRY, OSBORNE** Andalucia	Light and fresh with flor yeast aromas on the nose and a salty character on the persistent palate.	**£5.00**	HBJ
(S)	**WAITROSE SOLERA JEREZANA MANZANILLA SHERRY, LUSTAU** Andalucia	Refined wine with sea air aromas. The palate is well-balanced and fresh with yeasty characters.	**£5.60**	WTS
(B)	**WAITROSE SOLERA JEREZANA DRY OLOROSO SHERRY, LUSTAU** Andalucia	Rich and intense with raisined notes. The palate has nutty depth and good length.	**£5.60**	WTS
(G)	**WAITROSE SOLERA JEREZANA DRY AMONTILLADO SHERRY, LUSTAU** Andalucia	This dry, refreshing, hazelnut-scented wine has all the qualities of great sherry. Serve with roasted nuts.	**£5.60**	WTS
(S)	**WAITROSE SOLERA JEREZANA RICH CREAM SHERRY, LUSTAU** Andalucia	An opulent wine with caramel and hazelnut aromas. Rich and creamy with nougat nuances. Concentrated and very long.	**£5.60**	WTS
(B)	**LA GITANA MANZANILLA, VINÍCOLA HIDALGO** Andalucia	Dry and delicate. A perfect example of the genre; one can taste the tang of the seaside.	**£6.00**	SLT
(B)	**ELEGANTE FINO, GONZALEZ BYASS** Andalucia	Delicate, tangy aromas of flor, citrus blossom and almonds. A seam of chalky minerality adds power and interest.	**£6.20**	TOS WTS SAF ASD
(B)	**PEDRO XIMENEZ, EMILIO HIDALGO** Andalucia	Very rich with nut and caramel aromas and a sweet and creamy palate showing admirable persistence.	**£7.50**	SCA HRV
(B)	**DRY SACK FINO, WILLIAMS & HUMBERT** Andalucia	Refreshing wine with yeasty notes on the nose and a tangy palate.	**£7.50**	P&R

Pinpoint who sells the wine you wish to buy by turning to the stockist codes. If you know the name of the wine you want to buy, use the alphabetical index. If the price is your motivation, look out for the "Great Value Wine of the Year" symbol; the best red and white wines under £10, sparkling wines under £12 and champagne under £17.50. Happy hunting!

(S) EVA CREAM, BODEGAS BARBADILLO Andalucia	Honeyed and rich with balanced acidity and excellent length and complexity.	**£8.00**	DAM
(S) ALMACENISTA MANZANILLA PASADA DE SANLÚCAR, LUSTAU Andalucia	All the trademark seaside flavours of a traditional Manzanilla are here. Rich and mature.	**£8.40**	M&V RDS PGW
(G) ALMACENISTA AMONTILLADO DEL PUERTO, LUSTAU Andalucia	Powerful and concentrated, full of typical nut and raisined fruit flavours. Very clean and dry.	**£8.40**	M&V F&M
(S) ALMACENISTA MANZANILLA AMONTILLADA, LUSTAU Andalucia	Mature, elegant round fruit character, balanced by a firm seam of acidity.	**£8.60**	M&V P&S
(S) OLOROSO ANGEL ZAMORANO, LUSTAU Andalucia	Very rich with chocolate, dried fruits and roast nuts. Another winner from the towering talents at Lustau.	**£8.60**	M&V F&M OWC
(S) PUERTO FINO, LUSTAU Andalucia	Lengthy flor maturation lends this a yeasty nose. Almost salty, tangy, ripe round fruit on the palate.	**£9.60**	M&V RDS UBC SEL
(S) DON NUÑO DRY OLOROSO, LUSTAU Andalucia	The compellingly dry palate is tinged with sweetness and a whiff of roast nuts, raisins, and honeycomb.	**£9.60**	M&V BUT WRK
(S) CAPATAZ ANDRES DELUXE CREAM, LUSTAU Andalucia	Sweet yet not heavy, this fantastic wine is what cream sherry should taste like. Extremely fine and elegant.	**£9.60**	M&V F&M SEL
(G) GONZALEZ BYASS APOSTOLES, GONZALEZ BYASS Andalucia	Immensely powerful nose of roast nuts and dried figs. The fabulously rich tobacco-edged palate is massively unctuous.	**£10.70**	JSM
(G) GONZALEZ BYASS MATUSALEM, GONZALEZ BYASS Andalucia	Golden yellow with caramel and honeycomb aromas and a rich marmalade palate. Very complex and long.	**£10.70**	JSM
(G) OLD EAST INDIA SHERRY, LUSTAU Andalucia	Warming alcohol, rich molasses and raisined fruit aromas. Despite the sweet richness it still remains fresh and clean.	**£11.00**	JSM
(G) LA SACRISTIA DE ROMATE CREAM NV, SANCHEZ ROMATE Andalucia	Dark mahogany. Smooth, round and very profound. Clean and fresh yet rich and dark. A superb pudding wine.	**£12.30**	POR

(G)	**BARBADILLO OBISPO GASCON PALO CORTADO, BODEGAS BARBADILLO** Andalucia	A style somewhere between Amontillado and Oloroso. This wine combines nut and raisin notes with depth and style.	**£22.00**	G&M BCW RBS N&P
(G)	**SINGLE CASK AMONTILLADO, LUSTAU** Andalucia	Clean, fresh, and voluptuous with a piercing nose and a powerful palate. Complex and deep yet delicate.	**£29.00**	M&V
(G)	**VOS 20 YEAR OLD AMONTILLADO, LUSTAU** Andalucia	A concentrated nose showing nut, raisin, and burnt sugar aromas. The golden palate has good dried fruit intensity.	**£29.00**	M&V

USA

Only the most bigoted of Old Worlders would deny that the USA – which in wine terms effectively means the states on the west coast of North America – now produces some of the finest wines in the world. Unfortunately, that quality comes at a price that is often a lot higher than you might have to pay elsewhere. This helps to explain why a lot of top California wines rarely reach British shores these days. The award-winning wines on the following pages, however, should all be available in this country – and are very well worth buying.

USA • SPARKLING

(A)	**SPARKLING NV, BLOSSOM HILL** California	Floral, yet earthy. Light and quaffable.	**£6.00**	LON SPR CWS TOS

USA • WHITE

(A)	**OCEAN COAST CHENIN NV, CALIFORNIA DIRECT** California	Crisp yet waxy. Floral notes.	**£3.00**	ALD

Pinpoint who sells the wine you wish to buy by turning to the stockist codes. If you know the name of the wine you want to buy, use the alphabetical index. If the price is your motivation, look out for the "Great Value Wine of the Year" symbol; the best red and white wines under £10, sparkling wines under £12 and champagne under £17.50. Happy hunting!

(A)	**KALIFORNIA K BEACHFRONT WHITE NV, CDL** California	Sweetly scented with rose aromas.	**£3.50**	SAF
(A)	**SAINSBURY'S CALIFORNIAN COLOMBARD CHARDONNAY 2000, GOLDEN STATE VINTNERS** California	Leafy nose. Buttered apple palate.	**£4.00**	JSM
(S)	**ARROYO VISTA CHARDONNAY SINGLE VINEYARD 1999, J. LOHR** California	Complex and buttery wine with rich citrus fruit and lovely toasty oak and a long and concentrated finish.	**£7.50**	SWG
(G)	**CHATEAU STE MICHELLE EROICA ERNST LOOSEN RIESLING 2000, STIMSON LANE** Washington State	A fragrant bouquet of lemon blossoms and lime zest . The palate oozes ripe citrus flavours. Elegant and long.	**£16.00**	CAX PEA BAB COE
(G)	**CHARDONNAY RESERVE LE BOUGE D'À CÔTÉ 1999, AU BON CLIMAT** California	Light and lemony on the nose, this opens up in the mouth to reveal nutty, buttery roundness.	**£21.00**	M&V
(G)	**RAMEY HUDSON VINEYARD CHARDONNAY 1999, RAMEY** California	Concentrated fruit salad and passionfruit in a forward open style. Big and generous with ripe, fat fruit.	**£39.00**	M&V NYW

USA • ROSÉ

(G)	**VALLEY OAKS SYRAH ROSE 2001, FETZER VINEYARDS** California	Crushed raspberries, strawberries, and cream. Well-balanced. Peppery notes dance above the vivid fruit flavours.	**£6.00**	TOS WRC VGN ODD

USA • RED

(A)	**HERITAGE CALIFORNIAN RED 2000, SPAR UK** California	Soft with sweet, jammy fruit.	**£3.80**	SPR
(A)	**OAK RIDGE ZINFANDEL SYRAH 1999, LES GRANDS CHAIS DE FRANCE** Central Valley	Jammy berry and spice nuances.	**£4.00**	ALD
(A)	**RED NV, BLOSSOM HILL** California	Ripe, vivid, spiced raspberry fruit.	**£4.00**	PFC JSM ASD TOS

(A)	**GARNET POINT ZINFANDEL BARBERA 2000, GARNET POINT VINEYARDS** California	White pepper. Ripe red cherries.	**£4.00**	ASD BGN SAF TOS
(B)	**CABERNET SAUVIGNON 2000, BLOSSOM HILL** California	Not complicated but attractive sweet ripe fruit, soft tannin and juicy acidity.	**£5.00**	PFC
(S)	**CABERNET SAUVIGNON NV, BLACKWOOD CANYON** California	Notes of wild sage complement the rich cassis fruit palate.	**£6.00**	UNS
(S)	**RESERVE CABERNET SAUVIGNON 2001 PINNACLE ESTATES** California	A cassis and hedgerow nose precedes a palate of herb tinged fruit, buttressed by oak and firm tannins.	**£6.00**	SAF
(S)	**SHIRAZ 2001, DELICATO FAMILY VINEYARDS** California	Ripe black fruit, vanilla, and nutmeg lace the toasty nose. Well-integrated and balanced, soft and aromatic.	**£6.00**	EHL
(S)	**CAILFORNIA ZINFANDEL 1999, BERINGER VINEYARDS** California	Spices and toasty oak over a ripe fruit palate. Structured and powerful, with concentrated fruit for hearty drinking.	**£7.00**	BWC
(G)	**NUNS CANYON CABERNET SAUVIGNON RESERVE 1998, ST FRANCIS** California	A real green pepper and cassis style Cabernet with lots of opulence, ripe fruit and a long finish.	**£20.00**	WIM
(G)	**RESERVE SONOMA COUNTY CABERNET SAUVIGNON 1999, GEYSER PEAK** California	Inky black with heaps of peppery, ripe, forward fruit and generous vanilla oak . Concentrated and powerful.	**£20.00**	MAX
(G)	**KINGS RIDGE CABERNET SAUVIGNON RESERVE 1997, ST FRANICS** California	Showy Cabernet packed with tobacco, spice, and deep brambly fruit. Velvety texture and long finish.	**£35.00**	FWC WIM POR EVW
(G)	**KNOX ALEXANDER 1999, AU BON CLIMAT** California	Refined wine with a pronounced bouquet showing cherry and vanilla aromas. The peppery palate is ripe and chocolatey.	**£36.00**	M&V NYW

Pinpoint who sells the wine you wish to buy by turning to the stockist codes. If you know the name of the wine you want to buy, use the alphabetical index. If the price is your motivation, look out for the "Great Value Wine of the Year" symbol; the best red and white wines under £10, sparkling wines under £12 and champagne under £17.50. Happy hunting!

OTHER COUNTRIES

The International Wine Challenge has always attracted wines from vineyards across the planet – and this year it introduced us to the quality Gold Medal winning icewines of Canada, and Silver medallists from England, Greece, Lebanon, and Uruguay. There's no longer any reason to be surprised that unfamiliar countries and regions can produce good wines; the New World has proved that "terroir" – soil, aspect, and climate that suit particular kinds of vine – and highly skilled winemaking can both be found in places a long way from the classic wine regions of Europe.

AUSTRIA

AUSTRIA • RED

(B)	**SELECTION BLAUER ZWEIGELT 2000, LENZ MOSER** Rapel	Good colour and fragrant clean fruit nose. It has reasonable weight and earthy, dusty tannins.	**£4.00**	FTH

AUSTRIA • SWEET

(S)	**FISCHER TROCKENBEERENAUSLESE 1995, WEINGUT ALFRED FISCHER** Burgenland	This is a massively rich and concentrated wine with refreshing acidity and a finish reminiscent of clover honey.	**£9.50**	ALL
(G)	**WELSCHREISLING SAMLING 88 EISWEIN 1990, HELMUT LANG** Burgenland	Petrol aromas. Wonderfully mysterious and complex array of flavours. Smoke, marmalade and tea bags.	**£14.00**	EBA
(G)	**NOUVELLE VAGUE TROCKENBEERENAUSLESE NO. 2 1999, ALOIS KRACHER** Burgenland	This TBA is restrained, lean, and minerally on the nose with lychees and sherbet flavours.	**£23.00**	NYW J&B

Pinpoint who sells the wine you wish to buy by turning to the stockist codes. If you know the name of the wine you want to buy, use the alphabetical index. If the price is your motivation, look out for the "Great Value Wine of the Year" symbol; the best red and white wines under £10, sparkling wines under £12 and champagne under £17.50. Happy hunting!

CANADA

CANADA • SPARKLING

(G) **VIDAL SPARKLING ICE WINE 1999, INNISKILLIN** Ontario	Aromatic honeycomb and peach blossom. Flavours of ripe oranges, lime peel, and honey. Luscious yet delicate.	**£45.00**	AVB

CANADA • SWEET

(G) **PILLITTERI ESTATES VIDAL ICEWINE 2000, PILLITTERI ESTATES WINERY** Ontario	Fantastic honeycomb aromas. Great depth and intensity. Exceedingly complex, rounded, and altogether complete.	**£9.40**	VNE
(G) **SILVER RIESLING ICE WINE 1999, INNISKILLIN** Ontario	Classic Reisling with Icewine purity. Bright lemon nose, petrolly notes and peachy waxiness. An incredible finish.	**£45.00**	AVB

CYPRUS

CYPRUS • WHITE

(A) **CO-OP ISLAND VINES CYPRUS WHITE 2001, SODAP** Troodos South	Fresh with zesty citrus fruit.	**£3.50**	CWS
(A) **APHRODITE 2001, KEO**	Soft, fresh Granny Smith apples.	**£4.00**	TOS
(B) **CO-OP MOUNTAIN VINES SEMILLON 2000, SODAP** Troodos South	Rich and creamy with an oaky weight and honeyed, tangarine fruit profile. Excellent spice and ripe, grapefruit flavours.	**£4.30**	CWS

ENGLAND

ENGLAND • SPARKLING

CLASSIC CUVEE NV, THREE CHOIRS Gloucestershire	Pale straw yellow. Hawthorn aromas.	**£7.00**	TCV

ENGLAND • WHITE

COLERIDGE HILL 2000, THREE CHOIRS Gloucestershire	Mineral, pear, and spice palate.	**£4.00**	TCV

GEORGIA

GEORGIA • RED

Ⓐ CAUCASUS VALLEY MATRASSA 2000, GWS Kakheti	Fruity with a soft-centred palate.	**£4.00**	SAF
Ⓑ TELAVI WINE CELLAR SAPERAVI 2000, TELAVI WINE CELLAR Kakheti	Rich with a big attack, good acidity, and interesting herbal character. Fennel, liquorice, and plums.	**£5.00**	GEE

GREECE

GREECE • WHITE

Ⓢ DOMAINE GEROVASSILIOU WHITE 2001, EVANGELOS GEROVASSILIOU Macedonia	A rich, generous wine with a pronounced bouquet and a concentrated palate of ripe peach and apricot.	**£6.50**	ODD

GREECE • ROSÉ

(S)	**AMETHYSTOS ROSÉ 2001, DOMAINE CONSTANTIN LAZARIDIS** Macedonia	Currant bush and raspberry fruit flavours. Silver medal winning rose wines are few and far between.	**£6.50**	ODD

GREECE • RED

(A)	**MILL CREEK MERLOT 2001, DUNAVAR** Macedonia	Juicy, ripe, plummy wine.	**£3.50**	CWS

GREECE • FORTIFIED

(A)	**SAMOS MUSCAT SWEET WHITE NV, D KOURTAKIS** Samos	Fresh, lush mandarin orange aromas.	**£5.00**	UNS

LEBANON

LEBANON • RED

(G)	**HOCHAR PÈRE ET FILS 1999, CHÂTEAU MUSAR** Bekaa Valley	Juicy, spicy, chunky, and chewy with plenty of savoury, peppery fruit. A long finish.	**£8.00**	ANM BTH HOL

MALTA

MALTA • RED

(A)	**MEDINA VINEYARDS CABERNET SAUVIGNON 2000, EMMANUEL DELICATA**	Aromatic, structured, ripe cassis fruit.	**£4.00**	HWA

MEXICO

MEXICO • RED

	**PETITE SYRAH 2000, LA CETTO** Baja California	Sweet green pepper, blackcurrant, liquorice, and spice. This stunner is certain to draw attention to the region.	**£5.50**	WTS SMF UNS

MOROCCO

MOROCCO • RED

(A)	**ATLAS VINEYARDS MERLOT 2001, CASTEL FRÈRES** Beni M'tir	Sweet-fruited, soft and plummy.	**£4.00**	COX

ROMANIA

ROMANIA • RED

(A)	**RIVER ROUTE MERLOT VANJU MARE OREVITA 2000, CARL REH WINERY**	Round, yet firm, with juicy damson fruit.	**£3.50**	ASD WRC JSM

URUGUAY

URUGUAY • RED

(S)	**OAKED SAUVIGNON BLANC 2001, CASA FILGUEIRA** Canelones	A well-structured white from a country better known for its reds. Obvious oak well balanced by the fruit.	**£6.00**	WER VNO

CODE	COMPANY	TELEPHONE	E-MAIL
ABY	Anthony Byrne Wine Agencies	01487 814555	claude@abfw.co.uk
ADD	Allied Domecq	01403 222600	laura_rogers@adswell.com
ADN	Adnams Wine Merchants	01502 727222	wines@adnams.co.uk
ADS	Alldays Stores Ltd	023 8064 5000	cducann@alldays.co.uk
ADW	Andrew Darwin	01544 230534	
ALB	Albion Wines Ltd	01494 864 868	albionwines@aol.com
ALD	Aldi Stores Ltd	01827 710 871	
ALE	Alexander Wines	0141 882 0039	
ALI	Alivini Company Ltd	0208 880 2526	enquiries@alivini.com
ALL	Alliance Wine Company Ltd	01505 506060	info@alliancewine.co.uk
ASD	Asda Stores Ltd	0113 241 9172	gjrober@asda.co.uk
AUC	The Australian Wine Club	0800 856 2004	info@cellarmasters.com.au
AVB	Averys of Bristol	01275 811100	averywines@aol.com
AWS	Albion Wine Shippers	020 7242 0873	
BAB	Bablake Wines	02476 228272	mail@bablake-wines.co.uk
BBR	Berry Bros & Rudd	020 7396 9685	andrea.stewart@bbr.com
BBZ	Bargain Booze	01270 753001	
BCW	Brian Coad Fine Wines	01752 896545	
BEL	Bentalls of Kingston	020 8546 1001	
BEN	Bennetts	01386 840392	info@bennettsfinewines.com
BFD	Brian Fords Discount Stores	01271 327744	
BGL	Bottle Green Ltd	0113 205 4500	info@bottlegreen.com
BGN	Budgens Stores Limited	020 8864 2800	christine.sandys@budgens.co.uk
BLU	The Bluebird Store	020 75591156	
BMG	BMC Global	020 7702 1528	frankotten@bmcglobal.com
BOO	Booths of Stockport	0161 432 3309	johnbooth@lineone.net
BOR	De Bortoli Wines UK Ltd	01725 516467	debortoli@talk21.com
BRA	G. Bravo & Son Ltd	020 7836 4693	gbravo@gbravo.co.uk
BSE	Beer Seller	01305 751 399	
BSS	Besos (UK) Ltd	01243 575454	
BTH	Booths Supermarkets	01772 251701	info@booths-supermarkets.co.uk
BUT	The Butlers Wine Cellar	01273 698724	butlerwine.cellar@cwcom.net
BWC	Berkmann Wine Cellars	0207 609 4711	yasmin@berkmann.co.uk
BWL	Bibendum Wine Ltd	020 7722 5577	info@bibendum-wine.co.uk
C&B	Corney & Barrow	020 7251 4051	juliet.beeson@corbar.co.uk
C&D	C&D Wines Ltd	020 8778 1711	helen@canddwines.co.uk
CAX	Pernod Ricard UK Ltd	020 8538 4000	aluckes@pernodricard-uk.com
CER	Cellar 28	01484 710101	admin@cellar28.com
CFN	Carringtons Fine Wines	0161 446 2546	
CHA	Chalcot Wines	01372 468571	
CHC	Churchill Vintners Ltd	0121 4141719	info@churchill-vintners.co.uk
CHN	Charles Hawkins	01572 823030	
CHS	Champagne Shop	0870 0130105	info@thechampagneshop.co.uk

CODE	COMPANY	TELEPHONE	E-MAIL
CLA	Classic Drinks	01744 831 400	
CLW	Cellarmaster Wines UK	020 8843 8464	jp@madaboutwine.com
CMB	Colombier Vins Fins	01283 552 552	
CNL	Connolly's	0121 236 9269	connowine@aol.com
COC	Corks of Cotham	0117 973 1620	r@dandr.co.uk
COE	Coe of Ilford	020 8551 4966	
COX	Neville Cox Wines	01449 741855	nevillecoxwines@talk21.com
CPR	Capricorn Wines	0161 908 1360	natalief@cboutinot.com
CPW	Christopher Piper Wines	01404 814139	
CRS	The Co operative Society	01706 891628	
CSD	Peter Cossart Ltd	020 8749 6401	philipmuir@aol.com
CST	The County Stores	01823 272235	
CTL	Continental Wine & Food	01484 538333	vickyswalescwf@lineone.net
CWS	Co-operative Group	0161 827 5492	carole.nicholson@co-op.co.uk
D&D	D&D Wines International	01565 650952	ddwi@ddwinesint.com
D&F	D & F Wine Shippers Ltd	020 8838 4399	info@dandfwines.fsnet.co.uk
DAM	The Dram Shop	0114 268 3117	info@thedramshop.co.uk
DBO	Boyar International Ltd	020 7537 3707	info@domaineboyar.co.uk
DBY	D Byrne & Co	01200 423152	
DIK	Dickens Kimbell Ltd	020 7600 1111	dave@mustards.demon.co.uk
DIW	Direct Wine Importers	01481 726747	
DVY	Davy & Co Ltd	020 7407 9670	tlh@davy.co.uk
EBA	Ben Ellis Wines (FWW)	01737 842 160	vincent@benelliswines.com
EHL	Ehrmanns Ltd	020 7418 1800	toby.hancock@ehrmanns.co.uk
ELD	Eldridge Pope	01305 751 300	
EOO	Everton's of Ombersley	01905 620282	sales@evertons.co.uk
EOR	Ellis of Richmond Ltd	020 8943 4033	mcooper@ellis-wines.co.uk
ESL	Edward Sheldon Ltd.	01608 661409	info@edward-sheldon.co.uk
EUR	Europa Foods Ltd	020 8845 1255	info@europafoods.com
EUW	Eurowines	020 8747 2107	ellie@eurowines.co.uk
EVW	everywine.co.uk	0800 072 0011	
EWD	Euro World Wines	0141 649 3735	
F&M	Fortnum & Mason	020 7734 8040	info@fortnumandmason.co.uk
FCA	Fraser Crameri Assoc.	01580 200 304	fraser@fraserfinewines.co.uk
FEN	Fenwick Ltd	0191 232 5100	
FOL	Folio Wines	01305 751399	sheila.bednall@beerseller.co.uk
FRI	Friarwood Limited	020 7736 2628	edward@friarwood.com
FSW	Frank Stainton Wines	01539 731886	admin@staintom-wines.co.uk
FTH	Forth Wines Ltd	01577 866001	davidr@forthwines.com
FUL	Fuller Smith & Turner	020 8996 2000	
FWC	Four Walls Wine Company	01243 535360	fourwallswine@aol.com
G&M	Gordon & MacPhail	01343 545111	info@gordonandmacphail.com
GAR	Garland Wine Cellar	01372 275247	

CODE	COMPANY	TELEPHONE	E-MAIL
GCF	Les Grands Chais de France	+33 557 981 214	Timcdluk@cs.com
GEE	Georgian Embassy	020 7603 7799	geoemb@dircon.co.uk
GHL	George Hill of Loughborough	01509 212717	info@georgehill.co.uk
GNW	Great Northern Wine Co	01765 606767	info@greatnorthernwine.com
GON	Gauntleys of Nottingham	0115 911 0555	rhone@gauntleywine.com
GPA	Grapevine (Andover)	01264 737658	
GPW	GP Wines	01403 891 396	ian@gpwines.com
GRT	Great Western Wine	01225 322800	info@greatwesternwine.co.uk
GWI	The General Wine Company	01428 722201	angus@thegeneralwine.co.uk
GYW	Guy Anderson Wines	01935 817 617	@guyandersonwines.co.uk
H&H	H&H Bancroft	0870 444 1700	dross@opus-trust.com
HAR	Harrods Wine Shop	0207 730 1234	nick.attfield@harrods.com
HAY	Hayward Bros (Wines) Ltd	0207 237 0567	
HBJ	Heyman, Barwell Jones Ltd	01473 232322	paul.gow@heyman.co.uk
HDS	Hedley Wright Wine Merchants	01279 465 818	wine@hwcg.co.uk
HDY	Hollywood & Donnelly	01232 799335	
HMC	Hermitage Cellars	01243 373363	hermit@mcmail.com
HME	Haslemere Wine Merchants	0208 880 9200	
HOH	Hallgarten Wines Ltd	01582 722538	cliff@vitisvinifera.demon.co.uk
HOL	Holland Park Wine Co	020 7221 9614	info@handford-wine.demon.co.uk
HOT	House of Townend	01482 326891	info@houseoftownend.co.uk
HOU	Hoults Wine Merchants	01484 510700	sales@houltswinemerchants.co.uk
HRV	Harrison Vintners	020 7236 7716	sales@harrisonvinters.co.uk
HVB	John Harvey & Sons	0117 927 5010	
HVN	Harvey Nichols	020 7235 5000	
HWA	Heritage Wines	01454 294099	
HWL	HWCG Wine Growers	01279 873471	wine@hwcg.co.uk
HZW	Hazeley Wines Ltd	01244 332 008	simonely@hazely.u-net.com
IRV	Irvine Robertson	0131 553 3521	irviner@nildram.co.uk
IVY	Ivy Wines	01243 377883	
IWS	International Wine Services	01494 680857	info@intwine.co.uk
J&B	Justerini & Brooks	020 7484 6400	justmarketing@justerinis.com
JAS	Jascots Wine Merchants Ltd	020 7749 0022	jack@jascots.co.uk
JBR	Eldridge Pope Fine Wines	01305 751306	sue.longman@beerseller.co.uk
JEF	John E Fells & Sons	01442 870900	art@fells.co.uk
JKN	Jackson Nugent Vintners	020 8947 9722	
JMC	James E McCabe	02838 333102	
JNW	James Nicholson	02844 830091	info@jnwine.com
JOV	Jolly Vintner	01884 255644	
JSM	Sainsbury Supermarkets Ltd	020 7695 6000	info@sainsburys.co.uk
KJW	Kendall Jackson Europe Ltd	020 8747 2841	carol.sturch@kjmail.com
L&S	Laymont & Shaw Ltd	01872 270 545	info@laymont-shaw.co.uk
L&W	Lay & Wheeler Ltd	01206 764446	hugo.rose@laywheeler.com

CODE	COMPANY	TELEPHONE	E-MAIL
LAI	Laithwaites (Direct Wines)	0118 903 0903	info@directwines.co.uk
LEA	Lea & Sandeman	020 8244 0522	info@leaandsandeman.co.uk
LIB	Liberty Wines	020 8720 5350	sara.muirhead@libertywine.co.uk
LLW	Lloyd Taylor Wines	01738 444994	
LOH	Larners of Holt	01263 712323	
M&S	Marks & Spencer	020 7268 4605	info@marks-and-spencer.com
M&V	Morris & Verdin	020 8921 5300	sales@m-v.co.uk
MAC	Makro UK	0161 786 2256	kevin.wilson@makro.co.uk
MAE	Mandarine	0777 9246198	winery@tuscali.co.uk
MAK	Makro Self Service	01372 468571	info@tonystebbings.co.uk
MAX	Maxxium UK	01786 430500	susan.ralston@maxxium.com
MBW	Mounts Bay Wine Co.	01736 364118	
MCD	Marne & Champagne Ltd	020 7499 0070	
MCO	Malcolm Cowen	0208 965 1937	rupert.wilkins@cowen.co.uk
MCT	Matthew Clark	01275 890357	
MER	Meridian Wines	0161 908 1330	natalief@boutinot.com
MEW	Medina Wines	01983 761 058	
MFS	Martinez Fine Wine	01422 320022	davidlawson@martinez.co.uk
MHV	Booker Cash & Carry	01933 371363	info@boozer.co.uk
MHW	Mill Hill Wines	020 7959 6754	millhillwines@compuserve.com
MKV	McKinley Vintners	020 7928 7300	info@mckinleyvintners.co.uk
MNH	Manor House Wine Merchants	029 2040 3355	denisewhite@sab.com
MON	Mondial Wine Ltd	020 8335 3455	marketing@mondialwine.co.uk
MOR	Moreno Wine Importers	020 8960 7161	abbi@moreno-wines.co.uk
MRN	Morrison Supermarkets	01924 875234	
MSF	Milton Sandford Wines	01628 829 449	
MWW	Majestic Wine Warehouses	01923 298200	agilson@majestic.co.uk
MYL	Myliko International	01204 392222	aruna@myliko.co.uk
MYN	Myndtown Wines	01588 650516	philip@myndtownwines.co.uk
N&P	Nickolls & Perks	01384 394518	sales@nickollsandperks.co.uk
NEG	Negociants UK Ltd (Yalumba)	01582 462859	neguk@negociants.com
NIC	Nicolas UK Ltd	020 8964 5469	dhanns@nicolas-wines.com
NTD	Nisa Today's	01724 282028	david@drinks-marketing.com
NWG	New World Wines Ltd	020 8877 3450	matt@newworldwines.co.uk
NYW	Noel Young Wines	01223 566 744	noel.young@dial.pipex.com
ODD	Oddbins	020 8944 4400	karen_wise@oddbins.com
ODF	Oddbins Fine Wine	020 8944 4400	karen_wise@oddbins.com
OWC	The Oxford Wine Company	01865 301144	info@oxfordwine.co.uk
P&R	Peckham & Rye	0141 445 4555	sbatpeck@aol.com
P&S	Philglass & Swiggot	020 7924 4494	
PAT	Patriarche Père et Fils Ltd	020 7381 4016	felicity@patriarchewines.com
PBA	Paul Boutinot Agencies Ltd	0161 908 1370	natalief@boutinot.com
PEA	Peake Wine Assocs	01329 822733	

CODE	COMPANY	TELEPHONE	E-MAIL
PEF	Southcorp Wines Europe Ltd	020 8917 4600	
PFC	Percy Fox & Co	01279 633863	
PGR	Patrick Grubb Selections	01869 340229	
PGW	Peter Graham Wines	01603 625657	
PHR	Phillip Russell	01232 707755	
PIM	Pimlico Dozen	020 7834 3647	john@pimlicodozen.com
PLA	Playford Ros Ltd	01845 526777	sales@playfordros.com
PLB	Private Liquor Brands	01342 318282	claire.summersby@plb.co.uk
PLF	Peter Lehmann Wines	01227 731353	admin@lehmannwines.com
POR	Portland Wine Company	0161 928 0357	portwineco@aol.com
QRW	Quellyn Roberts Wine	01244 310455	qrwines@chesternet.co.uk
RAM	Ramsbottom Victuallers	01706 825070	rammy.vics@which.net
RAV	Ravensbourne Wine	020 8692 9655	
RBS	Roberts & Speight	01482 870717	
RCH	Le Riche	01534 811049	
RDS	Reid Wines	01761 452645	
REY	Raymond Reynolds Ltd	01663 742 230	info@raymondreynolds.co.uk
RHC	Reh Kendermann UK	01295 760000	richardnjones@btinternet.com
RIL	Alex Riley Wines	01954 208000	alex.riley.wines@dial.pipex.com
ROD	Rodney Densem Wines Ltd	01270 212200	sales@onestopwine.com
ROG	Roger Harris Wines	01603 880171	clare@rogerharriswines.co.uk
RWM	Roberson Wine Merchant	020 7371 2121	wines@roberson.co.uk
SAF	Safeway Stores Plc	020 8970 3506	tim_ranscombe@safeway.co.uk
SBS	Sainsbury Brothers	01225 460981	
SCA	Scatchard Ltd	0151 709 7073	info@scatchard.com
SCK	Seckford Wines Ltd.	01394 446629	meg@seckfordwines.co.uk
SEL	Selfridges Ltd	020 7318 3730	
SGL	Stevens Garnier Ltd	01865 263300	info@stevensgarnier.co.uk
SLT	Sanlucar Trading	020 7627 8985	santradco@aol.com
SMF	Somerfield Stores Ltd	0117 935 9359	nicola.anthony@somerfield.co.uk
SOM	Sommelier Wine Co	01481 721677	
SPR	Spar (UK) Ltd	020 8426 3700	williamsa@spar.co.uk
STN	Southern Wine Brands Ltd	01484 608898	swbltd@aol.com
SWB	Satchells	01328 738272	satchellswines@btinternet.com
SWG	SWIG	020 7903 8311	
SWS	Stratford's Wine Agencies	01628 810606	hayley@stratfordwine.co.uk
TAN	Tanners Wines Ltd	01743 234500	sales@tanners-wines.co.uk
TCV	Three Choirs Vineyards Ltd	01531 890555	nick@grape2wine.f9.co.uk
THI	Thierry's Wine Services	01794 507100	
THO	Thomas Peatlings	01925265689	
TOS	Tesco Stores Ltd	01992 632222	
TRI	Trinity Vintners	020 7493 6165	
UBC	Ubiquitous Chip	0141 334 5007	mail@ubiquitouschip.co.uk

CODE	COMPANY	TELEPHONE	E-MAIL
UNS	The Unwins Wine Group	01322 272711	brolfe@unwins.co.uk
UWM	United Wine Merchants	01232 231231	
VER	Vinceremos Wines	0113 244 0002	info@vinceremos.co.uk
VGN	Virgin Wine Online Ltd	01603 886 688	nicola@virginwines.com
VHW	Victor Hugo Wines	01534 507977	
VIN	Vinum	020 8840 4070	vinum@vinum.co.uk
VKW	Vickery Wines	01582 456180	islay@vickerywines.co.uk
VLW	Villeneuve Wines	01721 722500	wines@villeneuvewines.com
VNE	Vine to Wine	07041 514053	
VNO	Vinoceros (UK)Ltd	01209 314 711	lucy.rowe@vinoceros.com
VRA	Vranken UK Limited	020 7304 7012	lefevre.vrankenuk@cclgb.co.uk
VRT	Vintage Roots	0118 976 1999	sarah@vintageroots.co.uk
VSE	The Vintners Selection Ltd	01476 550476	vintners@hampers.co.uk
VTH	Vintage House	020 76372592	
WAV	Waverley Wines & Spirits	01738 472028	info@waverly-group.co.uk
WAW	Waterloo Wine Co	020 7403 7967	sales@waterloowine.co.uk
WBC	Whitbread Beer Co	01582 391166	
WBR	Wadebridge Wines	01208 812692	wadebridgewines@eclipse.co.uk
WCR	Wine Cellar Ltd (Parisa)	01925 454702	david.vaughan@parisa.com
WEP	Welshpool Wine Company	01938 553243	
WER	Wine Cellar (Douglas)	01624 611793	
WIE	Wine Importers Edinburgh	0131 556 3601	reception@wine-importers.net
WIM	Wimbledon Wine Cellars	020 8540 9979	info@wimbledonwinecellar.com
WNS	Winos	0161 652 9396	
WOW	Wines of Westhorpe	01283 820285	wines@westhorpe.co.uk
WRC	First Quench (Wine Rack)	01707 387200	jonathan.butt@firstquench.co.uk
WRK	Wine Raks	01224 311460	mike@wineraks.co.uk
WRT	Winerite Ltd	0113 283 7649	jeni.bailey@winerite.co.uk
WRW	The Wright Wine Co	01756 700886	bob@wineandwhisky.co.uk
WSG	Walter S Siegel Ltd	01256 701101	info@walter-siegel.co.uk
WSO	The Wine Society Ltd	01438 761190	info@thewinesociety.com
WST	Western Wines Ltd	01952 235 726	katherine@western-wines.com
WTL	Whittalls Wines	01922 36161	
WTS	Waitrose Ltd	01344 424680	gareth_strange@waitrose.co.uk
WWT	Whitebridge Wines	01785 817229	sales@whitebridgewines.co.uk
YWL	Yates Brothers Ltd	01204 391777	julie.waterfield@yates-bros.co.uk

RETAILERS

WHAT THIS CHAPTER CONTAINS

The following chapter has been conceived in order to help you to find almost everything – short of a congenial companion – you are likely to need to enjoy wine. If you are looking for a good local retailer, a wine from a specific region/country, or perhaps a wine course/school, vacation, tour, cellar, rack, or chiller, this is the place to look.

MAIN LIST OF RETAILERS

3D Wines ★★★★
1-2 North End, Swineshead,
Lincolnshire PE20 3LR.
℡ 01205 820745 FAX 01205 821042
@ www.3dwines.com
Credit cards, delivery, tastings, mail order.
French specialists who rent rows of vines to customers (who are known as partners). Great trips.

Addison Wines ★★★★
Horton House, Hailesfield 19, Telford,
Shropshire TF7 4QT
℡ 01952 686500 FAX 01952 686505
@ sales@addisonwines.com
W www.addisonwines.com
Credit cards, delivery, tastings, en primeur, cellarage, mail order.
French wines and good examples from Australia and Chile.

Adnams ★★★★★
Sole Bay Brewery, East Green,
Southwold, Suffolk IP18 6JW
℡ 01502 727222 FAX 01502 727223
@ wines@adnams.co.uk
W www.adnams.co.uk
Credit cards, accessories, delivery, tastings, en primeur, glass hire, mail order.
Innovative brewer and wine merchant.

The Antique Wine Co. ★★★★
Portland House, Station Road, Ballasalla,
Isle of Man IM99 6AB
℡ 01624 824771 FAX 01624 824837
@ info@antique-wine.com
W www.antique-wine.com
Mail order only, credit cards, accessories, delivery, tastings, cellarage, en primeur, internet sales.
Specialist in fine and rare wines. GiantBottles.com is their large format bottle supply arm.

John Armit Wines ★★★★★
5 Royalty Studios, 105 Lancaster Road,
London W11 1QF
℡ 020 7908 0600 FAX 020 7908 0601
@ info@armit.co.uk
W www.armit.co.uk
By the case only, mail order only, credit cards, free delivery, tastings, en primeur, cellarage, internet sales.
Superb clarets, Burgundies, Italians and own-label Champagne.

Asda Stores ★★★★
Asda House, Southbank,
Great Wilson Street, Leeds LS11 5AD
℡ 0113 241 9172 FAX 0113 241 7766
W www.asda.co.uk
Credit cards, selected delivery, tastings, glass loan, Internet sales.
The UK face of US supermarket giant Walmart with a mixture of big-saver lines by the case only, and big-name "icon" wines.

Australian Wine Club ★★★★★
3rd Floor, Regal House, 70 London
Road, Twickenham, Middx. TW1 3QS
℡ 0800 856 2004 FAX 0800 856 2114
@ orders@austwine.co. uk
W www.austwine.co.uk
Mail order only, by the case only, credit cards, delivery, tastings, internet sales.
Pioneers of Australian wines in the UK.

Averys of Bristol ★★★★
Orchard House, Southfield Road,
Nailsea, Bristol BS48 1JN
℡ 08451 283797 FAX 01275 811 101
@ averywines@aol.com
Credit cards, delivery, tastings, en primeur, cellarage, glass hire/loan, mail order.
Great wines from traditional as well as up-and-coming areas.

Ballantynes of Cowbridge ★★★★

3 Westgate, Cowbridge, Vale of
Glamorgan, Wales CF71 7AQ
☎ 01446 774 840 FAX 01446 775 253
@ richard@ballantynes.co.uk
w www.ballantynes.co.uk
Credit cards, accessories, delivery, tastings, en
primeur, cellarage, glass loan, mail order.
*Dynamic list, featuring small high
quality growers from Italy, Australia,
Burgundy and the Languedoc, with some
serious Californian wines. New store
opening in Cardiff.*

Balls Brothers ★★★★

313 Cambridge Heath Road,
London E2 9LQ
☎ 020 7739 1642 FAX 0870 243 9775
@ wine@ballsbrothers.co.uk
w www.ballsbrothers.co.uk
Credit cards, delivery, tastings, glass hire/loan, mail
order, internet sales.
Good French wines.

Bennetts Fine Wines ★★★★★

High Street, Chipping Campden,
Glos GL55 6AG
☎ 01386 840 392 FAX 01386 840 974
@ charlie@bennettsfinewines.com
w www.bennettsfinewines.com
Credit cards, accessories, delivery, tastings, cellarage,
en primeur, glass hire/loan, mail order.
*Specializing in the top end of the market
with a terrific selection of classic French
and Italian wines.*

Berkmann Wine Cellars ★★★★★

10/12 Brewery Road, London N7 9NH
☎ 020 7609 4711 FAX 020 7607 0018
@ info@berkmann.co.uk
w www.berkmann.co.uk
Credit cards, accessories, delivery, glass hire/loan,
tastings, cellarage, mail order.
*Focus on France, but the list has
expanded with strengths across the globe.
Recently amalgamated with Brian Coad
Fine Wines.*

Berry Bros. & Rudd ★★★★★

3 St. James's Street, London SW1A 1EG
☎ 0870 900 4300 FAX 0870 900 4301
@ orders@bbr.com
w www.bbr.com
Credit cards, accessories, delivery, en primeur,
cellarage, tastings, glass hire, mail order worldwide,
internet sales.
*Award-winning wine merchant with
fantastic French and New World wines.*

Bibendum ★★★★★

113 Regents Park Road, London
NW1 8UR
☎ 020 7449 4120 FAX 020 7449 4121
@ sales@bibendum-wine.co.uk
w www.bibendum-wine.co.uk
By the case only, mail order only, credit cards,
delivery, tastings, glass loan, en primeur, internet
sales.
*Excellent range of individual Old and
New World wines.*

Booths Supermarkets ★★★★★

4–6 Fishergate, Preston PR1 3LJ
☎ 01772 251 701 01772 255 642
Credit cards, accessories, tastings, glass hire/loan.
*One of Britain's most enterprising
supermarket groups.(Also owns
everywine.co.uk)*

Bordeaux Index ★★★★★

6th Floor, 159-173 St John Street,
London EC1V 4QJ
☎ 020 7253 2110 FAX 020 7490 1955
@ sales@bordeauxindex.com
w www.bordeauxindex.com
By the case only, credit cards, delivery, en primeur,
cellarage, mail order.
*Dynamic Bordeaux and Burgundy
merchants with good Italian, Spanish,
New World, Champagne and Port.*

Bottoms Up ★★★★

Enjoyment Hall, Bessemer Road,
Welwyn Garden City, Herts AL7 1BL
☎ 01707 387263 FAX 01707 387200
w www.firstquench.co.uk
Credit cards, delivery, tastings, glass hire/loan.
*Oddbins-lookalike under same ownership
as Thresher and Victoria Wine.*

La Bouteille d'Or ★★★★

Queens Lodge, Queens Club Gardens,
London W14 9TA
☎ 020 7385 3122 FAX 020 7385 3122
@ labouteilledor@newbury.net
By the case only, mail order, delivery, tastings.
*Focus on Champagne from small
growers.*

The Burgundy Shuttle ★★★★

168 Ifield Road, London SW10 9AF
☎ 020 7341 4053 FAX 020 7244 0618
@ info@bygneatwines.com
w www.burgundyshuttle.co.uk
By the case only, credit cards, accessories, en
primeur, cellarage, glass loan, delivery, internet sales.
Excellent Burgundy specialist.

The Butlers Wine Cellar ★★★★
247 Queens Park Road, Brighton,
East Sussex BN2 9XJ
☎ 01273 698724 FAX 01273 622761
W www.butlers-winecellar.co.uk
Credit cards, accessories, delivery, tastings, glass
hire/loan, mail order, internet sales.
Great range from the classic to the eclectic.

Anthony Byrne Fine Wines ★★★★★
Ramsey Business Park, Stocking Fen
Road, Ramsey, Cambs PE26 2UR
☎ 01487 814555 FAX 01487 814962
@ claude@abfw.co.uk
W www.abfw.co.uk
Delivery, en primeur, cellarage, tastings.
*An amazing choice of more than 2500
quality wines from 17 countries.*

Cave Cru Classé ★★★★
Unit 13, Leathermarket, Weston Street,
London SE1 3ER
☎ 020 7940 5112 FAX 020 7378 8544
W www.cave-cru-classe.com
By the case only, accessories, cellarage, credit cards,
delivery, en primeur, tastings.
*Top vintages of top wines from Rhône,
Bordeaux and Burgundy.*

Les Caves de Pyrene ★★★★
Pew Corner, Old Portsmouth Road,
Artington, Guildford, Surrey GU3 1LP
☎ 01483 538820 FAX 01483 455068
W www.lescavesdepyrene.com
By the case only, credit cards, delivery, tastings and
wine dinners, mail order, internet sales.
*Quirky and traditional French wines with
some good New World fare.*

The Cellar d'Or ★★★★
37 St Giles, Norwich NR2 1JN
☎ 01603 626246 FAX 01603 667848
@ wine@cellardor.co.uk
W www.cellardor.co.uk
Credit cards, accessories, delivery, tastings, en
primeur, cellarage, glass loan, internet sales.
*Their fine and rare wine branches trade
as The Antique Wine Company of Great
Britain.*

Charterhouse Wine Co. ★★★★
82 Goding Street, London SE11 5AW
☎ 020 7587 1302 FAX 020 7587 0982
@ norman@charterhousewine.co.uk
Credit cards, delivery, en primeur, cellarage, tastings,
glass loan, mail order.
*Good wines from Australia, Chile, and
Spain.*

Brian Coad Fine Wines ★★★★
Grape Expectations Wine Warehouse,
Stray Park, off Park St., Ivybridge,
Devon PL21 9DW
☎ 01752 896 545 FAX 01752 691 160
@ briancoadfinewines@lineone.net
Mail order, by the case only, credit cards, delivery,
tastings, en primeur (Port and Beaujolais only), glass
loan, cellarage..
See Berkmann Wine Cellars.

Cockburns of Leith ★★★★
7 Devon Place, Edinburgh,
Scotland EH12 5HJ
☎ 0131 346 1113 FAX 0131 313 2607
@ jhogg@winelist.co.uk
W www.winelist.co.uk
Credit cards, delivery, tastings, en primeur, glass loan,
cellarage, mail order, internet sales.
*Reliable, traditional merchant. Good for
Claret and Burgundy.*

Compendium Wine Merchants
★★★★
Alanbrooke Road, Castlereagh, Belfast,
N. Ireland BT6 9PR
☎ 028 9079 1197 FAX 028 9079 8001
@ info@compendiumwines.com
W www.compendiumwines.com
Credit cards, delivery, glass loan/hire, tastings,
mail order, internet sales.
*An exciting portfolio and an
approachable manner. Australian,
Spanish and Southern French range is
particularly impressive.*

Corkscrew Wines ★★★★
Arch 5, Viaduct Estate,
Carlisle CA2 5BN
☎ 01228 543033 FAX 01228 543033
@ wines@corkscrewwines.demon.co.uk
W www.corkscrew-wines.com
Credit cards, delivery, tastings, en primeur,
glass hire/loan, mail order.
*Small merchant with a big list. Good
Australian wines across the board.*

Corney and Barrow ★★★★
12 Helmet Row, London EC1V 3TD
☎ 020 7539 3200 FAX 020 7608 1373
@ wine@corbar.co.uk
W www.corneyandbarrow.com
Credit cards, accessories, delivery, en primeur,
cellarage, glass hire/loan, tastings, mail order, internet
sales.
*Fine wine specialists with an eye for the
world's most desirable wines from small
producers across the globe.*

Croque-en-Bouche ★★★★★
221 Wells Road, Malvern Wells,
Worcester WR14 4HF
☎ 01684 565612 **FAX** 0870 7066282
@ mail@croque-en-bouche.co.uk
W www.croque-en-bouche.co.uk
By the case only, accessories, credit cards, delivery,
cellarage, mail order, internet sales.
*Now that they are closing their Michelin
star restaurant after more than 20 years
they are to concentrate their efforts on
expanding the wine business.*

deFine Food & Wine ★★★★★
Chester Road, Sandiway,
Cheshire CW8 2NH
☎ 01606 882101 **FAX** 01606 888407
@ office@definefoodandwine.com
Credit cards, accessories, delivery, tastings,
cellarage, glass loan, mail order.
*Merchants bursting with enthusiasm.
Strong on Italy and the leading Soave
specialists. Now with in-store deli.*

Direct Wine Shipments ★★★★★
5/7 Corporation Square, Belfast,
N. Ireland BT1 3AJ
☎ 028 9050 8000 **FAX** 028 9050 8004
@ enquiry@directwine.co.uk
W www.directwine.co.uk
Credit cards, accessories, delivery, tastings, en
primeur, cellarage, mail order.
*Merchant offering tastings and courses.
Generally very recommendable but
especially strong on Spain and Australia.*

Domaine Direct ★★★★★
6-9 Cynthia Street, London N1 9JF
☎ 020 7837 1142 **FAX** 020 7837 8605
@ info@domainedirect.co.uk
W www.domainedirect.co.uk
By the case only, credit cards, delivery, tastings,
en primeur, mail order.
*A serious list with brilliant Burgundy
and New World estates (e.g., Leeuwin)
often at surprisingly competitive prices.*

English Wine Centre ★★★★
Alfriston, East Sussex BN26 5QS
☎ 01323 870164**FAX** 01323 870005
@ bottles@englishwine.co.uk
W www.englishwine.co.uk
Credit cards, accessories, delivery, tastings, glass
hire/loan, mail order, internet sales.
*Home to the English Wine Museum, with
daily tastings of a good range of wines
from various parts of the UK. Wines from
other countries are available too.*

Farr Vintners ★★★★★
19 Sussex Street, Pimlico,
London SW1V 4RR
☎ 020 7821 2000 **FAX** 020 7821 2020
@ sales@farr-vintners.com
W www.farr-vintners.com
By the case only (min. order £500), cellarage, delivery,
en primeur, internet sales, worldwide shipping.
*The reference point for the world's finest
and rarest wines.*

Fine & Rare Wines ★★★★★
Unit 17–18 Pall Mall Deposit, 124–128
Barlby Road, London W10 6BL
☎ 020 8960 1995 **FAX** 020 8960 1911
@ wine@frw.co.uk
W www.frw.co.uk
Mail order, delivery, en primeur.
*Specialists in the world's fine and rare
wines; from en primeur to the oldest
vintages.*

Irma Fingal-Rock ★★★★
64 Monnow Street, Monmouth,
Wales NP25 3EN
☎ 01600 712372 **FAX** 01600 712372
@ irmafingalrock@msn.com
W www.pinotnoir.co.uk
Credit cards, delivery, tastings, glass hire/loan,
mail order.
*Originally a food shop, wine now
constitutes 80 per cent of turnover.
Emphasis is on interesting, characterful
wines from small producers in Burgundy.*

Flagship Wines ★★★★
3 Keys Parade, Eagle Way, Warley,
Brentwood, Essex, CM13 3BP
☎ 01277 203420 **FAX** 01277 203421
@ sales@flagshipwines.co.uk
W www.directwineline.com
Accessories, credit cards, delivery, tastings, glass
loan/hire, mail order, Internet sales.
*Innovative company with distinctive
wines from all around the world,
although they specialise in New World
wines. Wine on Tap is part of the business
that "makes wine buying easy".*

Forth Wines ★★★★
Crawford Place, Milnathort,
Kinross-shire, Scotland KY13 9XF
☎ 01577 866000 **FAX** 01577 866010
@ enquiries@forthwines.com
W www.forthwines.com
By the case only, credit cards, delivery, en primeur.
*Wines from first rate producers in the Old
as well as the New World.*

Fortnum & Mason ★★★★★
181 Piccadilly, London W1A 1ER
☎ 020 7734 8040 ℻ 020 7437 3278
@ info@fortnumandmason.co.uk
ⓦ www.fortnumandmason.co.uk
Credit cards, accessories, delivery, tastings, en
primeur, mail order, internet sales.
Ultra-smart store with classic wines.

Four Walls Wine Co. ★★★★★
1 High Street, Chilgrove, Nr Chichester,
W. Sussex PO18 9HX
☎ 01243 535360 ℻ 01243 535418
@ fourwallswine@aol.com
Credit cards, accessories, delivery, en primeur,
tastings, cellarage, glass hire/loan.
*A super list of 3,500 blue-chip Bordeaux,
Burgundies, Germans, and Loires.*

Frank Stainton Wines ★★★★
3 Berry's Yard, Finkle Street, Kendal,
Cumbria LA9 4AB
☎ 01539 731886 ℻ 01539 730396
@ admin@stainton-wines.co.uk
Credit cards, delivery, tastings, mail order.
*Broad range. Good Rieslings, Bordeaux,
New World and half-bottles.*

Gauntleys of Nottingham ★★★★★
4 High Street, Exchange Arcade,
Nottingham NG1 2ET
☎ 0115 911 0555 ℻ 0115 911 0557
@ rhone@gauntleywine.com
ⓦ www.gauntleywine.com
Credit cards, accessories, tastings, mail order, en
primeur.
Superb on Alsace, Rhône and Languedoc.

Goedhuis & Co. ★★★★★
6 Rudolf Place, Miles Street,
London SW8 1RP
☎ 020 7793 7900 ℻ 020 7793 7170
ⓦ www.goedhuis.com
By the case only, delivery, en primeur, cellarage, glass
loan.
*Source of Old and New World wine. En
primeur, Bordeaux, and Burgundy.*

Gordon & MacPhail ★★★★
58–60 South Street, Elgin, Moray,
Scotland IV30 1JY
☎ 01343 545 110 ℻ 01343 540 155
@ info@gordonandmacphail.com
ⓦ www.gordonandmacphail.com
Credit cards, accessories, delivery, tastings, en
primeur (ports), glass hire/loan, mail order.
*Brilliant malt whisky from your birth year
and a good range of French country wines.*

Great Northern Wine Co. ★★★★
The Warehouse, Blossomgate, Ripon,
N. Yorks. HG4 2AJ
☎ 01765 606767 ℻ 01765 609151
@ info@greatnorthernwine.com
ⓦ www.greatnorthernwine.com
Credit cards, accessories, delivery, tastings, cellarage,
en primeur, glass loan, mail order, internet sales.
*One of the best merchants between
Edinburgh and Watford. Friendly service.*

Great Western Wine Co. ★★★★
Wells Road, Bath BA2 3AP
☎ 01225 322800 ℻ 01225 442139
@ davidl@greatwesternwine.co.uk
ⓦ www.greatwesternwine.co.uk
By the case only, accessories, credit cards, delivery,
tastings, cellarage, glass loan, en primeur, mail order,
internet sales.
*Great range, especially good French
country wines. Plenty of half-bottles, too,
and an enticing diary of tastings.*

Alexander Hadleigh ★★★★
19 Centre Way, Lock's Heath,
Southampton, Hampshire SO31 6DX
☎ 01489 885959 ℻ 01489 885960
@ info@ahadleigh-wine.com
Credit cards, accessories, delivery, tastings, glass
hire/loan, mail order.
*Good stock of organic wines, Armagnacs,
Cognacs and malts. They also have
gourmet food.*

Roger Harris Wines ★★★★★
Loke Farm, Weston Longville,
Norfolk NR9 5LG
☎ 01603 880 171 ℻ 01603 880 291
@ sales@rogerharriswines.co.uk
ⓦ www.beaujolaisonline.co.uk
Mail order only, by the case only, credit cards,
delivery, internet sales.
*The best of Beaujolais and the Mâconnais
with the promise of next-day delivery.*

Harrods Ltd ★★★★★
87–135 Brompton Road, Knightsbridge,
London SW1X 7XL
☎ 020 7730 1234 ℻ 020 7225 5823
@ food.halls@harrods.com
ⓦ www.harrods.com
Credit cards, accessories, delivery, en primeur,
tastings, mail order.
*State-of-the-art wine shop, with some
1,600 wines in stock. Still, predictably,
hot on the classics of the Old World, but
there are plenty of big-name New World
stars too.*

Haynes Hanson & Clark ★★★★
25 Eccleston Street,
London SW1W 9NP
☎ 020 7259 0102 FAX 020 7259 0103
@ london@hhandc.co.uk
Credit cards, accessories, delivery, tastings, cellarage,
en primeur, glass loan, mail order.
France is the area of focus here, and
Burgundy the particular strength.

Hedley Wright ★★★★
Twyford Business Centre, London Road,
Bishops Stortford, Herts CM23 3YT
☎ 01279 465818 FAX 01279 465819
Credit cards, delivery, tastings, en primeur,
cellarage, glass loan, mail order.
A good country merchant offering classy
New World wines and Old World stars.
They have an excellent range from Chile.

Douglas Henn-Macrae ★★★★
61 Downs View, Burnham, Rochester,
Kent ME1 3RR
☎ 01634 669394 FAX 01634 683096
@ drhm@clara.co.uk
W www.drhm.clara.co.uk
By the case only, mail roder only, delivery, tastings.
German specialists with a good selection
of US wines, including examples from
hard-to-find unknown regions such as
Texas and Colorado. They boast that if
you have heard of a wine you probably
won't find it on their list.

Hayman Barwell Jones ★★★★
24 Fore Street, Ipswich,
Suffolk IP4 1JU
☎ 01473 232322 FAX 01473 212237
@ paul.gow@hbjwines.co.uk
W www.hbjwines.co.uk
By the case only, credit cards, delivery, tastings, en
primeur, mail order.
A very good range from all corners of
the globe with especially interesting
Burgundy.

George Hill of Loughborough ★★★★
59 Wards End, Loughborough,
Leicestershire LE11 3HB
☎ 01509 212717 FAX 01509 236963
@ sales@georgehill.co.uk
W www.georgehill.co.uk
Credit cards, en primeur, cellarage, glass hire/loan,
delivery, tastings, mail order.
Informative, easy to follow list
representing each primary winemaking
region across the globe. Grapewise is
their wine appreciation arm.

House of Townend ★★★★
Red Duster House, 101 York Street,
Hull HU2 0QX
☎ 01482 586582 FAX 01482 587042
@ sales@houseoftownend.co.uk
W www.hotwines.co.uk
Credit cards, delivery, en primeur, mail order,
cellarage, glass loan, tastings, internet sales.
Burgundy, Champagne, and Australia
are particular strengths, with a good
South African range.

Inspired Wines ★★★★
West End, High Street, Cleobury
Mortimer, Shropshire DY14 8DR
☎ 01299 270064 FAX 01299 270064
@ info@inspired-wines.co.uk
W www.inspired-wines.co.uk
Credit cards, accessories, delivery, tastings, en
primeur, glass hire/loan, mail order.
A warehouse with good New World wines
but concentrating on Italy, Spain and the
Rhône.

Jeroboams ★★★★
8–12 Brook Street, London W1Y 2BH
☎ 020 7288 8888 FAX 020 7495 3314
@ sales@jeroboams.co.uk
W www.jeroboams.co.uk
Credit cards, accessories, delivery, en primeur,
cellarage, delivery, glass hire, tastings, mail order,
internet sales.
Specialists in wine and cheese from claret
to Caerphilly. Now also incorporates
Laytons.

S.H. Jones & Co. ★★★★
27 High Street, Banbury, Oxon OX16
5EW
☎ 01295 251177 FAX 01295 272352
@ shjonesbanbury@aol.com
Credit cards, accessories, delivery, tastings, en
primeur, cellarage, glass loan, mail order.
Dependable for Spanish, South American,
and south Italian wines. Top end French
are good.

Justerini & Brooks ★★★★★
61 St. James's Street,
London, SW1A 1LZ
☎ 020 7484 6400 FAX 020 7484 6499
@ justorders@justerinis.com
Credit cards, accessories, delivery, tastings,
en primeur, cellarage, glass loan, mail order.
Second-to-none in the quality of the
range and in the service offered.
Unfortunately, closed both its shops in
2002. Now mail-order only.

Richard Kihl ★★★★

142 The High Street, Aldeburgh, Suffolk,
IP15 7AQ.
📞 01728 454455 FAX 01728 454433
@ sales@richardkihl.ltd.uk
W www.richardkihl.ltd.uk
Credit cards, delivery,, en primeur, cellarage, glass
hire, mail order.
*Top class classicists, whose name is
familiar to wine enthusiasts in the UK
and overseas.*

Laithwaites ★★★★★

New Aquitaine House, Exeter Way,
Theale, Reading, Berkshire RG7 4Pl
📞 0870 444 8383 FAX 0870 444 8182
@ orders@laithwaites.co.uk
W www.laithwaites.co.uk
Credit cards, accessories, delivery, glass hire/loan,
en primeur, tastings, mail order, internet sales.
*Highly innovative mail-order sister-firm
to The Sunday Times Wine Club.*

Lay & Wheeler ★★★★★

Gosbecks Park, Gosbecks Road,
Colchester, Essex CO2 9JT
📞 01206 764446 FAX 01206 560002
@ sales@laywheeler.com
W www.laywheeler.com
Credit cards, accessories, delivery, tastings, en
primeur, cellarage, glass loan, mail order, internet
sales.
*One of the best regional and mail-order
sources of Old and New World classics.*

Laymont & Shaw ★★★★★

The Old Chapel, Millpool, Truro,
Cornwall TR1 1EX
📞 01872 270 545 FAX 01872 223 005
@ info@laymont-shaw.co.uk
W www.laymont-shaw.co.uk
Mail order, by the case only, delivery,
tastings, glass loan.
*A treasure trove of both new wave and
traditional wines from Spain and
Portugal that are often hard to find. They
now also offer a good South American
range.*

Lea & Sandeman ★★★★★

170 Fulham Road, London SW10 9PR
📞 020 7244 0522 FAX 020 7244 0533
@ sales@leaandsandeman.co.uk
W www.londonfinewine.co.uk
Credit cards, accessories, delivery, en primeur,
cellarage, tastings, glass loan, mail order.
*First class London merchant with shops
in Fulham, Notting Hill, and Barnes.*

Liberty Wines ★★★★★

Unit A53, The Food Market,
New Covent Garden,
London SW8 5EE
📞 020 7720 5350 FAX 020 7720 6158
@ info@libertywine.co.uk
By the case only, credit cards, delivery, mail order.
*One of the leading Italian specialists in
London, with a growing range from
France, Australia, South Africa and
California.*

O.W. Loeb & Co. ★★★★

82 Southwark Bridge Road,
London SE1 OAS
📞 020 7928 7750 FAX 020 7928 1855
@ finewine@owloeb.com
W www.owloeb.com
Credit cards, delivery, by the case only, en primeur,
tastings, cellarage, mail order.
*A well-chosen list with some superstars
from Burgundy, Germany and the Rhône.
Alsace and Spain are also good. Friendly
service.*

Magnum Fine Wines ★★★★

43 Pall Mall, London SW1Y 5JG
📞 020 7839 5732 FAX 020 7321 0848
@ wine@magnum.co.uk
W www.magnum.co.uk
Credit cards, delivery, en primeur, tastings, cellarage,
mail order.
*Impressive selection of French fine wines,
especially Bordeaux.*

Majestic Wine ★★★★★

Majestic House, Otterspool Way,
Watford, Herts WD25 8WW
📞 01923 298200 FAX 01923 819105
@ info@majestic.co.uk
W www.majestic.co.uk
By the (mixed) case only*, credit cards, accessories,
delivery, tastings, en primeur, glass loan, mail order,
internet sales.
*A generally good range of wines, with
bargain one-off purchases and the
opportunity to taste before you buy. *The
Vinopolis shop (020 7940 8313) also
sells by the bottle.*

Marks & Spencer ★★★★

46–47 Baker Street,
London W1A 8EP
📞 020 7935 4422
W www.marksandspencer.com
Credit cards, delivery, tastings, mail order.
*New World and Champagne are the
stars in this expanding range.*

Martinez Fine Wines ★★★★
35 The Grove, Ilkley, W. Yorks LS29 9NJ
☎ 01943 603241 FAX 01943 816489
@ martinez@martinez.co.uk
W www.martinez.co.uk
Credit cards, accessories, delivery, tastings,
en primeur, cellarage, glass hire/loan.
*Independent merchant specializing
in small boutique wineries and hard-to-
find buys.*

Mayfair Cellars ★★★★
203 Seagrave Road, Fulham, London
SW6 1ST
☎ 020 7386 7999 FAX 020 7386 0202
@ sales@mayfaircellars.co.uk
W www.mayfaircellars.co.uk
Mail order, credit cards, delivery, tastings,
en primeur, cellarage, internet sales.
*Small mail order, fine wine merchant
which, like, Berry Bros, boasts an office
in Hong Kong. Champagne is their
speciality with a wide offering from
Burgundy.*

The Moffat Wine Shop ★★★★
8 Well Street, Moffat, Dumfriesshire,
SW Scotland DG10 9DP
☎ 01683 220 554
@ moffwine@aol.com
W www.moffattown.com
Credit cards, accessories, delivery, tastings, cellarage,
glass loan, en primeur, mail order.
*Independent merchant with a unique
range and interesting wines from
Uruguay.*

Montrachet ★★★★★
59 Kennington Road, Waterloo,
London SE1 7PZ
☎ 020 7928 1990 FAX 020 7928 3415
@ charles@montrachetwine.com
By the case only, by mail only, credit cards, delivery,
tastings, en primeur.
*Superb domaine Burgundies and classic
Bordeaux. They source top wines from
various areas in France with the best
German estates.*

Moreno Wine Merchants ★★★★★
11 Marylands Road, London W9 2DU
☎ 020 7286 0678 FAX 020 7286 0513
@ morenowi@dialstart.net
Credit cards, tastings, delivery, mail order.
*Dynamic Spanish and South American
specialist. A good Fine and Rare Wine list
with some of the finest Spanish wines
available from as far back as the 1800s.*

Morris & Verdin ★★★★★
Unit 2, Bankside Industrial Estate,
Sumner Street, London SE1 9JZ
☎ 020 7921 5300 FAX 020 7921 5333
@ info@m-v.co.uk
W www.morris-verdin.co.uk
By the case only, delivery, tastings, en primeur,
cellarage, mail order, internet sales.
*Brilliant Burgundies, sublime sherries,
and "new classic" Californians. Recent
developments include a passion for
Riesling from Alsace, Austria, and the
Mosel. Now also have a selection of
Australian antiquities to complement
their Old World selection.*

Morrisons Supermarkets ★★★
Hilmore House, Thornton Road,
Bradford, West Yorkshire BD8 9AX
☎ 01924 875234 FAX 01924 875300
W www.morereasons.co.uk
Credit cards, accessories, glass hire/loan.
*Unashamedly discount-focused
supermarket chain (with special offers on
up to half the wines).*

New Zealand Wines Direct ★★★★
PO Box 476, London NW5 2NZ
☎ 020 7482 0093 FAX 020 7267 8400
W www.fwnz.co.uk
By the case only, credit cards, delivery, tastings,
mail order, internet sales.
*Exclusive New Zealand specialist
who arranges wine tours to the area.
Wines that are otherwise hard to find.*

Harvey Nichols ★★★★★
109–125 Knightsbridge,
London, SW1X 7RJ
☎ 020 7201 8537 FAX 020 7235 5020
Credit cards, accessories, delivery, tastings, mail order.
*A great collection of both Old World and
New World classics which can also be
enjoyed in the fifth-floor restaurant.*

James Nicholson ★★★★★
27a Killyleagh Street, Crossgar, Co.
Down, Northern Ireland BT30 9DQ
☎ 028 44 830091 FAX 028 44 830028
@ shop@jnwine.com
W www.jnwine.com
Credit cards, accessories, delivery, tastings, en
primeur, wine club, glass loan, mail order, internet
sales.
*Superb growers' wines from California.
List is expanding with some good French
country and Rhône wines. Friendly,
knowledgable and unstuffy staff.*

Nickolls & Perks ★★★★
37 High Street, Stourbridge, West
Midlands, DY8 1TA
☎ 01384 394518 FAX 01384 440786
@ sales@nickollsandperks.co.uk
W www.nickollsandperks.co.uk
Credit cards, delivery, tastings, mail order, en primeur,
cellarage, glass hire, accessories.
*One of the best sources of wine in the
heart of England.*

Nicolas UK ★★★★
Unit 1, Gateway Trading Estate,
Hythe Road, London NW10 6RJ
☎ 020 8964 5469 FAX 020 8962 9829
W www.nicolas-wines.com
Credit cards, delivery, cellarage, tastings, glass hire,
en primeur, cellarage.
*Reliable range from little-known French
regional wines to top-flight clarets. Now
linked to Oddbins.*

Noble Rot ★★★★
18 Market Street, Bromsgrove,
Worcs B61 8DA
☎ 01527 575 606 FAX 01527 833 133
@ info@nrwinewarehouse.co.uk
W www.nrwinewarehouse.co.uk
Credit cards, delivery, tastings, glass loan, wine club,
mail order..
*Majestic-style warehouse emporium with
a good range.*

The Nobody Inn ★★★★★
Doddiscombsleigh,Near Exeter,
EX6 7PS
☎ 01647 252394 FAX 01647 252978
@ info@nobodyinn.co.uk
W www.nobodyinn.co.uk
Credit cards, delivery, tastings, mail order, cellarage,
glass hire, accessories.
*A lovely country pub with an
extraordinary range of wine and malt
whisky.*

Oddbins ★★★★★
31–33 Weir Road, Wimbledon,
London SW19 8UG
☎ 020 8944 4400 FAX 020 8944 4411
W www.oddbins.com
Credit cards, accessories, delivery, tastings,
glass loan, en primeur, mail order, internet sales.
*The recent takeover by by the French
owners of Nicolas may affect the range
here. For the moment there's still a good
range with wine-mad staff. Those
wanting more should try Oddbins Fine
Wine shops. Also in Calais and Ireland.*

Ceci Paolo ★★★★
The New Cook's Emporium,
21 High Street, Ledbury,
Herefordshire HR8 1DS
☎ 01531 632976 FAX 01531 631011
@ patriciaharrison@compuserve.com
W www.cecipaolo.com
Credit cards, accessories, delivery, tastings,
mail order.
*Italian specialists with a Caffe Bar where
you can choose wines off the shelf to
drink with your lunch. Food and wine go
hand in hand here. They also have
expanded their range with some good
Australian wines and other New world
fare.*

Thos. Peatling Fine Wines ★★★★
Westgate House, Westgate Street,
Bury St Edmunds,
Suffolk IP33 1QS
☎ 01284 755948 FAX 01284 714483
@ sales@thospeatling.co.uk
W www.thospeatling.co.uk
Credit cards, accessories, cellarage, en primeur,
delivery, glass loan, tastings, mail order.
*Bordeaux specialist stocking over 50 malt
whiskies. Under new ownership which
has seen over 300 new wines introduced
to their existing list, including
considerable depth to the Italian wines.
They also stock an excellent selection of
fine and rare wines in their cellar.
Knowledgeable staff.*

Penistone Court Cellars ★★★★
The Railway Station, Penistone,
South Yorkshire S36 6HP
☎ 01226 766037 FAX 01226 767310
@ pcwc@dircon.co.uk
By the case only, credit cards, accessories,
delivery, glass loan, mail order.
*They specialise in Austrian wines, but
boast an excellent range from around the
world.*

Philglas & Swiggot ★★★★
21 Northcote Road, Battersea,
London SW11 1NG
☎ 020 7924 4494 FAX 020 7924 4736
@ philandswig@aol.com
Credit cards, accessories, tastings, delivery, glass
loan, mail order.
*Antipodean specialists par excellence who
also stock great Italians and good
Spanish wines. The shop has doubled in
size over the last year expanding the
range of wines.*

Christopher Piper ★★★★★
1 Silver Street, Ottery St. Mary,
Derbyshire. EX11 1DB
☎ 01404 814139 ℻ 01404 812100
@ sales@christopherpiperwines.co.uk
🗑 www.christopherpiperwines.co.uk
Credit cards, delivery, tastings, mail order, cellarage,
glass hire, accessories.
*Good across-the-board merchant with a
loyal local and mail-order following.
France remains a key strength.*

Terry Platt Wine Merchants
★★★★★
Council St. West, Llandudno, Conwy,
North Wales LL30 1ED
☎ 01492 874099 ℻ 01492 874788
@ plattwines@clara.co.uk
🗑 www.terryplattwines.co.uk
Credit cards, accessories, delivery by the case,
tastings, glass hire/loan, mail order.
*A range to satisfy bargain-seekers and
enthusiasts alike with many new
offerings.*

Playford Ros ★★★★
Middle Park House, Sowerby, Thirsk,
North Yorkshire YO7 3AH
☎ 01845 526777 ℻ 01845 526888
@ sales@playfordros.com
🗑 www.playfordros.com
By the case only, credit cards, accessories, delivery,
tastings, en primeur, ceelarage, glass hire/loan, mail
order, internet sales.
*Good Bordeaux, Burgundy and
Australian.*

Le Pont de la Tour ★★★★★
Butlers Wharf Building, 36d Shad
Thames, Butlers Wharf, London SE1
2YE
☎ 020 7403 2403 ℻ 020 7403 0267
@ patriceg@conranrestaurants.co.uk
🗑 www.conran.com
Credit cards, delivery, tastings, glass loan, mail order.
*The Pont de la Tour restaurant's excellent
and in some cases exclusive wine list.*

Arthur Rackham ★★★★
216 London Road, Guildford, GU1 1XR.
☎ 0870 870 1110 ℻ 0870 8701120
@ cellars@ar-emporia.com
🗑 www.ar-emporia.com
Credit cards, accessories, delivery, tastings, glass loan,
mail order, internet sales.
*A gourmet wine merchant that
concentrates on food and wine matching
with tastings on-site.*

Raeburn Fine Wines ★★★★★
21/23 Comely Bank Road,
Edinburgh, Scotland EH4 1DS
☎ 0131 343 1159 ℻ 0131 332 5166
@ sales@raeburnfinewines.com
🗑 www.raeburnfinewines.com
Credit cards, delivery, tastings, en primeur,
glass hire/loan, cellarage, mail order.
*Still enjoying a cult following both sides
of the border. Hard-to-find wines from the
New and Old worlds, with a good
selection from Burgundy.*

Reid Wines ★★★★★
The Mill, Marsh Lane, Hallatrow,
Bristol BS39 6EB
☎ 01761 452 645 ℻ 01761 453 642
Credit cards, delivery, tastings, en primeur, glass loan,
mail order.
*Eccentric merchant with a witty list
brimming with classic and rare wines.*

La Réserve ★★★★★
56 Walton Street, Knightsbridge,
London SW3 1RB
☎ 020 7589 2020 ℻ 020 7581 0250
@ realwine@la-reserve.co.uk
🗑 www.la-reserve.co.uk
Credit cards, accessories, delivery, tastings, en
primeur, cellarage, glass loan, mail order, internet
sales.
*Impeccable Burgundies and top wines
from most other regions.*

Richards and Richards Fine Wines
★★★★
6 Hebburn Drive, Brandlesholme,
Bury, Lancs, BL8 1ED
☎ 0161 762 0022 ℻ 0161 763 4477
@ fine.wines@btconnect.com
Credit cards, accessories, delivery, tastings, mail
order.
*A very good list of fine and rare wines
with an excellent variety of Portuguese
wines.*

Howard Ripley ★★★★★
25 Dingwall Road,
London SW18 3AZ
☎ 020 8877 3065 ℻ 020 8877 0029
@ info@howardripley.com
🗑 www.howardripley.com
By the case only, delivery, tastings, en primeur,
mail order and internet service only.
*Dentist-turned-specialist wine merchant.
Lists 50 of the best Burgundy domaines
with one of the most comprehensive
German ranges in the UK.*

Roberson Wine Merchant ★★★★★
348 Kensington High Street,
London, W14 8NS
☎ 020 7371 2121 FAX 020 7371 4010
@ wines@roberson.co.uk
w www.roberson.co.uk
Credit cards, delivery, tastings, cellarage,
glass loan, mail order, internet sales.
*An eclectic range of young and mature
wines from all over the world. They also
have an excellent selection of "antique
wines".*

Irvine Robertson ★★★★
10–11 North Leith Sands,
Edinburgh, Scotland EH6 4ER
☎ 0131 553 3521 FAX 0131 553 5465
@ irviner@nildram.co.uk
w www.irwines.co.uk
By the case only, credit cards, delivery,
glass loan, mail order.
*Traditional Scottish independent
merchant with a list featuring good range
and depth.*

Safeway ★★★★
6 Millington Road, Hayes,
Middlesex UB3 4AY
☎ 020 8970 3821 FAX 020 8756 2910
w www.safeway.co.uk (e-commerce:
www.safewaywinesdirect.co.uk)
Credit cards, accessories, tastings, glass loan,
internet sales.
*Improving range of good-value wines in
all sectors.*

Sainsbury ★★★★
Stamford House, Stamford Street,
London SE1 9LL
☎ 020 7695 7416 FAX 020 7695 6416
w www.sainsburys.co.uk
Credit cards, accessories, en primeur, glass hire/loan.
*Improving and increasingly customer
focused chain. Now runs
tasteforwine.co.uk (qv).*

Satchells of Burnham Market
★★★★
North Street, Burnham Market,
Norfolk PE31 8HG
☎ 01328 738272 FAX 01328 730727
@ satchellswines@btinternet.com
Credit cards, accessories, delivery, tastings,
glass hire/loan, mail order.
*Small traditional merchant with over
1,000 lines and a new wine club. They
now also boast a specialist room reserved
for claret.*

Savage Selection ★★★★
The Ox House, Market Place,
Northleach, Cheltenham,
Gloucestershire GL54 3EG
☎ 01451 860896 FAX 01451 860996
@ wine@savageselection.co.uk
w www.savageselection.co.uk
Credit cards, accessories, delivery, tastings,
en primeur, cellarage, glass hire/loan, mail order.
*Unashamedly esoteric list selected from
individual producers for their originality.*

Scatchard ★★★★
Kings Dock Street, Wapping,
Liverpool L1 8JS
☎ 0151 709 7073 FAX 0151 709 1500
@ info@scatchard.com
w www.scatchard.com
Credit cards, accessories, delivery, tastings, glass loan,
mail order.
Spain is the specialist subject.

Sebastopol Wines ★★★★
Sebastopol Barn, London Road,
Blewbury, Oxfordshire OX11 9HB
☎ 01235 850 471 FAX 01235 850 776
@ infosebastopol@aol.com
By the case only, credit cards, accessories, delivery,
glass hire.
Australia and Bordeaux specialists.

Seckford Wines ★★★★★
Dock Lane, Melton, Suffolk IP12 1PE
☎ 01394 446622 FAX 01394 446633
@ marcus@seckfordwines.co.uk
w www.seckfordwines.co.uk
By the case only, credit cards, delivery, en primeur,
cellarage, mail order and internet sales only.
A fine range of classic wines.

Selfridges ★★★★★
400 Oxford Street, London W!A 1AB
☎ 020 7318 3730 FAX 020 7318 3042
@ wine.club@selfridges.co.uk
Credit cards, tastings, en primeur, accessories,
delivery.
*Department store with one of the best
ranges in London.*

Edward Sheldon ★★★★
New Street, Shipston on Stour,
Warwickshire CV36 4EN
☎ 01608 661409 FAX 01608 663166
@ finewine@edward-sheldon.co.uk
w www.edward-sheldon.co.uk
Credit cards, accessories, delivery, tastings, en
primeur, cellarage, glass loan, mail order.
Strong on Bordeaux and Burgundy.

Somerfield ★★★

Somerfield House, Whitchurch Lane,
Bristol BS14 OTJ
☎ 01179 359359 FAX 01179 357826
W www.somerfield.co.uk
Credit cards, accessories, delivery, tastings.
*Price-conscious supermarket chain with a
good range.*

Sommelier Wine Co. ★★★★

The Grapevine, 23 St. George's
Esplanade, St. Peter Port,
Guernsey GY1 2BG
☎ 01481 721 677. FAX 01481 716 818.
Credit cards, accessories, delivery, tastings,
glass hire/loan, mail order.
*Great New World and sweet wines
available. Individually described and –
agreeably – VAT-free.*

Stevens Garnier ★★★★

47 West Way, Botley, Oxford
OX2 0JF
☎ 01865 263303 FAX 01865 791594
@ sales@stevensgarnier.co.uk
W www.stevensgarnier.co.uk
Credit cards, accessories, delivery, glass loan,
tastings, mail order.
*A good range (Loire, Burgundy, Portugal,
South Africa, South America) benefits
from this firm's other role as an importer-
wholesaler. Look for "niche" wines from
places like Savoie and Ontario.*

Stratford's Merchants ★★★★

High St, Cookham-on-Thames,
Berks SL6 9SQ
☎ 01628 810606 FAX 01628 810605
@ sales@stratfordwine.co.uk
W www.stratfordwine.co.uk
Credit cards, accessories, delivery, tastings, glass loan,
mail order, internet sales.
*A good international range, with some
particularly inspiring bottles from Chile
and Australia.*

The Sunday Times Wine Club
★★★★

New Aquitaine House, Exeter Way,
Theale, Reading, Berks RG7 4PL
☎ 0870 220 0010 FAX 0870 220 0030
@ orders@wine-club.co.uk
W www.sundaytimeswineclub.co.uk
Credit cards, accessories, delivery, tastings, en
primeur, cellarage, glass hire/loan, mail order, internet
sales.
*Laudable wine firm linked to Laithwaites
(qv).*

Tanners Wines ★★★★★

26 Wyle Cop, Shrewsbury,
Shropshire SY1 1XD
☎ 01743 234455 FAX 01743 234501
@ sales@tanners-wines.co.uk
W www.tanners-wines.co.uk
Credit cards, accessories, delivery, tastings, en
primeur, glass hire/loan, regional chain, mail order.
*First class traditional chain of shops
straddling the Welsh borders but
frequently a contender for best merchant
in the Heart of England*

Tasteforwine.co.uk ★★★★

FAX 0208 272 4210
@ sales@tasteforwine.co.uk
W www.tasteforwine.co.uk
Credit cards, mail order.
*Sainsbury's mail order and web-based
offspring. (Still associated with Oddbins
which once owned half of this business).*

Tesco Stores ★★★★

PO Box 18, Delemare Road, Cheshunt,
Herts EN8 9SL
☎ 0800 505555.
@ customer.service@tesco.co.uk
W www.tesco.co.uk
Credit cards, accessories, delivery, tastings, glass loan.
Ultra-dynamic supermarket chain.

Thresher Wine Shop ★★★★

Enjoyment Hall, Bessemer Road,
Welwyn Garden City, Herts AL7 1BL
☎ 01707 387263 FAX 01707 387350
Credit cards, delivery, tastings.
Britain's largest high-street chain.

Turville Valley Wines ★★★★★

The Firs, Potter Row, Great Missenden,
Bucks HP16 9LT
☎ 01494 868818 FAX 01494 868832
@ info@turville-valley-wines.com
W www.turville-valley-wines.com
Delivery, en primeur, cellarage, mail order.
*Classic Bordeaux, Burgundy (Domaine de
la Romanee Conti), and port.*

Unwins Wine Merchants ★★★

Birchwood House, Victoria Road,
Dartford, Kent DA1 5AJ
☎ 01322 272 711 FAX 01322 294 469
@ info@unwins.co.uk
W www.unwins.co.uk
Credit cards, accessories, delivery, en primeur, glass
hire/loan, tastings.
*Home Counties chain, in a state of flux,
having laid off a large number of staff.*

Valvona & Crolla ★★★★★
19 Elm Row, Edinburgh, EH7 4AA
[C] 0131 556 6066 [FAX] 0131 556 1668
[@] sales@valvonacrolla.co.uk
[W] www.valvonacrolla.co.uk
Credit cards, accessories, delivery, tastings,
glass hire/loan, mail order, internet sales.
*Stunning Italian wines and an expanding
range from elsewhere in the world.
Tutored tastings.*

Victoria Wine ★★★
Enjoyment Hall, Bessemer Road,
Welwyn Garden City,
Herts AL7 1BL
[C] 01707 387263 [FAX] 01707 387350
Credit cards, delivery, glass loan.
*Once-dynamic part of the same First
Quench group as Thresher. Now, sadly,
short of personality.*

La Vigneronne ★★★★★
105 Old Brompton Road,
London SW7 3LE
[C] 020 7589 6113 [FAX] 020 7581 2983
[@] lavig@aol.com
[W] www.lavigneronne.co.uk
Credit cards, accessories, delivery, tastings,
en primeur, mail order.
*Specialists in fine and rare wines from
around the world and strong on French
country wines. Frequent tastings and
dinners are informative. Their staff is
friendly.*

Villeneuve Wines ★★★★
One Venlaw Court, Peebles,
Scotland EH45 8AE
[C] 01721 722 500 [FAX] 01721 729 922
[@] wines@villeneuvewines.com
[W] www.villeneuvewines.com
Credit cards, accessories, delivery, tastings, glass loan,
mail order, internet sales.
*Three shops, with a range including rare
vintages of Château Musar and other
hard-to-find buys. Knowledgable and
friendly staff.*

Vin du Van ★★★★★
Colthups, The Street,
Appledore, Kent TN26 2BX
[C] 01233 758727 [FAX] 01233 758389
By the case only, mail order only, delivery,
credit cards, glass loan.
*Australian specialist merchant with an
emphasis on quality and hard-to-find
sought after wines. Wacky, unpretentious,
yet informative list.*

Vinceremos Wine & Spirits ★★★★
74 Kirkgate, Leeds LS2 7DJ
[C] 0113 244 0002 [FAX] 0113 288 4566
[@] info@vinceremos.co.uk
[W] www.vinceremos.co.uk
By the case only, glass loan, credit cards, delivery,
internet sales.
*One of the best sources for organic wines,
not to mention new Moroccan wines with
which to surprise your friends.*

Vino Vino ★★★★
Freepost, SEA 5662, New Malden,
Surrey KT3 3BR
[C] 07703 436949 [FAX] 020 8942 4003
[@] vinovino@macunlimited.net
Mail order only, credit cards, delivery.
*Merchants pecializing in wonderful
classic and new Italian wines. They
recently launched a good Spanish list.
Regular, informative mailings are
welcome too.*

Vintage Roots ★★★★★
Farley Farms, Reading Road, Arborfield
RG2 9HT
[C] 0800 980 4992 [FAX] 0118 976 1998
[@] info@vintageroots.co.uk
[W] www.vintageroots.co.uk
By the case only, credit cards, delivery, tastings, en
primeur, glass hire/loan, mail order and internet sales
only.
*All wines 100 per cent certified organic,
some biodynamic, all full of character,
and now on-line.*

Vintage Wines ★★★★
116–118 Derby Road,
Nottingham, NG1 5FB
[C] 0115 947 6565 [FAX] 0115 950 5276
[W] www.vintagewinesltd.co.uk
Credit cards, cellarage, en primeur, delivery, tastings,
glass hire/loan, mail order, internet sales.
*Good broad list to pick from. France,
Germany, and Australia are explored in
some depth.*

The Vintry ★★★★
Park Farm, Milland, Liphook,
Hants GU30 7JT
[C] 01428 741 389 [FAX] 01428 741 368
[W] www.vintry.co.uk
By the case only, glass loan/hire, en primeur,
credit cards, delivery, tastings.
*Eight outlets offering exclusively French
wine, with a good general selection,
including British-made French wines
such as Ch. Méaume.*

Waitrose ★ ★ ★ ★ ★
Duncastle Rd., Southern Industrial Area,
Bracknell, Berks RG12 8YA
☎ 01344 424680 FAX 01344 825255
W www.waitrose-direct.co.uk
Credit cards, accessories, delivery, tastings, en
primeur, cellarage, glass hire/loan, mail order, internet
sales.
*A well balanced list with good traditional
wines and plenty of innovative bottles to
look out for. Waitrose Wine Direct is their
first class mail order arm.*

Waterloo Wine Co. ★ ★ ★ ★
61 Lant Street, London, SE1 1QN
☎ 020 7403 7967 FAX 020 7357 6976
@ sales@waterloowine.co.uk
W www.waterloowine.co.uk
Credit cards, delivery, tastings, glass hire/loan,
mail order.
*Their list features some smaller
independent producers from around the
world. Focus on New Zealand. Great
Loire, German, and Midi offerings too.*

Waters of Coventry ★ ★ ★ ★ ★
Collins Road, Heathcote,
Warwick, CV34 6TF
☎ 01926 888889 FAX 01926 887416
@ rc@wildbunch.co.uk
W www.waters-wine-merchants.co.uk
Credit cards, delivery, tastings, mail order.
*Top Rhônes, Burgundies, Spanish. New
World offerings include fine olive oils.*

Weavers of Nottingham ★ ★ ★ ★
Vintner House, 1 Castle Gate,
Nottingham NG1 7AQ
☎ 0115 958 0922 FAX 0115 950 8076
@ weavers@weaverswines.com
W www.weaverswines.com
Credit cards, accessories, delivery, tastings,
glass hire/loan, mail order, internet sales.
*Traditional merchant who supplies a
creative and comprehensive range of
wines, accessories, malts, and liqueurs.*

Whitebridge Wines ★ ★ ★ ★
Unit 21, Whitebridge Estate, Stone,
Staffs ST15 8LQ
☎ 01785 817229 FAX 01785 811181
@ sales@whitebridgewines.co.uk
W www.whitebridgewines.co.uk
Credit cards, accessories, delivery, tastings,
cellarage, glass hire/loan, mail order.
*Good wines from Australia and France.
Their fine wine arm trades as The
Peckwater Wine Company.*

Whiteside's of Clitheroe ★ ★ ★ ★ ★
Shawbridge Street, Clitheroe,
Lancs BB7 1NA
☎ 01200 422281 FAX 01200 427129
@ wine@whitesideswine.co.uk
Credit cards, accessories, delivery, tastings,
cellarage, glass loan, mail order.
*An unusually good selection of wines
(especially from the New World) coupled
with an equally unusually fine range of
whiskies.*

Wine Cellar ★ ★ ★ ★
PO Box 476, Loushers Lane,
Warrington, Cheshire WA4 6RR
☎ 01925 444 555 FAX 01925 413 474
@ sales@winecellar.co.uk
W www.winecellar.co.uk
Credit cards, accessories, delivery, tastings, en
primeur, cellarage, glass loan, mail order.
*An independently-owned chain of shops
which had the clever idea of combining
wine retailing with cafes and micro-
breweries. Seems to have lost some of its
early momentum.*

The Wine Cellar ★ ★ ★ ★
10 Station Parade, Sanderstead Road,
South Croydon, Surrey CR2 0PH
☎ 020 8657 6936 FAX 020 8657 9391
@ woodgeraldine@aol.com
Credit cards, accessories, delivery, tastings,
en primeur, cellarage, glass loan, mail order.
*This independent merchant offers a
commendable selection.*

Winefinds ★ ★ ★ ★
Unit A, Dinton Business Park, Dinton,
Wilts SP3 5SR
☎ 01722 716916 FAX 01722 716179
@ sales@winefinds.co.uk
W www.winefinds.co.uk
By the case only, mail order only, credit cards,
free delivery.
*An original notion: a team of Masters of
Wine that works together to seek out high
quality wines from both the Old and New
Worlds.*

Wine Rack ★ ★ ★ ★
Enjoyment Hall, Bessemer Road,
Welwyn Garden City, Herts AL7 1BL
☎ 01707 387263 FAX 01707 387350
Credit cards, delivery, tastings, glass hire/loan.
*The up-market, high-street face of the
First Quench (Thresher, Victoria Wine)
empire. Making big efforts to improve the
range after a fairly dull patch.*

Wine Raks (Scotland) ★★★★
21 Springfield Rd, Aberdeen AB15 7RJ
📞 01224 311460 FAX 01224 312186
@ enq@wineraks.co.uk
w www.wineraks.co.uk
Credit cards, accessories, delivery, tastings,
en primeur, glass hire/loan, cellarage.
*This Scotish merchant has an interesting
list of Old World growers' wines with a
range of exciting efforts from the New
World.*

The Wine Society ★★★★★
Gunnels Wood Road, Stevenage,
Hertfordshire, SG1 2BG
📞 01438 740222 FAX 01438 761167
@ memberservices@thewinesociety.com
w www.thewinesociety.com
Mail order only, credit cards, delivery, tastings, en
primeur, cellarage.
*Britain's best mail-order only merchant
with an extensive range.*

The Wine Treasury ★★★★
69–71 Bondway, London, SW8 1SQ
📞 020 7793 9999
@ julian@winetreasury.com
w www.winetreasury.com
By the case only, credit cards, en primeur, delivery,
tastings, cellarage, mail order.
*An esoteric range with plenty of excellent
premium Californian, Italian and
Australian wines.*

The Winery ★★★★
4 Clifton Road, Maida Vale, London W9
1SS
📞 020 7286 6475. FAX 020 7286 2733.
@ dmotion@globalnet.co.uk
Credit cards, delivery, tastings, mail order, glass hire,
accessories.
*Composer David Williams has introduced
a great selection of quirky wines
(especially from France, California and
Italy) to this friendly shop near Lord's
Cricket Ground.*

Wines of Westhorpe ★★★★
Marchington, Staffs ST14 8NX.
📞 01283 820285. FAX 01283 820631.
@ wines@westhorpe.co.uk
w www.westhorpe.co.uk
By the case only, credit cards, delivery, tastings, mail
order.
*Experts on Hungary, with good South
African and New World wines. New
ranges from Argentina and Romania are
exciting.*

The Wright Wine Co. ★★★★
The Old Smithy, Raikes Road, Skipton,
N. Yorks BD23 1NP
📞 01756 700886 FAX 01756 798580
@ bob@wineandwhisky.co.uk
w www.wineandwhisky.co.uk
Credit cards, accessories, delivery, cellarage, glass loan.
*Great wines from Alsace, South Africa,
and Australia, including many halves.
Two rooms are devoted to whisky.*

Wrightson & Company ★★★★
Manfield Grange, Manfield, Darlington,
N. Yorks DL2 2RE
📞 01325 374134 FAX 01325 374135
@ ed.wrightson.wines@onyxnet.co.uk
w www.thatwineclub.co.uk
By the case only, credit cards, accessories, delivery,
tastings, en primeur, cellarage, glass loan, mail order,
internet sales.
*Independent specialist wine importer
expanding into mail order. Developing its
list of South African boutique wines and
those from other New World areas.
Friendly staff.*

Peter Wylie Fine Wines ★★★★★
Plymtree Manor, Plymtree, Cullompton,
Devon EX15 2LE
📞 01884 277 555 FAX 01884 277 557
@ peter@wylie-fine-wines.demon.co.uk
w www.wyliefinewines.co.uk
Mail order only (visitors by appointment), delivery
(worldwide), en primeur, cellarage, internet sales.
*A veritable treasure-trove of rare and fine
wines.*

Yapp Brothers ★★★★★
The Old Brewery, Mere,
Wiltshire BA12 6DY
📞 01747 860423 FAX 01747 860929
@ sales@yapp.co.uk
w www.yapp.co.uk
Credit cards, delivery, tastings, cellarage,
glass hire/loan, mail order, internet sales.
*Britain's most faithful and probably best
Loire and Rhône specialists, with a good
selection from all over.*

Noel Young Wines ★★★★★
56 High Street, Trumpington,
Cambridge CB2 2LS
📞 01223 844 744 FAX 01223 844 736
w www.nywines.co.uk
Credit cards, accessories, delivery, tastings,
en primeur, glass hire/loan, mail order.
*Good broad range with some brilliant
Austrian wines.*

RETAILERS IN BRIEF

A&A Wines
  [C] 01483 274666
  [W] www.spanishwinesonline.co.uk

A&B Vintners Ltd
  [C] 01892 724 977
  [W] www.abvintners.co.uk

Allez Vins!
  [C] 0800 096 6587
  [W] www.allezvins.co.uk

Amps Fine Wines
  [C] 01832 273502

Arriba Kettle
  [C] 01386 833 024

Bacchus Fine Wines
  [C] 01234 711140
  [W] www.bacchus.co.uk

H & H Bancroft
  [C] 0870 444 1700

Barrels & Bottles
  [C] 0114 2556611

Bat & Bottle
  [C] 01785 284495

Booths of Stockport
  [C] 0161 432 3309

The Bottleneck
  [C] 01843 861095

Cape Province Wines
  [C] 01784 451860

The Celtic Vintner
  [C] 01633 430055

Châteaux Wines
  [C] 01454 613 959

Colombier Vins Fins
  [C] 01283 552552

Connolly's Wine Merchants
  [C] 0121 236 9269
  [W] www.connollyswine.co.uk

Rodney Densem Wines
  [C] 01270 212200
  [W] www.onestopwine.com

Eckington Wines
  [C] 01246 433213

Edencroft Fine Wines
  [C] 01270 629975

El Vino Co.
  [C] 020 7353 5384

European Wine Growers Associates
  [C] 01524 703003

Evington's Wine Merchants
  [C] 0116 254 2702

Falcon Vintners
  [C] 020 7388 7055

Ferrers Le Mesurier & Son
  [C] 07771 676367

John Frazier
  [C] 0121 704 3415

Friarwood
  [C] 020 7736 2628

Garrards Merchants
  [C] 01900 823592

Charles Hennings
  [C] 01798 872 485

Hicks & Don
  [C] 01380 831234

High Breck Vintners
  [C] 020 8340 1848

Hopton Wines
  [C] 01299 270734

Ian G. Howe
  [C] 01636 704366

Victor Hugo Wines
  [C] 01534 507977

Mayor Sworder
  [C] 020 8686 1155
  [W] www.mayorsworder.co.uk

Mills Whitcombe Wine Merchants
  [C] 01981 550028

Mitchell's Wine Merchants
  [C] 0114 2745587

Thomas Panton
  [C] 01666 503088

Parfrements
  [C] 024 7650 3646

R.S. Wines
  [C] 0117 963 1780

The Rogers Wine Co
  [C] 01473 748464

Ashley Scott
  [C] 01244 520655

Smithfield Wines
  [C] 0161 273 6070

John Stephenson & Sons
  [C] 01282 614 618
  [W] www.thewinemill.co.uk

Transatlantic Wines
  [C] 01664 565013

Trout Wines
  [C] 01264 781472

Uncorked
  [C] 020 7638 5998
  [W] www.uncorked.co.uk

Vine Trail
  [C] 0117 921 1770

Vintage Cellars
  [C] 020 7630 6254
  [W] www.vintagecellars.co.uk

York Wines
  [C] 01347 878716.
  [W] www.yorkwines.co.uk

COUNTRY & REGION SPECIALISTS

THE AMERICAS

NORTH AMERICA
Adnams (see page 372)
The Antique Wine Co. (see page 372)
Asda Stores (see page 372)
Averys of Bristol (see page 373)
Bennetts Wines (see page 373)
Bibendum (see page 373)
Booths Supermarkets (see page 373)
The Bottleneck (see page 387)
Corkscrew Wines (see page 374)
Gordon and MacPhail
(see page 376)
Great Northern Wine Co.
(see page 376)
Charles Hennings
(see page 387)
Inspired Wines (see page 377)
Lea & Sandeman (see page 378)
Lay & Wheeler (see page 378)
Morris & Verdin (see page 379)
James Nicholson (see page 380)
Oddbins (see page 380)
Terry Platt (see page 381)
R.S. Wines (see page 387)
Raeburn Fine Wines
(see page 381)
Sommelier Wine Co.
(see page 383)
Stevens Garnier (see page 383)
Stratford's (see page 383)
The Wine Treasury
(see page 386)

SOUTH AMERICA
Booths of Stockport
(see page 387)
The Bottleneck (see page 387)
Charterhouse Wine Co.
(see page 374)
Ben Ellis Wines (see page 272)
Forth Wines (see page 375)
Hedley Wright (see page 377)
Moreno Wine (see page 379)
Stevens Garnier (see page 383)
The Wine Society
(see page 386)
The Wright Wine Co.
(see page 386)

AUSTRALIA
Addison WInes (see page 372)
Adnams (see page 372)
Amps Fine Wines (see page 387)
Australian Wine Club

(see page 372)
Bennetts (see page 373)
Booths of Stockport
(see page 387)
The Bottleneck (see page 387)
Corkscrew Wines (see page 374)
Charterhouse Wine Co.
(see page 374)
Direct Wine Shipments
(see page 375)
Domaine Direct (see page 375)
Eckington Wines (see page 387)
Edencroft Fine Wines
(see page 387)
Great Northern Wine Co
(see page 376)
H.& H. Fine Wines
(see page 273)
Jeroboams (see page 377)
Mills Whitcombe (see page 387)
Philglas & Swiggott
(see page 380)
Christopher Piper (see page 381)
R.S. Wines (see page 387)
Vin du Van (see page 384)
Vintage Wines (see page 384)

AUSTRIA
Bacchus Fine Wines (see page 387)
Ben Ellis Wines (see page 272)
Forth Wines (see page 375)
Morris & Verdin (379)
Penistone Court (see page 380)
Noel Young Wines
(see page 386)

EASTERN EUROPE
Wines of Westhorpe (see page 386)

ENGLAND
Stratford's Wine Shippers
(see page 383)

FRANCE

ALSACE
Amps Fine Wines (see page 387)
Ballantynes of Cowbridge
(see page 373)
Anthony Byrne (see page 374)
Gauntleys (see page 376)
O.W. Loeb (see page 378)
Scatchard Wines (see page 382)
Tanners Wines (see page 383)
Wine Rack (see page 385)
The Wine Society (see page 386)

BEAUJOLAIS
Berkmann Wine Cellars (see page 373)
Colombier Vins Fins (see page 387)
Roger Harris (see page 376)
Domaine Direct (see page 375)

BORDEAUX
Addison Wines (see page 372)
The Antique Wine Co. (see page 372)
John Armit Wines (see page 372)
Averys of Bristol (see page 372)
Balls Brothers (see page 373)
Berry Bros. & Rudd (see page 373)
Bibendum (see page 373)
Bordeaux Index (see page 373)
The Butlers Wine Cellar
(see page 374)
Anthony Byrne (see page 374)
Cave Cru Classé (see page 374)
Brian Coad (see page 374)
Colombier Vins Fins (see page 387)
Connolly's (see page 387)
Corney and Barrow (see page 375)
Direct Wine Shipments (see page 375)
Farr Vintners (see page 375)
Forth Wines (see page 375)
Fortnum & Mason (see page 376)
Four Walls Wine Co. (see page 376)
Friarwood (see page 387)
Goedhuis & Co. (see page 376)
Harrods (see page 376)
Harvey Nichols (see page 379)
Justerini & Brooks (see page 377)
Richard Kihl (see page 378)
Laithwaites (see page 378)
Lay & Wheeler (see page378)
O.W. Loeb (see page 378)
Magnum Fine Wines (see page 378)
Montrachet (see page 379)
Nicolas (see page 380)
Oddbins (see page 380)
Thos. Peatling (see page 380)
Le Pont de la Tour (see page 381)
Reid Wines (see page 381)
Roberson (see page 382)
Edward Sheldon (see page 382)
Tanners Wines (see page 383)
Turville Valley Wines (see page 383)
Wilkinson Vintners (see page 282)
The Wine Society (see page 311)
Peter Wylie Fine Wines
(see page 386)
Yapp Brothers (see page 386)

BURGUNDY
3D Wines (see page 372)
A & B Vintners (see page 387)
The Antique Wine Co. (see page 372)
John Armit Wines (see page 372)
Averys of Bristol (see page 372)
Bibendum (see page 373)
The Burgundy Shuttle
(see page 373)
The Butlers Wine Cellar
(see page 374)
Anthony Byrne (see page 374)
Cave Cru Classé (see page 374)
Brian Coad (see page 374)
Colombier Vins Fins (see page 387)
Connolly's (see page 387)
Corney and Barrow (see page 375)
Domaine Direct (see page 375)
Farr Vintners (see page 375)
Irma Fingal-Rock (see page 375)
Fortnum & Mason (see page 376)
Four Walls Wine Co. (see page 376)
Goedhuis & Co. (see page 376)
Harrods (see page 376)
Harvey Nichols (see page 379)
Haynes Hanson & Clark
(see page 377)
Heyman Barwell Jones (see page 377)
House of Townsend (see page 378)
Ian G. Howe (see page 387)
Jeroboams (see page 377)
Justerini & Brooks (see page 377)
Lay & Wheeler (see page 378)
Lea & Sandeman (see page 378)
O.W. Loeb (see page 378)
Montrachet (see page 379)
Morris & Verdin (see page 379)
James Nicholson (see page 379)
Oddbins (see page 380)
Christopher Piper (see page 381)
Le Pont de la Tour (see page 381)
Raeburn Fine Wines (see page 381)
Howard Ripley (see page 381)
Stevens Garnier (see page 383)
Turville Valley Wines (see page 383)
La Vigneronne (see page 384)
The Wine Press (see page 282)

CHABLIS
Ball's Brothers (see page 373)
Ian G. Howe (see page 387)

CHAMPAGNE
3D Wines (see page 372)
Amps Fine Wines (see page 387)
Addison Wines (see page 372)
Bordeaux Index (see page 373)
La Bouteille d'Or (see page 373)
Connolly's (see page 387)
Farr Vintners (see page 375)
Fortnum & Mason (see page 376)
Marks & Spencer (see page 378)

Harrods (see page 376)
Majestic Wine (see page 378)
Oddbins (see page 380)

COUNTRY WINES
A & B Vintners (see page 387)
Allez Vins! (see page 387)
The Great Western Wine Co.
(see page 376)
Laithwaites (see page 378)
Mills Whitcombe (see page 387)

LOIRE
Brian Coad (see page 374)
Colombier Vins Fins (see page 387)
Corkscrew Wines (see page 374)
Four Walls Wine Co.
(see page 376)
Yapp Brothers (see page 386)

RHONE
A & B Vintners (see page 387)
Bibendum (see page 373)
Connolly's (see page 387)
Corkscrew Wines (see page 374)
Croque-en-Bouche (see page 375)
Farr Vintners (see page 375)
Gauntleys (see page 376)
Waters of Coventry (see page 385)
Yapp Brothers (see page 386)

GERMANY
Adnams (see page 372)
Four Walls Wine Co. (see page 376)
Justerini & Brooks (see page 377)
O.W. Loeb (see page 378)
Majestic Wine (see page 378)
Tanners Wines (see page 383)

ITALY
John Armit (see page 372)
Averys of Bristol (see page 372)

Berkmann Wine Cellars (see page 373)
Bordeaux Index (see page 373)
Ceci Paolo (see page 380)
Colombier Vins Fins (see page 387)
Connolly's (see page 387)
Inspired Wines (see page 377)
Liberty Wines (see page 378)
Philglass & Swiggot (see page 380)
Valvona & Crolla (see page 384)
Vino Vino (see page 384)
Winefinds (see page 385)

NEW ZEALAND
Vin du Van (see page 384)
Waterloo Wine Co. (see page 385)

PORTUGAL
Forth Wines (see page 375)
Moreno Wine Importers
(see page 379)
Raeburn Fine Wines (see page 381)

SOUTH AFRICA
Cape Province (see page 387)
Forth Wines (see page 375)
Heyman Barwell Jones (see page 377)
Irvine Robertson (see page 382)

SPAIN
A & A Wines (see page 387)
Arriba Kettle (see page 387)
Bordeaux Index (see page 373)
Charterhouse Wine Company (see page 374)
Direct Wine Shipments (see page 375)
S. H. Jones (see page 377)
Laymont & Shaw (see page 378)
Moreno Wine Importers
(see page 379)
Oddbins (see page 380)
Scatchard (see page 382)
Waters of Coventry (see page 385)

FORTIFIED WINE SPECIALISTS

PORT & MADEIRA
Ballantynes of Cowbridge
(see page 373)
Farr Vintners (see page 375)
Fortnum & Mason (see page 376)
Moreno Wine Merchants
(see page 379)
Thos. Peatling (see page 381)
Reid Wines (see page 381)
Turville Valley Wines
(see page 383)
Peter Wylie (see page 386)

SHERRY
Ballantynes of Cowbridge
(see page 373)
Fortnum & Mason (see page 376)
Laymont & Shaw (see page 379)
Lea & Sandeman (see page 379)
Martinez (see page 379)
Moreno Wine Merchants
(see page 379)
Morris & Verdin (see page 379)
Reid Wines (see page 381)
Scatchard (see page 382)

BEER SPECIALISTS

Adnams (see page 372)
Majestic Wine (see page 379)
Mitchells Wine Merchants
(see page 387)

Oddbins (see page 380)
Unwins (see page 384)
Wine Cellar
(see page 385)

SPIRIT SPECIALISTS

ARMAGNAC & COGNAC

Justerini & Brooks (see page 378)
Nicolas (see page 380)

WHISKY

Berry Bros. & Rudd (see page 373)

Harrods (see page 376)
Charles Hennings (see page 387)
S.H. Jones (see page 378)
Oddbins (see page 380)
Pallant Wines (see page 387)
La Réserve (see page 381)

FINE AND RARE WINE SPECIALISTS

John Armit Wines (see page 372)
Bennetts Wines (see page 373)
Berry Bros. & Rudd
(see page 373)
Bibendum (see page 373)
Bordeaux Index (see page 374)
Anthony Byrne (see page 374)
Cave Cru Classé (see page 374)
Corney and Barrow
(see page 375)
Farr Vintners (see page 375)
Fine and Rare Wines
(see page 376)
Fortnum & Mason
(see page 376)
Four Walls Wine Co.
(see page 376)
Goedhuis & Co. (see page 376)
Harrods (see page 377)
Harvey Nichols (see page 380)
Lay & Wheeler (see page 378)
Nicolas (see page 380)
The Pavilion Wine Co.
(see page 387)
Oddbins Fine Wines
(see page 380)
Thos. Peatling (see page 381)
Raeburn Fine Wines
(see page 381)
Reid Wines (see page 381)
La Réserve (see page 381)
Roberson (see page 382)
Tanners Wines
(see page 383)
Turville Valley Wines
(see page 383)
Whiteside's of Clitheroe
(see page 385)

Peter Wylie Fine Wines
(see page 386)
Yapp Brothers (see page 386)
Noel Young Wines (see page 386)

LIVE AUCTIONEERS

Bigwood Auctioneers
☎ 01789 269 415 FAX 01789 294 168
W www.bigwoodauctioneers.co.uk
Christie's
☎ 020 7839 9060 FAX 020 7839 1611
W www.christies.com
Lithgow
☎ 01642 710 158 FAX 01642 712 641
@ lithgows.auctions@onyxnet.co.uk

Morphets
☎ 01423 530030 FAX 01423 500717
Phillips
☎ 01225 310 609 FAX 01225 446 675
Sotheby's
☎ 020 7293 6423 FAX 020 7293 5961
W www.sothebys.com
J. Straker Chadwick & Sons
☎ 01873 852 624 FAX 01873 857 311

WINE COURSES

Association of Wine Educators
☎ +FAX 020 8995 2277
Challenge Educational Services
☎ 01273 220 261 FAX 01273 220 376
@ enquiries@challengeuk.com
Christie's
☎ 020 7839 9060 FAX 020 7839 1611
German Wine Institute
☎ (0049) 6131 282918
Grape Sense
☎ +FAX 01359 270318
@ grapesense@aol.com
International Wine Academy of Rome
☎ +39 06 6990878
Kensington & Chelsea College
☎ 020 7573 5333 FAX 020 8960 2693
W www.kcc.ac.uk
Leicestershire Wine School
☎ 0116 254 2702 FAX 0116 254 2702
Leith's
☎ 020 7229 0177 FAX 020 7937 5257
Maurice Mason
☎ + 01480 896 416 FAX 01480 896424

North West Wine and Spirit Assoc.
☎ +FAX 01244 678 624
Plumpton College
☎ 01273 890 454 FAX 01273 890 071
@ enquiries@plumpton.ac.uk
Scala School
☎ 020 7281 3040 FAX 020 7281 3001
@ scalawine@cs.com
Sotheby's
☎ 020 7293 6423 FAX 020 7293 5961
Wensum Lodge
☎ 01603 666 021 FAX 01603 765 633
Wine Associates Ltd. (in UK & France)
☎ 01803 299292 (UK)
☎ 0033 553 588 148 (France)
W www.wineassociates.co.uk
Wine & Spirit Education Trust
☎ 020 7236 3551 FAX 020 7329 8712
@ wset@wset.co.uk
Wine Education Service
☎ 020 8423 6338 FAX 020 8723 3751
Wine Wise
☎ 020 7254 9734 FAX 020 7249 3663

WINE HOLIDAYS

Allez France & Great Escapes
☎ 01903 748 100 and 748 138
Arblaster & Clarke Wine Tours
§ 01730 893 344 ` 01730 892 888
W www.winetours.co.uk
Le Baccanti
☎ 020 7272 5592 FAX 0116 271 6016
@ info@lebaccanti.com
Country Lanes
☎ 01425 655 022 FAX 01425 655 177
DER Travel
☎ 020 7290 1111 FAX 020 7629 7442
Edwin Doran Travel
☎ 020 8288 1000 FAX 020 8288 2955
Fine Wine Travel Company
☎ 020 7229 1243

Francophiles Discover France
☎ +FAX 01362 851 076
HGP Wine Tours
☎ 01803 299 292 FAX 01803 292 008
KD River Cruises Europe
☎ 01372 742 033 FAX 01372 724 871
Moswin Tours
☎ 0116 271 4982 FAX 0116 271 6016
Ski Gourmet and Winetrails
☎ 01306 712 111 FAX 01306 713 504
The Sunday Times Wine Club Tours
☎ 01730 895 353 FAX 01730 892 888
Tanglewood Wine Tours
☎ 01932 348 720 FAX 01932 350 861
Wessex Continental Travel
☎ +FAX 01752 846 880

ACCESSORIES

GLASSES
Conran Shop (Riedel range)
[C] 020 7589 7401
Dartington Crystal
[C] 01805 626 262
FAX 01805 626 267
Equinox (Belfast) (Riedel range)
[C] 01232 230 089
Oneida/Schott UK
[C] 01753 212500

CORKSCREWS
Screwpull
[C] 01264 343 900
FAX 01264 356396

STORAGE
Access Storage Space
[C] 020 8991 9717
Consort Wine Care Systems
[C] 01635 550055
FAX 01635 41733
Euro-cave
[C] 020 8200 1266
[W] www.artofwine.co.uk
Smith & Taylor
[C] 020 7627 5070
FAX 020 7622 8235
Vin-Garde
[C]+FAX 01926 811 376

WINE RACKS
A.&W. Moore
[C] 0115 944 1434
FAX 0115 932 0735
R.T.A Wine Racks
[C] 01328 829 666

Spiral Cellars
[C] 01372 279 166
The Wine Rack Company
[C]+FAX 01243 543 253

ANTIQUES
Bacchus Gallery
[C] 01798 342 844
FAX 01798 342 634

Jasmin Cameron
[C]+FAX 020 7351 4154

GENERAL WINE ACCESSORIES
Most independent wine merchants also
stock a good range of accessories.
Birchgrove Products Ltd.
[C] 01483 533 400 FAX 01483 533 700
The Hugh Johnson Collection
[C] 020 7491 4912 FAX 020 7493 0602

CHILLING DEVICES
Chilla
[C] 0181 891 6464
Coolbags & Boxes UK
[C] 0118 9333 331 FAX 0118 9333 579
Vacu Products
[C] 01299 250 480 FAX 01299 251 559

BOOKS
Books for Cooks
[C] 020 7221 1992
[W] www.booksforcooks.com
Cooking the Books
[C]+FAX 01633 400 150
Richard Stanford
[C] 020 7836 1321

WINE CLUBS

Académie du Vin
[C] 01803 299 292
FAX 01803 292 008
[@] hgpwine@aol.com
Alston Wine Club
[C] 01434 381 338
Amersham
[C] 01494 771 983
Association of Wine Cellarmen
[C] 020 8871 3092
Barrels and Bottles
[C] 0114 255 6611
FAX 0114 255 1010
Charlemagne
[C] 020 8567 1733

Cirencester
[C] 01285 641 126
Confrérie Internationale de St. Vincent
[C] 0113 267 9258 FAX 0113 228 9307
[@] sh.smalley@ntlworld.com
Cornwall
[C] 01872 223 570
Decant & Taste
[C] 01507 605 758
Eastbourne
[C] 01323 727675
Goring & Streatley
[C] 01491 873 620
Guild of Sommeliers
[C] 0161 928 0852

Harrogate Medical
📞 01423 503 129 FAX 01423 561 820
Herefordshire
📞 01432 275 656
Hextable Wine Club
📞 01732 823 345
Hollingworth
📞 01706 374 765
@ peter-l@msn.com
Ightham Wine Club
📞 01732 885 557
Institute of Wines & Spirits
(Scotland) 📞+FAX 01324 554 162
The Interesting Wine Club
📞 020 7272 2457 FAX 020 7272 4312
International Wine and Food Society
📞 020 7495 4191 FAX 020 7495 4172
@ iwandfs@aol.com
Leicester Evington
📞 0116 231 4760
FAX 0116 287 5371
Leicester Grand Union
📞 0116 287 1662
Lincoln Wine Society
📞+FAX 01522 680 388
London Branch of IWFS
📞 0208 349 2260
FAX 0208 346 4360
Manchester
📞 01706 824 283
Moreno
📞 020 7286 0678

Myster Wine Club
📞 01633 893 485
Notting Hill
📞 020 8969 9668
Preston
📞 01772 254 251
FAX 01772 203 858
Rochester
📞 01634 848 345
Scottish
📞 0131 664 8855
Tanglewood Wine Society
📞 01932 348 720
FAX 01932 350 861
West Hampstead
📞 020 7794 3926
Windsor and Eton
📞 01753 790 188 FAX 01753 790 189
@ enquiries@etonvintners.co.uk
Wine and Dine
📞 020 8673 4639
FAX 020 8675 5543.
@ bensonwines@connectingbusiness.com
Wine Collectors (WineShare)
📞 01306 742 164
Wine Schoppen
📞 0114 255 6611
FAX 0114 255 1010
The Winetasters
📞 01753 889 702
York
📞+FAX 01904 691 628

CROSS-CHANNEL SHOPPING

EastEnders Bulk Beer Warehouse
14 Rue Gustave Courbet, 62100 Calais,
France
📞 (33) 3 21 34 53 33
FAX (33) 3 21 97 61 22
Normandy Wine Warehouse
(4 branches – 2 in Cherbourg, 2 in
Ouistreham) 71 Avenue Carnot, 50100
Cherbourg, France
📞 (33) 2 33 43 39 79
FAX: (33) 2 33 43 22 69
Oddbins
Cité Europe, 139 Rue de Douvres,
62901 Coquelles, Cedex, France
📞 (33) 3 21 82 07 32
FAX (33) 3 21 82 05 83
Perardel Wine Market
Z.A. Marcel Doret, Calais, France
📞 (33) 3 21 97 21 22
Sainsbury's Wine Store
Centre Commercial Auchon, Route de
Boulogne, Calais, France

📞 (33) 3 21 82 38 48
FAX (33) 3 21 36 01 91
Le Tastevin
9 Rue Val, 35400 St.-Malo,
France
📞 (33) 2 99 82 46 56
FAX (33) 2 99 81 09 69
Tesco Vin Plus
Espace 122, Boulevard du Kent, Cité
Europe, 62231 Coquelles, France
📞 (33) 3 21 46 02 70
FAX (33) 3 21 46 02 79
The Wine & Beer Company
Rue de Judée, Zone Industrielle Marcel
Doret, 62100 Calais, France
📞 (33) 3 21 97 63 00
FAX (33) 3 21 97 70 15
The Wine Society
1 Rue de la Paroisse, 62140 Hesdin,
France
📞 (33) 3 21 86 52 07
FAX (33) 3 21 86 52 13

The world of wine online is changing so rapidly that the following list can only offer a snapshot of what you may find if you go looking for wine on the web. But it should give you a pretty good start.

ONLINE RETAILERS

Apart from the specialist online retailers listed here, you will also find websites for many of the companies profiled on pages 372–387.

www.a-bestfixture.com
Wine accessories, supplies, and gifts.
www.auswine.com.au
Australian wines shipped worldwide.
www.bbr.co.uk
Traditional merchant. Worldwide delivery.
www.cawineclub.com
California wine club.
www.chateau-online.com
French wines shipped throughout Europe.
www.clarets.com
Not just claret. Ship worldwide.
www.connseries.com
US site with limited-production wines.
www.esquin.com
Superstore and wine club.
www.everywine.co.uk
UK site offering 30,000 wines.
www.finestwine.com
Global supply of collectable wines.
www.libation.com
Wine and beer delivered worldwide.

www.madaboutwine.com
UK-based general retailer. Informative.
www.vintageandvine.com
Links to good retailers in Australia.
www.virginwine.com
Top UK-based site.
www.wineaccess.com
Links to independent US wine retailers.
www.winelert.com
60 000 wines from 100 US retailers
www.wineandco.com
French-based retailer. Delivers to UK.
www.wine.com (includes evineyard.com).
Wines, gifts, accessories, and wine links
www.winesearcher.com
Impressive international wine-tracker
www.winebroker.com
Fine wine specialists.
www.thewinebrokers.com
Worldwide delivery and online wineclub.
www.winex.com
A good general catalog of wine.

ONLINE AUCTIONEERS

www.auctionvine.com
A central online auction site.
www.amazon.com
Online giant associated with Sotheby's.
www.brentwoodwine.com
Auction site with fixed price sales, too.
www.tcwc.com
The Chicago Wine Company.
www.internetauctionlist.com
Network of auction company websites.
www.magnumwines.com
Speciality wines.

www.uvine.com
Online wine exchange.
www.wine-auction-gazette.com
Calendar of wine auctions.
www.winebid.com
Auctions in the US, UK, and Australia.
www.winetoday.com
Updated archive of articles on auctions.
www.vines.netauctions.net.au
Five annual auctions in Australia.
www.winesonauction.com
Wine sold by producers.

ONLINE WINE EDUCATION

www.WineEducation.com
Certified Wine Educator, Stephen Reiss.
www.wine.gurus.com
Society of Wine Educators'
home page.

www.wine-school.com
An online diploma wine course.
www.wineprofessor.com
Food and wine pairing, wine
labels, etc.

NEWS, REVIEWS, & GENERIC SITES

www.4wine.com
US-dominant link to worldwide wines.

www.ambrosiawine.com
Vinous search engine and chatroom.

www.bestwinesites.com
Good source of wine on the web.

www.decanter.com
The UK wine magazine online.

www.erobertparker.com
The guru Robert Parker @ home.

www.connectingdrinks.com
The route to WINE Magazine online.

www.drinkwine.com
All about wine.

www.food-and-drink.com
Links to food and drink sites.

www.foodandwine.com
Food and Wine Magazine online.

www.gangofpour.com
Loads of information about wine.

www.grapevineweekly.com
An online magazine with lots of links.

www.hotwine.com
A link to winesites, plus poetic quotes.

www.interaxus.com/pages/wine.html
Wine reviews.

www.intlwinechallenge.com
The wine competition's official website.

www.intowine.com
Winemaking and wine-and-the-Bible.

www.jancisrobinson.com
The UK-based wine authority's site.

www.purplepages.com
Directory of wine-related websites.

www.smartwine.com
Market news for the investor.

www.thewinenews.com
News and reviews.

www.vine2wine.com
Links to over 2,000 wine sites.

www.winebrats.org
New-wave and emphatically unstuffy.

www.winecellar.com
A complete source of wine links.

www.wine-collector.com
Swap and chat about collectable bottles.

www.wineculture.com
A hip guide to wine on the web.

www.wineenthusiastmag.com
Articles and the latest news.

www.wineinfonet.com
A multilanguage portal.

www.wine-investor.com
How to spend your cash.

www.wineplace.com
Winemaking galore.

www.wineontheweb.com
The talking online wine magazine.

www.winepros.com
Experts including James Halliday.

www.wineratings.com
Wine reviews and advice.

www.wine-searcher.com
Search the web for all aspects of wine.

www.winesense.com
Wine appreciation and women in wine.

www.winexwired.com
Online presence of *Wine X* Magazine.

www.winetoday.com
News from the *New York Times*.

www.thewinenews.com
Features, reviews, recommendations.

www.winespectator.com
The *Wine Spectator's* online magazine.

www.worldwine.com
A website dedicated to wine links.

WINERIES

www.bestwinesites.com
Links for N. America and Europe.

www.cawinemall.com
Comprehensive directory of California web wineries by region or grape variety.

www.champagnes.com
An introduction to Champagne.

www.edgamesandart.com/wine.html
A database of wine and wineries.

www.hiddenwineries.com
Lesser-known US wineries.

www.vinosearch.com
Wines and wineries across the globe.

www.winecollection.com
An online collection of France's wineries.

www.wines.com
Details of over 1 400 Australian and New Zealand wineries.

www.winetitles.com
Selected wineries.

www.winetoday.com
A comprehensive list of wineries.

www.wineweb.com
Wines and wineries across the world.

www.worldwine.com
Lots of links.

REGIONAL SITES

www.argentinewines.com
Argentina's new-wave wines.
www.bordeaux.com
A virtual tour of the wine and wineries
of Bordeaux.
www.coonawarra.com
Australia's most famous region.
vino.eunet.es
The Spanish wine page.
www.germanwines.de
Multilingual official site.
www.indagegroup.com
Promoting India's wine.
www.ivp.pt
The Port Wine Institute's official
website.
www.liwines.com
Long Island wine country.
www.napawine.com
Visit Napa wineries and wine sites.
www.madeirawine.com
All about Madeira's wines and history.
www.nywine.com
New York uncorked.
www.nzwine.com
The official site of New Zealand wine.

www.portwine.com
Everything you need to know about port.
www.sonomawine.com
Sonoma County Wineries Association.
www.washingtonwine.org
All about wine in Washington.
www.wine.ch
The Swiss wine page.
www.wine.co.za
A guide to South African wines.
www.winecountry.com
The gateway to wines of California.
www.winesofchile.com
Ever-expanding guide to Chilean wines.
www.wineinstitute.com
Californian wineries with lots of links.
www.wine.it
Wines of Italy.
www.wineoftheweek.com
Great commercial New Zealand site.
www.wines-france.com
User-friendly guide to French wines
www.winetitles.com.au
A complete guide to wine Down Under.
www.winetour.com
A guide to Ontario's wineries.

ONLINE CHATROOMS & CLUBS

www.4wine.com
Lists a multitude of chat rooms.
www.auswine.com.au/cgi-bin/
auswine/browse
The Australian Wine Centre's virtual
shop with a forum, and a chat room.
www.drinkwine.com
Bulletin board and extensive listing of
associations.
www.evineyard.com
Offers live talk and a lively wine club.
www.iglou.com/wine/chat
Join a crowd of other wine lovers and
compare notes.
www.nobilevineyards.com
International wine club and
chat room.
www.secretcellars.com
A virtual wine club that brings
California's small vineyards to your door.
www.vineswinger.com
Plentiful chat rooms and busy forums.
www.winebrats.org
Access to various wine chat rooms.
www.wineculture.com
A resource of various chat rooms.

www.wineinstitute.org
Lists discussion groups and chat rooms
focusing on California wine.
www.wine-lovers-page.com
Wine chat room.
www.wine rave.com
Website with its own wine chat
room – arguably the liveliest on
the net.
www.wines.com
Bulletin board where questions can be
posed to wine experts.
www.winesite.com
Extensive list of links to international
wine clubs.
www.winespectator.com
Forum and online interviews.
www.zinfans.com
For lovers of the Zinfandel – in its every
form.

Please email recommendations of other sites
to robertjoseph@robertjosephonline.com.
In return, I will send copies of my book
French Wines *to senders of the most*
useful tips.

INDEX

This index can be used as a supplement to the A–Z of Wine (pages 97–262).

C

Clos de Paulilles 108, 135

Clos de Tart 313

Clos des Mont-Olivet 130

Clos des Mouches 148

Clos des Papes 130

Clos du Bois 101

Clos du Roi 128

Clos Floridène 165

Clos la Coutale 121

Clos Nicrosi 123

Clos Salomon 162

Clos Ste. Magdeleine 126

Clos Triguedina 121

Closel, Dom. du 103

Clusel-Roch 139

Co-op Australian Grenache 281

Co-op Australian Merlot 281

Co-op Cape Chenin Blanc Oak-Aged 341

Co-op Côtes du Rhône Reserve 308

Co-op Explorers Vineyard Sauvignon Blanc 329

Co-op Island Vines Cyprus White 361

Co-op Late Bottled Vintage Port 335

Co-op Montepulciano d'Abruzzo 322

Co-op Mountain Vines Semillon 361

Co-op Orvieto Classico 320

Co-op Primitivo Sangiovese 323

Co-op Puglia Chardonnay Bombino 321

Co-op Ruby Port 334

Co-op Sweet Asti 319

Co-op Tawny Port 334

Co-op Tierra Sana Tempranillo Organic 351

Co-op Vin de Pays d'Oc Cabernet Sauvignon 306

Co-op Vin de Pays d'Oc Chardonnay 301

Co-op Vin de Pays d'Oc Syrah 306

Co-op Vin de Pays du Jardin de la France 299

Co-op Vintage Character Port 335

Coche-Dury 106

Cocument, Cave de 140

Codex, Martin 100

Codorniu Brut Cava 34/

Cognard 117

Col d'Orcia 119

Col di Sasso 108, 325

Col Solare 103

Colin, Marc 129

Colin-Deleger 110, 129

Collards 106

Collier Falls 148

Colombier 142

Colombo, Jean-Luc 137

Colstream Hills Pinot Noir 285

Columbia Crest 135

Columbia Winery Syrah 135

Combier 142

Cometa 2001, Planeta 321

Commanderie e Peyrassol 140

Comte Armand 106

Concha y Toro, 99, 125

Concha y Toro Casillero del Diablo 294

Concha y Toro Casillero del Diablo Merlot 294

Concha y Toro Trio Merlot 295

Condamine, de 140

Confuron, Jean-Jacques 133

Cono Sur 113, 136

Cono Sur 20 Barrel Pinot Noir Limited Edition 296

Cono Sur 20 Barrel Pinot Noir Limited Edition 296

Cono Sur Merlot 294

Contea di Castiglione 105

Conterno 153

Conterno, Aldo 109, 147, 158

Conterno Fantino 109

Conterno, Giacomo 109

Conti 100

Contratto 105

Coopers Creek 106

Copper Crossing Bulgarian Medium Dry White 288

Copper Crossing Bulgarian Red Wine 289

Coppermine Road, The 104

Corbans 162

Corbieres Terra Vitis 309

Cordon Negro Brut 348

Corelli's Ribola 161

Cortaccia, Cant. Prod. di 102

Corte Gardoni 131

Corte, Quinta da 145

Corte Sant' Alda 102

Cortes de Cima 101

Cortes de Cima Reserva 333

Cortese 147

Corton Bressandes, Cossart Gordon 119

Cossart Gordon's Five Year Old Malmsey 337

Costanti 119

Coste Rubin 108

Côte Montpezat 140

Cottage Block 137

Cotto, Quinta do 147

Cotton 119

Coulaine, Ch. de 103

Couly-Dutheil 131

Courbis 137

Couret 140

Court-les-Muts, Ch. 112

Courtade, la 140

Coutet, Ch. 109

Coyeux, Dom. de 111

Cranswick, The Cocoparra Vineyard Shiraz 284

Cranswick, Zirilli Botrytis Semillon 287

Crasto, Quinta do 147

Crawford, Kim 162

Croft Late Bottle Vintage Port 336

Croix Vieilles Vignes 120

Croze de Pys, Ch. 121

Crozes-Hermitage, E Guigal 312

WINE ON THE WEB

Apart from our lists of recommended websites
on pages 16–17 and 395–397,
if you enjoy

the Robert Joseph Good Wine Guide

visit

vintage-intelligence.com

for news, comment, tasting notes, competitions, an electronic
Wine Atlas, and links to over 200 wineries and retailers
throughout the world,

www.wine-school.com

and, of course,

www.dk.com

for details of other
Dorling Kindersley titles.